Transforming Public Education

Transforming Public Education

Cases in Education Entrepreneurship

Edited by

Stacey M. Childress

Harvard Education Press
Cambridge, Massachusetts

Library of Congress Control Number 2009942744

Paperback ISBN 978-1-934742-42-6
Library Edition ISBN 978-1-934742-43-3

Published by Harvard Education Press,
an imprint of the Harvard Education Publishing Group

Harvard Education Press
8 Story Street
Cambridge, MA 02138

Cover Design: Sarah Henderson

The typefaces used in this book are Bitstream Aldine 401 for text
and Univers for diplay.

Contents

1 Introduction

MODULE I

Understanding the Context of Urban Schooling in the United States

11 **Case 1** KIPP National (A) (Abridged)
Stig Leschly

35 **Case 2** Thurgood Marshall High School
John J. Gabarro

44 **Case 3** Finding a CEO for the School District of Philadelphia: Searching for a Savior?
Stacey Childress, Purnima Kochikar, Stig Leschly

MODULE II

Tackling the People Problem

76 **Case 1** Teach For America 2005
Stacey Childress

105 **Case 2** Boston Teacher Residency: Developing a Strategy for Long-Term Impact
Stacey Childress, Geoff Marietta, Sara Suchman

137 **Case 3** New Leaders for New Schools
Stig Leschly, Jessica Boer

168 **Case 4** Memphis City Schools: The Next Generation of Principals
Stacey Childress, Robert Peterkin, Tonika Cheek Clayton

MODULE III

Focusing on Performance

194 **Case 1** Learning to Manage with Data in Duval County Public Schools: Lake Shore Middle School (A)
Allen Grossman, James P. Honan, Caroline King

223 **Case 2** SchoolNet: Pursuing Opportunity Beyond Federal Mandates
Stacey Childress, Kristen Campbell

246 **Case 3** Wireless Generation
Stacey Childress, Sophie Lippincott

267 **Case 4** Focusing on Results at the New York City Department of Education
Stacey Childress, Tonika Cheek Clayton

MODULE IV
Launching and Growing New Schools

303 **Case 1** If We Blew It Up, Then We Could . . . A Thought Experiment for Students of Entrepreneurship in Education
Stacey Childress

306 **Case 2** Launching the Bronx Lab School
Stacey Childress

328 **Case 3** Codman Academy: Beyond the Start-Up Phase
Stacey Childress, Tiffany K. Cheng

358 **Case 4** Frederick Douglass Charter School: The Renewal Decision
Stacey Childress, Debbie Kozar

384 **Case 5** New Schools for New Orleans 2008
Stacey Childress, Scott Benson, Sarah Tudryn

411 **Case 6** St. HOPE Academy: The Expansion Decision
Stacey Childress, Alison Berkley Wagonfeld

443 **Case 7** Green Dot Public Schools: To Collaborate or Compete?
Stacey Childress, Christopher C. Kim

465 **Case 8** KIPP 2007: Implementing a Smart Growth Strategy
Stacey Childress, Maura Marino

487 Acknowledgments

488 About the Editor

489 Permissions

Introduction

For nearly two decades, education entrepreneurs have been working to transform the K–12 public education system in the United States. What is an education entrepreneur? The term can mean many things, but in this book, it is used in a very specific way. Howard Stevenson of the Harvard Business School defines entrepreneurship as *the pursuit of opportunity regardless of the resources currently controlled*.[1] This definition describes a *behavior*, not a particular type of organization such as a start-up, or a type of person with particular characteristics or motives such as a risk-taker who exploits opportunity for financial gain. Entrepreneurial behavior is in contrast to an administrative approach in which a manager first assesses the resources he has at his disposal and then attempts to make the most of them in service of an organization's goals. Rather, an entrepreneur starts with the identification of an opportunity and then mobilizes the resources (people, money, time, technology) she needs to pursue it. Entrepreneurship, the pursuit of opportunity, can happen in organizations of all stages of development and by people with a variety of motives and goals.

In fact, "social entrepreneurship" has become part of the language of a new generation of idealists who are committed to solving social problems, and many social entrepreneurs are focused on education. One way to define social entrepreneurship is to adapt Stevenson's definition to capture its distinctive characteristics: the pursuit of an opportunity *to create pattern-breaking social change* regardless of the resources currently controlled. The education entrepreneurs you will encounter in this book fit this definition. All of them are pursuing an opportunity to create social change in the form of high-quality educational opportunities for low-income and minority students who are dramatically underserved by the current public education system. The change they seek is "pattern-breaking" for two reasons. First, it is aimed at improving the lifelong prospects of the children they directly serve by providing them with an excellent education, thereby breaking the cycle of poverty that is perpetuated by the limited access to opportunity that results from a low-quality education. Second, they are focused on entirely transforming the way the education system works through their collective efforts and influence so that *all* children have access to high-quality educational opportunities, regardless of the zip code they live in or their family background.

For social entrepreneurs, opportunities come disguised as entrenched, complex problems. The first step in tackling these problems is to understand the factors that contribute to them. In U.S. K–12 education, one of the biggest problems is the performance gap between African American, Hispanic, and low-income students and their white, Asian, and more affluent counterparts. By the time they are in third or fourth grade, on average these students are already nearly three grade levels behind in reading and math. The vast majority of them never catch up. Only half eventually graduate from high school, and of the 40% of graduates who enroll in college, two-thirds need extensive remediation before they are ready for basic courses. No wonder then that a student from a low-income zip code is seven times less likely to graduate from college than a student from a more affluent neighborhood. Taken together, these achievement and opportunity gaps are the overarching problem that drives the education entrepreneurs in the cases that follow. The problem has many contributing factors, but as you will see, the entrepreneurial activity in the sector is increasingly aggregated around opportunities related to three of them: (1) creating and preparing new pools of talent; (2) developing and managing effective performance tools; and (3) launching and growing new schools. These three areas of entrepreneurial activity represent levers that together could force dramatic change in the sector: people, performance tools, and schools. *Transforming Public Education* includes cases organized into modules on each of these opportunity areas, and four central questions run throughout:

1. Why are there opportunities for entrepreneurs in a sector that is funded primarily with public dollars and historically has been predominantly delivered by public agencies?
2. Why is entrepreneurial activity aggregating around certain opportunities?
3. What are the possibilities and constraints faced by entrepreneurs as they attempt pattern-breaking change in each opportunity area?
4. How might the direct and systemic impact of the approaches taken by education entrepreneurs be evaluated?

The book begins with a brief module on the context of U.S. public education, followed by modules for each opportunity area: "Tackling the People Problem," "Focusing on Performance," and "Launching and Growing New Schools."

Module I: Understanding the Context of Urban Schooling in the United States

As mentioned earlier, the public education system in the United States has profound performance challenges. Low-income, Hispanic, and African American students have predictable and significant differences in achievement and access to subsequent opportunities relative to their white, Asian, and more affluent peers. In international comparisons, American 15-year-olds rank 25th in math, 18th in science, and 15th in reading compared with their peers in 29 other developed economies. These performance disparities create opportunities for entrepreneurs to provide some of the basic functions of education such as recruiting and preparing a new pipeline of talent to work in the system, designing new ways to manage performance, and creating new schools that compete with the existing system. But the disparities also create opportunities for education entrepreneurs to influence the incumbent system so that its performance dramatically improves.

Because public education is not explicitly identified as a responsibility of the federal government in the Constitution of the United States, the responsibility for educating 50 million K–12 students falls to the 50 states. For the most part, the states create a regulatory environment and then devolve education decision-making to local communities, resulting in 15,000 separately governed districts operating 100,000 schools. Of the $500 billion in annual expenditures, 43% comes from local taxes, 48% from state coffers, and 9% from the federal government. Each state has its own performance standards and accountability regime as well as its own regulatory structure that defines the rules of the game. This operational, financial, and regulatory fragmentation presents enormous challenges to education entrepreneurs in their own organizations as well as in their efforts to have systemic impact. Module I includes three cases and supplemental readings that will set the context of public education so that the discussions in the ensuing modules about entrepreneurial opportunities in the sector are grounded in a basic understanding of it.

Module II: Tackling the People Problem

Public education is fundamentally a people enterprise. Of the $500 billion in annual public spending on K–12 education, nearly 80% is allocated to salary and benefits. The nearly $2 billion of education philanthropy is similar—most grants are used to fund staff positions to carry out a program or project. Given the large percentage of total spending on people, improvements in the quality, knowledge, and skill of the individuals who work in the system could have huge effects on performance. Another aspect of the people problem is that children in low-income neighborhoods tend to have the least prepared teachers. Teachers in these schools come from the least competitive colleges and scored below average on the SAT—in fact, 34% score in the bottom quartile. As the Education Trust put it, "we consistently assign teachers whose performance lags on important tests to low-income and minority students, whose performance in turn lags on important tests."[2] The national data for principals is similar. As the conception of the principal's role has shifted from building manager to instructional leader, the types of individuals self-selecting into administrative preparation programs and the quality of those programs have not kept up with the change.[3]

This module will give you an opportunity to analyze and discuss four cases focused on the "people problem": "Teach For America 2005," "Boston Teacher Residency: Developing a Strategy for Long-Term Impact," "New Leaders for New Schools," and "Memphis City Schools: The Next Generation of Principals." This combination of cases will introduce new approaches to preparing teachers and principals, nonprofit organizations that provide services to public school districts, a joint venture between a district and a nonprofit, and the district superintendent as a customer of entrepreneurial organizations. Evaluating the various approaches will allow you to develop your own point of view about effective ways to tackle the "people problem" in K–12 education.

Module III: Focusing on Performance

In 2002, the No Child Left Behind (NCLB) Act went into effect, and though it allowed states to set their own standards and benchmarks for acceptable performance on annual tests, it required them to track and publish student performance data disaggregated by subgroups such as race and ethnicity, English proficiency, and low-income status. The intent of this aspect of the law was to increase the level of accountability for student performance in every school and to spotlight the long-standing achievement and opportunity gaps for certain groups of students. The law prompted states and districts to build or buy technology systems that could collect, disaggregate, and analyze performance data on an enormous scale. It also created demand for new processes and systems that could help principals, teachers, and others diagnose student learning needs and implement new practices that would help their students improve.

In the performance module, you will be exposed to four cases that highlight organizations focused on performance management tools and systems. A case about technology and data use in Duval County Public Schools will allow you to get a broad understanding of the sector-wide problem that leads to opportunity for entrepreneurs, followed by cases about two technology companies—SchoolNet and Wireless Generation—that are pursuing an opportunity to meet the needs highlighted in the Duval case by using the power of the market to increase the sector's capacity to use data to improve performance. The module closes with an examination of efforts at the New York City Department of Education to implement a variety of performance systems and tools to support a decentralized structure in which principals are expected to behave entrepreneurially. Discussing these four cases will introduce you to a variety of managerial issues related to performance and accountability, as well as to the particular market opportunities and challenges faced by for-profit education companies.

Module IV: Launching and Growing New Schools

Another area of entrepreneurial activity being driven by legislation and philanthropy is the creation and growth of new schools, some within school districts but most incorporated separately as public charter schools. Much of the new school activity within districts is a result of the small high schools movement fueled largely by more than $1.5 billion in funding from the Bill & Melinda Gates Foundation from 2002 to 2007. Other in-district school start-up activity is taking place because of compliance with NCLB, which requires districts to take dramatic action to address chronically low-performing schools. Often, these schools are "reconstituted," with new leadership and new staff taking over to implement a new instructional strategy. These schools remain governed and funded by their local school districts. Charter schools, by contrast, are independently organized, governed, and managed but are funded with public dollars and are open to all students at no charge. Minnesota passed the first charter school law in 1992, and by 2008, 45 states and the District of Columbia had followed suit. The vast majority of the more than 4,000 charter schools are incorporated as nonprofit organizations, but more than 10% are run on a for-profit basis. A number of school networks have also sprung up and operate as multi-site enterprises.

The module has two parts—creating new schools and growing networks of schools. The module begins with an exercise—a thought experiment—that will provoke you to imagine what a new system might look like if designed from scratch. The exercise sets the stage for discussions of single-site start-up schools both inside a district and as charters, through discussions of the Bronx Lab School, Codman Academy, and Frederick Douglass Charter School. This set of cases will allow you to see a range of models and performance as well as analyze the drivers of success or failure. After laying a foundation for evaluating entrepreneurial efforts to start schools, the second part of the module includes cases about New Schools for New Orleans, St. HOPE Academy, Green Dot Public Schools, and KIPP (Knowledge Is Power Program). This series of discussions will give you an opportunity to evaluate expansion decisions facing school operators, as well as the opportunities and constraints related to influencing systemwide change through these models.

Analytical Frameworks

As you move through the cases in the various modules, you will have a chance to understand and practice three analytical frameworks that will help you make sense of the material. These frameworks will also be useful to you outside of the cases if you engage in some aspect of education entrepreneurship or social entrepreneurship more generally. The first is a framework for creating or evaluating social ventures. The next framework is a way of evaluating expansion decisions, and the final tool is an approach to building or analyzing the potential effectiveness of school models. The overviews for Module II and IV will briefly describe these frameworks, but your primary exposure to them will come from your instructor's use of them to organize the case discussions. Below are the guiding questions that are at the heart of each framework.

Creating and Evaluating Social Entrepreneurial Ventures

1. What is the **problem** the venture is designed to solve? What are the **contributing factors** to the problem?
2. What is the entrepreneur's **theory of change** about how to solve the problem? In other words, what beliefs about cause and effect are reflected in the approach? Is the theory grounded in one or more of the contributing factors to the problem? Is the theory aimed at creating direct change, systemic change, or both?
3. How does the entrepreneur plan to put the theory into practice? In other words, what is the **strategy** for producing results?
4. Is the **organization** that will implement the strategy designed in such a way that it is likely to execute successfully?
5. How does the organization define **success**? What indicators are appropriate for evaluating whether it is achieving its mission? Whether its theory of change is valid?

Evaluating Growth Opportunities

1. Given the overall goals of the organization, what are the likely effects of the various growth options on its ability to increase its direct and systemic **impact**?
2. What are the **market** conditions in the areas being considered as growth options?
3. How does the organization's **capacity** match up with the demands of growth options?
4. What are the key **risks** inherent in each of the growth options? How does the organization plan to mitigate these risks?

Building and Analyzing Effective School Models

1. What **learning model** has the school team adopted? Is it grounded in a rigorous **theory of action** about how student learning improves?
2. Does the **culture** of school (the beliefs and behaviors of staff and students) match the theory of action and instructional strategy?
3. Are the **systems and structures** of the school likely to accelerate the effectiveness of the instructional strategy, or do they constrain it?
4. Are the **resources** (people, money, time) allocated in ways that are consistent with the instructional strategy?
5. Are **stakeholder relationships** built and managed in a way that supports the instructional strategy?
6. How does the team evaluate and communicate **success**?

The social entrepreneurship framework will be introduced in Module II and reinforced in Modules III and IV. The growth framework is also introduced in Module II and reinforced in the second part of Module IV. The school effectiveness framework is mainly explored in Module IV. As you use them to analyze actual organizations and to put yourself in the shoes of real entrepreneurs facing real decisions, you will develop a more practical understanding of the frameworks than you would by simply reading a theoretical description of them. This approach is at the heart of the case-based pedagogy practiced at the Harvard Business School and is the underlying architecture of the flow of modules and cases in this volume.

Learning and the Case Method[4]

For many students, learning by the case method is a new experience. Rather than studying theories or research findings, this approach immerses the learner in real-world situations. Each case has been included because it illustrates important problems, practices, or concepts. By reading and discussing a case in the context of these larger ideas, you are able to see the relationship between theory and practice. Importantly, when you read and discuss the case, you are not asked to be an interested bystander. Rather, you will be challenged to diagnose the situation presented by the case and to propose a course of action as if you were the protagonist. Since many cases hinge on an important decision that must be made, this approach will give you the opportunity to develop recommendations consistent both with the facts of the case and with the larger concepts or theories it illustrates, as well as to test out your ideas with others.

Unlike case studies that are included in many textbooks on education administration, those in this book are not meant to be examples of either best or worst practice. Many include some promising practices, but none should be seen simply as a template to be taken and applied to another setting. Like the real world they come from, the cases often are messy, with seemingly irrational people and unexpected complications. Thus, thinking like an entrepreneur in one of these cases requires coping with the limitations and realities of everyday life in public education, diagnosing what works well, what does not, and what an entrepreneur who is trying to create change in the education system might do about it. Together, the cases and readings are designed to help you build a habit of mind of diagnosing the causes of performance problems, developing theories of change for solving the problems, and converting those theories into action through an organization.

It is important to leave yourself plenty of time to prepare for a case discussion. Each case includes discussion questions to serve as guides for your analysis. Typically, good preparation requires reading the case more than once. First, you might read to understand the central issue, the actors, and the chronology of events. Then, you might examine the materials in the exhibits to see how they are relevant to the events and decisions of the case. Next, you might read the case again and focus on the decision or action that is called for. Many students find it helpful to discuss their ideas about the case with a small group of colleagues (a study group) before the in-class case discussion. This allows students to verify their understanding of the facts of the case and to give their proposals for action a trial run in a small setting.

In a class discussion, you are a member of a learning community that works together to examine the facts, consider the underlying concepts, and explore and assess alternative actions. Finding the "right" answer or "cracking the case" is not the goal of good case discussion, since there is little to be learned from such an approach. Rather, the goal is to practice informed diagnosis, thoughtful planning, and critical reflection on what works and why. By using this approach with the cases in this book, you and your classmates will build the collective capacity to discuss the issues and concepts related to transforming public education through entrepreneurship.

Notes

1. Howard Stevenson, "Entrepreneurship: What Is It?" in *The Entrepreneurial Venture*, ed. William Sahlman, Howard Stevenson, Michael Roberts, and Amar Bhidé (Boston: Harvard Business Press, 1999), 9–10.

2. The Education Trust, "The Opportunity Gap: No Matter How You Look at It, Low-Income and Minority Students Get Fewer Good Teachers," *Thinking K–16* (winter 2004): 36–37.

3. Arthur Levine, *Educating School Leaders* (New York: Education Schools Project, 2005).

4. This section is adapted from the introduction to Stacey Childress, Richard F. Elmore, Allen S. Grossman, and Susan Moore Johnson, *Managing School Districts for High Performance: Cases in Public Education Leadership* (Cambridge, MA: Harvard Education Press, 2007).

Understanding the Context of Urban Schooling in the United States

In order to create fundamental change in any sector, entrepreneurs must understand how it works. How is performance measured, and how is the sector currently doing on these indicators? How are the various organizations regulated and governed? How is the sector structured and managed? How do revenues flow? What are the major drivers of costs, and how do these match with the levers of performance improvement? Which stakeholder groups have power, and what are their vested interests? Are there significant areas of unmet needs for basic services? In this opening module, you will discuss three cases and a number of readings that touch on these areas and help sketch a picture of how schools and school systems work. The cases and supplemental readings will also demonstrate the level of student outcomes in various content areas and the constraints that make it difficult to improve outcomes at scale.

As mentioned in the introduction, the 50 state governments are responsible for educating the 50 million K–12 students in public schools in the United States. Local communities (and a few mayors) govern 15,000 separate districts with 100,000 schools. The sector spends $450 billion annually, with 43% provided by local taxes, 48% by state revenues, and 9% by the federal government. Each state has its own performance standards, accountability system, and regulatory structure. This operational, financial, and regulatory fragmentation is a hallmark of the sector and will reemerge as a challenge repeatedly throughout the book. Module I will briefly set the context so that the discussions in the ensuing modules about entrepreneurial opportunities in the sector are grounded in a basic understanding of it.

The first case tracks the evolution of the Knowledge Is Power Program (KIPP) from its inception as a class of 50 fifth graders in an impoverished section of Houston through its growth into two middle school academies to the cusp of nationwide expansion. As students explore KIPP's characteristics and achievements, they also learn about the problems KIPP was designed to remedy and the barriers it had to overcome. The case allows for a discussion of the performance problems in the U.S. public education sector that have created entrepreneurial opportunities for private sector actors—in this case, a nonprofit organization. It also raises questions about the contributing factors to low performance in certain subgroups of students, the barriers that entrepreneurs face in the space, and the impact that new people, new ideas, and new money can have when deployed through the act of social entrepreneurship. Your instructor might also assign the "Note on Student Outcomes in U.S. Public Education," HBS No. 9-307-068, which breaks down national student performance statistics in a variety of ways. Used together, the case and the supplemental reading expose the widespread performance challenges in the K–12 education system and illustrate one of the ways that entrepreneurs launch organizations to combat these challenges.

The Thurgood Marshall High School case provides a powerful counterpoint to the KIPP case by challenging the notion that being new and innovative guarantees success. The case illuminates how a learning model can be strengthened or constrained by a leader's choices about organizational design and staffing issues as well as by the organizational culture that emerges out of those choices. With a bias for action, the case provides an opportunity for you to put yourself in the shoes of new principal David Kane to diagnose the situation in this struggling two-year-old school and to create a plan for action that takes into account the staff dynamics, student needs, and the external environment in which the school is operating.

In "Finding a CEO for the School District of Philadelphia," the discussion will explore the challenges of leading a large urban public school district that is in crisis. The case focuses on the extent to which contextual challenges can either enable or constrain change efforts focused on improving student achievement. It opens up many topics for discussion, including student performance, governance, politics, stakeholder relations, unions, education finance, entrepreneurial opportunities, and leadership turnover, all of which will be pursued throughout the remaining cases in this book. Education finance is one of a number of complicated topics covered briefly—and the extensive financial statements in the case allow for a deeper look at this area. Your instructor might assign two short companion pieces to enhance the discussion: "Note on U.S. Public Education Finance (A): Revenues," HBS No. 9-307-069, and "Note on U.S. Public Education Finance (B): Expenditures," HBS No. 9-307-070. The case, anchored in a hiring decision for a new superintendent, allows for an analysis of all the contextual and historical information about the district in order to inform a decision about which of three candidates is best suited to lead this district.

Obviously, it is impossible to acquire a full understanding of a complex sector such as public education in a few sessions. The goal of the cases and readings in Module I is to cover the basics so that the remaining cases in the book can build on this foundation. By the time you reach the end of the 20 sessions in this book (and other content that your instructor might assign), you should have a working understanding of how the sector operates and the various entrepreneurial opportunities. The course is not intended to make you an expert, but rather to give you an overview of the sector's leverage points, challenges, and opportunities, along with some analytical tools to help you make sense of the way education entrepreneurs attempt to create pattern-breaking change through their efforts.

Module Questions

Each case has its own questions to consider, but as you work through the cases and readings in this opening module, the questions below will help you make sense of them as a whole:

1. Why is there an entrepreneurial opportunity in public education?
2. What are the structural and institutional barriers that make it difficult to create large-scale change?
3. What are some of the key leverage points that entrepreneurs might tackle in order to create pattern-breaking change?

Stig Leschly

KIPP National (A) (Abridged)

On an icy January afternoon in 2000, Mike Feinberg, David Levin, and Scott Hamilton landed at Chicago O'Hare Airport. The trio had flown in from different corners of the United States to meet urgently for a day in a nearby hotel before flying home again in the morning. The purpose for the meeting was to discuss the design and potential launch of a national network of high-performing middle schools for poor and minority students. The network would be modeled on two schools, known as the KIPP academies, which had been founded by Feinberg and Levin.

Feinberg arrived from Houston, where he was the principal of the Houston KIPP Academy, a public middle school that he had launched in 1995 and which had achieved remarkable academic results with some of Houston's most disadvantaged students. Levin landed from New York where he ran the second KIPP academy, also a public middle school and the sister school to Feinberg's school in Houston. Like Feinberg, Levin had founded his school in 1995 and seen dramatic success with his students, almost all of whom lived in the impoverished neighborhoods of the South Bronx section of New York City.

Levin and Feinberg were old friends and trusted colleagues. Before opening their middle schools, the duo had met and served together in the early 1990s as Teach for America corps members in Houston's public school system. During this time, as idealistic and determined entry-level teachers in their early 20s, Feinberg and Levin cofounded the original KIPP program in a distressed Houston elementary school. From their early collaboration and experimentation as teachers in Houston, Feinberg and Levin set out in 1995 to launch two distinct public middle schools. One school would be in Houston, another in New York. Both would be named KIPP Academy, and both would serve the fifth through the eighth grades. KIPP was an acronym for Knowledge Is Power Program.

Feinberg and Levin's schools contrasted sharply with their inner-city counterparts. For example, the KIPP academies stayed in session from 7:30 a.m. to 5 p.m. each weekday, for half the day on Saturday, and for a month each summer. Teaching in the schools, most of which was done by young and tireless teachers in the mold of Feinberg and Levin, stressed mastery of core academic subjects. Despite the statistics that normally characterized inner-city students, KIPP pupils excelled on state-administered standardized exams, maintained nearly perfect attendance records, and regularly won scholarships to the most selective private, parochial, and public high schools in the United States.

Hamilton reached Chicago from San Francisco where he worked as the managing director of the Pisces Foundation, an education-related philanthropy funded by Donald and Doris Fisher, the founders of Gap Inc. Prior to managing the Pisces Foundation, Hamilton had served as associate commissioner of education in Massachusetts where, among various job responsibilities, he oversaw the state's first wave of investments in charter schools. Hamilton had met Feinberg and Levin in the fall of 1999 and, impressed with their schools, had begun talks with the two principals about financing a national replication of their schools.

Through the fall of 1999, Hamilton, Levin, and Feinberg had communicated regularly about expansion possibilities. The threesome was interested in the possibility of demonstrating on a wider scale that poor and minority students could excel in rigorous academic settings. They believed that the KIPP schools exemplified school-design principles that, if adopted widely, could improve dramatically the academic prospects of disadvantaged children. Their early talks about expansion centered on launching hundreds of middle schools nationwide in the mold of Levin and Feinberg's schools.

The immediate goal for their meeting in Chicago was for Hamilton, Levin, and Feinberg to push their initial talks toward an actionable proposal for the launch of a national network of schools. This proposal would need, at a minimum, to identify the essential attributes of Levin and Feinberg's schools and, from there, to address the rich mix of operating challenges that would accompany a national expansion.

With a written proposal in hand, Hamilton could return to San Francisco to propose an investment to the Fishers, and Feinberg and Levin could evaluate clearly the professional reorientation and personal commitment required of them in a replication effort.

The Early Years: 1992–1995

Levin and Feinberg met in the summer of 1992 in Los Angeles as enlistees with Teach for America (TFA), the legendary teacher-training program that, since its founding in 1990, had placed thousands of college graduates in two-year teaching positions in disadvantaged rural and urban schools. Levin joined TFA directly from his graduation at Yale University in 1992. Feinberg graduated in 1991 from the University of Pennsylvania and enrolled with TFA after a yearlong internship for a senator in Washington.

Like most TFA recruits, Levin and Feinberg joined out of an idealistic and urgent sense of public service. "TFA is the Peace Corps of my generation," explained Feinberg. "Every year it attracts another class of idealistic and committed young people. Many of them stay on in education after their TFA experience." Levin continued, "I needed a job out of college and had an interest in education policy. An advisor of mine told me to get teaching experience before I began working on policy."

At the close of their summer training with TFA, Levin and Feinberg shared a long car ride from Los Angeles to Houston where both had drawn teaching assignments in disadvantaged Houston elementary schools. On the desert highways from Los Angeles to Houston and fresh from their TFA initiation, the duo fashioned their first intuitions about strong teaching and effective schools. Feinberg recalled:

> We drove an old Ford Taurus across the Southwest in August of 1992. We had big ideas and big plans. We talked the whole drive about the perfect school and the perfect system and what it would take to create them. Even then, before we had taught, we had the right instincts, I think, about the nature of good teaching, the need for hard work, and the effect on kids of high expectations.

Feinberg and Levin landed hard in Houston, harder than either ever expected. Feinberg was assigned to Garcia Elementary School, a struggling primary school located in one of Houston's poorest neighborhoods. His task was to teach an English-Spanish bilingual class of fifth graders. "I walked into my first classroom in 1992," remembered Feinberg, "and, to be honest, got my ass kicked. I'm embarrassed to admit it, but I actually handed out lollipops and invited the kids to call me Mr. F in hopes of getting them to like me."

Nearby, Levin met an equally difficult task. He had been assigned to Bastian Elementary School, Houston's lowest-performing elementary school, and charged with leading a self-contained class of sixth graders. "The senior teachers in the school," said Levin, "were taking bets, actual bets, on how long I would survive. They were sure that the day would come when I would simply stop showing up. It was complete chaos initially. I was lost. The kids were out of control."

In the ensuing two years, exhaustion, professional solitude, and frustration followed Levin and Feinberg as they fought to master their craft. Their persistent search for mentors and master teachers helped their cause. Harriet Ball, a fellow elementary school teacher in Houston, figured prominently in Levin's and Feinberg's development.

"Mike and I met Harriet Ball during our first year in Houston," explained Levin. "In our free periods, we would sit in on her class. She taught us almost everything we know about teaching. We adopted her use of chants and rhymes, her ways of relating to kids, and her views of discipline and community accountability."

In addition to Ball, Rafe Esquith influenced Feinberg and Levin. A fifth- and sixth-grade teacher in Los Angeles, Esquith had achieved standout results with poor and minority students. His approach to teaching involved a combination of extended day schooling, demanding expectations, and total commitment by teachers, students, and parents. Feinberg recalled the duo's encounter with Esquith:

> Dave and I saw Rafe Esquith speak in the fall of 1993 just as we were beginning our second year in Houston. He preached longer days, hard work, high expectations, and college entry for all kids. His fifth and sixth graders, almost all of whom were poor and spoke a language other than English as their primary language, were reading Shakespeare, doing advanced math, and coming back year after year to study with him. Everything he described resonated with what we were beginning to learn firsthand. He was speaking right to us. Our jaws were on the floor.

Levin went on: "Rafe didn't claim he was a better teacher than anyone. He just said he worked harder than most. That was helpful to Mike and me because, however good or bad we were at the time, we knew we had stamina and grit. Over and over, he repeated that good teaching was built on simple ideas, reflected in aphorisms like, 'Work hard. Be nice' and 'There are no shortcuts.'"

The First KIPP Classroom, 1994–1995

In their second year of teaching, as they improved and deepened their insights about effective schooling, Feinberg and Levin grew increasingly dissatisfied with the common run of schools around them. They resolved to launch a self-contained classroom program for fifth graders and, in the fall of 1993, wrote a formal proposal to Houston district officials. In their proposal, Levin and Feinberg offered to coteach a fifth-grade classroom in a format that stressed high expectations and hard work. Levin and Feinberg requested permission to keep their students in class from 7:30 a.m. to 5 p.m. on weekdays, for half the day on Saturdays, and for one extra month of summer school. They would require parents and students to sign commitment contracts. To run their program, Levin and Feinberg also petitioned for freedom to manage their own materials budget and curriculum. Levin and Feinberg promised academic results to the district.

At the school district headquarters in Houston, the proposal stalled for months.

"When one senior manager finally read the report," noted Levin, "she asked us why we had picked such a small font size for our document. After reading our request, another district leader didn't understand what was new about KIPP since we weren't proposing some new curriculum. Our plan was to teach harder and longer and to expect more from students. We admitted that we do it with hodgepodge of existing materials and teaching techniques that we had lifted and modified from others."

Levin and Feinberg pushed on in the face of the district's indifference. "By April of 1994," said Levin, "our proposal had languished for seven months at district central offices. In that time, while teaching full time, Mike and I had scraped together $3,000 in donations to supplement whatever funding we might get from the district, and we had gathered significant interest from parents."

In the spring of 1994, the district finally relented and assigned the young teachers to a vacant art room in the elementary school where Feinberg was working. With a green light from central, Feinberg and Levin raced in the late spring of 1994 to enroll students and to prepare for their launch the following September. To recruit students, Levin and Feinberg walked house to house in Houston's poorest Hispanic neighborhoods. Feinberg recalled:

> Here came two tall white guys with bad Spanish. When we knocked, parents thought we had taken a wrong turn and were looking for directions back to our part of town. We'd sit in modest living rooms and talk to first-generation Hispanic immigrants about how all kids could learn, about how to succeed in America, and about how their child could climb the mountain to college. We would tell them about the work that was needed and promise them that it was worth the effort. I'll never forget those initial house calls. When you look people in the eye and make them a promise, you better honor your part of the deal.

In the summer of 1994, Levin and Feinberg opened the doors of their single classroom to 50 fifth graders, almost all of whom were poor and Hispanic and two-thirds of whom arrived from bilingual programs with limited English skills. An intense and formative year followed for Levin and Feinberg, one marked both by deep trust and collaboration and by constant and sometimes heated debate. Feinberg remembered:

> Dave and I taught our hearts out that year. We were in our mid-20s, and the district had given us our own group of kids. They were ours to teach. We were working out how to make operational the principles in which we believed so strongly. We had deep beliefs about the capacity of our kids and about the consequences of hard work and high expectations, but we were only just beginning to translate them into successful and practical teaching.

Levin continued:

> We were responsible for our own fate and had to figure out precisely how to grab and hold these kids, how to build a predictable and controlled environment around them, and how to teach them. We worked until we dropped. After the KIPPsters went home, we spent nights figuring out what we could do better. I remember one entire evening spent arguing with Mike over how best to write an equation on the board. We couldn't let up. We had asked these kids and their parents to believe, to make a commitment, and to join the KIPP family. We had painted them a picture of the mountaintop. We had to deliver.

And deliver they did. By year's end, Levin and Feinberg joined ranks with master teachers like Esquith and Ball. Half of their students began the year with failing scores on the math and English sections of the Texas Assessment of Academic Skills (TAAS), a set of state-administered standardized tests. By the summer of 1995, after a year under Levin and Feinberg's tutelage, 98% of the students passed both tests.

In testing their students and reporting their results, Levin and Feinberg purposefully claimed no exemptions for any of their students, a policy that ran counter to the common practice among principals of excluding students with special education status, bilingual status, and other learning impairments from school-level achievement reports. Levin and Feinberg maintained this stance even though a majority of their students qualified as bilingual students and even though many of their students initially exhibited behavioral patterns consistent with low-level special education diagnoses.

Feinberg and Levin succeeded with their first group of KIPP students despite continued interference from administrators. "At one point," recalled Levin, "they moved us without warning from our single classroom to two smaller, adjacent classrooms. They didn't realize or didn't care that we couldn't split the kids up. To coteach these kids, we had to keep them together and monitor them constantly. So we crammed all of our babies into one room and taught all 50 of them in one regularly sized classroom."

Planning the KIPP Schools

Energized by their success, Levin and Feinberg set their sights on launching a full middle school program. Loyalty to their students explained Levin and Feinberg's determination to develop a full school. Levin reflected:

> We didn't want to create a situation where, year after year, we sent our fifth graders back out there after just one year with us. We saw what happened to them. They sank back into apathy or, worse, into crime, gangs, drugs, and teenage pregnancy. In 1994, the elementary school that housed us fed its students to a nearby middle school where only 17% of the students progressed through high school and applied to college. Those few that applied to college had an average combined SAT score of 700. We couldn't sacrifice our kids to that future.

In late 1994, while coteaching their first KIPP classroom, Levin and Feinberg approached the district to negotiate for the expansion of their KIPP program into a full middle school from fifth to eighth grade. Levin and Feinberg proposed opening their school with a single class of fifth graders and adding a grade each year so as to reach a full middle school over several years.

Like their proposal to open their first classroom, Feinberg and Levin's pitch to start a full middle school met a cool reception at headquarters. So slow was the response in Houston that Feinberg and Levin initiated conversations with district officials in New York, Levin's hometown, about opening a KIPP middle school in the Bronx. Unlike Houston, New York seemed interested, a development that caught press coverage in a local Houston newspaper. With the press involved, the Houston school district engaged Feinberg and Levin and offered to support their middle school plan.

Consequently, by the spring of 1995, Feinberg and Levin held offers to open schools in both New York and Houston. Levin and Feinberg accepted both. "We took both deals," explained Feinberg, "because we were young and dumb. Somehow, after three years of working together, Dave and I thought we had enough momentum and confidence to step into running two schools. So that's what we did." In finalizing their negotiations in New York and Houston, Feinberg and Levin insisted on and won significant control over their schools' academic schedule, hiring and firing decisions for their classroom staff, and curriculum design.

With their approvals in place, Levin and Feinberg stepped up the pace in the spring and summer of 1995 to prepare for their school openings. Feinberg received classroom space in modular trailers stationed in the parking lot of Lee High School, in the Gulfton section of Houston. Lee High was one of Houston's most feared schools. The school had the highest ratio of English-deficient students of any school in the city, and its zip code had one of the worst juvenile crime profiles in Texas.

To recruit a fresh batch of fifth graders, Feinberg picked up where he and Levin had left off the prior summer. Walking door to door in Gulfton, Feinberg visited with immigrant families. Sharing stories of the prior year and the success he and Levin had seen, Feinberg won the confidence of almost all the families he met and, within months, had assembled a class of 72 fifth graders.

To teach them, Feinberg recruited three full-time teachers. Two of them were fellow TFA graduates. The third was the twin sister of a former girlfriend. "I didn't know anything about hiring or managing teachers, nor did I really have any time to think about it," mused Feinberg. "I hired a few and figured that if things didn't work out I would just teach all 72 kids myself and get new teachers for the next year."

In the summer of 1995, only months before opening his school, Feinberg received news that he had been evicted from his modular classrooms in the parking lot of Lee High School. The principal of Lee High School had reclaimed the space to meet an unexpected surge in enrollment. Feinberg scrambled to save his plans and was reassigned to classroom space in a school located 40 minutes by bus from Lee High School and the Gulfton neighborhood in which he had recruited most of his students. "It was hectic," remembered Feinberg. "One of the hardest parts of the move was my having to go back to my KIPPsters and convince them to ride the bus for hours every day to our new location."

At the same time, in New York, Levin worked with equal determination. Because of his teaching commitments in Houston, Levin arrived in New York in June of 1995 with less than two months to organize his school. Levin was granted space in an existing school complex in the Bronx, just north of the Harlem River. Levin shared space in the complex with several other schools.

To recruit his students, Levin resorted again to door knocking. This time, Levin's travels required him to communicate to a predominantly African-American constituency of parents and students who, unlike the first-generation Hispanic immigrants in Houston, had often endured multiple generations of poverty and racism and who harbored deep skepticism toward appeals by outsiders. To staff his school in its first year, Levin hired one full-time teacher who, like Feinberg's initial hires, had graduated from TFA.

The KIPP Academies, 1995–1999

From their launch in 1995, the KIPP academies grew steadily. By the fall of 1998, the Houston and New York schools enrolled approximately 300 and 220 students, respectively. KIPP students were almost universally poor and nonwhite. Each year from 1995 to 1999, the percentage of students in the schools who were poor and minority hovered north of 90%.

The KIPP schools were public schools. Revenue for both schools came from public funds controlled either by school districts or state agencies. Both schools admitted children by blind lottery and without regard to prior achievement, special education needs, or bilingual status. The only unusual attribute of the schools admission policy was the requirement that parents and students sign KIPP commitment forms, documents that delineated clearly the roles and responsibilities of teachers, parents, and students in KIPP schools.

From 1995 to 1999, the KIPP schools operated variously as district contract schools and as charter schools. Initially, both schools held contracts with the school districts in Houston and New York. These contracts, backed by various verbal agreements and understandings, defined the relationship between the Houston and New York districts and the schools, including the districts' obligation to fund the schools and provide various services, including food and transportation.

Later, in the late 1990s, both schools converted to charter schools. In 1998, KIPP Houston became a state charter school and, as such, received funding and oversight directly from the Texas Education Agency on the basis of state law. In 1999, KIPP New York converted to a district charter school. As a district charter school, KIPP New York was granted special financial and staffing freedoms from the superintendent's office in New York. In negotiating the various contracts and charter agreements that authorized and governed their schools, Levin and Feinberg sought to maximize their managerial freedom.

As a state charter school beginning in 1998, KIPP Houston operated independently of human resource and financial policies of the Houston school district. Moreover, since Texas did not sanction collective bargaining by teachers, Feinberg worked without the typical constraints of union contracts. Feinberg was free to dismiss teachers without compliance with lengthy legal processes, to compensate teachers as he saw fit, and to hire teachers without regard to detailed teacher-credentialing rules.

By contrast, KIPP New York, both as a contract school and a district charter school, employed teachers who were protected, at least nominally, by the district's contract with the teachers union. As a result, Levin was required technically to match the seniority-driven pay scales defined in the union contract, to hire only legally credentialed teachers, and to honor the extensive contract provisions that protected teachers identified for dismissal. In practice, though, Levin did not feel unmanageably inhibited by the union status of his school. This was so partly because of his well-developed ability to pressure underperforming teachers to self-assign out of his school.

Culture

Explicit and sustained commitments by students, teachers, and parents were the hallmark of the KIPP schools. All parents, teachers, and students signed commitment contracts that made explicit a variety of KIPP policies, notably the schools' extraordinarily long school day and year. Keeping with what they had begun in Houston, Feinberg and Levin ran their schools from 7:30 a.m. to 5 p.m. on weekdays, for several hours on Saturdays, and for a month over the summer. In the evenings, they kept their buildings open for students who preferred or needed to study away from home.

Commitment contracts asked parents to check homework every night, to read to their children whenever possible, and to accept general responsibility for the consequences, which could include expulsion, of failing to honor their contract. Students, in addition to accepting the long KIPP school day and year, agreed to help one another, to ask questions in class if they were confused, and to take responsibility for their own actions and their place in their KIPP community. Teachers promised in writing "to do whatever it takes" for their students to learn. This commitment included carrying pagers and cell phones 24 hours per day to answer homework questions from students. (See **Exhibit 1** for excerpts from KIPP contracts.)

KIPP schools exhibited unusually high levels of discipline. In both schools, when visitors entered classrooms, students remained unwaveringly focused on their work. Between classes,

KIPP students walked in neat lines. Over lunch, they ate with the manners of adults. In New York, Levin barred students from wearing baseball caps, makeup, artificial nails, baggy pants, and hoop earrings.

KIPP teachers in both schools could share endless anecdotes about discipline. One teacher in Houston offered:

> The other day, an argument broke out on the school bus about a Game Boy console. One student called the other a mother f—— within earshot of the bus driver. When the kids came off the bus, I sat them down and reminded them that they had failed to live up to the KIPP maxim, "Work hard. Be nice." I told them that they had ignored the KIPP rule for riding the bus, which is, "Sit back and enjoy the ride." I had them write essays about how to ride on the bus. I called home to talk with their parents. I suspended them both from several weekend field trips. And I porched them both.

At KIPP Houston, misbehaving students were often porched. A porched student was required, for some period of days or weeks, to wear his school uniform inside out, to refrain from any conversation with other students, and to eat and study on the porches. Porches were isolated areas of chairs and tables in each classroom and in the school lunchroom. Above each porch hung a banner that read, "If you can't run with the big dogs, stay on the porch." When porched, students were required to write individual letters of apology for their behavior to classmates in their homerooms.

In another story of student discipline, a KIPP New York teacher recalled:

> Our kids know to start their work if a teacher is late. Yesterday, I purposefully waited outside my classroom after the beginning of class to see how my students would act. A few of them slacked off and talked instead of staying on task. Worse yet, when I walked in and asked the class if everyone had begun their work in my absence, one of the misbehaving students didn't volunteer that he had been talking. I called him out and explained that he had broken my trust and the trust of his peers, including his classmates who had been honorable enough to admit their mistake. I reminded him that he had the mountain of college to climb, and I told him that he would need months to win back my trust in him as an honest KIPPster.

Occasionally, transgressions required expulsion. Feinberg elaborated:

> One year in Houston, we had a boy who joined the school in seventh grade. That's unusual since we don't admit many kids in the later grades. In the first few weeks of school, this boy was caught stealing a toy from another student. He eventually admitted to the theft and was given a chance to apologize to his fellow KIPPsters and to make the case for why he should stay in the KIPP family. Afterwards, I let the students vote on whether to expel him. They didn't believe he was sincere in his apology, and they believed he would steal again. They voted to expel him. So, that's what I did. I think the kids knew what was at stake for the boy and what was likely to happen to him out there. I also think they realized the effect that a bad element could have on their team. Expelling a student is extremely hard on everyone. But the good of the entire team must come first.

The KIPP schools coupled tough discipline with strong positive incentives. For example, students who completed their work and behaved well were eligible for monthly field trips to museums, sports events, and historic sites. At the end of each year, students in good standing were invited on a long-distance field trip. On this trip, fifth graders went to Washington, D.C., sixth graders to the national parks in Utah, seventh graders to the East Coast for a college and city tour, and the eighth graders to Yosemite National Park and the West Coast for a college and city tour. Moreover, KIPP students received weekly school paychecks by which they accumulated credits to purchase T-shirts, books, and other goods from KIPP school stores. The size of KIPP paychecks depended on the degree to which students mastered their weekly workload and followed KIPP rules.

To communicate the KIPP culture, Levin and Feinberg constantly promoted slogans and rhymes that captured the KIPP model. These included the original phrases "There are no shortcuts" and "Work hard. Be nice" that the duo had borrowed from Esquith. These aphorisms appeared ubiquitously on classroom walls and hallways. They also adorned school uniforms and all official school communications. The KIPP culture was also reflected in the chants and rhymes that teachers regularly integrated into their teaching plans. KIPP students knew these chants from memory. One frequently recited rhyme ran, "How do we make good grades? We bring our tools and follow the rules. It might sound square, but we're going somewhere." (See **Exhibit 2** for selected KIPP aphorisms and rhymes.)

Teachers

KIPP teachers were, in many cases, in their 20s, unmarried, and without children. Feinberg and Levin staffed their schools heavily with recruits from the TFA alumni network. Teachers averaged less than five years of experience. In New York, where Levin had purposefully sought more senior teachers, two-thirds of the staff had more than five years experience, and several teachers had over 20 years experience.

Though they worked long days, often arriving at the school at 7 a.m and working into the evening, KIPP teachers invested their time heavily in professional development and preparation. In New York, for example, teachers averaged only five hours in the classroom each day. Much of the remaining time was spent on lesson planning, often supervised by Levin.

KIPP teachers earned approximately 25% more than they would in the regular public schools of New York and Houston. Extra pay resulted primarily from extended hours. Levin and Feinberg also distributed small performance bonuses to teachers. In New York, annual salaries averaged $45,000. The most senior teachers in New York, some of whom had 15 years' experience, earned $70,000. The KIPP schools funded their operating costs, almost all of which were salary related, from standard per pupil allocations that they received under their contractual and charter agreements.

By 1999, teacher turnover in the KIPP schools ranged annually from 15% to 20%. Each school maintained staffs of fewer than 20 teachers. In the opinion of Feinberg and Levin, KIPP's demanding work ethic did not cause turnover. Rather, according to the school founders, teachers often left KIPP because they did not have the skills to teach. "Some new teachers just don't have the confidence and charisma it takes to lead these kids," explained Levin. In addition, teachers occasionally left KIPP out of irreconcilable differences with Feinberg and Levin over the KIPP program.

Instruction

The KIPP academies emphasized mastery of core academic subjects, particularly reading, writing, and math. The schools' long hours were central to their academic mission. KIPP students spent approximately 66% more time in class than their peers in regular public schools. The extra time was needed, in part, to compensate for incoming students' academic deficits. Tutoring and one-on-one instruction featured prominently in the KIPP program. (See **Exhibit 3** for an overview of courses at KIPP Houston.)

KIPP teachers shared common approaches to classroom discipline and, especially in New York, followed schoolwide norms about structuring lesson plans around consistent openings and board plans. Within those parameters, however, teachers were free to develop their own instructional styles and techniques. The KIPP schools, for example, had no fixed stance on how to teach reading. Levin commented:

> If teachers approach their work coherently and show results, then they can operate freely in our classrooms. There is no religion here about this or that curriculum. We teach what works. What emerges across our classrooms is an eclectic and integrated set of techniques and instructional approaches. For example, we teach reading by combining the best elements of direct instruction, whole language instruction, and reader's workshop.

Feinberg echoed Levin, "Our curriculum is not rocket science. We lengthened the day, and we work hard. That creates more time for reading and math, and we use that time to teach in ways that work. That's the story, basically. It's not flashy."

Leadership

From their beginning, the KIPP schools reflected the relentless and passionate leadership of Levin and Feinberg. Both principals lived by the KIPP work ethic and regularly arrived at school at 6 a.m. and left close to midnight. "You can't expect people to be on time if you're not on time," summarized Levin. "You can't expect people to be consistent if you're not consistent. You can't expect people to be humble and honest and hungry if you're not honest and humble and hungry."

Levin and Feinberg tended carefully to their star teachers. One year, for example, Levin convinced a supporter of KIPP New York to donate frequent flier miles so that an exhausted teacher could take a hiking vacation in Colorado. Another year, Levin accompanied some of his teachers to Atlantic City to listen to their concerns regarding the school.

A teacher in Houston recalled a memorable episode involving Feinberg:

> By 1997, we had reached 230 students in Houston. We were running three grades and had about a dozen teachers. One day that year, Mike walked into a classroom where a couple of teachers had seventh and eighth graders watching a movie clip from ***West Side Story.*** I think the students had been reading the book and were watching the movie in parallel. Some of the students were talking, rather than paying attention, and the teachers weren't intervening. Mike saw this and was incredibly upset. He walked out of the room and spent the rest of the day thinking about what to do. The next day, he called the students and teachers together and, for a while, just stood quietly in front of them. The teachers and students figured out pretty quickly that something was up. After sitting in silence for a while, Mike explained to the kids that they had been merely regular students the day before, not KIPPsters, and that they had broken their promise to each other, their parents, and the school. He asked each student to write an essay for the next day about the difference between watching a movie as a regular student and as a KIPPster. The next day, one kid had blown off the assignment and turned in a three-line essay. Mike was so disappointed and angry that, in full view of the teachers, he threw a chair out the window. He then assigned the student a daily 10-page essay for two weeks.

Academic Results

From 1995 to 1999, students in Levin and Feinberg's schools excelled academically. Each year in Houston, for example, almost 100% of Feinberg's students, in all grades, passed all sections of the state-administered Texas Assessment of

Academic Success. These success rates applied even to KIPP Houston's fifth graders, many of whom entered the school in need of remediation, and even during the 1995 school year, Feinberg's first as a solo principal. In 1995, only one-third of Feinberg's first incoming class of fifth graders had passed both the math and reading section of the state exams in the prior year. By the summer of 1996, more than 90% of pupils in KIPP Houston passed both halves of the test. (See **Exhibit 4** for schoolwide test results in KIPP Houston.)

In addition to monitoring performance on standardized tests, Feinberg tracked the grade-level improvement of his students. KIPP Houston's first batch of fifth graders arrived at the school in 1995 with fifth-grade math skills and approximately fourth-grade reading and writing skills. Four years later, as they completed eighth grade in the summer of 1999, these students had progressed an average of 7.3 grade levels in each major subject area. In math alone, Feinberg's first graduates had advanced 10 grade levels and were more skilled in math than an average American high school graduate. (See **Exhibit 5** for data on grade-level proficiency in KIPP Houston and **Exhibit 6** for data on KIPP Houston's performance relative to other Texas middle schools.)

Levin had also achieved strong academic results in New York. In 1999, for example, KIPP New York was selected as the best-performing public middle school in the Bronx for the second year in a row. Approximately one-third of the fifth graders admitted to his school each year met grade-level proficiency standards in reading and math. Typically, by the time these fifth graders entered seventh grade at KIPP New York, two-thirds of them were functioning at or above grade level in both math and science. That all but a third of Levin's students were fully remediated by eighth grade was notable. In adjacent Bronx middle schools, schoolwide failure rates regularly surpassed 80%. In each of KIPP New York's first four years of operation, Levin and his teaching team had improved the rate and frequency with which their students reached grade-level mastery in core subjects.

The KIPP schools excelled at more than standardized tests. For example, from 1995 to 1999, daily attendance and annual promotion rates hovered near 100% at both schools, and both schools maintained waiting lists with hundreds of students. Early data also indicated that KIPP graduates would succeed in high school. In 1999, over 95% of Levin's first graduating class in New York gained admission to top New York parochial and magnet schools. High school admission results were equally impressive in Houston. KIPP graduates often earned scholarships to attend selective private and parochial schools. The 1999 graduating class in Houston, for example, had earned more than $1 million in academic scholarships to private, parochial, and boarding schools. (See **Exhibit 7** for a sample of high schools attended by graduates from KIPP Houston. See **Exhibit 8** for national data on the effect of family, community, and school variables on student outcomes.)

The KIPP schools flourished from 1995 to 1999 despite ongoing school district intransigence and neglect. For example, in its first four years, KIPP Houston moved five times. At one point, Feinberg set up school in unused administrative offices at district headquarters, a situation that required him and his team to use kitchenettes as classrooms.

By 1999, school-wide student attrition at the KIPP Academies in Houston and New York had stabilized at approximately 3% per year. Accordingly, approximately 12% of students in an entering cohort of 4th graders left the schools before graduation 4 years later. Feinberg and Levin testified that, with the exception of an occasional expulsion, attrition occurred primarily in situations where families needed to move away from Houston and New York.

The National Spotlight and New Aspirations

As Levin and Feinberg developed their schools from 1995 to 1999, public interest in their work grew steadily. During this period, for example, every major newspaper in the United States covered KIPP. Some publications, including *The New York Times*, the *Los Angeles Times*, and *The Washington Post* repeatedly wrote about the program. Journalists as far away as Japan, Mexico, and France had picked up KIPP.

Politicians from both sides of the ideological spectrum embraced KIPP. By 1999, for example, the Children's Defense Fund had honored the KIPP schools. Concurrently, Texas Governor Bush had visited KIPP Houston in 1998 and mentioned it by name in his first campaign speech for president in September 1999.

In the spring of 1999, CBS television journalist Mike Wallace visited the Houston and New York schools to film a segment on KIPP for the program *60 Minutes*. When the piece aired in September 1999, Levin, Feinberg, and their KIPP schools became subjects of national interest. Feinberg remembered the aftermath of his and Levin's prime-time television debut:

> Press coverage and public interest in KIPP had been building for some time. But when the ***60 Minutes*** piece ran in the fall of 1999, the lid blew off. The phones were ringing all day long in our offices. I was taking calls from foundations, reporters, superintendents, and politicians. You name them. They were calling. One day, I picked up my cell phone, and it was the superintendent of a California school district. He said, "Mr. Feinberg, please, I want to order 15 KIPP schools for next year."
>
> Independent of their newfound celebrity, Levin and Feinberg had been pondering for some time the possibility of national expansion. Both were ready again for a new challenge.

Scott Hamilton and the Rendezvous in Chicago

In the fall of 1999, the two principals met Hamilton, an introduction that would speed them on their way to national expansion. Hamilton was the managing director of the Pisces Foundation, an education-related philanthropy in San Francisco. Funded by Donald and Doris Fisher, the founders of Gap Inc., the foundation made strategic investments in education reform.

Hamilton visited Feinberg's school in Houston in the fall of 1999 and, soon thereafter, paid Levin a visit in New York. His reaction was immediate, and he quickly sought out Feinberg and Levin about the possibility of the Pisces Foundation investing in the national expansion of the KIPP schools. Levin recalled, "We were approached by a variety of investors and sponsors in the fall of 1999, but most had little idea about what it takes to build a school, much less a series of schools. Scott, on the other hand, immediately understood the KIPP schools, and he had deep experience with start-up schools. We were also intrigued by working with the Fishers who, from building the Gap, understood how to replicate an organization."

Through the fall of 1999, Levin, Feinberg, and Hamilton communicated regularly about a national strategy for the KIPP academies. With a growing sense of progress, the threesome agreed to convene in Chicago for an intense working session. Their aim would be to push their talks toward a finite proposal, one to which Feinberg and Levin could consider committing and one which Hamilton could present formally to the Fishers. The proposal would include, at a minimum, the rationale for expanding nationally and a first draft of an implementation plan.

From their informal talks through the fall, Hamilton, Levin, and Feinberg shared a common strategic outlook. For example, all three were interested in long-term and lasting reform.

Whatever shape their school network might take, Levin, Hamilton, and Feinberg sought meaningful, national impact. They were particularly interested in demonstrating nationally the academic potential of poor and minority students and in promoting a wider understanding of the essential attributes of successful schools. Each of the trio had an approximate sense that their ambitions required rolling out hundreds of schools across the country over a decade or more.

The threesome also agreed that the core attributes of Levin and Feinberg's schools would serve as a starting point for expansion and as a constant in their work. They had generated a list, titled the "KIPP five pillars," of the defining attributes of their schools. These five features were more time on task for students, strong principals with the power to lead, high expectations of students, a school culture focused on objective measures of success, and clear commitments from students, parents, and teachers. (See **Exhibit 9** for details on the KIPP five pillars.)

The Challenges of Scale

These points of clarity aside, Feinberg, Levin, and Hamilton faced a variety of open issues related to the proposed expansion. For starters, to move forward, the threesome would need to develop a clearer view of the role and reach of the national office that would orchestrate the national expansion. The trio agreed that the national office would be located in San Francisco, near the headquarters of the Gap and the Pisces Foundation, and that its primary purposes would be to recruit, train, place, and support principals who would operate KIPP schools. These recruits would need to share Feinberg and Levin's unusual talent for teaching and leading. Exactly how this recruitment and training program would function and how likely it would be to succeed were topics of considerable debate.

Also unclear was the degree to which the national office would take responsibility for the mundane but critical operating challenges of opening and sustaining schools. For example, the trio would need to discuss their approach to winning approvals for new KIPP schools. These schools would presumably be a mix of state charter schools and district contract schools.[1] Hamilton, Levin, and Feinberg appreciated the difficulty of negotiating into district contracts and state charter agreements the financial, regulatory, and personnel autonomy that KIPP schools required.

Facilities issues, especially in the context of charter schools, also ranked high on the trio's list of implementation issues. Charter school operators faced notoriously intractable challenges in locating, financing, and improving leased or owned building space for their schools. The national office would face a choice of how heavily to invest in supporting school leaders in their facilities efforts.

Funding questions were also sure to arise in Feinberg, Levin, and Hamilton's working session. From Levin and Feinberg's experience as principals, the trio had accurate cash flow forecasts for new KIPP schools. These schools, once opened, would collect cash from public sources (i.e., school districts, state legislatures, and the federal government) and from charitable contributions, and they would use cash primarily on teacher salaries and materials. While KIPP schools would receive all manner of technical assistance from the KIPP national office and while KIPP national would seek to retain certain control rights over the schools (e.g., the right to revoke the use of the KIPP brand name and the right to veto a new principal appointment), they would operate as distinct legal entities governed by local boards of trustees and would not receive significant direct cash subsidies from KIPP national. (See **Exhibit 10** for a model KIPP school budget.)

The cashflow model of the national office was heavily dependent on philanthropy. To push their conversations on this point, the trio had drafted a financial forecast for a national office stretching to 2012. This scenario contemplated opening 235 KIPP schools, at a pace of 25 per year, and called for approximately $150 million in cash. Most of this cash would be used to recruit and train principals, conduct outreach to win district contracts and state charters for KIPP schools, and support sitting KIPP principals. Headcount in the national office, under this scenario, would stabilize at 60 within a few years of launch.

One-third of the $150 million needed at KIPP national would come from fees assessed to KIPP schools once they matured. The remaining two-thirds would come from foundations, notably the Pisces Foundation. Hamilton had briefed the Fisher family on the size of the investment that would likely be required to launch and support a national chain of KIPP schools. From this information, the Fishers were not deterred in their potential role as lead investors. That said, the Fishers had cautioned Hamilton, in partnership with Levin and Feinberg, to deliver a thoughtful implementation plan and to articulate opportunities to stage investment, look for partner investors, and reassess operating plans and financing requirements as events unfolded. (See **Exhibit 11** for details on the financial model of KIPP national.)

The question of who would lead KIPP national would also surface in the trio's deliberations. Feinberg and Levin were, on the one hand, obvious candidates to lead the expansion. They had conceived of and built the flagship KIPP schools. On the other hand, neither had run non-school organizations, neither lived in San Francisco, and neither could predict for sure whether they would enjoy leading KIPP national.

Finally, Hamilton, Feinberg, and Levin would need to discuss the path by which they hoped to influence national education reform. That influence would be hard to acquire even under the rosiest of scenarios. The public bureaucracies that operated US public schools and the maze of legal regulations that governed them were profoundly resistant to change. This reality had already led the trio to an uncompromising view that each new KIPP school would need to rival the academic results of KIPP Houston and KIPP New York. Anything short of an undiluted record of break-through success would, in the trio's opinion, expose their efforts to criticism and politicized attack.

Feinberg summarized with his characteristic candor:

> If we want to have national impact, if we want to KIPP-notize the country, then we have to answer the "yes buts." People always say, "Yes, that might work over there, but it won't work here." They make excuses for themselves to avoid making change. There are no excuses. To get that message across, we need to show that we can lead kids up the mountain to college in many places and under many circumstances just as we have in Houston and New York.

Notes

1. Charter schools were sanctioned by state law, and state education agencies (or their nominees) usually approved, funded, and regulated charter schools. State charter school statutes generally funded the operating costs of charter schools without any subsidies for facilities or capital investments. By the end of 1999, 37 states had passed charter school statutes, and 1,700 charter schools served some 350,000 children (less than 2% of US public school students). District contract schools were operated on the basis of contracts issued by public school districts. These contracts typically set districts' per-pupil funding obligations to contract schools, clarified districts' role in providing non-financial assistance to contract schools (for facilities, busing, food services, etc.), and enumerated the degree to which contract schools would by exempt from traditional district oversight and labor contracts.

Exhibit 1

KIPP Academies, Excerpts from Commitment to Excellence Contracts

Contract	*Excerpts*
Teacher Commitment Contract	• We will arrive at KIPP every day by 7:25 a.m. (Monday to Friday). • We will remain at KIPP until 5 p.m. (Monday to Thursday). • We will come to KIPP on appropriate Saturdays at 9 a.m. and remain until 1 p.m. • We will teach at KIPP during the summer (July 17 to August 4). • We will always teach in the best way we know how, and we will do whatever it takes for our students to learn. • We will always make ourselves available to students, parents, and any concerns they might have. • We will always protect the safety, interests, and rights of all individuals in the classroom. • Failure to adhere to these commitments can lead to our removal from KIPP.
Parent Commitment Contract	• We will make sure our child arrives at KIPP every day by 7:25 a.m. (Monday to Friday). • We will make arrangements so our child can remain at KIPP until 5 p.m. (Monday to Thursday). • We will make arrangements for our child to come to KIPP on appropriate Saturdays at 9 a.m. and remain until 1p.m. • We will ensure that our child attends KIPP summer school (July 17 to August 4). • We will always help our child in the best way we know how, and we will do whatever it takes for him/her to learn. This also means that we will check our child's homework every night, let him/her call the teacher if there is a problem with the homework, and try to read with him/her every night. • We will always make ourselves available to our children, the school, and any concerns they might have. This also means that if our child is going to miss school, we will notify the teacher as soon as possible, and we will read carefully all the papers that the school sends home to us. • We will allow our child to go on KIPP field trips. • We will make sure our child follows the KIPP dress code. • We understand that our child must follow the KIPP rules so as to protect the safety, interests, and rights of all individuals in the classroom. We, not the school, are responsible for the behavior and actions of our child. • Failure to adhere to these commitments can cause my child to lose various KIPP privileges and can lead to my child's expulsion from KIPP.
Student Commitment Contract	• I will arrive at KIPP every day by 7:25 a.m. (Monday to Friday). • I will remain at KIPP until 5 p.m. (Monday to Thursday). • I will come to KIPP on appropriate Saturdays at 9 a.m. and remain until 1 p.m. • I will attend KIPP during summer school (July 17 to August 4). • I will always work, think, and behave in the best way I know how, and I will do whatever it takes for my fellow students and me to learn. This also means that I will complete all my homework every night. • I will call my teachers if I have a problem with the homework or a problem with coming to school, and I will raise my hand and ask questions in class if I do not understand something. • I will always make myself available to parents, teachers, and any concerns they might have. • I will always behave so as to protect the safety, interests, and rights of all individuals in the classroom. This also means that I will always listen to all my KIPP teammates and give everyone my respect. • I will follow the KIPP dress code. • I am responsible for my own behavior. • Failure to adhere to these commitments can cause me to lose various KIPP privileges and can lead to my expulsion from KIPP.

Source: Organization documents.

Exhibit 2

KIPP Academies, Selected Chants, Rhymes, and Aphorisms

Topic	*Words*
School Culture[1]	If there's a problem, we look for a solution. If there's a better way, we try to find it. If we need help, we ask. If a teammate needs help, we give. There are no shortcuts. It's not a KIPP thing. It's a life thing. Knowledge is power. Power is freedom. And I want it. Work hard. Be nice.
Academics[2]	The more that you read, The more things you will know. They more you learn, The more places you'll go. This is the room That has the kids Who want to learn To read more books To build a better tomorrow! No need to hope For a good-paying job With your first-grade skills You'll do nothing but rob You got to read, baby, read! You got to read, baby, read! How do we make good grades? We bring out the tools and follow the rules. It might sound square, but we're going somewhere.
Discipline[3]	If you can't run with the big dogs, stay on the porch.

Source: Organization documents.

[1] Statements of culture were continually repeated by staff, displayed ubiquitously inside of the KIPP schools, repeated on school uniforms, and promoted on all KIPP correspondence.

[2] Teachers integrated chants and rhymes in daily teaching plans, often at the beginning of teaching sessions, to captivate and focus students.

[3] The "If you can't run with the big dogs, stay on the porch" slogan hung above the "porches" in KIPP Houston's cafeteria and classrooms, areas where misbehaving students would eat and study alone and in forced silence while wearing their T-shirts inside out.

Exhibit 3

KIPP Houston, Course Offerings

Courses[1]		*Grade 5*	*Grade 6*	*Grade 7*	*Grade 8*[2]
English	English	X	X	X	X
	Independent Reading Workshop	X	X	X	X
	Study Skills	X	X		
	Verbal SAT classes			X	X
History	U.S. History	X			
	Ancient Civilizations		X		
	Current Events	X	X		
	American History (pre-1865)			X	
	American History (post-1865)				X
Math	Math Survey	X			
	Thinking Skills	X			
	Technology	X	X		
	Pre-Algebra		X	X	
	Algebra 1 (A)			X	X
	Algebra 1 (B)				X
	Math SAT classes			X	X
Science	General Science	X			
	Earth Science		X		
	Life Sciences			X	
	Physical Science				X
Spanish	Native Spanish			X	X
	Non-Native Spanish			X	X
Other[3]	Music	X	X		
	Band			X	X

Source: Organization documents.

[1] KIPP Houston graduation requirements included four years of English, history, math, and science and two years of Spanish and art.

[2] In some cases, KIPP schools offered a postgraduate year for students who, after finishing eighth grade, needed another year of study and maturity before advancing to a college preparatory high school. During this year, postgraduates studied, among other courses, biology, geometry, and world history.

[3] In addition to the courses listed here, KIPP Houston offered daily enrichment classes (such as dance, drama, yearbook, baseball, basketball, technology, and ultimate Frisbee) and Saturday enrichment classes (such as chess club, guitar lessons, swimming, self-defense, ballet, and computers).

Exhibit 4

KIPP Houston, Texas Assessment of Academic Skills (TAAS)

	Schoolwide Percentage of Students Passing TAAS[1]			
	1995	*1996*	*1997*	*1998*
Math	96%	95%	97%	99%
Reading	93%	98%	96%	98%
Writing	n/a	n/a	n/a	100%
Science	n/a	n/a	n/a	100%
Social Studies	n/a	n/a	n/a	96%

Source: Organization documents.

[1] In computing these passing rates, KIPP Houston claimed no exemptions for students with learning disabilities or English deficiencies.

Exhibit 5

KIPP Houston, Improvement in Grade Level Proficiency, Class of 1999

	Grade Level Proficiency for Graduating Class of 1999[1]				
	Entering 5th Grade, Summer of 1995	*Entering 6th Grade, Summer of 1996*	*Entering 7th Grade, Summer of 1997*	*Entering 8th Grade, Summer of 1998*	*At Graduation, Summer of 1999*
Reading	4.8	7.0	8.4	9.7	11.7
Math	5.3	7.3	11.4	13.3	15.3
Writing	4.1	5.6	6.3	9.2	9.7

Source: Organization documents.

[1] KIPP Houston tracked grade-level proficiency progress by students' scores on the Woodcock-Johnson test of grade-level proficiency. KIPP Houston administered the test each summer.

Exhibit 6

Texas Middle Schools, 1999[1]

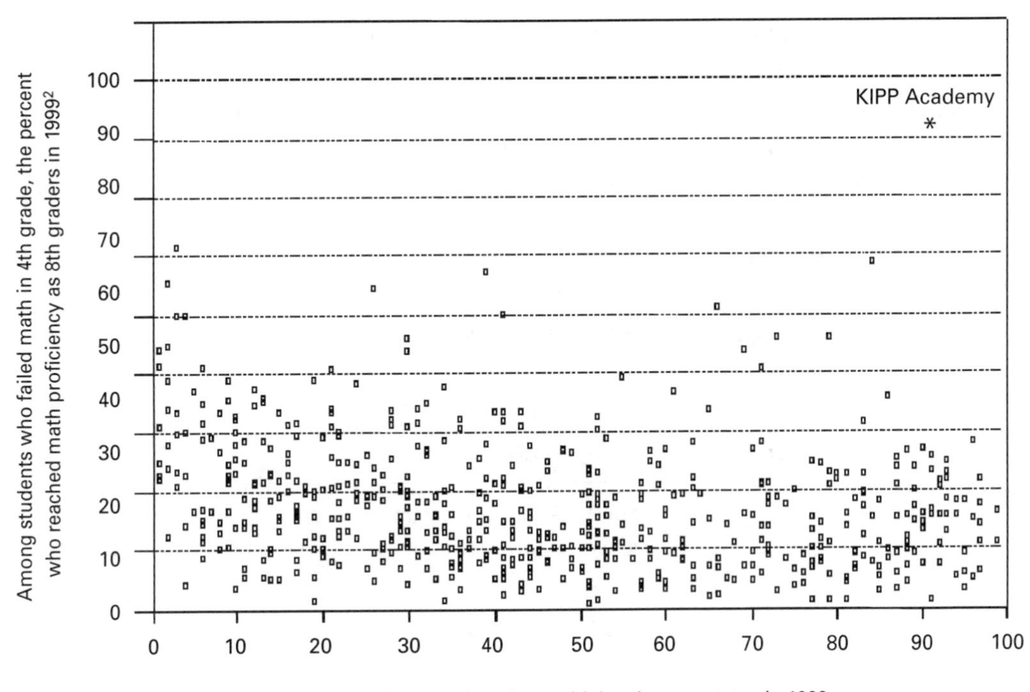

Source: Adapted from Chrys Dougherty, "Mathematics Proficiency of Texas Public Schools Students," Houston Mathema tics Workshop, January 24, 2000.

[1] The sample includes Texas middle schools that had at least 200 students in 1999, that had less than 15% of their students classified as special education students in 1999, and that had at least 15 8th graders in 1999 who had been in the school for two or more years and who had failed math in 4th grade.

[2] The percentage on this axis is equal to the number of 8th graders in a school who reached proficiency in math in 1999 after failing math in 4th grade divided by the number of students in a school who failed math in 4th grade. Failure is defined as a math score of 69 or less on the Texas Learning Index (TLI), an index derived from scores on the math section of the Texas Assessment of Academic Skills (TAAS). Proficiency is defined as a TLI math score of 85 or more.</TFN>

Exhibit 7

KIPP Houston, Selected High Schools Attended by Graduates

Type	*Location*	*Name*
Public Schools	Houston, TX	Bellaire Foreign Language Magnet High School
	Houston, TX	DeBakey Health Professions Magnet High School
	Houston, TX	High School for Performing and Visual Arts
	Houston, TX	YES College Preparatory High School
Private Schools	Houston, TX	Duchesny Academy
	Houston, TX	The Kinkaid Academy
	Houston, TX	St. John's School
	Houston, TX	Strake Jesuit College Preparatory
	Houston, TX	The Awty International School
	Houston, TX	St. Thomas High School
	Houston, TX	St. Agnes Academy
Boarding Schools	MA	Phillips Andover Academy
	MA	St. Mark's School
	MA	Concord Academy
	CT	The Hotchkiss School
	CT	Pomfret School
	NH	Phillips Exeter Academy
	RI	St. Andrews School
	TX	Chinquapin
	TX	Hockaday School
	TX	Saint Mary's Hall
	TX	Texas Military Institute
	CA	Thatcher School
	CA	Cate School
	TN	Baylor School
	NC	The Asheville School
	VA	Foxcroft School
	PA	George School
	IL	Lake Forest Academy

Source: Organization documents.

Exhibit 8

Variations in Student Outcomes

	Percentage of Variation Explained By:		
	Family Variables	*Neighborhood Variables*	*School Input Variables*
Variations in 12th Grade Math Scores	93.4%	3.8%	2.8%
Variations in Income at Age 33	89.8%	6.3%	3.9%
Variations in Education Attainment at Age 33	91.5%	4.8%	3.7%
Illustrative Variables	Parental education level, family income, number of siblings, family ethnicity, parental attendance at school events, parental knowledge of graduation requirements, number of books at home, family visits to museums.	Mean household income and other household income measures, income inequality index, ethnicity of population, education level of adult population.	Per-pupil spending, average class size, teacher salary measures (minimums, maximums, and average), teacher attributes (specialization level, education level, experience level).

Source: Adapted by case writer from Caroline Hoxby, "If Families Matter Most, Where Do Schools Come In," in *A Primer on America's Schools*, edited by Terry Moe (Stanford, CA: Hoover Institution Press, 2001).

Note: Hoxby analyzed data from the National Educational Longitudinal Survey, which began following 25,000 eighth graders in 1988, and data from the National Longitudinal Survey of Youth, which began following 13,000 teenagers in 1979. Neighborhood variables refer variously to census regions, school districts, and metropolitan areas.

Exhibit 9

KIPP Academies, Five Pillars

Pillar	*Explanation*
More Time	KIPP schools know that there are no shortcuts when it comes to success in academics and life. With an extended school day, week, and year, students have more time in the classroom to acquire the academic knowledge and skills that will prepare them for competitive high schools and colleges, as well as more opportunities to engage in diverse extracurricular experiences.
Choice and Commitment	Students, their parents, and the faculty of each KIPP school choose to participate in the program. No one is assigned or forced to attend these schools. Everyone must make and uphold a commitment to the school and to each other to put in the time and effort required to achieve success.
Power to Lead	The principals of KIPP schools are effective academic and organizational leaders who understand that great schools require great school leaders. They have control over their school budget and personnel. They are free to swiftly move dollars or make staffing changes, allowing them maximum effectiveness in helping students learn.
High Expectations	KIPP schools have clearly defined and measurable high expectations for academic achievement and conduct that make no excuses based on the background of students. Students, parents, teachers, and staff create and reinforce a culture of achievement and support through a range of formal and informal rewards and consequences for academic performance and behavior.
Focus on Results	KIPP schools focus relentlessly on high student performance on standardized tests and other objective measures. Just as there are no shortcuts, there are no excuses. Students are expected to achieve a level of academic performance that will enable them to succeed in the nation's best high schools, colleges, and the world beyond.

Source: Organization documents.

Exhibit 10

KIPP Model School Budget

	Entire School				Per Student	
	Year 1		*Year 5*		*Year 1*	*Year 5*
Number of Students	80		320			
Revenues						
Local Funds[1]	$415,840	56%	$1,663,360	72%	$5,198	$5,198
Federal Funds[2]	191,280	26%	365,120	16%	2,391	1,141
Grants[3]	130,000	18%	275,000	12%	1,625	859
Total Revenues	737,120	100%	2,303,480	100%	9,214	7,198
Expenses						
Salaries and Benefits						
Instructional Staff	280,440	39%	1,011,211	44%	3,506	3,160
Administrative Staff	24,600	3%	86,100	4%	308	269
Extended Time	38,192	5%	152,767	7%	477	477
	343,232	47%	1,250,078	54%	4,290	3,906
Instruction						
Supplies and Materials	91,170	13%	122,530	5%	1,140	383
Motivators and Rewards	44,000	6%	130,000	6%	550	406
Extended Time Materials	18,263	3%	39,810	2%	228	124
	153,433	21%	292,340	13%	1,918	914
Other						
Administration	48,560	7%	48,480	2%	607	152
Insurance	25,000	3%	55,000	2%	313	172
Food Service	84,480	12%	337,920	15%	1,056	1,056
Rent	54,000	7%	283,179	12%	675	885
Building Operations	19,659	3%	29,459	1%	246	92
	231,699	32%	754,038	33%	2,896	2,356
Total Expenses	728,364	100%	2,296,456	100%	9,105	7,176
Surplus	8,756		7,024		109	22

Source: Organization documents.

[1] Local funds are per-pupil revenues received by schools under their contracts and charter agreements with districts and states.

[2] Federal funds include receipts under various federal education programs paid directly to schools, including aid for schools with high concentrations of poor students.

[3] Grants include funding from foundations and other donors.

Exhibit 11

KIPP National, Cash Flow and Operating Projections, 2002–2012 ($ millions)

	2002	*2003*	*2004*	*2005*	*2006*	*2007*	*2008*	*2009*	*2010*	*2011*
Sources of Cash										
Support from schools[1]	$0.02	$0.6	$1.5	$2.7	$4.0	$5.3	$6.6	$7.9	$9.2	$10.6
Donations and grants[2]	13.6	15.1	14.7	12.4	11.6	10.3	9.0	7.8	6.5	5.3
Total Sources	13.6	15.7	16.2	15.1	15.6	15.6	15.7	15.7	15.8	15.8
Uses of Cash										
Leadership Development										
Selection and Training	1.3	1.6	1.6	1.6	1.6	1.6	1.6	1.6	1.6	1.6
Guides and Other	2.3	2.5	2.5	2.5	2.5	2.5	2.5	2.5	2.5	2.5
Subtotal	3.6	4.1	4.1	4.1	4.1	4.1	4.1	4.1	4.1	4.1
School Development										
Trailblazing and Recruiting[3]	1.7	1.9	1.9	1.9	1.9	1.9	1.9	1.9	1.9	1.9
Other	.8	1.2	1.4	1.6	1.8	1.8	1.9	1.9	2.0	2.0
Subtotal	2.5	3.1	3.3	3.5	3.7	3.7	3.8	3.8	3.9	3.9
National Office										
National Staff	0.8	0.8	0.8	0.8	0.8	0.8	0.8	0.8	0.8	0.8
Office Rent and Equipment	1.3	1.2	1.3	1.3	1.3	1.3	1.3	1.3	1.3	1.3
Finance and Development	0.6	0.6	0.7	0.7	0.7	0.7	0.7	0.7	0.7	0.7
Other	0.9	1.2	1.2	1.2	1.2	1.2	1.2	1.2	1.2	1.2
Subtotal	3.6	3.9	4.0	4.0	4.0	4.0	4.0	4.0	4.0	4.0
Other										
School Evaluation	1.5	1.5	1.8	0.9	0.9	0.9	0.9	0.9	0.9	0.9
Fellow Compensation[4]	1.2	1.5	1.5	1.5	1.5	1.5	1.5	1.5	1.5	1.5
Annual Operating Reserve	1.2	1.6	1.6	1.2	1.5	1.4	1.5	1.5	1.5	1.5
Subtotal	4.0	4.6	4.9	3.6	3.9	3.9	3.9	3.9	3.9	3.9
Total Uses of Cash	13.6	15.7	16.2	15.1	15.6	15.6	15.7	15.7	15.8	15.8
Operating Forecasts										
# of fellows in training[5]	20	25	25	25	25	25	25	25	25	25
# of school in 1st year	10	20	25	25	25	25	25	25	25	25
Total # of schools[6]	15	35	60	85	110	135	160	185	210	235
Total students[7]	1,920	4,560	9,200	15,600	23,200	31,200	39,200	47,200	55,200	63,200

Source: Organization documents.

[1] Schools contribute 1% of school revenues in year 1 and 3% of school revenue per year subsequently. Accordingly, in fiscal year 2011–12, 25 new schools contribute 1% of revenues and 215 other schools contribute 3% of revenues.

[2] Donations and grants are primarily from the Fisher family and their foundation, the Pisces Foundation.

[3] Trailblazing staff complete early preparation work for launching KIPP schools, including developing relationships with district and state education leaders, negotiating contracts and charter agreements, locating facility sites, and establishing community relationships.

[4] During their training year, fellows receive $60,000 in salary and benefits.

[5] This forecast anticipates 20 principals in training from September 2002 to September 2003.

[6] The calculation of total number of schools includes the two original KIPP schools and 3 new schools opened in 2001–02, and it assumes no school closures.

[7] Total students served by KIPP schools = [number of new schools * 80 students] + [number of 2nd-year schools * 160 students] + [number of 3rd-year schools * 240 students] + [number schools in 4th or later year * 320 students].

John J. Gabarro

Thurgood Marshall High School

On July 15, David Kane became principal of the Thurgood Marshall High School, the newest of the six high schools in Great Falls, Illinois. The school had opened two years earlier amid national acclaim for being an important breakthrough in inner-city education. Among its many features, the school was specially designed and constructed for the "house system" concept. Marshall High's organization was broken down into four "houses," each of which contained 300 students, a faculty of 18, and a housemaster. The Marshall complex was designed so that each house was in a separate building connected to the "core facilities" and other houses by an enclosed outside passageway. Each house had its own entrance, classrooms, toilets, conference rooms, and housemaster's office. (See **Exhibit 1** for the layout.)

Kane knew that Marshall High was not intended to be an ordinary school. It had been hailed as a major innovation in inner-city education, and a Chicago television station had made a documentary about it shortly after it opened. Marshall High had opened with a carefully selected staff of teachers; many were chosen from other Great Falls schools and at least a dozen had been especially recruited from out-of-state. Indeed, Kane knew his faculty included graduates from several East and West Coast schools such as Stanford, Yale, and Princeton, as well as several of the very best Midwestern schools. Even the racial mix of students had been carefully balanced so that African-Americans, whites, and Hispanics each constituted a third of the student body (although Kane also knew—perhaps better than its planners—that Marshall's students were drawn from the toughest and poorest areas of the city). The building itself was also widely admired for its beauty and functionality and had won several national architectural awards.

Despite these careful and elaborate preparations, Marshall High School was in serious difficulty by the time Kane became its principal. It had been wracked by violence the preceding year, having been closed twice by student disturbances and once by a teacher walkout. It was also widely reported (although Kane did not know for sure) that achievement scores of its ninth and tenth grade students had actually declined during the last two years, while no significant improvement could be found in the scores of eleventh and twelfth graders' tests. Marshall High School had fallen far short of its planners' hopes and expectations.

David Kane

An athletic man who stood over 6 feet 4 inches tall, David Kane was born and raised in Great Falls, Illinois. His father was one of the city's first African-American principals; thus Kane was not only familiar with the city but with its school system as well. After serving a tour of duty with the U.S. Marine Corps in Viet Nam, Kane decided to follow his father's footsteps and went to Great Falls State College, from which he received both his bachelor's and master's degrees in education. Kane was certified in elementary and secondary school administration, English, and physical education. Kane had taught English and had coached in a predominantly African-American middle school until ten years ago, when he was asked to become the school's assistant principal. After five years in that post, he was asked to take over the George La Rochelle Middle School, which had 900 pupils and was reputed to be the most difficult middle school in the city. While at La Rochelle, Kane gained a citywide reputation for being a gifted and popular administrator and was credited with turning La Rochelle around from the worst middle school in the system to one of the best. He had been very effective in building community support, recruiting new faculty, and raising academic standards. He was also credited with turning out basketball and baseball teams that won state and county middle school championships. Kane knew that he had been selected for the Marshall job over several more senior candidates because of his ability to handle tough situations. The superintendent had made that clear when he offered Kane the job.

The superintendent had also told him that he would need every bit of skill and luck he could muster. Kane knew of the formidable credentials of Dr. Louis Parker, his predecessor at Marshall High. Parker, a white, had been the superintendent of a small, local township school system before becoming Marshall's first principal. He had also written a book on the house system concept as well as a second book on inner-city education. Parker had earned a Ph.D. from the University of Chicago and a divinity degree from Harvard. Yet despite his impressive background and obvious ability, Parker had resigned in disillusionment and was described by many as a broken man. In fact, Kane remembered seeing the physical change that Parker had undergone over that two-year period. Parker's appearance had become progressively more fatigued and strained until he developed what appeared to be permanent dark rings under his eyes and a perpetual stoop. Kane remembered how he had pitied him and wondered how Parker could find the job worth the obvious personal toll it was taking.

History of the School

The First Year

The school's troubles became apparent in the school's first year. Rumors of conflicts between the housemasters and the six subject area department heads were widespread by the middle of the first year. The conflicts stemmed from differences in interpretations of curriculum policy on required learning and course content. In response to these conflicts, Parker had instituted a "free market" policy by which department heads were to encourage housemasters to offer certain courses, while housemasters were to convince department heads to assign certain teachers to their houses. Many observers in the school system felt that this policy exacerbated the conflicts.

To add to this climate of conflict, a teacher was assaulted in her classroom in February. The beating frightened many of the staff, particularly some of the older teachers. A delegation of eight teachers asked Parker to hire security guards a week after the assault. The request precipitated a debate within the faculty about the desirability of having guards in the school. One group felt that the guards would instill a sense of safety within the school and thus promote a better learning climate, while the other group felt that the presence of guards would be repressive and would destroy the sense of community and trust that was developing. Parker refused the request for security guards because he believed that symbolically they would represent everything the school was trying to change. In April a teacher was robbed and beaten in her classroom after school hours and the debate was rekindled, except this time a group of Latino parents threatened to boycott the school unless better security measures were instituted. Again Parker refused the request for security guards.

The Second Year

The school's second year was even more troubled than the first. Because of budget cutbacks ordered during the previous summer, Parker was not able to replace eight teachers who resigned during the summer; it was no longer possible, therefore, for each house to staff all of its courses with its own faculty. Parker therefore instituted a "flexible staffing" policy whereby some teachers were asked to teach students from outside their assigned house; thus, students in the eleventh and twelfth grades were able to take some elective and required courses in other houses. During this period, Wesley Chase, one of the housemasters, publicly attacked the move as a step toward destroying the house system. In a letter to the *Great Falls Times*, he accused the Board of Education of subverting the house concept by cutting back funds.

The debate over the flexible staffing policy was heightened when two of the other housemasters joined a group of faculty and department chairpersons in opposing Wesley Chase's criticisms. This group argued that the individual house faculties of 15 to 18 teachers could never offer their students the breadth of courses that a schoolwide faculty of 65 to 70 teachers could offer and that interhouse cross registration should be encouraged for that reason.

Further expansion of a cross-registration or flexible staffing policy was halted, however, because of difficulties encountered in the scheduling of classes in the fall. Several errors were found in the master schedule that had been planned during the preceding summer. Various schedule difficulties persisted until November, when the vice principal responsible for the scheduling of classes resigned. Burt Wilkins, a Marshall housemaster who had formerly planned the schedule at Central High, assumed the scheduling function in addition to his duties as housemaster. The scheduling activity took most of Wilkins's time until February.

Security again became an issue when three sophomores were assaulted because they refused to give up their lunch money during a "shakedown." It was believed that the assailants were from outside the school. Several teachers approached Parker and asked him to request security guards from the Board of Education. Again he declined, but he asked Bill Jones, a vice principal at the school, to secure all doors except the entrances to each of the four houses, the main entrance to the school, and the cafeteria. This move appeared to reduce the number of outsiders in the school.

In May a disturbance occurred in the cafeteria that grew out of a fight between two boys. The fight spread and resulted in considerable damage to the school, including the breaking of classroom windows and desks. The disturbance was severe enough for Parker to close the school. A number of teachers and students reported that outsiders were involved in the fight and in damaging the classrooms. Several students were taken to the hospital for minor injuries but all were released. A similar disturbance occurred two weeks later and again the school was closed. The Board of Education then ordered a temporary detail of municipal police to the school despite Parker's advice to the contrary. In protest of the assignment of the police detail, 30 of Marshall's 68 teachers staged a walkout that was joined by over half the student body. The police detail was removed from the school, and an agreement was worked out by an ad hoc subcommittee of the Board of Education with informal representatives of teachers who were for and against assigning a police detail. The compromise called for the temporary stationing of a police cruiser near the school.

Kane's First Week at Marshall High

David Kane arrived at Marshall High on Monday, July 15, and spent most of his first week interviewing individually the school's key administrators. (See **Exhibit 2** for a listing of Marshall's administrative staff as of July 15.) He also had a meeting with all of his administrators and department heads on Friday of that week. Kane's purpose in these meetings was to familiarize himself with the school, its problems, and its key people.

His first interview was with William Jones, who was one of his vice principals. Jones, an African-American, had previously worked as a counselor and then as vice principal of a middle school. Kane knew that Jones had a reputation as a tough disciplinarian and was disliked by many of the younger faculty and students. However, Kane had also heard from several teachers, whose judgment he respected, that Jones had been instrumental in keeping the school from blowing apart in the preceding year. It became clear early in the interview that Jones felt more stringent steps were needed to keep outsiders from entering the building. In particular, Jones urged Kane to consider locking all of the school's 30 doors, except for the front entrance, so that everyone would enter and leave through one set of doors. Jones also told him that many of the teachers and pupils had become fearful of being in the building and that "no learning will ever begin to take place until we make it so people don't have to be afraid anymore." At the end of the interview, Jones told Kane that he had been approached by a nearby school system to become its director of counseling but that he had not yet made up his mind. He said he was committed to Marshall High and did not want to leave, but that his decision depended on how hopeful he felt about its future.

As Kane talked with others, he discovered that the "door question" was one of considerable controversy within the faculty and that both pro and con feelings ran high. Two of the housemasters in particular—Wesley Chase, an African-American, and Frank Kubiak, a white—were strongly against closing the house entrances. The two men felt that such an action would symbolically reduce house autonomy and the feeling of distinctness that was a central aspect of the house identity and pride they were trying to build.

Wesley Chase, master of C House, was particularly vehement on this issue as well as on the question of whether students of one house should be allowed to take classes in another house. Chase said that the flexible staffing program introduced the preceding year had nearly destroyed the house concept and that he, Chase, would resign if Kane intended to expand the crosshouse enrollment of students. Chase also complained about what he described as interference from department heads in his teachers' autonomy.

Chase appeared to be an outstanding housemaster from everything Kane had heard about him—even from his many enemies. Chase had an abrasive personality but seemed to have the best operating house in the school and was well liked by most of his teachers and pupils. His program also appeared to be the most innovative of all. However, it was also the program that was most frequently attacked by the department heads for lacking substance and for not covering the requirements outlined in the system's curriculum guide. Even with these criticisms, Kane imagined how much easier it would be if he had four housemasters like Wesley Chase.

During his interviews with the other three housemasters, Kane discovered that they all felt infringed upon by the department heads, but that only Chase and Kubiak were strongly against locking the doors and that the other two housemasters actively favored crosshouse course enrollments. Kane's fourth interview was with the housemaster of A House, Burtram Wilkins, an African-American in his late forties who had been an assistant to the principal of Central High before coming to Marshall. Wilkins spent most of the interview discussing how schedule pressures could be relieved. Wilkins was currently involved in developing the schedule for the new school year until an administrative vice principal was appointed. (Marshall High had allocations for two vice principals and two assistants in addition to the housemasters. See **Exhibit 2**.)

Two pieces of information concerning Wilkins came to Kane's attention during his first week there. The first was that several teachers were circulating a letter requesting Wilkins's removal as a housemaster because they felt he could not control the house or direct the faculty. This surprised Kane, since he had heard that Wilkins was widely respected within the faculty and that he had earned a reputation for supporting high academic standards and working tirelessly with new teachers. However, as Kane inquired further he discovered that although Wilkins was greatly liked within the faculty, he was generally recognized as a poor housemaster. The second piece of information concerned how Wilkins's house compared with the others. Although students had been randomly assigned to each house, Wilkins's house had the largest absence rate and the greatest number of disciplinary problems. Jones had also told him that Wilkins's drop-out rate for the previous year was three times that of any other house.

While Kane was in the process of interviewing his staff, he was called on by Francis Harvey, chairman of the social studies department. Harvey was a native of Great Falls, white, and in his late forties. He was scheduled for an appointment the following week but asked Kane if he could see him immediately. Harvey had heard that a letter was being circulated asking for Wilkins's removal and therefore wanted to present the other side of the argument. He became very emotional during the conversation and said that Wilkins was viewed by many of the teachers and department chairpersons as the only housemaster who was making an effort to maintain high academic standards; his transfer would be seen as a blow to those concerned with quality education. Harvey also described in detail Wilkins's devotion and commitment to the school and the fact that Wilkins was the only administrator with the ability to straighten out the schedule, which he had done in addition to all his other duties. Harvey departed by saying that if Wilkins was transferred, then he, Harvey, would write a letter to the regional accreditation council telling them how standards had sunk at Marshall. Kane assured him that it would not be necessary to take such a drastic measure and that a cooperative resolution would be found. Kane was aware of the accreditation review that Marshall High faced the following April, and he did not wish to complicate the process unnecessarily.

Within 20 minutes of Harvey's departure, Kane was visited by a young white teacher named Tim O'Reilly, who said he had heard that Harvey had come in to see Kane. O'Reilly said he was one of the teachers who organized the movement to get rid of Wilkins. O'Reilly said he liked and admired Wilkins because of his devotion to the school, but that Wilkins's house was so disorganized and discipline so bad that it was nearly impossible to do any good teaching. O'Reilly said that it was "a shame to lock the school when stronger leadership is all that's needed."

Kane's impressions of his administrators generally matched what he had heard about them before arriving at the school. Wesley Chase seemed to be a very bright, innovative, and charismatic leader whose mere presence generated excitement. Frank Kubiak seemed to be a highly competent though not very imaginative administrator, who had earned the respect of his faculty and students. John Di Napoli, a housemaster who was only 26, seemed very bright and earnest but unseasoned and unsure of himself. Kane felt that with a little guidance and training, Di Napoli might have the greatest promise of all. At the moment, however, Di Napoli appeared to be uncertain, and tentative, and Kane suspected that Di Napoli had difficulty simply coping. Wilkins seemed to be a sincere and devoted person who had a good mind for administrative details but an incapacity for leadership.

Kane knew that he would have the opportunity to make several administrative appointments because of three vacancies that existed. Indeed, should Jones resign as vice principal, Kane could fill both vice principal positions. He knew that his recommendations for these positions would carry a great deal of weight with the central office. The only constraint Kane felt in making these appointments was the need to achieve some kind of racial balance among the Marshall administrative group. With his own appointment as principal, the number of African-American administrators exceeded the number of white administrators by a ratio of two to one, and Marshall did not have a single Latino administrator, even though a third of its pupils had Hispanic surnames.

The Friday Afternoon Meeting

In contrast to the individual interviews, Kane was surprised to find how quiet and conflict-free these same people were in the staff meeting he called on Friday. He was amazed at how slow, polite, and friendly the conversation appeared to be among people who had so vehemently expressed negative opinions of each other in private. After about 45 minutes of discussion about the upcoming accreditation review, Kane broached the subject of housemaster–department head relations. The ensuing silence was finally broken by a joke Kubiak made about the uselessness of discussing that topic. Kane probed further by asking whether everyone was happy with the current practices. Harvey suggested this was a topic that might be better discussed in a smaller group. Everyone in the room seemed to agree with Harvey except for Betsy Drobna, a white woman in her late twenties who chaired the English department. She said that one of the problems with the school was that no one was willing to tackle tough issues until they exploded. She said that relations between housemasters and department heads were terrible, and it made her job very difficult. She then attacked Wesley Chase for impeding her evaluation of a nontenured teacher in Chase's house. The two argued for several minutes about the teacher and the quality of the experimental sophomore English course that the teacher was giving. Finally, Chase, who by now was quite angry, coldly warned Drobna that he would break her neck if she stepped into his house again. Kane intervened in an attempt to cool both their tempers and the meeting ended shortly thereafter.

The following morning, Drobna called Kane at home and told him that unless Wesley Chase publicly apologized for his threat, she would file a grievance with the teachers' union and take it to court if necessary. Kane assured Drobna that he would talk with Chase on Monday. Kane then called Eleanor Dodd, one of the school's math teachers whom he had known well for many years and whose judgment he respected. Dodd was a close friend of both Chase and Drobna and was also vice president of the city's teachers' union. He learned from her that both had been long-term adversaries but that she felt both were excellent professionals.

She also reported that Drobna would be a formidable opponent and could muster considerable support among the faculty. Dodd, who herself was African-American, feared that a confrontation between Drobna and Chase might create tensions along race lines within the school even though both Drobna and Chase were generally quite popular with students of all races. Dodd strongly urged Kane not to let the matter drop. She also told him she had overheard Bill Jones, the vice principal, say at a party the preceding night that he felt Kane didn't have either the stomach or the forcefulness necessary to survive at Marshall. Jones further stated that the only reason he was staying was that he did not expect Kane to last the year. Should that prove to be the case, Jones felt that he would be appointed principal.

Exhibit 1

Thurgood Marshall High School Complex Layout

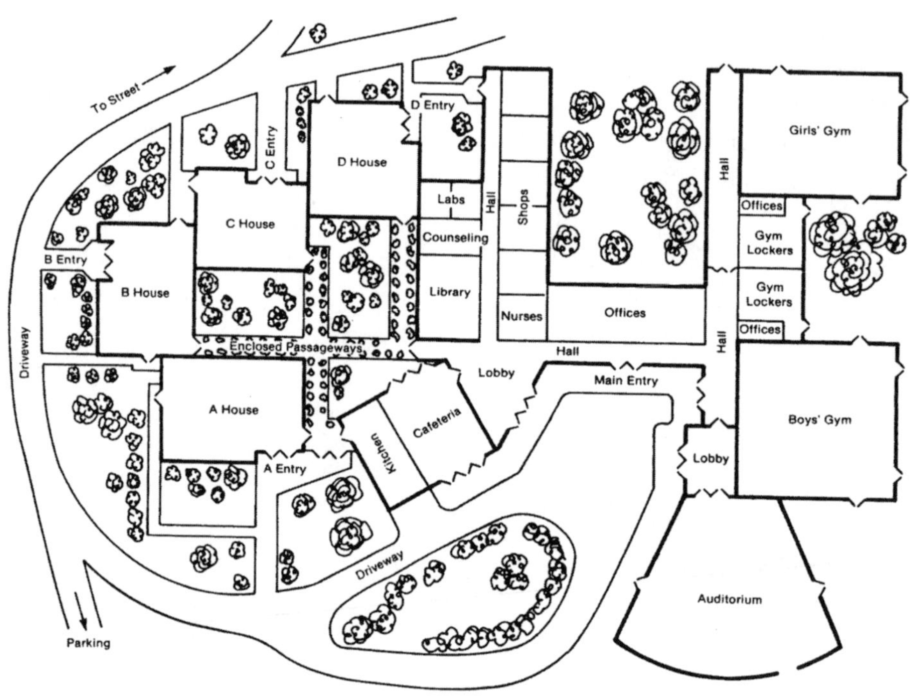

The core facilities included the cafeteria, nurses' room, guidance offices, the boys' and girls' gyms, the offices, the shops, and auditorium.

Exhibit 2

Administrative Organization, Thurgood Marshall High School, Great Falls, Illinois

Principal	David Kane, 42 (African-American) B.Ed., M.Ed., Great Falls State College
Vice Principal	William Jones, 44 (African-American) B.Ed., Breakwater State College M.Ed. (counseling), Great Falls State College
Vice Principal	Vacant
Housemaster, A House	Burtram Wilkins, 47 (African-American) B.S., M.Ed., University of Illinois
Housemaster, B House	Frank Kubiak, 36 (white) B.S., University of Illinois M.Ed., Great Falls State College
Housemaster, C House	Wesley Chase, 32 (African-American) A.B., Wesleyan University B.F.A., Pratt Institute M.A.T., Yale University
Housemaster, D House	John Di Napoli, 26 (Italian-American) B.Ed., Great Falls State College M.Ed., Ohio State University
Assistant to the Principal	Vacant
Assistant to the Principal (for community affairs)	Vacant

CASE 1.3

Stacey Childress ■ Purnima Kochikar

Finding a CEO for the School District of Philadelphia: Searching for a Savior?

"Only a fool would turn down this opportunity," James Gallagher counseled himself in late December 2001 when the Republican governor of Pennsylvania invited him to be a member of the Philadelphia School Reform Commission (SRC). Gallagher, also a Republican, had a distinguished track record in Pennsylvania higher education and currently served as president of Philadelphia University. As a 60-year resident of Philadelphia, he saw the opportunity to serve on the SRC as more than simply his civic duty: "The crisis in our schools was one of the biggest problems facing our city, and I knew that being in a position to work on the solution could be the zenith of my career."

Governor Mark Schweiker created the SRC, a five-member independent governing body, under the authority of Act 46, a piece of legislation that allowed the state to take over the School District of Philadelphia from the city's Democratic mayor and his appointed board of education. He appointed James Nevels as chair. Nevels, a Republican, was the veteran of another state takeover commission in a smaller Pennsylvania school district. He was also the cofounder, chair, and CEO of the Swarthmore Group, one of the largest minority-owned investment management firms in the United States with over $1 billion in assets under management.

Given the district's decade-long downward spiral in fiscal and academic performance, the SRC had a mandate to govern a dramatic turnaround. However, given the crisis—two CEO resignations in two years, a $200 million operating deficit, dismal academic performance, a contentious privatization debate, and escalating school violence—the SRC risked being dragged indefinitely into daily operations unless it quickly found the right CEO.

Nevels and Gallagher agreed the CEO search was the SRC's most important task. "I knew that if we found the right leader, we could set the schools up for success for years," Gallagher explained. Few were surprised when Nevels asked Gallagher to lead the search process. While commissioner of higher education for Pennsylvania, he had run searches for seven university and college presidents, and as a university president he had successfully hired numerous deans and other senior administrators.

On a snowy, blustery day in February 2002, Gallagher paced the length of his impressive wood-paneled office at Philadelphia University, as was his habit when thinking through tough issues. He knew that this search was going to be more complex than any he had led in the past. The standard job description for superintendents seemed inadequate, politically motivated stakeholders from both parties were clamoring to influence the decision, and the futures of tens of thousands of students seemed at stake. Gallagher felt he was looking for a savior, not simply a CEO. Moreover, a recent trend toward hiring big-city superintendents from outside the education establishment meant the field of candidates was wide open. (**Exhibit 1** contains selected superintendent backgrounds.)

Stopping for a moment before his smoldering fireplace, Gallagher jotted down three burning questions the SRC needed to answer: What capabilities and experience would the ideal CEO need to succeed in this difficult context? How should the search be structured not only to identify an attractive set of candidates but also to build public confidence in the fairness of the process? What steps were needed to ensure that the CEO was in place and positioned to succeed before the new school year began in September 2002?

Crisis in Philadelphia

The School District of Philadelphia was the eighth-largest public school system in the United States in the academic year ending 2001. The district had a $1.8 billion annual budget and a preK–12 student population of approximately 205,000. The estimated per student operating expenditure was $7,543, compared with the average Pennsylvania suburban spending of approximately $13,000 per student.[1]

The district employed 11,141 teachers and operated 264 schools. Thirty-eight charter schools also operated within the district. Under the contract of the Philadelphia Federation of Teachers, the powerful teachers' union, seniority and teacher preference were the key determinants in the assignment of educators to school buildings rather than capabilities, fit, or need.

The district operated the fourth-largest security force in Pennsylvania, which responded to a wide range of violations, including the seven felonious assaults per day committed by students against teachers, administrative staff, and other students. (**Exhibits 2, 3,** and **4** contain additional enrollment and demographic data for the district.)

Changing Demographics

Like the populations of many other urban areas in the United States, Philadelphia's population of poor and immigrant children had grown at the same time as middle-class families had moved out of the city. Between 1995 and 2001, the number of students in the district with a primary language other than English increased from 5,600 to 13,200.

Eighty-three percent of the district's students qualified for free or reduced-price meals in 2001, up from approximately 55% in 1997. In fact, this percentage was so high in some areas that 230 of the 264 schools served free breakfast and lunch to all students because doing so cost less than the administrative burden of filing for federal subsidies on an individual student basis.

Growing Financial Troubles

Throughout the 1990s the district's financial troubles escalated as it fought a losing battle for increased state funding. By 2001, the district faced an annual operating deficit of over $200 million. The city's changing demographics combined with a change in the state's education funding policy contributed to this shortfall. The state provided 52% of the total district budget. In 1993 the legislature had frozen the state's school-aid formula, which was computed on a dollars-per-student rate. As a result, the funding failed to keep pace with inflation—had state support grown at the rate of inflation, the district would have received an additional $51 million from the state in 2001.

Approximately 12% of district revenues came from federal sources. The remaining 36% came from the city of Philadelphia's budget because the mayoral-appointed board of education, unlike those of many school districts in the United States, had no independent taxing authority. During the 1980s, the flight of residential and commercial property owners from Philadelphia to the suburbs created a dramatic decline in the city's tax base. Philadelphia already had one of the highest local tax burdens in the United States for individuals and businesses, so it was politically unfeasible for city officials to raise the rates to compensate for the declining base. The district was forced to borrow from banks, the state, and its own pension fund to finance school operations. By 2001 the district was strapped, with $1.5 billion in long-term debt, and financial projections estimated a $1.5 billion cumulative operating deficit by 2005. (**Exhibit 5** contains selected district financial data.)

Disappointing Student Performance

Student performance on the Pennsylvania System of School Assessment (PSSA), a set of criterion-referenced tests, was disappointing to district stakeholders. The state implemented the PSSA in 1996 to evaluate Pennsylvania students in grades 5, 8, and 11 in reading and math and grades 6, 9, and 11 in writing. The test judged student performance as advanced, proficient, basic, or below basic in each of the categories.

From 1996 to 2001, Philadelphia students showed slight gains on the PSSA. However, these gains paled in comparison to the low absolute scores. Each year, a combined average of over 50% of the district's students scored in the bottom quartile statewide. In 2000, only 17.8% of the district's students scored above the state median. Local critics also pointed to the dismal performance of the district relative to other schools in the state. Only 0.6% of Pennsylvania school districts performed worse than Philadelphia's. (**Exhibit 6** shows selected PSSA data.)

Prior Reform Efforts: Big Ideas, Little Improvement[2]

Between 1994 and 2001, the district embarked on two significant reform efforts. The first was an ambitious 10-point plan for revitalizing the district under Superintendent David Hornbeck entitled "Children Achieving." The second was the School District Improvement Plan developed under the auspices of the state's Education Empowerment Act. Also known as Act 16, this legislation required districts with over 50% of students scoring in the bottom quartile on the PSSA in two consecutive years to submit improvement plans aimed at raising test scores.

Children Achieving: 1994–2000

In 1994, Hornbeck arrived in Philadelphia as superintendent determined to transform the schools. He had been active in national education reform and child advocacy, had served as state superintendent of schools in Maryland, and was widely acknowledged as the author of a sweeping overhaul of Kentucky's public education system. He was also an Oxford-trained theologian with a law degree from the University of Pennsylvania. A charismatic leader, Hornbeck quickly articulated his vision for reform—Children Achieving. The fundamental premise of Children Achieving was that all children could learn at high levels and that low achievement levels resulted from the low expectations of the adults responsible for educating and motivating children. Hornbeck articulated the 10 points that formed the foundation for Children Achieving in a comprehensive public document called the "Children Achieving Action Design":

1. Set high expectations for everyone.
2. Design accurate performance indicators to hold everyone accountable for results.
3. Shrink the centralized bureaucracy and let schools make more decisions.

4. Provide intensive and sustained professional development to all staff.
5. Make sure that all students are ready for school.
6. Provide students with the community support and services they need to succeed in school.
7. Provide up-to-date technology and instructional materials.
8. Engage the public in shaping, understanding, supporting, and participating in reform.
9. Ensure adequate resources and use them effectively.
10. Be prepared to address all of these priorities together and for the long term—starting now.

At the core of the 10-point plan were standards, accountability, and decentralization. Hornbeck's premise was that incremental change was not enough; rather, the entire system needed to be changed. He backed up each of the 10 components with goals and extensive action plans developed collaboratively with 1,000 administrators, teachers, and parents from the city's schools, as well as over 2,500 citizens who attended 22 community meetings. He restructured the district into 22 clusters, each with a cluster leader with operating responsibility for a set of schools. He also issued a challenge to the citizenry to get involved to help make Philadelphia the first major American city to succeed in having *all* its children achieve at high levels. Hornbeck exhorted, "Timid, little steps won't do it. Changes at the margins only delay a continuing decline. We must all do our part for bold, comprehensive reform. The time is now. The place is Philadelphia."[3]

Hornbeck's ambitious vision and charismatic style initially won him the support of the business community, Democratic Mayor Ed Rendell, parents, and teachers. His reform efforts attracted many who had previously been disengaged in the problem of the schools. The Annenberg Foundation awarded Philadelphia a $50 million challenge grant in 1996, and Hornbeck leveraged this to raise an additional $100 million from other private foundations and corporations to create the Children Achieving Challenge, a separately incorporated nonprofit that served as a fiscal agent to channel private money into the reform of the public school system.

Comprehensive change required substantial funding, and the private donations were not sufficient. Hornbeck maintained that Pennsylvania's 1993 state education funding freeze not only adversely affected the district and his ability to implement Children Achieving successfully but also was inherently discriminatory against minority students in poor rural and urban areas. By contrast, New Jersey had implemented a funding model in which high-poverty districts actually spent $324 more per student than high-income districts. This formula was the result of 30 years of litigation and court rulings requiring the state to equalize school spending.[4]

Hornbeck made it his mission to get adequate funding from the state of Pennsylvania. In 1998 he threatened to submit an unbalanced budget that would lead to the shutdown of the schools if the state refused to adjust its aid formula. Legislators countered by passing Act 46, a law authorizing a state takeover of the district if it fell into financial or academic distress. A series of legal battles ensued, including a federal civil-rights suit filed by the district against the state alleging that Pennsylvania's school funding formula discriminated against schools with a high number of nonwhite students. The Pennsylvania Supreme Court ruled in 1999 that the state legislature was required to develop an equitable school funding formula. Lawmakers continued to stall on the issue of equitable funding for poor rural and urban schools.

In order to ease the escalating tensions and avert an imminent state takeover of the district, John F. Street, the newly elected Democratic mayor of Philadelphia, started a parallel negotiation with Republican Governor Tom Ridge in summer 2000. Street dropped the pending federal lawsuit and committed to significant cuts in school operating expenses, thereby convincing the governor to allocate an additional $45 million to the district and averting a state takeover. Unable to accept these terms, Hornbeck resigned in July 2000 after six years of acrimonious battles, with little of his vision accomplished.

Reviewing Hornbeck's tenure, some local civic and business leaders believed that his initial support began to erode as he elevated financial disputes with the state to a moral level. He further alienated many important stakeholders by characterizing criticism against him and elements of Children Achieving as evidence that those who questioned the plan did not believe that all children could achieve at high levels. One group of researchers concluded:

> The superintendent's posture of "You're either for me or against me" compounded the problem. Important decisions and the discussions and debates leading to them were located in a handful of people and were therefore invisible to front-line educators, parents, the general public, and central office administrators not part of the inner circle. The moral dimensions of the reform's message and their close association with Hornbeck were barriers to principled discussions of important values, beliefs, and ideas underlying the reform. Hornbeck's ownership of the reform and the reform's dependence on him as its leader and visionary permeated [local perceptions of its effectiveness].[5]

Not everyone agreed on the reason for Hornbeck's lack of effectiveness. One longtime Philadelphia civic leader noted:

> David was controversial because of his evangelical approach. But the truth is he was an innovative, talented educator. Test scores actually increased every year he was superintendent. Unfortunately, he was an awful politician and an ineffective manager. As his tenure unfolded, the mayoral-appointed board of education trusted him with less and less of the authority related to those elements of his leadership. He lost Mayor Rendell's personal support because he alienated the state over the funding formula. By the time he resigned, he had little influence on or visibility into the budget; a CFO who reported to the board was responsible for the financials. The board minimized his role in union negotiations by putting the school attorneys in charge of the bargaining process. He couldn't even hire and fire his own senior team—they all reported directly to the board. He definitely made mistakes, but the board of education shares the blame for not creating an environment in which he had a chance to succeed.

School District Improvement Plan: 2000–2001

After Hornbeck's departure in 2000, the state Department of Education, under the authority of a piece of legislation known as Act 16 (The Education Empowerment Act), declared Philadelphia an Empowerment District because a combined average of 50% or more of its students scored in the bottom quartile of the PSSA in two consecutive academic years. The local board of education appointed a 12-member Education Empowerment Team made up of parents, principals, teachers, administrators, and community members. The team was charged with developing and submitting a School District Improvement Plan to the state Department of Education in November 2000. The district hoped to receive a state grant to implement the plan with a goal of raising PSSA scores to such a level over the next three to four years that the district could be removed from the empowerment list. (**Exhibit 7** outlines the main elements of the School District Improvement Plan.)

Mayor Street appointed Philip Goldsmith, a successful banker and management consultant, to be the interim CEO. Goldsmith focused on executing the school improvement plan and rolled back many of the structural changes and programs implemented under Children Achieving to reduce expenses. By summer 2001, however, the district still faced a $200 million operating deficit.

In August 2001, Republican Governor Ridge awarded a controversial $2.7 million no-bid consulting contract to Edison Schools, a for-profit educational management organization. Edison's task was to conduct an evaluation of the district and recommend improvements should the governor trigger Act 46 and implement a state takeover. In early October 2001, following the terrorist attacks of September 11th, President George W. Bush tapped Governor Ridge to lead the new Homeland Security efforts; Republican Lieutenant Governor Mark Schweiker, seen as a supporter of Edison Schools and privatization, succeeded Ridge as governor.

Edison issued its findings in November 2001 with a sweeping set of recommendations for turning around the district, including a suggestion to hire Edison to run 45 low-performing schools and the district's central administration. Under the proposal, the senior leadership of the district would be Edison employees who would not be accountable to the board of education. Philip Goldsmith, the interim CEO, lashed out against the report in a speech to the board of education: "Edison says there has been a brain drain at the district and a lack of management talent. To an extent that is true. But it is not because a private company does not run the school district—it is because we are a district on the ropes. It is hard to retain or recruit talent when you don't know the future of the district."[6]

Livid that Governor Schweiker would likely relinquish central administration to Edison Schools if the state took over the district, Goldsmith resigned in protest on December 14, 2001.

State Takeover and the Creation of the State Reform Commission

Governor Schweiker and Mayor Street emerged from their negotiations about the impending change in district control at 5 p.m. on December 21, 2001—just seven hours before the midnight deadline for a hostile state takeover as mandated by Act 46. They hugged repeatedly and expressed optimism about the future. "We want to assure the students of this city that we have your best interests at heart," said Mayor Street. The negotiations had been tough, and as part of the compromise the governor abandoned his commitment to award Edison Schools a contract to run the district's central administration. Nonetheless, Schweiker expressed high expectations for the new partnership between the city and state, saying, "I believe we will give rise to the finest urban school system in the country."[7]

Although Pennsylvania and other states had intervened in a small number of local districts since the late 1980s, the Philadelphia takeover was by far the largest, and therefore the highest profile. (See **Exhibit 8** for data on previous state takeovers.) Under the agreement, the district was transferred officially to state control, but the governor and the mayor would both have a stake in the turnaround effort through the five-member SRC. The creation of the SRC effectively disbanded Mayor Street's appointed board of education. Act 46 gave the governor four appointees and the mayor one appointee. However, as part of the December 21 negotiation, the governor agreed to appoint only three commissioners, including the chair, making it possible for Mayor Street to fill two positions. Act 46 chartered the SRC as an independent body, although lawmakers gave it a fiduciary responsibility to the state and required the commission to submit occasional reports to the state and the city. They did not, however, empower the governor, the state legislature, or the mayor with the ability to remove a commissioner before the end of his or her term except in the event of ethical misconduct.

Membership and Goals

Governor Schweiker immediately named James Nevels to a seven-year term as chair of the SRC. Nevels, a Republican, was a prominent African-American business executive in Pennsylvania with a JD/MBA from the University of Pennsylvania. He immediately began functioning as interim CEO while the governor and the mayor finalized their remaining appointees. Mayor Street appointed two members of his now defunct board of education, Democrats Sandra Dungee Glenn and Michael Masch. Governor Schweiker appointed two additional Republicans—Dan Whelan and James Gallagher. (See **Exhibit 9** for SRC bios.)

As chair, Nevels aspired to create an agenda for the SRC that focused on governance rather than operational issues:

> I am committed to the SRC being a governing board, not a management committee. Our discourse must be at the policy level. For instance, if 40% of our fourth graders can't read, we should adopt a policy that will facilitate a systemwide response to the problem, rather than dictating the details of which curriculum or what classroom schedule is best to improve the literacy rates. Then we should support and evaluate one person and hold him or her accountable for the results—that person is the CEO. Not other senior administrators, not principals and teachers, but the CEO. The CEO should have operational latitude at the strategy and implementation level and hold everyone else in the system accountable. The intercession of external forces to distract superintendents and school leaders from their primary mission to educate kids is rampant. This is a big problem in many urban districts, and it has been debilitating in Philadelphia in the past. Hopefully, we will effect a sea change regarding that problem.

One researcher echoed Nevels's articulation of the governance challenges in urban schools:

> Traditional school boards, especially in large cities, are increasingly seen as a large part of the problem. Their tendency toward micromanaging; their factionalization along ethnic and political lines; the political ambitions of individual members; their use of the school system as a candy store for their families and friends—all are seen as needlessly distracting the superintendent and the school system from their main goal, academic excellence.[8]

In order to minimize the politicization of the SRC, Nevels was inclined to avoid for as long as possible votes on fractious issues that would publicly split the commissioners. His aim was to present a united front to the public in the face of dramatic differences of opinion among stakeholders on contentious issues. While the other commissioners were supportive of Nevels's intentions, some privately worried that politically motivated groups might use this as leverage to influence the SRC to delay or forgo decisions on tough issues.

Priorities

The SRC faced a number of urgent issues that needed attention. As chair, Nevels continued to function as interim CEO, and the SRC identified a set of priorities to work on in tandem with the CEO search in an effort to create an environment for success for the new leader. Nevels reflected on these priorities:

> We had to tackle three key problem areas as we were conducting the CEO search. First was the financial situation. We had a $200 million annual operating deficit, and when I stepped in as chair, we had 45 days of cash and the financial office couldn't even provide me with actual-to-budget information. Continuing to fund operations by issuing bonds was not an option. Also, school safety was a huge issue. Violence was out of control. Students committed an average of seven felonious assaults per day in our school buildings. It is unrealistic to expect teachers to perform well or students to achieve at their full potential when they are in constant fear for their personal safety.
>
> Finally, the ongoing privatization debate threatened to consume our entire agenda. When the SRC was formed, a group of anti-privatization folks were staging a sit-in at the district headquarters. Because the governor was a supporter of privatization, many in the public assumed that his three appointees would rubber-stamp his views. We had to convince parents, teachers, and others that we could make an independent decision.

The financial problems required complex negotiations with the state, city, and other funding sources. Members of the SRC immediately began working on this issue. School safety required tough action, including the creation of crisis intervention task forces and the permanent removal of repeatedly violent students from mainstream schools. Broad agreement existed about the need to act on these two issues; the privatization question was another matter.

Privatization advocates believed that introducing market forces such as competition, accountability, and profit incentives—by contracting companies to operate schools and allowing families to choose which schools their children attended—would change the monopoly structure of public education and lead to dramatic improvements in educational outcomes. They also argued that third-party providers should be free from union agreements with teachers and other bargaining units. Principals could then select teachers for their buildings based on capabilities and attitude rather than seniority and save money by eliminating some nonteaching positions currently mandated by unions. The elevator operators' union was a favorite example of privatization supporters. Thirty-one well-paid elevator operators worked in school buildings with no functioning elevators because their assignments were dictated by a contract.

One local education activist summed up the argument against privatization:

> The state underfunded public education in Philadelphia for years, which led to a steady decline in student achievement. Now the state cites poor student achievement as the primary reason for turning over our tax dollars to profit-making companies. These companies will be motivated to provide even less to our children so that they can provide a better return to shareholders. Public education should be public. Besides, private-sector managers can be just as incompetent as public-sector managers. Management problems are only a part of what's wrong with the schools. The real issue is more money—specifically more money focused on what happens at the classroom level. Privatization is not the magic bullet.

The Privatization Vote

"We are an independent commission, not the Edison commission," Gallagher asserted above the rumble of the 500 attendees at an April 2002 public meeting of the SRC. As the debate over awarding management contracts to third parties for the lowest-performing elementary and middle schools gathered steam, the commissioners had difficulty reaching consensus on the details of the privatization plan. Gallagher prepared to move for a vote.

Suddenly, a commissioner's cell phone rang at the head table. The chief of staff of an influential elected official was on the other end of the line. He said, "You guys are about to make a big mistake! Do me the courtesy of calling a recess, and let me speak privately with you and the other commissioners before you vote." The commissioner obliged, and the SRC filed out of the meeting room and squeezed into a nearby janitor's closet. An assistant to the chief of staff followed the group and patched in her boss using the hands-free feature on her cell phone. During the heated debate as they stood among the brooms and mops, the chief of staff made it clear that because his boss and other influential political stakeholders were against privatization, the SRC faced the unattractive option of presenting a divided front to the public. Nevels took the phone and conveyed in strong terms his intention as chair to take a vote, even if it meant a split decision. The SRC filed back in to the meeting room and reconvened.

Within the hour, the SRC voted three to two to award contracts to a combination of seven private companies, nonprofits, universities, and community groups to run 45 of the city's worst schools. The commission authorized an additional 48 schools for either reconstitution or conversion to charter or independent status.[9] The split vote fell along party lines and was the first time the SRC failed to reach unanimity on a public decision. As part of the plan, the state committed an additional $55 million for use in these 90 schools. Among the seven contractors was Edison Schools, a polarizing symbol of the privatization debate. The decision marked the beginning of the largest privatization experiment in U.S. public education. (See **Exhibit 10** for privatization plan details.)

The Search and the Decision

"We need a 'Tiffany' name to build the public's confidence in the fairness of the search. If we try this on our own without the insulation of a respected executive search firm, we run the risk of this decision becoming as politicized as the privatization debate," Gallagher explained to Nevels. Even though Nevels trusted him to run a clean process, he knew Gallagher's concern was legitimate.

In the past, Philadelphia had incorporated town-hall meetings into its hiring process for superintendents. Finalists for the position were subjected to a series of public meetings at which they would present their qualifications, position themselves against other candidates, and take questions from the audience. Commissioner Whelan described it as more like a political primary than a recruiting process. The SRC was under external pressure to follow this precedent, but Whelan and others held firm against it. They opted for a more corporate-style recruiting and decision process. Commissioner Dungee Glenn agreed to work closely with Gallagher in coordinating the search effort. The SRC decided to issue a request for proposal to attract high-caliber executive search firms to the project. After presentations from a variety of firms, the SRC voted unanimously in March 2002 to retain Heidrick & Struggles, a leading international executive search firm, to work with it.

Gallagher immediately worked with Heidrick & Struggles to develop a schedule with a goal of having the new CEO in place to open school in September—only five months away. The SRC worked on defining the leadership criteria that were important to it and its stakeholders, and the Heidrick & Struggles team began identifying potential candidates. (**Exhibit 11** contains a timeline of the search.)

Capabilities and Characteristics

The SRC was interested in the accepted notions of the skills and capabilities necessary for superintendents but worried these might not be adequate for the scale of the district and the scope of its challenges. Some scholars identified the generic attributes of the traditional superintendency as personnel management, school finance, curriculum development, school board relations, public and community relations, district operations, policy formulation and implementation, collective negotiations, and school construction.[10] (**Exhibit 12** contains additional superintendent leadership theories.)

Leadership Profiles Based on Search Committee Member Preferences

Heidrick & Struggles used their expertise to develop a set of capabilities to guide their initial search for candidates that included a superb reputation for leadership in a highly complex operating environment, a demonstrated capacity for strategic thinking and implementation, goal- and objective-setting skills combined with the achievement of measurable results, strong financial and other business skills, and the communication skills necessary to advocate effectively and forcefully for the district's vision. (See **Exhibit 13** for Heidrick & Struggles's position description.)

The SRC members each had views about the ideal CEO informed by their own backgrounds and experiences. Some commissioners thought the new leader should have a depth of financial and political skills combined with the ability to build a team of experts to handle the educational leadership functions. They preferred someone experienced in managing large, complex public budgets. One cited the university practice of having both a provost and a president as a possible model for the district.

Another preferred profile was someone with experience in the education sector. The ability to inspire confidence in the district's educators seemed to depend on this. However, the ability to manage a large, complex budget and deal with city and state politics was also important. One commissioner worried that hiring a candidate who had been successful as a superintendent in a more stable, less complex district would be like hiring a dermatologist to work in an emergency room.

Yet another commissioner sketched out the ideal candidate as a person of color who was a one- or two-star general who had held successful training commands with entry-level enlisted troops. Realizing there might be public concern about a command-and-control model of leadership in a situation that called for community building and collaboration, the commissioner clarified that the model was Colin Powell, not George Patton.

Other school districts had followed various leadership models, including hiring a corporate executive, former attorney, local community leader, or retired military officer as CEO and pairing this leader with a chief academic officer or chancellor of instruction with deep educational expertise. The SRC knew that among other cities, New York, Los Angeles, Chicago, Miami, San Diego, Jacksonville, and Seattle had pursued and hired nontraditional candidates.

One school reform advocate in a Texas urban district has suggested that in districts with a high percentage of minority students, minority superintendents are more likely to succeed.[11] The SRC was under public pressure to hire a minority candidate, and members discussed this openly in their search meetings. They agreed that hiring a qualified minority candidate was ideal, but they were also open to a candidate of any race who had succeeded in a high-minority urban environment.

The Candidates

On May 3, 2002, Heidrick & Struggles presented the SRC with a resume book of 15 diverse candidates with backgrounds from education, the military, business, and government. (**Exhibit 14** contains information about the 15 candidates.)

The commissioners quickly reduced the pool to seven and held in-depth interviews at Heidrick & Struggles's offices with each of these candidates. After spirited conversations about the strengths and weaknesses of all seven, the SRC narrowed the field to three outstanding candidates and brought each of them back to Philadelphia for another round of interviews.[12] Each finalist not only had a unique skill set and background, each represented a particular candidate model for urban superintendent positions.

The Superintendent

As superintendent of an urban district, David Fernandez managed a school system with over 20,000 students and a $300 million budget. In three years under Fernandez's helm, district reading scores increased 63%, and graduation rates and advanced placement participation both rose. In addition, he implemented comprehensive teacher guides for all curricular areas and introduced pre-kindergarten programs in all schools. Fernandez also successfully drove a $75 million bond issue as the first phase of a large construction plan.

Previously, Fernandez spent over 25 years in one of the largest urban districts in the United States. He started as a teacher and progressed to area superintendent with 30,000 students. Fernandez earned his bachelor's and master's degrees in bilingual education from a university in the Northeast.

In addition to the Philadelphia position, Fernandez was evaluating a number of other opportunities, including staying at his current district. SRC members described him as bright, articulate, and focused. They were impressed with the depth of his vision for a turnaround in Philadelphia and believed he was a proven instructional leader who had a track record of improving student achievement. Some commissioners questioned his readiness to step up to a district 10 times the size of his current assignment with the political and financial complexities of Philadelphia. Others found the number of opportunities he was considering unsettling and questioned his genuine interest in the Philadelphia job.

The General

A veteran of over 30 years in the United States Armed Services, Major General Kent Williams held two roles at the time of the search. Based in the Washington, D.C. area, he was responsible for all training and education programs for over 211,000 active and reserve personnel for the Marine Corps. In addition, he oversaw the operations of a 60,000-acre base and the living and working conditions for over 20,000 military members, family members, and civilian workers. He managed a budget of $133 million and supervised a staff of 300.

Previously, he provided leadership for over 12,000 military personnel on a base in California and managed an annual budget of over $100 million. Earlier in his career, he served as the leader of all public and media relations and as a Capitol Hill liaison for the Marine Corps. Williams started his military career in 1969 after graduating from a university in the Southeast. He was a White House Fellow and received a master's degree in counseling from a university in the Mid-Atlantic area. Williams expressed a strong passion for public education and had family in the Philadelphia area.

The SRC considered the general to be an extremely attractive nontraditional candidate who would be a fantastic role model for young

African-Americans in the district. His presence and demeanor inspired confidence. Some believed that the capabilities needed to prepare entry-level Marine recruits from all backgrounds to operate at high skill levels were transferable to public education. They also thought that his financial and human resource management skills and community and public relations experience would be invaluable. However, some worried that his lack of experience in K–12 education meant that his learning curve would be too steep to effect change as quickly as needed and that he would fail before he had time to grasp the complexities of the context.

The Urban Public Servant

John Kring campaigned unsuccessfully for his state's Democratic gubernatorial nomination from 2001 through early 2002. Prior to running for governor, he had served from 1995 to 2001 as superintendent of a large Midwestern urban school district with over 400,000 students. During his tenure he eliminated a projected shortfall of $1.3 billion within the first two years and balanced the budget thereafter, implemented a capital improvement program, streamlined the system's administrative organization, ended social promotion and extended the school day until 6 p.m., created 15 charter schools and 50 neighborhood and school-based magnet program options, and negotiated two consecutive four-year contracts with the teachers' unions. Test scores improved by most academic indicators every year from 1996 to 2000. He reported directly to the city's mayor.

Earlier in his career, Kring spent 10 years in public finance in city government both as a budget and a revenue director. Prior to entering city government, Kring served as a policy advisor on elementary and secondary education for a state senator. He earned his bachelor's and master's degrees from a university in the Midwest.

Some SRC members felt that Kring's public finance expertise and tenure as an urban superintendent in a mayoral-controlled district made him an ideal candidate. He was high energy, confident, and passionate about public education. Although not a minority himself, he had succeeded in a high-minority school district. Some were concerned about the leveling off of test scores at the end of his term at his former district and his break with the city's mayor that led to his departure. Another concern was that his confidence in his ability to turn around the district seemed to lack a pragmatic optimism about a realistic time horizon for change and the differences in the political landscape between Philadelphia and his former city.

The Decision

The SRC met to discuss the final three candidates on June 13, 2002. In approximately nine weeks, over 200,000 students were scheduled to begin the new school year in Philadelphia.

"Let's outline the characteristics we agreed were important, rate each candidate against those, and see where we come out. We'll go around the room and score each candidate on a scale of one to five for each of the criteria, five being the highest, and justify our ratings," Gallagher suggested as he drew a matrix on the whiteboard and listed nine criteria:

1. Most qualified "as is"
2. Good fit with the SRC
3. Ability to deal with scale
4. Viewed as a change agent
5. Ability to assemble team quickly
6. Ability to establish public trust
7. Ability to produce midterm results (two years)
8. Ability to lead from mediocrity to excellence
9. Potential for long-term results

Even though the finalists were all strong leaders, none was the perfect candidate. As they moved through the rating process, Nevels realized there were risks associated with each of the finalists and that no matter whom they chose, as a governing body they would need to create an environment of support for their new CEO.

Notes

1. Operating expenditures are the sum of instruction, support, and administrative costs.

2. In addition to casewriter interviews, this section relies on background information from a number of public sources including various articles from *Education Week* and *The Philadelphia Inquirer,* as well as a number of research reports from The Consortium for Policy Research in Education. Attributions are used for direct or adapted quotations from sources.

3. See "Children Achieving Action Design Document," School District of Philadelphia Web site, http://www.philsch.k12.pa.us/Children_Achieving/exec_summary.html, accessed October 28, 2002.

4. See Dale Mezzacappa, "Study Finds Pennsylvania School-Spending Gap," *The Philadelphia Inquirer*, August 9, 2002.

5. Adapted from J. B. Christman and A. Rhodes, "Civic Engagement and Urban School Improvement: Hard-to-Learn Lessons from Philadelphia," paper published by the Consortium for Policy Research in Education, 2002, pp. 30–31.

6. From remarks by Philip Goldsmith to Philadelphia Board of Education, November 5, 2001, School District of Philadelphia internal documents.

7. For more detail, see Jacques Steinberg, "In Largest Schools Takeover, State Will Run Philadelphia's," *The New York Times*, December 22, 2001; and Catherine Gewertz, "It's Official: State Takes Over Philadelphia Schools," *Education Week*, January 9, 2002.

8. Paul Hill, "Hero Worship," *Education Next,* Vol. 1, No. 4 (March 2001): 26.

9. Reconstitution allows for the complete turnover of all teachers and administrators at a public school. Charter schools have public school status but are free from many of the regulations and union contracts in force in the district. Independent schools are separately incorporated, privately run, and operate outside the public system.

10. Compiled from a literature review in Cryss C. Brunner, "Taking Risks: A Requirement of the New Superintendency," *Journal of School Leadership,* 9 (July 1999): 291–292.

11. See Donald R. McAdams, *Fighting to Save Our Urban Schools and Winning: Lessons from Houston* (New York: Teachers College Press, 2002).

12. Candidate profiles are disguised for confidentiality reasons.

Exhibit 1

Leadership of 10 Largest and Selected Other Local School Districts in the United States, December 2001

Rank	*District*	*State*	*# Students*	*Chief Executive*[1]	*Background*	*Sector*	*Since*
1.	New York City Public Schools	NY	1,050,000	Harold O. Levy	Corporate Executive, Attorney	Business, Law	2000
2.	Los Angeles Unified School District	CA	736,700	Roy Romer	Governor of Colorado	Government	2000
3.	City of Chicago School District	IL	420,000	Arne Duncan	Pro Athlete, Nonprofit Leader	Sports/Nonprofit	2001
4.	Miami–Dade County School District	FL	370,000	Merrett R. Stierheim	City Manager, Nonprofit Leader	Government/Nonprofit	2001
5.	Broward County School District	FL	255,000	Franklin Till, Jr.	Educator and Administrator	Education	1999
6.	Clark County School District	NV	231,125	Carlos A. Garcia	Educator and Administrator	Education	1999
7.	Houston Independent School District	TX	210,670	Kaye Stripling	Educator and Administrator	Education	2000
8.	Philadelphia City School District	PA	204,851	Philip Goldsmith[2]	Management Consultant	Business	2000
9.	Hillsborough County School District	FL	183,000	Earl J. Lennard	Educator and Administrator	Education	1996
10.	Detroit City School District	MI	162,200	Kenneth Burnley	Educator and Administrator	Education	2000
15.	San Diego Unified School District	CA	140,000	Alan Bersin	United States Attorney	Law	1998
18.	Duval County School District	FL	128,000	John Fryer	Major General, US Air Force	Military	1998
89.	Seattle Public Schools	WA	46,800	Joseph Olschefske	Investment Banker	Business	1999

Source: National Center for Education Statistics Web site, <http://nces.ed.gov>, accessed December 16, 2002; various school district Web sites; case writer analysis.

[1] Titles vary by district, including superintendent, CEO, and chancellor.

[2] Philip Goldsmith was serving as interim CEO in 2001.

Exhibit 2

Selected Enrollment Data, School District of Philadelphia, 1997–2001

	1997	*1998*	*1999*	*2000*	*2001*
Total number of students[1]	212,150	212,865	207,465	205,199	204,851
Receiving free or reduced-price meals	55%	55%	82%	83%	83%
Limited English language proficiency	4%	4%	5%	6%	6%
Total special education students	14%	14%	13%	16%	16%
Gifted as % of total special education	20%	21%	11%	28%	28%
Student mobility[2]	n/a	n/a	n/a	41%	43%

Source: School District of Philadelphia Web site < http://www.phila.k12.pa.us/>, accessed October 10, 2002; Standard & Poor's School Evaluation Services Web site, <http://www.ses.standardandpoors.com/>, accessed October 10, 2002; case writer analysis.

[1] Does not include charter school enrollment.

[2] Student mobility is the sum of the number of students entering any district school after the start of the school year and the number of students leaving any district school before the end of the school year and is expressed as a % to total students.

Exhibit 3

Racial/Ethnic Distribution, School District of Philadelphia and Citywide, 2000

Race /Ethnicity	*District*	*Citywide*
African-American	65%	43%
Asian	5%	4%
Hispanic	13%	8%
Native-American	0.2%	0.3%
White	16%	45%
Total	100%	100%

Source: Adapted from Standard & Poor's School Evaluation Services Web site, <http://www.ses.standardandpoors.com/>, accessed October 10, 2002; and U.S. Census Bureau.

Exhibit 4

Dropout Rates, School District of Philadelphia, 1997–2000

Class	*1997*	*1998*	*1999*	*2000*
Grade 8 (%)	0	0	0	0
Grade 9 (%)	10.1	10.6	9	8.4
Grade 10 (%)	12.9	12	11.3	14
Grade 11 (%)	14.8	11.9	10	12.1
Grade 12 (%)	11.8	10.8	10	12.8
High School Dropout Rate (%)	11.4	10.8	9.7	11.1

Source: Standard & Poor's School Evaluation Services Web site, http://www.ses.standardandpoors.com, accessed October 10, 2002.

Exhibit 5

Selected Financial Information, School District of Philadelphia, 1996–2001

5a Revenues by Source, 1996–2001

(Amounts in millions of dollars)	*1996*	*1997*	*1998*	*1999*	*2000*	*2001*
Revenues by Source						
Local						
Taxes						
Real Estate	$401.9	$420.7	$403.2	$413.4	$414.8	$427.6
Use and Occupancy	84.5	81.4	80.8	82.9	90.6	94.7
Other[1]	42.1	85.3	45.4	48.0	51.9	50.6
Total Taxes	$528.5	$587.4	$529.4	$544.3	$557.3	$572.9
City Contributions	15.0	15.0	15.0	30.0	0.0	15.0
Other[2]	47.3	56.1	67.9	58.3	70.1	54.1
Total Local	590.8	658.5	612.3	632.6	627.4	642.0
State Subsidies[3]	834.7	851.0	848.7	854.1	896.4	942.6
Federal Grants	132.8	144.9	151.5	161.7	189.0	211.4
Total General Revenues	1,558.3	1,654.4	1,612.5	1,648.4	1,712.8	1,796.0
Other Financing Sources[4]	213.1	154.5	0.0	257.4	177.5	157.5
Total General Revenues and Other Sources	$1,771.4	$1,808.9	$1,612.5	$1,905.8	$1,890.3	$1,953.5

Source: School District of Philadelphia, comprehensive annual financial report year ended June 30, 2001; case writer analysis.

[1] Other Local Taxes include Liquor tax, School (non-business) Income Tax, and Public Utility tax.

[2] Other Local Non-Tax Revenues include Interest Income, Legal Settlements, Voluntary Contributions, Grants from Private Foundations, and miscellaneous other non-tax income.

[3] State Subsidies include grants for General Instruction (70%), and categorical grants for Special Education Instruction (10%), General and Special Education Transportation (5%), Employee Social Security (4%), and miscellaneous categorical funds including Health Service, Non-public school services, Vocational Education and Charter Schools (11%). (Percentages are for 2001.)

[4] Other Financing Sources include General Obligation (GO) Bonds and Loans Payable. GO Bonds are unsecured municipal bonds that are backed by the full faith and credit of the municipality, and generally have maturities of at least 10 years and are paid off with funds from taxes or other fees. They are exempt from federal taxes, and when purchased by state and local residents of the issuing municipality are also exempt from state and local taxes. However, capital gains are taxable. Yields are often lower than corporate or treasury bonds with comparable maturities because of the tax savings. In 2001, the district issued GO Bonds totaling a net $133.5 million, and borrowed an additional $24 million from the state of Pennsylvania.

5b Expenditures by Use, 1996–2001

(Amounts in millions of dollars)	*1996*	*1997*	*1998*	*1999*	*2000*	*2001*
Expenditures by Use						
Instructional[1,3]	$1,085.9	$1,145.2	$1,111.1	$1,125.1	$1,050.4	$1,150.7
Support and Administration[2,3]	231.8	236	257.5	269.4	380.2	395.6
Basic Building Services[4]	234.7	284.2	289.5	311.4	366	382.3
Debt Service and Temporary Borrowing	72.4	83.6	43.9	84.5	89.6	77.9
Net Transfers/Uses[5]	56.7	51	0	103.7	74.9	0
Total General Expenditures	$1,681.5	$1,800.0	$1,702.0	$1,894.1	$1,961.1	$2,006.5
Operating Surplus/(Deficit) before Other Financing Sources	$(123.2)	$(145.6)	$(89.5)	$(245.7)	$(248.3)	$(210.5)

Source: School District of Philadelphia, comprehensive annual financial report year ended June 30, 2001; case writer analysis.

[1] Employee payroll and benefits account for approximately 90% of Instructional expenses

[2] Employee payroll and benefits account for approximately 84% of Support and Administration expenses

[3] Total Special Education spending accounts for 11.5% of the combined Instructional, Support and Administrative expenses

[4] Basic Building Services include both maintenance and capital expenditures. In 2001, Maintenance expenses were $217.7 million and Capital Expenditures were $164.6 million for a total of $382.3 million.

[5] Net Transfers/Uses are bond defeasement costs.

5c Changes in Long-Term Obligations Payable, FY 2001

(Amounts in millions of dollars)	*Balance July 1, 2000*	*Additions*	*Deletions*	*Balance July 30, 2001*
Termination Compensation Payable	256.5	36.1	19.7	272.9
Severance Payable	147.3	6.9	5.2	149
General Obligation Bonds	891.4	154	27.6	1,017.8
Loans Payable				
Federal Asbestos	2.1	0	0.4	1.7
Commonwealth	21.3	24	0	45.3
Other Liabilities	56.5	35.4	44.3	47.6
Total Liabilities	1,375.1	256.4	97.2	1,534.3

Source: School District of Philadelphia, comprehensive annual financial report year ended June 30, 2001; case writer analysis.

[1] The district's borrowing base is an average of the net revenue for the prior three fiscal years, or approximately $1.5 billion in 2001. The statutory nonelectoral debt limit is 100% of the borrowing base. The available nonelectoral borrowing capacity was $496 million at fiscal year ending 2001.

[2] All outstanding general obligation bonds as of June 30, 2001 were insured and carried the highest rating of "AAA," "Aaa," and "AAA" from Standard & Poor's, Moody's, and Fitch IBCA, respectively.

Exhibit 6a

Average PSSA Scores by Subject and Grade, Philadelphia and Statewide, 1996–2001[1]

		1996	*1997*	*1998*	*1999*	*2000*	*2001*
Reading							
Grade 5	Philadelphia	1090	1110	1090	1120	1140	1140
	Pennsylvania	1300	1310	1310	1310	1320	1310
Grade 8	Philadelphia	1080	1140	1120	1130	1120	1130
	Pennsylvania	1300	1300	1300	1310	1310	1310
Grade 11	Philadelphia	1160	1140	1140	1140	1140	1180
	Pennsylvania	1300	1300	1300	1310	1300	1300
Math							
Grade 5	Philadelphia	1100	1130	1140	1140	1140	1150
	Pennsylvania	1300	1300	1310	1300	1310	1310
Grade 8	Philadelphia	1070	1110	1120	1120	1130	1150
	Pennsylvania	1300	1300	1300	1300	1310	1310
Grade 11	Philadelphia	1170	1130	1120	1140	1160	1190
	Pennsylvania	1300	1300	1300	1300	1310	1310

Source: "School District of Philadelphia Announces PSSA Results," School District of Philadelphia press release, October 17, 2002.

[1] Participation in the writing portion of the PSSA was optional until 2000 and therefore not included in the table for comparison.

Exhibit 6b

PSSA Results by Score Distribution Group, Philadelphia and Statewide, 2001

		Advanced	*Proficient*	*Basic*	*Below Basic*
Reading					
Grade 5	Philadelphia	3%	15%	22%	59%
	Pennsylvania	29%	26%	23%	22%
Grade 8	Philadelphia	3%	20%	25%	52%
	Pennsylvania	25%	29%	23%	24%
Grade 11	Philadelphia	7%	27%	22%	44%
	Pennsylvania	26%	25%	25%	24%
Math					
Grade 5	Philadelphia	4%	13%	25%	57%
	Pennsylvania	27%	25%	26%	22%
Grade 8	Philadelphia	3%	13%	21%	63%
	Pennsylvania	25%	27%	26%	23%
Grade 11	Philadelphia	8%	15%	20%	56%
	Pennsylvania	25%	26%	23%	25%

Source: "Philadelphia School Profile," Pennsylvania Department of Education Web site, <http://www.paprofiles.org/pa0001/pdf/DIST7256.pdf>, accessed December 16, 2002; "Pennsylvania State Profile," Pennsylvania Department of Education Web site, <http://www.paprofiles.org/pa0001/state20002001.pdf>, accessed December 16, 2002.

Exhibit 7

School District Improvement Plan Highlights

Date: November 27, 2000

Major Objective: To ensure that less than 50% of the students in the School District of Philadelphia will perform in the bottom quartile in the Pennsylvania State Skills Assessment (PSSA) by the school year ending June 30, 2004.

Four cornerstones of the improvement plan

1. High standards and expectations
2. Accountability and assessment
3. Intensive intervention for students not meeting high standards
4. Enhancing organization, order, and efficiency

Nine goals stated to improve student performance across the district

1. The district will develop and mandate uniform curricula that are based on state and local standards.
2. The district will maximize instructional time for reading, math, and science.
3. The district will provide effective instructional programming and support.
4. The district will assure a healthy, safe, and secure learning environment.
5. The district shall endeavor to attract, develop, and retain a qualified professional for every position.
6. The district will assure that the assessment process will accurately measure student performance and will not detract from instructional time.
7. The district will ensure that local decisions will reflect districtwide policy, be data driven, and include the participation of parents and the community.
8. The district will hold each school accountable for increased student achievement.
9. The district will provide meaningful choice to every student in the district.

Clear strategies and time frames were set up for achieving these goals. The team communicated to each school a set of quarterly objectives to be met until the overall goal was achieved.

Source: "School District Improvement Plan," School District of Philadelphia Web site, <http://www.phila.k12.pa.us/executiveoffices/pps/edemp1116.htm>, accessed November 11, 2002.

Exhibit 8

Comprehensive State Takeovers of Local School Districts, 1989–2000[1]

District	*State*	*No. of Students[2]*	*Total Expenditures[2]*	*Takeover Year*
Jersey City	NJ	31,347	$386,432,000	1989
Paterson	NJ	24,629	$303,267,000	1991
Compton	CA	31,037	$187,779,000	1993
Newark	NJ	42,150	$616,379,000	1995
Hartford	CT	22,543	$315,605,000	1997
Lawrence	MA	12,634	$113,588,000	1999
Chester-Upland	PA	6,491	$66,000,000	2000

Sources: Kenneth Wong and Francis Shen, "Does School District Takeover Work?" paper presented at the annual meeting of the American Political Science Association, September 2001; National Center for Education Statistics Web site, <http://nces.ed.gov>, accessed December 16, 2002; case writer analysis.

[1] Of the over 40 city and state takeovers of local districts that occurred from 1989 to 2000, only 15 were complete takeovers of all academic, management, and financial aspects of the districts. Of those, eight were city takeovers, and seven were the state takeovers, reflected in the table above.

[2] Number of students and expenditures are from academic year ending 2001.

Exhibit 9

Biographical Information of School Reform Commissioners

James Nevels, an African-American, serves as board chair of the Philadelphia School Reform Commission. He is Chairman and CEO of the Swarthmore Group, one of the largest minority-owned investment firm in the United States. Nevels previously served on the Pennsylvania governor's school reform commission in the Chester-Upland school district. He earned a JD/MBA from the University of Pennsylvania.

James Gallagher, a white native Philadelphian and president of Philadelphia University, served as a member of the Pennsylvania State Board of Education from 1996 until the time of his appointment to the SRC and as the former commissioner of higher education for Pennsylvania. He had held a number of administrative leadership positions with colleges and universities around the state. Gallagher, a Ph.D., had degrees from St. Francis College, Duquesne University, and the Catholic University of America. Like Nevels, Gallagher received a seven-year appointment.

Sandra Dungee Glenn, an African-American and president of the American Cities Foundation, was a well-known political force and community organizer in Philadelphia. She had served on the mayoral-appointed board of education and managed multiple local political campaigns. A cum laude graduate of Pennsylvania State University, she had also served as the NAACP Voter Fund's state director and as chief of staff for a Democratic state senator. She received a three-year appointment.

Michael Masch, a white native Philadelphian, had also served on the mayoral board of education and was the vice president of budget and analysis for the University of Pennsylvania. Prior to this, he was the city budget director under Democratic Mayor Rendell. He did coursework in urban studies at Temple University and public policy analysis at the University of Pennsylvania. He received a three-year appointment.

Dan Whelan, also a white native of Philadelphia with degrees from La Salle College and Temple University School of Law, was the CEO of Verizon Pennsylvania, where he had spent most of his career. Whelan also served on the executive committees of Greater Philadelphia First and the Philadelphia Chamber of Commerce and on the boards of prominent arts and culture organizations such as the Free Library of Philadelphia, The Historical Society of Pennsylvania, and the Regional Performing Arts Center. He received a five-year appointment.

Source: School District of Philadelphia.

Exhibit 10

Private Management Contracts Awarded by School Reform Commission

Educational Management Organizations	*Per Pupil Teacher Differential*	*Per Pupil "Equity Grant"*	*Dollar Value of Reduced HQ Admin. Cost*	*Negotiated Per Pupil Subsidy*	*Student Enrollment*	*Total Cost*	*Total Schools*
Chancellor Beacon (For Profit)	$259 +	$438 +	$106 =	$803 x	4,448 =	$3,571,744	5
Edison (For Profit)	$337 +	$438 +	$106 =	$881 x	13,377 =	$11,785,137	20
Foundations (Nonprofit)	$123 +	$438 +	$106 =	$667 x	2,351 =	$1,568,117	4
Universal (Nonprofit)	$112 +	$438 +	$106 =	$656 x	654 =	$429,024	3
Victory (For Profit)	$313 +	$438 +	$106 =	$857 x	3,132 =	$2,684,124	4
Pickett MS - to be assigned	$262 +	$438 +	$106 =	$806 x	664 =	$535,216	1
				Subtotal	24,626	$20,573,362	37
SRC Discretionary Funds for Start-Up Costs, EMOs to submit proposals						$2,473,888	
Total Funds for Managing 37 Schools						$23,047,250	
Partnership Universities							
Temple University				$450 x	2,243 =	$1,009,350	5
University of Pennsylvania				$450 x	1,652 =	$743,400	3
				Subtotal	3,895	$1,752,750	8
Total Funds for Managing 8 Schools						$1,752,750	
Total Private Contracts Assigned							45
Reconstituted and Neighborhood Charters							
Reconstituted	$112 +	$438 +	$0 =	$550 x	12,484 =	$6,866,200	19
Neighborhood	$112 +	$438 +	$0 =	$550 x	2,848 =	$1,566,400	6
				Subtotal	15,332	$8,432,600	
Total Funds for Managing 25 Schools						$8,432,600	
Other Reform Schools per SRC 10							
Other Reform Schools per SRC 10	$112 +	$438 +	$0 =	$550 x	7,879	$4,333,450	16
				Subtotal	7,879	$4,333,450	
Total Funds for Managing 16 Schools						$4,333,450	
Total for Reforming 86 Schools					51,732	$37,566,050	
Other districtwide reform efforts: student remediation, expanded summer schools, high school reform, etc.						$17,433,950	
Commonwealth of Pennsylvania Supplemental Funding						$55,000,000	

Source: "School Reform Commission Reaches Agreement with Education Management Organizations," School District of Philadelphia press release, July 31, 2002; Catherine Gewertz, "Philade lphia Panel Taps Temple University, Others to Run Troubled Schools," *Education Week,* April 17, 2002; case writer analysis.

[1] Under agreement with the Commonwealth of Pa $24,800,000 is being dedicated to the EMO and University schools.

[2] The "Per Pupil Cost" does not include extraordinary start-up costs and summer school costs. Startup costs will be paid from the $2,473, 888 balance of the $24,8000,000 dedicated to the EMO and University schools, on a case by case basis by the District. Summer School costs will be paid from $17,433, 950 allocated for that purpose. All Partnership schools are eligible to apply for summer school grants.

[3] "Per Pupil Teacher Differential" is the difference between average teacher salary in the District and the teacher salary in the low performing school. All Partnership schools will be eligible to receive these funds in order to provide support and training to less experienced teachers in those schools.

[4] Equity Grant: Funds to ensure that students in the lowest performing schools receive additional supports and services including reduced class size, extended day programs, and summer school. Equity grants were calculated based on the costs of: ensuring a full complement of staff at each school (e.g., full-time librarian, full-time nurse, permanent long-term substitute teacher); providing on-site academic coaching and mentoring for teachers; enhancing student support services such as behavior intervention and case management; and purchasing enhanced classroom materials and technology. All partnership schools are eligible to receive the equity grant.

[5] Administrative Support: The School District will not to provide the same level of admin support for EMO-managed schools. For example, EMOs will be providing curriculum development, teacher and principal development and other technical assistance. Consequently, EMOs will receive their fair share of the costs the District would normally expend on these administrative supports. Other partnership schools will continue to receive services from central and academic area offices in lieu of a cash payment.

Exhibit 11

School District of Philadelphia CEO Search Time Line

Time Period	*Activity*
Mid-March	The School Reform Commission (SRC) awards Heidrick & Struggles (H&S) the search.
Late March	SRC approves description for the CEO position. H&S solicits nominations from each SRC member.
Early–mid April	H&S begins outreach activity by sending letters and calling individuals directly. Advertisements are run in The New York Times, Chronicle of Higher Education, and Education Week.
Mid–late April	H&S interviews candidates in person or via videoconference. H&S gives a formal update to the full SRC via conference call. H&S is in weekly, often daily, contact with James Gallagher.
May 3	H&S meets with the SRC to discuss a diverse slate of 15 candidates. SRC agrees to meet with seven candidates for first-round interviews.
May 10–16	SRC interviews candidates.
May 23	SRC selects three finalists.
May 29–June 6	SRC interviews three finalists a second time.
June 13	SRC and H&S meet formally for four hours to discuss the merits of each candidate. In advance of the meeting, H&S provides full reference report and newspaper articles on each candidate. SRC then grades each one against a set of nine criteria. Consensus emerges around a lead candidate.

Source: Heidrick & Struggles internal documents.

Exhibit 12

Summaries of Selected Research on Superintendent Leadership Attributes

In a longitudinal study of 12 superintendents, **Susan Moore Johnson** of the Harvard Graduate School of Education identified a collaborative leadership model in which superintendents work with their constituents to improve public education. She categorized the three types of leadership functions of successful superintendents as educational, political, and managerial. As educators, the leaders instilled trust among principals, teachers, and parents with a vision and a plan for educating students and evaluating their performance. As politicians, the superintendents dealt with various political interest groups, influenced policies, and secured resources to support the educational plan. Finally, as managers, the leaders ensured the smooth working of the complex system by implementing creative organizational structures and processes, managing finances, and implementing policies that encouraged communication, the sharing of information, and learning within the organization. Johnson identified these as three separate leadership functions but noted that they must be integrated for a superintendent to be successful.

Richard Elmore, also of the Harvard Graduate School of Education, has suggested that the purpose of school leadership at any level is the improvement of instructional practice and performance because improvement in student achievement is driven by the effectiveness of what happens in classrooms between teachers and students. Under Elmore's model of school leadership, superintendents should have the capability to operate as agents of large-scale instructional improvement and the skills and knowledge to create learning environments focused on clear expectations for instruction. Many superintendents have been adept political or managerial leaders without effecting what Elmore terms the instructional core of schooling and therefore have been ineffective in driving improvement.

Elmore defined a set of leadership functions for each role in public education, from school boards and policymakers to teachers, and recommended that at the superintendent level the leader should design system improvement strategies; design and implement incentive structures for schools, principals, and teachers; recruit and evaluate principals; provide professional development consistent with the improvement strategy; allocate system resources toward instruction; and buffer non-instructional issues from principals and teachers.

Sources: Susan Moore Johnson, *Leading to Change: The Challenge of the New Superintendency* (San Francisco, CA: Jossey-Bass, Publishers, 1996); Richard F. Elmore, "Building a New Structure for School Leadership," paper published by The Albert Shanker Institute, 2000.

Exhibit 13

Heidrick & Struggles Position Description for CEO Search, School District of Philadelphia

The Chief Executive Officer should have:

Competencies

- A superb reputation for leadership, characterized by one or more successful change-management initiatives achieved in a large, highly complex operating environment.
- Demonstrated capacity for strategic thinking and implementation in a large organization with multiple operating sites, programs/activities, diverse constituencies, and multiple decision makers and decision-making processes. Proven capability to establish, negotiate, and oversee outsourcing and partnership relationships will be evidence of relevant competency.
- Effective manager who is successful in a large organization, skilled in goal/objective setting and the achievement of measurable results; experience in diverse constituent management; experience in leadership in a unionized environment is preferred, as is experience in public/private issues gained in more than one sector of the economy.
- Strong financial and other business skills to maintain effective oversight of the CFO and to oversee district financial conditions.
- Communication skills to be an effective spokesperson and an articulate, forceful advocate for a guiding vision for the district, in the media and in multiple decision forums, public and private.

Characteristics

- Passion for the rights and learning potential of all students, together with a deep commitment to the principle that parents are equal and accountable partners in improving student achievement and that their views and priorities must be solicited and respected.
- Sound judgment, informed by common sense, and an uncommon degree of self-knowledge and personal security.
- Intellect and determination to understand and evaluate the technical merits of key education issues.
- Orientation, when defining success, toward practical results achieved more than processes completed or installed, with commitment to student achievement as the ultimate goal.
- The ability to recruit, retain, and motivate excellent people.
- Demonstrated ability to creatively increase the productivity of human and material resources.
- Highly developed interpersonal skills suited to effective dealings with a very wide variety of kinds of individuals and constituencies.
- Keen sense of the workings of political systems and the ability to devise and execute effective strategies and tactics in such systems.
- The ability to analyze problems quickly, identify their core causes, and craft effective remedies.
- Willingness to take risks where there is reasonable promise of high reward and the danger is not prohibitive.
- Willingness to work with commission members to achieve common goals.

Source: Heidrick & Struggles internal documents.

Exhibit 14

Demographics of 15 Initial CEO Candidates, School District of Philadelphia[1]

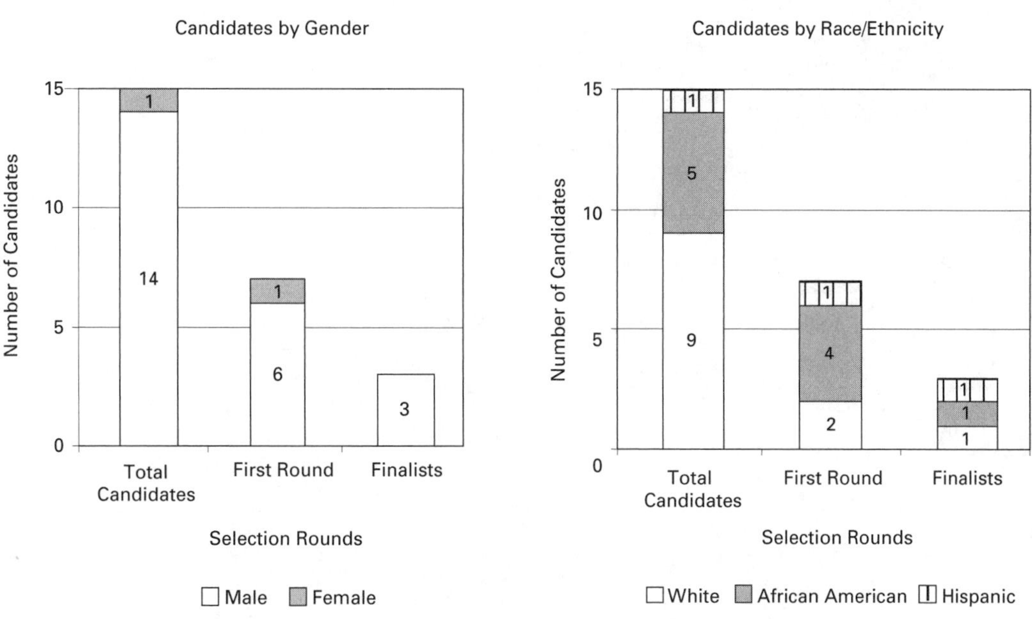

Candidates By Sector

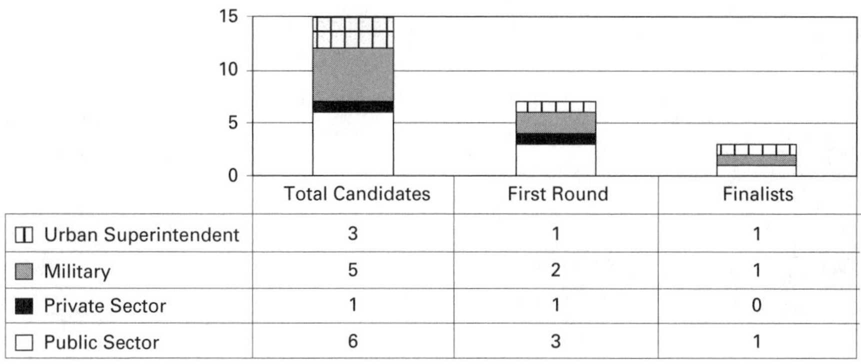

	Total Candidates	First Round	Finalists
Urban Superintendent	3	1	1
Military	5	2	1
Private Sector	1	1	0
Public Sector	6	3	1

Selection Rounds

Source: Heidrick & Struggles internal documents.

[1] Candidates by Sector chart refers to the most recent position or affiliation of the applicants.

Tackling the People Problem

At its most basic level, the success of public education hinges on the interaction between teachers and their students. The rest of the activities—leadership, policymaking, operations management—are only successful to the degree that they strengthen and support what happens in classrooms. Increasingly, research studies show that the quality of teaching has the most impact on a student's academic success and that the quality of leadership in a school has the most impact on the willingness of effective teachers to work there. Because of this, focusing on ways to increase the quality and preparation of the three million teachers and 100,000 principals in public education is a compelling opportunity. Also, with 80% of the $500 billion in public education spending allocated to salaries and benefits, improvements in the sector's human capital are a highly leveraged way to have an impact.

This is especially true in urban areas. Although there are 15,000 school districts in America, the largest 100—mostly urban—enroll more than 20% of all students and approximately 40% of all minority and low-income students. One in four high school courses nationwide are being taught by a teacher who did not major in that subject in college. In high-poverty schools, the ratio jumps to one in three. Low-income students are 77% more likely to be taught a course by someone without a degree in the content area.[1] Nationwide, low-income and minority students are twice as likely to be taught by a novice teacher, and schools with high percentages of these students are more likely to attract teachers with subpar academic credentials. Only 8% of teachers in high-poverty and high-minority schools scored in the top quartile on the SAT, while 34% scored in the bottom quartile. By contrast, 23% of teachers in low-poverty, low-minority schools scored in the top quartile, with only 9% scoring in the bottom quartile. Nearly 40% of teachers in high-poverty schools went to a noncompetitive college, while only 20% of teachers in low-poverty schools graduated from a similar institution. [2]

As for principals, their role has changed dramatically in the last 20 years, and the institutions that prepare the vast majority of them have not adapted to the present realities of the job. No longer merely supervisors of employees and facilities, school leaders are increasingly expected to set goals for student achievement and other outcomes and to redesign and manage their schools to meet those goals. They have to find and hire staff who fit their vision for success, and they must build relationships with parents and community leaders so that all these adults support the work of the school. And with the advent of state accountability regimes and No Child Left Behind, principals must work with teachers to continuously improve the performance of all subgroups of students so that their schools meet expectations and avoid the consequences of underperformance. Unfortunately, the preparation that the vast majority of principals have received is not up to the challenge of helping them successfully meet their new responsibilities. In 2005, Arthur Levine, then president of Teachers College at Columbia University, conducted a study of education school degree programs that prepare 88% of the nation's principals. He found that "the overall quality of educational administration programs in the United States [is] poor. The majority of programs range from inadequate to appalling, even at some of the country's leading universities."[3]

Because of these statistics, education entrepreneurs are increasingly pursuing opportunities that are aimed at strengthening human capital in the sector. This module explores three of these efforts—two focused on teachers and another on principals—plus a district superintendent as a customer trying to analyze the value of two external providers that prepare principals for her district. Through discussions of these cases, you will begin to build your own point of view about the "people problem" and theories of change for addressing it, as well as a familiarity with various approaches to building and growing social enterprises focused on human capital.

The first case in the module is "Teach For America 2005," which describes the challenges facing the organization as the team considers how to realize the aggressive goals its board has just approved. As the first in a series of cases that explore entrepreneurial ventures focused on improving the pipeline of human capital for public education, the case prompts a discussion of the complexities of developing and growing an organization focused on eliminating the achievement gap by placing graduates of competitive colleges as teachers in low-performing schools. The case raises issues of strategy, organizational capacity, and success indicators, as well as the forces affecting the supply and demand of teachers around the country and the ways in which Teach For America (TFA) aims to have an impact on the larger problem of student performance in the long term. The discussion will introduce the first three steps of a framework for idea development for social entrepreneurs: identifying a problem and analyzing its contributing factors, developing a theory of change, and designing and implementing a strategy that puts the theory into action. It also raises the issue of organizational growth as a tool for system-level change.

The next case covers the Boston Teacher Residency (BTR), a joint venture between a local nonprofit and the Boston Public Schools. As a contrast to TFA, the BTR case allows you to consider a different theory of change for increasing the supply of quality teachers who are well prepared for urban classrooms and to evaluate the implications the theory has for a strategy for long-term impact. The case allows for an evaluation of the ability of an innovative model of teacher preparation to have an impact on the lowest-performing schools in a district. It also provokes discussion about the challenge of reevaluating an approach that seems to be working in the face of new market dynamics, such as a new decision maker and new competitors.

"New Leaders for New Schools" (NLNS), the third case in the module, is a nonprofit organization that recruits and prepares new principals in a full-year residency model and then places them in full-time positions in urban public schools. The case examines the creation and development of NLNS, the group's theory of change and strategy, and the competing notions of how best to grow the operation. Discussing the case provides an opportunity to practice problem identification and contributing factor analysis, development of a theory of change and a strategy for putting the theory into action, as well as a frame for analyzing an early-stage social venture's approach to decisions about growth. The NLNS case also allows for a debate about the possibility of creating system-wide change through an entrepreneurial organization.

"Memphis City Schools" examines a district's efforts to strengthen and support the development of new principals as instructional leaders. It highlights challenges posed by an influx of new first-year principals and the looming retirement of more than half of the district's principals, as well as the district's partnership with two principal development programs. The case is an effective tool for exploring the definition of an "instructional leader" and what it takes to prepare people for the role. Since most entrepreneurs focused on the people problem must sell their services to district superintendents in order to implement their theories of change, the case challenges students to put themselves in the shoes of a superintendent as a "customer" of two external providers and explore ways to assess the value of each service beyond its price tag.

Creating and Evaluating Social Ventures

Module II introduces a way of thinking about the creation and evaluation of social ventures, a framework that will be useful throughout all the modules. In order to pursue an opportunity to create pattern-breaking social change, social entrepreneurs

1. identify the problem that presents an opportunity and analyze its contributing factors;
2. develop a theory of change for addressing one or more contributing factors in order to solve the problem and analyze the assumptions about how the world works that are embedded in the theory;
3. design a strategy to put the theory of change into action (this includes who will be served and how);
4. implement the strategy and build and manage an organization that supports it; and
5. monitor results and adapt the strategy as you learn more about the problem, contributing factors, and theory of change.

Social entrepreneurs must develop a deep understanding of the problem they propose to address including its contributing factors. For example, entrepreneurs in this module have identified the current state of human capital, particularly at the teacher and principal level, as a contributing factor to achievement and opportunity gaps among low-income and minority students. The various organizations in the module are driven by different theories of change. A theory of change is simply a belief about cause and effect, directed at addressing one or more of the contributing factors to the problem. As with any kind of theory, it can be phrased as if-then statements.

As an example, let's look at an organization outside the human capital area. The Posse Foundation is focused on opening up access to elite networks that influence business, government, and civil society to low-income students. The organization's theory of change is that *if* groups of low-income students attend and finish top-tier colleges, *then* they will naturally become part of these networks, and that *if* they enter college with a group of friends (a posse), *then* they will be more likely to graduate. One benefit of a theory of change is that it helps narrow the range of possibilities for a strategy, helping an organization focus on activities that are most likely to lead to impact. In the theory of change in the Posse Foundation example, an effective strategy must focus on recruiting groups of high-potential students (not individuals) who are likely to do well in college and partner with top-tier colleges (not less competitive ones) that will be willing to admit students in groups. If the organization focuses on individuals, students who are less prepared, or colleges that are less competitive, it will not be enacting its theory of change. In order to implement its strategy, Posse must build an organization that is good at recruiting high-potential students, placing them into posses, working with top-tier colleges to admit them, and supporting the posses throughout their time in college. In order to measure its progress and learn from its work so that it constantly improves, the organization must pick a few interim and long-term metrics that are core to the effectiveness of its model. This social entrepreneurship framework is a useful tool for entrepreneurs planning their ventures as well as for funders and stakeholders (and education entrepreneurship students!) attempting to evaluate the ventures.

Evaluating Growth Options

In the cases in this module, TFA, BTR, and NLNS are each facing growth decisions, giving you an opportunity to practice using a framework for thinking about expansion that will also be used in Module IV. Social entrepreneurs seldom have a "right or wrong" choice about the growth of their model; rather, they must try to make the best decision possible by balancing a number of factors that can be categorized as the potential for *impact*, the attractiveness of the *market*, *organizational capacity*, and *risks*. In each category, a number of questions are helpful in evaluating growth opportunities:

- *Impact:* Is the growth opportunity consistent with the organization's theory of change? Is the expanded footprint critical for demonstrating that the model works for different populations? A different geography? Or does it increase the number of students served in a particular market in order to create momentum for change in the broader system in that market? How are the organization's current results likely to be affected by growth?
- *Market:* Do the demographics fit the population the model is designed to serve? Is there sufficient demand to absorb the entry of a new provider? Is the regulatory and policy environment hospitable to the entrepreneur's model? How about the funding environment? Will the entrepreneur's efforts be part of a larger strategy of change for a superintendent, a mayor, or an existing coalition of education reformers?
- *Organizational capacity:* Does the leadership team have the necessary skills and network (or ready access to them) to successfully execute the expansion plan? Is the organization good at the things it must be good at in order to be successful in more than one location? Is the program model sufficiently proven and stable to be replicated? Are the operating systems of the organization well enough established—hiring, training, financial management, etc.—to support operations in additional sites?
- *Risks:* What could go wrong—contextually, strategically, programmatically, and financially? How might these risks be mitigated?

Again, there is no formula for determining the perfect answer—in some situations, the market dynamics will be so compelling that the organization can scramble to build the capacity it needs to make expansion work. In others, the risk assessment will outweigh the opportunity for impact.

Module Questions

Each case has its own set of assignment questions, but as you move through the module, keep these overarching questions in mind:

1. Are the education entrepreneurs in the cases acting on an implicit or explicit theory of change? If so, what are the underlying assumptions they are making about the sector, the people working in it, and how organizations work? In other words, what would you have to believe about the way the world works for their theories of change to have merit?
2. How likely is the strategy of each organization to lead to the results the entrepreneurs aim to achieve?
3. Are there elements of these ventures that could lead to system-wide change?

Notes

1. The Education Trust, "The Opportunity Gap: No Matter How You Look at It, Low-Income and Minority Students Get Fewer Good Teachers," *Thinking K–16* (winter 2004: 36–37).

2. Ibid.

3. Arthur Levine, *Educating Leaders* (New York: Education Leadership Project, 2005).

Stacey Childress

Teach For America 2005

In the spring of 2005, as Teach For America's (TFA) national board meeting adjourned, Chief Operating Officer Jerry Hauser considered the opportunity before the organization. The board had approved a new strategic plan for 2006 through 2010. The aspirations were ambitious, and if they succeeded in reaching the goals set out in the plan, TFA would take its place among the country's most enduring institutions.

TFA was a national teacher corps of recent college graduates who committed to teach for two years in under-resourced urban and rural public schools in the United States. The organization's mission was two-fold—corps members would first work hard to expand the educational opportunities of their students during their two-year commitment, and would subsequently become a force of leaders in education and other sectors such as law, business, politics, and medicine to accomplish systemic changes to expand educational opportunity. With an FY04 operating budget of $39 million, a total corps of 3,000, and a talented national and regional staff of approximately 300, TFA pursued its vision that "one day all children will have the opportunity to attain an excellent education." (See **Exhibit 1** for TFA financial data.)

Hauser knew that the key to converting the plan into success was ensuring the organization had the right strategy and the capacity to execute effectively. As he looked toward the future, he reflected on the opportunities and challenges that TFA had faced in its first 15 years to identify lessons that might be useful for its next phase of growth.

The Need

Achievement rates for low-income and minority students in the United States significantly trailed that of white, middle class, and affluent students. Results on the National Assessment of Educational Performance revealed that by age nine, low-income students were already on average more than three grade levels behind their wealthier peers in reading ability and on average more than two grade levels behind in math and science. The gap widened as students progressed through school. Students in low-income communities were seven times less likely to graduate from college than those from higher-income neighborhoods. (See **Exhibit 2** for national achievement data.)

Education researchers consistently found that high-quality teaching was one of the most important elements in raising the achievement level of all students, and several studies indicated that teachers with strong academic skills tended to have more success with students than those with weaker academic skills. In a report in Winter 2004, the Education Trust reported that 39% of teachers in high-poverty schools had attended "non-competitive" colleges, as compared to 21% of teachers in low-poverty schools. Additionally, 34% of new teachers in high-poverty schools had SAT scores in the bottom quartile, while only 8% had scores in the top quartile. By contrast in low-poverty schools, only 9% of new teachers had scores in the bottom quartile, and 23% scored in the top quartile. The report concluded that as a nation "we consistently assign teachers whose performance lags on important tests to low-income and minority students, whose performance in turn lags on important tests."[1]

Public schools in the United States employed approximately three million teachers, and compensated them on average $42,912 annually. Between 2000 and 2010, approximately 50% of the nation's teachers were eligible for retirement. Increased birth and immigration rates coupled with recent policy mandates requiring class size reductions in a number of states increased the national demand for teachers. Taken together, these factors prompted education observers to forecast the need for U.S. public schools to hire over two million new teachers in the first decade of the 21st century.[2]

Looking Back: Teach For America, 1989–1999[3]

By 2004, TFA recruited, trained, and placed approximately 1,600 incoming corps members in some of the lowest-performing schools in 22 areas of the United States. In 2005, TFA was on track to increase placements to at least 2,000 incoming members for a total corps size of approximately 3,600. Corps members were recruited from hundreds of colleges and universities, and were hired directly by school districts and paid the same salary as other beginning teachers. Over 9,000 TFA alumni had worked with over 1.75 million students, 95% of whom were African-American or Hispanic. To reach this point, TFA had progressed through periods of opportunity, challenge, and growth. The journey had not been easy.

Getting Started: 1989–1992

Wendy Kopp founded Teach For America in 1989 after graduating from Princeton University. In writing her senior thesis on educational inequality, Kopp came to believe that one approach to addressing this problem was recruiting top graduates from some of the best universities in the United States to teach for two years in areas of great need, who would then go on to lead the systemic change necessary to end educational inequality. She believed that many of these talented young people were looking for post-college options that provided more meaningful work than they could find in the typical private sector companies that recruited on their campuses. After her own graduation, Kopp worked with a small team of fellow recent graduates to recruit 2,500 college seniors to apply to the program, from which they chose 500 corps members, none of whom were formally trained as teachers before joining TFA. As Kopp recalled,

> If we were going to get the kind of people we really wanted—the most talented, dedicated college graduates who were already demonstrated leaders on their campuses—we needed to surround this initiative with a sense of national importance. To me, this meant we needed to begin on a certain scale. I felt that the minimum number that would convey the appropriate sense of urgency was 500. In fact, in the research for my thesis, I discovered that the Peace Corps had also determined to start with no fewer than 500 corps members for the same reason.[4]

After completing a seven-week summer training institute in Los Angeles and passing the National Teacher's Exam, corps members dispersed to high-need schools in North Carolina, Georgia, Los Angeles, New York City, and New Orleans. The first year was not without challenges. Some districts failed to meet their staffing commitments because of budget cuts and personnel changes, but overall the program was up and running. After raising $2.5 million for the first year from foundations, corporations, and philanthropists, Kopp and her team raised an additional $5 million to expand operations in the second year. They entered Houston, Oakland, the Texas Rio Grande Valley, and the Mississippi Delta, and selected 700 corps members from a pool of 3,000 applicants.

Stabilizing the Model: 1993–1995

By 1995, TFA had expanded to 13 urban and rural areas, with an annual operating budget of approximately $7 million and 55 full-time staff. Regional directors managed school district relationships and corps members, and raised funds from local supporters. Regional support directors provided ongoing professional development. Senior teachers filled these positions and functioned as mentors and coaches for corps members. The incoming corps remained at approximately 500 members, and TFA ran an annual five-week summer institute, now located in Houston, to prepare new members. The recruits participated in training sessions and taught summer school to students from some of the city's lowest-performing schools.

Between 1993 and 1995, the traditional teacher education community presented a number of obstacles. In 1994, a professor at Columbia Teacher's College blasted TFA in a leading education journal. In an article titled "Who Will Speak for the Children? How TFA Hurts Urban Schools and Students," she called TFA a fly-by-night organization that was bad for its corps members, bad for schools, bad for children, and bad for the teaching profession.[5] The repercussions were significant. Although TFA had evidence from a survey that indicated 95% of principals who had corps members in their schools considered them at least as effective as other beginning teachers, the organization had difficulty responding to the concerns the article generated among its supporters.

The pace of growth caused constant financial stress, particularly in generating a stable cash flow to meet the bi-weekly $200,000 payroll. In order to match expenses with their ability to generate donations, the senior team made a number of cuts. In addition to shutting down non-core activities that had sprung up along the way, they reorganized the staff, and deleted the regional position of support director, which meant laying off 60 employees. Because the role was the primary support for corps members, many felt that the organization was abandoning them. Nonetheless, the senior team had determined that this model of support did not work well and that they needed to redesign ongoing professional development for both financial and programmatic reasons.

The stress of financial instability and organizational restructuring, the pressure of last-minute crises, and the overwhelmed leadership team contributed to a deterioration of the organizational culture. In an effort to explicitly address this emerging culture problem, Kopp created a set of core values to guide the organization. (See **Exhibit 3** for core values.)

Strengthening the Organization: 1996–1999

TFA emerged from the restructuring of 1995 stronger and better positioned to increase its impact on public education. In early 1996, the senior team created a three-year plan to transform TFA into a stable, thriving institution. The plan had five priorities: 1) gaining financial stability; 2) bolstering core programmatic activities with a focus on training and supporting corps members; 3) building capacity by recruiting high-quality staff and supporting them with effective management and development; 4) strengthening its reputation with the public and the education community; and 5) strengthening its national board and building regional boards.

According to staff members, specific measures for each priority helped clarify the roles of staff in the field and at headquarters, and subsequently drove the activities and tasks of the organization. As one senior manager recalled, the measures allowed the organization to delegate significant autonomy to the regional executive directors, and prompted the national office to think more about how to develop and support the field managers in meeting their targets.

Regional offices developed local boards of advisers to help with fundraising, program support, and public relations. Kopp remade the national board to infuse the body with expertise in recruitment, marketing and fundraising. In 1997, TFA ran a financial surplus for the first time in its history. The organization had doubled regional donations since 1994, contributing to a more diversified and stable funding base. The national development staff was overhauled, and became more efficient and effective. By 1999, TFA had paid down $1.2 million in debt, and had accumulated a cash reserve of $1 million and an endowment of $3.5 million.

In 1997, Kopp and a group of veteran TFA staff created a separate organization called The New Teacher Project (TNTP), to influence more broadly the way teachers were brought into the public school system by providing consulting services to help school districts increase their capacity to recruit, hire, and develop teachers. TNTP launched with four one-year contracts to provide services, and doubled its volume in its second year.[6]

Also in 1999, Kopp promoted Jerry Hauser, a charter corps member, to become TFA's first chief operating officer. Hauser was a Yale Law School graduate and former McKinsey consultant who had been serving as vice president of programs. He assumed responsibility for managing the regions and the national staff, allowing Kopp to focus primarily on vision and strategy development and external affairs, as well as engaging strategically in high-impact internal issues. Hauser described his task as working with the staff to build a high-performance organization, saying:

> In the start-up days, there was so much to do that we were a fly-by-the-seat-of-your-pants, entrepreneurial organization. Ten years later, we do some things much more effectively, but there's a fear that we might become too bureaucratic and "professional", and lose some of the passion that comes from being grass-roots and entrepreneurial. As we move on, we need to find ways to combine the benefits of those approaches.[7]

Beginning the Second Decade: 2000–2005

The first half of TFA's second decade was characterized by dramatic growth in size, quality, and operating capacity. At the beginning of 2000, TFA was a $10 million organization with a national and regional staff of 90, and a corps of 1,300 serving in 15 regions. By early 2005, TFA was a $39 million[8] organization with 300 employees and a corps of 3,000 in 22 regions. TFA continued to pursue its theory of change—corps members would help close the achievement gap for their students during their two-year commitment, and at the same time gain the "insight, outrage, and added commitment" necessary to become a leadership force for long-term systemic change from both inside and outside the education establishment.

To map its next five years, the team developed a new strategy with five priorities: growing the size and diversity of the corps; increasing corps member effectiveness; strengthening the TFA alumni network; improving financial sustainability; and deepening organizational capacity. Setting goals and executing against the five priorities drove the organization's overall growth between 2000 and 2005. (**Exhibit 4** contains performance data.)

Size and Diversity

Recruitment

TFA planned to increase its impact by growing in size while maintaining a focus on the quality of the corps. TFA doubled the number of recruitment offices in 2001 to cultivate applicants on more than 100 college campuses. Experience showed that it took time to build relationships and awareness on a new campus, so the team did not expect an increase in applications commensurate with the investment for two years. In addition to marketing activities designed to drive quantity (such as an upgraded website, collateral material, and advertising campaigns), TFA developed a set of focus schools at which they focused on attracting student leaders who demonstrated the characteristics of the most successful corps members. Recruiters "headhunted" top prospects rather than relying solely on mass marketing and discovered that these targeted prospects were accepted into the corps at a much higher rate than the general applicant pool.

By 2005, TFA saw a dramatic increase in its recruitment results. TFA received 17,000 applications, up from 4,000 in 2000, and an overall increase of 29% from 2004. Applications among college seniors in particular, the target group, grew 39%. Between 2000 and 2005, TFA also saw a dramatic increase in its market share on top campuses, as defined by the percentage of the senior class that applied for the corps. At Spelman College, market share grew from 4% to 12%; at Harvard and Princeton, market share increased from 2.2% to 8%, and from 1.4% to 8%, respectively. At Dartmouth and Amherst, 11% of the graduating classes applied to TFA in 2005.

Because 95% of the students taught by corps members were African-American or Hispanic, TFA also focused specifically on recruiting candidates of color, then used a race-blind admissions process in selecting corps members. African-Americans represented 11% of TFA recruits but only 8.5% of all graduating seniors in the U.S., and Hispanics represented 6% of both the corps and the total population of college seniors. Even so, the results in each of these areas fell short of TFA's diversity goals. For instance, as a proxy to measure socio-economic diversity, TFA tracked the parental educational attainment of its corps. First-generation college graduates were 43% of the U.S. total, but only 25% of new TFA corps members.[9] (**Exhibit 5** displays diversity goals.)

The recruitment staff noted a number of challenges in attracting diverse, talented individuals, including intense competition for this desirable candidate pool from other job, graduate school, and fellowship options. High-caliber candidates from minority and low-income backgrounds often faced self-imposed, societal, and family pressure to get "on track" with their first post-graduate job. The staff cited similar obstacles for men and math and science majors.

Additionally, economic considerations tended to play more of a role in the decisions of low-income candidates. Corps members were required to pay for their travel to the summer training institute, relocate themselves to the areas where they had received teaching assignments, and in some cases pay testing and certification fees—all out of their own pockets. In response, TFA invested more resources into "transitional assistance" in the form of need-based financial aid made up of interest-free loans and grants for incoming corps members. By 2005, TFA awarded aid totaling $4 million.

Placement

In order to place a larger corps, TFA focused on deepening its influence in existing cities. Executive directors were charged with developing strategic plans that specified both the number of corps members and where they should be placed to have a "catalytic" impact in their areas, as well as how the regional office would generate the revenue necessary to meet these goals.

Beyond deepening its influence in existing sites, TFA also created a new national position to lead its expansion to new sites. The director of new site development would work with Kopp to select new sites, raise start-up funding, and recruit and support new executive directors in each new area. The growth plan formalized the criteria for selecting new sites: 1) low student achievement rates in high-poverty areas; 2) ability of the site to appeal to potential applicants; 3) feasibility of placing a critical mass of corps members given district needs and certification requirements; and 4) interest from local institutions in funding the costs of recruiting, training, and supporting corps members.

The existing demand to enter new areas was more than enough to meet the growth target of 25 total sites, but the national management team was committed to following the selection criteria closely to ensure a strong environment for success, and thereby increase the probability of having significant impact in the new sites. By 2004, TFA was operating in 22 regions around the country.

Corps Member Effectiveness

The second priority in the five-year plan was to increase the number of corps members able to demonstrate a dramatic impact on their students' academic achievement. To pursue this priority, TFA refined its selection criteria and process, redesigned pre-service training, developed a measure to track corps members' progress in advancing their students academically, and strengthened ongoing professional development.

Refining the Selection Criteria and Process

Applicants submitted a written application that included their academic record, resume, and an essay in advance of participating in a day-long selection process that included a personal interview, role play, problem-solving exercise, group discussion, and sample teaching session. Around 150 selectors were trained annually to assess applicants on seven criteria: achievement, perseverance, critical thinking, organizational ability, influencing/motivating, respect for others, and fit with TFA's mission.

With help from outside consultants, TFA analyzed data from past corps members who had achieved both high and medium levels of performance, as well as those who resigned from the corps. Reviews of application files and interviews with corps members and regional staff led to a refinement of the selection process to focus on identifying the personal characteristics of candidates that matched those of former corps members who had achieved classroom success. In particular, TFA found that a pattern of past demonstrated achievement and perseverance[10] was predictive of success, while prior experience in a low-income environment was not necessary. A belief in TFA's vision was found to be necessary, but the intensity of this belief did not necessarily distinguish top performers from others. Because variation in quality across the large number of selectors could have significant impact on corps quality, the TFA staff used this information to create successful selection profiles for use in selector training seminars.

Redesigning Training

TFA developed a new curriculum to prepare corps members with the skills, tools and knowledge to be effective teachers. Based on pedagogical research, evaluation of corps member effectiveness, and feedback from staff and corps members, the curriculum was strengthened to help accelerate the learning curve that new teachers encountered in the classroom. The redesigned program included: 1) six research-based education courses; 2) full (and intensely supervised) teaching responsibility for a class of summer school students; 3) weekly content- and pedagogy-based institute learning teams; and 4) content- and grade-level-specific workshops.

Courses in the summer institute included: Teaching as Leadership; Learning Theory; Literacy (Elementary and Secondary); Instructional Planning & Delivery; Classroom Management & Culture; and Diversity, Community and Achievement. Teaching as Leadership helped corps members internalize the instructional strategies used by teachers who demonstrated dramatic gains in student achievement. Among these were: establishing ambitious goals for student achievement; investing students and their families in the idea that hard work will lead to success in school; working purposefully and relentlessly to overcome obstacles and progress toward their goals; and improving their instructional practice over time through a constant process of self-evaluation and learning. The other courses included exposure to a number of topics, such as creating a classroom environment that fostered a culture of achievement; developing literacy skills at all grade levels; developing a goal-oriented, standards-based approach to instructional design; child development theories; motivational theory; and working effectively within a new community.

TFA added two institute locations to accommodate the growing corps. In 2005, TFA planned to conduct summer institutes in Philadelphia and Los Angeles, in addition to Houston. This required hiring additional staff to plan and execute the program at the additional locations. Early in TFA's history, the availability of high-quality faculty members to serve in the summer institute presented a challenge, given the competing opportunities available to outstanding corps members and alumni who were ideal candidates for these opportunities. TFA repackaged the faculty positions as a selective leadership opportunity, and increased the stipend from $2,500 to $5,000 in order to increase the attractiveness of the roles. By 2004, the faculty positions were highly competitive. Over 240 corps members and alumni applied for 72 faculty positions at the Houston institute. TFA invested in bringing in the best people through a rigorous application process that included observations of applicants' teaching as well as an examination of their students' academic progress.

Measuring Corps Member Performance

Setting expectations for corps members' impact on student achievement and tracking their performance over time was critical to ensuring TFA was delivering on its mission, improving its organizational effectiveness, and garnering the support necessary for building a sustainable enterprise. Hauser noted, "Corps member effectiveness is a top priority. We developed the 'significant gains' metric to reflect the level of performance necessary for our corps members to meet the goal of helping their students 'catch-up.' Our students come to us behind their peers in terms of achievement, so they must make gains well above what you would normally expect in one school year."

In short, the significant gains metric aimed for students to perform better than simply advancing one grade level during an academic year. Depending on subject and grade level, achieving significant gains meant that, on average, students in a corps member's classroom progressed 1.5 or 2 grade levels in a single year, as measured by an external benchmark such as a district or state achievement test. (See **Exhibit 6** for explanation of significant gains and targets.)

In 2003, 22% of corps members were able to demonstrate evidence of significant gains. In 2004, TFA fell short of its goal of 33% of corps members reaching this milestone, but was encouraged by the increase to 27%. Additionally, the national staff attempted to better norm the results across the country by monitoring the data coming from the regions to ensure that a consistent standard was being used. Hauser clarified the measure:

> People often misunderstand the metric, and therefore think a goal of having 33% of teachers reach it is way too low. But really what we're saying is that in the immediate term we want at least a substantial minority of our teachers—and in the longer run the vast majority—to move their students forward much more than would normally be expected in the course of a single academic year, despite all the obstacles. Beyond that, the rest should have students making at least "normal" progress—that is, growth of at least one full year.

Gathering and interpreting the necessary data across the number of states and districts in which corps members were teaching was difficult given the range of assessments used in various states. While TFA acknowledged that this was not a perfect measurement system, they were confident that it allowed them to usefully assess their corps members' performance in the classroom. The national staff also used the data to improve the selection process, and attempted to identify best practices that could be disseminated throughout the network and built into the summer training. TFA believed it was the only teacher preparation program in the nation, traditional or alternative, that set specific student achievement targets for its teachers, monitored their performance, and used the data to improve its selection criteria, pre-service training, and ongoing professional development model.

Ongoing Professional Development

The regional program staff was ultimately responsible for determining whether corps members met the "significant gains" standard, as well as observing and providing feedback on classroom practice. All of TFA's regional program activities were designed to support corps members in setting and pursuing clear and ambitious goals and then to serve as a resource to them as they pursue these goals. To accomplish this, the regions maintained a ratio of one program director for every 50 corps members. The regional training and support structure was driven by a cycle of classroom observation and feedback at four key points during the year. Through these cycles of observations and discussions, program staff acted as guides to keep corps members focused on of the larger goal of achieving significant academic gains in their classrooms, while helping them access resources to improve their ability to handle day-to-day classroom challenges.

Alumni Leadership

Kopp, Hauser, and the senior team recognized the full importance of TFA's alumni in putting their theory of change into practice, and implemented a strategy of engaging them in a network to catalyze their ongoing leadership in education and other fields. Although TFA's theory of change did not require that 100% of its alumni remain in the education sector, the organization estimated that 86% of the total alumni population were having an impact on education or low-income communities either through full-time work or on a volunteer basis. The organization publicized its claim that 63% of the 9,000 alumni since 1990 were still working in or studying education full-time, and approximately 40% were still teaching. TFA estimated that of this group, 94% were either working directly with low-income students or with an organization focused on low-income communities. Although most were still in their twenties and thirties, many alumni were running traditional and charter schools and others had started nonprofit education organizations, such as The New Teacher Project. In addition, they won accolades as teachers, including an alumnus from the 1996 corps who won the 2005 National Teacher of the Year award. Former corps members had also gone on to attend some of the nation's top graduate schools, and had assumed a variety of leadership roles in nonprofit management, law, government and business. (**Exhibit 7** contains alumni information.)

As with any network, the larger and more connected the membership, the more valuable the network. TFA built an alumni team that focused on ways to keep alumni connected to the movement to end educational inequality, such as building an alumni database, sending out regular content-rich email communications, and sponsoring periodic events in cities with a critical mass of alumni. A new Office of Career and Civic Opportunity developed a job bank and partnerships with graduate schools to permit corps members to defer their admissions and take advantage of dedicated scholarship opportunities. By the end of 2004, this roster consisted of more than 65 schools including Harvard Business School, Stanford Law School, and the University of Michigan Medical School. Additionally, in 2004 a growing number of graduate schools offered benefits ranging from fellowships to course credits to waived application fees for Teach For America alumni.

Financial Sustainability

TFA's cost per corps member was approximately $11,000 annually. In addition to fundraising at the national level, the organization relied heavily on the regional executive directors' abilities to raise local money to sustain their activities. Overall, private donors provided 72% of total revenue, with public sources accounting for the remainder. One source of public funds was the majority of the public school districts that hired corps members. On average, districts paid TFA $1,500 each year for each corps member they hired. By 2004, TFA had accumulated an operating reserve of approximately $17 million. Although the growth plan developed in 2000 projected a budget of approximately $26 million by 2004, the actual budget that year was $39 million. Hauser addressed the variance:

> We underestimated the number of staff it would take to reach the goals we set out in our original plan. One thing we learned was that, in growing, there may not be huge economies of scale. One reason for this is that we, like many non-profits, were probably "under capacity" when we started growing, so even at our existing scale our costs may not have been sustainable. Additionally, we were in some respects already serving the "cheapest" part of the market, so going deeper meant investing more on a per unit basis. For instance, in our recruitment efforts, we were already attracting the "easiest" applicants who would have found Teach For America with relatively little effort on our part, so growing meant having to expend more energy to go after people who did not initially seek us out. Nor are there enormous savings from scale—for instance, in program elements like professional development support, we have to scale up proportionately with the number of corps members to maintain a consistent ratio between trainers and program directors and corps members.

In addition, TFA was affiliated with AmeriCorps, the national service organization that operated with federal funds as part of the Corporation for National and Community Service. TFA received operating funds, and corps members were eligible for a package of federal educational grants in addition to their teaching salaries.[11] In 2003, due to mismanagement and accounting irregularities, the national AmeriCorps budget fell by $200 million, and TFA did not receive a renewal of its funding.

Although its recruiting materials had always indicated that it could not guarantee the educational awards, TFA immediately committed to provide the equivalent of an education award to each eligible corps member, as well as cover the costs of qualified student loan deferment—a liability of approximately $10 million. Kopp commented on this decision:

> We felt we had some moral obligation to [cover the awards and deferment], despite the fact that there was a qualifier noting that [education] awards are contingent on federal funding in our materials. Also, we felt that we would lose some corps members as well as a lot of trust among the others if we did not make this commitment, and that the fallout would hurt our reputation on college campuses in the future; we didn't want our organizational focus taken away from our growth/quality objectives and felt that making an early commitment to corps members was the only way to achieve that.[12]

After an active lobbying effort from TFA and other affected organizations, Congress eventually authorized $100 million in emergency funding to keep AmeriCorps operational. However, the decrease in funding meant that only 22,000 of the usual 50,000 AmeriCorps slots were funded in 2003. The TFA development staff, with the help of Board member contacts, quickly raised millions from a combination of federal and private sources to cover the lost awards and operating support, representing $6 million of the total $39 million budget that year. Congress reauthorized funding for 55,000 members in 2004. However, the government's commitment to AmeriCorps in the long term was unclear, and although it had regained its grantee status, TFA's ability to rely on education awards for all of its corps members as it grew remained uncertain.

Organizational Capacity

Growing from 15 to 22 regions between 2000 and 2004 forced TFA to think strategically about how to give regional executive directors the level of autonomy they needed to effectively lead their operations, while at the same time ensuring consistent quality and outcomes across the sites. Hauser reflected:

> We started by establishing clear, shared goals that stemmed from our theory of change and were backed up by discussions, critical thinking, and data. We then developed local and regional goals that roll up to senior management goals, so everyone is invested in the same targets. One of the most important things we learned from this process is that clarifying and communicating targets and plans at all levels that are aligned with our organizational priorities is a key to delivering our mission across our diverse sites. We can look back at our results and see in areas where we made less progress than we would have liked, our goals weren't as clear or aligned as they could have been.

TFA developed a rubric of best practices for regional offices that included summaries of guidelines for supporting and developing corps members during their two-year service, nurturing local relationships, and fundraising. (See **Exhibit 8** for an excerpt from the rubric.) Executive directors were expected to follow these general approaches in meeting their goals, unless they could make a case for why another approach would be more effective. The national office also developed more detailed tools and processes that executive directors could use in implementing these practices.

Hauser commented on the relationship between the field offices and the national team:

> We have occasional tensions between the field and headquarters that are similar to those of many multi-site organizations. One thing we have found is that when there are areas where regional offices are resistant to input from national teams we need to look as much at the quality of the services from the national teams as the abstract questions about decision rights.

> That is, many tensions between national and regional control disappear or are minimized when our national teams are providing high quality services and providing the regions with good support and good tools that make their lives easier and help them to their goals.

Hauser believed that effective execution depended on having the right people in the right places at headquarters and in the field, explaining, "We are always aware of our revenue needs, but our biggest constraint isn't money, it's people. We are committed to building an organization that talented leaders want to work for, but we also have to get better at finding and developing these folks." TFA focused on its corps members as a pool of future leadership talent for the organization. Many of the senior managers were former corps members, as were many of the regional executive directors. Between 2000 and 2005, the senior team expanded to include vice presidents of program design, program execution, and alumni affairs, each of whom was a former corps or staff member. However, Hauser felt that the organization could still do a better job of deliberately cultivating promising corps members to take on leadership roles in the organization. (See **Exhibit 9** for organization charts.)

TFA also focused on retention of current employees as part of its talent strategy. As Hauser described it, the goal was retention of high-performers, not retention of everyone. Hauser explained TFA's philosophy of retaining high-performers:

> We believe that the most effective way to keep our best people is to invest them in exciting, ambitious goals—these appeal to high-achievers by engaging them in something important that is larger than themselves. We also offer positions with more responsibility than people typically get at comparable organizations early in their careers. Another component is recognition and compensation. We are working on ways to more effectively acknowledge high-performers. While our salaries may be lower than in similar private sector roles, we are committed to staying highly competitive with the public and nonprofit sectors.

Impact

In 2002, TFA agreed to an external, independent evaluation of its program.[13] In 2003, Mathematica Policy Research, Inc., conducted the study by asking the question "Do TFA teachers improve (or at least not harm) student outcomes relative to what would have happened in their absence?"[14] The researchers compared outcomes of students in grades one through five taught by TFA teachers with those in the same schools and at the same grades taught by other teachers, whom they designated as "control teachers." The comparison was done in six of the 15 active TFA sites at the time of the study. Before the beginning of the school year, students were randomly assigned to TFA and control teachers to ensure comparable classes. All students were given the Iowa Test of Basic Skills in reading and math at the beginning of the year to establish a baseline, and again at the end of the year to determine progress. The researchers further refined the study by comparing outcomes between TFA students and the entire control group, and between TFA students and those of novice teachers in the control group.[15]

The study provided insight into both the makeup of the teacher force in schools where TFA corps member teach and their students' outcomes. While 75% of TFA members graduated from a "most competitive," "highly competitive," or "very competitive" college or university, only 4% of control group teachers had the same background.[16] Additionally, although the 51% of TFA teachers who earned teacher certification by the end of their first year was lower than the 67% of total control group, this percentage was comparable to that of the control group novices.

In a report issued in 2004, Mathematica concluded that the TFA and control group students showed no statistically significant differences in their reading achievement gains. However, TFA teachers had a positive impact on the math achievement of their students relative to those of control group students. The researchers found a statistically significant difference in achievement growth that was roughly equivalent to an increase of about 10% of one grade level, or one additional month of math instruction. The report noted that TFA corps members' impact on math achievement in comparison to the entire control group was analogous to 65% of the positive impact that could be gained by reducing class size from 23 to 15. When compared to only novice control group teachers, the TFA teacher gains were even higher—for these students, the result was similar to the full impact of reducing class size by eight children. The researchers concluded that given the comparisons in both student achievement and educational and certification profiles, TFA offered school districts an appealing pool of teacher candidates, and was making progress toward its mission. (See **Exhibit 10** for selected data from the Mathematica report.)

As an additional measure of effectiveness, Kane, Parsons & Associates, Inc., conducted a periodic telephone survey of principals who hired TFA corps members. Interviewing approximately 50% of principals who had hired corps members in 2004, researchers found that nearly 95% of responding principals reported that they would hire another Teach For America corps member if given the opportunity. Seventy-two percent considered the Teach For America teachers more effective than other beginning teachers, and 70% rated corps members' training as better than that of other beginning teachers in their buildings.

Envisioning the Future: 2006–2010

Throughout 2004, TFA conducted a strategic planning process that involved staff members, regional executive directors, and the national management team. The organization created a seven-member strategy committee, which included Kopp, Hauser, Vice President of Development Kevin Huffman, two regional executive directors, and two management team members who were former executive directors. The committee integrated input from the participating staff, and developed the assumptions and framework for a plan that would chart TFA's growth through the end of its second decade. They developed four strategic priorities: 1) growing to scale while increasing diversity, 2) maximizing the percentage of corps members achieving significant academic gains, 3) fostering an unrivaled alumni network, and 4) building an enduring American institution. (**Exhibit 11** contains growth projections.)

Scale and Diversity

In reflecting on the lessons of the last phase of growth in terms of the new goals, Hauser said, "We've had no substantive challenge harder than recruitment." Even so, TFA received 17,000 applications for the 2005 corps, a 29% increase over the prior year and a 325% increase over the 2000 corps. Looking forward, the draft strategic plan called for 6,000 total corps members by 2010 although, given the success of the 2005 recruitment season, TFA pondered whether 6,000 was ambitious enough or whether they should increase their target to 8,000 total corps members. At this scale, approximately 500,000 students around the country would have a TFA teacher. In order to gain more leverage and impact in existing cities, TFA envisioned 5,400 total members in its current sites. As Huffman explained:

> As we explored the scale question, we saw that we could go big in a few places, or grow incrementally in many. For us, "going big" means reaching 200 incoming corps members in a site. One way to do this is to focus heavily on sites where we already place significant numbers—New York, Philadelphia, Los Angeles, and Houston. In our next tier of sites, such as Chicago, New Orleans, and Atlanta we'll grow to 100-plus incoming corps members. When we reach critical mass in a location, it changes the development game. We can approach new board members and engage new donors to provide major support if we become that kind of presence in their cities.

To create an additional 750 placements, TFA needed to cultivate seven new sites. TFA believed that reaching a certain scale in all of its sites would engender a feeling among corps members and alumni that they were having a collective impact on the student achievement of their districts. This would address the isolation that corps members sometimes felt when they were one of a few in a location.

Building deep relationships within their partner districts was critical to the "go big" strategy. District human resources offices placed a high value on teacher retention, a goal TFA was not best positioned to meet. However, the organization positioned their corps members as a leadership pipeline for the districts, as well as with local nonprofits and other influential stakeholders.

As the corps grew, the organization intended to achieve greater socio-economic, racial, ethnic, and gender diversity in the membership in order to better reflect the students they served. TFA had been successful in attracting a corps that reflected the overall composition of college graduates, but envisioned a corps with twice the representation of African-Americans and Latinos as compared to the overall graduation population. While maintaining a race-blind admissions process, TFA set a 2010 goal of a corps that was approximately 14.8% African-American and 10.4% Latino, with 35% overall coming from low-income family backgrounds, as measured by the proxy of first-generation college graduates. They also targeted more math and science majors, as well as men.

The organization considered a number of tactics to meet these goals. TFA was exploring ways to better position itself as a "prestigious, once-in-a-lifetime" leadership opportunity. This positioning included partnerships with leading private sector corporations and graduate schools that would consider TFA alumni attractive candidates, and communicating to applicants that, besides being an incredibly challenging, high-impact opportunity, participating in TFA could help open doors in the future. Additional recruiting teams would be established, particularly to focus intense, personalized cultivation efforts on colleges with high concentrations of diverse candidates.

Corps Member Effectiveness

Fundamentally, TFA believed that increased corps member effectiveness changed the lives of more students, and that effective corps members were more likely to learn lessons that would inspire them to become social change leaders throughout their lives. Therefore, setting ambitious targets was critical. In 2004, the overall significant gains rate for the corps was 27%, and a higher percentage of elementary teachers (37%) than secondary teachers (24%) met the benchmark. The senior team believed that with access to enhanced tools such as effective diagnostic assessments, performance tracking tools, and year-end assessments, all first-year corps members, including secondary and special education teachers, could affect significant gains at a rate of 50% by 2010. Over that same time horizon, they believed second-year teachers could achieve significant gains at an 80% rate.

Although TFA had created a high-performance culture with a focus on student achievement, a number of obstacles existed. Even with improved tools and systems for organizational learning, the inherent difficulties in the selection process, condensed pre-service training, limited opportunities for in-service development, and school-specific factors all presented challenges in reaching the corps effectiveness goals.

Alumni Network

Given the long time horizon involved in realizing alumni impact, TFA resisted pressure from some stakeholders to focus management attention on creating social impact measures that would track the year-by-year impact of alumni, and instead set specific, clear goals that staff could directly effect each year, such as annual giving and a feeling of connection to the TFA network. TFA believed that when alumni felt more connected, they were more willing to help recruit, support, and train new corps members; join the full-time staff; and help secure funding, support, and policy changes that were beneficial to the organization. Using strong university and corporate alumni networks as benchmarks, the senior team set goals for alumni connection and involvement to measure the strength of the network. By 2010, they aimed for 75% of alumni to feel strongly connected to the TFA network, and for 50% to make an annual donation. In 2005, 7% of former corps members contributed to the organization, and no hard data existed on the "connection" metric.

Enduring American Institution

The senior team described a number of benefits and challenges to becoming an "enduring American institution." Strengthening TFA's brand would have a positive effect on recruiting the nation's top graduates, attracting district partners, increasing the caliber and depth of staff, securing sustainable funding, and quieting detractors. Senior managers envisioned building a similar level of brand-awareness as the Peace Corps, the United Negro College Fund, and the Rhodes Scholarship Program.

Growing the corps to 6,000 required a significant increase in funding. With costs per member expected to grow with inflation and modest increases to $14,000 by 2010, the annual budget would grow from $39 million to over $84 million in five years. This figure would be higher if TFA decided to expand its goal beyond 6,000 corps members. Huffman explored a number of scenarios, and determined that it was unlikely that TFA could raise the entire amount necessary from individuals, foundations, and corporate donors. One option was to pursue an annual "carve-out" in the federal budget, similar to the Peace Corps, to fill the gap between private donations, earned revenues, and projected expenses. Strengthening the national and regional boards was an important element of reaching all of the 2010 goals. The national body had 16 members, but the senior team wondered if they should expand the number to add new directors with bi-partisan political access. Many of the regional boards had committed members, and TFA planned to build their capacity to further tap into the high-net-worth individuals and corporations in their communities to fund the projected growth in the corps.

The team also wanted to increase the perception of TFA as a great place to work. To scale the organization quickly, TFA needed to attract significant management talent to the national and regional staffs. The senior staff felt they had much work ahead in strengthening the culture and management systems so that talented managers who traditionally had not viewed TFA as a long-term option were more likely to do so.

Senior staff members also expressed a desire to strengthen TFA such that uninformed criticisms of the organization's model would seem illegitimate. As one put it, "The people who have been most publicly critical of us in the past have been isolated as we have demonstrated our effectiveness, but it still happens occasionally. We need to get to a place where you seem 'silly' if you disregard our results and take shots at us solely on ideological grounds."

Looking Ahead to 2010

As he thought about the road ahead, Hauser knew that some observers would wonder if the sheer ambition of the 2010 goals was outrageous or simply the next step in realizing the full potential of TFA. Attracting the corps members, general managers, board members, financial resources, and political support to achieve the targets would be an enormous undertaking. Some staff and supporters wondered if the rapid pace of growth over the last five years called for a period of stabilization before launching another significant expansion. The leadership team understood this position and had discussed a more moderate growth option. Nevertheless, the leadership team felt tremendous urgency to grow TFA's impact. Hauser recalled a recent conversation with Kopp in which she observed that in the previous era, the ambitious goals had attracted new allies, talent, and resources. Because of this it seemed almost easier to imagine achieving dramatic growth than modest growth, even though it would be difficult. The next five years promised to be both challenging and exciting.

Notes

1. "The Opportunity Gap," *Thinking K-16*, Volume 8, Issue 1. The Education Trust, Winter, 2004. pp. 36–37.

2. Johnson, Susan Moore. *Finders and Keepers: Helping New Teachers Survive and Thrive in Our Schools,* Jossey-Bass, San Francisco, 2004. pp. 3–4.

3. The Looking Back section draws heavily on "Teach For America," Harvard Business School Case 9-300-084, by John Sawhill and Sarah Thorp, 2000. Direct quotes from the case are noted for attribution as they occur.

4. Sawhill and Thorp, p. 8.

5. See Linda Darling Hammond, "Who Will Speak for the Children?" *Phi Delta Kappan,* September 1994, p. 33.

6. For more information on The New Teacher Project, see their website at www.tntp.org.

7. Sawhill and Thorp, p. 15.

8. Total operating expenses in FY04 included the one-time addition of $6 million in replacement education award costs. See Financial Sustainability for further details.

9. After reviewing research about this topic, TFA determined that the best metric for socio-economic diversity was parental educational attainment. According to researchers, tracking income was unreliable (people tend to not know or misreport their parents' actual incomes). Even if such self-reporting data were accurate, regional variations and differences in family size and timing skewed the results.

10. TFA roughly defined perseverance as "When challenged, remains optimistic about own ability to reach goals through effort, and works through obstacles purposefully and relentlessly."

11. As AmeriCorps members, TFA corps members were eligible to receive forbearance and interest payment on qualified student loans during their two years of service, as well as an education award of $4,725 at the end of each year of service (a total of $9,450 over the two years), which could be used towards future educational expenses or to repay qualified student loans.

12. From an internal monthly staff bulletin in July 2003.

13. The study was funded by The Smith Richardson Foundation, The William and Flora Hewlett Foundation, and The Carnegie Corporation. Hewlett and Carnegie were also financial supporters of Teach For America.

14. To download a copy of the Mathematica Report, go to ww.teachforamerica.org/documents/mathematica_results_6.9.04.pdf.

15. The study defined novice teachers as those in their first three years of teaching.

16. The categories "most competitive," "highly competitive," or "very competitive" are from *Barron's Profile of American Colleges.*

Exhibit 1a

TFA Statement of Activities, Years Ending September 30, 2000–2004

Changes in unrestricted net assets:					
Operating revenue, gains, and other support:					
Contributions	$14,059,440	$11,282,415	$9,131,644	$8,758,574	$6,527,712
Contributed goods and services	476,925	1,001,781	755,734	1,538,842	854,108
Fee income	-	-	-	137,687	139,372
Interest income	586,531	528,303	293,071	491,561	270,326
Net appreciation (depreciation) in fair value of investments	(91,695)	213,089	(420,054)	(299,625)	(88,566)
Other revenue	17,398	11,398	4,186	24,073	5,406
Net assets released from restrictions	32,264,639	16,736,105	13,516,324	8,715,329	2,848,613
Total operating revenue, gains, and other support	$47,313,238	$29,773,091	$23,280,905	$19,366,441	$10,556,971
Operating expenses:					
Program services:					
Teacher recruitment and selection	$7,995,181	$6,437,810	$6,355,495	$4,475,512	$2,003,880
Pre-service institute	6,255,780	5,587,645	4,803,100	3,319,289	1,876,699
Placement, professional development, and other	19,358,885	12,018,943	8,456,921	6,135,750	4,177,311
Total program services	33,609,846	24,044,398	19,615,516	13,930,551	8,057,890
Supporting services:					
Management and general	1,843,197	1,218,657	1,329,601	969,968	727,945
Fundraising	3,956,339	3,682,189	2,335,788	1,683,815	1,094,460
Total supporting services	5,799,536	4,900,846	3,665,389	2,653,783	1,822,405
Total operating expenses	$39,409,382	$28,945,244	$23,280,905	$16,584,334	$9,880,295
Increase in unrestricted net assets from operating activities	7,903,856	827,847	-	2,782,107	676,676
Nonoperating activity					
Net assets designated for reserve purposes	1,519,397	2,730,980	2,471,896	5,700,000	2,900,000
Increase in unrestricted net assets	9,423,253	3,558,827	2,471,896	8,482,107	3,576,676
Changes in temporarily restricted net assets:					
Contributions	14,900,410	19,572,276	8,889,371	15,700,749	15,238,177
Federal grants	8,041,000	7,340,300	5,633,000	1,633,000	1,632,970
Net assets released from restrictions	(33,784,036)	(19,467,085)	(15,988,220)	(14,415,329)	(5,748,613)
(Decrease) increase in temporarily restricted net assets	(10,842,626)	7,445,491	(1,465,849)	2,918,420	11,122,534
Changes in permanently restricted net assets:					
Contributions	-	54,366	-	449,999	361,094
Increase in permanently restricted net assets	-	54,366	-	449,999	361,094
(Decrease) increase in net assets	(1,419,373)	11,058,684	1,006,047	11,850,526	15,060,304
Net assets at beginning of year	46,739,299	35,680,615	34,674,568	22,824,042	7,763,738
Net assets at end of year	$45,319,926	$46,739,299	$35,680,615	$34,674,568	$22,824,042

Source: TFA audited financial reports and case writer analysis.

Exhibit 1b

TFA Balance Sheet, Years Ending September 30, 2003 and 2004

	2004	*2003*
Assets		
Cash and cash equivalents	$4,667,370	3,428,196
Federal grants receivable	8,060,390	6,074,398
Prepaid expenses and other assets	416,908	289,513
Contributions receivable, net	13,995,043	17,153,302
Other receivables	1,099,680	890,000
Loans receivable from corps members, net of allowance of $428,000 in 2004, and $277,000 in 2003	2,766,067	2,636,072
Investments	20,581,349	17,582,941
Fixed Assets, net	1,778,034	1,389,347
Total assets	$53,364,841	49,443,769
Liabilities and Net Assets		
Liabilities		
Accounts payable and accrued expenses	$2,604,894	1,792,620
Education Awards due to Core Members	$4,424,859	-
Other liabilities	1,015,162	911,850
Total liabilities	8,044,915	2,704,470
Net assets:		
Unrestricted:		
Available for operations	11,650,582	4,135,413
Invested in fixed assets	1,778,034	1,389,347
Board designated for reserve purposes	16,522,273	15,002,876
	29,950,889	20,527,636
Temporarily restricted	11,796,226	22,638,852
Permanently restricted	3,572,811	3,572,811
Total net assets	45,319,926	46,739,299
Total liabilities and net assets	$53,364,841	49,443,769

Source: TFA audited financial reports and case writer analysis.

Exhibit 2

Student Outcomes in the United States, 2002

Achievement on the National Assessment of Educational Performance by Race, 2002

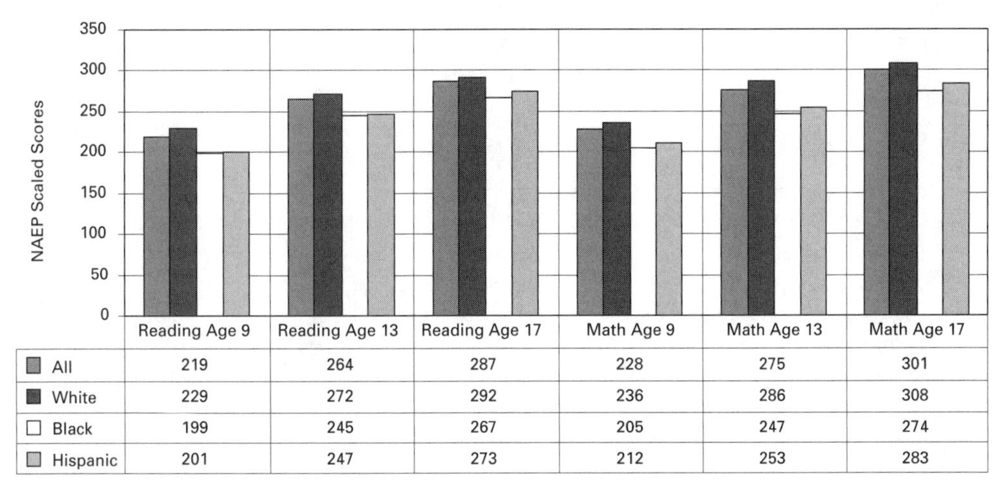

	Reading Age 9	Reading Age 13	Reading Age 17	Math Age 9	Math Age 13	Math Age 17
All	219	264	287	228	275	301
White	229	272	292	236	286	308
Black	199	245	267	205	247	274
Hispanic	201	247	273	212	253	283

Note: Each 10 points on the NAEP represents approximately one grade level.

Educational Attainment, White vs. Nonwhite by Highest Level of Education Completed

	Less than High School	*High School or Associates Degree*	*Bachelor's, Master's, Professional, or PhD*
White	5%	69%	28%
Black	7%	81%	12%
Hispanic	12%	78%	10%
Asian and Pacific Islander	1%	54%	64%
American Indian and Alaskan Native	18%	75%	7%

Source: National Center for Education Statistics.

Achievement on the National Assessment of Educational Performance by Socioeconomic Status, 2002

	Poor (A)	*Not Poor*
Reading Age 9	203	230
Reading Age 13	249	272
Reading Age 17	273	289
Math Age 9	210	236
Math Age 13	255	285
Math Age 17	280	305

Notes: Each 10 points on the NAEP represents approximately one grade level.

(A) The term "poor" refers to students who qualify for free and reduced-price lunch under the National School Lunch Act of 1946. For the school year 2002–2003, a four-person family salary at or below $23,530 qualified a student for free lunch. A four-person family salary at or below $33,485 qualified a student for reduced-price lunch.

Highest Level of Education Completed by U.S. Socioeconomic Status

	Lowest SES Quartile	*Middle 2 SES Quartiles*	*Highest SES Quartile*
Less than High School	9%	4%	1%
High School Degree	65%	54%	33%
High School Certificate	12%	12%	7%
Associate's Degree	7%	9%	8%
Bachelor's Degree	6%	19%	41%
Master's Degree	1%	2%	7%
Professional Degree	0%	1%	3%

Source: National Center for Education Statistics.

Exhibit 3

TFA Core Values

Relentless Pursuit of Results

We are determined to achieve ambitious, measurable results in working toward our vision. As a result, we continue pursuing our end goals despite the constraints or obstacles we encounter along the way, and we work toward these goals with a sense of urgency.

Good Thinking

We push ourselves to think critically about all that we do, approaching each issue and decision with rigor and always searching for the best idea.

Constant Learning

We reflect on and draw lessons from previous experiences and apply them to do even better in future endeavors. We also seek out feedback and resources to help meet our goals.

Personal Responsibility

We do our best in all that we take on and assume ownership for producing the best possible result in our area of work.

Respect and Humility

We approach others in a way that demonstrates that we value them and their contributions and have high expectations of what they can contribute. We keep in mind always the limitations of our own experience and value others' perspectives and experience.

Positive Outlook

We establish big goals and greet new ideas with a sense of possibility. We also assume the best in others and treat them with a generosity of spirit.

Integrity

We are honest and ethical in all that we do. In making choices, we aim to do what's best for the broader good.

Collective Impact

We assume responsibility for the success of our broader movement and contribute toward increasing our collective impact.

Source: Teach For America.

Exhibit 4

TFA Performance, 2000–2004

Projected vs. Actual Annual Performance on Key Indicators, 2000–2004

	2000		*2001*		*2002*		*2003*		*2004*	
	Projected	*Actual*	*Projected*	*Actual*	*Projected*	*Actual*	*Projected*	*Actual*	*Projected*	*Actual*
Applicants	4000	4068	5250	4946	6700	13877	8000	15698	8000	13378
1st year corps	1000	900	1310	951	1670	1731	2000	1719	2000	1661
Attrition (A)	10%	13%	10%	14%	10%	18%	10%	TBD	10%	TBD
Total corps	1691	1490	2210	1710	2849	2504	3503	3078	3800	3026
Sites	15	13	19	16	23	18	25	20	25	22
Total budget	$9,319,000	$10,287,538	$20,342,000	$17,019,652	$24,421,000	$23,845,679	$25,669,000	$29,601,797	$26,262,000	$39,751,280

(A) Attrition represents the percentage of corps members who fail to meet their full two-year commitment and therefore is undetermined for 2003 and 2004.

Incoming Corps by Site, 2000 and 2004

Sites	*Incoming Corps 2000*	*Incoming Corps 2004*
Atlanta	58	72
Baltimore	61	57
Bay Area	69	73
Chicago	41	73
Houston	70	120
Los Angeles	110	84
Mississippi Delta	36	71
New Jersey	47	76
New Orleans	58	72
New York City	114	328
North Carolina (Eastern)	36	49
Phoenix	33	75
Rio Grande Valley	35	85
South Louisiana	41	37
Washington, D.C.	65	47
Charlotte, North Carolina		42
Las Vegas		62
Miami		60
New Mexico (Navajo Nation)		25
Philadelphia		102
South Dakota		19
St. Louis		32
Total incoming corps size	874	1661
Number of sites	15	22

Source: TFA internal documents and case writer analysis.

Exhibit 5

Diversity Measures, 2004 and 2010

Metric	*All Graduating Seniors*[a]	*2004 Incoming Corps Actual*	*2010 Goal*
African-American corps members are twice as represented in our corps as they are among college seniors	8.50%	11.00%	14.80%
Latino corps members are twice as represented in our corps as they are among college seniors	5.90%	6.00%	10.40%
Percent of corps members from a low-income family background	43%	25%	35%

Source: Internal TFA documents.

[a] All graduating seniors column is derived internally by TFA staff.

[b] Low-income family background is measured by using being a first-generation college graduate as a proxy.

Exhibit 6

Significant Gains Definition, Standards, and Goals, 2004

Significant Gains Expectations by Grade Level and Content Area

For Elementary Teachers:	*For Secondary Content Area Teachers (and Math and Language Arts Teachers if Appropriate):*	*For Special Education Teachers:*
• Class average gains ≥ 1.5 grade levels in math AND literacy (reading or writing) *Or* • Class average gains ≥ 2 grade levels in math OR literacy (reading or writing) *And* • Gains ≥ 1 grade level in the other subject	• Mastery of ambitious grade-level content area goals (class average ≥ 80%) *For Secondary Math and Language Arts Teachers if Appropriate:* • Average class gains of ≥ 2 grade levels	• Meets criteria listed for other elementary or secondary teachers as appropriate *Or* • On average, class meets 80% of Individual Educational Plan goals

Significant Gains Results for 2002–2004; Goals for 2010

	2002	*2003*	*2004*	*2010 projected*[a]
% Corps achieving significant gains	11%	22%	27%	50%—1st year corps; 80%—2nd year corps

[a] TFA based this projection on the fact that just under 50% of first year teachers in the highest-performing regions made significant gains (Houston 40%, Phoenix 45%, New Mexico 55%, and Rio Grande Valley 67%).

Source: Internal TFA documents.

Exhibit 7

TFA Alumni Achievement Information

As a result of our increased ability to remain connected with alumni, we know that alumni are working from inside education and from all sectors to effect the fundamental changes needed to truly expand opportunity for children.

- More than 60% of alumni dating back to 1990 are still working in or studying education; around 40% of alumni are still teaching. Of those who have left the field of education, the majority have jobs that impact education or low-income schools or volunteer in low-income schools or communities. Overall, 86% of alumni remain actively committed to public service through their work or volunteer activities.
- Many of our alumni in education are assuming school leadership roles, within the traditional system and within the charter system. Our alumni run some of the country's most acclaimed charter schools including more than twenty KIPP Academies and Texas' YES College Preparatory Academy, which is the state's highest performing public high school. The KIPP Academies, which were started by Teach For America alumni, have proliferated from a single classroom in Houston in 1994 to 38 public charter and contract schools in 26 cities. Our alumni run 24 of the KIPP Academies across the nation and staff the vast majority of them.
- The New Teacher Project (TNTP), a non-profit organization whose mission is to assist school districts and states with the recruitment and retention of teachers, is working with some of the largest school districts nationally. Once Teach For America opened the door for alternative routes to certification, organizations such as TNTP were created as spin-offs to bring top individuals into the teaching profession. The current CEO of TNTP is also an alumna of Teach For America.
- TFA corps members receive the highest honors teachers can win. For instance, Jason Kamras, a 1996 corps member in Washington, D.C., who in December was named the 2005 District of Columbia Teacher of the Year, was selected as the 2005 National Teacher of the Year by the Council of Chief State School Officers. Kamras is a mathematics teacher at Sousa Middle School in Washington, D.C., his original placement school through TFA.
- Outside of education, our alumni continue to lead key reform efforts. For example, in the policy arena, three alumni are serving as policy advisors to Governors; two have been elected to school boards; and several others are working as advisors on Capitol Hill. In public interest law, three of this year's 25 prestigious Skadden Fellowships were awarded to Teach For America alumni.
- The Gleitsman Foundation awarded its national "Citizen Activist Awards" in 2004 to individuals who have had an impact in education; of the 12 winners, 4 were Teach For America alumni. As further testament to the fact that Teach For America's alumni are assuming leadership roles in the realm of education, there are five Teach For America alumni out of 33 members of the new National Council on Teacher Quality Advisory Board, which includes such prominent individuals as Harvard professor Ron Ferguson, former Georgia Governor Roy Barnes, and San Diego Superintendent Alan Bersin.

Source: Internal TFA document.

Exhibit 8

Example of TFA Regional Directors' Performance Rubric

The region has a diversified base of community and financial support, sufficient to sustain and grow Teach For America's regional presence.

	1	*2*	*3*
Clear Strategy	• There is not a strategy for maximizing the site's funding potential that makes sense given the site's unique dynamics and resources.	• There is a strategy to raise funds that makes sense, but that doesn't fully maximize the site's funding potential.	• There is a solid strategy for maximizing the site's funding potential that makes sense given the site's unique dynamics and resources.
Strong Champions	• There is not a core group of champions or supporters within the region who understand the strategy and are helping the region make it happen.	• There is a core group of supporters within the region who understand our mission and strategy and are somewhat helpful, but they either are not fully committed or don't have the capacity to help to the extent that we need. • Supporters could be further cultivated to become champions.	• There is a core group of champions within the region who understand our mission, strategy, and challenges, and are helping the region make it happen. • Our supporters and champions feel connected to and updated on Teach For America at all times, not only when we are seeking funds.
Sustainability	• The region is not on a path to sustainability, because we are not tapped into all resources in all possible sectors and have overly concentrated on one. • The region is not receiving the right amount of public funding (given the specifics of the region), and the process of obtaining such funds has not been demystified.	• The region has a somewhat balanced fundraising portfolio, given the particulars of the region, but there is still too much reliance on one fundraising sector despite the fact that there are other possible resources to tap into. • The region is working towards receiving the right amount of public funding (given the specifics of the region), and the process of obtaining such funds has been successfully demystified, though there is still work remaining to secure support.	• The region is on a path to sustainability as we have tapped into resources in all possible sectors, and not overly concentrated on one. • The region is receiving the right amount of public funding (given the specifics of the region), and the process of obtaining such funds has been demystified. • Our public funders have become champions of the organization.
Effective External Meetings	• Meetings are not utilized to effectively sell or re-sell Teach For America's mission or to accomplish a strategic purpose, and the ED does not have a solid Teach For America pitch and regional story.	• Meetings accomplish a strategic purpose, and the ED has a solid Teach For America pitch and regional story. • Meetings may result in funding, but our mission may not be fully sold or understood by the funder.	• Meetings are utilized to effectively sell or re-sell Teach For America's mission and to accomplish a strategic purpose, and the ED has perfected his or her Teach For America pitch and regional story, which summarizes where we are headed and why we need the funder's (or other meeting attendee's) support to get there.
Organization and Strong Written Communication	• The region is often operating at the last minute, as evidenced by mistakes in written work and tactical errors in meetings or proposals, or in being slow to follow up on leads and with funders.	• Written communication from the region to funders and possible supporters is solid: generally based on a template, well-constructed, professional, timely, and generally effective (e.g., letters, e-mails, proposals, reports).	• Written communication from the region to funders and possible supporters is excellent: very well written, thoughtfully tailored to the right audience, well-constructed, professional, timely and effective (e.g., letters, e-mails, proposals, reports).
Utilizing Resources	• The ED, DD, SAED, etc., do not reach out for help when needed or do not utilize the resources that are available.	• The ED, DD, SAED, etc., reach out for help when needed, but may not effectively maximize the resources that are available.	• The ED, DD, SAED, etc., reach out for help and resources when needed (e.g., Diane, Aimee, Wendy, Kevin, etc.), and effectively utilize the resources available.

Source: Internal TFA documents.

Exhibit 9a

National Organization Chart

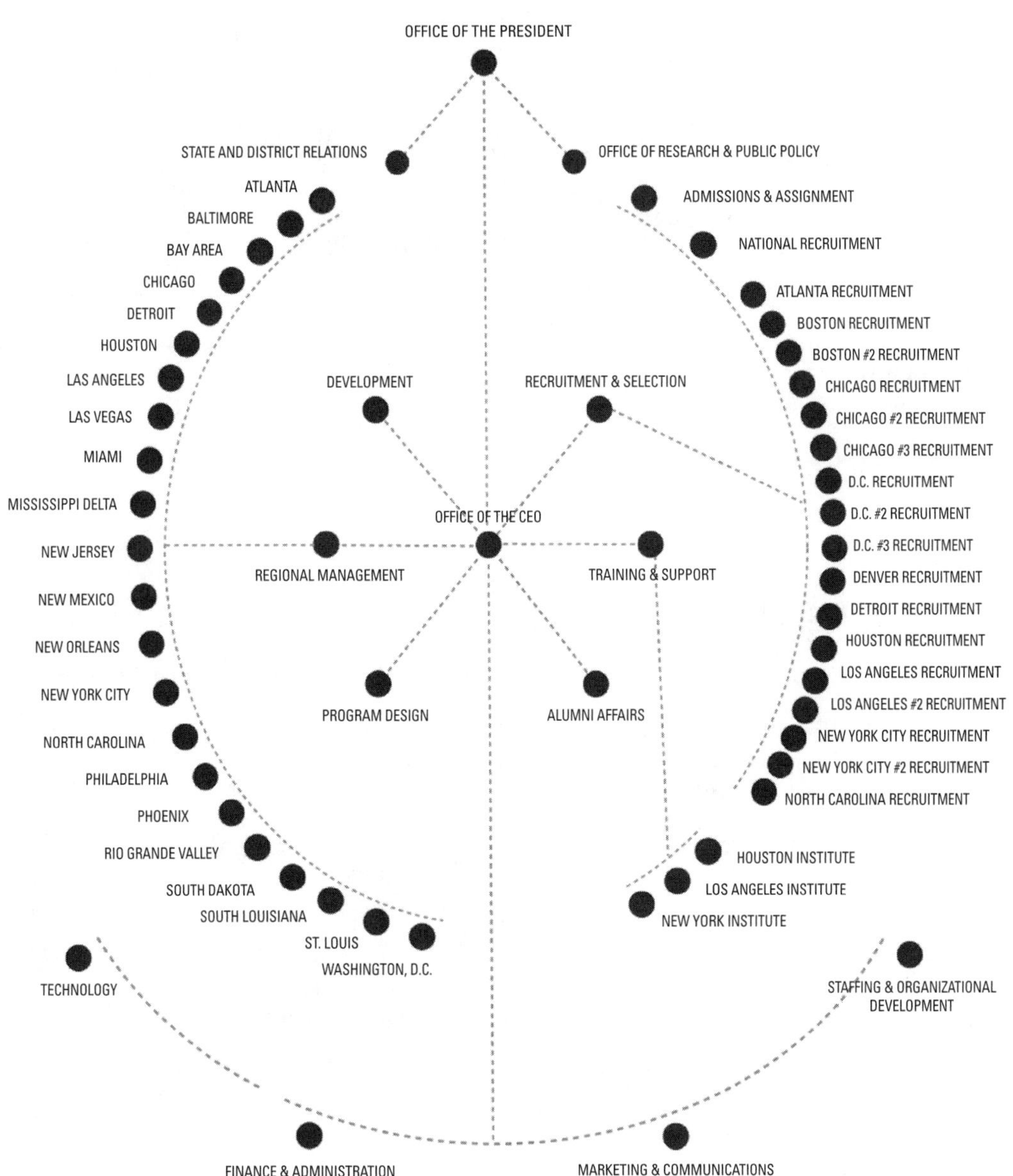

Source: Internal TFA document.

Exhibit 9b

Sample Regional Organization Chart

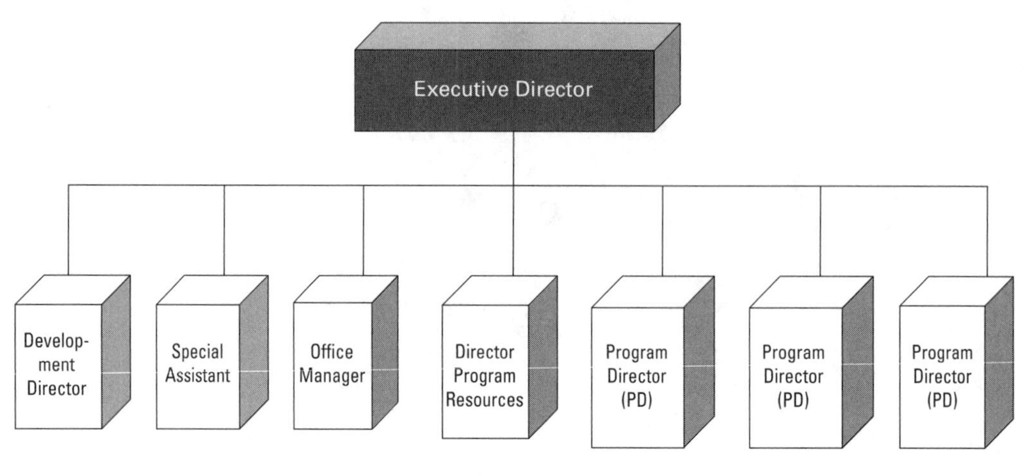

Source: Internal TFA document.

Exhibit 10

Selected Data from Mathematica Survey, 2004

Study Design and Participant Data

			Number of Classes Taught by:			*Number of Students Taught by:*		
Region	*Number of Schools*	*Number of Comparison Blocks*	*TFA Teacher*	*Novice Control Teacher*	*Veteran Control Teacher*	*TFA Teacher*	*Novice Control Teacher*	*Veteran Control Teacher*
Baltimore	3	6	7	1	8	137	18	147
Chicago	3	7	7	2	5	139	42	105
Houston	3	7	7	3	7	126	56	114
Los Angeles/ Compton	2	6	6	6	4	97	111	72
Mississippi Delta	3	6	12	2	10	201	31	146
New Orleans	3	5	5	1	7	85	21	117
Total	17	37	44	15	41	785	279	701

Educational Background of TFA and Control Group Teachers

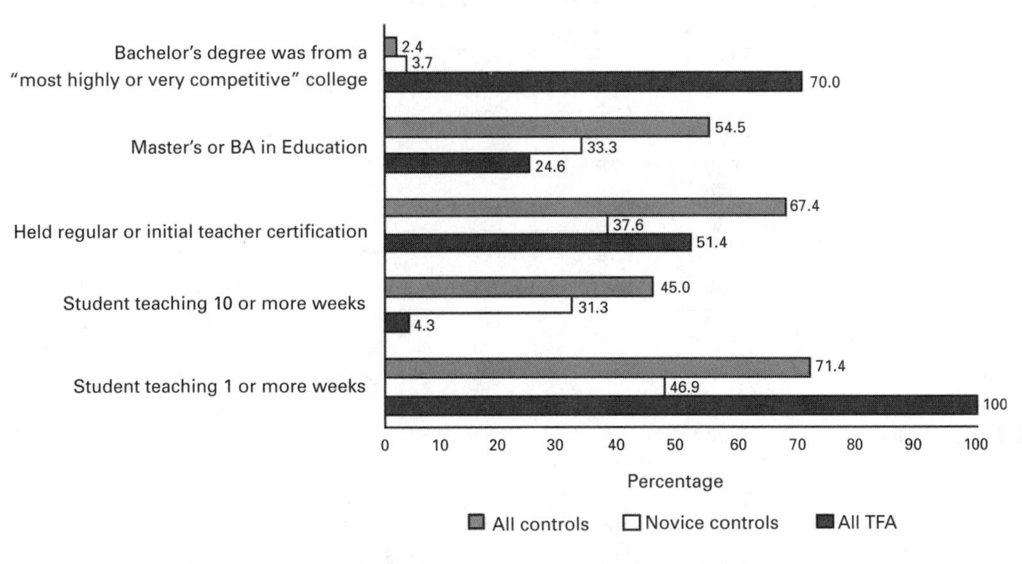

Source: Decker, Paul T., Daniel P. Mayer, and Stephen Glazerman. "The Effects of Teach for America on Students: Findings from a National Evaluation"; Mathematica Policy Research, Inc. June, 2004, funded by the Corporation for the Advancement of Policy Evaluation through grants from the Smith Richardson Foundation, the William and Flora Hewlett Foundation, and the Carnegie Corporation.

Changes in Achievement in Math and Reading in TFA and Control Classrooms

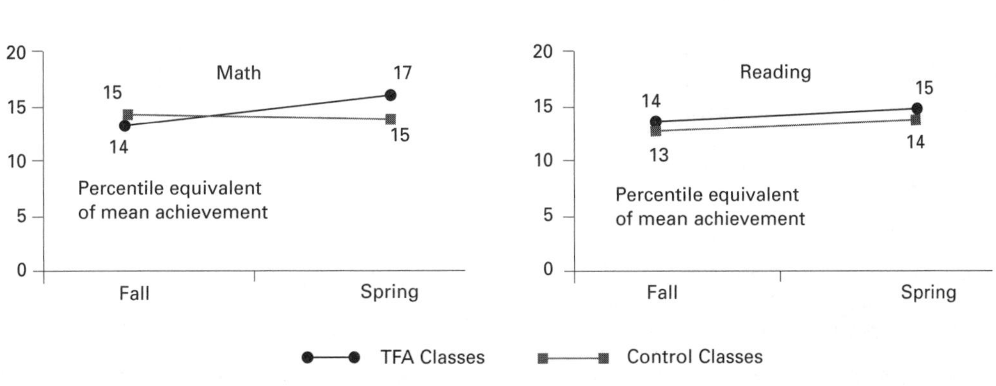

Source: Decker, Paul T., Daniel P. Mayer, and Stephen Glazerman. "The Effects of Teach For America on Students: Findings from a National Evaluation" Mathematica Policy Research, Inc. June, 2004.

Exhibit 11

TFA Preliminary Growth Projections, 2005–2010 ($ thousands)

Sites	*2005 Projected Revenue*	*2010 Incoming Corps*	*2010 Total Corps*	*2010 Projected Costs (A)*	*2010 Projected Revenue (B)*	*2010 Subsidy Needed*
Atlanta	$1,500	100	190	$2,660	$1,900	$760
Baltimore	$1,050	100	190	$2,660	$1,500	$1,160
Bay Area	$1,750	125	238	$3,325	$2,750	$575
Charlotte		75	143	$1,995	$1,100	$895
Chicago	$1,500	150	285	$3,990	$2,850	$1,140
Houston	$2,150	200	380	$5,320	$3,800	$1,520
Las Vegas	$1,100	175	333	$4,655	$3,000	$1,655
Los Angeles	$2,300	250	475	$6,650	$4,000	$2,650
Miami	$500	100	190	$2,660	$1,000	$1,660
Mississippi Delta	$800	85	162	$2,261	$1,000	$1,261
New Jersey	$1,400	80	152	$2,128	$1,500	$628
New Mexico	$200	50	95	$1,330	$500	$830
New Orleans	$875	100	190	$2,660	$1,000	$1,660
New York	$5,300	500	950	$13,300	$9,500	$3,800
North Carolina (rural)	$1,050	60	114	$1,596	$750	$846
Philadelphia	$1,900	200	380	$5,320	$3,500	$1,820
Phoenix	$1,000	100	190	$2,660	$1,500	$1,160
Rio Grande Valley	$800	100	190	$2,660	$1,000	$1,660
St. Louis	$675	60	114	$1,596	$1,100	$496
South Dakota	$75	20	38	$532	$250	$282
Southern Louisiana	$575	60	114	$1,596	$900	$696
Washington DC	$650	75	143	$1,995	$1,000	$995
Expansion sites		400	760	$10,640	$7,500	$3,140
Total Local	$27,150	3,165	6,016	$84,189	$52,900	$31,289
Other Sources						
Federal	$5,200				$20,000	
Private						
Foundations	$4,250				$5,000	
Corporations	$1,000				$5,000	
Individuals	$850				$1,000	
Alumni	$50				$750	
Total Private	$6,150				$11,750	
Total Other Sources	$11,350				$31,750	
Grand Total	$38,500				$84,650	

Source: Internal TFA documents and case writer analysis.

(A) Assumes $14,000 fully loaded cost per corps member, including all local, regional, and national expenses. (B) Projected local revenues include regional fundraising targets and placement fees from school districts at $1500 per corps member.

CASE 2.2

Stacey Childress ■ Geoff Marietta ■ Sara Suchman

Boston Teacher Residency: Developing a Strategy for Long-Term Impact

In June 2008, Jesse Solomon, the founding director of the Boston Teacher Residency (BTR), faced an important decision about the organization's strategic direction. Since its founding in 2003, 125 of its graduates had joined the Boston Public Schools (BPS) and BTR had established a reputation as a provider of some of the district's best-prepared new teachers. The program had been hailed as one of the 10 best teacher preparation programs in the nation by an industry journal, and a number of cities around the country had expressed interest in replicating the BTR model. Yet Solomon wondered if their approach so far was optimal going forward.

BTR had been created in partnership with former BPS superintendent Thomas Payzant with a mission to "recruit, prepare, and sustain excellent teachers in and for the Boston Public Schools." After a rigorous recruiting and selection process, residents started two months of training in July before spending from September to June working four days week in the classroom of a mentor teacher in a Boston public school. On Fridays, the only day outside of their classrooms, residents attended graduate classes and learned about instructional practices and behavior management techniques that they could apply with their students the following week. Upon successful completion, residents earned their master's degree and teaching certification, along with credits toward licensure in special education. With 84 residents in 2008, BTR was on track to meet its annual growth targets.

Carol Johnson, the new superintendent for BPS, was developing a district-wide improvement strategy that prioritized accelerating the performance of the district's lowest-performing schools. Many of these reflected the national trends in low-performing schools: less experienced teachers and high turnover. Relatively few BTR graduates joined these schools—they were free to pursue teaching openings at any school in the district, and often the principals of higher-performing schools had more aggressive recruiting approaches. However, the need for effective teachers in high-priority schools prompted Solomon to wonder if they should be an explicit part of BTR's strategy.

Solomon knew the potential to partner more closely with the new superintendent was a time-sensitive opportunity with a number of questions. What were the implications of moving from an open hiring market to the placement of cohorts of BTR graduates in high-priority schools? Was BTR's model sufficient to prepare new teachers to join struggling schools in the absence of a comprehensive turnaround strategy? How could BTR continue to strengthen the quality of its program while supporting the new superintendent's priorities?

Jesse Solomon and the Creation of the Boston Teacher Residency

Before starting his career in education, Jesse Solomon attended Massachusetts Institute of Technology (MIT), where he majored in mathematics. He then entered the Harvard Graduate School of Education's teacher education program and earned both a master's degree and a teaching license in hopes of launching a career in urban education. Upon finishing the program in 1992, Solomon tried to secure a job with BPS:

> All I wanted to do was teach in Boston. For what it's worth, I had a bachelor's degree in math from MIT and a master's from Harvard and I couldn't even get an interview. The district has dramatically improved its recruiting and hiring processes in the last 15 years, but back when I finished graduate school, you basically had to know someone and I didn't know how to work the system. So, I finally took a job in Cambridge in August because I couldn't hold out for BPS any longer.

After two years in Cambridge, Solomon finally made the move to Boston, first to Brighton High School and then as one of the founding teachers at City on a Hill Charter School in 1995.

As one of Boston's first charter schools, City on a Hill was started during an era when charter schools were seen as laboratories through which to introduce new and effective practices and strategies back into the public school systems. Solomon's experiences with new teachers at City on a Hill solidified his frustration and disappointment with the preparation offered by traditional teacher education programs. With the help of a federal grant designed to facilitate cross-fertilization between charters and districts, Solomon was part of partnership with a BPS high school called the Urban Calculus Initiative in which mathematics teachers from both schools worked together on professional development. Based on this experience, Solomon and others at City on a Hill began to think about how a charter could influence educational improvement more broadly. This led them to create the Teachers' Institute at City on a Hill, which was in many ways a forerunner of BTR. Aspiring teachers spent a year at the school, working four days a week in the classroom with a mentor teacher and taking courses towards a state teaching license on Fridays. After running the institute for two years, Solomon began a series of informal discussions that stretched over two years with BPS deputy superintendent Tim Knowles and assistant superintendent Rachel Curtis about how the City on a Hill model could be applied to the district's approach to teacher recruitment, preparation, and support.

Strategic Grant Partners

In the fall 2002, Joanna Jacobson (HBS 1987) of Strategic Grant Partners began talking with Knowles and Superintendent Tom Payzant to identify the right opportunity to help BPS improve student achievement. Strategic Grant Partners (SGP) was a newly formed coalition of 13 family foundations "working to affect systemic change in the areas of education and family services in Massachusetts." SGP functioned more like venture philanthropy than a traditional foundation, and as a result did not accept unsolicited applications or use a written grantmaking process. Rather, the Managing Partner and staff actively searched out opportunities with senior public-sector executives, non-profit leaders, and community stakeholders to find opportunities to invest in projects that were in line with its mission of systemic change. Jacobson explained:

> SGP starts with a nine- to twelve-month planning process with a potential grantee, during which we try to figure out how we might help

> an organization start-up, strengthen their work and/or increase capacity. Our grants typically range from one [to] four million dollars and we favor those opportunities that act as catalysts to change entrenched systems and are demonstrations of how to take entrepreneurial ideas to scale. We pride ourselves on our ability to get the key stakeholders at the table together and make agreements so that everyone has skin in the game. This is supported by a legal contract, which means we can hold the grantee's and institutional key stakeholders' feet to fire if necessary.

Payzant and Knowles convinced Jacobson that the best opportunity for dramatic impact was to focus on finding, training, and keeping good teachers. Payzant believed that for students to learn, teachers had to know how to teach and that required a rigorous training program, which most certification programs did not offer. Knowles believed that teacher preparation should resemble a medical residency. Together they developed a formal plan to create a teacher residency for BPS.

Jacobson presented the idea to SGP's partners in February 2003. In the presentation, she highlighted the crisis in Boston's public schools that one local foundation executive called a "morally unacceptable status quo." Though improvement has been made in recent years, state assessments showed that only 24% of 4th graders in BPS were proficient in language arts and only 15% were so in math (**Exhibit 1**). When the results were disaggregated by race and income they were even worse (**Exhibit 2**). In addition, fewer than 65% of BPS students graduated from high school. On top of this, more than 50% of BPS's teachers were expected to retire within the next five years and close to half of Boston's new teachers quit within their first three years.

SGP agreed to fund the creation of the Boston Teacher Residency, and Jacobson worked with Payzant and Knowles to organize the new venture. Some BPS stakeholders felt that the program should be housed within the district. But Payzant and Knowles disagreed. As Payzant said, "BTR needed to be outside of the system so it could do its own recruitment and have independence in day-to-day operations." At the same time, both knew that the program would need some connection to BPS because of the complexity of teacher recruitment and hiring in the district. Knowles elaborated:

> Districts have a habit of eating their young and converting interesting entrepreneurial ideas into not-so-interesting ones, so keeping one foot outside allowed some focus and independence for an idea that was clearly going to be unusual. But one foot in is equally important because we wanted it to be imbedded in the DNA or the daily diet of the system and not be just an entrepreneurial outside-in reform.

However, the decision to create a "one foot in, one foot out" structure for BTR meant that Payzant, Knowles, and Jacobson needed a partner to house the fledgling program. Payzant suggested that they discuss the idea with Ellen Guiney, the executive director of the Boston Plan for Excellence.

Boston Plan for Excellence

Boston Plan for Excellence (BPE) had been established in 1984 as a locally focused education fund and reorganized in 1995 to work in close partnership with the BPS. BPE's mission was to be a "catalyst and support to the Boston Public Schools in transforming instruction to improve the performance of every student." BPE considered itself a partner on all aspects of BPS's school reform work and even staffed a team dedicated to solving operational problems in the district. BPE also conducted and distributed research intended to help build an understanding of BPS's reform efforts.

Because Payzant had a productive relationship with executive director Guiney, he saw BPE as the perfect partner to house BTR. Payzant commented on their relationship:

> Ellen and I knew each other's strengths and weaknesses, and we agreed 85–90% of the time. But when we disagreed, she was comfortable pushing me and I was comfortable telling her to back off, so it worked. But it's one of those tricky things because the partnership between BPS and BPE was based on the relationship between a couple of key players.

Being housed within BPE also had an added benefit for BTR. Private foundations and other funders leery of giving money directly to a large urban district or to an unproven start-up might be more willing to give to BPE.

Payzant, Knowles, and Jacobson brought the idea of forming BTR within BPE to Guiney, who needed little convincing. Guiney remarked, "One of the things that BPE recognized in its work with BPS was a lack of shared expertise and continuous learning in teaching. We saw BTR as really focused on this problem." After a series of discussions with BPE's board, a plan was worked out whereby BPE would provide BTR with office space, back office support, and assistance in fundraising.

Given his experience at City on a Hill and his conversations with Knowles and Curtis, Solomon was quickly targeted as the person to lead the new venture. SGP provided the seed money to hire Solomon for three months to create a detailed business plan for BTR. As a result of Solomon's business plan, a contract was drawn up between SGP, BPE, and BPS (see **Exhibit 3** for funding arrangement).

Officially, Solomon was accountable both to BPS's deputy superintendent of teaching and learning and to Guiney at BPE (**Exhibit 4**). Jacobson felt that the dual reporting line was critical to the success of BTR because it provided a tight link to the district and gave BTR access to its top administrators while also making Solomon a member of Guiney's team at BPE. Because BTR operated as a program within BPE, a steering committee was formed as opposed to a governing board. The steering committee consisted of Guiney, Jacobson, and two BPS executives—the deputy superintendent of teaching and learning and director of human resources.

Designing and Implementing the Program

From the beginning, the founders saw BTR as more than just a teacher training program for BPS. Local colleges and universities such as Simmons, Boston College, and Boston University already filled that role through traditional undergraduate and graduate teacher certification programs. But BPS felt that the new teachers coming through these traditional routes were not prepared for the challenging and resource-scarce environment of an urban school district where a vast majority of students came from low-income backgrounds and nearly one in five had a home language other than English (**Exhibit 5**). Guiney remembered the reaction from one professor from a local school of education:

> By starting BTR, we were essentially telling all the schools of education in the area that they weren't doing a good enough job preparing teachers for Boston's public schools. When we presented the idea to the BPE board the first time, I thought that one of our members, an ed school professor, would be resistant. But after the presentation he just said, in a positive way, "There goes the cartel!"

Most of the traditional certification programs had a 13- to 15-week student-teacher component, which the founders of BTR saw as an insufficient amount of time to be prepared as a first-year teacher. There was also evidence that many teacher education schools emphasized theoretical and generic pedagogy instead of giving teachers the practical skills and content knowledge to teach in urban classrooms. BTR would be a teacher residency program that addressed these shortcomings through an intensive program of a yearlong student-teacher mentorship combined with rigorous graduate coursework.

Knowles continued to advocate for designing BTR on the medical residency model and saw the teachers' institute that Solomon had created at City on a Hill as a perfect example of how it could work in education. Knowles commented: "We don't let doctors who have only finished their coursework immediately perform surgery. First, they must go through a residency where they learn how to be surgeons by working side-by-side with experienced surgeons." A yearlong teacher residency—a rigorous training program that values practice along with content and theory and where future practitioners would apply what they were learning by working in the field alongside an experienced professional—would ensure that when new teachers stepped into the classroom alone for the first time, they would be effective teachers. As Guiney explained:

> The whole reason to do a residency program is that you believe that you learn how to teach by teaching. It is not a crash course in the summer. It's not an eight-week practicum. It is the dailyness of being there a week before the school year opens and watching what you have to do to prepare for the roster of students that you have. And then it's watching, trying it out, getting feedback, working it through. That's how you learn to be a good teacher.

Implementing the Model

The 13-month program started in July with a two-month summer institute followed by ten months in a classroom four days a week with a mentor teacher, and was capped at the end with a month of coursework necessary to finish the master's degree. During the year, residents did not earn a salary but instead received a stipend of $10,000. In addition, they were responsible for $10,000 in tuition for the residency and coursework. In return for completing three years of teaching in BPS after finishing the residency, BTR would forgive the tuition. Also, because BTR was part of the federal AmeriCorps program, residents who successfully finished the year also received an educational voucher for nearly $5,000 that they could use to pay off any student loans they had, including those incurred to cover the BTR tuition.

Recruitment and Selection

Solomon and BTR recruiter Monique Davis defined three types of potential BTR candidates (**Exhibit 6**). Candidates applied to BTR through an online application that included essay questions such as "What are your thoughts about the opportunities and challenges in urban schools?" and "How do you think current movements in education affect urban schools?" Staff at BTR and the BPS human resources department evaluated the applications and invited a group of finalists to attend a daylong selection process at a BPS school.

During the day, each candidate taught a mini-lesson to students at the school, participated in a group problem-solving activity, wrote a response to a classroom observation, and was interviewed by multiple raters. Applicants were then rated by teachers, BTR staff, BPS human resource staff, and course instructors. By the end of the day, each candidate had been evaluated performing multiple activities by 15 to 20 people. The selection day also offered an opportunity for mentors to look for a fit with prospective residents. (See **Exhibit 7** for biographies of successful applicants.)

At first, it was difficult to predict exactly what types of teachers BPS would need 18 months later, given that BTR began recruiting six months before residents started their year-long residency. Working with BTR, the BPS human resources department built a model that could better predict the district's future teacher needs. Bill Horwath, director of staffing for BPS, explained, "What we try to do is align the supply and demand of teachers in BPS. We consider retirement and attrition trends in the district as well as the need to recruit a diverse group of teachers." As a result of the new forecasting model, the BPS human resource department could let BTR know at the beginning of each recruiting cycle the composition of the new resident cohort that would best meet the district's needs.

Teaching Sites and Mentor Teachers

The 14 schools that hosted residents during their residency year were called teaching sites. To have their school become a teaching site, principals and potential mentor teachers filled out a lengthy application answering questions such as "How do teachers collaborate to improve instruction at your school?" and "What is your vision of the role of a mentor teacher?" The BTR team visited all of the interested schools to make sure the principal and faculty could meet the expectations of a teaching site (**Exhibit 8**).

From the beginning, Solomon felt that it was important that residents be placed as a group of at least six in teaching sites. By participating as a cohort during their preparation year, residents had a built-in support system of colleagues and the teaching sites were more likely to integrate the practices of the residency into their cultures rather than treating it as a side activity. However, placing groups of residents in schools presented challenges. This approach required that there would be at least six qualified mentors in each school. As of 2007, only half of the 14 sites hosted six or more residents, and around a third hosted four or fewer.

Hollee Freeman, the field director for BTR, worked with principals of teaching sites to select mentors to work with the residents. BTR staff interviewed prospective mentor teachers and observed them teaching a lesson. Mentors received a $3,000 stipend for the year and often found the experience rewarding, but finding enough quality mentors could be difficult. Some veteran teachers were hesitant to open their classrooms to outsiders, and the time commitment required to be a mentor was tremendous. Mentors not only had to ensure that their own students succeeded, but also that the resident was prepared to teach by the end of the year.

For some, the demand was too much to continue on as a mentor for consecutive years. As one mentor said, "I've thought about whether I would be a mentor again next year. I enjoy it and have really been able to tighten up my own practice. But, the amount of time it takes to support the resident and still do justice to your kids—I don't feel like there's enough time in the day." But others were willing to serve as mentors for an extended period. As one explained, "I love being a BTR mentor. I can see doing it every year for as long as I teach. It forces me to reflect on my own teaching practice and I really feel like I am helping people become better teachers."

Finding enough quality mentors had been a challenge from BTR's inception. Many of those recruited for the role had never mentored prior to BTR. Even those with mentoring experience had never served full-time for an entire school year. Freeman realized that mentors would need professional development on the BTR mentoring model and designed "Dimensions of Effective Mentoring" (**Exhibit 9**). They also instituted contracts that required mentors to commit to specific expectations. Mentors kicked off the year with a two-day training program that was followed by monthly all-mentor training sessions and weekly on-site check-ins.

During these meetings mentors were briefed on requirements that their residents were expected to complete and received training on how to differentiate their mentoring approach to meet individual resident needs.

Site Directors

To help coordinate between the mentors, residents, principals, and BTR, Solomon created the position of site director. Site directors were hired collaboratively by BTR, and the principal at the school and their salaries were split equally between BTR and BPS. Most were teachers or instructional coaches in the school with half-time assignments as site directors. They were expected to play a coordinating and support function, but more importantly to help residents connect theory and practice. Site directors across all schools were expected to keep track of the BTR curricular focus month to month and ensure that residents and mentors were focused on putting those concepts into practice in their daily work.

Solomon felt that it was important for the site directors to be school staff in order to best understand the school and the day-to-day challenges faced by residents and mentors. He explained:

> Most traditional preparation programs hire program supervisors from outside the host school. We wanted to place the supervision in the school with someone one knows the context—the kids, culture, other teachers etc. We also thought they would be better positioned to build the capacity of the school to effectively incorporate the ideas of mentoring and collaboration more broadly.

The site directors were critically important to the overall quality of the residency experience. As one recent graduate reflected:

> Our site director was key in fostering an environment in which we could really focus on learning to be good teachers. She created a place where we could grow. And there were seven of us, so she was able to accomplish that even with very, very different personalities. I think that's at least in part due to her hard work, compassion, and commitment to us.

Site directors attended twice a month training meetings with their peers focused on how best to work with mentor teachers and residents. BTR devised a rubric that identified the characteristics of a successful site director, and measured the performance of site directors against it (**Exhibit 10**).

Coursework

While the 1993 Massachusetts Education Reform Act allowed BTR to operate a certification program, the classes that residents took outside their schools needed to be accredited in order to count towards a master's degree. BTR partnered with UMass Boston to provide accreditation for the courses, which were designed and taught by instructors hired by BTR. UMass Boston played a very limited role in overseeing and delivering the coursework and allowed BTR to hire instructors for its classes from the multitude of colleges and universities in the Boston area, as well as from a large group of knowledgeable practitioners and experienced coaches. This meant that BTR was able to recruit top talent to teach its residents. Marcie Osinsky served as BTR's curriculum director, and worked to develop a rigorous set of courses and experiences for residents.

BTR delivered a two-month summer institute to give residents the necessary background to be prepared for the start of the school year. Mornings during the first month were fit to the needs of individual residents. For residents with limited classroom experience, this meant working in a summer school classroom while others with more experience but who had been out of college longer took prep classes for the state licensing exam. The July afternoons were reserved for basic classes on lesson planning and classroom management. In August, classes on teaching in specific content areas started (**Exhibit 11**). Once the academic year began, residents attended class for one three-hour session during the week and then two three-hour blocks on Friday.

Because BTR attempted to link what the residents learned in the classroom to what they were working on with their mentor, the graduate coursework had to be aligned with the BPS curriculum and the rhythms of the school year. To ensure the relevance of the coursework, the BTR curriculum and resident portfolios were centered on BPS's existing Dimensions of Effective Teaching (**Exhibit 12**). BTR instructors were trained to develop their syllabi around this framework and focus on content that could be directly applied to teaching.

There were two exceptions to the typical schedule of a resident (**Exhibit 13**). In January, BTR pulled residents out of their schools for an intensive one-and-a-half-week training session on special education and to conduct a midyear portfolio evaluation. As a requirement for the BTR program and master's degree, residents were required to develop a portfolio to demonstrate their progress toward mastering the Dimensions of Effective Teaching. The portfolios included examples of lesson and unit plans, videos of their teaching practice, and examples of rigorous evaluation of their students' work. The portfolio evaluation also provided an opportunity for residents to think about their teaching over the first half of the year and create an action plan to improve in the second half.

Another important part of the curriculum explored beliefs about intelligence. As Solomon explained:

> We have to understand that there are lots of achievement gaps, what they look like and what they mean. And we must know what the gaps have to do with the history of our city and the history of our country, and then think about the causes and our role in it. This has to happen at the same time a resident is starting to think about how to teach reading, math, history or science.

After successfully completing the 13-month program, residents earned a teacher license in their primary academic content area and a master's degree in education. Residents also received credit towards a dual licensure in special education, which they could fulfill by completing future classes offered through the UMass Boston/BTR partnership the following year for $4,000 in tuition.

Hiring and Placement

BTR was committed to having all of its graduates teaching in a BPS classroom the fall after completing their residencies. The hiring process in BPS, unlike some large urban school districts, was decentralized. Essentially, the BPS human resource department (HR) acted as a pipeline to schools for a pool of applicants that included BTR graduates. Principals posted positions on a central portal managed by the human resource department. Candidates applied for the open positions on the portal, and then principals could download all the submitted applications and cover letters for the jobs they had posted. HR provided online screening tools that could sort by certification level or degrees earned and BPS staffing specialists screened applications themselves to highlight top candidates for principals. Some positions, such as math, science, and special education, were harder to fill and required more involvement from HR staff.

Once a principal identified a group of potential hires, the teacher's union contract specified that the interview process be conducted by a hiring committee that included teachers and the principal. This committee was also responsible for making the final hiring decision, though in practice it was usually made by the principal. For BTR, the decentralized system meant that the organization had little influence over where its residents ended up. By 2007, 55 of the 144 BPS schools had hired residents; only six schools had hired five or more, 80% had hired three or fewer, and around half had hired only one.

Ongoing Support

The first year of teaching was very challenging for all teachers, and even though they felt well prepared, BTR graduates were no exception. During their residency, they could rely on the support and knowledge of their mentor teacher, but once in their own classrooms, some residents felt isolated. A growing number of graduates asked BTR to do more to support them once they began teaching. Solomon recounted, "Residents were telling us, 'When I went through BTR, there was someone in my classroom all the time. They were giving me feedback and talking to me about my teaching. Now, I started teaching on my own and nobody's ever in my classroom.'"

To give residents continuing support through their initial teaching years, BTR hired induction coaches. Some induction coaches were retired teachers while others had worked as instructional consultants in BPS schools. They visited the classrooms of first-, second-, and third-year BTR teachers to provide support, give feedback on lessons, or serve as a general sounding board for school challenges. One graduate explained, "The coaches give you suggestions on your teaching. They also point you to helpful resources, and when you really need help they are there to support you."

By the 2007–2008 school year, BPS had launched a similar support program for all first-year teachers in the district. "New teacher developers" were deployed around the district to assist first-year teachers. With a BPS support network in place for first-year teachers, BTR moved its support to a hybrid model of BTR and BPS coaches. BTR graduates were supported by the district's new teacher developers in their first year and by BTR induction coaches in their second and third years. To prevent problems arising from the amalgamated support system, BTR's induction coordinators worked closely with BPS's new teacher support team.

Impact and Challenges

BTR had evolved into BPS's "grow your own" teacher program in its first five years and provided around 10% of all the teachers BPS hired in 2007 and more than a quarter of its new math and science teachers. Administrators within BPS saw the program as a way to access a predictable number of the teachers it needed without having to rely solely on local universities. Before they started their first year of teaching, BTR residents already knew the BPS curriculum and culture. Most importantly they were prepared for the specific challenges of an urban district. As one BTR graduate commented, "I was very well prepared for my first year of teaching. I don't know if I could have survived this if I had done another program." A current resident emphasized the reputation of the program, saying, "When principals see BTR on our resumes, their reaction is, 'Wow, you are highly qualified. You clearly have the skills to handle teaching, especially at BPS.' And at hiring fairs, we're competing with people from Harvard and getting the advantage. That says a lot about this program."

Because over 50% of its total graduates since 2003 were black or Hispanic, BTR had brought greater diversity into BPS's teacher ranks. In 2007, over 50% of BTR graduates hired were minorities compared with 21% of all new teachers. Also, retention of BTR graduates compared favorably to other first-year teachers—nearly 80% of BTR graduates were likely to complete their third year of teaching compared to 53% of other BPS teachers (**Exhibit 14**). Not only were they staying longer, BTR graduates also had a strong reputation within the district. In a 2006 survey of principals, 88% viewed BTR teachers the same as or more effective than other first-year teachers at their school, and the majority (55%) believed them to be "significantly more effective."

However, BTR still faced challenges. As of yet, no empirical data existed to show that the students of BTR teachers outperformed those of other teachers. In 2007, BTR had enlisted the help of a team of Harvard researchers to measure its residents' effectiveness, but the results were not yet available. Individual classroom data had been hard to gather and it was difficult to control for differences in student background, school environment, and teacher characteristics. This was true for all BPS teachers, not just BTR graduates. Nevertheless, BTR could not yet claim that its graduates' impact on student achievement was significantly better than candidates the district hired from other sources, only that principals liked them and they stayed longer.

Solomon also saw variability in the experience of residents across the 14 teaching sites. His initial belief that it was more effective to have a minimum of six residents in any one site had been confirmed by experience, but this was the case in only half of the sites. He wondered if it made sense to work with fewer teaching sites that would each host a larger group of residents. As he explained, "Sometimes we are stretched thin trying to manage relationships across 14 schools—a teaching site with four residents requires about the same attention from us as one that hosts seven. I sometimes think that with fewer schools we would have more time to build deeper relationships and increase the quality of the residency year at the same time."

In addition, Solomon wondered if the potential to change school cultures and have a dramatic impact on student performance was being diluted by following the district's decentralized hiring and placement approach. A BTR graduate reflected on how he thought about working in the same school with residents from his cohort:

> I really wanted there to be other BTR people in the school because of the camaraderie, mutual support, mutual philosophies, and the way we communicate with each other. At first I was just worried about getting the job, but after I was hired I emailed the principal and told him that he really should hire another BTR person.

Residents usually accepted their first offers, which tended to be from principals who were the most organized and deeply understood how the system worked. Guiney elaborated:

> The sharpest principals who run the best schools have figured out how to say in February or March, "I don't have a job open right now but I promise you a job. You're going to have to wait to sign the contract until May but it will be in fourth grade and I can guarantee you it's going to happen." And residents will accept that if the principal has a reputation for delivering. So, residents end up in really good schools because they have offers early.

In fact, of the 55 schools that had hired BTR graduates only six employed five or more former residents. Most of these schools had higher historical levels of student achievement than the district average (**Exhibits 15** and **16**).

Yet some district staff questioned the notion that BTR graduates could change a school's culture, even if they went in as a group. Without corresponding changes in school leadership and central office supports, this line of thinking was skeptical about whether placing cohorts of residents in low-performing schools would make any difference, and worried that it would lead to higher turnover among BTR graduates because their early teaching experiences would be negative. As one senior manager at BPS remarked:

> The cultures in our struggling schools are so complex and so entrenched that to ask a small group of BTR graduates to take them on would be unfair. You're going to put the burden of changing the dysfunctional culture of a broken school on the backs of a handful of first year teachers? It would be smarter to think of BTR as one piece of what comprehensive school reform looks like, not the entire answer.

In the midst of these challenges, Superintendent Johnson began discussions with Teach For America (TFA) about entering Boston for the first time in its history. Johnson had partnered with TFA in her former districts and had a good relationship with the organization. TFA teachers would cost BPS around $3,000 each, which was less than the district's cost for each BTR teacher (**Exhibit 17**). Similar to TFA's arrangement with other urban districts, BPS could potentially direct TFA corps members to principals who had hard-to-fill openings in high-priority schools, which was in alignment with the mission of TFA. In addition, TFA might compete with BTR for qualified candidates at universities around Boston since its corps members could receive a full teacher's salary right away and did not have to train under a mentor teacher.

TFA also had its drawbacks. Corps members only received eight weeks of preparation the summer before they began teaching for the first time. Also, since TFA recruited nationally and only asked for a two-year commitment, there was no guarantee that teachers would stay in Boston as long as BTR teachers. In fact, only about one-third of TFA corps members nationwide remained in classrooms after their initial service. The national footprint also meant that BPS would have little influence over the content of corps members' training or which ones chose to teach in Boston.

Shaping the Future

For Solomon, the real measure of effectiveness for BTR over the long term would be whether or not the students of BTR teachers were achieving up to their potential. Even though he could envision ways to improve BTR, he deeply believed that the residency prepared teachers better than other options, and he wanted its graduates in classrooms with students who needed them the most.

He and his team engaged in a business planning process with the Bridgespan Group to develop a set of strategic options for increasing BTR's impact. In addition to BTR staff, the process included Guiney and other BPE staff, Jacobson, BPS's directors of HR and professional development, as well as a few trusted external advisors. The process yielded options for a new strategy that centered on three key activities: strengthening teaching sites, creating partner schools, and measuring impact.

Strengthening Teaching Sites

In order to increase the quality of the residency year, BTR considered partnering more closely with BPS to identify schools with the capacity to host as many as 12 residents per year. Rather than spreading 120 residents across more than 14 sites, BTR would focus on deeper relationships with 10 sites that would become known throughout the district as places in which the next generation of BPS teachers was being developed. This approach could also create a network of model schools that set the standard for how to create environments that valued continuous improvement and collaboration among professionals. With a critical mass of 12 mentors and 12 residents, BTR could invest in a full-time site director and make the on-site professional development available to all teachers in the school, not just those formally participating in BTR. Solomon described the option:

> Basically we would move from loose affiliations with 14 sites to deep partnerships with 10 over the next four years. A few of our schools are ready to make the leap to 12 residents now, but others will have to be cultivated and developed to a point where they have 12 high-quality mentors. It requires a big commitment from a principal, but the benefits could be significant in terms of resources, recognition as a model school, and a lever for building a deep culture of professional collaboration. From our standpoint, we expect more consistent quality because of the critical mass of professionals involved at each site and the increased standardization of the model across the schools.

This option required agreement from BPS to formally recognize teaching sites as model schools and give them some flexibility around key policies related to daily scheduling and formal roles to accommodate the residency model. This would signal to schools a more "official" tie between BPS and BTR than in the past when principals were welcome to participate but not formally recognized by the district for doing so. From a budget perspective, because BTR would be reducing the number of sites even as it invested more in each, the incremental annual cost of investing in training sites at full deployment would be approximately $350,000 over the current model (**Exhibit 18**).

Creating Partner Schools

A parallel option that BTR could pursue was to create closer linkages with a group of high-priority schools that would agree to hire a critical mass of residents over time. Solomon imagined that nearly all BTR graduates would be eager to work in these schools, but with logistical hurdles such as the availability of positions in any given year, he estimated that 70% of graduates would join high-priority schools with the remaining 30% going to work in other schools in the district. Within five years, BTR projected that it could grow from eight partner schools to twenty-four, requiring an incremental annual cost of around $700,000 over the current model (**Exhibit 18**).

BTR would work closely with BPS to identify and select partner schools so that the increased presence of its graduates would be an integral piece of the district's strategy to accelerate the performance of particular schools. Principals in partner schools would hire several graduates over three to four years in order to build a critical mass of teachers specifically prepared to work in those types of schools who also had a deep understanding of how to nurture and participate in organizational cultures that valued professional collaboration.

Given the latitude principals currently had in identifying candidates for positions in their buildings, asking them to commit to hiring a certain number of teachers from the BTR pool over a number of years was a significant shift. In order to make this option a reality, BPS would have to agree to work closely with BTR to select partner schools and make the case to principals of low-performing schools that hiring residents was an integral part of the district's overall approach to supporting leaders attempting to turn around their schools.

For BTR graduates, the opportunity to work with former residents who shared a common experience and point of view about teaching would provide the critical support and camaraderie necessary to sustain their commitment in the early years of teaching in a difficult school. Solomon elaborated on the attractiveness of moving to a partner school model, saying, "By working more closely with a finite number of high-need schools, BTR will have the potential to significantly impact student achievement in BPS."

BTR would invest in a coordinator for every four partner schools who would serve as a liaison between the program and the principals. In addition, the ongoing training and support that BTR offered to its graduates on topics such as special education and English as a second language would be available to all teachers in a partner school. Over time as performance in these schools accelerated, Solomon envisioned that rapidly improving partner schools could also serve as teaching sites, so that residents would have an opportunity to work side-by-side with mentors who were BTR graduates involved in turning around struggling schools.

Measuring Impact

Solomon had always been committed to delivering results, but the strategic planning process provided an opportunity to put a stake in the ground on a few areas of leverage and identify indicators that BTR could track over the coming five years. The four areas were recruitment, retention, graduate development, and teacher effectiveness.

Recruitment

In this area, BTR would track the number of residents, the number of graduates, the percentage of first-year graduates to the total of BPS new hires who were Hispanic or African-American and who taught math, science, special education, or English as a second language.

Retention

Under the retention category, BTR would track the percentage of graduates who became teachers and the percentage of graduates who stayed in BPS for three and five years.

Graduate Development

BTR would make a more concerted effort to develop BTR graduates to become mentors and site directors in the program after a few years of teaching, as well as track the percentage of its graduates that took on other types of leadership roles in BPS.

Teacher Effectiveness

In order to measure the effectiveness of its graduates, BTR would compare their student results with all first-year teachers in BPS. In years three and beyond it would track how its graduates performed relative to teachers from other preparation programs. It would continue to track BTR graduate turnover compared to other BPS teachers, as well as principals' impressions of their effectiveness through an annual survey.

As Solomon weighed the new strategic options against simply working on making the current model of preparation and placement as powerful as it could be, he was committed to choosing the path that would most support the goal that every student in BPS would have an effective teacher who gave them the opportunity to learn at high levels every day. He believed that in the long run, that would be the true test of BTR's impact.

Exhibit 1

Boston Public Schools MCAS Results 1999–2007

Percent of Students by Performance Level

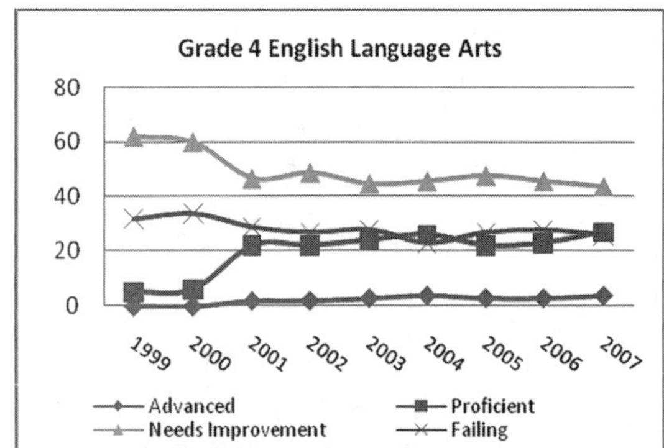

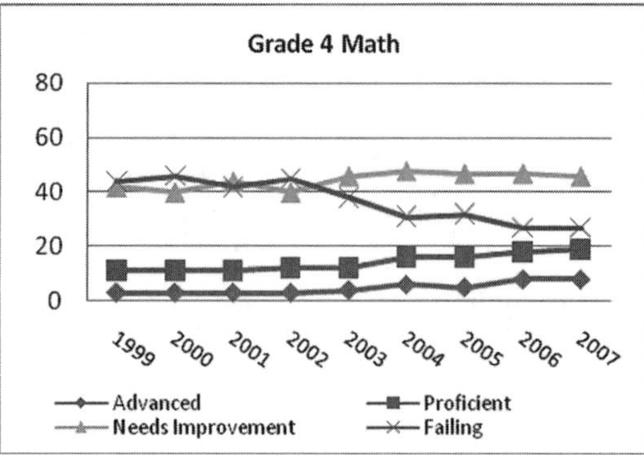

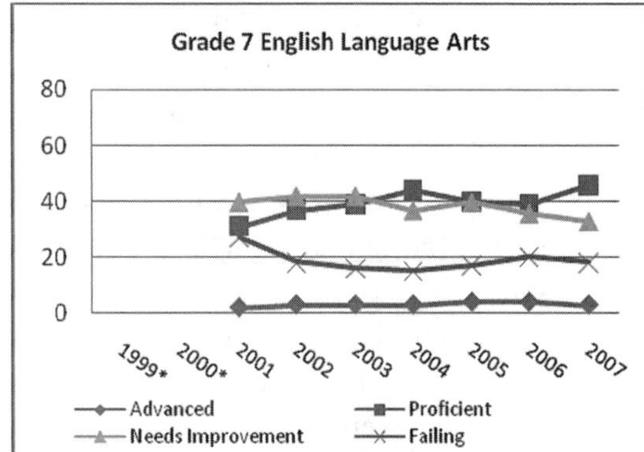

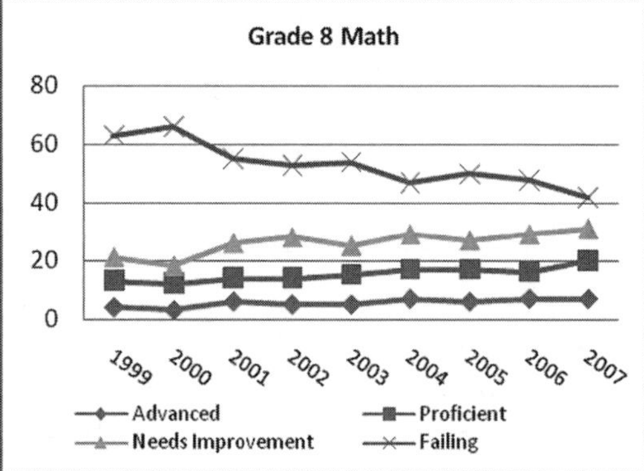

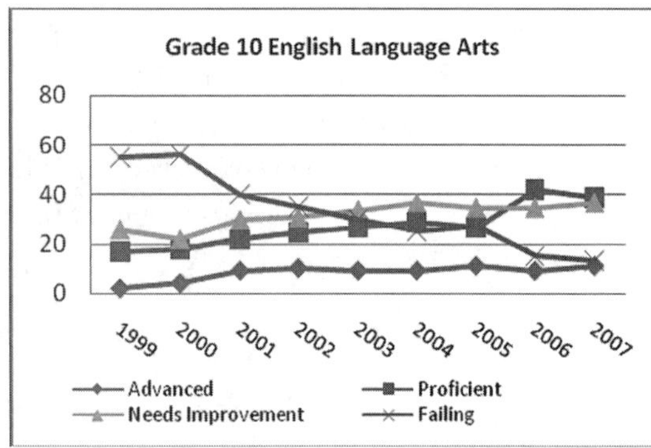

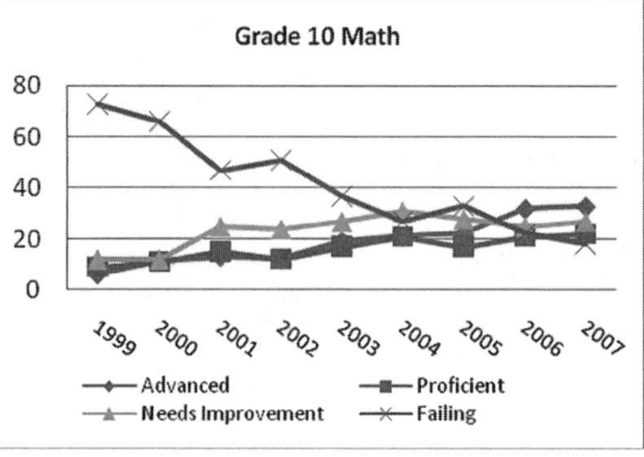

*Massachusetts did not assess 7th grade language arts proficiency before 2001.

Source: Massachusetts Department of Education, "MCAS Annual Comparisons for Boston," Massachusetts Department of Education web site, http://profiles.doe.mass.edu/mcas, accessed February 2008, and case writer analysis.

Exhibit 2

Boston Public Schools MCAS Results by Subgroup 2001–2007

Percent of Students Testing Proficient or Advanced

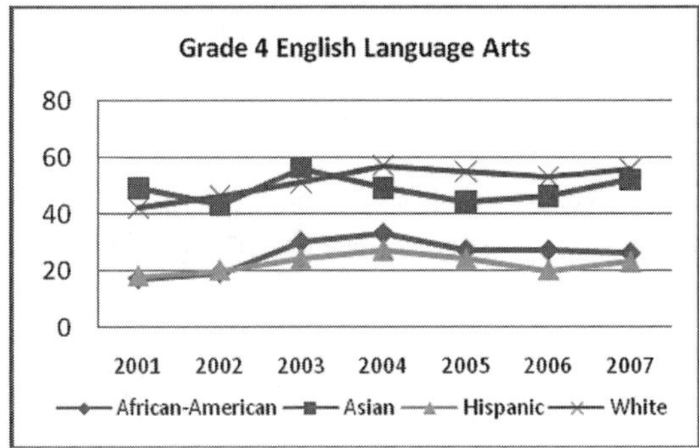

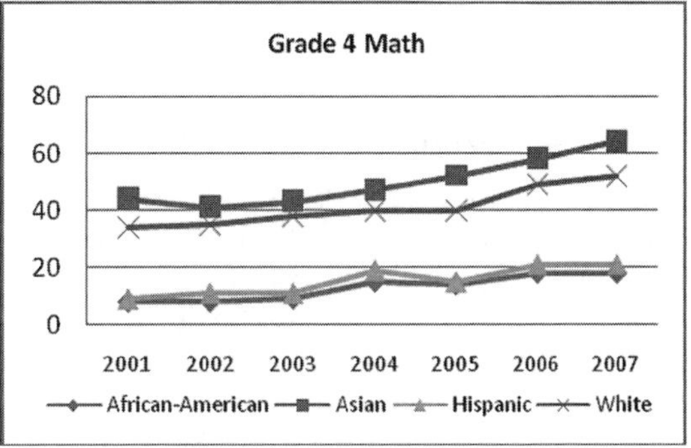

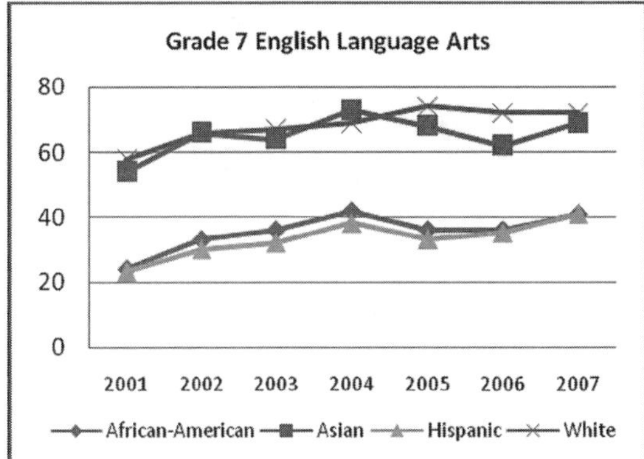

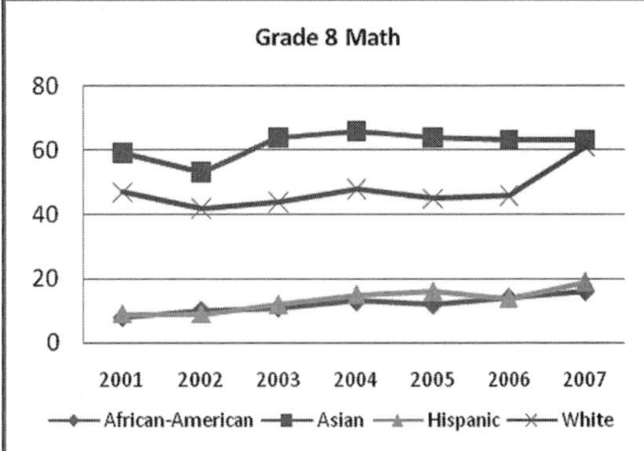

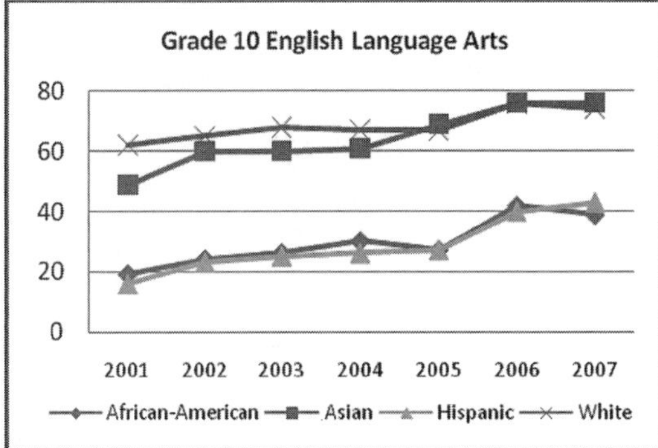

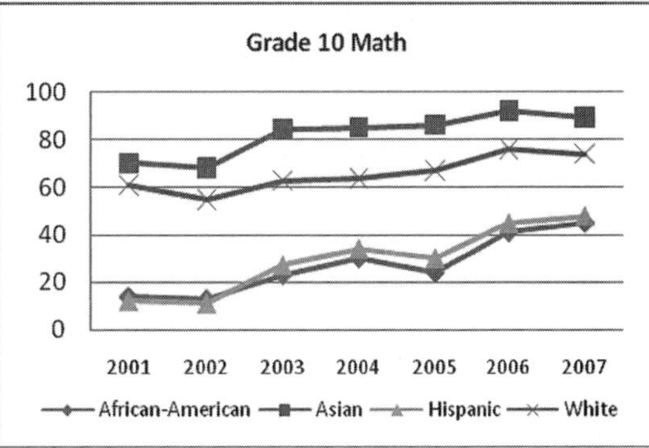

Note: MCAS data by subgroup do not exist prior to 2001.

Source: Massachusetts Department of Education, "MCAS Results by Subgroup," retrieved February 2008 from http://profiles.doe.mass.edu/mcas/subgroups2.aspx?district=035&school=&mcasyear=2002, and case writer analysis.

Exhibit 3

Boston Teacher Residency Funding Agreement

	03–04	*04–05*	*05–06*	*06–07*	*07–08*	*08–09*	*09–10*
Strategic Grant Partners	100%	100%	—	—	—	—	—
Boston Public Schools	—	—	20%	40%	60%	51%	51%
Private Sources	—	—	80%	60%	40%	49%	49%

Source: Internal BTR Documents and case writer analysis.

*Beginning with the 08–09 SY and continuing forward, BPS would become a "majority funder," likely supplying 51% of BTR's total budget, which had to be approved by the BPS superintendent and deputy superintendent of teaching and learning.

Exhibit 4

Boston Teacher Residency Organization Chart

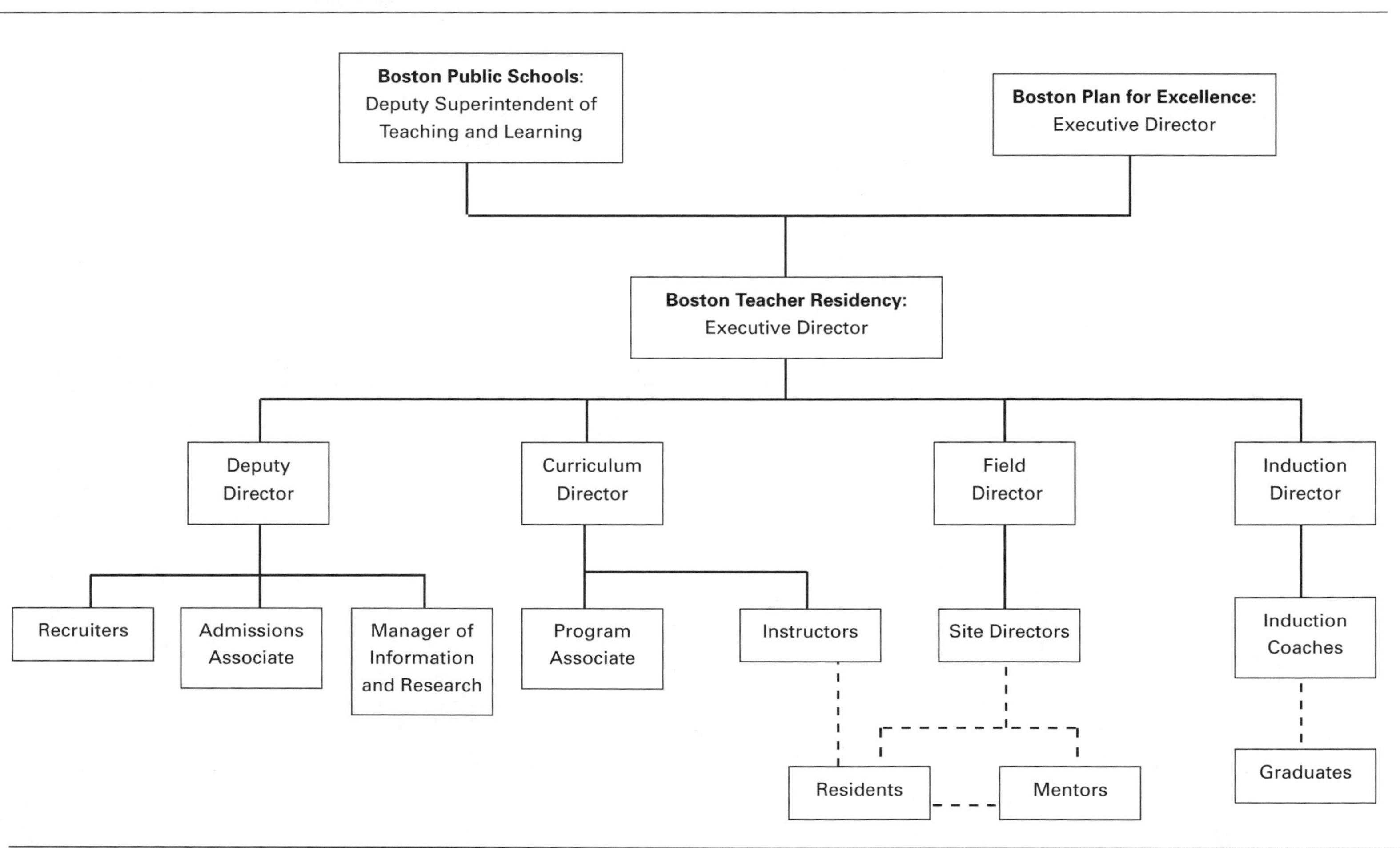

Source: Internal BTR documents and case writer analysis.

Exhibit 5

2007–2008 Boston Public Schools Student and Staff Data

Student Demographics	
Total enrollment	56,190
Black	41%
Hispanic	35%
White	14%
Asian	9%
Multi-racial, non-Hispanic	1%
American Indian	<1%
Students receiving free and reduced meals	71%
Students with disabilities	20%
English language learners	18%
Home languages of English language learners	
Spanish	58%
Haitian Creole	9%
Chinese	8%
Cape Verdean Creole	7%
Vietnamese	5%
Other*	13%

Staff Demographics	
Total staff positions	9,412
Teachers	53%
Administrators	8%
Support personnel	5%
Aides and monitors	13%
Secretaries and clerical	4%
Custodial/safety/technical	13%
Part-time and summer	5%
Teacher demographics	
Black	25%
Hispanic	9%
White	61%
Asian	5%
Administrator demographics	
Black	46%
Hispanic	33%
White	17%
Asian	4%

Source: Compiled from Boston Public Schools, "Boston Public Schools at a Glance," Boston Public Schools web site, http://boston.k12.ma.us/bps/bpsglance.asp, accessed February 2008.

*BPS English Language learners come from more than 40 different countries.

Exhibit 6

Potential Boston Teacher Residency Candidate Types

Candidate Type	*Characteristics*	*Marketing Approach*
Recent college graduate	Good GPA, youth-focused community service, demonstrated leadership	College campus representatives, career fairs, campus career offices
Midcareer switcher	Business, engineering or similar background, more than 10 years of work experience, looking for a job that "makes a difference"	Website, subway ads, radio, newspaper, social enterprise job search engines
Community connected	Worked in a community service role, such as a domestic violence officer in a police department or church leader	Recruiters visit churches, community centers, nonprofits, and schools networking and handing out informational pamphlets

Source: Case writer analysis.

Exhibit 7

Biographies of Selected Boston Teacher Residency Graduates

Neema Avashia. Ms. Avashia brings to Boston's schools her experience working with students as a tutor and mentor in elementary and secondary schools in Pittsburgh (PA) and Madison (WI). A graduate of Carnegie Mellon University with degrees in anthropology-history and professional writing and a minor in teaching English to speakers of other languages, Ms. Avashia also earned a master's degree in educational policy studies from the University of Wisconsin–Madison.

Sheila Brown. After graduating from Boston State College with a BA in mathematics, Ms. Brown spent over 28 years working at Verizon Communications in various positions, ranging from engineer to human resources business partner. For more than a decade now, Ms. Brown has demonstrated her commitment to youth and community by volunteering at St. Catherine of Sienna in Charlestown as a First Communion teacher, a CYO advisor, and a softball coach. In 1997 she received the Charlestown Community Unsung Hero Award.

Amit Gupta. Mr. Gupta holds a bachelor's degree in electrical engineering from Boston University and an MBA from the Olin Graduate School of Business at Babson College. He worked for 11 years in the technology field and volunteered for Babson's Coaching and Leadership program.

Jane Long. A graduate of Boston Latin School and Boston College with a bachelor's in communications, Ms. Long has been an active volunteer at the Gate of Heaven CYO, where she coached, mentored, and refereed girls' basketball. Ms. Long received the Gate of Heaven Catholic Youth of the Year award in 1999.

Henry Paige. Mr. Paige graduated from South Carolina State University with a BA in English. He worked as a head teacher counselor at the Boys Club of New York, supervising counselor and camper daily activities, mentoring inner-city middle school students, and tutoring students in social studies, mathematics, and English. As a junior researcher for the department of transportation in Orangeburg (SC), he prepared and conducted educational activities for fifth through eighth grade classes, and wrote, designed, and edited a monthly newsletter highlighting African-American inventors.

Julie Perry. Ms. Perry holds a bachelor's degree in management from the University of Massachusetts/Amherst. After a career in recruitment and staffing for corporations such as Fidelity Investments and Shawmut Design and Construction, Ms. Perry joined the Somerville Public Schools last year as a substitute and assistant site coordinator for the city's 21st Century Community Learning Center program.

Nicole Tabolt. Before joining BTR, Ms. Tabolt worked as a curriculum planning coordinator and classroom aide with the America Reads program in Philadelphia. In her undergraduate summers, she also worked with youth as a dance and art teacher at the Cambridge Family YMCA. Ms. Tabolt received a bachelor's degree in English and minor in Hispanic studies from the University of Pennsylvania. She also received her diploma from the Boston Latin School. She completed her English residency at Brighton's Edison Middle School. Ms. Tabolt speaks Spanish.

Source: Boston Teacher Residency, "FAQs," Boston Teacher Residency web site, http://www.bpe.org/btr/.html, accessed March 2008.

Exhibit 8

Expectations of a Boston Teacher Residency Teaching Site and Principal, 2007

Overall Expectations

BTR is seeking Principals who:

- Support the collegial analysis of instructional practice,
- Are instructional leaders.
- See the work of BTR and of the Mentor Teachers as integral to the successful operation of the school, and ensure that all involved have time to do it.
- Champion BTR.

BTR is seeking schools which:

- Have a developing culture of inquiry and improvement.
- Have a critical mass of teachers willing and qualified to serve as mentors.
- Will share the responsibility for the success of the Residents.

More Specifically

A BTR host school principal commits to:

- Ensure that Mentor Teachers are available and scheduled to meet with Residents for at least *two hours per week.*
- Ensure that Mentor Teachers have sufficient time to fulfill mentoring duties.
- Make teaching public. Support and build a culture which encourages and facilitates the discussion and analysis of faculty members' teaching.
- Ensure that every Mentor Teacher identifies and makes public at the beginning of the year an instructional strength that they are willing to allow observers to see during the year.
- Ensure that every Mentor Teacher identifies and makes public an area of instructional focus which they will work on throughout the year.
- Attempt to hire teachers who are or who will soon be Mentor Teachers.
- Support good teachers who are not currently ready to be Mentors to develop into Mentor Teachers. This may involve collaborating with BTR to involve these teachers in selected BTR activities.
- Participate in an Annual School Review with all involved school personnel to identify strengths and areas of need.
- Identify teachers who are qualified to be Mentors: who are both excellent teachers skilled in the district's work, and are willing and able to coach an adult learner.
- Identify a teacher or other faculty member willing and qualified to serve as Site Director.
- Support the Site Director in the fulfillment of both BTR and school-based duties.

Source: Internal BTR documents.

Exhibit 9

Dimensions of Effective Mentoring

1. Mentor holds high expectations for Resident
   - Shows through words and actions the belief that Resident can meet high expectations
   - Supports Resident to problem-solve in challenging situations
   - Builds on Resident's strengths and identifies areas of challenge with clear accountability and support mechanisms
2. Mentor reflects on own practice as a Mentor
   - Regularly reflects on mentoring strengths, skills and areas of weakness; sets and assesses progress against learning goals with Site Director, Resident and other Mentors
3. Mentor uses data to inform instruction
   - Works with Resident to use a variety of formal and informal assessments to evaluate student learning and needs and uses that information to individualize instruction
4. Mentor works to communicate effectively with Resident
   - Uses appropriate communication techniques with Resident to discuss practice and to address conflicts
   - Engages in inquiry-based conversations with Resident around practice
   - Matches coaching approach with Resident's need for support and structure
5. Mentor provides daily opportunities for Resident to practice teaching
   - Encourages Resident to implement ideas from coursework and practicum; holds Resident accountable for careful implementation and assessment of effectiveness
   - Fully participates in the structured release of responsibility by allowing and demonstrating to Resident how to take over specific portions of classroom instruction and activities
   - Explicitly discusses with Resident philosophical approach and reasoning behind instructional decisions; maintains focus on student achievement
6. Mentor models professional behavior
   - Fully participates in BTR activities by being punctual and prepared; fulfills BTR commitments in the face of conflicting priorities
   - Uses respectful language and discretion when discussing challenging situations; maintains confidentiality
   - Routinely analyzes professional interactions and serves as a model for resolving concerns and issues in a timely and constructive manner
7. Mentor functions effectively in a multilingual, multicultural and economically diverse classroom and school community
   - Engages in two-way conversations with Resident around issues of equity, achievement, experience, race, class, and ability, and how these issues intersect with teaching and learning for the Resident and Mentor
8. Mentor displays a commitment to implementation of BTR and BPS initiatives
   - Effectively implements BPS instructional and curricular initiatives (e.g. Readers/Writers Workshop, LASW, CCL and other PD opportunities)
   - Effectively uses BTR structural and curricular initiatives (e.g. Lesson Planning, two hours of sacred-time meetings, Monthly Mentor professional development meetings, documentation of Resident progress and goals)

Source: Internal BTR documents.

Exhibit 10

Dimensions of Effective Site Directorships

1. Site Director demonstrates excellence, equity and high expectations for Mentors and Residents
   - Fosters and encourages Resident and Mentor learning
   - Plans instruction

2. Site Director reflects on own practice as a Site Director and makes work public
   - Invites Residents, Mentors, BTR, principal, and other colleagues to observe her/himself in a professional setting (i.e. teaching, observing, debriefing, facilitating school-based PD, etc.) and uses feedback to improve
   - Communicates with Field Director and other Site Directors regarding strengths, challenges, and progress

3. Site Director uses data to inform work with Residents and Mentors
   - Works with residents to assess progress during their practicum experience
   - Works with mentors to assess development as mentors during the school year
   - Works with Residents and Mentors to thoroughly analyze student data to identify trends and areas of continuing challenge

4. Site Director models professionalism
   - Ensures that all Site Director responsibilities are met (as outlined in the SD job description)
   - Functions effectively in a multicultural and economically diverse community of adults through the use of respectful language and discretion when discussing challenging situations and maintains confidentiality

5. Site Director establishes a safe, respectful, and culturally sensitive learning community
   - Works to manage the Site Director relationship to maximize learning for mentor and resident through effective communication, respect of differences and management of conflicts
   - Provides daily/weekly opportunities for residents and mentors to explain their thinking and ask questions that deepen their learning

6. Site Director partners with school, BTR, and BPS community
   - Works with the whole school community to provide a rich learning experience for Residents
   - Makes resources available to Residents and Mentors, which will aid their work
   - Understands BTR and BPS curricular initiatives
   - Engages in collaborative problem solving and decision-making based on what is in the best interest of the program
   - Reflects on the successes and challenges of BTR and uses that information to improve the program

Source: Internal BTR documents.

Exhibit 11

Sample Boston Teacher Residency Course Offerings for High School Residents

Summer

- Becoming an Educator in Boston
- Reflective Seminar: Building a Culture of Achievement
- Curriculum Design; Backwards Design
- Community; Neighborhoods, Families, Schools

Fall

- Reflective Seminar/Pre-Practicum—Residency
- Content Methods Courses for Middle/High School (choose one):
    - Teaching Mathematics
    - Teaching Science
    - Teaching Language Arts
    - Teaching History

Winter—mini courses

- Special Education: Introduction to SPED: IEP's and Categories for Disabilities
- Literacy Across the Curriculum

Spring

- Practicum—Residency
- Reflective Seminar
- Inclusive Education

Summer

- Special Education: Differentiated Instruction
- Working with ELL's: Language Acquisition

Source: Internal BTR documents.

Exhibit 12

Boston Public Schools Dimensions of Effective Teaching

Equity and High Expectations: Demonstrate a commitment to excellence, equity, and high expectations for all students with an emphasis on building on the strengths that students bring to the teaching/learning process and closing the achievement gap between subgroups within the school.

Professionalism: Model professional behavior that addresses job responsibilities, district policies and procedures, and the expectations of professionals working in a multi-lingual, multi-cultural, and economically diverse community.

Safe, Respectful, and Culturally Sensitive and Responsive Learning Communities: Build and maintain safe, fair, and respectful learning environments that celebrate the diversity of the student population.

Partnerships with Family and Community: Initiate and maintain consistent communication and develop constructive partnerships with families, community members, and agencies, building on their strengths and recognizing them as co-educators.

Instructional Planning and Implementation: Plan instruction and employ strategies that address the wide range of learning, behavioral, and communication styles of the student population.

Content Knowledge: Have extensive knowledge of the content including, but not limited to, key concepts and facts, relevant research, methods of inquiry, and communication styles specific to the respective discipline(s).

Monitoring and Assessment of Progress: Use a variety of assessment tools and strategies to gather data to monitor student mastery of instructional content, to improve instruction, and to assess the comparative performance of subgroups within the classroom.

Reflection, Collaboration, and Personal Growth: Reflect on practice in collaboration with administrators and colleagues, monitor personal and professional growth, and pursue professional development in needed areas.

Source: Boston Public Schools, "Dimensions of Effective Teaching," Boston Public Schools web site, http://www.boston.k12.ma.us/teach/dimensions.pdf, accessed March 2008.

Exhibit 13

Typical Schedule of Elementary School Residents

	Monday	Tuesday	Wednesday	Thursday	Friday
7:30	Arrive at school. Prepare for the day.	Arrive at school. Prepare for the day.	Arrive at school. Prepare for the day.	Arrive at school. Prepare for the day.	
8:00					
8:30	School starts.	School starts.	School starts.	School starts.	BTR Course: Reflective Seminar
9:00	Readers Workshop	Readers Workshop	Readers Workshop	Readers Workshop	
9:30					
10:00	Writers Workshop	Writers Workshop	Writers Workshop	Writers Workshop	
10:30					
11:00	Math	Math	Math	Math	
11:30					
12:00	Lunch	Lunch	Lunch	Lunch	
12:30	Specialist	Social Studies	Specialist	Social Studies	BTR Course: Elementary Literacy
1:00					
1:30	Science	Collaborative Coaching & Learning	Science	Science	
2:00					
2:30	After-school tutoring		Meet with mentor teacher	After-school tutoring	
3:00	Meet with mentor teacher				
3:30		BTR Course: Elementary Mathematics			
4:00				BTR Course: Designing Curriculum	
4:30					
5:00					
5:30					
6:00					
6:30					
7:00					

Source: Boston Teacher Residency, "FAQs," Boston Teacher Residency web site, http://www.bpe.org/btr/faq.html, accessed March 2008.

Exhibit 14

Boston Teacher Residency Recruitment, Admissions, and Retention Data

Class of	*Applied*	*Enrolled in Program*	*Ratio Applied: Enrolled*	*% of People of Color*	*% of Math/ Sci at MS/ HS Level*	*Completed Program Success-fully*	*Accepted Hiring Offer by BPS*	*Finished 1st Year in BPS**	*Finished 2nd Year in BPS**	*Finished 3rd Year in BPS**	*Finished 4th Year in BPS**	*Currently Teaching in BPS**
2004	149	16	9.31	75%	71%	12	12	12	12	11	6	6
2005	300	39	7.69	41%	38%	36	31	31	31	27		27
2006	325	57	5.70	51%	55%	48	46	44	40			40
2007	408	65	6.28	53%	70%	58	56	53				53
2008	450	84	5.36	57%	57%	77	74					
2009	479	75	6.39	57%	68%							
Total	2,111	336	6.28	54%	62%	239	219	140	83	38	6	126

Source: Internal BTR documents.

*As of June 30, 2008.

Exhibit 15

2007 MCAS Performance of Schools That Hired Five or More BTR Graduates Since 2005

Mathematics

School	*BTR Graduates*	*% Proficient & Advanced*	*% Needs Improvement*	*% Failing*
Murphy (K–8)	9	53	41	5
McCormick (Middle)	8	25	35	40
Parkway (HS)	7	49	36	15
Charlestown High (HS)	6	67	21	12
Boston Community Leadership Academy (HS)	5	59	36	5
Gavin (Middle)	5	19	34	47

Language Arts

School	*BTR Graduates*	*% Proficient & Advanced*	*% Needs Improvement*	*% Failing*
Murphy (K–8)	9	32	39	29
McCormick (Middle)	8	44	38	18
Parkway (HS)	7	34	49	16
Charlestown High (HS)	6	44	44	12
Boston Community Leadership Academy (HS)	5	53	39	7
Gavin (Middle)	5	29	42	28

Source: Massachusetts Department of Education and case writer analysis.

Exhibit 16

Past Performance of Students Entering Non-Specialized Boston High Schools

Percentage of First-Time 9th Graders in 2006 Who Had Scored in the Bottom Quartile on the English Language Arts MCAS in 7th Grade

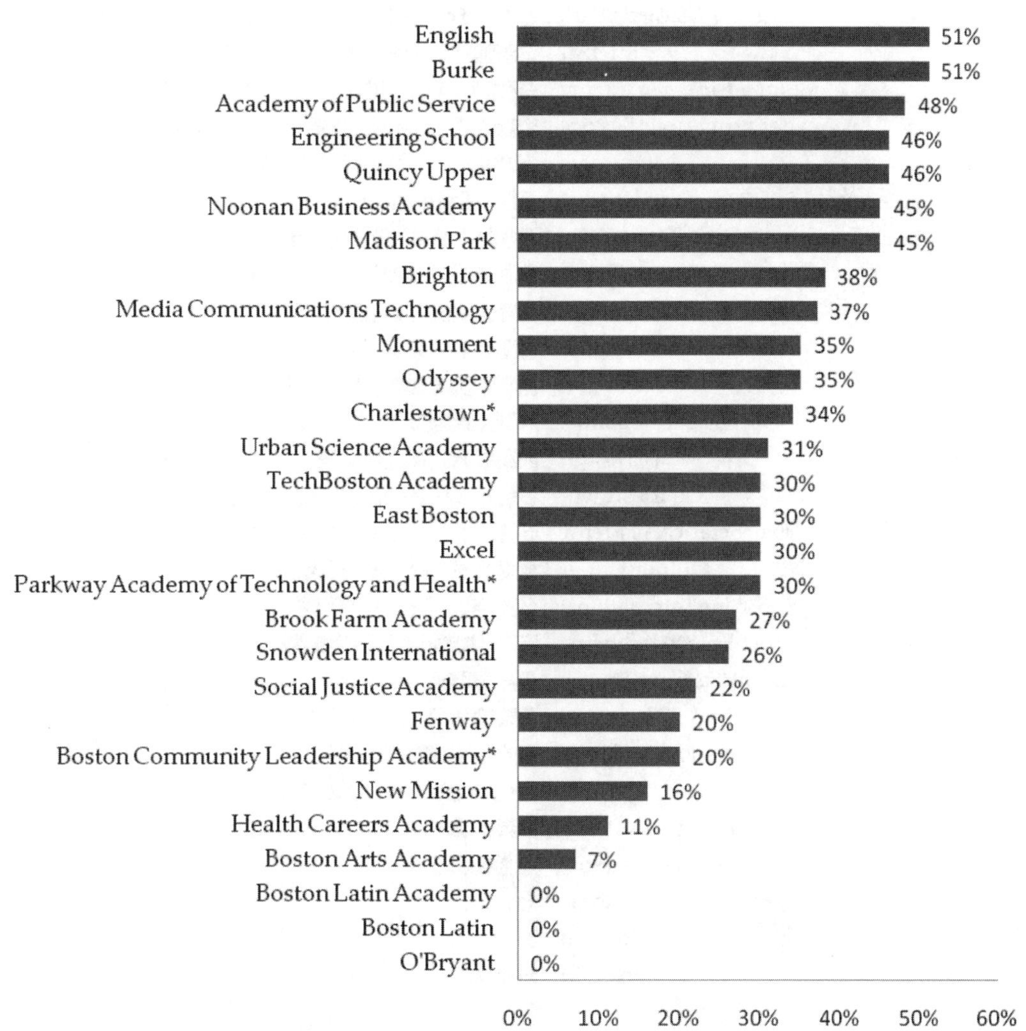

Source: Internal BTR documents.

*High schools with 5 or more BTR graduates.

Percentage of First-Time 9th Graders in 2006 Who Had Scored in the Bottom Quartile on the Mathematics MCAS in 7th Grade

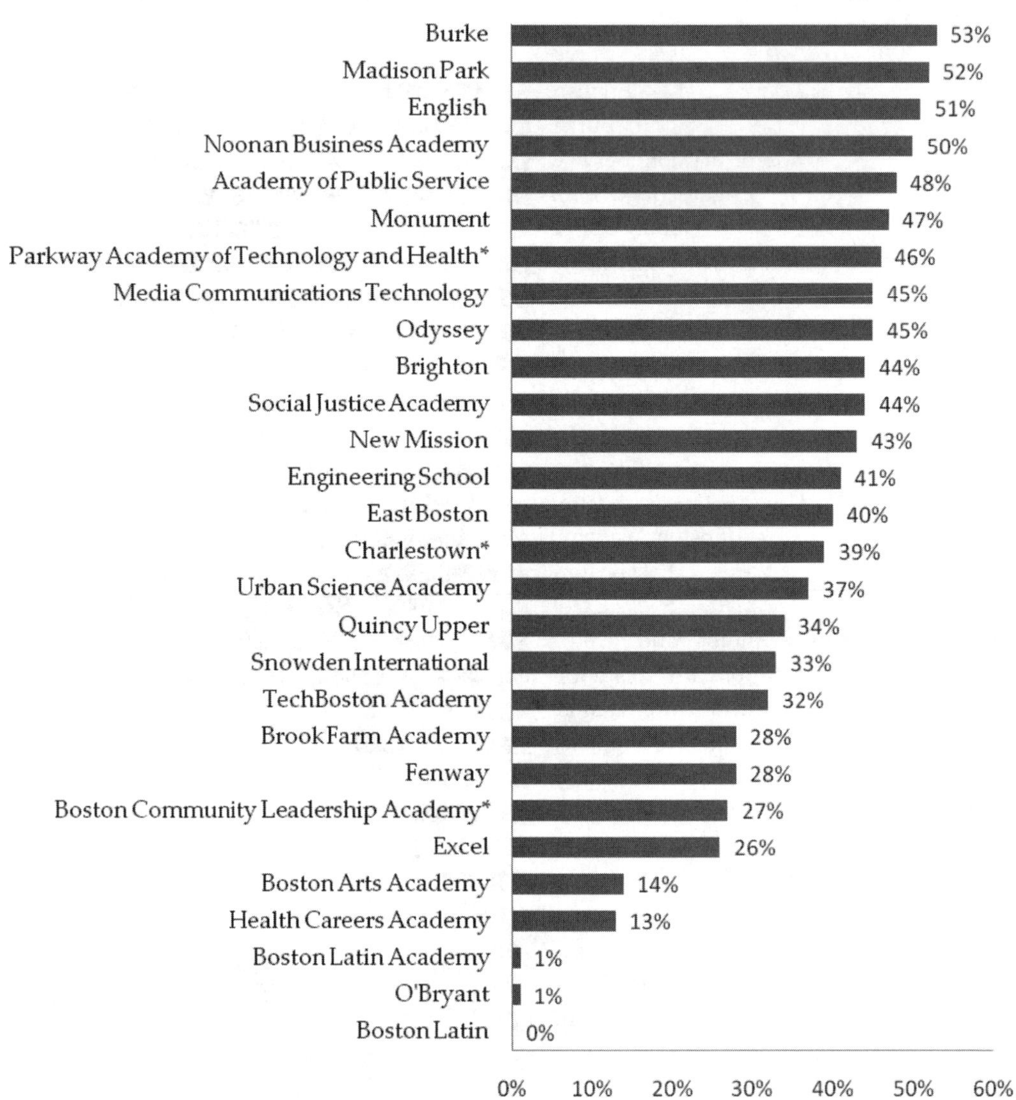

Source: Internal BTR documents.

*High schools with 5 or more BTR graduates.

Exhibit 17

BTR's 2007–2008 Annual Budget

	Total	*By Function*		
	2007–08 Total Budget	*Recruitment*	*Preparation*	*Induction*
		100 residents	84 residents	125 graduates
Expenditures				
Program				
Personnel (Salary and Benefits)				
Total Salary & Benefits	$775,498	$243,998	$368,873	$162,628
Recruitment & Admissions				
Advertising & Communications	$60,000	$60,000		
Events and Travel	$32,500	$32,500		
Selection Events	$10,798	$10,798		
Field Department				
Site Director Salaries	$465,864	$23,293	$442,571	
Mentor Teacher Stipends/ Training	$313,900		$313,900	
Induction Coaches/ Classroom Supplies	$133,020			$133,020
Curriculum Department				
Preparation Courses	$203,000		$203,000	
Induction Courses	$44,350			$44,350
Space/materials/logistics	$56,000		$42,000	$14,000
Textbooks	$52,749		$47,474	$5,275
Supplies & Equipment	$21,557	$4,311	$12,934	$4,311
Resident Expenses				
Stipends	$901,900		$901,900	
Resident's Health Insurance	$126,400		$126,400	
Scholarship Fund	$50,000		$50,000	
Evaluation	$50,000	$5,000	$20,000	$25,000
Online Capability	$39,280	$19,780	$11,250	$8,250
Administrative				
Administrative Expenses				
Telephone/Postage	$6,536	$3,922	$1,307	$1,307
Events	$10,000		$4,000	$6,000
Travel	$6,154		$4,123	$2,031
Total Expenditures	$3,353,354	$403,603	$2,545,610	$404,141
		$4,036 per Accepted Resident	$30,305 per Resident	$3,233 per Graduate

Source: Internal BTR documents.

Exhibit 18

Budget Implications for Proposed BTR Strategy

	2007–08	*2008–09 (e)*	*2009–10 (e)*	*2010–11 (e)*	*2011–12 (e)*	*2012–13 (e)*
Budget (m)	$3.4	$4.7	$5.6	$6.7	$6.9	$7.3
# of Residents	80	80	100	120	120	120
# of Students Taught	5,546	7,078	8,931	11,318	13,398	15,632
Cost per Resident (k)	$34	$40	$41	$41	$41	$43
Cost per Retained Grad (k)	$44	$56	$58	$59	$58	$59
Cost per Student (k)	$613	$664	$627	$592	$515	$467

Source: Internal BTR Documents.

Abbreviations: e = estimate; m = millions; k = thousands.

Stig Leschly ■ Jessica Boer

New Leaders for New Schools

> Among the legacies of New Leaders for New Schools should be the transformation of adults' expectations about our children's potential and the reshaping of adults' sense of responsibility for helping our children achieve that potential. In far too many places, the unstated belief is that we really should have pretty low expectations of our children and that we shouldn't hold ourselves accountable if they don't succeed. A measure of our success will be whether people across America look at underperforming schools and stop asking "What's wrong with those kids?" and start asking "What's wrong with us adults?"
>
> —*Jon Schnur, CEO, New Leaders for New Schools*

On a hot and humid Saturday morning in the summer of 2002, Jon Schnur, CEO of New Leaders for New Schools, waited in his cramped New York office for his cofounders, Monique Burns and Ben Fenton. Burns and Fenton rounded out New Leaders' executive team as chief curriculum officer and chief operating officer, respectively. Schnur looked forward to the arrival of his cofounders. Their morning meeting promised to be pivotal.

Two years earlier, as graduate students at Harvard University, Schnur, Burns, and Fenton had launched New Leaders. Their purpose was to improve the U.S. system of public education by transforming its approach to school leadership. To that end, New Leaders recruited outstanding principal prospects, trained them, and placed them in full-time positions in public schools through partnerships with urban school districts and charter school organizations.

In the short span of two years, New Leaders had evolved from a start-up idea long on aspirations and short on resources to a credible, funded, and nationally discussed nonprofit education reform initiative. New Leaders' early accomplishments included raising $5 million in early-stage financing, hiring an initial staff of 16 people, and launching principal recruitment and training programs in partnership with the Chicago and New York public school systems and a nonprofit charter school management organization.

As he waited for his colleagues to arrive, Schnur reflected on the agenda for their morning meeting. Having reached important early milestones with unusual speed, New Leaders now confronted the task of making the transition from an entrepreneurial venture to a mature and fully stabilized company. With that transition came a dizzying set of management challenges. One of them was defining New Leaders' expansion plan.

The cofounders were considering two 10-year growth strategies. One plan called for New Leaders to expand aggressively to open recruitment and training programs across the country. By this plan, the company would graduate thousands of principals and reach millions of students. An alternative growth plan envisioned New Leaders as a smaller and more focused organization that worked intensively with particular school districts and charter school operators. In contrast to the expansive reach of the first option, this second plan stressed close partnerships with schools and sought on the basis of clearly documented results to influence national leadership reform.

As they began their meeting, the cofounders paused to note the complexity and importance of the issues before them. They recognized that New Leaders' chances of long-term success depended on their selecting an optimal growth plan for their young company and on their managing effectively the organizational transition that lay ahead.

Origins Of New Leaders

Schnur, Burns, and Fenton met in the fall of 1999 while they were graduate students at Harvard University. At the time, Fenton was completing an M.B.A, and Schnur and Burns were both enrolled at the Graduate School of Education. Schnur was completing an M.A. in education, and Burns was working on a Ph.D. in education to complement the M.B.A. that she had earned from Harvard Business School five years earlier. (**Exhibit 1** includes details on the cofounders' professional and educational backgrounds.)

The three met while enrolled in a class at Harvard Business School on entrepreneurship in the social sector. From their chance encounter as students, they quickly discovered a remarkably complementary mixture of backgrounds, influences, and convictions.

Shared Interests and Insights

Schnur's interest in founding New Leaders dated to his term in the first Clinton administration, where he had served variously as the White House's associate director for educational policy, as Vice President Gore's senior policy advisor on education, and as special assistant to the U.S. Secretary of Education. Schnur commented on his work and its relevance to New Leaders:

> One of my main responsibilities in the White House and Department of Education in the 1990s was to advise the Clinton administration on charter schools, a new movement in school reform at that point, and to oversee federal investments in early charter schools. In that capacity, I visited schools and communities across the United States to gather input from a wide array of reformers, educators, business leaders, parents, and students.
>
> While I learned a great deal about charter schools and other efforts to reform public education, I came away with a basic insight that ensuring high-quality education for all of our children means placing a highly effective teacher in every classroom and an outstanding principal in every school. The two go together. Great principals get and keep great teachers. Dramatic change in our public schools will simply not happen without systemic efforts to improve school leadership.

Like Schnur's background, Burns's work experience explained her interest in education reform and dedication to leadership reform. Burns reflected:

> I finished my M.B.A. at Harvard Business School in 1993 and went to work for four years in the D.C. and Philadelphia public schools as a consultant, school founder, assistant principal, and district administrator. By the late 1990s, I returned to Harvard to get my doctorate in education, to reflect on what I had experienced, and to research successful leadership and management practices in education. Throughout my work and research, I have been interested in how quality management can support quality teaching.

Fenton completed the founding team and, like Schnur and Burns, perceived New Leaders as a compelling personal and professional opportunity. Fenton explained:

> I became interested in education during college when I did a lot of research on economic development and the relationship between economic and social change. Since then, I have thought a lot about the American Dream and whether it still is, or ever was, a reality. So many of my peers at McKinsey and Harvard Business School seemed to believe that the game was fair and that everyone achieved according to their effort and abilities in the U.S. Considering the incredible and often inequitable challenges that so many children face across our country, I don't believe that's true.

My goal in helping to start New Leaders was to use my business training to improve the quality of education that we provide, particularly in underresourced urban and rural areas, and to improve the return on investment of the additional money that I believe our society should invest in education. I unfortunately believe that many of our large urban school districts are bad investments today, but my sincere belief is that improved ideas about school leadership, and therefore district leadership, can change this substantially.

I turned down other job offers quite simply because I doubted that I would learn anywhere near as much as I have learned while starting and running a new organization and because, after meeting and working for three months with Jon and Monique on the New Leaders mission and business plan, I could not imagine a more exciting and rewarding way to spend 100 hours a week. I could have returned to McKinsey, but I felt like I had learned much of what I could there, regardless of the incredibly attractive financial package.

Early Results and Entrepreneurial Risk

New Leaders launched at a feverish pace. In the spring of 2000, while still enrolled as graduate students at Harvard, Schnur, Burns, and Fenton developed a formal business plan for New Leaders and entered it in the annual Harvard Business School business plan contest. In writing the business plan, the cofounders worked closely with Michael Johnston and Allison Gaines, two highly experienced teachers. Johnston, for example, was a former member of Teach For America's teaching corps and the coauthor of *In the Deep Heart's Core*, a best-selling book on education in America.[1]

The results of New Leaders' entry in the business plan contest were clear and groundbreaking. "We were the first nonprofit entry to reach the semifinals of the contest," explained Schnur, "and we did this at a time when the Internet bubble was in full effect and the competition was filled with dozens of for-profit businesses that would go on to attract venture funding. Even though we had no plans to earn a classic financial return, the judges were impressed by the depth and diversity of our team and the potential impact of our idea." Encouraged by the feedback, Schnur, Burns, and Fenton began full-time work on the project.

By the summer of 2002, two years after its official launch, New Leaders employed 16 full-time staff, maintained offices in Boston, New York, and Chicago, and had secured $5 million in investment from a variety of respected venture philanthropists and national foundations. Most importantly, by the summer of 2002, New Leaders had launched operations in Chicago, New York, and California's Bay Area. The introduction of these programs had required New Leaders to meet complex start-up challenges under intense time pressure, including recruiting principals, training them, and securing placements for them through negotiated partnerships with charter schools and school district administrations in New York and Chicago.

Two years into their work, the cofounders had a new appreciation for entrepreneurship. Schnur spoke for the trio:

> Founding an organization is, at times, grueling. Monique, Ben, and I work extremely hard. The same is true for the whole team at New Leaders. Many on our team work here at considerable personal and professional sacrifice. Some have deferred completing their graduate degrees. Others have forgone lucrative private-sector careers. And all of our personal lives have been affected by the demands of the work. Nevertheless, it's a thrill and an awesome responsibility to work for an organization devoted to the potential of millions of overlooked and underserved children.

Establishing a Management Culture

From the beginning, the cofounders of New Leaders carefully developed their management practices, communication style, and organizational values. Schnur commented:

> I often remind myself that New Leaders has virtually no physical assets. We're an enterprise exclusively of people. Our primary task is to build an organization that can consistently attract and retain talented and relentless employees, partners, and advisors. Keeping the organization and our culture on that track to do this is constant work, especially with our expanding geographic reach and our growing team. One very helpful fundamental, I think, is that our entire leadership team works with similar energy, commitment, and decisiveness. As it grows, New Leaders will continue to reflect those values.

Early on, Schnur, Burns, and Fenton decided on their roles as chief executive officer, chief curriculum officer, and chief operating officer, respectively. Burns reflected on each of the cofounders' skills and on their efforts to strike a balance between consensus and individual action:

> When we hit a strategic issue, one that affects the whole of New Leaders, the three of us spend a lot of time debating and searching for consensus. In every other way, though, we aim to operate as independently and efficiently as possible. Like many CEOs, Jon lives on airplanes and, among his leadership tasks, focuses on establishing and managing partnerships and on concentrating NLNS' many internal and external stakeholders—including district and city partners, employees, and fellows—on a common mission and shared goals. Jon is an exceptional communicator, listener, and compromise broker. As our COO, Ben is an outstanding manager and operator, and he's exceptionally methodical and analytical. He drives much of the organization on the inside. My priority is to design and deliver our core curriculum and training program for principals. One of my main contributions, drawn from my dual business and education background, is my understanding of what school leaders need to know and be able to do.

As they looked ahead, the cofounders recognized the need for continually reevaluating their own roles and, as necessary, modifying their management styles and priorities to suit the needs of their growing organization. "Monique, Ben, and I," explained Schnur, "need to manage towards a more decentralized organization and to cede control as we expand. To do that, we have been focused from the start on hiring a great team at New Leaders. We have been especially determined to build the organization around instructional leaders, principals, and urban educators who bring critical insight into the realities of urban education."

(See **Exhibit 2** for profiles of select New Leaders managers.)

To illustrate New Leaders' commitment to expanding and reorganizing its management ranks as needed, Schnur went on:

> We are about to announce the addition of Cami Anderson to New Leaders' executive team. Cami is a nationally recognized nonprofit executive and most recently the executive director of Teach For America's New York division. Cami will lead our national efforts to recruit and select candidates and to provide our fellows with support during and after their yearlong apprenticeships. We will consider Cami a fourth officer at New Leaders, an equal colleague to Ben, Monique, and me. Hiring Cami is a major development for us and exemplifies our commitment to organizing ourselves in whatever way makes sense for our growth.

New Leaders Mission and Strategy

New Leaders' vision and mission statements spoke of "fostering high academic achievement for every child through successful school leadership" and of "attracting, preparing, and supporting the next generation of outstanding school leaders in our nation." Fenton characterized New Leaders' goals:

> Our long-term goal is to effect systemic change in public education in the U.S. and to improve academic achievement for all students. In the near term, that implies setting a new standard for selecting principals, creating breakthrough training programs for principals, and placing principals in schools with the decision-making authority that makes it possible for leadership to have an impact.

The relationship between school leadership and student achievement was evident to the cofounders of New Leaders, first of all, from their work experiences. Burns commented: "From what I saw in school turnarounds in D.C., school leadership predicted the success or failure of a school. I worked in middle schools with similar staff, resources, and student populations. Some could absorb change. Some couldn't. The difference was the quality of the principal and school leadership team."

In their work and research, the cofounders of New Leaders had identified and categorized the attributes of an outstanding principal. Fenton summarized:

> First, a principal must be a leader of change and a builder of a culture that sets high expectations for all members of the school community. Second, a principal must be a skilled instructional leader who improves instructional quality by giving insightful and actionable feedback to teachers. Finally, a principal must have the management, operational, and political skills needed to work with internal and external constituents effectively.

A growing number of academics were studying the nature of effective school leadership and its impact on academic outcomes. Like any effort to explain academic achievement, their work met with frequent criticism. Nevertheless, the link between school leadership and student performance commanded important scholarly attention and, though not without its skeptics, generally supported the contention of the New Leaders management team that school leadership practices significantly determined the academic prospects of students.

Existing Principal Programs and the Principal Shortage

State laws required principals to earn and maintain licenses in educational administration and supervision. To obtain these certificates, principals typically attended training programs at one of approximately 370 accredited graduate schools of education in the United States.

Tuition at these programs ranged from $5,000 to $25,000 annually. Programs were structured variously as part-time, weekend, and full-time formats.

Burns commented on the inadequacy of existing principal training programs:

> Unfortunately, most principal training programs are designed to comply with certification statutes and regulations, and they focus incorrectly on classroom-based educational theory rather than practical skill development that working principals need. For example, internships are an effective way to train principals, but they are rarely included in any meaningful way in traditional principal training programs. Housed generally in universities, these principal training programs are deeply resistant to change.

Fifty distinct bodies of state law codified principal certification requirements. These statutes described a variety of requirements for principals, including minimum prior teaching and work experience, mandatory completed coursework and degrees, and required ongoing certification training.

Schnur criticized principal certification laws:

> Obviously, states have an interest in assuring principal quality. But the particulars of state certification laws and their notions of how to legally codify the definition of a competent principal are misguided. For example, detailed certification laws often discourage promising candidates with important management and leadership experience outside of K–12 education and, ironically, often certify mediocre candidates simply on the basis of classroom credit.

In the opinion of New Leaders' cofounders, a dramatic principal shortage compounded the effects of inadequate leadership training and overly bureaucratic certification laws. Schnur commented:

> Nearly 40% of our country's approximately 90,000 principals are eligible to retire within four years. Because of this retirement wave, new school openings, and the movement to break larger schools into smaller schools, studies predict a demand for 50,000 new principals over the next decade. Sadly, the problem is most acute in urban areas, where principal turnover regularly reaches 10% per year. By leading studies, 12,000 new principals will be needed by 2006 in urban settings alone.

Fenton elaborated on the role of existing principal training programs:

> A handful of prestigious programs, often at elite universities like Harvard and Stanford, train principals well. But, for a variety of reasons, these programs have little bearing on the larger principal and leadership problem. For example, these programs are not designed to attract and prepare candidates other than those coming directly from the classroom, and they are not focused on training leaders for work in large, urban school districts.

Stand-alone efforts by school districts to establish their own principal recruiting and training programs testified to the principal shortage and to the relevance of New Leaders' vision. For example, in response to its principal shortage and concerns about its ability to develop strong instructional leaders, District 2 in New York City had created its own Aspiring Leaders Program, which sought to identify and support principal candidates. Similar programs had emerged in dozens of school districts across the country.

Additionally, a variety of small nonprofit organizations supported alternative recruiting, training, and placement models for principal candidates. These programs, like start-up initiatives by districts, were generally regional or local efforts designed to supply principals for a particular district. Modest in size, they often involved school district collaborations with universities, advocacy groups, and professional organizations.

New Leaders' Operating Model

New Leaders' operating activities were grouped into four categories. These categories covered New Leaders' recruiting and admissions process, training programs, job-placement policies, and performance-evaluation functions. (**Exhibit 3** summarizes New Leaders' operating model.)

Recruiting and Admissions

New Leaders considered its ability to recruit talented principal candidates a vital component of its operating model. The company deliberately targeted its recruiting efforts to both traditional principal candidates with strong teaching backgrounds and to nontraditional candidates with managerial, advocacy, and other professional backgrounds outside the education sector.

To solicit principals, New Leaders canvassed national and local professional conferences in the education sector, including those hosted by the dominant teachers unions. Additionally, the organization used personal networks to identify candidates and invite applications. The cofounders in particular sought nominations from their colleagues in the business, civic, and education sector. New Leaders also organized an annual series of in-person regional orientation sessions for interested candidates. Finally, it actively sought and managed mass-media exposure. New Leaders had attracted coverage from important print publications, including national newspaper dailies such as *The New York Times*, the *Chicago Tribune*, and *The Wall Street Journal*.

New Leaders required applicants to submit extensive references, transcripts, and personal statements. Staff reviewed applications for evidence of outstanding personal qualities and of exemplary instructional, organizational, and community leadership potential. (**Exhibit 4** describes New Leaders' recruiting profile.) The selection process culminated with a full-day assessment session that, in addition to interviews, involved role plays related to instructional leadership and a case study on a school turnaround. A panel of New Leaders staff members, outside educators, and business and nonprofit leaders participated in this final evaluation process.

Once admitted, candidates were termed "fellows" for the duration of New Leaders' 12-month training program. New Leaders admitted its first class of 15 fellows in the summer of 2001. The cofounders considered their initial recruiting effort a success. Fenton commented:

> We admitted 15 fellows for our first class. They entered our training program in the summer of 2001 after a recruiting and admission process that significantly exceeded our expectations. To select the first 15 fellows, we responded to 750 requests for information about the program and received over 200 completed applications, 50 more than we planned. We made 19 offers, of which 15 were accepted.

The first group of fellows was split almost evenly by gender and represented diverse minority backgrounds. With few exceptions, the fellows had strong teaching backgrounds. Several also brought significant professional experience from noneducational settings. (**Exhibit 5** summarizes the work experiences and educational backgrounds of fellows in New Leaders' first class.)

New Leaders considered its second class of fellows, admitted in the spring of 2002, at least as strong as the first one. For its second class, the organization received 400 applications, a doubling of the applicant pool for its first class, and admitted 33 fellows. Schnur reflected on New Leaders' first two recruiting seasons:

> I think that we've proven that we can reach, solicit, and admit exceptional principal candidates. We never really doubted that personally because of the opportunity that we present to the many talented people who care about public education, who want to serve as school leaders, and who are put off by traditional principal certification programs and career paths. Still, we can now point skeptics to real data that suggests that we will be able, on an ongoing basis, to be extremely selective in our admissions process.

Training

New Leaders structured its yearlong training program around an initial two-month summer institute and a subsequent 10-month in-school residency. Burns summarized the three design principles of the training program:

> The first design principle of our training program is usefulness. I have no tolerance for theories unless they function in practice. Principals go to work every day to motivate, support, and guide teachers, teachers who actually teach in real classrooms with real children with real learning needs. Principals need practical skills that will allow them to diagnose the needs of their school, support and develop the teachers, and continually manage with a focus on student achievement.
>
> Second, we teach interactively and by the case method. Adults learn best by engaging material hands-on and by making it their own. Participation-based learning allows us to teach decision-making skills and methods of analysis, in addition to content. Our fellows don't need answers to today's problems as much as they need to learn approaches to tomorrow's problems.
>
> Third, we have designed our training program for continual improvement. Right now, our fellows learn what our research and our collective experiences convince us they should learn. That's a fine start, but over time it's not good enough. In the next few years, as we train more fellows and as our fellows graduate to lead schools, we will gather feedback, analyze our efforts, and, as necessary, adapt our training.

Fellows began their training by completing an intensive, classroom-based summer institute. (**Exhibit 6** summarizes New Leaders' summer institute curriculum.) Taught over two months, the institute's curriculum stressed two themes. Burns explained:

> The institute's curriculum focuses, first of all, on helping our fellows develop as instructional leaders. We build on our fellows' teaching backgrounds and push them to reflect on and analyze generally how to evaluate teachers, give feedback to teachers, and guide and lead teachers in instruction. A great principal, for example, understands how to influence teachers to believe that all children can learn. Similarly, successful principals can leverage academic data effectively to evaluate and mentor teachers.
>
> Second, the summer institute challenges fellows to see themselves as general managers. As principals, our fellows will need to define and sustain mission-driven organizations. They will need to manage people skillfully and negotiate complex stakeholder environments. They will need to run budgets and allocate resources. They will need to lead change. And so on. Principals need to thrive as entrepreneurial managers.

Prior to the launch of the first summer institute, Burns and Gail Parson, New Leaders' deputy director of curriculum, invested a full year in researching and developing the institute's curriculum. To design it, Burns and Parson systematically sought input from topical experts.

State law considered New Leaders a non-accredited institution and prohibited it from granting principal certificates. To solve this problem, New Leaders partnered with accredited universities in Chicago and New York. These universities housed its summer institute, approved its training program, and extended legally valid principal certificates to its fellows. "Finding universities with whom we can partner," Burns explained, "is an important challenge for us. We need university partners to oversee and validate the quality of our curriculum and to certify our fellows. But we are insistent on not relinquishing control over what or how we teach."

Even with its university partners, New Leaders operated within important constraints of state certification laws. For example, New Leaders could not guarantee certification to fellows who had not completed a master's degree, a consistent requirement under state certification statutes. Fellows who were ineligible for formal state certification remained qualified for principal placements in charter schools. Charter schools generally operated independently of state licensing laws.

In the spring of 2002, as she prepared for the second iteration of the summer institute, Burns reflected on the organization's continuous improvement:

> Looking back, I think we got the curriculum 65% right the first time around. We needed more organizational behavior cases on change management and working with difficult individuals. We also needed a course on the school start-up process, since over 25% of our fellows will join new charter schools or start-up schools within districts. And, finally, we needed better ways to gather real-time feedback on our curriculum modules and faculty.

After completing the summer institute, New Leaders' fellows entered a 10-month, in-school residency during which they shadowed sitting principals. Fellows received a stipend during their residency. Stipends varied depending on the organization with which fellows were placed, but they averaged $27,500 per year, a compensation level similar to that of a typical first-year teacher.

New Leaders bore the cost of stipends for fellows who completed residencies at charter schools.[2] When fellows undertook residencies in district schools, the districts themselves covered stipend costs. In either case, New Leaders' stipend policy differed dramatically from typical principal training programs that, far from paying their trainees, charged tuition. In addition to paying fellows a stipend, New Leaders funded certain housing and travel costs incurred by fellows during their summer institute training.

In organizing its residency program, New Leaders carefully matched fellows with mentor principals. For its first residency program, New Leaders interviewed and visited 30 potential mentors before selecting the 15 they needed to match each fellow. Burns commented on these efforts:

> Principals, especially the really good ones, are always in demand, and they are wary of new commitments, especially ones that might detract from their work in schools. We emphasize that our fellows will help, not hinder, principals in their work, and we offer principals a $5,000 mentor stipend. Principals agree to be mentors, I think, partly because they find satisfaction in passing on knowledge and partly because our fellows really add capacity to their teams.

While working with mentors, fellows completed a variety of projects designed to apply in practice concepts from the summer institute. For example, during the residency and with guidance from their mentors, fellows conducted actual teacher observations, worked with teachers to create teacher development plans, and coached teachers.

During the residency period, New Leaders organized several multiday workshops designed to allow fellows to reflect as a group on the progress of their residencies. Also, at the end of the 10-month residency, the organization hosted a weeklong retreat that brought closure to the training year and allowed fellows to interact before assuming permanent positions.

Placement

After completing their training, New Leaders fellows assumed permanent principal positions in schools. New Leaders expected to place approximately 25% of its fellows in charter schools and the remaining 75% in traditional public schools.[3] Placement negotiations with school districts and charter organizations occupied a central role in the organization. Schnur explained:

> If our principals are to succeed, we need to locate them in schools where they have a chance to succeed. That means schools where they and their teams have authority to make the important decisions. Specifically, in negotiating with districts and charter school operators, we stress the need for our principals and their teams to control staffing and budget decisions. While that level of authority generally exists in charter schools, it's not as common in schools that operate inside of traditional school districts. Even where superintendents support school-level autonomy, union contracts, regulations, and other institutional attributes often constrain what is possible.

Eleven of New Leaders' first 15 fellows would be placed in Chicago or New York public schools under agreements that New Leaders had negotiated with each district. Remaining fellows would be placed with charter schools. New Leaders worked for almost a full year, starting in September of 2000, to reach agreement with district leaders in Chicago and New York for placements for the 2002 school year. Schnur elaborated:

> I started conversations with the leadership of Chicago and New York schools in the fall of 2000, as we launched New Leaders. I naively thought it would take a few weeks to sign an agreement. Well, it took almost a full year to complete these agreements. At one point in the spring of 2001, we had admitted our first class of fellows, were about to launch the summer institute, and still needed to finalize a number of placement agreements in Chicago and New York. We were stressed.
>
> Large school districts, like Chicago and New York, are often change resistant and unaccustomed to responding systemically to new opportunities and challenges. They have traditionally had few clear lines of accountability and few reliable decision-making processes for evaluating a proposal like ours. There are highly capable superintendents out there, like Arne Duncan, the recently appointed CEO of Chicago's public schools, but superintendents like Arne and their senior team members are incredibly busy in their attempts to alter the course of giant school systems, weighed down by slow-moving bureaucracies, complicated organizations, and a web of competing and often important stakeholders.

Schnur recalled the means by which he succeeded in closing New Leaders' placement agreements in Chicago and New York:

> I spent a lot of time with top and mid-level school district leaders in Chicago and New York, especially the regional superintendents in those cities. I knew the only way to make an agreement work was to address the needs of these leaders. They felt genuine responsibility for turning around their troubled schools, and we needed to make them see how New Lead-

> ers could be a solution to their problems. Creating real partnerships takes time.
>
> At times in the negotiation process, it was helpful to mobilize outside support. For example, New Leaders won financial and political support from the Chicago Public Education Fund, an organization with immense influence in Chicago. Their endorsement and credibility in the eyes of district decision makers helped us finalize the right kind of agreement and partnership in Chicago.

In contrast to districts, charters school operators negotiated at a far more rapid pace. "High-quality charter school operations," explained Schnur, "work at our tempo, share our entrepreneurial culture, and support our commitment to principal empowerment." New Leaders' first charter school partner, Aspire Public Schools, was developing a chain of charter schools in California.

Schnur reflected on New Leaders' relative focus on charter and in-district schools:

> Our mission to foster high levels of academic achievement for every child requires us to work inside the traditional public schools system that educates 90% of America's children. We absolutely value, support, and work with charter schools. But we can't focus on charter schools to the exclusion of district schools. We need great principals and leadership teams in all public schools. We will learn much in the next few years about the impact that we can have in various districts and charter school settings.

As the fall of 2002 approached and as the first set of fellows prepared to take up full-time principal positions, the New Leaders staff began to design actively an ongoing professional development program for its alumni. The program would include a variety of support services, including participation in regular professional seminars, membership in a network of educators and experts facilitated by New Leaders, and access to *pro bono* consultants and expertise.

Performance Measurement

New Leaders' fourth primary operating activity was performance measurement. Schnur commented on the company's preoccupation with performance:

> We focus on impact as much as we do partly because of who we are. Monique, Ben, and I don't want to do this unless we can track our progress. Our investors, all of whom focus on systemic impact, share that attitude and press us continuously on our theory of change and how we will monitor our progress. Our mission drives us. But so does performance. And what gets measured gets improved.

The team members at New Leaders understood the difficulty of designing and implementing a workable measurement model for a project as ambitious as theirs. In their deliberations on how to measure progress, the staff had defined two categories of success metrics that reflected the goals of the organization as a whole. One sought to measure academic results by students in schools led by New Leaders' principal corps. Fenton described the challenges of measuring academic success:

> Few topics are more contentious in the education establishment than how to measure student learning. Our performance-measurement effort inherits the full complexity of that debate. For example, we debate the appropriate balance in our measuring program between test-based assessments and portfolio assessments. We also think about whether we should seek to measure the absolute academic results of our students or their incremental performance over a control group. And finally, we analyze the appropriate time frame for seeking results and what, if any, incremental measures we should track as indicators of future success.

New Leaders had won a grant from the Casey Foundation to research and design its academic measurement policy. The grant would fund a forum in the summer of 2002 of 25 national education experts who would debate and help draft New Leaders' approach to student-outcome measurement.

A second category of metrics measured New Leaders' impact on systemwide reform. Fenton explained:

> In addition to improving student learning, we seek to influence sectorwide policy and practices by pressuring the system to improve the conditions and quality of school leadership. We debate continuously the precise meaning of that goal and how to measure it. Indicators could include policy reforms by districts and legislatures in support of leadership improvements. They could also include the emergence of organizations with missions similar to ours or innovation in university training programs for educators. What's clear is that New Leaders alone cannot address directly the leadership of nearly 100,000 U.S. public schools. Our work must result in a broader and more systemic correction in leadership development and support in public education.

New Leaders' Financial Model

Like most nonprofits, New Leaders managed its finances primarily on a cash basis and sought annually to match sources and uses of cash. (**Exhibit 7** details New Leaders' cash flow for the first two years of its operations.)

Sources of Cash

New Leaders generated cash from three sources. The first was investment from national foundations and venture philanthropists of various kinds. In its first two years of operations, New Leaders had received investment commitments for approximately $5 million, of which roughly $1.5 million had been collected and spent in its first year of operations. In its second year, New Leaders expected to draw down an additional $1.6 million of its national funding commitments.

New Leaders' national investors included New Schools Venture Fund, a venture philanthropy fund founded and financed in part by John Doerr, a partner at the venture capital firm Kleiner Perkins Caufield & Byers and a legendary Silicon Valley start-up investor. New Leaders had also won endorsements from other respected venture philanthropy funds and national foundations, including New Profit Inc., a Boston-based venture philanthropy fund; and the Broad Foundation, a national foundation focused on human resources reform in public education. (**Exhibit 8** profiles select New Leaders investors.)

A second source of cash was local, city-specific fund-raising. New Leaders raised money locally mostly by marketing individual fellow sponsorships to local corporations and organizations. Fellow sponsorships cost $20,000. In its first year, New Leaders raised nearly $300,000 in local fellow sponsorships.

New Leaders structured local fund-raising as the responsibility of city directors and their staff. City officers were burdened with raising $40,000 per fellow. At scale, New Leaders expected to graduate at least 30 fellows annually in each of its cities. As a result, city directors would eventually be responsible for raising at least $1.2 million annually in fellow sponsorships. The Broad Foundation had agreed initially to match dollar for dollar any fellow sponsorships raised by New Leaders' city operations. Schnur commented on the challenges of local fund-raising: "Because we cannot rely forever on national investment, local fund-raising is vital to our sustainability. As we expand, it will become a major responsibility of our city management teams. That the Broad Foundation has agreed to match local sponsorships is an enormous benefit to us as we build out our local fund-raising capacity."

Placement fees paid by charter schools constituted New Leaders' third source of cash. Charter schools paid New Leaders $15,000 for each permanent principal placement. New Leaders estimated that it would place 25% of its fellows at charter schools. The traditional school districts that would hire the remaining 75% of New Leaders' graduates did not pay placement fees because, unlike charter schools, districts covered the full cost of fellows' residency stipends.

Uses of Cash

In its initial year of operations, New Leaders spent approximately $1 million, primarily to staff its national office. For its second year, the organization budgeted $2.7 million in expenses, as it began to invest more heavily in its city-specific operations and expansion of its training programs. It expected to close 2002 with a cash balance of approximately $250,000 and to have in reserve roughly $1 million of funding commitments from existing investors.

New Leaders conceived of and tracked its cost structure in three distinct ways. The first organized costs by operating function. The second examined variable and fixed costs. The third monitored costs per fellow.

Functional Costs

New Leaders' functional cost structure was divided, first of all, between national and local offices. At each of these levels, New Leaders tracked its investments in various functions and activities, including executive salaries, curriculum development, recruiting, and training.

In its initial year, as it built its reach and organization, New Leaders invested strategically in national executive and administrative staff. Beginning in its second year, it budgeted increased local expenditures related to the management of city-specific operations. (See the notes accompanying **Exhibit 7** for details on the functional cost structure of New Leaders' national and local operations.)

Variability of Costs

New Leaders' cost structure included a mix of fixed, variable, and semivariable costs. At one extreme, certain national expenses, including executive salaries and centralized curriculum development costs, remained fixed regardless of the size of New Leaders' training operation. By contrast, certain local costs, such as stipends paid to fellows during charter school residencies and fees paid to mentors, varied directly with the number of fellows enrolled. A third category of semivariable costs varied primarily with the number of cities in which New Leaders operated. For example, setup costs for summer institutes and overhead staff in city offices varied with the organization's regional expansion.

New Leaders expected its mix of fixed, variable, and semivariable costs to vary with time as the focus of the organization changed. Its long-term financial plans relied heavily on stabilizing its fixed national investments and amortizing them across multiple city organizations and a large number of fellows.

Per-Fellow Costs

New Leaders tracked carefully its costs per fellow. During its first year of operations and because of heavy early investments in national operations, it spent over $100,000 per graduating fellow. Over time, New Leaders targeted dramatic reductions in its costs per fellow. Conceptually, it sought reductions by spreading its fixed and semivariable costs across a growing number of fellows.

New Leaders believed that city operations could become self-sustainable and operate without funding from the national office at approximately 30 fellows. This break-even target assumed that each city office raised $40,000 locally for each fellow.

Growth Options

In the spring of 2002 and with the benefit of two years of operating experience, the cofounders of New Leaders faced a crucial choice between two growth options. "We're faced with a strategically vital growth question," Schnur explained, "which we have to answer correctly if we're going to succeed."

The first growth option involved expanding aggressively to maximize the number of principals New Leaders could graduate and the number of students it could reach through its alumni. This option, which the cofounders termed the "go-broad" option, had been the forecast in the original New Leaders business plan. A second option, referred to as the "go-deep" option, called for a significantly smaller principal corps than the go-broad option and for partnering closely with selected districts and charter school operators. (**Exhibits 9** and **10** include 10-year cash flow projections and operating statistics for the two growth options.)

The Go-Broad Option

The go-broad option envisioned operations in 15 cities by 2012 and projected spending over $100 million to train approximately 1,500 principals. With these principals in place and on the assumption that they would manage schools with an average of 650 students, the go-broad option forecasted reaching 1 million students annually by 2012. Schnur commented:

> The go-broad option emphasizes reach and relevance. If we grow to a point where our principal corps serves 1 million students annually, then we'll be reaching approximately 10% of urban public school students in the U.S. Our student population would be larger than every urban school system in the country, including Los Angeles and New York. The raw scale of this direct impact on children is appealing.
>
> In addition to maximizing our absolute student reach, the "go broad" optimizes our general relevance to policymakers and districts with which we don't work by forcing us to implement our model in a wide variety of settings. A unique set of circumstances and constituents characterizes every state, city, district, and school. The more diversity we have in our school and district settings, the more relevant our results and message will be to a national audience.

The go-broad growth option involved a variety of operating challenges. For example, it required New Leaders to identify 13 new cities that met its strict criteria for partners. In the course of establishing initial training programs in Chicago and New York, it had defined nine requirements for partnering with school districts. Criteria included the size of a city's talent pool of fellows and mentors, the presence of local sponsors and partners, and the commitment level among district leaders to school autonomy and innovative reform. (**Exhibit 11** summarizes New Leaders' partnership criteria for school districts.)

The cofounders agreed unanimously that they could not simply enter 13 new markets in the way that they had opened operations in New York and Chicago. Many urban school districts simply failed to meet their criteria. Moreover, according to their calculations, fewer than five large urban school districts could support an entire New Leaders city office by absorbing 30 principals annually.[4]

Schnur commented on the complications of finding district partners under the go-broad option:

> There are currently nowhere near 13 cities, in addition to New York and Chicago, which meet our criteria and which can hire a full annual load

> of graduates from a New Leaders training program. Consequently, if we are to reach 15 cities under the go-broad option, one of our tasks will be to make a market for ourselves through advocacy and consulting. This could involve lobbying legislatures and influencing districts to adopt new school reform agendas.

Even with such lobbying efforts, New Leaders expected, under the go-broad option, to serve clusters of smaller districts. Fenton explained:

> We can't locate a New Leaders training program in San Francisco alone, even if San Francisco met our criteria perfectly. San Francisco is just not big enough, even with demand among its charter schools. We could, however, open a program in San Francisco if it served a cluster of districts that included San Francisco, Oakland, and San Jose. Similarly, we could open a program in Boston if it also served satellite districts in Worcester, Lowell, and Providence, in a sort of hub-and-spoke constellation.

Fenton commented further on the management and control issues that came with the go-broad option:

> With every new city comes the challenge of negotiating and establishing a new set of relationships with universities, mentors, districts, and so on. Creating and maintaining these networks, we have learned, requires immense time, thought, and effort. Moreover, at some point, probably once we grow beyond half a dozen cities, we will need regional staff to intermediate and coordinate between local city operations and our national office.

The cofounders also paused on the funding requirements, both locally and nationally, of the go-broad option. Schnur elaborated:

> If we expand to 15 cities and strive to reach a million students annually, we need to raise nearly $100 million over 10 years, half of which would come from local sponsorships and one-third of which would come from national fund-raising. In the year 2012, for example, the go-broad option forecasts us raising and spending $15 million. That's a serious fund-raising challenge, especially for local city operations.

The Go-Deep Option

Considerably more modest in its expansion goals, the go-deep option committed New Leaders to opening training programs in seven cities and to investing approximately $60 million over 10 years. Fenton commented on the vision of the go-deep option:

> The go-deep option, by placing us in only seven cities over the next 10 years, allows us to focus and control our impact more precisely. Under this option, we would become an integral partner to a select number of districts and would work closely with their management teams to implement and measure leadership reform. If we go deep, we need to invest heavily in measuring and documenting our impact and, on that basis, influencing other districts and policymakers to adopt our message of leadership reform.

The go-deep option appealed to the New Leaders management team in part because of its manageability. Fenton explained: "We've learned that it takes laser-like focus by management to open a new city. The go-deep option limits our operating challenge and our exposure to execution risk. Compared to the go-broad option, it simply involves fewer problems—fewer cities to deal with, fewer relationships to manage, fewer investors to persuade, and so on."

The cofounders shared a variety of concerns about the go-deep option. For example, they wondered if its narrower student and district reach jeopardized the long-term goal of influencing systemic and national change. "With the go-deep scenario," Schnur explained, "we need to be especially confident that breakthrough results in particular districts will breed change in others. We think a lot about this."

For the time being, New Leaders' board was divided on the merits of the go-deep option and on the growth question in general. Some on the board favored the go-deep option and its reduced financial and operating risk. By contrast, certain board members advocated strongly for staying with the go-broad option. One board member argued:

> New Leaders needs, as it originally intended, to roll out as quickly and as widely as possible. The alternative, this notion of influencing change by creating an example that others can copy, just doesn't work in the education sector. Public education is not like the private sector where firms, as a matter of survival, study and repeat innovations by competitors. Inertia dominates in education. If you want to change a school district, you need to go shake it up, from the inside. Publishing a white paper, no matter how compelling, won't do it.

Business Model Expansion

As they considered their growth plans, the cofounders understood that the core business model of New Leaders, like that of any start-up organization, might evolve beyond its initial scope. In fact, they had begun to contemplate a variety of activities that expanded on New Leaders' core recruiting, training, and placement model. These activities included consulting to large districts, copyrighting and leasing New Leaders' documented curriculum, and operating schools directly with the benefit of New Leaders' leadership expertise. (**Exhibit 12** lists select New Leaders expansion opportunities.)

Schnur, Burns, and Fenton wondered if they should consider augmenting either or both of their growth options with additional activities. Notably, they considered whether to expand the reach and impact of the go-deep option by matching it with one or more of the expansion activities under consideration.

Looking Ahead

As their meeting came to a close, Schnur, Burns, and Fenton had made progress toward resolving New Leaders' growth dilemma. In the weeks ahead, they would continue their consultations and, in a push to reach closure on the growth issue, complete a series of meetings with their investors and most respected advisors. At summer's end, the cofounders were scheduled to present to their board a final view of New Leaders' growth plan and associated management issues.

As they worked on, the cofounders took pride and confidence from the already significant track record of their company. Whatever lay ahead, they would continue to approach their work with commitment and a large vision of change. One advisor to New Leaders, moved by the determination of its cofounders and the magnitude of their goal, recalled anthropologist Margaret Mead's famous and controversial definition of social change, "Never doubt that a small group of thoughtful, committed citizens can change the world. Indeed, it's the only thing that ever has." As they left their morning meeting and planned for the management challenges ahead, the cofounders of New Leaders were determined to prove Margaret Mead right.

Notes

1. Michael Johnston and Robert Coles, *In the Deep Heart's Core* (New York, NY: Grove Press, September 2002).

2. Charter schools that hired New Leaders' graduates for full-time principal positions paid New Leaders a $15,000 placement fee. This fee, in effect, allowed New Leaders to recoup approximately half of its investment in residency stipends.

3. Frequently, fellows assumed full-time positions and completed residencies in the same schools. For example, New Leaders generally negotiated with school districts to both mentor and hire fellows.

4. In the spring of 2002, New Leaders believed that Los Angeles, Miami, and San Antonio were the only large urban districts, other than New York and Chicago, that could host an entire New Leaders city operation. New Leaders reached this conclusion by analyzing principal turnover rates in urban districts and by making informed assumptions about the willingness of district management teams to hire principals from a single outside training program.

Exhibit 1

Biographies of New Leaders Cofounders

Founder	*Education*	*Work Experience*
Jon Schnur, CEO	2002: M.A. candidate, Harvard Graduate School of Education 1989: B.A., Politics, Princeton University	2000–2002: CEO, New Leaders for New Schools 1997–2000: Senior Advisor on Education to U.S. Vice President Gore 1998–1999: Associate Director for Domestic Policy, Domestic Policy Council, White House 1993–1997: Special Assistant to Secretary of Education Riley and Deputy Secretary Kunin, U.S. Department of Education 1991–1993: Staff, Clinton for President campaign and Presidential Inaugural Committee 1989–1991: Legislative Aide, U.S. House of Representatives
Monique Burns, President & Chief Curriculum Officer	2002: Ph.D. candidate, Harvard Graduate School of Education 1993: M.B.A., Harvard Business School 1989: B.A., Drama, Dartmouth College	2000–2002: President and Chief Curriculum Officer, New Leaders for New Schools 1998–2000: Leadership Coach, Massachusetts Charter School Resource Center 1995–1997: Special Assistant for Management and Productivity to the Superintendent of the Philadelphia Public School District 1994–1995: Assistant Principal, Roper Middle School, District of Columbia School District 1993–1995: Education Consultant, McKenzie Group 1989–1991: Assistant Brand Manager, Quaker Oats Company
Benjamin Fenton, COO	2000: M.B.A., Baker Scholar, Harvard Business School 1996: B.A., Social Studies, Harvard College	2000–2002: COO, New Leaders for New Schools 1999: Manager, Fisher Scientific 1996–1998: Consultant, McKinsey and Company

Source: Company documents.

Exhibit 2

Profiles of Select New Leaders Managers

Name	*Title*	*Start Year*	*Prior Experience*
Cami Anderson	National director of recruiting and professional development	2002	Executive director, Teach For America, New York
Jann Coles	Residency director, New York	2001	Head of education programs, Colgate Palmolive. School leadership coach, New York City.
Sylvia Gibson	Executive director, Chicago	2001	Principal, Cregier Multiplex. Selected by *Time* Magazine as one of the leading principals in the United States.
Evelyn Gonzalez-Spivey	Residency director, New York	2001	Founder and principal, Zora Neale Hurston Academy
Todd Kern	Executive director, New York	2002	Vice president, Knowledge Quest Ventures. Former acting director of the Institute on Education and Government, Columbia University.
Kim Marshall	Graduate support consultant	2002	Principal of the Mather School, Boston. During Marshall's tenure as its principal, the Mather School was Boston's most improved public school.
Gail Parson	Deputy curriculum director	2000	Award-winning teacher and curriculum developer

Source: Company documents.

Exhibit 3

New Leaders' Operating Model

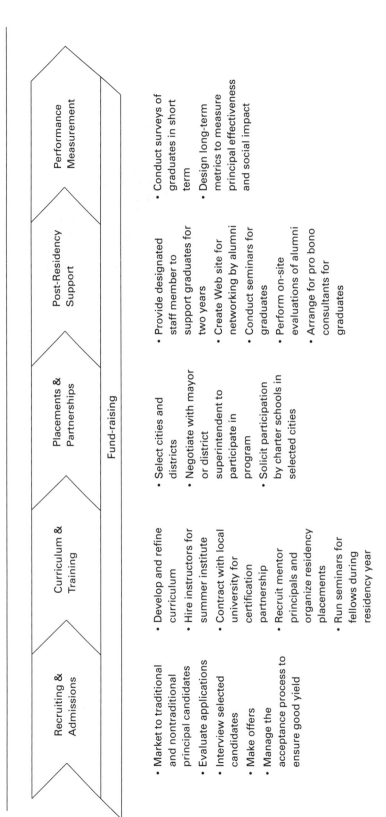

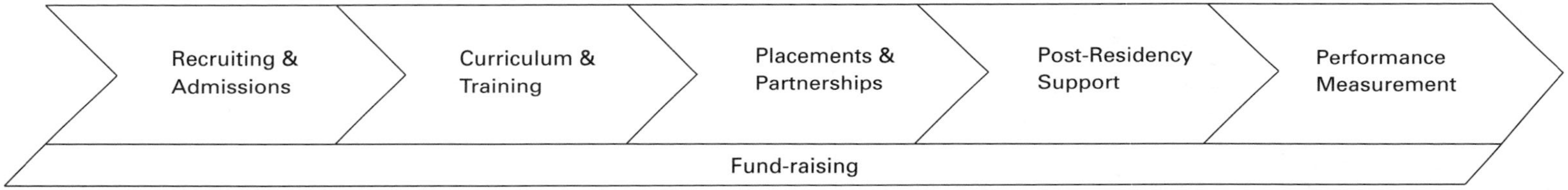

Recruiting & Admissions	Curriculum & Training	Placements & Partnerships	Post-Residency Support	Performance Measurement
Fund-raising				
• Market to traditional and nontraditional principal candidates • Evaluate applications • Interview selected candidates • Make offers • Manage the acceptance process to ensure good yield	• Develop and refine curriculum • Hire instructors for summer institute • Contract with local university for certification partnership • Recruit mentor principals and organize residency placements • Run seminars for fellows during residency year	• Select cities and districts • Negotiate with mayor or district superintendent to participate in program • Solicit participation by charter schools in selected cities	• Provide designated staff member to support graduates for two years • Create Web site for networking by alumni • Conduct seminars for graduates • Perform on-site evaluations of alumni • Arrange for pro bono consultants for graduates	• Conduct surveys of graduates in short term • Design long-term metrics to measure principal effectiveness and social impact

Source: Company documents.

Exhibit 4

New Leaders' Fellow Profile

Key Personal Attributes	*Relentless drive to help every child learn and succeed* • Believes that all children can and must learn at high levels • Has a record of sustained focus and energy in service of this commitment *Integrity and inner strength* • Adheres to deeply held beliefs and maintains focus on a mission when facing difficult circumstances or intense skepticism or opposition • Exercises leadership in a manner that is ethical and fair • Treats all people with respect and confronts people with dignity *Dedication to lifelong learning and continuous improvement* • Loves to learn and seeks opportunities for learning, reflection, and growth • Builds on individual strengths, addresses weaknesses, and accommodates style of working and learning • Strives for constant improvement, taking responsibility for failures and sharing credit for successes • Seeks new information and diverse opinions; willing to reexamine assumptions based on new evidence
Potential for Instructional, Organizational, and Community Leadership	*A record of successful leadership in bringing people together to accomplish a common mission or purpose* • Motivates people to define a problem or common vision, design solutions, and achieve shared goals • Builds teams that match individual strengths to appropriate challenges • Focuses on and achieves results • Creates and sustains productive working relationships with diverse groups of people • Supports the success of other team members and helps develop others' talents, skills, and knowledge *A record of effective teaching and success with young people* • Has helped young people succeed and learn at high levels • Demonstrates an understanding of what constitutes effective and ineffective teaching • Creates trusting relationships with children, ensures appropriate behavior, enforces high expectations • Demonstrates commitment and respect for children from diverse backgrounds *Outstanding communication skills* • Communicates with purpose and clarity both in person and in writing • Listens well and demonstrates willingness to ask for and act on others' opinion and help • Communicates in a way that builds shared vision *Problem-solving and other key skills needed for general management and leadership* • Thinks critically and analytically • Discerns the nature of problems and creatively finds available and new resources to solve them • Reads new situations quickly, identifies opportunities for learning and progress, and responds effectively • Understands reality of immediate environment while working with a sense of possibility • Takes appropriate risks on behalf of an important mission or goal • Maintains focus on long-term goals while successfully managing details and execution

Source: Company documents.

Exhibit 5

New Leaders Fellows, Class of 2001–2002

Fellow	*Gender*	*Minority*	*Placement*	*Education*	*Most Recent Work Experience*
1	M	N	Chicago Public Schools	M.A. Education, Seattle University M.A. Theology, Graduate Theological Union	Chicago Program Director, Facing History and Ourselves
2	M	Y	New York Public Schools	B.S. Education, Long Island University	Cofounder and Curriculum Developer, El Puente Academy for Peace and Justice in Brooklyn
3	M	Y	Chicago Public Schools	M.A. Education, DePaul University Ph.D. Candidate, DePaul University	Senior Pricing Analyst, CAN Insurance Companies
4	F	Y	New York Public Schools	M.A. Education, Columbia University Teachers College	Teacher and Staff Developer, New York Public Schools
5	F	N	Aspire Public Schools (charter)	B.A., University of the Pacific	Teacher, Aspire Public Schools
6	F	N	New York Public Schools	B.A., University of Arizona M.A. Candidate, Indiana University–Bloomington	Teacher, Indianapolis Public Schools
7	F	Y	Chicago Public Schools	B.A., San Francisco State University	Education Director, Chicago Urban League
8	F	N	Chicago Public Schools	M.B.A., Kellogg Graduate School of Management	Executive Director, Making Waves
9	F	N	Chicago Public Schools	B.A. Music, Northwestern University	Assistant Head, Triumphant Charter School
10	F	N	Chicago Public Schools	M.A. Education, University of Illinois–Chicago	Interim Director, Urban Education Program at the Associated Colleges of the Midwest
11	M	N	New York Public Schools	B.A., Yale University M.A. Education Candidate, Columbia University Teachers College	Teacher, Alternative High School District in New York City
12	M	Y	Chicago Public Schools	B.A., University of Illinois at Urbana–Champaign M.A. Education Candidate, University of Illinois–Chicago	Teacher, Telpochalli Elementary School in Chicago
13	M	N	Aspire Public Schools (charter)	Master's of Science, City College of New York	Teacher, The Lab School in the Bronx
14	M	Y	New York Public Schools	B.A., Wayne State University M.A. Education, University of Detroit-Mercy	Teacher, Paul Robeson Academy in Detroit
15	F	N	New York Public Schools	B.A., Amherst College M.A. Education, Columbia University Teachers College	Teacher, United Nations International School in New York City

Source: Company documents.

Exhibit 6

Summer Institute Curriculum, July 2001

Module	*Course*	*Description*
Instructional Leadership	Learning Theories and Instructional Planning	Explore current learning theories that pertain most to urban education.
	Curriculum, Standards, and Assessment	Cover state and national content and skill standards. Emphasizes alignment of standards with curriculum and pedagogy.
	Literacy	Review reading, writing, speaking, and listening processes. Understand the educational need of at-risk learners, English-language learners, and other special needs students.
	Numeracy	Survey developments and leading practices in mathematics education.
	Observation and Supervision of Instruction	Develop effective instructional supervision and observation skills through demonstrations, group discussions, role playing, and analysis of case studies and video.
Building Capacity and Accountability	Human Resources	Understand organizational support systems and related topics, including recruiting, hiring, supervision, evaluation, dismissal processes, and equity issues.
	The Power of Data	Learn to use data and related analysis tools to improve instruction and student learning and to support various other school goals.
School Climate and Culture	Building School Community and Mission	Create a mission-driven culture and organizational climate. Explore ways in which leaders can articulate and develop personal and shared visions.
	Models of Reform and Decision Making	Analyze several models of school reform and the decision-making skills and processes necessary to manage and implement change.
Management and Operations	Managing the Effective Facility	Integrate management of facilities, maintenance functions, and operations, and understand the relationship between learning and facilities.
	Budgeting to Support School Goals	Learn how to budget strategically and how to link budgets to goals and improvement plans.
External Relations	Engaging Community Resources	Learn how to engage and collaborate with a diverse group of educational stakeholders.
	School Law	Address a variety of legal issues that urban school leaders face, such as child abuse, harassment, free speech, and affirmative action.
School Internship	Mentoring	Prepare both principals and fellows to effectively enter and negotiate their formal mentoring relationship.

Source: Company documents.

Exhibit 7

New Leaders Cash Flow Statement, 2000–2002 ($ thousands)

	2000–2001 Actual	*2001–2002 Budget*
Sources of Cash		
Investment[1]	$1,581	$1,645
Fellow sponsorships[2]	278	423
Charter school placement fees[3]	0	53
Total Sources	$1,859	$2,121
Uses of Cash		
National Office		
Staff[4]	$519	$382
Rent, supplies, and travel	236	206
Curriculum development[5]	140	447
Fellow recruiting[6]	63	73
Performance evaluation[7]	0	52
Total national uses	$958	$1,160
City Offices		
Fellow recruiting[6]	$36	$188
Training[8]	5	763
Stipends[9]	0	208
Staff[10]	4	300
Rent, supplies, and travel	0	74
Total local uses	$45	$1,533
Total Uses of Cash	$1,003	$2,693
Net Cash Flow for Period	$856	($572)
Accumulated Cash Balance	$856	$284

Source: Company documents.

[1] Investment includes funding from venture philanthropists, foundations, and other institutions.

[2] Fellow sponsorships were raised in $20,000 increments from local foundations, businesses, and individuals. The Broad Foundation matched donations for fellow sponsorships.

[3] To hire a full-time principal, charter schools paid New Leaders a $15,000 placement fee. New Leaders expected to place 25% of its fellows with charter schools.

[4] National staff includes salaries and benefits associated with New Leaders' CEO, COO, and other centralized staff. From the 2000–2001 to the 2001–2002 budgets, the costs of curriculum development staff were moved from the national staff budget line to the curriculum development budget line.

[5] Curriculum development includes the costs of expert team meetings, outsourced course development, and faculty selection and training. The 2001–2002 curriculum development budget also includes the salaries and benefits of chief curriculum officer and related staff.

[6] Fellow recruiting includes costs associated with marketing to and admitting fellows. Recruiting and admissions costs were divided as appropriate between national and local offices.

[7] Performance evaluation includes primarily the cost of consulting contracts to design and implement New Leaders' formal evaluation process.

[8] Training includes summer institute faculty stipends and fees to university accreditation partners, course materials, and New Leaders staff dedicated to directing the residency program.

[9] Stipends covered $7,000 payments to mentors and $27,500 payments to fellows during residencies at charter schools. In-district fellows received equivalent $27,500 residency stipends directly from their host districts. New Leaders expected the fee to mentors to be reduced to $5,000.

[10] Local staff includes salary and benefits associated with city directors and related staff.

Exhibit 8

Profiles of Select New Leaders Investors

Investor	*Founders*	*Founded*	*Capital under Management*[1]	*Investment Strategy*	*Sample Investments*
Broad Foundation	Eli Broad	1999	$400 million	Invest in school leadership initiatives in large urban districts nationwide.	Broad Prize for Urban Education Broad Center for Superintendents
Chicago Public Education Fund	Corporate and civic leaders	1999	$14 million	Improve school leadership and student achievement in the Chicago area.	Principal training National certification of teachers Alternative teacher certification
New Profit, Inc.	Vanessa Kirsh	1998	$11 million	Invest in social entrepreneurs who generate social change.	The B.E.L.L. Foundation Citizen Schools Jumpstart Teach For America Working Today
New Schools Venture Fund	John Doerr (Partner, Kleiner Perkins) Brook Byers (Partner, Kleiner Perkins) Kim Smith (Managing Partner, New Schools Venture Fund)	1998	$70 million	Improve public K–12 education nationwide through investments in the 10–20 most promising, scalable entrepreneurial ventures.	Aspire Public Schools Carnegie Learning, Inc. Greatschools.net High Tech High LearnNow, Inc. Success for All Teach For America Teachscape

Source: Company documents.

[1] Figures for capital under management include certain estimates of the results of ongoing fund-raising efforts.

Exhibit 9

Go-Broad Option, Cash Flow Projection, 2002–2012 ($ thousands)

	2002–03	*2003–04*	*2004–05*	*2005–06*	*2006–07*	*2007–08*	*2008–09*	*2009–10*	*2010–11*	*2011–12*	*Total*
Sources of Cash											
Investment[1]	$2,217	$2,056	$2,575	$2,819	$3,021	$3,210	$3,745	$3,723	$3,833	$4,080	$31,279
Fellow sponsorships	1,400	3,000	3,800	4,240	5,240	6,240	7,240	8,360	9,360	10,000	58,880
Charter school placement fees	131	281	356	398	491	585	679	784	878	938	5,521
Total Sources	**3,748**	**5,337**	**6,731**	**7,457**	**8,752**	**10,035**	**11,664**	**12,867**	**14,071**	**15,018**	**95,680**
Uses of Cash											
National Office											
Staff	542	812	985	976	1,162	1,248	1,351	1,476	1,518	1,570	11,640
Rent, supplies, and travel	226	226	226	226	226	226	226	226	226	226	2,260
Curriculum development	354	354	374	354	354	374	354	354	374	354	3,600
Fellow recruiting	30	30	30	30	30	30	30	30	30	30	300
Performance evaluation	150	300	350	400	450	500	550	600	650	700	4,650
Total national uses	1,302	1,722	1,965	1,986	2,222	2,378	2,511	2,686	2,798	2,880	22,450
City Offices											
Fellow recruiting	84	102	131	178	212	240	287	323	357	375	2,289
Training	1,324	1,842	2,472	2,675	3,157	3,637	4,384	4,788	5,225	5,593	35,097
Stipends	411	881	1,116	1,246	1,540	1,833	2,127	2,456	2,750	2,938	17,298
Staff	496	637	850	1,107	1,307	1,588	1,930	2,143	2,424	2,691	15,173
Rent, supplies, and travel	131	153	197	265	314	359	425	471	517	541	3,373
Total local uses	2,446	3,615	4,766	5,471	6,530	7,657	9,153	10,181	11,273	12,138	73,230
Total Uses of Cash	**$3,748**	**$5,337**	**$6,731**	**$7,457**	**$8,752**	**$10,035**	**$11,664**	**$12,867**	**$14,071**	**$15,018**	**$95,680**
Net Cash Flow for Period	**$0**	**$0**	**$0**	**$0**	**$0**	**$0**	**$0**	**$0**	**$0**	**$0**	**$0**

	2002–03	2003–04	2004–05	2005–06	2006–07	2007–08	2008–09	2009–10	2010–11	2011–12	Total
Operating Statistics											
Number of cities	3	4	5	7	8	9	11	13	14	15	
New Leaders headcount	23	30	38	44	53	61	72	78	86	93	
Number of fellows admitted[2]	35	75	95	106	131	156	181	209	234	250	
Cumulative number of fellows[3]	50	125	220	326	457	613	794	1,003	1,237	1,487	
Student reach of current fellows[4]	22,995	49,275	62,415	69,642	86,067	102,492	118,917	137,313	153,738	164,250	
Cost per fellow[5]	$107,093	$71,167	$70,844	$70,350	$66,801	$64,328	$64,438	$61,564	$60,125	$60,065	

Source: Company documents.

[1] Investment projections are derived so that net cash flow tallies to zero in each period.

[2] Fellows admitted refers to the number of fellows accepted by New Leaders in a given year.

[3] Cumulative number of fellows adds up fellows admitted in the current year and fellows admitted in prior years.

[4] Student reach of current fellows computes the number of students that can be served by fellows admitted in a particular year. The calculation assumes that each admitted fellow will lead a school with 657 students.

[5] Cost per fellow divides total uses of cash by the number of fellows admitted in a given year.

Exhibit 10

Go-Deep Option, Cash Flow Projection, 2002–2012 ($ thousands)

	2002–03	*2003–04*	*2004–05*	*2005–06*	*2006–07*	*2007–08*	*2008–09*	*2009–10*	*2010–11*	*2011–12*	*Total*
Sources of Cash											
Investment[1]	$2,142	$1,673	$2,160	$2,067	$2,346	$2,064	$1,772	$1,885	$1,796	$2,191	$20,096
Fellow sponsorships	1,400	3,000	3,600	3,800	4,120	4,720	5,520	5,840	6,040	6,560	44,600
Charter school placement fees	131	281	338	356	386	443	518	548	566	615	4,182
Total Sources	**3,673**	**4,954**	**6,098**	**6,223**	**6,852**	**7,227**	**7,810**	**8,273**	**8,402**	**9,366**	**68,878**
Uses of Cash											
National Office											
National staff	467	602	879	896	914	932	951	1,003	1,023	1,043	8,710
Rent, supplies, and travel	226	226	226	226	226	226	226	226	226	226	2,260
Curriculum development	354	354	354	354	354	354	354	354	354	354	3,540
Fellow recruiting	30	30	30	30	30	30	30	30	30	30	300
Performance evaluation	150	300	450	450	450	450	450	500	500	550	4,250
Total national uses	1,227	1,512	1,939	1,956	1,974	1,992	2,011	2,113	2,133	2,203	19,060
City Offices											
Fellow recruiting	84	84	102	102	136	136	136	154	154	183	1,271
Training	1,324	1,815	2,209	2,259	2,474	2,652	2,921	3,044	3,093	3,541	25,332
Stipends	411	881	1,058	1,116	1,210	1,387	1,622	1,716	1,774	1,927	13,102
Staff	496	531	637	637	859	859	918	1,024	1,024	1,246	8,231
Rent, supplies, and travel	131	131	153	153	199	201	202	222	224	266	1,882
Total local uses	2,446	3,442	4,159	4,267	4,878	5,235	5,799	6,160	6,269	7,163	49,818
Total Uses of Cash	**$3,673**	**$4,954**	**$6,098**	**$6,223**	**$6,852**	**$7,227**	**$7,810**	**$8,273**	**$8,402**	**$9,366**	**$68,878**
Net Cash Flow for Period	**$0**	**$0**	**$0**	**$0**	**$0**	**$0**	**$0**	**$0**	**$0**	**$0**	**$0**

	2002–03	*2003–04*	*2004–05*	*2005–06*	*2006–07*	*2007–08*	*2008–09*	*2009–10*	*2010–11*	*2011–12*	*Total*
Operating Statistics											
Number of cities	3	3	4	4	5	5	5	6	6	7	
New Leaders headcount	22	24	28	28	33	33	35	37	37	41	
Number of fellows admitted[2]	35	75 •	90	95	103	118	138	146	151	164	
Cumulative number of fellows[3]	50	125	215	310	413	531	669	815	966	1,130	
Annual student reach[4]	22,995	49,275	59,130	62,415	67,671	77,526	90,666	95,922	99,207	107,748	
Cost per fellow[5]	$104,950	$66,061	$67,754	$65,511	$66,527	$61,242	$56,601	$56,661	$55,645	$57,107	

Source: Company documents.

[1] Investment projections are derived so that net cash flow tallies to zero in each period.

[2] Fellows admitted refers to the number of fellows accepted by New Leaders in a given year.

[3] Cumulative number of fellows adds up fellows admitted in the current year and fellows admitted in prior years.

[4] Student reach of current fellows computes the number of students that can be served by fellows admitted in a particular year. The calculation assumes that each admitted fellow will lead a school with 657 students.

[5] Cost per fellow divides total uses of cash by the number of fellows admitted in a given year.

Exhibit 11

New City and District Screening Criteria

1. Market Size, Customer Demand, and Talent Pool
   - Large absolute number of students, schools, and charter schools
   - Large pool of potential fellow applicants, mentor principals, and summer institute faculty
   - Presence of competitors to New Leaders
2. Potential Partners and Champions
   - High level of involvement of local nonprofit, business, and civic institutions in public education
   - Presence of organizations that could refer fellows, mentor principals, and summer institute faculty
3. Potential Funders
   - High availability of local education-related funding from corporations, foundations, and individual philanthropic organizations
4. Reform Agenda
   - Established standards-based goals, sanctions, and rewards for schools and districts
   - Positive charter school climate
5. City Director
   - Outstanding individual to manage city operations
6. Charter School and Education Management Organization (EMO) Presence
   - EMOs operating in metro area and forming potential clients for New Leaders
   - General interest in innovation and alternatives to district-run schools
7. School-Level Autonomy
   - School autonomy over budgeting and hiring practices, indications of interest in further decentralization
   - Union contracts allowing principals to evaluate teachers and take corrective action on underperforming teachers
8. Political and Structural Environment
   - Stability among key constituents, including superintendent, school board, and mayor's office
   - Stable regulatory and political environment
9. Principal Certification Requirements
   - Presence of an alternative certification program or the likelihood that New Leaders could negotiate a waiver from regulatory authorities

Source: Company documents.

Exhibit 12

Select New Leaders Expansion Activities

Activity	*Description*
Services	*Headhunting:* Provide principal and executive recruiting and evaluation services for urban and suburban school districts.
	Consulting: Consult districts on principal recruiting, training, and professional development.
	Training: Provide tuition-based training of principals on behalf of districts, EMOs, and other education employers.
	Advocacy: Lobby state boards of education and legislatures on principal leadership. Create and manage fund to reward excellent performance by principals.
Licensing	*Nonprofits:* Sell recruiting, curriculum, and training knowledge to other nonprofits focused on the principal shortage.
	Content Providers: License curriculum and other documented expertise to book publishers, traditional-education schools, and other content providers.
School Management	*EMO:* Operate charter and pilot schools with a focus on teacher and principal quality.

Source: Company documents.

Stacey Childress ■ Robert Peterkin ■ Tonika Cheek Clayton

Memphis City Schools: The Next Generation of Principals

On November 18, 2004, Memphis City Schools (MCS) Superintendent Carol R. Johnson waited in her office for a telephone call from the principal of Geeter Middle School (Geeter). That morning, Johnson had arrived to a flood of parental complaints and media calls regarding the principal's decision to suspend the entire eighth-grade class because students refused to apologize and clean up after a cafeteria food fight. The Geeter principal was leading a school for the first time, and while some parents supported the new principal's actions, many questioned her judgment and experience in maintaining an orderly learning environment. Johnson worried that the school's escalating disciplinary problems and the community's response would distract the principal from her role as an instructional leader. Before communicating with school board members, news reporters, and parents, Johnson wanted to speak directly with the principal to make sure she had all of the facts. The media frenzy had brought attention to the recent influx of first-time principals hired to turn around several of the district's underperforming schools.

In the four years leading up to the 2004–2005 (SY05), Geeter had been under heavy scrutiny by the district and the state for not meeting adequate yearly progress (AYP) targets. As with several other schools in a similar predicament, Johnson appointed a new principal to Geeter as part of the district's action plan to improve student achievement and to reverse the school's substandard record. Overall, MCS hired 31 new principals that year, 29 of whom had no prior experience as principals. Because 52% of MCS's 185 principals would be eligible to retire within three years, Johnson was preoccupied with developing new principals and expanding the pipeline of high-quality candidates.

Johnson reflected on her team's initial efforts to strengthen the pipeline of quality candidates, match newly hired principals to appropriate schools, and provide principals with the support and resources to be successful instructional leaders. The situation at Geeter raised questions concerning a new principal's capacity to carry out MCS's instructional agenda and the district's ability to effectively support the increasing number of inexperienced principals. She believed that high-performing principals were a key lever for improving student achievement across the district, and she wondered if her team had built the right foundation for identifying and preparing candidates.

Background

MCS Demographics and History

Serving over 119,000 students, MCS was the largest school district in the state of Tennessee (see **Exhibits 1** and **2** for MCS facts and figures). Shaped by a history of desegregation laws, busing integration policies, annexation, and racial tensions, MCS evolved over 50 years from a majority white student population[1] at the time of the 1954 *Brown vs. Board of Education* ruling to one in SY05 that was 86% black, 9% white, 4% Hispanic, and 1% other, including Asians and other ethnicities. Seventy-one percent of students qualified for free or reduced-price meals, 14% participated in special education programs, and 4% had limited English proficiency. In SY04, MCS showed modest gains in reading test scores and significant improvement in every subgroup on math test scores. In high school algebra, the percentage of students scoring at proficient or advanced increased from 42% in SY03 to 60% in SY04. Nevertheless, MCS still fell short of meeting state goals across several student achievement indicators assessed yearly by the Tennessee Department of Education (see **Exhibit 3** for MCS student achievement indicators).

In Tennessee, county governments typically ran school districts. However, MCS had special status as a city-operated district and was funded by the city, county, state, and federal government. The district was located in Shelby County, which independently operated a neighboring school district, Shelby County Schools (SCS), making Shelby County a rare dual-district county. Serving approximately 46,000 students, SCS catered to a predominantly white (68%), middle-class community with less than 13% of students eligible for Title 1[2] federal funds.[3] In recent years, conflicts between the two districts over county funds had escalated in part due to SCS's population influx as a result of suburban growth and MCS's request for more financial resources to fund student achievement initiatives. In contrast to MCS, SCS surpassed the majority of the state's student achievement goals in SY04 and was two percentage points short of reaching the state's graduation goal of 90%.[4]

Attempts to consolidate the two districts over the years (most recently in early 2003) were opposed by SCS leadership and residents who felt that consolidating the districts would bring down the quality of education in SCS schools. Some MCS board members and community leaders also publicly expressed skepticism at the proposed benefits of handing over the reins of MCS to SCS leadership. Proponents of consolidation argued that it would streamline the tax and budget process in the city and county, provide more equitable resources to schools across the county, and maintain the quality of education at any given school. Although the most recent push to dissolve the MCS charter had failed, this issue perpetually loomed over both districts.

Superintendent Carol Johnson

Originally from Brownsville, Tennessee, a town 63 miles outside Memphis, Johnson took the helm of MCS in the fall of 2003 following a six-year stint as the superintendent of Minneapolis City Schools. Highly respected and trusted in Minneapolis, Johnson built a strong reputation for working collaboratively with parents, board members, principals, teachers, and the external community to achieve results. After spending 30 years of her career in Minneapolis, Johnson chose to bring her skills and experience to MCS, a school district almost three times the student enrollment size of Minneapolis's with tighter financial constraints and a higher rate of poverty and illiteracy.

In her first 15 months, Johnson took action in a number of key areas. Forced to cut over $25 million from the proposed MCS SY05 budget in her first term, she eliminated over 90 central office positions and restructured the district's administrative departments. She also successfully campaigned to repeal the school board's policy for corporal punishment after a highly publicized community debate. MCS also won bids to partner with national programs, New Leaders for New Schools and the New Teacher Project, to raise the quality of its principals and teachers.

With 148 of 191 MCS schools on the state's No Child Left Behind (NCLB) watch list of failing schools at the start of SY04, Johnson's administration successfully worked to clear 77 schools from the list by the start of SY05. After assessing the 15 schools in the "corrective action" category under the NCLB guidelines,[5] Johnson decided to "fresh-start"[6] the five worst schools. She removed the principals in these five schools and replaced them with new leaders and instructional staffs. Fresh-start principals were given the autonomy to completely replace existing staff, from custodians to teachers. Johnson placed first-time principals in three of the five fresh-start schools. For the remaining 10 schools under corrective action, Johnson prescribed a mix of actions from replacing principals and/or selected teachers to reconfiguring grade structure and program designs. In total, Johnson assigned 11 of the 29 new first-time principals to underperforming schools labeled as "high priority" under NCLB guidelines.[7]

Johnson believed that principals were critical change agents because of their front-line interaction with teachers and students; therefore, an important component of her strategy focused on preparing and managing principals to be more effective instructional leaders. She noted, "In the schools where we've had progress, despite poverty and language barriers, it seems to be that the principal's leadership has created an environment where the staff believes in the notion that all students can learn and can achieve at higher levels."

Although the district mandated that principals adopt common literacy and math curriculums, they were give n some autonomy in the day-to-day management of when and how to deliver the content. As instructional leaders, they were expected to ensure that teachers effectively taught the curriculum set forth by MCS. Johnson described her view on instructional leadership:

> For awhile across the nation, we saw principals hired for their management skills so that buses ran on time, kids were served, the halls were clean, and the school had no major incidents. And that was what constituted good leadership. But I think in the new order of work, leadership around instruction takes center stage. We need principals who know what high-quality instruction looks like and how to work with teams of teachers to achieve it.

Principal Management and Support

In order to more effectively manage and support school leaders, Johnson hired Deputy Superintendent Bernadeia Johnson and appointed five academic directors to directly supervise principals (see **Exhibit 4** for organizational chart). Bernadeia Johnson oversaw both the academic directors and the academic leadership team (ALT), which included the academic directors, the associate superintendent of curriculum and instruction, and the district's NCLB representative. The ALT created the district's academic agenda each year and was responsible for carrying it out at the school level. Each week, the group met to report on the status of the current agenda, to refine the agenda for the upcoming year, and to discuss issues that had surfaced at the school level. By participating in the ALT, academic directors used the input they gleaned from daily interactions with principals to help steer the academic agenda and its implementation. At the same time, the ALT influenced the academic directors' management of principals by setting the district's instructional priorities, which informed decisions about resource allocation to and professional development for schools.

The Role of Academic Directors

Carol Johnson revised a long-standing organizational structure in which principals were geographically assigned to one of three zone directors whose primary function was operational support. Under the old system, one zone director supervised and evaluated principals across both elementary and secondary levels with less of a focus on the school's instructional agenda. The revised structure created an academic director for high schools, one for middle schools, and three for elementary schools. The number of schools managed by one academic director ranged from 25 to 38 schools. An academic director's main function was to drive the district's instructional agenda and to provide his or her principals with support and development opportunities (see **Exhibit 5** for a list of academic director responsibilities).

High school academic director James Bacchus explained some differences between the new and old roles:

> In the past, the zone directors were more or less operational managers involved in all the K–12 schools in their geography. A former zone director confessed he didn't know anything about elementary schools because his experience was in high schools. Every time he needed to address a situation at an elementary school, he had to talk to another director who had elementary experience. By being focused only on high schools, I can focus on all of a school's issues, not just the operations piece. I can support the principal by helping them focus on academic challenges and by assisting them with resource allocation issues such using staff and dollars more strategically.

In addition to providing support for individual schools, academic directors oversaw resource allocation across schools in an attempt to achieve a more equitable balance of resources. Under the old system, a principal's ability to garner resources from the central office often depended more on his or her personal relationships within the district than on the relative level of need compared with that of other schools. Consequently, some schools had the latest technology and renovations, while others operated with significantly fewer amenities. Elementary school academic director Virginia McNeil observed: "We try to make sure there's an equitable distribution of funds, personnel, grants, materials, and equipment. So each time we have a chance to allocate funds or distribute personnel, we take into consideration those schools with the highest rate of poverty and those schools listed under 'corrective action' or 'high priority.'"

Principal Support and Development

Bernadeia Johnson and the academic directors communicated with principals in a variety of ways. Before SY05 began, principals attended the Principal Leadership Academy (PLA), a three-day session hosted by the district designed to introduce principals to the new academic leadership team, review the MCS academic agenda, and provide them with some professional development tools for the upcoming year (see **Exhibit 6** for PLA agenda).

Each month, all principals convened for a mandatory four-hour meeting to get the latest district updates from Carol Johnson and other MCS central office administrators. These meetings also allocated time for the academic directors and principals to break into their subgroups to discuss issues or progress made at individual schools. Additionally, each academic director put together a principal advisory committee that helped determine the kind of developmental support principals within their subgroup needed. To make sure that the majority of interests were served, the academic director usually selected principals of varying experience levels and from different backgrounds to serve on the committee.

Support from academic directors varied across principal subgroups depending on the academic director's management style and the nature of the challenges facing the principals. Academic directors also differentiated the support they provided for schools based on the school's performance and the principal's experience. Underperforming schools and schools with first-time principals were subject to more instructional "walk-throughs" and visits than other schools. Academic directors typically required new principals to meet more frequently and participate in more development sessions than their more experienced peers. Also, first-time principals were paired with a mentor, a veteran principal whom they could rely on for guidance about building-level issues or help in navigating the larger system. Elementary school academic director Myra Whitney discussed the work she did with her principals:

> I've been working with my principals mainly on two things: school improvement plans and literacy. When I visit the schools, I have all of their data with me, and I take materials that can help them. They share with me and I share with them what I've thought of and what they might want to use. These visits are very focused. My next step is to help them see the impact that the learning environment can have on promoting our literacy initiative.
>
> My first-time principals and principals in their second and third years are participating in a book study. Everybody's reading a book on creating professional learning communities. I meet with them once a month. I'm constantly on the phone with them and going out to their schools. The new principals are also participating in a book study on emotional intelligence because I'm trying to stress the importance of relationships for first-time principals, especially relationships with families and the staff, before they make quick judgments.

Middle school academic director Brenda Cassellius described the kinds of support she provided to her group of principals:

> I love technology and I love data, so I contacted the IT Department and I said, "Look, I've got 11 schools on the [NCLB] list only because of attendance, and these 11 schools also have high suspension rates. For every meeting, I need to give my principals data on suspension and attendance and how their suspensions are affecting their attendance rate." And so at every principals meeting they got a packet with all that information and we talked about how to analyze what the data said and how to act on it.
>
> I meet with new principals every two weeks, and they drive the content of our meetings for the most part. I've also started meeting with assistant principals on a voluntary basis. These meetings are about professional development for them and how they can get to the next level. That serves two purposes. One is to give them tools so they support the current academic agenda, and the other is to identify those who are really interested in becoming leaders. Therefore, it's optional. And as we meet, I will get to know them better and will develop an understanding of their strengths as future leaders. So as I get to know them better, I'm not only growing the leadership pipeline but also am able to gather more accurate evidence to present to the superintendent for best fit and promotional opportunities.

Development opportunities for an individual principal were largely left up to the principal and his or her respective academic director. Academic directors had the autonomy to decide what their principal's developmental needs were and how to best supplement those needs to meet MCS's academic goals. Each principal's budget included a small amount for professional development that they could use at their own discretion. Although professional development for assistant principals was primarily managed by their principals, the new academic directors were committed to more actively engaging assistant principals at the district level to help develop them for the principal role.

Developing a Pipeline of Principals

With 52% of principals eligible for retirement in three years, MCS needed at least 96 new principals over the next three years, not counting normal attrition or terminations for poor performance. School board policy required new principals to have a minimum of three years' administrative experience as an assistant principal or instructional supervisor. Applicants were also required to receive principal certification from an accredited state program, which could be earned at a local university by enrolling in evening or summer courses.

Many current MCS principals had risen through this system, but many in the district were concerned that assistant principal experience combined with certification was not always adequate preparation for leading a school. While some principals had built a track record of developing their assistant principals into good leaders, others relegated their assistant principals to specific roles that failed to offer the leadership experience necessary to prepare them to be successful principals. First-time MCS principal Corey Harris remarked:

> I just don't feel like the average assistant principal gets that breadth of experience that I was able to get from my former principal. It seems that many deal primarily with the three Bs: the books, the butts, and the buses. That means textbooks, discipline, the cafeteria and those sorts of responsibilities. They don't really have an opportunity to immerse themselves in leading teachers, learning curriculum, and instructional leadership. My experience was not like that. I had responsibilities as it related to the curriculum, meeting with teachers in teams, working with parents, and participating in athletic activities. I got to see the good, the bad, and the ugly.

When Carol Johnson joined MCS, efforts were already under way to improve the quality of the pool from which new principals were chosen. The University of Memphis (U. Memphis) was in the first year of its Memphis Leadership Fellows Program (MLFP), a leadership development program targeted toward assistant principals aspiring to become principals. Separately, a push from community and business leaders had led to discussions between MCS and New Leaders for New Schools (NLNS), a national program that trained principals to lead in urban school districts. With MLFP and NLNS, MCS seemed poised to reach its goal of training at least 60 qualified principals over the next three years (see **Exhibit 7** for comparisons and costs of MLFP and NLNS).

Memphis Leadership Fellows Program—University of Memphis

Piloted in SY04, the Memphis Leadership Fellows Program (MLFP), a joint venture between the University of Memphis and MCS, allowed MCS assistant principals to develop leadership skills and become certified to assume a principal position in the state of Tennessee. The university redesigned its existing principal certification program, which was described as "a traditional program that adequately certified and licensed aspiring principals but did not prepare them to assume leadership roles that made a difference in an urban school district." MLFP bore little resemblance to its predecessor besides the requirement that participants had to have at least two years of administrative experience in a school district. The new program aimed to develop each fellow's unique leadership style and to cultivate the management and organizational skills needed to run a school. To evolve the program to better suit MCS's needs, U. Memphis was committed to adapting the curriculum and training for fellows "to prepare them to lead in different kinds of situations, such as taking over a 'fresh-start' school, following a low-performing principal, or following an exemplary principal."

Selection Process

In an attempt to raise the quality of candidates, the program required that applicants could not self-select into the program, unlike with other state certification programs, but instead had to be nominated by their supervisor. A selection committee that included MCS academic directors and U. Memphis faculty reviewed applications and decided which candidates to invite to the next phase. In the second screening, the selection committee judged the applicants' communication skills and leadership ability using interviews, role plays, and situational activities. Finalists were chosen using a composite scoring system that assigned varying weights to each component of the selection process (see **Exhibit 8**). During the program's first year, 23 of 51 nominated applicants were selected for the program, and in the second year 15 of 32 applicants were selected.

Program Components

To foster team unity among the cohort of fellows, MLFP's program introduction was Team Trek, a four-day outdoor orientation that included team-building activities with U. Memphis faculty and program coaches. Throughout the year, fellows attended seminars and workshops focused on instructional leadership, organizational management, school law, finances, and "principled leadership." Additionally, fellows would go on two-day site visits each month to schools and community businesses to gain exposure to different styles of leadership and to observe the different challenges across elementary, middle, and high schools.

Over a five-month period, fellows worked on a team project to address a district-wide issue facing MCS. Near the end of the program, fellows wrote a detailed report on the issue and presented their findings and recommendations to MCS administrators and MLFP faculty. Because MLFP fellows maintained their full-time positions at MCS schools, program components were usually scheduled outside of the school day. During site visits or other program activities that conflicted with school events, the program provided funding for the principal at each fellow's school to hire a substitute administrator, if requested.

Mentorship and coaching were also key components of the MLFP program. At the start of the program, each fellow was assigned an individual mentors and a program coach. There was also a shared pool of principal mentors, business coaches, and community organization mentors. The principal mentors were highly regarded MCS principals nominated by other principals and interviewed by the MLFP faculty. By exposing fellows to a variety of principals, one faculty member "hoped that fellows would experience the leadership style of at least 10 different stellar principals and use an eclectic approach to hone their personal leadership style." Business coaches, who held upper-level management positions in the Memphis business community, provided fellows assistance with management questions and networking. Program coaches were U. Memphis faculty members who followed each fellow's personal growth over the course of the program. Community organization mentors helped the fellows learn about challenges and benefits to schools partnering with community-based youth and family learning organizations.

Fellow Evaluations

At the beginning of the program, an individual profile compiling data from the selection process and Team Trek evaluations was made for each fellow detailing his or her strengths, weaknesses, and personal growth areas to focus on during the program year. Program assignments, site visits, and mentors were assigned specifically to address the needs outlined in the fellow's individual profile. Using the profile as a basis for evaluation, mentors, coaches, and the fellows themselves documented ongoing assessments. In the fellows' midyear reviews, program coaches collaborated with the mentors and the fellows to assess areas of improvement and to provide feedback. In the final evaluation, program coaches again consulted with mentors and the fellows to prepare a performance status report on each fellow and filed the report with MCS administration. Finally, MLFP faculty ranked the fellows according to their "readiness for principal leadership" and presented each candidate in rank order to MCS's principal selection committee.

Reactions from MLFP Fellows

Linda Campbell, an MCS assistant principal and MLFP fellow, described her experience in the program:

> I chose this program because I believe that someone coming straight from the classroom to the principalship misses an important middle piece of being an assistant principal. And there are some things that you're not going to get unless you've had to make certain on-the-job decisions at the spur of the moment, like when you're faced with that angry parent, faced with that child that's out of control, faced with that school emergency.
>
> I've learned that it's not enough to want to be a principal or to lead a school community. It's about self-analysis, self-assessment, and identifying who I am first. I can't lead anybody else unless I know who I am. I've engaged in a lot of discussions and reflection about why I want to be a principal, why I want to lead. Then once I'm there, how do I lead a school community? How do I develop teachers? How do I impact student achievement?

Cory Harris, a middle school principal and graduate of the MLFP program, explained the benefits and drawbacks of the program from his experience:

> I think the program was very effective in that you very seldom get an opportunity to leave your own school to go into another school to see some of the strategies and some of the best practices that they're using. A lot of graduate programs give you a lot of theory, but they don't really give you any application. The program was great because it gave me an opportunity to see theory in practice and to learn from more veteran administrators in the system. It also got me down the path of reading more for my own professional development as well as attending seminars. It also gave me a cohort of people that I can trust, that I can call on, and that I know are going through the same challenges that I'm going through.
>
> I think the one draw-back is that it's hard to fully benefit from the program and hold down a job. Whenever we were out to visit another school, there would be so much work left when we came back that it would be difficult to keep up with the new knowledge and the reading. In contrast, New Leaders for New Schools fellows are immersed 100% of the time and not trying to hold down other administrative duties at the same time.

New Leaders for New Schools (NLNS)

With wide support from local business and community leaders, MCS won a nationwide competition with other urban school districts to partner with NLNS to recruit, train, and support high-quality candidates for principal positions. Starting in February 2004, NLNS contracted with MCS to develop 60 new principals over a three-year period beginning with 10 principals the first year, 20 principals the second year, and 30 principals the third year, with an option to develop 30 more principals in a fourth year.

As part of the agreement, NLNS negotiated with the University of Memphis and the MCS Board of Commissioners to become an official alternative principal certification program, which allowed NLNS candidates to bypass the board policy requirement of having three years' administrative experience before obtaining principal certification. In exchange for services, NLNS would receive $2 million in private funding from local business and foundation donors to cover training expenses. MCS agreed to create a paid position for each "new leader" and pay each one a salary of $60,000 during the fellowship year. As part of its agreement with NLNS, MCS agreed to give more autonomy to high-performing principals starting in SY06, when the first cohort of "new leaders" would enter principal roles. MCS committed to interviewing each NLNS participant during the principal selection process, but not to hiring them.

Selection Process

In the program's first year of operation in MCS, NLNS chose nine of 250 applicants to become the first cohort of new leaders. Memphis NLNS Director Billy Kearney pared down the first wave of applications by assessing each candidate based on the NLNS selection criteria (see **Exhibit 9**). Candidates minimally demonstrating all components of the selection criteria in their applications and during a first round of interviews were invited back to "finalist day." "Finalist day" was a daylong intensive process in which a team of MCS administrators, NLNS staff, veteran principals, and business leaders evaluated the candidates on their instructional knowledge, case-study analysis, role plays, and interviews. Successful applicants exhibited a readiness to fill a principal position after a year of training in addition to "NLNS qualities" outlined in the selection criteria. Eight of the nine new leaders had prior experience working in MCS.

Program Components

The NLNS program began in the summer with an intense six-week national institute in Philadelphia where principals and faculty from education and business schools taught new leaders from all NLNS districts courses in instructional leadership and the management of systems, people, and financial resources. Though the participants came from all over the country, they lived with their city cohort for the institute's duration in order to foster a peer support group (see **Exhibit 10** for program content).

Following the summer institute, each new leader was assigned an MCS mentor principal in the school in which they would fulfill their full-time residency. The residency model was designed to enable the NLNS participants to apply the skills developed through the coursework to a real urban school under guidance from mentor principals. To select mentors, NLNS interviewed 35 self-selected principals who had records of effective instructional leadership and were willing to supervise and evaluate NLNS participants. During the residency, the NLNS participants worked with their mentor principals and NLNS leadership to define the projects on which they would be evaluated at the end of the academic year in addition to other managerial and operational tasks they would undertake as part of their role. NLNS participants met weekly with their mentor principal and their NLNS program coach for intensive coaching and feedback.

NLNS Evaluations

At the culmination of the residency, each new leader was evaluated using the "NLNS Principal Leadership Competencies Rubric" in Table A to assess their ability.

Taking into account the project and the work experience completed during the residency, mentor principals and Kearney gave each new leader a rating of expert, proficient,

Table A **NLNS Principal Leadership Competencies**

1. Lead Change	7. Nurture Excellent Teaching
2. Plan Strategically	8. Develop and Empower Teams
3. Distribute Leadership	9. Build a Safe and Supportive Culture
4. Manage Time and Priorities	10. Engage Parents
5. Focus on Student Outcomes	11. Schedule and Manage Effectively
6. Learn from Data	12. Network Outside the School

Source: New Leaders for New Schools.

developing, or novice in each competency area. The new leader's final evaluation would be made available to the MCS principal selection committee.

Reactions from NLNS fellows

Randy Thompson, an NLNS fellow in SY05, described his relationship with his mentor principal:

> My mentor principal involved me in virtually every decision he made to give me a real sense of everything I would be required to do as a principal. He even warned me that he would probably have to call me to meet him at 2 a.m. when the alarm is tripped at the school because that is all part of the job. During our conversations at the end of school days, he regularly asked me what I would do under different scenarios and gave me feedback on my decisions.

Another NLNS fellow, Tisha Stewart, explained the iterative process of crafting her role with her principal:

> Initially, I was not pleased with the level of work my mentor principal assigned to me due to a lack of communication and understanding between the both of us. However, my relationship with my mentor principal improved tremendously after the lines of communication were opened and we reached a level of understanding as to what my role entailed. We've since become a lot closer, and I've become much more involved in her day-to-day decision making.

Principal Placement

Participation in either the MLFP or NLNS program did not guarantee placement as a principal. The MCS principal selection committee, which included Bernadeia Johnson, the academic directors, and other executives, focused on selecting the candidate most qualified to match the specific needs of a school with a principal opening. Given Carol Johnson's focus on the principalship as a lever for change, she paid particular attention to principal placement and worked closely with the selection committee. As she explained,

> You don't want the candidate's first principal role to be a career-busting experience. In their first role, you want to make sure that they are successful and that they have an opportunity to see success in the role so that as they progress they know what skill sets worked. So what I'm always looking for is not just the best candidate. I want the best candidate for the particular kind of school and school environment. There's no perfect match, but you can make the best match possible. When you select someone who is not quite the right fit it forces you to put in fillers that compensate for their lack of experience or growth areas. It is nothing short of a miracle when it's done right, and nothing is more tremendously stressful for you for the rest of the year and years to come if it's done wrong. It has an impact on teaching and learning and on how confidently families view the school.

Out of 31 principals hired to start in August 2005, two had prior experience as principals and

29 would begin their first year as a principal. Of the first-time principals, three were assigned to "fresh-start" schools, and 11 were placed in "high-priority" schools. Twelve of the first-timers came through the MLFP program. During the hiring process, MLFP faculty presented a short vignette on each MLFP fellow that summarized their strengths, weaknesses, and overall rank relative to their peers. Carol Johnson recalled:

> They were pretty candid in their remarks, like, "This person needs more growth before she'll be ready to lead in these core areas," or "This guy might never be ready." And of the 12 assistant principals we promoted to principal from MLFP, I have to say that if they said a particular fellow was the best they had, what I've seen is of the principals I appointed, that fellow is the best I have.

In the coming year, NLNS fellows would be eligible for review by the MCS principal selection committee for the first time.

Challenges Ahead

After speaking with Geeter's principal, Carol Johnson immediately asked a retired veteran principal to go to Geeter and serve as an advisor to the principal, who had not participated in either the MLFP or NLNS programs. Then she released the following statement to the media: "Although we support the principal's actions, we acknowledge that there were other ways to send just as strong a message to parents and students."

Though Johnson did not second-guess the principal's decision, a few things still concerned her after their conversation. She wondered why more preventative measures had not been taken to avoid the escalation of events in the cafeteria. Furthermore, she knew from experience that the Memphis community could be harsh critics of principals and hoped that the principal could still garner sufficient community support. She also worried about the extent to which the instructional environment at Geeter had been irreparably compromised due to the events and the media attention.

As she watched the day's events unfold, she revisited her administration's work on principal leadership. Were they progressing toward systematically preparing principals to use good judgment, create the environment necessary to improve student achievement, manage instruction, and build successful partnerships with the community? What more should the district do to support its principals, especially the new ones? Did the district have the right long-term approach to recruiting and retaining qualified principals?

Notes

1. "City Schools Integration Timeline," *The Commercial Appeal*, May 16, 2004.

2. Federally funded programs in high-poverty schools that target children with low achievement (definition cited from the Tennessee Department of Education website, http://www.state.tn.us/education/Primer%20Terms%202.doc, accessed January 15, 2005).

3. "Shelby County Report Card 2004," Tennessee Department of Education website, http://www.k-1.state.tn.us/rptcrd04/system.asp, accessed January 15, 2005.

4. Ibid.

5. If after four years a school has still not improved, it is placed on the "corrective action" list and put on probation. At this stage, the State Department of Education may take action such as removing school staff, increasing the length of the school day or year, or decreasing the authority of local management (explanation cited from the MCS website, http://www.mcsk12.net/admin/communications/NCLB_Webpage/NCLB_frames.htm, accessed January 28, 2005).

6. "Fresh-start" schools were assessed as having no prior proven record of effectiveness. These schools were completely restructured and assigned new leadership and instructional staff.

7. Schools categorized as "high priority" have not met NCLB federal benchmarks for at least two consecutive years.

Exhibit 1

MCS Facts and Figures, SY05 MCS Overview

Student Demographics		
Number of students (K–12)	119,021	
African-American		86.1%
White		8.9%
Hispanic		3.7%
Asian/Pacific Islander		1.2%
Other		0.1%
Eligible for free and reduced-price lunch		71.0%
English-language learners		4.1%
Special education students [a]		14.4%
Graduation rate (SY04)		62.1%
Dropout rate (SY04)		19.8%
K–8 Attendance rate (SY04)		93.6%
9–12 Attendance rate (SY04)		87.2%
Schools and Staff		
Number of schools	191	
Elementary	112	
Middle	25	
Junior high	4	
Senior high	31	
Alternative	13	
Charter	6	
Number of principals [b]		
Principals	185	
Assistant principals	157	
New principals	31	
First-time principals	29	
Number of teachers	8,035	
African-American		59.0%
White		40.0%
Other		1.0%
Total full-time employees (FTEs)	16,500	

Source: Memphis City Schools.

[a] Twelve percent of the total number of special education students are enrolled in special programs for gifted students.

[b] Figures do not include charter school administrators. MCS did not pay or manage charter school administrators.

Exhibit 2

MCS Budget ($ millions)

	SY05	*% of Total*	*SY04*	*% of Total*	*SY03*	*% of Total*
Total Budget	773.6		737.3		731.3	
Revenue Sources						
State	346.5	44.7%	319.7	43.5%	309.8	42.4%
Shelby County	230.8	29.8%	222.8	30.3%	225.8	30.9%
Local sales tax	97.3	12.6%	92.1	12.5%	95.5	13.1%
City of Memphis	88.9	11.5%	89.5	12.2%	81.3	11.1%
Federal funds	8.3	1.1%	4.6	0.6%	3.4	0.5%
Local funds	3.4	0.4%	4.5	0.6%	5.5	0.8%
Transfer to charter schools	-6.7	-0.9%	-1.9	-0.3%	-	0.0%
Fund balance reserves	5.1	0.7%	4.1	0.6%	10.0	1.4%
Total Revenue	773.6		735.4		731.3	
Expenditures						
Salaries	515.6	66.6%	494.1	67.2%	491.6	67.2%
Employee benefits	147.6	19.1%	127.7	17.4%	122.5	16.8%
Professional services	21.9	2.8%	23.1	3.1%	23.7	3.2%
Property maint. services	28.3	3.7%	27.3	3.7%	26.8	3.7%
Contracted services	24.4	3.2%	20.7	2.8%	20.9	2.9%
Supplies and materials	14.9	1.9%	19.7	2.7%	19.7	2.7%
Travel	1.0	0.1%	1.0	0.1%	1.4	0.2%
Furniture/equipment/property	9.9	1.3%	11.5	1.6%	14.7	2.0%
Other	10.0	1.3%	10.3	1.4%	10.0	1.4%
Total Expenditures	773.6		735.4		731.3	

Source: Memphis City Schools.

Exhibit 3

Student Achievement Indicators Based on Tennessee Department of Education Standards, SY03–SY04

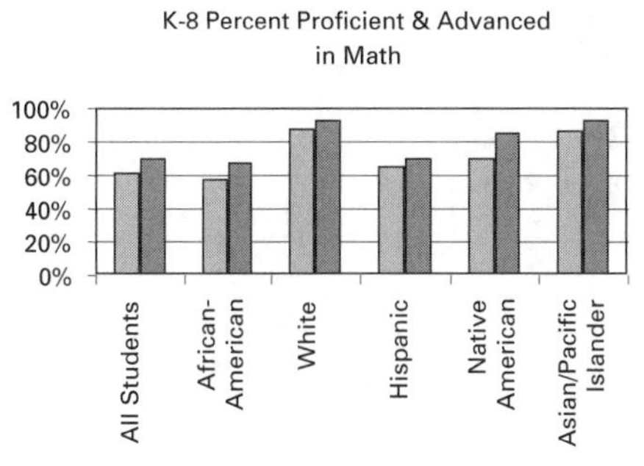

MCS Elementary & Middle Schools (TVAAS[a] Report Card Data)

Year-by-Year Breakdown	*Science*	*Social Studies*	*Reading/ Language Arts*	*Math*
School Year 2003-2004	A	B	D	D
School Year 2002-2003	D	F	F	F

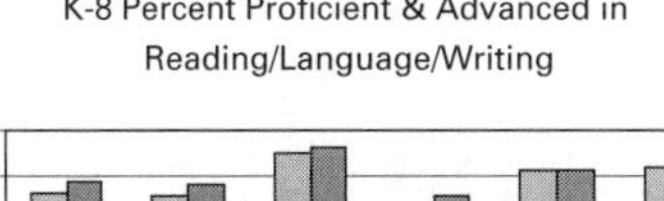

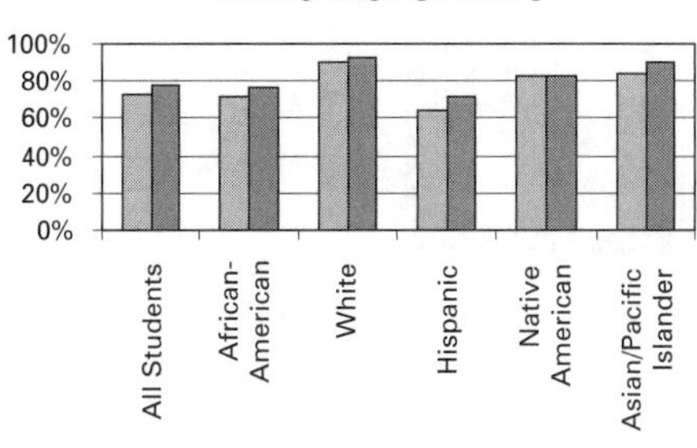

Additional Indicators

Indicator	*2002-2003*	*2003-2004*	*State Goal*
K-8 Attendance Rate	93.4%	93.6%	93.0%
K-8 Promotion Rate	91.1%	92.4%	97.0%
9-12 Attendance Rate	87.4%	87.2%	93.0%
Cohort Dropout Rate	19.9%	19.8%	10.0%
Graduation Rate	60.0%	62.1%	90.0%

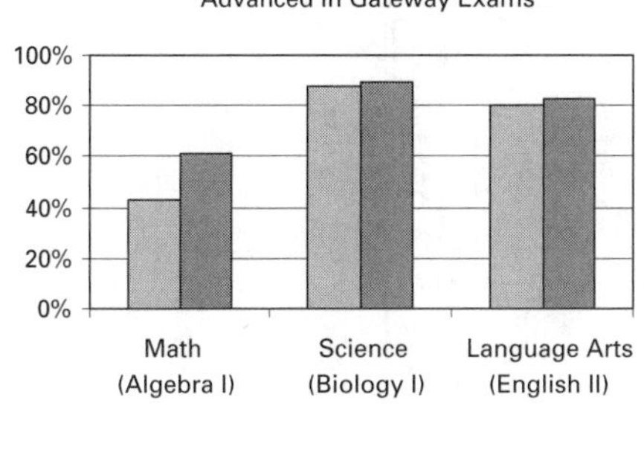

2003 2004

MCS High Schools (TVAAS[a] Data ACT Scores)

	Mean Student Score/2004	*Status/2004*	*Mean Student Score/2003*	*Status/2003*
Act Composite	17.4	Above State Expectation	17.2	(NDD) Met State Expectation
English	17.3	Above State Expectation	17.2	Above
Math	16.8	Above State Expectation	16.6	Above
Reading	17.4	(NDD) Met State Expectation	17.3	(NDD) Met State Expectation
Science	17.5	(NDD) Met State Expectation	17.3	Below

Source: Memphis City Schools.

[a] The Tennessee Value-Added Assessment System (TVAAS) is a diagnostic tool used by the state and school systems to measure the effectiveness of teachers and administrators in producing expected growth in student achievement. A grade of "C" means the school system has met the standards for average performance in that area. A grade of "A" or "B" represents exemplary or above-average performance for that system. A "D" is a below-proficient score, while an "F" deems that area of the school is deficient in meeting the students' needs. Grades are based on Normal Curve Equivalent (NCE) test scores.

Exhibit 4

MCS Organizational Chart

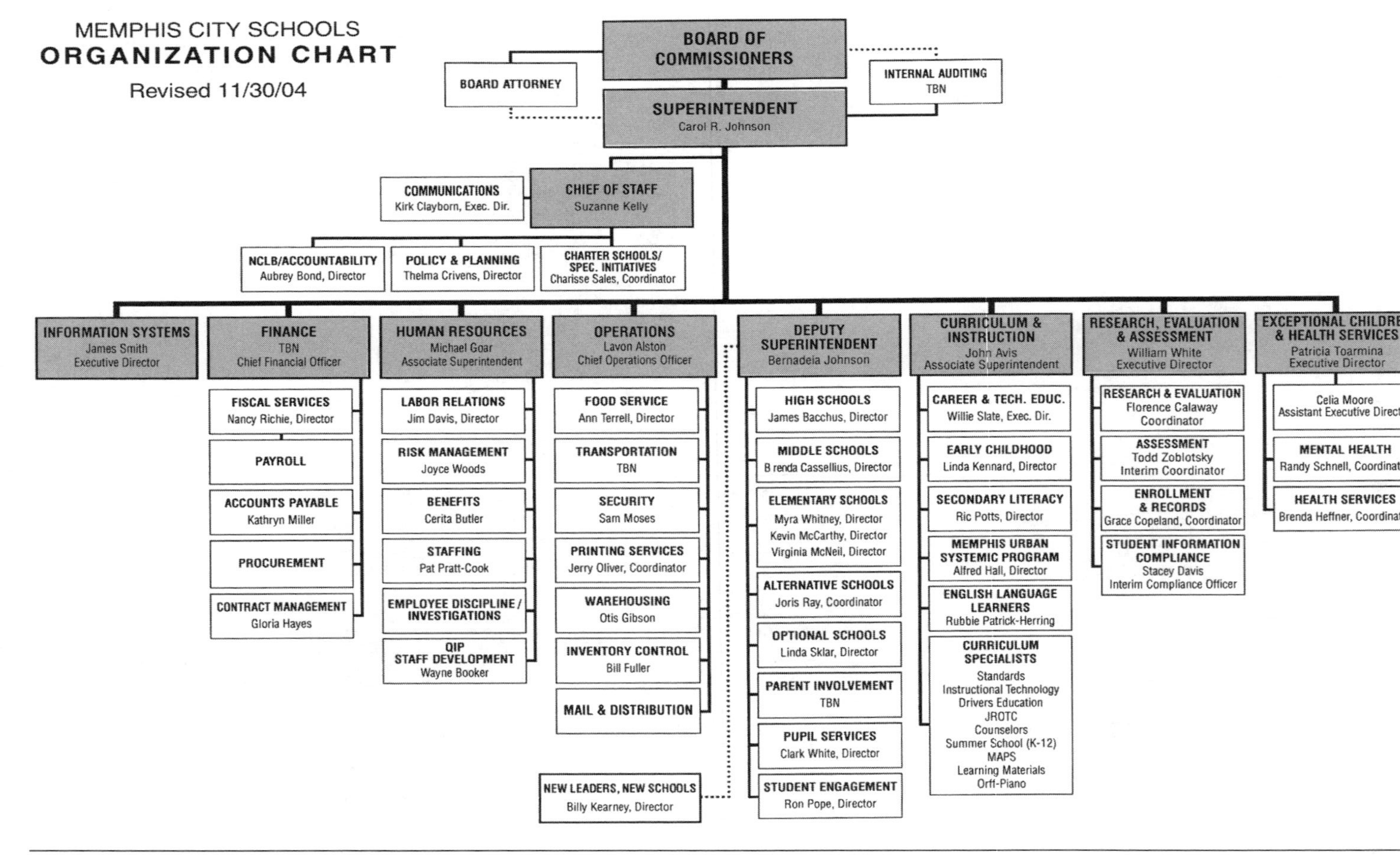

Source: Memphis City Schools.

Exhibit 5

MCS Academic Director Responsibilities

Academic Directors report directly to the Deputy Superintendent and are responsible for all MCS educational sites. They recognize that the most important work of education takes place at the school and classroom level, and that effective leadership provides instructional focus and necessary support and assistance to bring about school improvement. They directly supervise and support building administrators.

Responsibilities include:

- Work with schools to achieve the District's goals related to academic learning;
- Develop professional learning communities that will support student achievement;
- Assist and monitor each school in the development, implementation and assessment of individual school improvement plans; provide additional support for schools identified by the NCLB criteria;
- Serve as advocate and identify and coordinate school system and community resources for schools;
- Develop a network for increased parent-community awareness, involvement, and help the district to strengthen community confidence;
- Design and conduct regular meetings and professional development opportunities to address the instructional and management needs of principals and assistant principals (principals' professional development);
- Identify and help advocate for each school's financial, physical, and human resource needs;
- Evaluate principals using multiple indicators including leadership competencies;
- Create a process for supporting new principals' professional growth;
- With the assistance of human resources, establish a process for identifying potential principal candidates and support principals whose assignment has changed (reassignments);
- Work with the principal's advisory committee to increase communication between central office staff and school leaders;
- Identify and assign principal, assistant principal, and intern candidates;
- Support events and activities being sponsored by schools and the community;
- Collaborate and identify opportunities for schools to "spotlight" their success in the district and collaboration with communications;
- Visit school sites, attend school events, and continue to identify ways to build collegial relationships with principals and assistant principals;
- Liaison between the school community and the district leadership;
- Work with Deputy Superintendent to establish and implement a process for responding to parents, staff and community concerns and complaints.

Source: Memphis City Schools.

Exhibit 6

MCS Principal Leadership Academy Agenda

Wednesday, June 16		
8:00-9:30am	Introductions Reorganization of District Services Academic Achievement in MCS	Dr. Carol Johnson, Superintendent
9:30-9:45am	"The Spy Glass" by Richard Paul Evans	Principals - Marty Pettigrew, Peabody Kongsouly Jones, Rita White and Charles Newborn
10:00-11:30am	Focus on Instruction	
	Teaching and Learning Association	John Avis, Associate Superintendent
	Greater Memphis Art Council	Peggy Seessel, Dir. of Arts Education and Outreach
	Literacy, Pre K-12	Dr. Kathleen Cooter, Professor College of Education, University of Memphis
	Memphis Urban Systemic Program Update	Dr. Alfred Hall, Dir. of MUSP
11:30-12:30pm	Lunch	
12:30-3:30pm	Creating Professional Learning Communities	Academic Directors (Breakout sessions)
Thursday, June 17		
BREAKOUT SESSIONS (8:00-9:30am; 9:45-11:15am)		
8:00-11:15am	New District Policies & Grant Guidelines	Thelma Crivens, Dir. of Policy and Planning
	Communications: How to Handle the Media	Vincent McCaskill, MCS Communications Manager
	Secondary Special Education Transition Model	Pat Beane, Coordinator of Exceptional Children
	Legal Issues Update	Percy Harvey, Attorney
	Understanding NCLB, AYP, and TCAP Reports	William White, Exec. Dir. of Research and Assessment
	Parent Involvement/PTA/Memphis Urban League	Peggy Johnson, Coordinator of Special Projects
		Dr. Darryl Ukufu, President, Memphis Urban League (MUL)
		Susanne Jackson, Dir. of MUL Education & Youth Dev.
	NetTrekker	Kevin Reed, Coordinator of Staff Development
11:15-12:00pm	Lunch	
12:00-3:00pm	Human Resources Updates	Michael Goar, Assoc. Sup. of Human Resources
	Selection and Retention of Certified Section	Bob Mathes, Coordinator of Secondary Section
	(New) Teacher Performance	Dr. Lydia Abell, Quality Improvement Specialist
	Progressive Employee Discipline	Jim Davis, Dir. of Labor Relations
	Substitute Management System	Chanda Broosk, Coordinator of Special Projects
		Jerri Rudolph, Clerk of Human Resources
3:00-3:30pm	NCLB Update/Budget	Aubrey Bond, Dir. of NCLB Accountability

Friday, June 18, 2004		
8:00-9:00am	Focus on Literacy	Dr. Rick Potts, Dir. of Secondary Literacy
		Becky Bones, Scholastic
		John Avis, Associate Superintendent
		Dr. Linda Kennard, Dir. of Elem. Literacy/Early Childhood
9:00-9:15am		Bernadeia Johnson, Deputy Superintendent
9:30-10:30am	Secondary Literacy (All Secondary Principals)	Dr. Rick Potts, Dir. of Secondary Literacy
	Elementary Literacy (All Elementary Principals)	John Avis, Associate Superintendent
		Dr. Linda Kennard, Dir. of Elem. Literacy/Early Childhood
10:45-12:00pm	Breakout Sessions with Academic Directors	Academic Directors

Source: Memphis City Schools.

Exhibit 7

Comparisons of MLFP and NLNS Principal Development Programs

	Memphis Leadership Fellows Program (MLFP)	*New Leaders for New Schools (NLNS)*
Relationship with MCS		
Inaugural Year	SY04	SY05
Term Length	1 to 5 years[a]	3 years[b]
Target goal of principals developed	Unspecified	60 principals
Selection Process		
MCS staff on selection committee	Yes	Yes
Supervisor nomination required to apply	Yes	No
School administrative experience required	2 years minimum	No
Teaching experience required to apply	Yes	Yes
# applicants (SY04)	51	-
# participants selected (SY04)	23	-
# applicants (SY05)	32	250
# participants selected (SY05)	15	9
Program Components		
Full-time residency	No	Yes
Salary/stipend for participation	No[c]	$60,0000 plus benefits
Principal mentors	Yes	Yes
Leadership coach	Yes	Yes
Business coach	Yes	No
Community organization mentors	Yes	No
Ranked evaluation system	Yes	No
Job Placement in MCS		
# principals hired from first class of fellows	12	6[d]
MCS principal interview guaranteed	No	Yes
MCS job placement guaranteed	No	No
Program Costs		
Total cost per participant	$15,000	$100,000
Incremental cost to MCS per participant	$12,000	$60,000 plus benefits

Sources: Case writer created with information from Memphis Leadership Fellows Program, New Leaders for New Schools, and Memphis City Schools.

[a] The University of Memphis contracted with MCS on a yearly basis to operate MLFP, giving MCS the option to end the program at the end of each year. The program was designed to last for at least five years.

[b] The current contract includes an option to extend the program for a fourth year to develop 30 more principals.

[c] The average MCS assistant principal salaries are $64,511 for elementary schools and $66,163 for secondary schools.

[d] At the end of the case no NLNS fellows had yet been hired, but follow-up with the Memphis City Schools provided the updated information that they later hired 6 of the 9 fellows as principals. One became an assistant principal; two left MCS.

Exhibit 8

Memphis Leadership Fellows Program: Selection Evaluation Indicators

Letter of Application (Weight 1 Point)	• Expressed an in-depth level of interest in becoming an urban school leader • Expressed a desire to improve the human condition • Exhibited growth through professional development activities • Expressed a desire to foster learning opportunities for all children • Identified how participating in the Fellows program would strengthen his/her leadership ability
Resume (Weight 5 Points)	• Indicated three–five years of leadership experience in a variety of areas, indicating depth of experience • Demonstrated successful teaching experience and an understanding of global school issues • Provided evidence of effectively leading major schoolwide projects • Illustrated experience in using research to bring about change and making data-driven decisions
Essay (Weight 5 Points)	• Demonstrated excellent written communication skills • Demonstrated knowledge of at least three research-based instructional strategies • Described a method of influencing meaningful change in schools • Evidenced a belief that all children can learn • Described the use of a collaborative approach in addressing student needs • Demonstrated a willingness to assume responsibility for student learning
Letter of Nomination (Weight 10 Points)	• Noted specific leadership skills and contributions • Provided evidence of solid interpersonal relationships with various role groups • Identified specific projects led • Provided examples of the nominee's knowledge and understanding about research and change • Referred to nominee's success in at least three of the following areas: completion of instructional projects; collaboration; visionary leadership; professional development; inquiry; ethical behavior; and reflection
Interview (Weight 10 Points)	• Communicated a vision of urban leadership • Expressed a willingness to empower all stakeholders • Expressed the importance of the leader's understanding school culture • Demonstrated potential for visionary leadership, knowledge of school and classroom policies, and methods for improving student achievement • Demonstrated personal presence • Demonstrated effective oral communication skills; statements were clear, focused, and conveyed a strong belief system
Situational Activities (Weight 5 Points)	• Presented ideas in a clear manner • Expressed a willingness to take risks • Demonstrated the ability to analyze problems
Letter of Recommendation (Weight 5 Points)	• Noted specific leadership skills and contributions • Provided evidence of solid interpersonal relations with various role groups • Identified specific projects led • Provided examples of the nominee's knowledge and understanding about research and change
Leadership Inventory (Weight 5 Points)	• Demonstrated evidence of practical knowledge of leadership practice • Exhibited a belief that all children can learn

Source: Memphis Leadership Fellows Program.

Exhibit 9

New Leaders for New Schools: Selection Criteria

1. *Belief in the Potential of* All *Children to Excel Academically*
   - Believe each and every child can excel academically
   - Take personal responsibility for ensuring high academic achievement for every child
   - Demonstrate the personal drive and commitment to eliminate the disparity of educational quality that exists
2. *Commitment to Ongoing Learning*
   - Seek feedback and reflect on experiences to grow and develop
   - Demonstrate humility and willingness to continually improve
   - Commit to the coaching and the development of adults
3. *Communication and Listening*
   - Possess written and verbal skills to communicate with clarity, conciseness, and appropriateness to multiple audiences
   - Demonstrate poise and professionalism in diverse situations
   - Listen actively
4. *Interpersonal Skills*
   - Build successful one-on-one relationships
   - Value each person's perspective and treat people with respect
   - Relate to adults and children: understand where they are coming from, what they need, and how to meet their needs
   - Diffuse anger and find common ground to move people towards solutions
   - Exhibit confidence and competence under pressure
5. *Knowledge of Teaching and Learning*
   - Identify exemplary teaching
   - Provide feedback and guidance to improve instructional strategies
   - Enable students to attain results despite significant challenges
6. *Problem Solving*
   - Work proactively to solve problems and reach effective solutions
   - Analyze and diagnose complex issues to develop strategic plan
   - Identify concrete outcomes as a way to evaluate results
7. *Project Management to Deliver Results*
   - Articulate a clear vision, set agenda, and implement goals
   - Select, prioritize, and communicate strategies effectively to reach goals
   - Balance day-to-day tasks and urgent needs with progress towards goals
   - Delegate decision-making and authority in responsible manner
8. *Self-Awareness*
   - Identify accurately personal strengths and areas for development
   - Demonstrate integrity by acting in a manner that consistently reflects stated values and beliefs
   - Understand how you are perceived by and impact others
9. *Team Building*
   - Collaborate effectively
   - Read group dynamics accurately
   - Mobilize adults to take action and hold them accountable for reaching common goals
   - Engage and empower others to take responsibility in decision-making to achieve results
10. *Unyielding Focus on Goals and Results*
    - Confront difficult situations head-on and implement diverse solutions to get results
    - Achieve results despite obstacles by demonstrating persistence, determination, and relentless drive
    - Exhibit resilience to persevere and overcome setbacks
    - Take personal responsibility for finding solutions when faced with challenges
    - Be decisive and hold people to core values when it counts

Source: New Leaders for New Schools.

Exhibit 10

New Leaders for New Schools Program Content

Foundations is the year-long, academic core of the New Leaders for New Schools program. Designed to equip Residents with a comprehensive toolkit of knowledge and skills necessary to successfully lead and manage an urban public school, Foundations is best described as intense and inspirational. Foundations has two components: a six-week summer Foundations Institute and four five-day Foundations Seminars scheduled throughout the school year. (Residents who are developing new schools also attend a five-day New School Start-up Workshop.) Courses are taught by leading academics, thought leaders, experts, and master principals from around the country. They are case- and problem-based, using interactive pedagogy as much as possible and focusing on the acquisition of problem-solving skills and application of best practices.

Foundations Curriculum

Our curriculum is organized into four strands, while incorporating the common themes that impact urban school leadership: parent involvement, diversity, education policy and reform.

Transformational Leadership addresses the essence of leadership—the skills, insights, perspectives, personal voice and authority, and change management strategies necessary to lead a school that has high expectations for every child.

Instructional Leadership addresses high-quality instruction, thoughtful alignment of curriculum, standards, and assessment, effective use of data to drive student achievement, and high-functioning teacher teams.

Operational Leadership addresses building and organizational management that supports high student achievement and a positive school culture.

Local situation/job context addresses the local knowledge, networks, and skills a successful principal needs to support a high-quality school.

Residency Year

Principal Leadership Competencies (PLCs): Residents will demonstrate proficiency in the PLCs, the critical skills of successful principals as identified by New Leaders for New Schools.

Leadership Coaches & Weekly Meetings: Through direct coaching, support, and instruction on coursework and day-to-day challenges faced at Residency sites, Leadership Coaches help Residents to gain the PLCs. Coaches also lead the weekly meetings, a time for Residents to learn, reflect, problem-solve, develop skills, and support one another.

Mentor Principals & Residency Placements: Residents are in a formal mentor relationship with a highly-skilled, successful urban public school principal who shares our core beliefs, believes in our model, and is willing to train and empower aspiring leaders. If you know someone who would make a great Mentor Principal, please contact us.

Residency Project & Portfolio: Residents complete several major projects, based on their own development needs and the goals of the Residency schools. One project focuses on working with teacher teams to improve student achievement, while another focuses on the observation and supervision of instruction. In addition, each Resident compiles a portfolio of evidence that documents their fulfillment of the PLCs and serves as a resource for their future principalship.

Source: New Leaders for New Schools internal documents.

Focusing on Performance

Throughout Modules I and II, the cases and readings highlighted the performance disparities among students as the main driver of entrepreneurial opportunity in the public education sector. Over the past 30 years, scores in reading in mathematics on the National Assessment of Educational Progress (NAEP) have been flat, and the nearly three-grade-level gap between low-income and minority students and the rest of the population has remained stable. In international comparisons, although U.S. 10-year-olds score near the top, by the time they are 15, they perform near the bottom in math and science and in the middle of the pack in reading. In response to this data, states began to implement standards and mechanisms for measuring student performance in the late 1990s. Currently, nearly all states have developed common standards in some content areas and annual exams at various grade levels to assess students' mastery of those standards. When it went into effect in 2002, No Child Left Behind (NCLB) loosely gathered the separate state efforts into a national accountability system by establishing a common set of consequences for schools that persistently failed to meet their state's standards of performance overall and for specific categories of students (low-income, race/ethnicity, special education).

The combination of the state and federal regulatory mandates created a market for technology systems that could collect, disaggregate, and analyze performance data so that districts could track the outcomes of their students and make better decisions about interventions that would help them improve. Inundated with reams of data about student performance, the districts, schools, and education-related nonprofits also needed new processes and systems that could help them use the data effectively to diagnose and respond successfully to student learning needs to meet the requirements of state and federal legislation.

Module III includes four cases that highlight organizations focused on performance management tools and systems. Along with the cases, your instructor might assign an article by Amy Edmondson, "The Competitive Advantage of Learning," which explains some of the conditions necessary for organizational learning and the need to balance them with accountability for results to perform well and continuously improve. With the advent of the standards movement and No Child Left Behind, accountability for performance has increased dramatically for educators with a goal of improving student outcomes. Edmondson's research shows that high-performing organizations in several industries not only have accountability for demanding goals, but also have environments in which professionals are comfortable using performance data to collaboratively solve performance problems. The cases in this module will allow you to apply these ideas to education.

The first case is about Duval County Public Schools in Florida, a district committed to building a data system and holding principals accountable for using it to improve the performance of their schools. The new principal in the case works hard to meet all the superintendent's expectations for data use and requires her teachers to make "data-driven decisions." At the end of its first year, the school's scores actually get worse instead of better. The case provokes a discussion about the dual purposes of performance data: accountability and organizational learning. The case allows for an exploration of the conditions that must be in place for schools to be successful in a data-driven effort and introduces large districts as potential customers of technology companies with products designed to help them use data effectively.

The next two cases explore technology companies that provide tools to districts and schools that will help them use student information and performance data more effectively. SchoolNet has a content-neutral platform that allows districts to track multiple curricula and content standards across all grade levels to keep track of student performance and generate the reports necessary for state and NCLB compliance. The case "SchoolNet: Pursuing Opportunity Beyond Federal Mandates" allows for an analysis of the market dynamics that a company has to contend with when selling to school districts, and because the case is positioned at a time when the company must pitch a renewal of its contract with its largest customer, a review of the case allows for a discussion about how one might evaluate the success of a company such as this beyond its financial performance.

"Wireless Generation," written about the company of the same name, focuses on the company's product development strategy (rather than its sales strategy as in the SchoolNet case). The case raises important questions about the opportunities and constraints a company faces when partnering with specific states and districts to develop products that it hopes will be generic enough to address the needs of many districts in a fragmented market. The SchoolNet and Wireless Generation cases also allow for a comparison of products focused on accountability and organizational learning. Both cases raise questions about the importance of government regulation in creating and expanding product markets and the implications that changes in the regulatory environment can have for a company's product portfolio and growth prospects.

"Focusing on Results at the New York City Department of Education" explores the efforts of the largest school district in the United States as it implements a variety of performance systems and technology tools to support a decentralized structure in which principals are expected to behave entrepreneurially. The case allows for a healthy discussion about the difficulty in managing the tension between accountability for demanding goals and the supportive environment necessary for organizational learning. It also introduces an approach to shifting an organizational culture by implementing specific systems and structures that change the way people interact with the organization and with each other.

Module Questions

Each case has its own study questions, but below are some module-wide questions to consider as you work through the cases:

1. What are the implications of Amy Edmondson's work ("The Competitive Imperative of Learning," *Harvard Business Review*, July 2008) on the tensions between accountability and organizational learning for each case in the module?
2. What are the unique challenges of the education context for companies attempting to sell products and services aimed at improving performance?
3. How important are regulatory mandates in creating product markets and changing behaviors and beliefs about performance in U.S. public education? Specifically, if the regulations were removed, how confident are you that the leaders in the sector would continue to focus on accountability and organization learning as mutually reinforcing forces for improving performance?

CASE 3.1

Allen Grossman ■ James P. Honan ■ Caroline King

Learning to Manage with Data in Duval County Public Schools: Lake Shore Middle School (A)

As Lake Shore Middle School Principal Iranetta Wright drove toward Region III Superintendent Mary Brown's office in early June 2004, she felt both nervous and confident. As part of Wright's personnel evaluation, Brown had called a meeting with Wright to discuss Lake Shore's academic performance in SY04.[1] A lot was riding on the meeting for Wright, a first-year principal in the Duval County Public School (DCPS) district.

Wright knew that Brown would ask her to explain the school's 2004 Florida Comprehensive Assessment Test (FCAT) results. Nearly 70% of Lake Shore students had not met the state's rigorous standards in reading and math. Sixth and seventh graders' scores on the FCAT had declined substantially from SY03, while eighth graders made modest gains. At the end of SY04, the school's grade had dropped from a C to a D under Florida's high-stakes accountability system. Lake Shore was clearly falling further behind the district and state (see **Exhibit 1** for student achievement trends).

The SY04 results were far from what Wright had envisioned when she was appointed Lake Shore's principal in the summer of 2003. During her first staff meeting, Wright had announced her goal of making Lake Shore the first A school in Region III of DCPS. Wright recalled how much time and effort she, her leadership team, and teachers had invested in using data to identify students' needs and implementing strategies to increase achievement for every student. Clearly, the school had experienced some major challenges in SY04—a new and inexperienced principal, an influx of low-performing students, and one-third of the staff's being first-year teachers. But Wright was not one to look for excuses, and she knew Brown would not accept any. Wright was confident that she had made the best managerial and instructional decisions possible based on the available data, her staff's capacity, and the school's resources.

Wright also anticipated Brown asking her to evaluate her own effectiveness as an instructional leader and her ability to raise student achievement at Lake Shore in SY05. DCPS had developed a strong culture of accountability for results, and Wright knew she was not guaranteed a second chance at Lake Shore. Wright felt that she and her staff had learned a lot from SY04 that would help the school improve next year. And Wright remained committed to seeing Lake Shore earn Region III's first A. As she pulled into the parking lot outside Brown's office, Wright prepared to present her reflections and determination to Brown.

Duval County Public Schools

History and Demographics

Following the consolidation of the City of Jacksonville and Duval County governments in 1968, DCPS served the largest city in land area in the contiguous United States. In 2004, nearly 800,000 residents called Duval County home, with a population 74% white, 22% African-American, and 4% other minority groups. Approximately 47% of adults in the county were functionally illiterate.[2] At 18.16%, the county had the highest percentage of students attending private schools in Florida.[3]

In SY04, approximately 130,000 students attended the district's 166 schools, making DCPS the sixth-largest school system in Florida and the 20th-largest in the United States. DCPS was divided into five administrative regions. The district's coastal areas (Regions IV and V) were more affluent and higher performing academically than the inland communities to the north and west (Regions I, II, and III). Whites comprised 46% of the student body, African-Americans 43%, Hispanics 5%, Asians 3%, and other ethnic/racial groups 3%. Fifty-nine percent of DCPS students attended "racially diverse schools."[4] Nearly 50% of students were eligible for free or reduced-price meals, and 3,000 students were learning English for the first time (see **Exhibit 2** for DCPS demographics).

Governance

The Duval County School Board (the Board) was the official policymaking body for DCPS. County residents elected seven members to serve four-year terms. Prior to the late 1990s, the relationship between the Board and DCPS leadership was strained. According to a local reporter in 2003, "One of the biggest slashes to the school system's reputation over the past years has not even focused on the academic achievement of students, but rather on the once-dubbed dysfunctional relationship between the School Board and the superintendent."[5] Indeed, the Board had ousted two superintendents, Herb Sang (1976–1989) and Larry Zenke (1989–1996), prior to their contracts' expiration.

Beginning in 1991, the Florida legislature required a school advisory council (SAC) comprising the principal and elected parents, students, faculty, staff, and community members in every school. SACs assisted in the preparation, evaluation, and implementation of an annual state-mandated school improvement plan (SIP) designed to improve student achievement. SACs also helped prepare and approve a school's budget.

Superintendent John C. Fryer's Strategy: Aim High and Fryer's High Five

Background

By a 6–1 vote, the Board appointed John C. Fryer, Jr., a retired two-star U.S. Air Force general, DCPS superintendent in June 1998. Fryer sought out the new position, which he often referred to as "a calling," because he felt that he could contribute his leadership and management skills to the district.[6] When Fryer assumed the helm of DCPS in August 1998, he observed, "What I see now is a lot of individual programs and efforts. But I don't see a system, and I don't see a coherence to it all."[7] Reflecting back on his early days, Fryer recalled, "People warned me that I wouldn't find high-caliber employees in DCPS, but I found very hard-working and committed people. They just needed help thinking strategically."

Strategy: Fryer's High Five

Having spent nearly a year reading about education reform efforts nationwide, Fryer walked into DCPS with a strategy and a vision. Fryer adopted the Air Force motto "Aim High" and unveiled five strategic priorities that quickly came to be known as "Fryer's High Five":

1. Academic achievement
2. Safety and discipline

3. High-performance management
4. Learning communities
5. Accountability

Fryer described academic achievement as the overarching aim. In 1999, the Board formally adopted "Fryer's High Five," and in 2002, the Board enacted a five-year strategic plan with action strategies and performance metrics for the High Five. Fryer's team aligned the High Five metrics with Florida's Sunshine State Standards (SSS)[8] and internally developed student performance standards in an effort to drive a districtwide focus on results.

Stakeholder Relationships

Under Fryer's leadership, the Board–superintendent relationship transformed from adversarial to productive and focused on improving academic achievement. This shift occurred despite the fact that Fryer served under 13 different Board members from 1998 to 2004. In 2003, the Board awarded Fryer with his highest performance marks ever and a new three-year contract.[9]

After an initial period of distrust, Fryer also improved relations with the local collective bargaining unit, Duval Teachers United (DTU). By SY04, both DTU President Terrie Brady and Fryer described their organizations' relationship as "productive and collaborative." Fryer also mobilized the Jacksonville business community. In January 1999, area CEOs established the World Class Alliance for Education to coordinate financial and volunteer efforts with High Five goals.

High-Stakes Accountability: External and Internal Demands for Data

At the turn of the twenty-first century, DCPS had to respond to mounting external pressures to report student-achievement data. Concurrently, Fryer's commitments to standards-based education and developing a results-oriented system created an internal demand for data.

Federal and State Regulations

In January 2002, President George W. Bush signed into law the No Child Left Behind Act of 2001 (NCLB), a framework for improving the country's public schools driven by rigorous standards and high-stakes accountability. NCLB set a nationwide goal for all public school students to achieve proficiency in reading and mathematics by 2014 and established annual adequate yearly progress (AYP) targets to benchmark schools' progress. For the first time, states, districts, and schools were required to report a wide range of achievement data, and schools were rewarded or sanctioned based on their students' performance (see **Exhibit 3** for key NCLB provisions).

Concurrently, Florida boasted a rigorous standards-based state accountability system. The Florida A+ Accountability Plan (A+ Plan) rated each Florida public school annually with a letter grade, ranging from A to F, based on students' participation, performance, and growth on the Florida Comprehensive Achievement Test (FCAT).[10] School and district rankings quickly became front-page news and carried serious consequences. While high-performing schools earned monetary and other incentives, D and F schools, labeled "challenged schools," received school improvement funds and frequent state monitoring. If a school received two F grades in four years, districts had to provide students with an "opportunity scholarship"—the ability to transfer into a higher-performing public school or a voucher to attend a private school. In SY03, the Florida Department of Education aligned the A+ Plan with NCLB requirements.

Fryer's Drive for Data

Fryer quickly realized that the district lacked the information systems to track student, school, and district progress toward the High Five goals and state standards. Chief of Staff Nancy Snyder recalled the superintendent drawing an analogy to his military career: "Mr. Fryer often said, 'I could not have survived in air-to-air battle in my F-16 if my radar had only swept once a year. I need an instrument panel or a dashboard if I'm going to fly this plane at DCPS. We need real-time data about how our students, schools, and staff are doing if we're going to learn and continuously improve over time.'"

The nameplate outside Fryer's office, "Chief Learner," revealed his approach toward data as a resource for learning rather than for punitive or command-and-control purposes. Signaling his commitment to instilling data-driven decision making in DCPS, Fryer moved Director of Research and Evaluation Tim Ballentine and his team next door to the superintendent's office. When Fryer arrived, the district did not have its own infrastructure to house historical student data; instead, DCPS paid to use the City of Jacksonville's computer mainframe. Frustrated with the costs and inefficiencies of this arrangement, Fryer charged Ballentine with creating a data warehouse in SY00, enabling the district to store, update, and retrieve data daily. Fryer also directed staff to establish a mission control room (MCR) to graphically display the district's annual performance and progress toward the High Five goals (see **Exhibit 4** for MCR indicators). As a result of the district's new data investments, DCPS officials estimated that spending on research, evaluation, and technology increased from 1.3% to 2.1% of the annual budget between SY98 and SY04 (see **Exhibit 5**).

Developing the Data-Driven Principal

Fryer's own priority was to support his "core commanders," the principals, and specifically to strengthen their ability to use data to improve teaching and learning in the classroom. Fryer and his five regional superintendents revamped the recruitment, training, and evaluation procedures for principals to focus on instructional leadership and data-driven decision making. Principals visited the MCR during monthly principal conferences instituted in SY99, and many constructed similar rooms in their own schools. Starting in SY01, Ballentine's team created "research data affects change" (RESDAC) reports to provide every principal with student data; however, many principals viewed the 500-plus page RESDAC spreadsheets as more cumbersome than helpful.

Introducing the AIDE Data System

As DCPS struggled to provide actionable data to principals, the district drew upon the expertise of some data-savvy staff. Jill Budd, principal of Duncan Fletcher Middle School, and Patrick Barr, a district information technology staff member, began designing templates that Budd could re-create throughout the year. As news of Barr and Budd's innovations spread, Fryer asked Barr to build a user-friendly and interactive Web-based tool so that all principals could run similar reports. In response, Barr developed and piloted the Academic Interpretation and Data Evaluation (AIDE) system in SY03.[11]

AIDE allowed principals to view and analyze the RESDAC student data from their desktop computers. Like the RESDAC reports, AIDE student records contained demographic information (e.g., age, ethnicity) and achievement data (e.g., FCAT scores and course grades for the previous year). AIDE disaggregated students' FCAT scores by the subject tests' skill sets, called "strands" (see **Exhibit 6** for FCAT subject-test strands). AIDE also identified academically at-risk students by assigning one of five additional AIDE variables based on the student's FCAT performance. For example, AIDE assigned the variable "lowest 25%" to any student whose FCAT scale score fell in the school's bottom quartile.

Principals received AIDE datasets five times during the school year, one prior to the first day of class and updated versions at the end of each quarter, that included course grades and benchmark test results. Principals were able to create color-coded reports that sorted and presented student data for the entire school or by grade, subject, teacher, individual student, or FCAT achievement level, which ranged from a low of one to a high of five, with three considered "proficient." The colors reflected students' FCAT levels: red identified Level 1s and 2s; green Level 3s, 4s, and 5s; and yellow flagged students to monitor.

In SY04, all principals and their administrative leadership teams had access to and were expected to use AIDE. At the end of SY04, the district launched Managing Academic Progress (MAP), a management tool developed by Barr that contained 81 suggested AIDE tasks for principals to complete during the school year (see **Exhibit 7**). Barr also designed AIDE Express, a wizard-based report program that answered the 10 most frequently asked data questions in AIDE.

Reactions to AIDE

Principals voiced various opinions about how the RESDAC and AIDE data had changed their role and use of time. One middle school principal welcomed the ability to "see where my students are, where we want them to be, and key areas we need to improve in to get there." Others, like one challenged school principal, felt overwhelmed: "My education did not prepare me to be a data analyst. And if I cannot understand the data or figure out next steps, how can I expect that of my teachers?" Most principals agreed, however, that the availability of data was helpful, and one high school principal praised the AIDE program for making the data so accessible:

> The data is very friendly now, and now that it's color coded, you can pull it up and people see exactly what the data is saying. It's like a traffic light. Anything that shows up in red means that you're in trouble and you really need to look in those areas. If it has yellow, it means that you're cautious, and green means you're OK. It's really useful when you have conferences with teachers, parents, and students.

A challenged-school elementary principal noted the impact of data on her teachers:

> Data has been a powerful tool for changing teachers' beliefs. The data showed that some teachers who always believed they were the best in the school actually weren't making the highest gains, which devastated some of the teachers but also motivated them to learn new techniques. The data also dispelled the belief that some students just cannot learn at high levels—they can improve, they just need effective and differentiated instruction.

Managing with Data at Lake Shore Middle School

Principal Iranetta Wright

A graduate of Duval's William M. Raines High School, Wright joined DCPS in 1993 as a mathematics teacher at Douglas Anderson School for the Arts. After four years in the classroom, she left DCPS to become a successful senior salesperson for Mary Kay Cosmetics. After winning the Mary Kay pink Cadillac for her record high sales, Wright decided to return to her self-described "passion," teaching, and was hired as a special education teacher at Lake Shore Middle School in SY98. During the year, Wright assumed various leadership positions and earned her administrative credential. She served as assistant principal at Fletcher Middle School from SY99 to SY02 and was appointed vice principal in SY03. Wright flourished under Principal

Jill Budd's leadership in learning how to mine the RESDAC and AIDE data files. She recalled:

> When we piloted the AIDE program in SY03, our data-mining work became much less time consuming and tedious, which really allowed us to focus on being diagnostic and prescriptive as instructional leaders. In other words what's really important—what specifically were we going to do differently to help every student achieve at high levels. AIDE also made it easier to draw our coaches and teachers into the conversations about student performance. Finally, when everyone in the school had the data, we all had to take ownership of it and teachers started analyzing the data themselves. As our superintendent likes to say, "There's nowhere to hide."

In July 2003, Wright returned to Lake Shore, this time as a first-year principal. Region III Superintendent Mary Brown commented on Wright's selection: "We thought that Iranetta had the energy and experience—particularly the skills she developed using the AIDE data at Fletcher—to be a guiding light at Lake Shore and help move that school forward." Wright also considered her appointment to Lake Shore "a perfect match" given her prior experience in the school, expertise with the school's large special needs student population, and commitment to high performance.

Lake Shore Demographics and Achievement

In SY04, Lake Shore Middle School enrolled 1,293 students in grades six through eight. Fifty-two percent of Lake Shore's students were African-American, 38% white, 5% Hispanic, and 4% Asian. Nearly 60% received free or reduced-price meals, 20% participated in special education, and less than 1% were limited English proficient.

Lake Shore had enjoyed stable leadership, as Wright's predecessor served as the school's principal from SY95 through SY03. In concert with Fryer's districtwide reform efforts, Lake Shore had implemented standards-based reforms schoolwide, used mathematics and literacy coaches to help improve teachers' practice, and enrolled many veteran teachers in data analysis training workshops. Lake Shore students performed below district and state averages (see **Exhibit 1**), and the DCPS individual school profile demonstrated that a wide achievement gap divided white and minority students (see **Exhibit 8**). At the end of SY03, Lake Shore's state letter grade improved from a D to a C.

Lake Shore's Action Plan

Strategic Planning

Needs Assessment

Wright remembered her first days as the new Lake Shore principal. Excited, and a bit overwhelmed, she called Lake Shore's leadership team—comprising her vice principal, three grade-level or house administrators, mathematics and literacy coaches, department chairs, and lead teachers—together to start planning for SY04. Wright and her team assessed the overall needs of their sixth, seventh, and eighth graders by running the AIDE FCAT executive summary reports for reading and math (see **Exhibit 9**). Red dominated the color-coded reports, as about 70% of Lake Shore's students were performing below grade level as reflected by their Level 1 or 2 FCAT scores.

Next, the team generated the FCAT reading and math content score A+ reports to show how individual students scored on the different FCAT strands (see **Exhibit 10**). From these, Wright and her colleagues identified two major areas of weakness across all grade levels: words and phrases on the reading exam, and number sense in mathematics. Using the A+ report's real-time calculator, the team calculated that at least 50 students would need to move up to a

Level 3 on both the FCAT reading and math exams in order to improve Lake Shore's letter grade to a B. The companion FCAT reading and math content score NCLB reports showed that Lake Shore's African-American, Hispanic, and limited English-proficient students did not meet NCLB adequate yearly progress (AYP) goals in SY03. An NCLB calculator enabled the team to see the percentage of students in each ethnic or ability group that would need to make gains on the FCAT to meet AYP targets for SY04.

The team also looked at reports to see how students of different teachers in the same grade level and subject performed on the FCAT (see **Exhibit 11**). A teacher demonstrated "gains" if an average of his students' FCAT achievement level increased; a teacher showed "losses" if her students' achievement level declined. Wright also pulled student data from Lake Shore's eight elementary feeder schools to get a sense of the incoming sixth graders. While seven of the feeders were A schools, sixth graders' performance had often dropped once they came to Lake Shore in past years.

The school faced additional challenges. In order to comply with Florida's new class-size reduction amendment and fill vacant positions due to attrition, Wright had to hire 23 teachers (about a quarter of the teaching staff) before the first day of school.[12] Lake Shore was also scheduled to receive 112 opportunity scholarship students transferring out of low-performing schools.

Designing a School Improvement Plan

As required by state law, Wright met with her school advisory council (SAC) in August to design Lake Shore's school improvement plan (SIP). As with all schools in DCPS, the SIP articulated the school's targets and strategies to meet Fryer's High Five goals. The district set the school's annual academic achievement targets based on the long-range goal of having every student score a 3 or above on the FCAT and demonstrate at least one year's growth on the test. Based on their needs assessment and data analysis, Wright, her team, and the SAC established targets for the other four High Five goals and outlined strategies, timelines, and responsibilities for all five goals.

Organizing to Meet Students' Needs

Class Scheduling

Lake Shore's 85 teachers worked in teams of four (math, reading, social studies, and science teachers), with each team assigned between 85 and 100 students. Teachers "looped" or remained with the same students in seventh and eighth grades. Wright selected specific teachers to work with some of the more at-risk students in remedial math and reading classes, which enrolled approximately 450 students with Level 1 FCAT scores. She then distributed students by FCAT level proportionately across the other teams. When teachers arrived for their in-service planning day before the first day of school, they received AIDE data profiles on every student in their class and on their team, often referred to within the district as "the hand you've been dealt." A first-year sixth-grade math teacher recalled feeling "overwhelmed by the data at first. My class report was almost entirely red with every student scoring a Level 1 or 2. I was new, and they were deficient in almost every area; we were starting at ground zero together."

Schoolwide Interventions

Recognizing that nearly 70% of Lake Shore students were performing below grade level, Wright instituted a number of schoolwide interventions. Wright asked every student to read 25 books per year, a campaign originally introduced by Fryer in SY99, and continued the "Principal's Book of the Month" initiative, which began under her predecessor. During monthly department meetings, teachers and coaches selected a "reading strategy of the month" to reinforce literacy skills in the classroom. Wright also invited students' parents and family members to attend four family nights during the school year.

Safety Nets

Wright and her colleagues designed "safety net" programs to provide extra support to low-performing students. Safety nets were targeted at students scoring Level 1 or Level 2 on the FCAT, students performing in Lake Shore's lowest 25%, and bubble students, those scoring 10 points above or below a Level 3. Year-round safety nets included new remedial mathematics and reading classes and before- and after-school tutoring sessions. With the FCAT approaching in mid-February, Wright sent student profile reports (**Exhibit 12**) to the parents and family members of the Level 1 and 2 students in January. Wright sent the report with a cover note identifying the student's weakest strands and inviting the student to attend a two-week after-school "ramp-up" session focused on his or her specific strand(s) of weakness.

Supporting Teachers to Use Data

Given the high percentage of new teachers, Wright and her leadership team provided biweekly training sessions for teachers and staff on data analysis, FCAT strands, standards, and instructional strategies. Additional training was provided in mandatory grade-level meetings that took place monthly during teachers' free planning period and in quarterly "vertical breakouts," required meetings for teachers of the same subject across grade levels that occurred on paid professional development days. Teachers were also encouraged to attend monthly department meetings before school and to maintain and update data notebooks to track students' progress over the year.

In addition to making data more accessible, Wright tried to change teachers' attitudes, commenting, "I want our teachers and staff to understand that the data is here to help us learn how we can be more effective for our students. It's not an 'I got you.' We're all in this together because Lake Shore's test scores are public, everyone knows our business. We have to know why our students are struggling and what our challenges are in order to improve."

Monitoring Performance

Student Assessments

Lake Shore staff evaluated students' progress during the school year through two schoolwide assessments. In October, Lake Shore administered a prewriting assessment to all students in anticipation of the eighth graders' first FCAT writing exam in February. In early January, all students took an FCAT reading and mathematics practice exam prepared by Lake Shore's math and literacy coaches.

While teachers frequently asked for benchmark data, literacy coach Katrina Short observed that the practice exam had limited impact: "The students scored very low on the practice exams, but we didn't believe that those results adequately reflected their performance or all the work we had done in the fall to prepare them for the FCAT. Instead, we thought we had designed the test poorly. In retrospect, we know that what the test was telling us was more right than wrong." Wright shared the results of the practice exam with teachers and students, arguing that "I learned during my time at Fletcher that comparing teachers and classrooms fosters a healthy competition in the school, especially among the students. They start saying, 'We have to beat Ms. Green's class on this test or the FCAT.'"

Concurrently, individual teachers designed their own tests and projects to evaluate students, and departments administered common assessments at the end of each nine-week quarter. Teachers discussed student progress in weekly team meetings during their planning periods, their department and grade-level meetings, and oftentimes informally during breaks or after school. Using an AIDE quarterly tracking chart, administrators and teachers monitored students' course grades, compared student achievement across teacher teams, and identified students earning below a 2.0 grade point average (GPA).

However, the most intensive and anticipated student assessment was the FCAT 2004. All Lake Shore students took the FCAT reading and math exams over four days in mid-February. Eighth graders also took the FCAT science and writing tests.

Teachers' Performance

Wright and her administrative team developed the "quick peek" process to evaluate teaching and learning at Lake Shore. During a quick peek, Wright or another administrator observed a classroom for about 15 to 20 minutes and evaluated the teacher's implementation of the Sunshine State Standards and use of effective instructional strategies using a checklist aligned with the teachers' formal evaluation rubric (see **Exhibit 13**). The administrator left a copy of the quick peek checklist with the teacher, and either party could ask for a follow-up meeting to discuss the feedback. Administrators conducted about one quick peek per month for every teacher.

As needed, Wright and her administrators scheduled conferences with teachers performing below their expectations. Wright met with every teaching team at the end of each quarter to discuss its students' performance. If any student on the team was earning below a 2.0 GPA, Wright handed out a student profile report (see **Exhibit 12**) to each team member and asked the team to design a comprehensive strategy to help the student improve. Wright also used the opportunity to compare student achievement across teaching teams.

School Performance

Wright shared Lake Shore's challenges and current issues with other principals, Regional Superintendent Brown, and the regional director during the Region III monthly principal conferences. The SAC reviewed the school improvement plan twice during the school year. Two small teams of visiting principals and central office staff conducted a "snapshot"—a districtwide process used to observe the implementation of standards in schools—at Lake Shore. At the beginning of the year, a data-driven decision-making snapshot team met with Wright, observed classrooms, and evaluated Lake Shore using a districtwide rubric (see **Exhibit 14**). The snapshot team found Lake Shore to be in the lowest implementation level, or preparing stage. In March, a second snapshot team observed Lake Shore's implementation of reading standards and again found the school in the preparing stage. Wright remarked:

> The reading snapshot was a real eye-opener. Even with all the teacher training and observations we've done, we learned that our teachers were not connecting all of the dots—the standards, our students' areas of deficit on the FCAT, the instructional strategies our coaches try to model, etc. After the snapshot, I gave every teacher the implementation rubric and the observers' feedback. We met as a school and discussed teachers' questions, what each level on the rubric meant, and shared ideas about how to improve.

Measuring Results

Principal and Teacher Evaluations

In September, Wright entered her school improvement plan targets for each of the High

Five goals into the online Appraisal Plus system, the district's performance-evaluation tool for school administrators implemented in SY03. Administrators received points based on how many targets were achieved. The targets were weighted according to the High Five goals: academic performance (40%), safety and discipline (10%), high-performance management (25%), learning communities (10%), and accountability (15%). Based on the total score, administrators were recommended for *incentive, annual reappointment, probationary annual reappointment,* or *no reappointment*. During Wright's midyear review in January, she and Brown discussed Lake Shore's progress toward the school's academic targets established by the central office. Wright recalled that "In January, I still felt very optimistic that we would meet our academic performance targets."

Wright frequently discussed student-achievement data with teachers during quick peeks, conferences, quarterly meetings, and the districtwide teachers' evaluations that took place every March. She explained the role of student-achievement data in teachers' evaluations:

> I make reference to how students performed on the previous year's FCAT—if they made gains or losses—and how students are performing during the current school year, but we're not at the point yet where we use FCAT data alone to dismiss or reward someone. There are just too many other variables that impact how a student scored and other reasons why a teacher may not be effective for Lake Shore students. In fact, I dismissed one teacher this year whose students made quite high gains on the FCAT.

School Climate Survey

Administered in every DCPS school each spring, the SY04 school climate survey asked parents, employees, and students to rate their school's quality of instruction, staff, and safety. Compared to the SY03 survey results, Lake Shore students and staff gave higher marks for the principal's leadership, implementation of standards, and quality of instruction; however, parents' satisfaction declined slightly in these same areas.

FCAT 2004

In mid-May 2004, the Florida Department of Education released the 2004 FCAT results (see **Exhibit 1** for Lake Shore's results). Wright was clearly disappointed that the school had not met its academic performance targets. The percentage of Lake Shore's sixth and seventh graders scoring a Level 3 or above in reading had dropped between eight and 10 percentage points, while eighth graders made small gains. In math, sixth graders' performance also declined by five percentage points, while seventh and eighth graders' scores remained stagnant.

Wright also analyzed the data by teacher. Since the new FCAT data would not be uploaded into the AIDE program for a few more weeks, Wright created her own chart that showed students' gains and losses by teacher and distributed the chart to every teacher (see **Exhibit 15**). Wright explained her rationale for the transparency:

> Reporting the gains and losses by teacher helps us start very specific conversations with our teachers about their students' performance and to identify curriculum and instructional gaps. I expect teachers who are teaching the same subject, grade, and level kids to have gains within plus or minus 5% of each other. If one doesn't, we need to explore if there is an issue with that teacher's instructional strategies. On the other hand, if all the teachers have very low gains or losses, it may signal a curriculum issue—either something is getting taught out of sequence or not at all.

By Wright's calculations, Lake Shore's letter grade would drop to a D and the school would not demonstrate adequate yearly progress under NCLB. Wright shared her reaction:

> At first, I was deflated because we had put in so much time and hard work, and we felt we had been very strategic in our efforts. Then, I started looking at the results by grade level and strands, and the performance of specific students. I want our school to first celebrate what worked well. Then, we need to talk about what the data is telling us in order to start learning what we can do differently to improve next year.

Challenges For Continuous Improvement

Professional Development: Translating Data Analysis to Instructional Strategies

Teachers

Lake Shore's staff observed that teachers needed additional professional development to make their instruction more data driven. A veteran math teacher said, "We really needed more training up front about what content areas and skills are going to be tested in each FCAT strand." A remedial math teacher commented, "Over 75% of my Level 1 sixth graders made gains on the 2004 FCAT math exam. Some of my students went from a Level 1 to a Level 4 in one year! It is amazing, but I need help trying to figure out which instructional strategies had the most impact so that we can share them with other teachers and schools."

Wright observed that the "reading strategy of the month" professional development sessions had not been as effective as she had hoped. Wright also noted that she could have done a better job of sharing student data with teachers: "This year, we only gave teachers the student profile reports for students identified as at risk for failing at the end of each quarter. Otherwise, teachers never saw how their students performed in other subjects or content areas of the FCAT."

Administrators

Wright acknowledged that she was trying to build expertise on her leadership team: "Our coaches, department chairs, house administrators, even my vice principal and I, all need more training. We're all trying to learn how to learn from the data together." Fryer acknowledged that strengthening the capacity of principals and other administrators to analyze and use data proved an ongoing challenge for the entire district: "Learning how to support our new and experienced principals to use data more effectively is a constant training need. We reinforce the message that data-driven decision making is integral to being an effective instructional leader through our monthly principal conferences and the summer principal institute."

Training and Supporting New Teachers

Wright and others described the difficulties associated with providing adequate training and support to Lake Shore's high number of new teachers. By the end of SY04, Lake Shore had 35 first-year teachers—almost a third of its teaching force—who either started at the beginning of the school year or came midyear due to attrition, and the school expected to have about 20 new teachers in SY05. The impact on students was tangible, as one parent and member of Lake Shore's SAC commented: "My daughter had three different seventh-grade science teachers this year and a substitute for half the year."

Wright observed, "We need to figure out a way to help our new teachers develop a sense of community here at Lake Shore, connect with other teachers and administrators, and get the mentoring and ongoing support that they need. I know that some of our first-year teachers just felt lost in the shuffle, isolated, and sometimes, overwhelmed." However, Wright also was quick to defend the performance of her first-year teachers, noting:

> Our FCAT scores declined the most in the sixth grade, which was also the grade with most of our new teachers and transfer students from low-performing schools. However, when I compared students' gains and losses across teachers, I was surprised to find that some of the first-year teachers had even higher percentages of students that improved their FCAT achievement level compared to the veterans.

Wright had company, as principals throughout DCPS struggled to train and support the massive influx of new teachers required to comply with the state's new class-size reduction (CSR) amendment. "The CSR requirements have stretched the district's training capacity far beyond what we could have ever programmed in advance," noted Fryer. Indeed, the district estimated that the new hires would increase the district's teaching force from 6,000 in SY03 to over 8,500 by SY05.

Curriculum, Assessment, and Alignment

Curriculum

During the year, the Lake Shore staff identified some areas of misalignment among their curriculum, the state standards, and the FCAT. For example, a first-year sixth-grade math teacher recalled, "The FCAT practice exam at the end of January was a real wake-up call for me and the other math teachers. The test really pushed hard on fractions, but we had just started covering fractions in class. We switched gears and taught our students everything we could about fractions, but we really only had a few weeks before the FCAT."

Assessment

Almost every Lake Shore teacher and administrator talked about the need for more frequent benchmark data. A veteran math teacher commented:

> I really wish we administered a baseline test at the beginning of the year to capture what students learned between when they took the FCAT in February and the end of the school year in May. Sure, the FCAT AIDE data is useful, but it misses four months of learning. And we need quarterly or end-of-unit assessments so that we can evaluate if our curriculum and lesson plans are truly aligned with the state standards and the FCAT and so we can pinpoint students' areas of weaknesses on an ongoing basis.

Assistant Superintendent for Curriculum and Instruction Ed Pratt-Dannals noted that these issues were not unique to Lake Shore. Pratt-Dannals described the challenge of aligning standards, curriculum, instruction, assessments, professional development, and performance evaluation as "a constant work in progress in which data plays an integral role. We used data to set our High Five targets and develop a strategic plan to reach them, but we are also constantly collecting data on our students to measure our progress, learn, and fine-tune our work." Pratt-Dannals also noted that "Our principals and teachers are constantly asking for districtwide formative assessments and benchmark tests so that they can assess students' progress in real time and not have to wait for the FCAT scores to come back at the end of the year."

Sharing Best Practices Across Classrooms and Schools

The eighth graders' FCAT gains confirmed for Wright, her team, and teachers that "looping" was having a positive impact on student achievement. Wright commented, "By the time students reach eighth grade, their teachers already know their individual strengths and weaknesses and feel more ownership for their success. Unfortunately, we cannot start looping in the sixth grade because most of our sixth-grade teachers are only certified as elementary teachers and cannot teach seventh and eighth graders."

The availability of data also had the potential to galvanize discussions among teachers. A first-year math teacher said, "This year, 25% of my students improved on the FCAT. Next year, my goal is for 50% to make gains. I want to work with my team and other math teachers so I can figure out how to learn from my mistakes and know what questions to ask next year so that I can make that goal a reality." A veteran math teacher said that sharing teachers' gains and losses was sometimes uncomfortable, but useful:

> Two years ago, my students didn't improve and I was really embarrassed, but then I realized that I had to get over my pride and figure out my weak areas. We're all professionals, and we have to adopt the mind-set that we're all capable of learning how to learn from each other and improve. When I got Mrs. Wright's chart that showed the percentage of students who improved an FCAT level by teacher, I saw that 62% of my students made gains this year, but others teachers had over 80%, so I decided to ask those teachers what they did. We're all in this together, and it benefits me as much as another teacher to help each other.

However, a veteran social studies teacher observed, "We have a lot of support and training on data use this year, and we talk a lot about it as a team, but it's hard to find the time to analyze data in an in-depth way with other teachers and colleagues in an ongoing and meaningful way."

Creating a High-Performance Culture with Accountability

Cultural changes at Lake Shore proved difficult and were often met with skepticism. Literacy coach Short noted, "One of our greatest challenges is getting total buy-in about the importance of data use and then to actually train teachers how to analyze data. Most of our new teachers were not trained in a college of education, so they are basically teaching the way they were taught and do not know what to do differently. And some of our veteran teachers resist change." Some veteran teachers suggested that Wright's appetite for data, leadership style, and focus on accountability had changed Lake Shore's culture and affected morale. A social studies teacher commented that the administration's attitude toward data use and teacher practice had gone from "benign neglect under the previous principal to micromanagement at times under Mrs. Wright." A mathematics teacher added, "Wright was very up front about wanting Lake Shore to be the first A school in Region III, and her management style has been very aggressive. Administrators had never visited our classrooms so often; we started calling this the 'year of observation.'"

Communicating Performance to Students, Parents, and the Public

Lake Shore and the district struggled to communicate performance results to students, parents, and the community. A veteran science teacher noted, "The data is a real blur for students and parents. The terminology and format are really in a language only spoken by teachers and administrators." "Parent involvement is very low," commented one veteran math teacher, adding, "We need to do a better job helping parents understand their children's data so they can support our work at home and by sending them to the extra tutoring sessions we offer."

Superintendent Fryer concurred but remained committed to analyzing and reporting data:

> One of our greatest challenges is figuring out how to communicate our progress and our ongoing work to the public. . . . We want

people to look at our results, at what we've accomplished over the past five years. I feel comfortable showing the warts and all because I know what the warts mean—I can explain the data. We should be proud of where we've come, and it is OK to say we've still got a long way to go. My goal is the same as when I arrived in 1998, to make DCPS the highest-achieving urban school district in the country, and our data shows we're on our way.

Iranetta Wright Looks Ahead

Wright was cognizant of her leadership challenges and the district's expectations for results. She reflected, "We've done a lot at Lake Shore to promote rigorous standards, accountability for results, and high expectations for every student this year, so I think we'll be in a much better position to move forward next year. But I do feel like the pressure is on to make sure we show improvements next year." Wright entered the Region III office determined to communicate her vision to Regional Superintendent Brown.

Notes

1. SY is a PELP convention that denotes "school year." For example, SY04 refers to the 2003–2004 school year.

2. *Improving Adult Literacy* (Jacksonville, FL: Jacksonville Community Council, Inc., Spring 1999), p. 3.

3. Beth Kormanik, "How Well Has Duval Really Desegregated?" *The Florida Times-Union*, May 17, 2004.

4. "An agreement between the NAACP and DCPS defined 'racially diverse schools' as having between 20% and 55% black student enrollment," cited in Kormanik, "How Well Has Duval Really Desegregated?"

5. Cynthia L. Garza, "5 Years of Fryer," *The Florida Times-Union*, April 20, 2003.

6. Nancy Mitchell, "Fryer Says Yes to Schools Post," *The Florida Times-Union*, June 17, 1998.

7. Nancy Mitchell, "I Just Don't Quit," *The Florida Times-Union*, August 2, 1998.

8. Adopted in 1996, the Sunshine State Standards (SSS) specified the knowledge and skills students were expected to master in seven subjects in grades pre-K through 12.

9. Cynthia L. Garza, "Questions and Answers: John Fryer," *The Florida Times-Union,* April 20, 2003.

10. The FCAT measured students' progress toward meeting the Sunshine State Standards (SSS). The A+ Plan required annual FCAT testing in reading and math for every grade 3–10 student; writing in grades 4, 8, and 10; and science in grades 5, 8, and 10. See "A+ Plan for Education," Governor Jeb Bush's official Web site, http://www.myflorida.com/myflorida/ government/governorinitiatives/aplusplan/index.html, and "FCAT," Florida Department of Education Web site, http://fcat.fldoe.org/, accessed May 6, 2004.

11. Barr issued DCPS an unlimited free license to use AIDE from his private software company, Academic Performance Series.

12. In November 2002, Florida voters approved a constitutional amendment limiting class sizes to 18 students in grades K–3, 22 students in grades 4–8, and 25 students in grades 9–12 by SY11. Implementation began in SY04. See "Class Size Reduction Amendment," Florida Dept. of Education Web site, http://www.firn.edu/doe/arm/class-size.htm, accessed July 2, 2004.

Exhibit 1

Student Achievement Trends, SY01–SY04: Percentage of Students Meeting Florida State Standards in Reading and Math (FCAT Level 3 or Above)

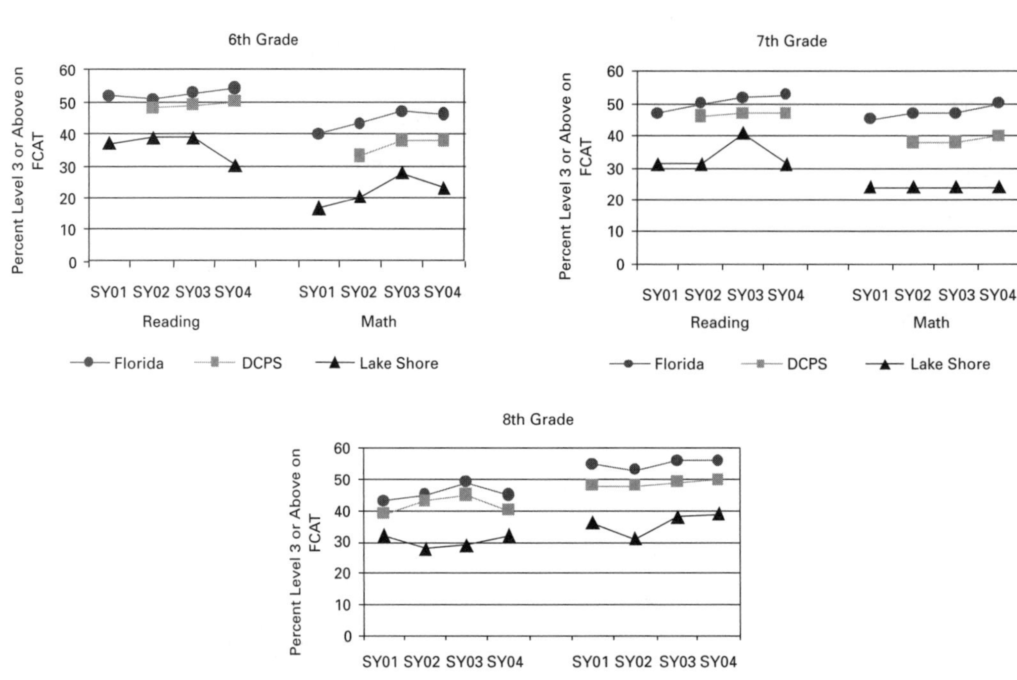

	FCAT Reading				FCAT Math			
	SY01	*SY02*	*SY03*	*SY04*	*SY01*	*SY02*	*SY03*	*SY04*
Grade 6								
Lake Shore	37	39	39	30	17	20	28	23
DCPS	a	48	49	50	a	33	38	38
Florida	52	51	53	54	40	43	47	46
Grade 7								
Lake Shore	31	31	41	31	24	24	24	24
DCPS	a	46	47	47	a	38	38	40
Florida	47	50	52	53	45	47	47	50
Grade 8								
Lake Shore	32	28	29	32	36	31	38	39
DCPS	39	43	45	40	48	48	49	50
Florida	43	45	49	45	53	53	56	56

Source: "Reading Scores Statewide Comparison for 2001 to 2004," "Mathematics Scores Statewide Comparison for 2001 to 2004," "Duval District (16) FCAT 2004 District Report," "Duval District (16) Lake Shore Middle School FCAT 2004 Report," Florida Department of Education Web site, http://fcat.fldoe.org, accessed May 24, 2004.

[a] Not available. DCPS was not required to test the sixth and seventh grade in every school until SY02.

Exhibit 2

DCPS Demographics: SY04 DCPS Overview

District Area Demographics (2000)	
Total population	778,879
Per-capita income	$20,753
Families below poverty level	203,225
Median household income	$40,539
Percent of county residents holding college degrees	21.9%
Unemployment (2004)[a]	4.9%
Student Demographics	
Number of students (K–12)	129,553
White	46.2%
African-American	43.0%
Hispanic	4.8%
Asian/Pacific Islander	3.1%
Other	2.9%
Eligible for free and reduced-price lunch	49.2%
English-language learners	2.7%
Exceptional-education students	18.3%
Graduation rate (SY03)	63.7%
Dropout rate (SY03)	4.6%
Schools and Staff (sixth-largest district in Florida)	
Number of schools	166
Elementary	106
Middle/Junior High	26
Senior High	19
Alternative	8
Charter	7
Total full-time employees (FTEs)	12,125
Average teacher salary	$40,335
Student/teacher ratio[b]	
Pre K–3	19.7:1
Gr. 4–8	21.4:1
Gr. 9–12	22.5:1

Source: District area demographics cited in "Duval County Public Schools," School District Demographics System, National Center for Education Statistics (NCES), U.S. Department of Education, Bureau of the Census, U.S. Department of Commerce. NCES Web site, http://www.nces.ed.gov/surveys/sdds/singledemoprofile.asp?county1=1200480 &state1=12, accessed June 2, 2004. Student, schools, and staff data from district files and "Duval County School District," Florida Department of Education Web site, http://www.firn.edu/doe/eias/flmove/duval.htm, accessed June 15, 2004.

[a]Data for January 2004: "Metropolitan Area at a Glance: Jacksonville, FL," U.S. Department of Labor, Bureau of Labor Statistics Web site, http://www.bls.gov.eag.fl_jacksonville.htm, accessed June 16, 2004.

[b]District files.

Exhibit 3

Key Provisions of the No Child Left Behind Act of 2001 (NCLB)

The No Child Left Behind Act of 2001 (NCLB) replaced the Elementary and Secondary Education Act first authorized in 1965 and dramatically expanded the federal government's role in public education. Key provisions of NCLB required:

- Approval of state accountability plans by the U.S. Department of Education
- Annual testing of at least 95% of all students in grades 3–8 on state reading and math exams aligned with state academic standards by SY06
- All students and student ethnic/racial and ability subgroups to score proficient or above on state tests by SY14, all schools to meet state adequate yearly progress (AYP) targets toward the 2014 goal beginning in SY03, and districts to allow students to transfer out of schools receiving federal Title I funds that failed to meet AYP goals
- States and school districts to issue report cards on district and school performance disaggregated by student ethnic/racial and ability subgroups by SY03
- All schools to have "highly qualified" teachers in all core content areas by SY06

Source: Information summarized from "No Child Left Behind," *Education Week* Web site, http://www.edweek.com/context/topics/issuespage.cfm?id=59, accessed May 12, 2004.

Exhibit 4

Mission Control Room Indicators

Goal 1: Academic Performance	*Goal 2: Safety and Discipline*	*Goal 3: High-Performance Management*	*Goal 4: Learning Communities*	*Goal 5: Accountability*
1. FCAT performance by grade level, subject, and ethnicity	1. Parent perception of safety	1. School employee turnover rate	1. School volunteerism	1. Individual school profiles
2. FCAT performance vs. satisfactory grades	2. Student perception of safety	2. Employee satisfaction	2. Business partnerships	2. School improvement plans
3. Parent satisfaction with quality of instruction	3. Employee perception of safety	3. Teacher training	3. Kindergarten readiness	3. School department profiles
4. Student satisfaction with quality of instruction	4. Student conduct	4. School technology deployment and training	4. % of teachers with advanced degrees	4. Central office department improvement plans
5. Scholastic Aptitude Test (SAT) scores		5. Business services and purchasing	5. % of National Board–certified teachers	5. RESDAC/AIDE data
6. American College Test (ACT) scores		6. Facilities and maintenance	6. Student attendance	6. Learner profiles
7. Promotion rate		7. Transportation	7. Staff diversity	7. FCAT five-year performance
8. Four-year graduation rate		8. Instructional materials		8. A+ school grades
9. College readiness		9. Research, evaluation, and assessment		9. NCLB adequate yearly progress
10. Exceptional student education		10. Information technology		
11. Title I		11. K–12 educational administration costs		
12. Community education		12. Media services		
13. Applied technology and career development				
14. Magnet programs/school choice				
15. Academic and special programs				
16. Student services				
17. Jacksonville Urban Systemic Initiative				

Source: District files.

Exhibit 5

DCPS Financials, SY98–SY04

A. Revenues and Expenditures SY98–SY04

	1997/98	*1998/99*	*1999/2000*	*2000/01*	*2001/02*	*2002/03*	*2003/04*
Revenues							
Federal	$ 1,721,281	$ 1,619,099	$ 4,287,934	$ 1,541,684	$ 1,640,600	$ 1,743,019	$ 1,597,309
State	405,778,561	412,743,414	409,843,999	423,450,174	409,067,682	417,428,037	429,206,973
Local	187,160,106	196,592,494	197,071,118	216,142,053	217,155,008	234,176,776	257,345,909
Private and/or Other	3,478,322	13,908,446	13,108,764	15,544,242	2,867,611	20,590,997	3,679,152
Total	**$ 598,138,271**	**$ 624,863,452**	**$ 624,311,816**	**$ 656,678,153**	**$ 630,730,901**	**$ 673,938,829**	**$ 691,829,343**
Expenditures							
Direct Instruction	363,552,785	372,711,276	363,641,381	380,952,747	395,325,301	413,925,275	434,618,373
Instructional Support[a]	59,973,787	62,576,686	64,771,606	70,116,037	70,319,321	76,658,127	73,757,071
General Admin[b]	27,084,187	35,776,189	38,162,097	44,482,311	38,675,947	42,701,352	39,799,010
School Admin	27,569,944	28,724,260	29,774,026	31,019,725	32,386,035	34,184,716	35,077,253
Facilities & Constr	2,452,295	3,209,306	4,458,630	6,099,265	1,467,344	895,049	937,633
Transportation	34,881,420	35,187,650	38,117,798	38,379,368	37,377,704	36,442,825	30,599,691
Plant Op/Maintenance	66,175,995	66,160,831	68,585,174	69,912,426	60,192,888	74,995,358	60,990,820
Community Services	6,828,555	7,463,490	7,829,456	8,017,213	544,311	657,150	641,617
Debt Service	531,160	547,267	489,982	479,277	1,394,863	1,392,447	942,700
Transfers	57,729	813,393	778,971	1,026,606	2,138,689	170,187	1,392,312
Total	**$ 589,107,857**	**$ 613,170,348**	**$ 616,609,120**	**$ 650,484,976**	**$ 639,822,403**	**$ 682,022,487**	**$ 678,756,480**
Surplus/Deficit	**$ 9,030,414**	**$ 11,693,105**	**$ 7,702,695**	**$ 6,193,177**	**$ (9,091,503)**	**$ (8,083,658)**	**$ 13,072,863**

B. Research, Evaluation, and Technology Expenditures as a Percentage of Total Budget

	1997/98	*1998/99*	*1999/2000*	*2000/01*	*2001/02*	*2002/03*	*2003/04*
Total Expenditures	$ 589,107,857	$ 613,170,348	$ 616,609,120	$ 650,484,976	$ 639,822,403	$ 682,022,487	$ 678,756,480
Research, Evaluation & Technology	$ 7,399,351	$ 11,503,959	$ 13,586,960	$ 14,353,852	$ 13,609,341	$ 14,762,472	$ 14,047,334
Research, Eval & Tech as a % of Total	**1.3%**	**1.9%**	**2.2%**	**2.2%**	**2.1%**	**2.2%**	**2.1%**

Source: District files.

Note: SY98–SY03 revenues and expenditures are audited, SY04's are unaudited.

[a] Includes pupil personnel, media services, curriculum, and instructional staff training.

[b] Includes central and boardadministration, fiscal services, and central services.

Exhibit 6

FCAT Subject-Test Strands

Reading	*Mathematics*	*Science*	*Writing*
1. Words and Phrases in Context 2. Main Ideas, Plot, and Purpose 3. Comparisons and Cause/Effect 4. Reference and Research	1. Number Sense and Operations 2. Measurement 3. Geometry and Spatial Sense 4. Algebraic Thinking 5. Data Analysis and Probability	1. Physical and Chemical Sciences 2. Earth and Space Sciences 3. Life and Environmental Sciences 4. Scientific Thinking	1. Expository or Narrative Essay (Gr. 4) 2. Expository or Persuasive Essay (Gr. 8 and 10)

Source: Florida Comprehensive Assessment Test, Florida Department of Education, http://www.firn.edu/doe/sas/fcat.htm, accessed May 6, 2004.

Exhibit 7

Managing Academic Progress (MAP) Management Tool

Lake Shore Middle Map Profile

MAP Corridor

All MAP Tasks | C and I | Scheduling | Safety Net | Accountability

Pre-School | Pre-Plan | Instruction | Summative

Print		Task	Component	Cycle	Report	Analyze
Task Report	1	Create cover sheet for MAP Profile	Accountability	Pre-School		NA
Task Report	2	Create school MAP Profile check list	Accountability	Pre-School		NA
Task Report	3	Create a demographic profile of your school	Scheduling	Pre-School		
Task Report	4	Print and complete the Curriculum and Instructional Gaps planning sheet	C and I	Pre-School		NA
Task Report	5	Determine the number of students in the five AIDE variable categories for reading and math	Scheduling	Pre-School		
Task Report	6	Develop an overview of student performance on FCAT A+	C and I	Pre-School		
Task Report	7	Present NCLB overview to Leadership Team for discussion and input	C and I	Pre-School		

Print | Close

Record: 1 of 81

Source: Management of Academic Progress (MAP) Administrative Guide.

The MAP corridor interfaced the MAP program with the Academic Interpretation and Data Evaluation (AIDE) system. MAP tasks were divided into four instructional components: (1) *Curriculum and Instruction* (C and I), (2) *Scheduling*, (3) *Safety Net*, and (4) *Accountability*. MAP tasks were also divided into four sequential cycles: (1) *Pre-School*: prior to the beginning of school, (2) *Pre-Plan*: began the first day teachers return to work and continued to the 10th instructional day, (3) *Instructional*: each 45-day instructional cycle, and (4) *Summative*: end of the school year.

Exhibit 8

Lake Shore Middle School Individual School Profile

2002-2003 School Profile
LAKE SHORE MIDDLE SCHOOL # 69
Region 3

Legend

N:	Number of students evaluated.
Pct:	Percentage of students achieving the standard for this criterion, by ethnicity. (N/S if N < 6 for a single grade or N < 10 for multiple grades.)
Yellow bars:	Performance of all schools on this criterion, ranked from low to high.
Heavy dark vertical segment:	Performance of all students at this school.
Red vertical line:	Performance of all students in the district at specified grade level.

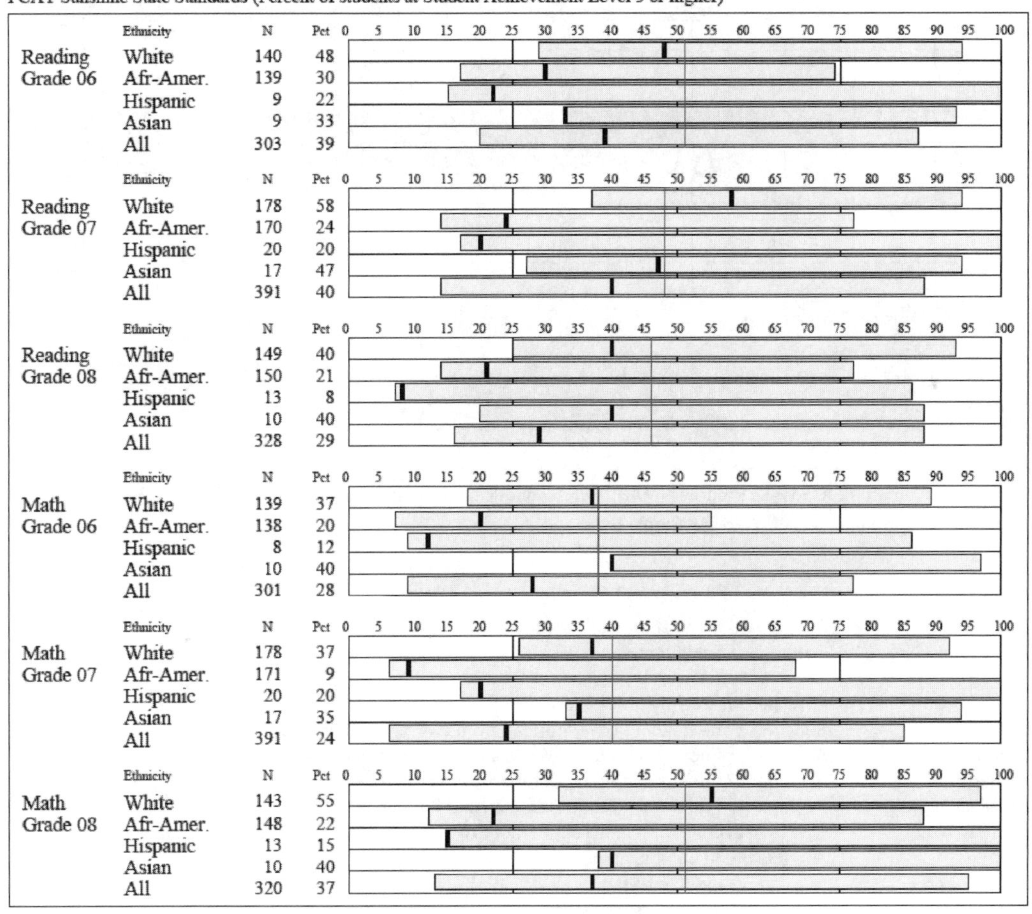

FCAT Sunshine State Standards (Percent of students at Student Achievement Level 3 or higher)
Ethnicity N Pct 0 5 10 15 20 25 30 35 40 45 50 55 60 65 70 75 80 85 90 95 100
Reading Grade 06
White 140 48
Afr-Amer. 139 30
Hispanic 9 22
Asian 9 33
All 303 39
Reading Grade 07
White 178 58
Afr-Amer. 170 24
Hispanic 20 20
Asian 17 47
All 391 40
Reading Grade 08
White 149 40
Afr-Amer. 150 21
Hispanic 13 8
Asian 10 40
All 328 29
Math Grade 06
White 139 37
Afr-Amer. 138 20
Hispanic 8 12
Asian 10 40
All 301 28
Math Grade 07
White 178 37
Afr-Amer. 171 9
Hispanic 20 20
Asian 17 35
All 391 24
Math Grade 08
White 143 55
Afr-Amer. 148 22
Hispanic 13 15
Asian 10 40
All 320 37

Source: District files.

Exhibit 9

FCAT Sunshine State Reading (SSR) Executive Summary for Lake Shore Middle School

Lake Shore Middle Students

FCAT SSR Executive Summary

All Students | FCAT Eligible

Sch	2003 FCAT Gr	SSR Level	Words Avg	Main Idea Avg	Comparisons Avg	Reference Avg	Raw Total Avg	GPA Avg	No of Students	No of Students %
69	6	1	38	37	40	36	38	2.21	186	45%
69	6	2	59	64	59	52	60	2.58	98	24%
69	6	3	73	78	76	73	76	2.78	86	21%
69	6	4	88	89	90	84	88	3.16	35	9%
69	6	5	93	93	100	100	96	3.56	4	1%
69	7	1	33	41	44	31	39	2.21	133	42%
69	7	2	54	60	67	49	59	2.38	85	27%
69	7	3	71	75	82	61	74	2.57	74	23%
69	7	4	86	85	95	84	87	2.77	23	7%
69	7	5	95	95	97	94	96	2.42	5	2%
69	8	1	46	36	46	21	38	2.32	147	38%
69	8	2	73	56	69	39	59	2.64	117	30%
69	8	3	86	65	82	57	71	2.79	83	22%
69	8	4	94	78	92	73	82	3.09	28	7%
69	8	5	95	86	100	85	90	3.25	9	2%
			72	69	76	63	70	2.72	1113	

Print Current Form | SSR Min/Max | Close

Record: 1 of 15

Source: Management of Academic Progress (MAP) and Academic Interpretation and Data Evaluation (AIDE).

Legend

All Students	Sorted data for all students in school
FCAT Eligible	Sorted data only for students eligible to take the FCAT
Sch	School number
2003 FCAT Gr	FCAT 2003 results by grade level
SSR Level	Sunshine State Reading Level (ranged from low of 1 to high of 5)
Words Avg	Average % of points scored on Words and Phrases strand
Comparisons Avg	Average % of points scored on Comparisons strand
Reference Avg	Average % of points scored on Research and Reference strand
Raw Total Avg	Raw total average of points scored on FCAT Reading test
GPA Avg	Average grade point average
No. of Students	Number of students tested
No. of Students %	Percentage of students represented
SSR Min/Max	Real-time calculator used to calculate minimum and maximum SSR level

■ Red

■ Yellow

Exhibit 10

FCAT Sunshine State Math (SSM) Content Score A+ Report for Lake Shore Middle School

Lake Shore Middle Students

FCAT SSM Math Content Scores - A+

All | FCAT Eligible | FCAT 3,4,5 | FCAT 1 and 2 | Lowest 25%

Sch	Stu Numb	Last Name	First Name	GPA	2003 FCAT Gr	SSM Level	SSM Scale	SSM Dev	Number #	Number %	Measure #	Measure %	Geometry #	Geometry %	Algebra #	Algebra %	Data Anal #	Data Anal %	NRM %ile
69	6779146	BEAL	GERARD	2.57	6	1	274	1519	3	33	2	22	5	56	3	38	4	44	20
69	8007817	BUCKMAN	SAMMIE	2.62	6	1	100	770	3	33	0	0	1	11	0	0	2	22	10
69	7850303	BROOKBAN	RODOLFO	2.62	6	1	209	1239	1	11	0	0	3	33	2	25	3	33	23
69	6715357	ATWOOD	DANNI	2.62	7	1	267	1631	2	22	2	22	3	38	6	67	4	44	31
69	8125777	BURRELL	TALIB	2.62	6	1	239	1368	1	11	3	33	6	67	2	25	4	44	6
69	6780071	BEALE	GERMAN	2.58	7	1	232	1490	2	22	1	11	2	25	3	33	2	22	21
69	6495283	MERRY	LESLI	2.58	6	1	274	1519	5	56	3	33	4	44	3	38	4	44	36
69	7436787	BOX	MYRICK	2.58	6	1	267	1489	2	22	5	56	2	22	2	25	5	56	44
69	6934997	BILOTTA	JONATHAN	2.58	6	1	278	1536	3	33	4	44	2	22	2	25	6	67	61
69	6748110	BANKS	ELIJAH	2.58	7	1	249	1559	1	11	0	0	3	38	4	44	4	44	16
69	6775220	BAWLI	GALE	2.58	6	1	243	1386	2	22	3	33	2	22	1	12	3	33	44
69	7616762	BRATCHER	PETER	2.12	7	1	100	958	1	11	1	11	1	12	0	0	2	22	
			Minimum	0.00		1	100	770		0		0		0		0		0	1
			Average	2.46		1.75	268	1557		41		34		49		36		48	48
			Maximum	4.00		5	401	2172		100		89		100		100		100	99
			Standard Dev	0.83		0.92	57	250		20		22		21		20		23	26

Biographical Data / AIDE Math

Last Name	S	E	Gr	HR	L	ESE	C	R	ESOL	DDP	CHO	PRSCH	BUB	25%	1+2	LOSS	CON
BEAL	M	B	6	609	F						T	143			X		
BUCKMAN	M	H	6	615	H	K	251	R	Y			0			X		
BROOKBAN	M	B	6	612	R							92		X	X		
ATWOOD	M	W	7	701							J	216			X	X	
BURRELL	M	H	6	615	F				Y			305			X		
BEALE	M	B	7	701	F						T	168		X	X		
MERRY	F	W	6	620	N	V	251					207			X	X	
BOX	M	W	6	604	F	K	251					256			X		
BILOTTA	M	W	6	608	F							18			X	X	
BANKS	M	B	7	705	F							21		X	X		
BAWLI	M	B	6	611	F							31		X	X		
BRATCHER	M	W	7	730	H	J	252					149			X		

SSS Math Content Possible Points	
Students in School	1232
Students on Screen	728
% on Screen	59%

SSM 3 - 5	178	24%
SSM 1 - 2	550	76%
SSM Tested	728	100%

Bubble	103
Lowest 25%	142
Levels 1 and 2	550
Level Loss	174
Conflict	106
Potential SSM Calculator	
SSM 3 - 5	24%
SSM 1 - 2	76%
Enter Number	0

Remove | Print | Bio | Aide | NCLB | Close

Record: 1 of 728 (Filtered)

Source: Management of Academic Progress (MAP) and Academic Interpretation and Data Evaluation (AIDE).

Note: Page 1 of a 728-page report. Student names have been changed. Data could be sorted by all students, FCAT eligible students, or by FCAT level (3–5, 1 and 2, or lowest 25%).

Legend

GPA	Grade point average	#	# of points correct	Gr	Grade	R	Retained	BUB	Bubble
2003 FCAT Gr	Grade tested	%	% correct	HR	Homeroom	ESOL	English Learner	25%	Lowest 25%
SSM Level	FCAT Math Level	NRM%ile	Norm Reference %	L	Lunch status	DDP	Dropout Prevention	1 + 2	Level 1 or 2
SSM Scale	Scale score	S	Sex	ESE	Special Ed	CHO	Choice (voucher)	LOSS	Loss
SSM Dev	Development score	E	Ethnicity	C	Cost	PRSCH	Prior School	CON	Conflict

Exhibit 11

FCAT Sunshine State Reading (SSR) Gain and Loss Report for Language Arts 3 by Teacher

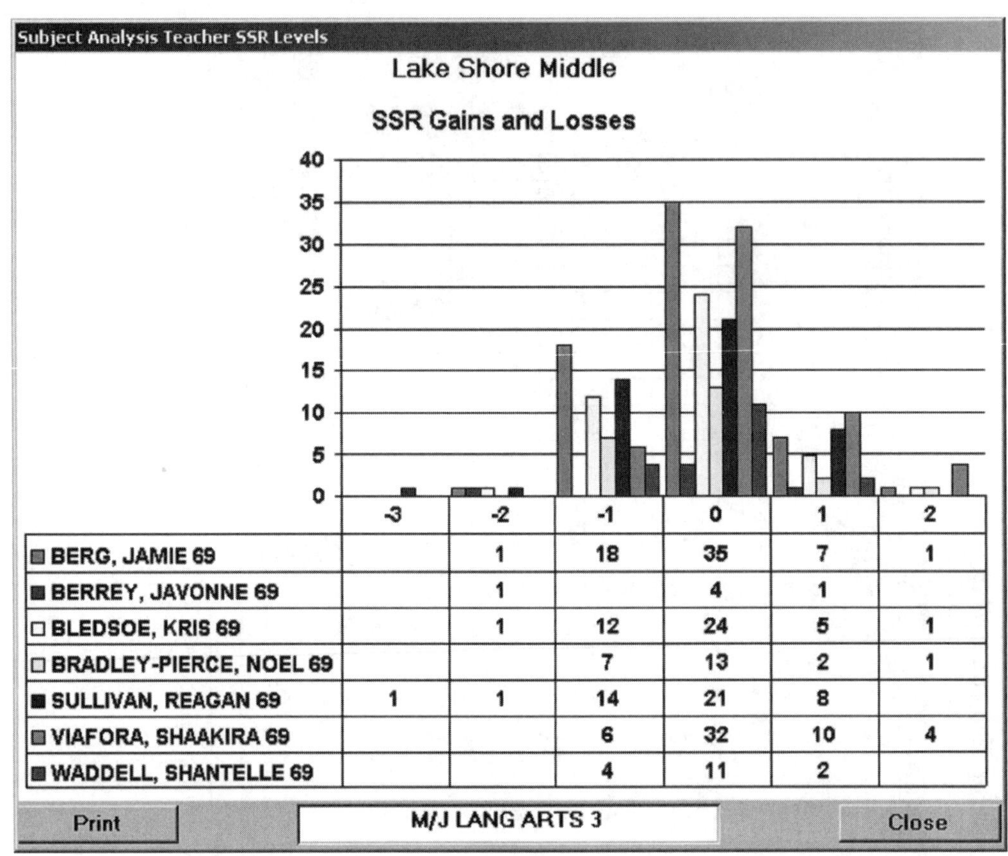

	-3	-2	-1	0	1	2
BERG, JAMIE 69		1	18	35	7	1
BERREY, JAVONNE 69		1		4	1	
BLEDSOE, KRIS 69		1	12	24	5	1
BRADLEY-PIERCE, NOEL 69			7	13	2	1
SULLIVAN, REAGAN 69	1	1	14	21	8	
VIAFORA, SHAAKIRA 69			6	32	10	4
WADDELL, SHANTELLE 69			4	11	2	

Source: Management of Academic Progress (MAP) and Academic Interpretation and Data Evaluation (AIDE). Copyright Accelerated Data Solutions 2002–2004. All Rights Reserved.

Note: Teachers' names have been changed.

Gain/Loss	*Students' Change in FCAT Level from Prior Year*
-3	# of students who dropped 3 FCAT levels
-2	# of students who dropped 2 FCAT levels
-1	# of students who dropped 1 FCAT level
0	# of students who maintained same FCAT level
1	# of students who increased 1 FCAT level
2	# of students who increased 2 FCAT levels

Exhibit 12

Student Profile Report

Lake Shore Middle Student Profile

CHRISTOPHER ARCHEVAL

Grade	Homeroom	GPA
7	704	2.41

Course Title	Qtr 1				Qtr 2				Qtr 3				Qtr 4				Exam	Final		
	Gr	A	T	C	Gr	A	T	C	Gr	A	T	C	Gr	A	T	C		Gr	A	T
M/J LANG ARTS 2	B-	0	0	IO	B	1	0	HM	B	0	0	M	A+	1	0	GM	87	B	2	0
M/J WORLD GEOG	[illegible]	0	0	OP	B+	1	0	GM	C+	0	0	HN	B	1	0	FN	73	C	2	0
M/J HEALTH 3		0	0			0	0		C+	0	0	O		0	0		65	C+	0	0
M/J COMP PHYS ED 2		0	0			0	0			0	0		A	1	0	M	100	A	1	0
M/J COMP PHYS ED 2	A	0	0	N	A	0	0	N	O	0	0	N		1	0				1	0
M/J MATH 2	D	0	0	N	C-	1	0	N	B	0	0	N	B-	1	0	N	100	C	2	0
M/J RESEARCH 3		2	0			1	0			2	0			3	0				8	0
M/J COMP SCI 2	D	2	0	NPT	C	1	0	N	C	2	0	N	C+	3	0	N	100	C	8	0
M/J READ I	B	1	0	N	B-	1	0	N	C	2	0	N	C-	0	0	N	70	C	4	0
M/J RESEARCH 4		2	0			1	0			2	0			3	0				8	0
Average	2.00				2.83				2.33				3.00					2.43		

Sunshine State Reading Scores

2003 FCAT Grade	7	2002 FCAT Grade	6	Gain/Loss
2003 SSR Level	2	2002 SSR Level	3	-1

Sunshine State Reading Content Scores

2003 Writing	Words and Phrases	Main Idea and Purpose	Comparisons	Reference and Research
2003 Content Score	50	50	58	71
Bench Mark 1				
Bench Mark 2				
Bench Mark 3				

SSR AIDE Variables

Scored 10 Points Over or Below Level 3 Cut Score	Scored in the lowest 25% of the class	Scored in SSR Level 1 or 2	Lost at least 1 SSR Level	GPA of 3.0 but scored SSR Level 1 or 2
		X	X	

Sunshine State Mathematics Scores

2003 FCAT Grade	7	2002 FCAT Grade	6	Gain/Loss
2003 SSM Level	2	2002 SSM Level	2	0

Sunshine State Mathematics Content Scores

	Number Sense	Measurement	Geometry	Algebraic Thinking	Data Analysis
2003 Content Score	78	33	50	33	44
Bench Mark 1					
Bench Mark 2					
Bench Mark 3					

SSM AIDE Variables

Scored 10 Points Over or Below Level 3 Cut Score	Scored in the lowest 25% of the class	Scored in SSM Level 1 or 2	Lost at least 1 SSM Level	GPA of 3.0 but scored SSM Level 1 or 2
		X		

Source: Management of Academic Progress (MAP) and Academic Interpretation and Data Evaluation (AIDE).

Note: Sample data, fictional student name.

Exhibit 13

Lake Shore Classroom Teacher Observation Rubric: Quick Peek

Lakeshore Middle School
2003-2004
Quick Peek

Name: ____________________ **Date:** ______________

Class Period: __________ **Subject:** ____________________

Observer: ______________ **Time began:** ______ **Time ended:** _____

- ☐ Performance standards posted (A, D)
- ☐ Word/Concept Wall (A, B)
- ☐ Rituals and Routines posted (A, B, C)
- ☐ Evidence of planner in use (A, C, F)
- ☐ Evidence of author's chair/sharing area (A, B, C)
- ☐ Evidence and advertisement of 25 Book Standard (D, I)
- ☐ Appropriate classroom management (C)
- ☐ Teacher actively teaching (B, D)
- ☐ Lesson plans available (A, B, G)
- ☐ Classroom orderly and inviting (I)
- ☐ Evidence of hands-on activities (A, B)
- ☐ Teacher interacting w/ students (D)
- ☐ Students on task (C)
- ☐ Standards based bulletin board *Standard, rubric and student work w/ commentary_____ Date of work (A, B, E, G)
- ☐ Utilization of student portfolio/notebook (B, E, G)
- ☐ Today's standard identified (A, D)
- ☐ Students can identify standard being addressed (C, D)
- ☐ Evidence of current reading strategy (D, G)
- ☐ Classroom library w/ ckout system (C)
- ☐ Teacher's booklist posted (D, I)
- ☐ Evidence of safety nets (E)

I thought:

____
____
____
____
____
____

I wondered:

____
____
____
____
____
____

Legend:
√- Observed Ø – Should have observed * - Did not observe/Did not ask

Source: Lake Shore Middle School files.

Note: The letters A through I corresponded to specific competencies in the DCPS teacher evaluation.

Exhibit 14

DCPS School Observation Rubric: Data-Driven Decision-Making Snapshot

Host Principal Rating:

1. Preparing	*2. Getting Started*	*3. Moving Along*	*4. In Place*
❑	❑	❑	❑

Your ratings (Mark all that apply, and then assess the overall phase of implementation):

Preparing	*Getting Started*	*Moving Along*	*In Place*
❑ The school improvement plan (SIP) contains measurable objectives that are based on data-driven needs. ❑ School leaders use aggregated school-level data to make decisions. ❑ At least some teachers use classroom tests at the end of an instructional unit to measure what students have learned. ❑ School leaders use state test results to identify professional development needs for faculty. ❑ School staff process some data in-house (either manually or electronically). ❑ The school provides parents with basic student achievement data such as quarterly report cards, standards mastery levels, and state assessment scores.	❑ School leaders conduct a yearly review of SIP objectives to determine adequate progress. ❑ School leaders use data disaggregated by subgroup to determine the current status of teaching and learning. ❑ At least some teachers use a variety of data sources to keep track of the standards their students have mastered. ❑ School leaders use a variety of disaggregated student performance data to plan professional development activities for faculty. ❑ At least one person in the school is able to use computer technology for effective data processing. ❑ Parents are provided with data concerning individual standards mastery, student achievement levels, and the means by which the levels are assessed.	❑ School leaders conduct both midyear and end-of-year review of SIP objectives to determine adequate progress. ❑ Disaggregated data are distributed at least quarterly to all faculty to highlight patterns, in order to inform practices. ❑ Most teachers use a variety of data sources to keep ongoing track of the standards their students have mastered in order to individualize and focus instruction. ❑ School leaders use a variety of data (e.g., disaggregated student achievement data, annual performance appraisal data for teachers and administrators, etc.) in order to plan schoolwide and individual professional development. ❑ School leaders demonstrate competency in the use of computer technology to manipulate data. ❑ Most teachers document individual student achievement by collecting and maintaining performance and standards mastery data from a variety of sources for use in communicating with parents.	❑ School leaders regularly revise their SIP as a result of data collection and analysis. Frequent measures of student achievement are used to set and refine a course of action and to improve instruction and student learning. ❑ The school has developed a climate of inquiry, supported by the allocation of time and resources, for individuals and teams of teachers to conduct ongoing explorations of student performance data in order to inform instructional decision making. ❑ All teachers regularly use a variety of data sources to keep ongoing track of the standards their students have mastered and use this information to provide differentiated instruction. ❑ Ongoing collection and analysis of student achievement data are used to adjust and refine schoolwide professional development based on current student needs and staff competencies. ❑ Teachers and administrators routinely use technology to gather, disaggregate, and analyze different achievement indicators from a variety of sources. ❑ All teachers regularly communicate with parents to ensure their understanding of their child's progress.

Source: District files.

Exhibit 15

Lake Shore FCAT 2004 Student Gains and Losses by Teacher

Grade and Level	*Total No. of FCAT Eligible Students*	*Math Teacher*	*No. of Students with Math Gains*	*% of Students with Math Gains*	*English/ Language Arts Teacher*	*No. of Students with Reading Gains*	*% of Students with Reading Gains*
6th Grade							
Standard	47	Wick	23	49%	Bushnell	30	64%
Standard	51	*Freund*[b]	12	24%	McDonald	19	37%
Standard	55	First	13	25%	*Cook*[b]	17	31%
Standard	76	*O'Hare*[b]	23	30%	*Kelly*[b]	19	25%
Standard	1	c			Hauser	1	100%
Standard[a]	30	*Magoon*[b]	7	23%	*Arroyo*[b]	8	27%
Advanced	30	Wick	20	67%	Bushnell	24	80%
7th Grade							
Standard	43	Sheffield	24	55%	Smith	17	40%
Standard	54	Quinn	20	37%	Jacobs	24	44%
Standard	81	Woodsome	50	62%	Bird	34	42%
Standard	62	*Upton*[b]	39	63%	*Richards*[b]	31	50%
Standard	13	c			Henry	8	62%
Advanced	15	Sheffield	11	73%	Smith	9	60%
8th Grade							
Standard	34	*Rupley*[b]	25	71%	Burnett	20	59%
Standard	51	Wigren	29	56%	*Joyce*[b]	21	41%
Standard	47	Ciampi	42	89%	Morrison	23	49%
Standard	50	Nicholas	40	80%	*Nelson*[b]	38	76%
Advanced	27	Nicholas	22	82%	*Nelson*[b]	16	59%
Advanced	34	*Rupley*[b]	30	89%	Burnett	22	65%

Source: Lake Shore Middle School files.

Note: "Gains" signified an increase of at least one achievement level on the FCAT math or reading test. Teacher names have been changed.

[a]Students in this homeroom were performing more than two years behind grade level.

[b]Denotes first-year teacher.

[c]Student(s) included in another class.

Stacey Childress ■ Kristen Campbell

SchoolNet: Pursuing Opportunity Beyond Federal Mandates

In early March 2005, Jonathan Harber, CEO and cofounder of SchoolNet, jumped into a cab headed toward Philadelphia's 30th Street Station with Andy Brenner, who managed the company's relationship with the School District of Philadelphia (SDP). SchoolNet's two-year, $5.7 million contract with SDP was up for renewal at the end of the academic year, and Harber and Brenner recognized that resting on their past success was not an option. The pair had just completed an encouraging meeting with key decision makers at SDP, but a number of factors presented challenges.

Even though SDP acknowledged the role that SchoolNet's Instructional Management Solution (IMS) had played in the district's improved student achievement results, the technology platform was fully deployed in only 168 of 273 district schools, and none of its high schools. SchoolNet IMS had been accepted by principals and teachers as the one-stop access point for instructional and performance information in schools in which it was installed, but Harber and Brenner recognized that implementation at the high school level could be more challenging because teachers had already been trained to use a proprietary technology solution linked to a well-known curriculum and materials provider.

Additionally, a number of large, established vendors had begun competing for SDP's limited technology budget, and the district representatives had informed Harber and Brenner that SDP was facing another year of deep budget cuts. SchoolNet was suddenly vying with other technology projects for a share of a shrinking wallet. The stakes were high; as an early adopter and SchoolNet's most extensive implementation, Philadelphia was an important reference account that represented nearly 15% of the young company's annual revenue.

Settling into his seat on the train bound for New York, Harber reflected on the evolution of SchoolNet's position in the educational technology market and its important relationship with Philadelphia. Specifically, how could they transition from a one-time project to a long-term technology partner in Philadelphia? More generally, though Philadelphia and other districts had been searching for technology solutions for several years, the federal No Child Left Behind Act of 2001 (NCLB) had accelerated the adoption rates of products designed to help districts manage performance data. How might SchoolNet continue to take advantage of this market dynamic, while extending its relevance to current and potential customers beyond the parameters created by the mandates?

Competing in an Emerging Industry

Founded in 1998, SchoolNet had a vision to improve the world's education systems by providing tools for using data to increase academic achievement. Based in New York City, the company served the K–12 public education market in the United States. SchoolNet offered technology solutions for the collection, analysis, and reporting of data about curriculum and instruction, student performance, and teacher professional development. By 2005, the company served 45 clients in 15 states representing over 1.1 million students, with annual revenues of approximately $15 million. (See **Exhibit 1** for financials and **Exhibit 2** for selected client list.)

In 1997, Jonathan Harber, a serial educational technology entrepreneur, and Denis Doyle, a thought leader in education reform, began exploring their common interest in the emerging opportunity to bring to public school districts the same tools that corporations had used for decades to gather and analyze data about their core business to increase their performance. (See **Exhibit 3** for Harber and Doyle biographies.) Both men believed that the nascent standards-based reform movement sweeping state education departments would create demand from school districts for technology solutions to manage student performance data. Additionally, they believed the very nature of education was changing and that access to performance data would become even more valuable. As Harber explained:

> Eventually, teachers will move from a "sage-on-the-stage" to a "guide-on-the-side." Students will become managers of their own education. Teachers will become portfolio managers of their students, principals will become portfolio managers of their schools, and administrators will become portfolio managers of their districts. For this to work, everyone in the system needs access to high-quality, timely data about the entire educational process.

In 1998 they launched SchoolNet, and began the product development process for a technology platform that would allow school districts to aggregate instructional content from multiple vendors and collect and manage student performance data for use at the district, school, and classroom level. In 2000, after funding the company with their own resources for two years, the founders raised $3 million in a Series A financing round. In addition to a number of angel investors, The Princeton Review, an established content company, participated as a strategic investor.

In late 2001, in order to fund aggressive growth opportunities created by the impending No Child Left Behind Act, SchoolNet raised a $5 million Series B round, led by Ascend Ventures.[1] A number of Series A investors participated in the follow-on round, including The Princeton Review. As a result of the round, investors owned approximately 45% of the company, while the founders held approximately 35%. The remaining 20% was available for stock options.

No Child Left Behind Act of 2001

In January 2002, President George W. Bush signed into law the No Child Left Behind Act, a framework for improving the country's public schools driven by rigorous standards and high-stakes accountability. NCLB reauthorized the Elementary and Secondary Education Act, which had first been authorized in 1965 and dramatically expanded the federal government's role in public education. For the first time, states, districts, and schools were required to report a wide range of demographic and achievement information at the end of each school year, and faced consequences such as loss of funding, and takeover or closure of underperforming schools.

Key NCLB Provisions Required

- Annual approval of state accountability plans by the U.S. Department of Education
- Annual testing of at least 95% of all students in grades 3–8 on state reading and

math exams aligned with state academic standards by 2006
- All students and student ethnic/racial and ability subgroups to score proficient or above on state tests by 2014, all schools to meet state adequate yearly progress (AYP) targets toward the 2014 goal beginning in 2003, and districts to allow students to transfer out of schools receiving federal Title I funds that failed to meet AYP goals
- States and school districts to issue report cards on district and school performance disaggregated by student ethnic/racial and ability subgroups by 2003
- Schools to have "highly qualified" teachers in all core content areas by 2006

Few school districts had the necessary technology infrastructure in place to meet the data and accountability demands imposed by NCLB. Even the most technologically advanced districts, which centrally purchased and supported business systems for the finance and human resource functions, tended to leave the instructional and student performance technology decisions to schools or district curriculum offices. In less technologically advanced districts, systems to track instruction and student performance were paper-based and were administered at the school or classroom level. As a result, NCLB created the need for districts to develop enterprise-wide technology strategies that could support the performance and reporting requirements of the law.

Industry Landscape

The K–12 public education industry in the United States was extremely fragmented, with approximately 15,000 school districts, 90,000 schools, and 3 million teachers serving nearly 50 million students. In 2004, over $450 billion was spent annually in the sector, of which approximately $8 billion was for technology-related purchases.[2] School districts typically funded technology spending out of their annual operating budgets, making it difficult to invest in large-scale installations or upgrades that required multiyear planning and financing. As with other capital investments such as building construction, large technology expenditures relied on special public bond issues or one-time grant programs from the federal or state departments of education, which were episodic and uncertain. (See **Exhibit 4**.)

Within K–12 technology spending, the enterprise software and services (ESS) market was approximately $2.5 billion and had initially accelerated as a result of the testing and reporting requirements created by NCLB. Funding for the new requirements was distributed under several federal grant programs and administered through state education departments. In 2004, the ESS market included the nearly $400 million that school districts spent on business systems to manage functions such as financial reporting, procurement, and human resources. The market also included the $2.1 billion spent on student information systems (SIS) and instructional management systems (IMS).

An SIS typically included a data warehouse that pooled individual student background and demographic data with student performance data from assessments, each of which were usually stored in separate data management systems. Most products also included tools for data analysis, and a portal through which district employees could easily access student information relevant to their jobs. An IMS was a platform that provided tools for developing, administering, and publishing course content and materials. Installing an SIS or IMS required districts to conduct extensive employee training. As a result, vendors in this market often competed for a portion of multiple district budget line-items, such as instructional software, administrative software, professional development, and services and support.

SchoolNet straddled the SIS and IMS categories. While the overall ESS market remained relatively flat between 2002 and 2004, the combined SIS and IMS categories grew by approximately 4% during the same period, and were projected to grow by $400 million to reach a total of $2.5 billion by 2007.[3]

Other significant players in the SIS and IMS categories included EduSoft (recently acquired by Houghton-Mifflin); Chancery Software (privately held, with an established SIS); Pearson PLC (a large educational publisher with SIS and IMS technology); PLATO Learning, Inc. (a public company, with tools for managing standards-aligned content and student performance); and Blackboard, Inc. (publicly held, with an online, content-neutral course platform).

The competitive environment for SIS and IMS products was complicated by a lengthy sales process. Even if account representatives were armed with timely, accurate, and specific market intelligence, the sales process could take anywhere from six months to a few years, depending on the manner in which a school district organized its decision-making and purchasing processes. Because SIS and IMS packages cut across multiple budget categories, the sales process was usually characterized by multiple in-person meetings with five to 25 district personnel, who jointly recommended a purchase decision to a superintendent, who often was required to obtain purchase approval from the school board, depending on the size of the contract.

SchoolNet Instructional Management Solutions

Historically, school districts purchased content from vendors, such as textbook publishers, which often required buyers to use proprietary content delivery technologies. Harber believed that districts would be better served by a single, content-neutral platform, with the freedom to select content and diagnostic assessments on an ongoing basis from multiple vendors. In addition to the flexibility this approach provided, district teachers and administrators would need training on only one technology instead of multiple solutions, and district IT departments could focus their support on one platform.

In keeping with this belief, the company launched SchoolNet Instructional Management Solutions (IMS).[4] SchoolNet's content-neutral platform consisted of six modules: Account, Align, Assess, Assign, Outreach, and PD Planner. These modules were designed to increase user effectiveness and efficiency within the district central office, the principal's office, and the classroom. SchoolNet did not embed pedagogy or policy into the modules, but rather supported the existing practices of a district by providing a solution that tied curriculum to instructional and assessment data. The Account, Align, and Assess modules were the foundation of SchoolNet IMS. (See **Exhibit 5**.)

The **Account** module was targeted toward district administrators, and allowed users to analyze student assessment data without requiring technical statistical methods. The data was primarily useful for analysis and accountability purposes. District users were able to access, analyze, and compare district data in order to understand trends, target remediation, and allocate resources. A suite of NCLB reports and data analysis tools assisted principals and superintendents in understanding the relationship between their assessment data and NCLB's AYP requirements. (See **Exhibit 6** for screen shots of Account.)

The **Align** module included a dashboard that allowed teachers to view differentiated student performance data and to plan individualized instruction that was responsive to the performance data. Through the module, teachers had access to academic standards, best practices, pacing calendars, lesson plans, and curricular materials. Teachers were able to use Align to monitor their coverage of required concepts, to access standards-aligned curriculum and materials, and to view student mastery of required academic standards. (See **Exhibit 7** for screen shots of Align.)

The **Assess** module was a benchmark testing administration system. Benchmark tests were delivered periodically, usually every three to six weeks, and were aligned to state-level standards that would later be tested on annual high-stakes tests. Benchmark tests allowed teachers to diagnose student progress and adapt their instructional practices to help students master concepts well in advance of standardized tests. Using Assess, districts could utilize and manage the data from any benchmark testing regime delivered by scan forms, plain paper forms, or online test entry. The module allowed principals and teachers to conduct item analysis to determine individual student or group performance on each question, and to identify institutional needs for teacher professional development or curriculum enhancement. Data from the assessment solution flowed into a data warehouse, where it was linked to individual student records containing demographic, achievement, and other historical information. (See **Exhibit 8** for screen shots of Assess.)

The three remaining IMS modules could be added to Account, Align, and Assess to enhance their features. The **Assign** module was designed to function as a course platform that allowed instructors to post assignments and related content that could be accessed by students at school or at home via the Web. Students were able to download homework, take quizzes, or access tutorials using Assign. The **Outreach** module provided districts with a tool to manage their external Web presence. The module could be used to provide community access to performance data, as well as information such as minutes from school board proceedings, sports team results, lunch menus, and school calendars. SchoolNet developed the **PD Planner** module in collaboration with Chicago-based AHA! interactive. PD Planner allowed districts to align teacher professional development with state standards and to tailor training to individual needs by cross-referencing student and teacher performance data. In 2005, SchoolNet purchased AHA! interactive, and kept the entire staff as part of a new human capital business unit based in Chicago.

SchoolNet realized that school improvement was complex, and that the company had a specific role to play. As Harber put it, "SchoolNet is a piece of a puzzle. You can look at IMS in terms of teacher time saved, satisfaction increased, attitudinal data—teachers and administrators feel more excited and prepared, and believe they can do more. Our IMS saves them the time of having to find the data on their own, and helps them better utilize the data to improve student results."

In particular, the company and its customers believed the product had the potential to dramatically affect the instructional practice of teachers. According to one SchoolNet client, "Time is a teacher's currency. We can't change the number of hours in a day so we have to create efficiencies. SchoolNet tools can help make stronger, quicker, instructional decision makers."

By 2005, SchoolNet had contracts with 45 school districts of various sizes, including Chicago, IL; Corpus Christi, TX; Atlanta, GA; Cleveland, OH; and Pittsburgh and Philadelphia, PA. The company's long-standing and evolving relationship with Philadelphia was not only important, but representative of the general opportunities and challenges associated with selling, implementing, and supporting IMS in complex public school districts.

Philadelphia: The Ultimate Reference Account

The School District of Philadelphia (SDP) was the eighth-largest school district in the United States and the largest in Pennsylvania, with an annual budget of $2 billion and a technology budget of $13.5 million.[5] SDP served over 200,000 students, employed over 12,000 teachers, and operated 273 public schools in 2005. Eighty percent of students were eligible for free or reduced-priced meals. Over 65% of students were African American, 14.5% were Hispanic, 14.2% were White, 5.3% were Asian, and the remainder Native American. Throughout the 1990s, SDP experienced significant financial troubles and posted disappointing results on the Pennsylvania System of School Assessment (PSSA), a statewide examination instituted in 1996.

During the fall of 2000, the Pennsylvania State Department of Education ("the State") began exploring the potential direct effect of technology on student achievement. The State pre-qualified 30 vendors (including SchoolNet) that districts could partner with in applying for a grant known as Students Achieving Standards (SAS), to pilot technology products linked to improving student performance. Each of the vendors offered a different approach to using technology. Concurrently, SDP had been exploring ways to use technology to enhance its instructional practices. The district took advantage of the SAS program and developed a cross-functional review team to consider proposals from the approved vendors, and recommend a small number of projects for pilot in SDP.

In order to better position itself with the State and SDP, SchoolNet brought KPMG and The Princeton Review into the bidding process as subcontractors to outline an integrated set of professional services and content-development capabilities in the product proposal. SchoolNet participated in multiple presentations and product demos throughout December 2000. The committee narrowed the selection process from 30 to eight vendors. In February 2001, the State awarded an SAS grant to SDP, which it split among two providers, SchoolNet and IBM. SchoolNet would install IMS, and IBM would install its Learning Village product. Each vendor was awarded four elementary schools for the pilot.

SchoolNet was viewed as nimble enough to provide the future capabilities that SDP might need. According to a key decision maker at SDP, "We didn't have faith in their current capacity, but we liked what they were offering and believed they would build the capacity to deliver if we contracted with them."

The Two-Year Pilot

In the first year of the pilot, SchoolNet's approach was to roll out all of the IMS modules to every teacher in each of the four pilot schools. Teachers went to intensive training sessions every Wednesday afternoon for two hours. According to Barbara Hockstader, vice president of professional development at SchoolNet:

> The pilot got off to a rocky start. Teachers didn't seem the least bit interested in learning to use IMS, nor could they be—we had been told there were T1 lines in all of the schools, which are critical to the speed and efficiency of our Web-based platform. As it turned out, the T1 lines were split among several schools. This meant that when teachers would go to SchoolNet training sessions, the site would be at a standstill. We'd have to send them home.

Eventually the technical problems were solved, and the pilot picked up momentum. As one SDP official explained: "We saw a number of 'easy-to-demo' products from the companies in the selection process, but during the pilot it became apparent that SchoolNet had more than that—an 'easy-to-use' tool for teachers. When I saw teachers who had been in the district for 30 years actually inputting lesson plans into IMS, I knew we were on to something."

During the pilot, SDP experienced a state takeover due to chronically low academic achievement and a $200 million operating deficit. In December of 2001, then Republican Governor Mark Schweiker and Democratic Philadelphia Mayor John Street brokered a shared governance agreement. The existing school board, which had been fully appointed by the mayor, was dismantled. Schweiker and Street created a new five-member governing board, the School Reform Commission (SRC), with three members appointed by the governor and two by the mayor. The superintendent resigned in protest of this exertion of state authority. The SRC was empowered to select SDP's new CEO, assumed fiduciary responsibility for SDP, and gained a number of extraordinary powers under Act 46 of the Pennsylvania School Code (see **Exhibit 9**).

One of the SRC's first decisions divided SDP's schools into four categories: (1) *Partnership Schools,* which were the 45 lowest-performing schools in the district. This set of schools was run under contract with SDP by for-profit and nonprofit organizations such as educational management organizations (EMOs), local universities, and community development organizations; (2) *Reconstituted Schools,* another group of extremely low-performing schools which were combined as one subdistrict, completely restarted with new staff and programs, but still under the full control of the District; (3) *Charter Schools,* operated by a number of outside providers under the Pennsylvania charter school code; and (4) *Regular Schools*, the remaining schools in the district, which would continue to operate under the same conditions as before.

During the second year of the pilot, SchoolNet expanded from the four original schools to 21 reconstituted schools, which represented a unique opportunity. The district's reconstitution guidelines imposed on these schools a common expectation and system for using data to influence instructional decisions. Consequently, SDP installed the necessary technology and network infrastructure to support the guidelines, which were also necessary for SchoolNet IMS to function optimally. Importantly, although these schools were classified as underperforming, they were still operated by SDP, as opposed to contracted out to private management. SDP central office and school staff were highly motivated to improve results in reconstituted schools to prevent them from being taken over by EMOs and other private managers in future years. As a result of this competitive mindset, SDP employees viewed the SchoolNet relationship in the reconstituted schools as a partnership that could help them meet their goals.

New Leadership in Philadelphia

After operating the district without a senior executive for six months, the SRC appointed Paul Vallas as CEO in July 2002. The former head of Chicago Public Schools from 1995 to 2001, Vallas enacted a series of large-scale reforms aimed at improving academic achievement throughout SDP. Under Vallas's strategic plan, "Students Succeeding 2002–2008," SDP standardized the K–9 curriculum, increased instructional time for literacy and mathematics, implemented six-week benchmark assessments, strengthened professional development, reduced class sizes in grades K–3, and earmarked $1.5 billion for capital improvements.[6]

In sharp contrast to his predecessors, Vallas provided District educators little instructional leeway. Because of high rates of student mobility and teacher attrition, Vallas believed that teachers needed real-time access to student data and a scripted curriculum on a daily basis, with the understanding that experienced teachers would be able to supplement the curriculum as needed. He also believed that in order for a standards-based, data-driven district to succeed, several steps were necessary. First, the district needed a curriculum that was explicitly aligned to state standards at a granular level. (SDP defined "curriculum" as a sequenced set of standards by grade level and content area [scope and sequence], which would grow over time to include more specific content.) Next, Vallas believed the district needed to implement benchmark assessments in reading and math, aligned to the state standards and delivered to every student, every six weeks, to allow teachers to diagnose and respond to individual learning needs. Finally, Vallas believed that SDP needed a consistent districtwide standards-based grade book and report card, to replace the myriad grade books and multiple report cards in use throughout the district.

In his first year, Vallas introduced sweeping changes, including districtwide benchmark assessment testing and a uniform, standards-aligned curriculum. He hired Princeton Review to provide benchmark assessment testing at the K–8 level, and Kaplan, Inc., to design the high school curriculum. As part of the new curriculum, teachers taught for five weeks, administered benchmark tests at the end of week five, and used week six to provide remediation based on areas of weakness uncovered by the test results. SchoolNet's 25 schools took tests online, while non-IMS schools used paper and pencil. As opposed to the weeks-long lead time to receive results in the paper and pencil schools, IMS school teachers received student results in two or three days. Also, the technology provided direct mapping to remediation for individuals as well as groups of students. As one SDP leader pointed out:

> With SchoolNet, every piece of data about schools now has a name and face attached to it. For example, when we received test scores that suggested our Hispanic students were underperforming in reading and language arts, our first assumption was that these students were English Language Learners. However, with SchoolNet, we were able to dig into the data further and uncover that the underperforming Hispanic students actually were not students learning English, which changed our approach to the problem. Armed with this data, we were able to make adjustments to instruction.

This confluence of new programs and practices during the pilot, along with the performance of the SchoolNet product, was instrumental to SDP's decision to roll out IMS as the technology solution that would allow the district to track and analyze individual student performance on an ongoing basis. This meant quickly growing SchoolNet's penetration from 25 to 273 schools. After investing a few hundred thousand dollars in the two-year pilot, SDP signed a two-year $5.7 million contract with SchoolNet in 2003 to accomplish this task. By early 2005, SchoolNet IMS was fully deployed in 168 schools. (See **Exhibit 10** for a time line.)

According to Harber:

> With Philadelphia, it's never done. IMS is implemented, but it's a living breathing thing. Scores have gone up in a big way across the board, but I think it's a mistake to look at a piece of software as the cause of success. You don't look to a measuring stick to increase length. That said, the fact that a measuring stick is in place may help provide focus to make something grow faster.

Impact on District Practices

Two years into the SchoolNet IMS rollout, SDP had become increasingly interested in evaluating the performance of technology vendors. The district developed criteria that evaluated the quality of the infrastructure, the effectiveness of user training, and the level of awareness the product had achieved with the relevant user groups. SDP also collaborated with Temple University to measure log-in and usage data. Ultimately, though, the district tried to assess the impact the technology had on student test results (**Exhibit 11**). According to a senior SDP official:

> SDP measures a technology provider's success based on alignment with the goals and the mission of the District, as well as results. We are interested both in what a vendor said they'd do, and how that manifests itself in student achievement. A lot is at stake here. This is a city where generation after generation has failed. I am impatient for results because I have to bring kids above the water line, and if I have to wait 10 years for results, another generation of kids will drown. As a result, out of the gate, a vendor has to be willing to show me data to demonstrate that their product works.

Implementing the SchoolNet IMS in the district required a significant change in behavior, especially for more experienced teachers. SchoolNet worked hard to ensure that everyone learned and adopted the technology. According to a member of SDP's educational technology group, "We had a lot of early adopters, and now we have a new cadre of teachers coming into the district who are comfortable with technology. However, right now we also still have data coaches printing out results for many teachers. Until all teachers are going into the IMS to print out reports themselves, we still have more work to do."

A number of SDP officials observed that the tool was taking hold both administratively and instructionally. At the district level, groups providing professional development in particular content areas and instructional techniques were becoming increasingly targeted in their offerings and their work with specific teachers. Additionally, teachers were increasingly using the data to adjust their instructional practice. As one principal described, "Before, a teacher might ask a class, 'did everyone get it?' Students would likely nod in approval whether they understood or not. Now, with the level of benchmark testing data available through IMS, teachers can see who really understands the material and who is struggling."

Given that up to 35% of students changed schools within the district in any given year, and annual teacher attrition remained high, IMS helped the district work toward its goal of creating seamless educational continuity and instructional consistency. An oft-cited example of this effect was the M. H. Stanton School, which had endured a fifth-grade teacher vacancy for most of the 2004 school year. Despite that fact, the fifth-grade PSSA scores at M. H. Stanton jumped from the 20th to the 70th percentile that year.

Looking Ahead: Philadelphia and the Broader Market

Philadelphia

> Every day is a new sales day for SchoolNet. Once you get beyond the pilot, beyond the initial rollout, once money has been spent, people really want to see proof of concept. To date, Philadelphia has been very forgiving of any challenges with implementation, training, and usage. Over time, they should expect more and be less forgiving. SchoolNet can no longer act like a start-up.
>
> —*Mindy Sinyak, Project Manager, SchoolNet*

SchoolNet's contract with SDP's educational technology group included installation and maintenance of IMS and the professional services required to train employees on its use. The contract was under review in 2005, with the potential for a three-year extension by the close of the school year. Contract negotiations were complicated by the current budget situation—SDP was running a deficit.

SchoolNet also faced the challenge of establishing itself as a legitimate player and a long-term technology partner, which was increasingly important as new leadership inevitably transitioned into and out of SDP.

Competition for District Mindshare and Share of Wallet

By 2005, SchoolNet interacted with the Education Technology Group, the Office of Assessment, the Office of Accountability, Curriculum and Instruction, and Professional Development. Sometimes these groups worked together and sometimes they were at odds. The challenge for SchoolNet going forward was to continue to garner district mindshare and share-of-wallet from the key internal constituents as an increasing number of larger, better-funded external vendors came into the District with potentially competing solutions.

The SchoolNet IMS maintained data from multiple sources. The solution provided the district with centralized storing and single sign-on for users. Every night, SchoolNet updated data feeds from various content and assessment vendors, such as The Princeton Review, which already worked with SchoolNet, and Kaplan, which had installed its own content-delivery system in SDP high schools.

Additionally, IBM played an increased role in the District. Long interested in the K–12 market, IBM began rollout of a data warehouse solution throughout SDP in the fall of 2004. This solution was designed to house all student and employee data for SDP and could feed data into IMS, if the district continued its relationship with SchoolNet. SDP increasingly saw SchoolNet as a general contractor. As one official explained, "With SchoolNet, we're not locked into one assessment, content, or professional development provide: we can plug multiple products into the IMS."

However, as more vendors entered, there was potential for overlap and the need to clarify and define the different roles of each project and provider. As Mindy Sinyak explained, "We have to help our contacts at SDP with internal marketing—say what IBM is for, say what SchoolNet is for, and distinguish who the most appropriate internal users are for each."

Transition from Project to Long-Term Partner

As SchoolNet entered year three of the rollout, Andy Brenner described SchoolNet's challenge in Philadelphia as "not wanting teachers and administrators to view the solution as simply a benchmark system or a one-time project. Rather, we want users to view this as 'our IMS'—as the de facto location to go for district resources."

Brenner and Sinyak had begun working with SDP in early 2005 to make this transition. SchoolNet had spent the last two years focused on "data." It had become increasingly important to ensure the message was refocused on "instruction." In particular, Brenner and Sinyak collaborated with internal teams to help them build a cohesive vision around the idea of "one-stop, seamless access to instruction." They also collaborated with the various constituents to identify the pieces of SchoolNet not yet rolled out, such as parent access, lesson banks, and other teacher tools. As one internal team member commented, "We're getting to the point where we have to help make the SchoolNet IMS all it can be or it will lose credibility as a total solution."

Beyond Philadelphia, Beyond NCLB

> NCLB guaranteed a small start-up from New York City a temporary seat at the table. Now we must position ourselves as a true platform. Any other vendor with a product that has value in terms of content or assessment should flow through the SchoolNet platform.
>
> —*Jonathan Harber, CEO, SchoolNet*

As Harber thought about acquiring new customers, he considered a number of strategic questions. How could SchoolNet position itself to prospects as a general contractor with a platform on which many applications could rest, similar to what they had accomplished in Philadelphia? What would it take for customers to see the value of the IMS beyond the reporting requirements of NCLB? And just how fast could SchoolNet take on new accounts, given the need to implement with a high standard of quality, combined with the current commitments it had to existing customers? What were the implications of all of these questions for SchoolNet's organizational capacity and capital needs?

As the train pulled into Penn Station, Harber pulled out his cell phone to call the office and ask people to gather for a brainstorming session the next morning. He was determined to build on the excitement and momentum of the Philadelphia meeting to kick-start the action planning for the larger questions facing SchoolNet.

Notes

1. Ascend Ventures was based in New York, NY, and primarily invested in early-stage education and applied technology ventures.

2. "K–12 Solutions, Learning Markets and Opportunities 2004," Eduventures, Boston, MA, 2004, p. 6.

3. Ibid, p. 27.

4. SchoolNet called its product "IMS"; and the remainder of the case will use these initials to stand for the specific SchoolNet product, rather than the market category referred to by the same acronym on pp. 3–4.

5. Comprehensive Annual Financial Report, School District of Philadelphia, year ending June 30, 2004.

6. This paragraph was adapted from "Reinventing Human Resources at the School District Philadelphia," by David Thomas and Caroline King, HBS Case PEL-029, June 2005, pp. 2–3.

Exhibit 1

SchoolNet Financial Information, 2001–2004

Exhibit 1a: Income Statement (in Thousands of Dollars)

	2001	*2002*	*2003*	*2004*
Revenue	$1,492	$1,759	$6,037	$14,881
Direct Costs				
Compensation	292	368	281	1,690
Hosting & Maintenance	71	60	44	76
Other	—	—	765	675
Total Direct Costs	363	428	1,091	2,441
Gross Profit	1,129	1,331	4,946	12,440
Operating Expenses				
Provision for Bad Debt	—	—	6	—
Compensation	1,831	3,653	4,255	6,721
Marketing	79	313	216	1,258
Office Administration	376	696	692	1,082
Professional Fees	100	227	236	479
Sales Commission	32	36	392	546
Travel & Entertainment	315	599	604	1,237
Total Operating Expenses	2,733	5,525	6,400	11,323
Operating Income (Loss)	(1,603)	(4,194)	(1,454)	1,117
Net Interest (Income)/Expense	918	(48)	(7)	48
Depreciation & Amortization	381	490	78	177
Total Other (Income)/Expenses	1,299	442	70	224
Net Income/(Loss)	($2,902)	($4,636)	($1,525)	$892

Exhibit 1b: Balance Sheet, Years Ending December 31 (in Thousands of Dollars)

	2001	*2002*	*2003*	*2004*
ASSETS				
Current Assets				
Cash	$1,897	$1,533	$550	$8,115
Accounts Receivable	37	312	2,115	2,266
Other Current Assets	4	298	25	387
Total Current Assets	1,938	2,143	2,691	10,769
Fixed Assets	180	166	242	545
Capitalized Software	379	—	—	—
	$2,497	$2,309	$2,933	$11,314
LIABILITIES & STOCKHOLDERS' EQUITY				
Current Liabilities				
Accounts Payable	$312	$205	$312	$827
Accrued Expenses	205	233	1,183	1,943
Credit Facilities	165	—	—	1,304
Deferred Revenue	107	483	1,565	6,380
Total Current Liabilities	789	921	3,059	10,453
Total Liabilities	789	921	3,059	10,453
Stockholders' Equity				
Common Stock/APIC	7,010	11,334	11,348	11,450
Retained Earnings	(5,302)	(9,946)	(11,474)	(10,589)
Total Stockholders' Equity	1,708	1,388	(126)	861
	$2,497	$2,309	$2,933	$11,314

Source: SchoolNet, Inc.

Exhibit 2

SchoolNet Selected Client Information

Client Name	*Students*	*Staff*	*Total Expenditures 2004*	*Initial Contract Date*	*# of Renewals to Date*	*Current Contract Term*	*# of Modules Purchased*
Philadelphia (PA)	189,779	22,554	$2,039,389,000	2001	4	3 years	3
Cleveland Municipal City (OH)	69,655	11,591	$808,400,000	2003	3	1 year	4
Corpus Christi (TX)	39,310	5,172	$291,647,000	2003	1	5 years	3
Pittsburgh (PA)	34,658	5,214	$547,636,000	2003	3	4 years	3
City of Chicago (IL)	434,419	27,582	$4,159,228,000	2004	1	2 years	4
Northside—San Antonio (TX)	56,914	7,877	$560,016,000	2004	1	4.5 years	4
Atlanta (GA)	52,103	7,310	$780,889,000	2005	n/a	1 year	3
District of Columbia	65,099	9,583	$1,105,963,000	2005	1	1 year	4

Source: National Center for Education Statistics and SchoolNet, Inc.

Exhibit 3

Biographical Information for Denis Doyle and Jonathan Harber

Denis Philip Doyle, Co-founder and Chief Academic Officer of SchoolNet, is a nationally and internationally known education writer, lecturer and consultant. After earning his BA (1962) and MA (1964) in political theory at the University of California at Berkeley, he worked for the California Legislature, where he was the architect of major education bills, including the Ryan Act, the major teacher licensing reform of the 1970s.

Moving to Washington, DC, in 1972, he became Assistant Director of the U.S. Office of Economic Opportunity, then Assistant Director of the National Institute of Education, where he ran the nation's two largest education demonstration projects, Education Voucher and Experimental Schools.

He has been associated with think tanks since 1980—Brookings, AEI, Heritage, and Hudson Institute, where he is presently a non-resident Fellow. He has written numerous scholarly and popular articles for *The Atlantic, The Public Interest, Change, Education Week,* and *The Phi Delta Kappan.* He has also published more than 150 op-eds in the nation's most prestigious newspapers: the *Washington Post, Wall Street Journal, Los Angeles Times,* and *Baltimore Sun.*

Three of his books in print are *Investing in Our Children: Business and the Public Schools (New York: CED, 1984); Winning the Brain Race: A Bold Plan to Make Our Schools Competitive,* with David T. Kearns, Xerox CEO (San Francisco: ICS Press, 1989 and 1991); and *Reinventing Education: Entrepreneurship in America's Public Schools,* with Louis V. Gerstner, IBM CEO, et al. (New York: E. P. Dutton, 1994). His most recent book is *Raising the Standard* (with Susan Pimentel), a how-to book for schools interested in standards-based reform.

Jonathan D. Harber, CEO, President, and Co-founder of SchoolNet, has extensive experience in the education technology market and has proven past success as an entrepreneur. Mr. Harber was the Co-founder and Chairman of NewKidCo (Nasdaq: NKCIF), a children's video game publishing company based on licenses such as Sesame Street, Disney, Tiny Toons, and Tom and Jerry. When NewKidCo was sold to SoftQuad in 1998, it had revenues of roughly $23 million and had just completed a $10 million secondary offering.

Previously, Harber founded the award-winning children's educational software company KinderActive. Harber was the Co-founder and President of Diva, a publisher of software to the multimedia and education markets. Diva was acquired by Avid Technology (Nasdaq: AVID), a world leader in digital media technology, concurrent with its IPO, led by Morgan Stanley, in 1993. Harber began his career as an investment banker working for Merrill Lynch in corporate finance and decision support.

Harber earned an MS in Management from MIT and completed a joint Master's thesis between the MIT Media Lab and the MIT Sloan School. Harber received a Bachelor of Arts with Honors in Cognitive Science from Wesleyan University. He currently sits on the Board of Trustees of Trail Blazers, a not-for-profit agency providing life skills for disadvantaged urban youths, and also sits on the Board of Outward Bound NYC, a non-profit organization that works with the NYC Department of Education, including managing schools and running supplemental educational services for disadvantaged students.

Source: SchoolNet, Inc.

Exhibit 4

Breakdown of Technology Spending in a Typical Public School District

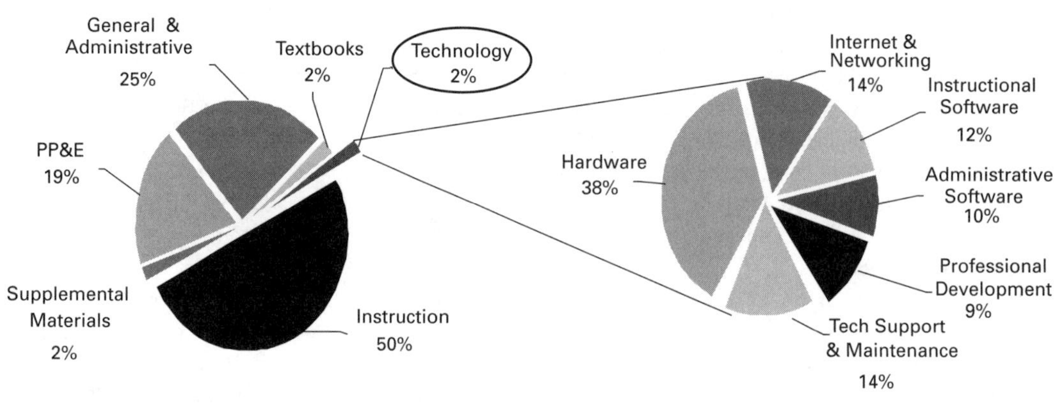

Source: National Center for Education Statistics, Common Core of Data (CCD), 2001–02; QED's 10th Annual Technology Purchasing Forecast: 2004–2005; and case writer analysis.

Note: PP&E: property, plant and equipment.

Exhibit 5

Graphic of IMS Product and Relationship to Other Technology

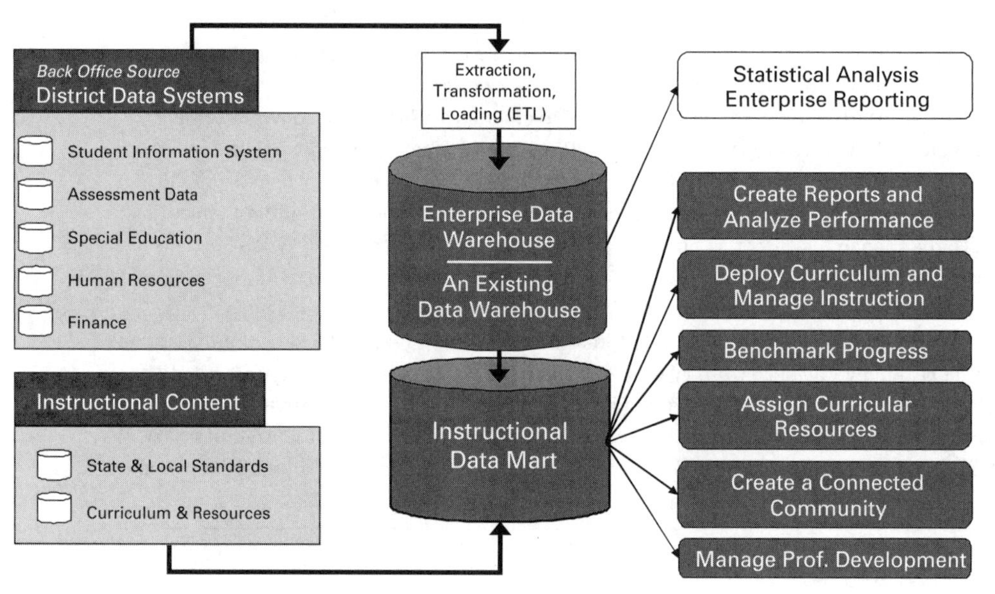

Source: SchoolNet, Inc.

Exhibit 6

Screen Shots for Account Module

NCLB Report: Performance by Subgroup

NCLB Category	Math	ELA
Summary	AYP Goals Not Met	AYP Goals Met
Male	AYP Goals Met	AYP Goals Met
Female	AYP Goals Met	AYP Goals Met
Ethnicity: African American	AYP Goals Met	AYP Goals Met
Ethnicity: Latino	AYP Goals Met	AYP Goals Met
Ethnicity: Caucasian	AYP Goals Met	AYP Goals Met
Ethnicity: Other/Multicultural	AYP Goals Met	AYP Goals Met Insufficient Data
Ethnicity: Asian	AYP Goals Met	AYP Goals Met
Ethnicity: American Indian	AYP Goals Met Insufficient Data	AYP Goals Met Insufficient Data
Special Education	32 Students Not Proficient	AYP Goals Met
LEP	Zero Data	Zero Data

Benchmark Performance Report: Results for Entire Grade 8

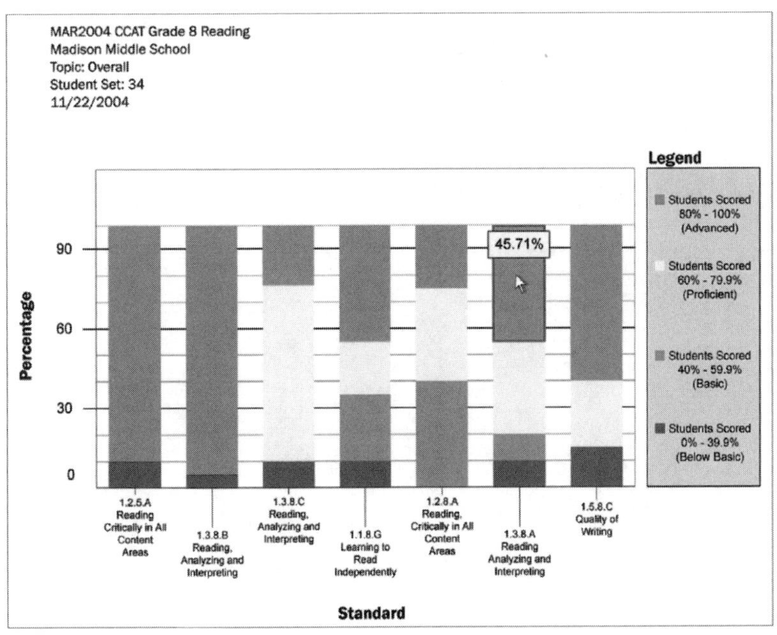

Source: SchoolNet, Inc.

Exhibit 7

Screen Shots of Align Module

Exhibit 7a: Item Analysis by Student

Standards Mastery | Skill Analysis | Item Analysis | Student List | Student Analysis

Test:	MAR2004 CCAT Grade 8 Math (2)	**Teacher:**	MAC RYBARCZYK
Test Date:	Wednesday, December 01, 2004	**Number of Students:**	20
Number of Questions:	Total Possible Points: 20	**Number of Students:**	Tested: 19
Section:	Homeroom 8th Grade - (87)		

Question	**1**	**2**	**3**	**4**	**5**	**6**	**7**	**8**	**9**	**10**	**11**	**12**	**13**	**14**	**15**	**16**	**17**	**18**	**19**	**20**	**Points Scored**
Standard	2.2.8. B.1	2.2.8. B.4	2.2.8. B.3	2.2.8. C.3	2.9.8. B.4	2.9.8. B.2	2.9.8. F.3	2.9.8. E.1	2.9.8. G.1	2.9.8. K.1	2.9.8. K.1	2.9.8. D.1	2.9.8. B.2	2.10. 8.B.1	2.3.8. A.2	2.3.D. 3	2.3.8. G.3	2.3.8. D	2.3.8. E	2.3.8. F	
Possible Points	1	1	1	1	1	1	1	1	1	1	1	1	1	1	1	1	1	1	1	1	
Correct Response	C	C	C	B	B	A	D	A	B	C	C	B	D	C	C	C	D	C	B	C	
BOUKNIGHT, KANISHA	✓	B	✓	D	✓	C	✓	✓	✓	B	✓	✓	A	D	A	✓	✓	✓	A	✓	11/20
BURGESON, ALVA	✓	✓	✓	✓	✓	C	B	✓	✓	✓	✓	✓	C	A	A	D	✓	✓	✓	✓	14/20
CHRISTLEY, ANTWAN	✓	A	✓	✓	✓	B	B	✓	C	✓	A	✓	B	✓	✓	✓	A	✓	✓	✓	11/20
DELANGEL, SCOTT	✓	✓	✓	A	✓	✓	✓	✓	✓	✓	✓	✓	✓	B	A	✓	✓	✓	✓	✓	17/20
DOEPKE, LELAH	✓	✓	✓	✓	✓	✓	B	✓	✓	✓	✓	✓	✓	✓	A	✓	B	✓	C	✓	15/20
EASTMAN, ISIAH	✓	✓	✓	✓	✓	✓	✓	✓	✓	✓	✓	✓	✓	✓	A	✓	✓	✓	✓	✓	20/20
ESSEX, WILLIS	✓	✓	✓	✓	✓	✓	B	✓	C	✓	✓	✓	✓	✓	A	✓	B	✓	✓	✓	17/20
FALLEN, ZITA	✓	✓	✓	✓	✓	C	✓	✓	✓	✓	A	C	✓	✓	A	✓	A	✓	A	✓	14/20
GOLSON, RAEANN	✓	✓	✓	✓	✓	B	✓	✓	D	✓	✓	✓	✓	D	✓	✓	✓	✓	✓	D	15/20
HEDRICK, JAMEL	✓	✓	✓	✓	✓	D	✓	✓	✓	✓	A	✓	✓	✓	A	✓	B	✓	C	✓	15/20
HOEL, ARDEN	✓	✓	✓	✓	✓	C	✓	✓	✓	✓	✓	✓	✓	✓	A	✓	B	✓	✓	✓	17/20
KALAR, MY	✓	✓	✓	✓	C	D	A	D	C	B	✓	✓	C	C	A	✓	A	✓	A	✓	10/20
KIRBY, WILLARD	✓	A	B	C	✓	D	B	✓	C	✓	✓	✓	B	A	A	✓	B	✓	C	✓	10/20
KOSS, TARI	✓	✓	✓	✓	✓	C	✓	✓	✓	✓	✓	✓	C	A	A	✓	✓	✓	A	✓	15/20
KUNDE, ALEISHA	✓	✓	A	✓	✓	C	B	✓	D	✓	D	✓	A	✓	A	✓	✓	✓	D	✓	11/20
LAMPMAN, THEODORE	✓	✓	✓	✓	✓	C	✓	✓	✓	✓	✓	✓	✓	A	✓	✓	✓	✓	✓	✓	16/20
MCDERMOTT, JENIFER	✓	✓	✓	✓	✓	C	B	✓	✓	✓	✓	✓	✓	D	✓	✓	B	✓	✓	✓	15/20
MCDONNELL, BILLY																					
PORTEE, GILBERTE	✓	✓	✓	✓	✓	C	✓	C	✓	✓	✓	✓	✓	A	✓	✓	✓	✓	✓	✓	16/20
RAU, KUM	✓	✓	✓	✓	✓	C	✓	✓	C	B	✓	✓	✓	D	✓	✓	✓	✓	A	✓	14/20
Summary	30/30	27/30	24/30	25/30	28/30	8/30	18/30	25/30	16/30	24/30	20/30	28/30	22/30	10/30	7/30	27/30	16/30	30/30	12/30	29/30	

Source: SchoolNet, Inc.

Exhibit 7b Item Analysis by Standard

Standards Mastery | Skill Analysis | Item Analysis | Student List | Student Analysis

Report Type: Individual Benchmark Test — Grade: 8

Subject: Mathematics — Benchmark Tests 12/01/04 MAR2004, CCAT Grade 8 Math

Tools	Standard		Students Scored 80%-100% Correct	Students Scored 60%-79.9% Correct	Students Scored 40%-59.9% Correct	Students Scored 0%-39.9% Correct	Times Taught	Times Sched.	Time Assessed
	2.10.8.B.1:	Use concepts of similarity, Pythagorean Theorem & Right Triangle relationships to find indirect measurements	10	5	4	1	3	1	1
	2.2.8.B.1:	Subtract Integers	28	1	1	0	5	2	2
	2.2.8.B.3:	Calculate a percent of a number (e.g., sales tax)	24	2	2	2	3	3	1
	2.2.8.B.4:	Demonstrate proficiency using all four operations with all types of real numbers.	25	4	1	0	9	4	3
	2.2.8.C.3:	Order a set of real numbers	25	3	1	1	2	2	1
	2.3.8.A.2:	Find the area of a triangle when given the base and the height	15	7	2	6	4	1	1
	2.3.8.D:	Estimate, use and describe measures of distance, rate, perimeter, area, volume, weight, mass and angles	10	9	8	2	8	4	3
	2.3.8.E:	Describe how a change in linear dimension of an object affects its perimeter, area, and volume	12	12	3	3	7	3	3
	2.3.8.F:	Use scale measurements to interpret maps or drawings	27	2	1	0	2	2	2
	2.3.8.G:	Create and use scale models	18	5	3	4	3	2	2

Key: Students Scored 80%-100% Correct: 80-100% — Students Scored 60%-79.9% Correct:60-80%

Students Scored 40%-59.9% Correct:40-60% — Students Scored 0%-39.9% Correct:0-40%

View Standard Detail — Schedule Standard — View Related Materials

Source: SchoolNet, Inc.

Exhibit 8

Screen Shot of Assess Module: Benchmark Test Archive

Test Name	Grade Level	Subject	Start Date - End Date	Status
Algebra 1 Block Schedule Benchmark Assessment D	9	Mathematics	Jan. 30, 2005 - Feb. 01, 2005	Testing: Complete Data Collection: In progress 380 of 1,996 Students Data Collection Report
Algebra 2 Benchmark Assessment 4	9	Mathematics	Jan. 30, 2005 - Feb. 15, 2005	Testing: Complete Data Collection: Completed 4,464 of 2,021 Students Data Collection Report
Algebra 2 Block Schedule Benchmark Assessment D	9	Mathematics	Jan. 30, 2005 - Feb. 01, 2005	Testing: Complete Data Collection: In progress 861 of 1,996 Students Data Collection Report
Biology Benchmark Assessment 4	9	Science	Jan. 30, 2005 - Feb. 15, 2005	Testing: Complete Data Collection: Completed 1,358 of 5,718 Students Data Collection Report
Biology Block Schedule Benchmark Assessment D	9	Science	Jan. 30, 2005 - Feb. 15, 2005	Testing: Complete Data Collection: Completed 1,358 of 1,358 Students Data Collection Report
Chemistry Benchmark Assessment 4	9	Science	Jan. 30, 2005 - Feb. 01, 2005	Testing: Complete Data Collection: In progress 1,358 of 3,759 Students Data Collection Report
Chemistry Block Schedule Benchmark Assessment D	9	Science	Jan. 30, 2005 - Feb. 01, 2005	Testing: Complete Data Collection: In progress 1,209 of 1,385 Students Data Collection Report
English 1 Benchmark Assessment 4	9	Language Arts	Jan. 30, 2005 - Feb. 15, 2005	Testing: Complete Data Collection: Completed 2,021 of 6,421 Students Data Collection Report
English 1 Block Schedule Benchmark Assessment D	9	Language Arts	Jan. 30, 2005 - Feb. 01, 2005	Testing: Complete Data Collection: Completed 351 of 1,996 Students Data Collection Report

Source: SchoolNet, Inc.

Exhibit 9

School Reform Commission (SRC) Powers under Act 46

The SRC was created under Act 46 of the Pennsylvania School Code. The SRC acts in place of the Philadelphia Board of Education and has complete control of every aspect of Philadelphia Public Schools. Under the Act 46, the SRC can:

- Suspend the Pennsylvania School Code
- Suspend the State Board of Education regulations
- Hire, or delegate its power to, for-profit corporations to manage the school district
- Turn over public schools to private groups and corporations
- Hire noncertified teachers and managers
- Reassign, suspend, or dismiss professional employees
- Terminate collective bargaining agreements
- Levy taxes and incur debts

Source: The General Assembly of Philadelphia Senate Bill No. 640, http://www2.legis.state.pa.us/WU01/LI/BI/BT/2001/0/SB0640P1473.pdf; and http://www.savephillyschools.org/schoolboard/, accessed July 27, 2004.

Exhibit 10

Time Line of SchoolNet's Relationship with the School District of Philadelphia

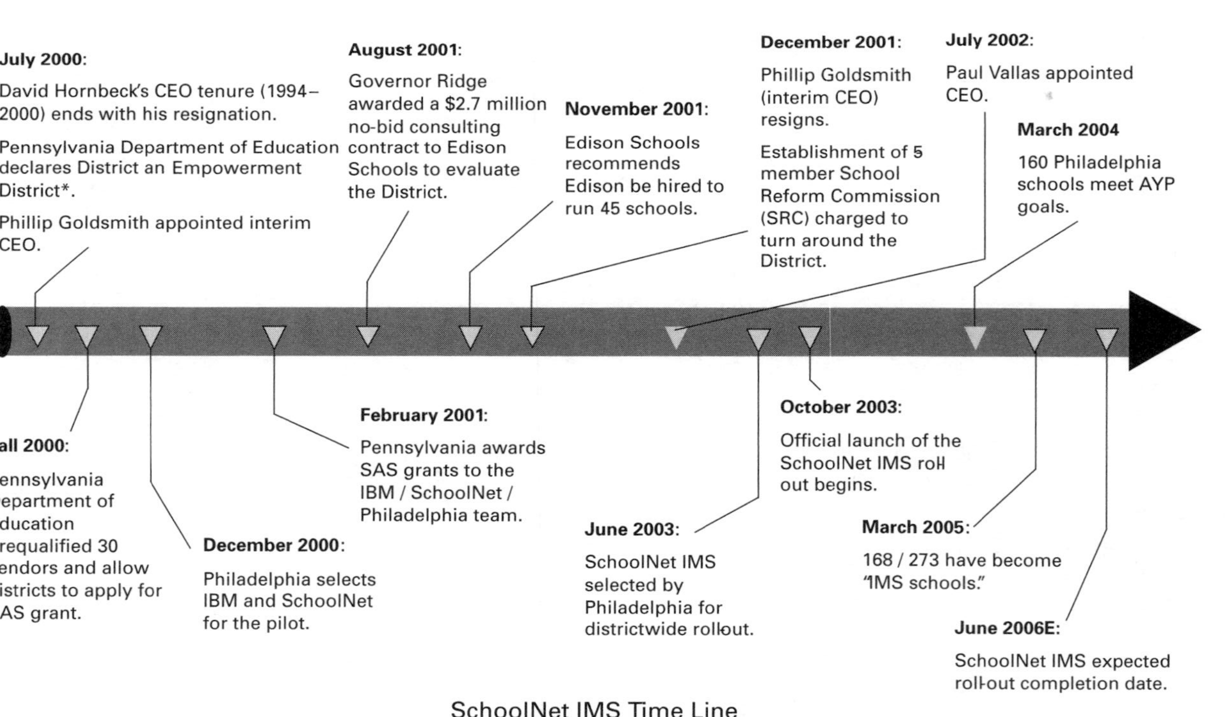
Philadelphia Governance Time Line
July 2000:
David Hornbeck's CEO tenure (1994–2000) ends with his resignation.
Pennsylvania Department of Education declares District an Empowerment District*.
Phillip Goldsmith appointed interim CEO.
August 2001:
Governor Ridge awarded a $2.7 million no-bid consulting contract to Edison Schools to evaluate the District.
November 2001:
Edison Schools recommends Edison be hired to run 45 schools.
December 2001:
Phillip Goldsmith (interim CEO) resigns.
Establishment of 5 member School Reform Commission (SRC) charged to turn around the District.
July 2002:
Paul Vallas appointed CEO.
March 2004
160 Philadelphia schools meet AYP goals.
Fall 2000:
Pennsylvania Department of Education prequalified 30 vendors and allow districts to apply for SAS grant.
December 2000:
Philadelphia selects IBM and SchoolNet for the pilot.
February 2001:
Pennsylvania awards SAS grants to the IBM / SchoolNet / Philadelphia team.
June 2003:
SchoolNet IMS selected by Philadelphia for districtwide rollout.
October 2003:
Official launch of the SchoolNet IMS roll out begins.
March 2005:
168 / 273 have become "IMS schools."
June 2006E:
SchoolNet IMS expected roll-out completion date.
SchoolNet IMS Time Line

*Empowerment District: status signified that a combined average of 50% or more students had scored in the bottom quartile of the PSSA over two consecutive academic years.

Source: Case writer analysis and SchoolNet, Inc.

Exhibit 11

Pennsylvania System of School Assessment Results for School District of Philadelphia and Pennsylvania

Percentage of Students Scoring Proficient or Advanced

	Grade	*2001*	*2005*	*Change*
Reading				
Philadelphia	5	18.8	35.1	16.3
Pennsylvania	5	56.1	64.2	8.1
Philadelphia	8	23.0	39.4	16.4
Pennsylvania	8	60.1	64.1	4.0
Philadelphia	11	34.0	30.6	–3.4
Pennsylvania	11	58.1	65.0	6.9
Math				
Philadelphia	5	17.5	45.8	28.3
Pennsylvania	5	53.0	69.0	16.0
Philadelphia	8	16.2	39.4	23.2
Pennsylvania	8	51.0	62.9	11.9
Philadelphia	11	23.8	23.1	–0.7
Pennsylvania	11	47.9	50.9	3.0

Source: Pennsylvania Department of Education, "PSSA Results," Pennsylvania Department of Education Web site, http://www.pde.state.pa.us/a_and_t/cwp/view.asp?a=3&q=115272, accessed August 2008.

Stacey Childress ■ Sophie Lippincott

Wireless Generation

On a sweltering morning in the middle of a New York heat wave in July 2006, Larry Berger made his way to Wireless Generation's new headquarters at the foot of the Manhattan Bridge in Brooklyn. He and cofounder Greg Gunn had just moved the company from a cramped office in Manhattan to a sprawling space with a deck and a fantastic view of the city across the East River. Since 2001, Wireless Generation had grown from a small education technology shop to a $22 million company nearing profitability. A number of private investors owned approximately 60% of the company, with the remaining 40% held through stock and options by the founders and employees.

The company had created a number of products under its mCLASS[1] brand that were designed to assess students' acquisition of early-literacy skills. Wireless Generation's success to date was partially due to federal legislation that mandated early-reading assessment in low-performing schools and provided the funds for schools to implement it. In 2004, Wireless Generation had developed a product called the mCLASS:Reading 3D solution in an unusual joint venture with Montgomery County Public Schools (MCPS) in Maryland. The Chicago Public Schools and the Fort Worth Independent School District in Texas had recently purchased Reading 3D, providing revenue for Wireless Generation and royalties for MCPS. (See **Exhibit 1** for Wireless Generation products.)

Emerging from the subway station into the 93-degree morning, Berger thought about the strategic questions the company faced as it strove for profitability. Could lessons from the MCPS partnership be applied to future product development and marketing efforts? Did Wireless Generation have the capacity to continue improving and selling its reading products, while broadening its product mix to include math assessments and other tools that would help districts and schools develop the capacity of teachers and administrators to use data for continuous improvement?

The Education Products and Services Industry

Wireless Generation competed for revenues across multiple categories in the education products and services industry. Its reading products were based on formative assessments, which represented $150 million of the $3.5 billion supplemental content market in 2005. The company was also part of the enterprise software and technology segment, a $1.7 billion market. It also generated approximately 15% of its sales from training services, which were part of the $3.3 billion professional development market.

Launching the Company

Gunn and Berger met as Rhodes Scholars at Oxford in 1992 where they bonded over a shared passion for education technology. After Oxford, they both moved to Washington, D.C. Berger was a White House Fellow, where he worked for NASA developing its twenty-first century educational technology agenda. Gunn joined the Carlyle Group, a private equity firm, and focused on investments in new media, health care, and systems integration businesses. During their time in D.C., they stayed in touch through regular lunches and were fascinated by the new opportunities created by the Internet. Berger recalled they each discovered the Mosaic Web browser around the same time in 1994:

> Greg and I sat together and paged through the 50 or 60 Web sites that were out there and thought it was pretty great. I remember being involved that day in an online discussion about what the metaphor should be for exploring the Web. Some said "surfing," others thought "weaving." I enthusiastically championed "weaving" because I thought it described a proactive, participatory meeting in which people would actually make stuff together instead of just skimming across the top alone.

In 1996 an opportunity arose to collaborate on a freelance project to develop "The Hole in the Web," an online extension of Paul Newman's "Hole in the Wall Gang" camp for children with cancer and blood diseases. Berger and Gunn jumped at the chance. The Internet was still new, and when the duo demonstrated an early version of the site to the camp's board, several members looked perplexed. One finally summoned the courage to ask, "So, how far from the camp is the Internet?" The project was a success, though, and by 2006, the Hole in the Web was an online community of over 10,000 children with cancer.

As the Internet boom heated up, Berger and Gunn pursued opportunities at separate start-ups in New York but remained in touch. As the boom turned to bust and Gunn's e-commerce start-up faltered, Berger persuaded Gunn to join him at the Web solutions firm where he worked. Although they both enjoyed Web development, they realized that they wanted to focus exclusively on educational technology that would improve teachers' lives. Gunn, who had taught middle school math, explained: "We wanted to build technology that would help teachers and students interact in a more productive way. We saw a need for tools that would deliver measurable time savings over all the paper-based tasks that teachers had to do." Berger recalled a seminal moment spurred by Gunn's love of the *Star Trek* television series:

> Early in our brainstorming, Greg said, "We need to build a tricorder for teachers." On nearly every episode of "Star Trek," the crew uses this handheld device with three buttons to get out of a jam—it's different every time but always has the right three things they need to survive. You know, fix a broken leg, beam to another planet, call for help. Greg's image of a teacher's tricorder was the first moment that it really popped into my consciousness what we were going to try to do.

Palm Pilots were becoming increasingly accepted and affordable, and Berger and Gunn decided the wireless handhelds would be the perfect vehicle for their technology. In March 2000, armed with "50 ideas" for Palm applications for education and a $150,000 investment from Irwin Jacobs of Qualcomm, they decided to form their own company called Wireless Generation.

The Early Days

Through their New York contacts, Berger and Gunn formed a relationship with the Center for Children and Technology (CCT), a nonprofit research group. CCT gave Wireless Generation space in its facility and access to cutting-edge educational research and connected them with schools in its network that needed consulting services for technology projects. Berger noted that for a start-up, the arrangement was ideal: "We didn't have enough confidence in any one of our ideas to invest heavily in product development, and the consulting projects helped us understand the market better." One of these engagements proved fortuitous for the young company. In 2001, CCT introduced Wireless Generation to the public school district in Mamaroneck, New York. Gunn recalled:

> Mamaroneck said, "We like the reading assessment in our elementary schools [called running records], but it takes a lot of time. We know it's valuable, but the information takes a huge amount of effort to get into a form we can use. It's on paper and ends up in file drawers. If you can put it on a Palm Pilot, maybe that would be useful." So we studied what was going on in the reading assessment field and spent hours and hours observing Mamaroneck teachers conducting the assessments, and after some trial and error, we created an application that they adopted—it was an early version of what we later called mCLASS:Reading.

Berger and Gunn soon realized that Mamaroneck was not an isolated case: nearly half of the elementary school teachers in the United States were using the running-record method, which entailed observing a student reading a text designed to diagnose his or her reading level and marking every word as either correct or incorrect. If the child read the word incorrectly, such as saying "horse" when the printed word was "house," the teacher made a note describing the error and then kept track of overall metrics like "self-correction rate." Over time, the teacher had a running record of each child's reading ability and could use it to target reading instruction to individual students' needs. But the data collection and analysis were incredibly time-consuming. Berger and Gunn expanded their vision for the mCLASS:Reading product to pursue this market opportunity. As Gunn recalled:

> We realized that we could capture all the data for every student in every classroom and create a centralized database that could generate reports enabling teachers to see student progress over time, dive into the details, and print it out in a format that they could share with parents. We made the leap in our thinking from individual tools to an enterprise assessment application that schools and districts could use to better understand children's learning needs, deliver the right instruction for each child, and improve their reading scores.

The team decided that rather than build a sales force, they would partner with a large publisher such as McGraw-Hill or Scholastic to fully develop the product, then license it and take a royalty on the sales made through the publisher's existing distribution channels. This would allow Wireless Generation to continue developing new product ideas without the burden of building a sales and distribution infrastructure. In 2001, they began demonstrating a prototype to publishers and practitioners at education technology conferences. School districts began calling to purchase mCLASS right away. The publishers were more cautious, but eventually Berger and Gunn began negotiations with a well-known player. The longer the negotiations took, the worse the deal became. With only two months of cash left in the bank in late 2001, Berger and Gunn made a fateful decision—rather than sign over the intellectual property rights for $50,000, they would try to take the product to market themselves. Berger explained, "Even with our cash crunch, our intuition was that this idea was worth far more than $50,000. These districts were calling, asking to buy the product, and our confidence was waning that the publisher could really focus on selling it as effectively as we could ourselves. So we walked away."

One Thing Leads to Another: Texas, DIBELS, and No Child Left Behind

One week later, Berger and Gunn got a call from their contact at Palm, Inc., about an opportunity in Texas that had the potential to make the company. The Texas Education Agency (TEA) had been in talks with Palm about handheld applications for students in Texas schools, but the conversations had stalled. Palm sensed the state was not interested in spending the kind of money it would require to outfit a critical mass of students with the devices. In a last-ditch effort to interest the TEA in Palm-based applications, company officials invited Wireless Generation to join them in a meeting with agency executives. Berger recalled the December 2001 meeting:

> We told them about the application the Mamaroneck teachers were using, and they got very excited. Texas had been using an assessment developed by the University of Texas called the Texas Primary Reading Inventory [TPRI] but was trying to improve the quality of their statewide rollout—and they wanted to respond to concerns that the assessment took too long to administer. They agreed to fund a small pilot of the mCLASS application on Palm Pilots loaded with an electronic version of the TPRI. Shortly after the pilot was off the ground, we got another call saying that Governor Rick Perry had seen the product in use and made a public statement [that] every elementary teacher should have tools like this. Before we knew it, we were back in Texas negotiating a big, big contract.

Wireless Generation signed a seven-year contract worth $1.7 million annually to roll out the product across the state. In the early years of the contract, the company would be overpaid, and in later years it would be underpaid, but the revenue would be smoothed across the term of the contract. At the contract-signing ceremony, Berger asked a TEA official why the agency had been willing to take a chance on a start-up company from New York City, and the answer surprised him:

> The director of textbooks, technology, and assessments told me that I had answered The Question correctly. When I asked her "which question?" she said she always asks vendors what they can do to help Texas. They usually launch into their prepared pitch about their product or service. Of course, I really didn't have a product yet, so my response to her was "What does Texas need?" But in her mind, I was willing to listen and meet her needs rather than pitch something off the shelf. I still tell this story to new employees—as our products become more mature, we never want to lose our focus on understanding customer needs.

DIBELS

As word of the Texas contract spread, other states began to contact Wireless Generation for help because Texas was licensing the TPRI (and a Spanish-language sister assessment called Tejas LEE) to other departments of education. New Mexico was immediately interested, but in addition to the TPRI, they wanted to use an assessment developed by the University of Oregon called the Dynamic Indicators of Basic Early Literacy Skills (DIBELS). DIBELS had been developed in alignment with the recommendations of the National Reading Panel in 2000 and predicted how three basic literacy skills correlated to later reading proficiency in students from kindergarten through third grade.[2] In practice DIBELS was a series of timed, one-minute measures delivered to students in order to aid teachers in identifying students who were not progressing as expected. The University of Oregon made the assessment available for download from the Web at no charge.

Gunn explained Wireless Generation's willingness to incorporate DIBELS into the mCLASS system: "I don't think we fully appreciated DIBELS at first, but New Mexico wanted it, and we wanted another state besides Texas, so Larry flew to Oregon and talked to the creators. We struck an agreement with them for an exclusive license to adapt DIBELS to a mobile computing device." Wireless Generation created a version of its product called mCLASS:DIBELS software and signed up New Mexico, but the DIBELS exclusive license turned out to significantly accelerate the company's growth.

No Child Left Behind: Reading First

As part of the federal No Child Left Behind Act of 2001 (NCLB), which went into effect in January 2002, the U.S. Department of Education established the Reading First program. States were required to submit detailed plans about how they would remedy schools that failed to have sufficient numbers of students reach proficiency on the annual state reading assessments required by NCLB. As part of the plans, states were required to indicate which formative reading assessment their schools would adopt to screen children for reading difficulty, monitor progress, and measure annual outcomes. If its application was approved, a state would receive a grant based on its number of low-income children. The state agency could use 20% of the grant for statewide efforts but would be responsible for redistributing the remaining 80% to local school districts that qualified as "Reading First districts."[3] In 2002, the U.S. Congress allocated $900 million for Reading First grants to states.

Because of a short time frame, states were scrambling to put together plans with budgets, and because DIBELS was research based and available at no charge, many states incorporated it into their plans. Several other states chose the TPRI. Suddenly, Wireless Generation was the sole handheld technology solution for the most-sought-after early-reading assessments in the country. Berger and Gunn began contacting state education offices to persuade them to write mCLASS into their funding requests to the federal government. When the dust settled, Wireless Generation was part of the Reading First plans of 20 states.

Staying Neutral in the Reading Wars

The field of literacy could be organized along a continuum, and at the poles were two basic ideologies about the best way to teach children to read: phonics and whole language. While there were various subcategories and labels along the continuum (balanced literacy, guided reading, etc.), most points of view could be grouped under one of those two headings. In very general terms, the phonics camp emphasized a bottom-up approach in which mastering letters and their sounds would lead to reading skills. The whole-language adherents believed in a top-down approach that focused on building recognition of words and their meaning in context, similar to the way children learn to speak their first language.

Gunn explained how Wireless Generation's early products mapped to the two poles: "DIBELS and TPRI were closely identified with phonics even though they had elements of other methods, and the running-records approach was closer to the balanced-literacy camp. So the way our products evolved, we ended up with tools that served both approaches."

Each assessment approach had its strengths and limitations. DIBELS was considered an excellent way to identify a student's skills at a point in time and specifically to highlight what he or she *could not* do. The running-records approach focused on what a student *could* do and how his or her mastery was progressing over time. Rather than endorse one or the other, Berger and Gunn saw value in both approaches and became interested in developing an integrated product that could follow a student's progress from core skills acquisition all the way through to fluency and comprehension. Gunn described their evolving vision, saying:

> We felt that our understanding of reading instruction was increasing, and we began looking for an opportunity to develop a product that would bring together the best of both worlds. The schools and teachers we were working with wanted a blended approach to reading instruction, while the universities and researchers were fighting it out at the poles. We believed that the market would eventually support a quality product that could follow a student all the way from being a pre-reader to a fluent, comprehending reader.

Partnering with the Montgomery County Public Schools

Montgomery County Public Schools in Maryland (MCPS) was considered a high-performing district by experts and its peers (**Exhibit 2**). As part of their strategy to close the achievement gap, the senior leadership team had divided the district into green and red zones, with the majority of minority and low-income students residing in the red zone (**Exhibit 3**). This area of the district received more financial and human investments in order to help accelerate the performance of students who were further behind. Superintendent Jerry Weast and Chief Information Officer John Q. Porter were widely known for their innovative use of technology and performance data to drive improvement in student outcomes. NCLB required testing in grades 3 through 11, but Weast wanted an assessment for the earlier grades that would show how students were progressing on the way to the third-grade test. MCPS developed its own predictive assessment for kindergarten through second grade called the MCPS Assessment Program Primary Reading (APPR). Weast explained:

> There was a debate among psychometricians about whether you could measure the acquisition of reading knowledge by young children. They knew it had something to do with vocabulary and something to do with sounds—phonemic awareness—but nobody wanted to enter the reading wars by trying to develop a valid assessment. So we asked ourselves if we could do it in-house, which led to our own instruments that used the running-records approach. In the beginning, the stumbling block was that many of our employees thought it was not age appropriate for K–2 kids to be tested. But once the assessments were in use for awhile, people began to believe in their validity and see their value in the classroom.

By 2002, the district was using the homegrown APPR in all 129 of its elementary schools. In addition, it had purchased and was piloting mCLASS Reading in 19 of its red zone elementary schools and was using mCLASS DIBELS in its four red zone elementary schools that were designated Reading First schools. Pleased with the Wireless Generation tools, Weast and Porter approached the company in early 2004 about developing a custom application that would put APPR on Palm handheld devices for all of their teachers. Porter explained their motivation:

> Automating our internal assessment on a handheld device meant that teachers didn't have to manually juggle a pencil, paper, and a stopwatch while listening to readers. It would free up time for teachers to do higher-level tasks with students. It also meant that we could electronically capture all the assessment data on every child in every classroom and analyze it. This would not only help teachers differentiate their instruction for their students but allow the

district to differentiate professional development for teachers.

The Deal

Weast had formed a number of public-private partnerships in his career, including joint ventures that resulted in curricular and professional development products, while serving as a superintendent in public districts in Montana, North Carolina, and South Dakota. He explained:

> I had learned that the best entrepreneurial partnerships happen when both parties have a common interest in creating a product. We knew that automating APPR would save an enormous amount of time that teachers could reinvest in their students and would allow us to be more sophisticated in our data collection and analysis, but we did not have the capacity to develop it ourselves. Wireless Generation saw a viable market opportunity in developing an automated K–2 product that blended phonics and whole language. We saw an opportunity to help our teachers improve their instruction.

Wireless Generation was interested in the proposal but estimated that, at more than a million dollars, the cost of developing and installing the custom application was higher than either the company or MCPS could bear alone. Berger recalled:

> We considered Weast and Porter's proposal and realized that this was an opportunity to create an assessment that used the best of both sides of the reading wars by combining what we knew worked well from DIBELS with the APPR. Developing it solely for MCPS was not compelling economically, but creating a product that had nationwide potential was exciting. We would not do it with every district, but Jerry and John had already proven to be sophisticated customers who understood instruction, assessment, technology, and the dynamics of working productively with vendors.

Weast asked Porter to spearhead the negotiation on behalf of MCPS. Porter had a solid track record of striking mutually productive agreements with vendors, and Berger described him as one of the most innovative school district executives he had worked with, saying:

> John Porter spoke at a conference recently and said, "I like to buy things." The person sitting next to me said, "I can't believe he said that!" She thought it suggested looseness with money and coziness with vendors—a consumer attitude about education instead of a traditional public-agency mind-set. But he really meant that he values the engagement with companies who are thinking about a particular problem of his that MCPS doesn't have the internal capacity to solve. He meant "buy" instead of "build." It makes him a savvy negotiator, too. I think Weast and Porter were way ahead of us most of the time.

Porter crafted a deal that required Wireless Generation and MCPS to each contribute development dollars to the new product and to share the revenues generated by future sales to other school districts. MCPS had an established "enterprise fund" into which earned income from a variety of revenue-generating activities flowed, and the royalties from the new product would flow into this pot. As the enterprise fund grew, MCPS planned to use the pool of money to invest in additional innovative projects. MCPS would also receive a discounted pricing structure as it rolled out the completed product in all of its schools. (See **Exhibit 4** for contract highlights.)

Weast explained the importance of transparency when setting up revenue-sharing arrangements with for-profit companies:

> The first criterion of a good business partnership is that the affected stakeholders understand why the product is valuable and why the partnership makes strategic sense for the

> district. Second, everyone has to be absolutely certain that no one on the district side is personally deriving any financial benefit—of any kind, in any way. Third, the district leaders have to have confidence in the integrity of the private-sector partner, since public money is involved. Fourth, and most importantly, the board of education has to be fully informed, and all agreements and transactions have to be publicly recorded and available for review.

The company and the district agreed that during the fall of 2004 they would adapt the APPR to a Palm application and combine it with mCLASS:DIBELS software to cover the full range of reading assessment. They planned to pilot it with teachers in 19 schools beginning in January 2005. Contingent upon a successful pilot, the district would roll out the application to all 129 elementary schools over two years. Once the product was stable, the company would begin selling it to other school districts.

Development and Pilot

To reflect the multidimensional approach to reading assessment, Wireless Generation and MCPS agreed to call the new product mCLASS:Reading 3D. Each dedicated a point person to the project—Producer Jodi Rothstein organized the company's efforts, and Anne Bedford, the director of curriculum projects for MCPS, coordinated the district involvement. Rothstein described the early task:

> When we began the product design phase with MCPS, we looked closely at the APPR and our existing assessments to identify redundancy and determine how the measures could work together as a well-integrated whole. If we simply bolted DIBELS and APPR together we would have created a monster assessment that would have required hours to administer—counter to the goal of saving teachers time. Together we selected measures from their existing battery of assessments and from DIBELS to create a blended, effective assessment that was also efficient to administer.

Bedford added:

> We had deep discussions about each piece of our respective assessments and came to agreement about what we would keep and what we would each give up. MCPS had enough data on APPR to know that each portion was valid, but the company also had a strong research base. We ultimately decided on a combination of 10 measures as well as a writing portion to assess reading comprehension.

From a technology standpoint, Bedford observed, "Wireless Generation had to get into our heads to understand the logic flow of the APPR, and we had to get into their heads to understand the logic of their technology platform." Because the APPR had been developed as a paper-based test, it did not fit naturally with the requirements of the technology.

By October they agreed on the design of the assessment, and the Wireless Generation technical staff began building the application and creating a data bridge that would allow for a transfer of all MCPS teacher and student enrollment data into the company's Web-based data warehouse. Wireless Generation and Bedford's team created a training program for teachers and introduced staff from the 19 pilot schools to the new product throughout November and December in anticipation of a January launch. Meanwhile, MCPS technical staff installed Palm sync stations in classrooms and prepared the district's teacher and student data for transfer via the data bridge.

In January, teachers began using the product to assess students' reading skills in kindergarten through second grade in 19 schools. Teachers listened to each student read aloud from hard-copy stand-alone passages or "leveled readers"[4] and tracked the results through a corresponding electronic version of the text on a Palm handheld device. The assessments were timed, and the application tracked the elapsed time and automatically scored the students' performance. Teachers then uploaded the results into the central data base using a sync station in their classroom and could then access online reports by student, groups of students, or their entire classroom (**Exhibit 5**).

Aside from a number of routine problems such as defective synching stations and duplicate records in the database, the technical aspects of the implementation reportedly were smooth. Teachers in the 19 schools had already used mCLASS:Reading, so they were familiar with the Palm technology but now had to adjust to using the device instead of the paper-based APPR. The culture shift that was required for this transition was bumpy. As Bedford explained, the paper-based APPR "relied on teachers' professional judgments about each student, but Reading 3D made some of those judgments irrelevant, and this was more difficult than I think we originally anticipated."

For example, one of the measures, Text Reading and Comprehension, contained 22 levels of difficulty. The APPR had allowed teachers to decide at which level to stop assessing a student, but the mCLASS:Reading 3D software automatically determined the stopping point for each student based on his or her performance in order to pinpoint the student's instructional reading level. The mCLASS:Reading 3D software might require a teacher with a student who performed well at level nine to continue assessing that student at level ten, even if the teacher believed the higher level was too difficult. This caused understandable frustration for many experienced teachers but also challenged the assumptions that some had about particular types of students. Bedford explained:

> I had a series of difficult conversations with a second-grade teacher who was having trouble accepting the judgments of the software. He kept arguing with me that he knew a particular kid couldn't perform at the level the technology required. He said, "Why should I even waste my time and waste his time? I know he can't do it." Finally after several conversations, I looked at him and said very firmly, "No matter what you believe about this student, at some point in time when you administer the test he *is* going to be able to do it, and you're not going to know that until you try it." And he didn't have any response to that.

Nevertheless, the district agreed to slight adaptations in the product that allowed teachers some flexibility in determining the appropriate level for their students, easing some of the tension.

Accelerating the Rollout

In March, Weast was so pleased with the progress of the pilot that he decided to accelerate the rollout schedule. Instead of migrating half of the schools in the next academic year and the remaining half the year after that, he decided that the product would be up and running in all elementary schools by the time school opened in September, only five months away. He explained:

> I didn't believe we had the option to wait. Every day, every year that we delay, we're impacting children's lives, particularly those children most in need of assistance in literacy development. Once John told me the pilot was working, then I wanted teachers to have it right away, as many teachers as possible, both as a function of continuous improvement and as function of our responsibility to do everything we can, as quickly as we can, to improve the instructional capabilities of our teachers and the academic opportunities for our most vulnerable children.

With the decision made, the project teams at Wireless Generation and MCPS were suddenly under enormous pressure to work out minor product glitches and to figure out how to equip thousands of teachers with the tool and the training. As Porter described it:

> We were already moving at a fast pace, and then suddenly we had to shift into warp speed. It was stressful, but I agreed with Jerry's decision. Sometimes you have to keep moving and correct mistakes along the way; otherwise you'll never get anywhere. The alternative is to slow down, evaluate how it's going, spend a lot of time talking about the plan—believe me, we could have talked it to death.

Berger described the impact the accelerated schedule had on Wireless Generation:

> In the education industry you spend a lot of time wishing that districts would move more quickly. I've seen good education companies get piloted to death by districts that decide to do one school this year, then two schools the next year. But Weast and Porter went from 0 to 19 to 129 in the course of a year—all with a new product we were still getting our heads around. It was exciting—I remember Josh Reibel, our COO, giving the software development version of the Henry V Crispin's Day speech to cheer the team through the last 10 days of all-nighters.[5]

Throughout the spring and summer, teachers attended training sessions for the mCLASS:Reading 3D solution while the MCPS technology team installed the necessary hardware in classrooms. MCPS staff also rushed to prepare staff and enrollment data for every elementary school for transfer to Wireless Generation via the data bridge. When school opened in September 2005, every elementary school in the district was required to use the mCLASS:Reading 3D software to assess and diagnose the reading skills of all students in kindergarten through second grade.

Porter described a snag created by the accelerated schedule:

> Remember that we had a goal of saving teachers time. But because every child needed a baseline assessment and because every teacher was using the technology for the first time, it was a pretty slow process. We hadn't really experienced this in the 19 pilot schools because those teachers were already familiar with Palm Pilot technology. In the full rollout, the teachers said the tool was too slow, and my tech staff thought that the users were the primary reason everything moved so slowly. Initially we thought more training would solve the problem. Finally we just brought everything to a halt and went into classrooms and watched what was going on. Turns out, it did take 20 to 30 minutes for a new user to develop the baseline for each child—you multiply that by 23 students in a class, and you quickly realize it eats up a lot of instructional time. So we agreed with our teachers union that the district would provide a high-quality substitute teacher to cover the classroom while teachers delivered the baseline assessments.

Bedford also reflected on the consequences of moving so quickly:

> With more time maybe we could have communicated more fully and clearly with stakeholders—teachers and principals. Much of the push back in the rapid rollout came—I believe—because we didn't take the time to explain well enough how it was linked to instructional improvement. Our teachers and administrators are great and they are focused on their students' learning, but many are naturally intimidated by technology. Maybe if we had moved more slowly we could have built the buy-in at the school level for why this product was so important for students.

Throughout the 2005–2006 school year, Wireless Generation and MCPS worked through the technical and cultural issues and ended the year satisfied that the product could save teacher time and improve the accuracy of the reading assessments. As its staff became more comfortable with the product, MCPS believed that they would embrace it and differentiate their instruction more effectively based on the data the tool provided. Wireless Generation believed it had a new product that school districts all over the U.S. could use to improve the reading skills of students.

Going to Market with mCLASS:Reading 3D

Wireless Generation publicly launched the mCLASS:Reading 3D product in 2005 and began the sales process with a number of large districts. Vice President of Sales Jim Mylen described the process the company used to identify high-potential prospects:

> There are districts where we know they are working on narrowing the achievement gap by investing in supports for their youngest learners. Many are committed to using both DIBELS and balanced-literacy measures such as running records. So we knew immediately that there would be an opportunity to talk to them about how mCLASS:Reading 3D software lets them easily and accurately use both kinds of assessments and have the data presented to teachers and administrators in one place, for that whole picture.

In the sales process, the company worked to balance the benefits and risks of offering a product that was so closely identified with one well-known school district. On the plus side, the assessment embedded in mCLASS:Reading 3D had been developed and validated over a number of years in a successful district, and the technology had been tested and adopted by practicing teachers in real classrooms. On the minus side, school districts often thought of themselves as idiosyncratic, with performance problems that were unique to their students and communities. Embracing a product that grew out of a partnership with one district with demographics that were substantially different could be problematic both practically and politically. Berger described Wireless Generation's approach to this marketing challenge:

> We downplay the centrality of MCPS in the generic marketing material, but if we have a receptive audience in a face-to-face presentation, then we rely on the Montgomery County story to make the product features come alive. If we are in a district whose identity includes having its own way of doing things, we might need to focus more on how similar their homegrown assessments are to the APPR and be willing to customize to reflect their variants. But we never leave the MCPS story out entirely because it's part of the distinctiveness of the product and, for the most part, people in education are so hungry for something that's been validated somewhere.

Berger continued, describing the power of the MCPS student performance data:

> The notion that this is actually working in a large district with 129 elementary schools is a useful part of the story for any potential customer that knows how to evaluate a new technology. And you can't argue with results—a lot of districts struggle with "the second-grade wall," the time when kids need to start comprehending what they are reading and suddenly the scores start to flat line. But the second-grade wall doesn't exist in the MCPS data—the kids just keep growing. That gets people's attention.

Wireless Generation priced the product by the student, charging $21 for each student assessed. This included the necessary hardware and software, as well as the installation of the product and the creation of the Web-based data files for each teacher and student. The pricing included basic training materials about how to use the application but did not include the instructor-led training sessions that most districts request or the ongoing professional development for teachers and administrators in how to use the mCLASS:Reading 3D data to improve classroom instruction.

In July 2005, Chicago Public Schools (CPS) purchased the product for use in first grade in approximately 450 elementary schools. In June 2006, the Fort Worth Independent School District in Texas signed a contract to implement mCLASS:Reading 3D software in 48 elementary schools. In each case, the district purchased the "shrink-wrapped" product, but Wireless Generation agreed to customize a number of features to fit existing practices and cultures. The product was flexible enough to make front-end adaptations easily, but this could create maintenance challenges down the road. As one employee described, "If mCLASS:Reading 3D is hugely successful, and we sell it to, let's say, 100 districts and are willing to modify it for each one, it will be difficult to provide high-quality technical support over the long term because each customer will have unique problems."

Berger agreed, saying, "This is one of the distinctive challenges of the K–12 market—there are 15,000 school districts, and each has discovered a particular way of doing things—it is hard to find economies of scale. That's what makes large, ahead-of-the-curve districts like MCPS so important to innovation in our industry—they know how to do things at the kind of scale that can support ongoing product improvement."

Extending the Product Line

With the mCLASS:Reading 3D solution, Wireless Generation solidified its position as a market force in formative assessment for literacy. But the company had aspirations beyond the reading market. Because NCLB and state accountability systems placed a heavy emphasis on math as well as reading, Wireless Generation was developing a math assessment product (**Exhibit 6**). However, there was no analogous provision to Reading First to drive states and districts to adopt formative assessments for math, and there was no widely accepted assessment that Wireless Generation could license to break into the market the way it did with DIBELS and running records. Berger explained:

> mCLASS:Reading 3D was an important inflection point for us as a company—before 3D, all of our reading products were automating an assessment that already had a large installed base on paper. mCLASS:Reading 3D was the first chance to build a new mix of assessment content that would have to earn its own base of users. Once we had that under our belt, a flurry of original products and services followed. Our math product is designed entirely from scratch.

Berger, Gunn, and their senior team were also spending considerable time and resources developing products that extended their market beyond Palm applications. As Vice President of Marketing Andrea Reibel explained:

> The handheld technology is important because it helps streamline the administration and scoring of assessments, but we're not just about making the assessment process easier and faster. We're about helping districts to use the data thoroughly and at every level, from the classroom up to the central office, to get continuous improvements in student achievement. The mobile computing device as the means of data capture is an important part of the value we offer, so we don't want to eliminate that from our messaging, but we also don't want to be known as the "Palm guys." The mobile

> data capture is an enabler, but it's all the things enabled by it that really drive change and improvement.

Wireless Generation had begun building a professional services division to provide consulting and advanced professional development focused on using student performance data to improve performance. As Gunn explained, "We saw that in many districts they have plenty of data, but they don't know how to weave it into their daily lives, which is tough. Through our work in hundreds of schools, we've built a strong knowledge base about how to do this effectively, and we think we can build a solid business around this" (**Exhibit 7**).

With the expanding portfolio of product types, many employees at Wireless Generation felt they were beginning to "define our own future" rather than always reacting to customer requests. But Berger described a recent encounter with Weast that added a wrinkle to that notion:

> Dr. Weast strolled into our recent quarterly meeting at MCPS—he wasn't on the agenda—and drew a diagram on his yellow pad, then said, "What we've built so far is the prism that pulls the different elements of a child's development apart so that we can see them—and that's good—but now we need to get to work on the prism that puts it all back together again so that we can see and understand the child as a whole. And I need us to do it in reading *and* in math, and it needs to be one coherent assessment from pre-K through third grade, and it needs to predict how students are going to do in middle school. And I want it in 18 months. We don't have time to waste. The country needs this."

We thought we'd have the next five years to start working these things out—but it's hard to say no to Jerry.

Notes

1. mCLASS is an acronym for "mobile classroom assessment."

2. The three skills assessed in DIBELS were phonological awareness, the alphabetic principle, and fluency with connected text. The National Reading Panel (convened by President George W. Bush) identified a total of five skills; the two not tested by DIBELS were fluency with vocabulary and comprehension.

3. Criteria for being categorized as a Reading First district include having schools with among the highest percentages of K–3 students reading below grade level in its state along with at least one of the following: a geographic area that includes an empowerment zone or enterprise community; a significant number of schools designated for Title I school improvement; or significant number or percentage of children who are counted for funding under Title I, Part A.

4. A leveled reader is a developmentally appropriate book that is written to match a specific level of reading proficiency. Publishers create leveled-reading series that follow students from the building blocks of literacy knowledge through fluency. Sequenced with a numeric or an alphabetical designation, leveled readers help teachers, students, and parents track the progression of reading skills.

5. The Saint Crispin's Day speech was given by King Henry V to motivate his outnumbered troops before the Battle of Agincourt in William Shakespeare's *Henry V*, Act 4, Scene 3. The closing lines read, "And gentlemen in England now-a-bed will think themselves accurs'd they were not here, and hold their manhoods cheap whiles any speaks that fought with us upon Saint Crispin's day."

Exhibit 1

Wireless Generation Literacy Product Descriptions

All assessments available on the mCLASS platform share the same basic use case: the teacher administers the assessment using the handheld for directions and guidance on administration protocols and to record students' responses. Results are delivered immediately on the handheld and are securely transferred to the mCLASS Web site when the teacher "syncs" the handheld. On the Web, educators can access a range of reports about the individual student, class, school, and district and activate features that support planning and delivery of differentiated instruction. Beyond the basic use case, each of the mCLASS assessments described below has unique features and nuances.

mCLASS®:DIBELS® software—An mCLASS handheld computer-to-Web version of the Dynamic Indicators of Basic Early Literacy Skills (DIBELS™), a nationally normed research-based assessment. DIBELS offers standardized, individually administered measures of early literacy for students in grades K–6 and enables educators to follow up with short, frequent progress monitoring assessments that track student growth. The mCLASS:DIBELS Act feature recommends instructional activities linked to DIBELS results. The software was developed in collaboration with DIBELS authors Roland Good, Ph.D., and Ruth Kaminski, Ph.D.

mCLASS:DIBELS *Reading Street* Edition—Developed through a partnership with Pearson Scott Foresman, mCLASS:DIBELS *Reading Street* Edition guides teachers who use the *Reading Street* preK–6 curriculum to specific lessons based on mCLASS:DIBELS results.

mCLASS:DIBELS Small Group Advisor—Web-based reporting that creates up to nine instructional groups based on DIBELS key skills, enabling teachers to target multiple skills simultaneously and each skill at the appropriate level of challenge and intensity.

mCLASS:DIBELS Item-Level Advisor—Web reporting that helps teachers understand students' answers on each DIBELS probe and what these responses reveal about each student's reading development. The Item-Level Advisor automatically detects, highlights, and clearly explains significant patterns in the students' responses based upon analysis and observations from Dr. Roland Good, DIBELS coauthor.

mCLASS® Home Connect™—Customized letters from the district or school to parents that explain DIBELS measures and the child's results and suggest appropriate at-home learning activities. Available in English or Spanish, or other languages for an additional fee.

mCLASS®:TPRI® software—A handheld-to-Web version of the TPRI®, a scientifically based K–3 assessment for screening and diagnosis of early-reading skill development. Wireless Generation developed mCLASS:TPRI software in partnership with the Texas Education Agency and the Center for Academic and Reading Skills at the University of Texas Health Science Center at Houston.

mCLASS®:Tejas LEE® software—A handheld-to-Web version of the Tejas LEE, a proven, research-based assessment for K–3 students who receive primary literacy instruction in Spanish. Used for screening and diagnosis. The mCLASS solution was developed in collaboration with the Texas Institute for Measurement, Evaluation, and Statistics (TIMES, University of Houston).

mCLASS:TPRI and mCLASS:Tejas LEE Progress Monitoring Tools—The mCLASS system fully supports a suite of instruments that enables teachers to closely track the progress of their students between benchmark assessments. These include mCLASS:TPRI Progress Monitoring for Emergent Readers and mCLASS:Tejas LEE Monitoreo del Progreso para Lectores Emergentes; and mCLASS:TPRI Progress Monitoring for Beginning Readers and mCLASS:Tejas LEE Monitoreo del Progreso para Lectores Principiantes.

mCLASS®:Reading software—A handheld-to-Web version of a suite of formative early-reading assessment tools, including reading records, an accuracy/fluency assessment, and a comprehension rubric. The mCLASS:Reading solution allows teachers to track students' reading levels using four different, commonly used leveling systems. Selecting from thousands of leveled readers from 15 of the leading education publishers, teachers can download actual text of books in their classroom libraries from Wireless Generation's mCLASS:Reading Web site and then follow along on the handheld as the child reads aloud from the book, marking different kinds of errors and self-corrections and making handwritten notes.

mCLASS®:Reading 3D™ software enables K–2 teachers to use a handheld computer to give two different kinds of assessments commonly relied upon to evaluate young students' reading development: the scientifically based DIBELS for screening and progress monitoring in the five Big Ideas in Beginning Reading; and diagnostic inventories based on balanced literacy, which blends phonics instruction with holistic activities emphasizing understanding meaning through context. mCLASS:Reading 3D software allows teachers to easily capture data from these different assessments in one central place for a complete, detailed view of a student's reading development and to support both the needs of students at risk and students achieving at benchmark. Once the handheld is "synched" to a computer, data is uploaded to the secure mCLASS Web site, where educators access rich reports on an individual student, class, school, and district for further analysis and instructional planning. Wireless Generation developed the software in collaboration with Montgomery County Public Schools in Maryland, one of the nation's highest-performing districts.

mCLASS®:CIRCLE™ software, developed by Wireless Generation in collaboration with Dr. Susan Landry and her team at the Center for Improving the Readiness of Children for Learning and Education (CIRCLE) from the University of Texas Health Science Center–Houston, helps early childhood educators to observe and understand each child's ongoing early-literacy, social, and emotional development and to be thoughtful and intentional in planning activities for 3-,4-, and 5-year-olds. While children do fun, age-appropriate assessment tasks, teachers record children's responses on the handheld and then receive immediate feedback and suggested activities for fostering development based on the needs of the whole class, groups of children, and individual children. By "synching" the handheld to a computer, the tool uploads information about each child to a secure Web site, where teachers can view a portfolio of reports that assist in classroom planning.

mCLASS®:PALS™ software—An mCLASS version of the University of Virginia's Phonological Literacy Awareness Screening (PALS), the scientifically based assessment currently used in 98% of Virginia school districts, as well as in other states.

Source: Wireless Generation.

Exhibit 2

Montgomery County Public Schools Student Performance Data

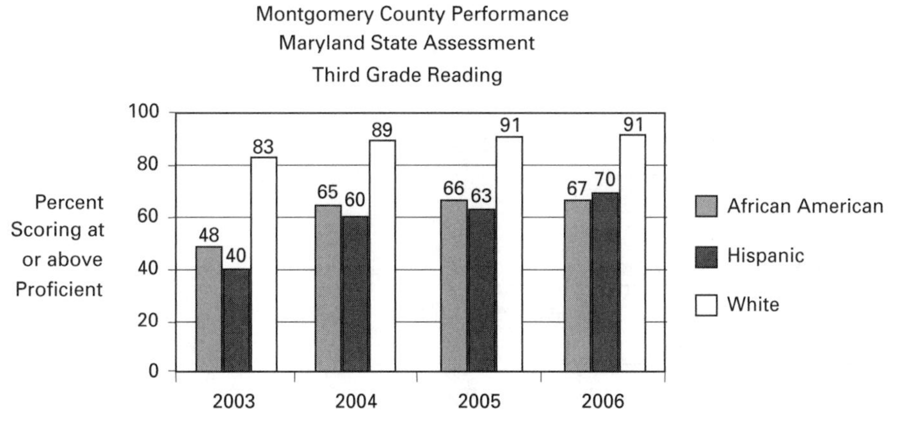

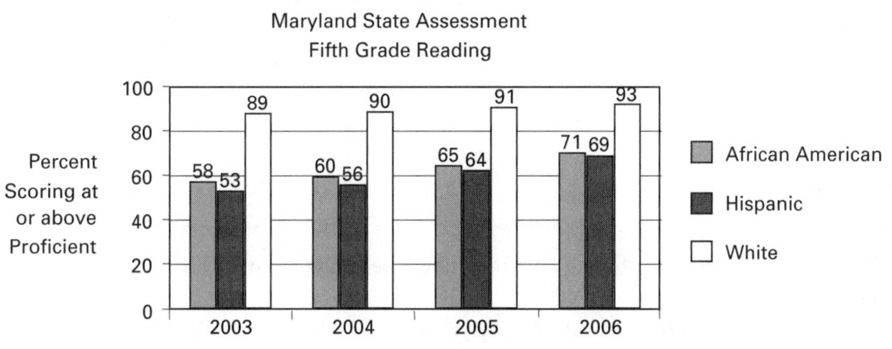

Source: Maryland Department of Education.

Exhibit 3

Montogomery County Public Schools Selected Statistics

MCPS Financial Statistics 2005

Total Budget	$1.6 billion
$ per student	~$11,500
Tech Spending	~2%

Student Demographics

	MCPS	*K–2*	*Green K–2*	*Red K–2*
Total	138,000	31,000	15,000	16,000
Minority	56%	62%	42%	80%
Low income	24%	33%	14%	50%

Source: Maryland Department of Education.

Exhibit 4

Contract Highlights

- MCPS and Wireless Generation collaborated on the product development work for mCLASS:Reading 3D.
- Parties shared estimated development costs equally (although Wireless Generation absorbed any over-runs).
- MCPS maintained ownership of the content it contributed as well as all intellectual property rights related to that content and granted Wireless Generation the rights to use it in the jointly developed product royalty free. Similarly, Wireless Generation maintained ownership and IP rights to content it contributed and granted its use to MCPS.
- Legally, MCPS and Wireless Generation were each independent contractors under the terms of the contract. The contract did not create a new legal entity in the form of a partnership or joint venture, and each party was solely responsible for all of its own employees and labor costs connected with the development of mCLASS:Reading 3D.
- MCPS secured platform and product services for use in its schools at a significant discount.
- MCPS receives a per-student royalty on all national sales of mCLASS:Reading 3D software by Wireless Generation. MCPS may not independently sell, loan, or rent the combined product to third parties.
- MCPS must approve any marketing materials developed by Wireless Generation for mClass:Reading 3D.

Source: Wireless Generation.

Exhibit 5

mCLASS:Reading 3D Product Screenshots: Handheld Device

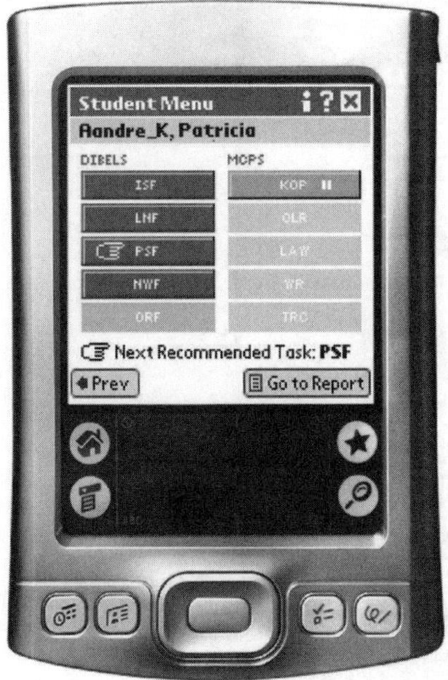

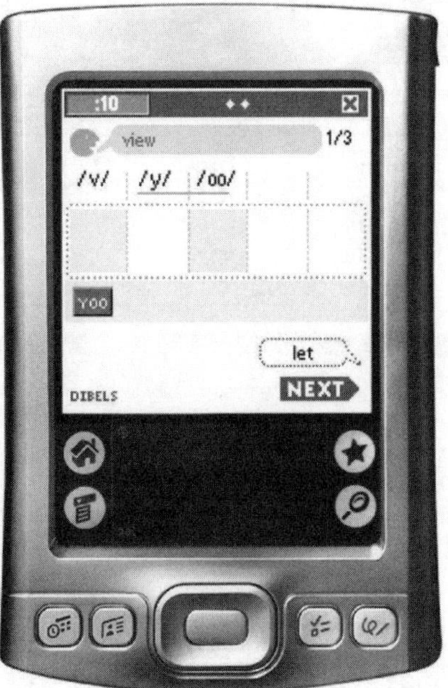

Source: Wireless Generation.

mCLASS: Reading 3D Product Screenshots: Web Application, Student Data

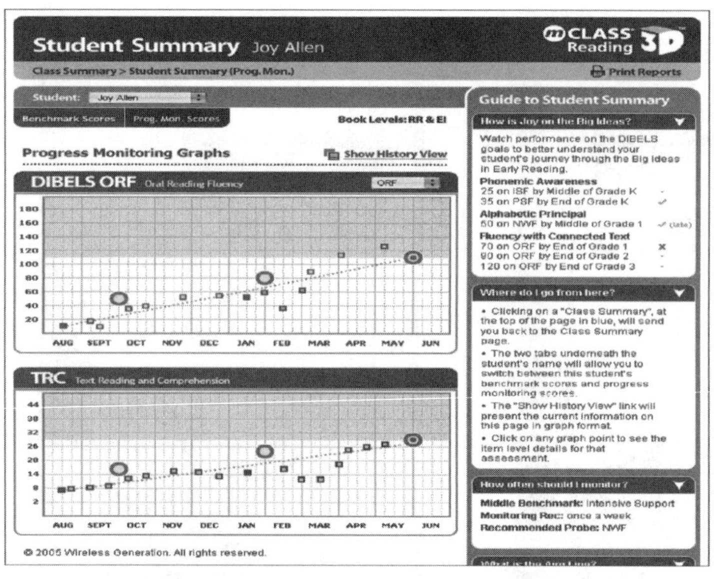

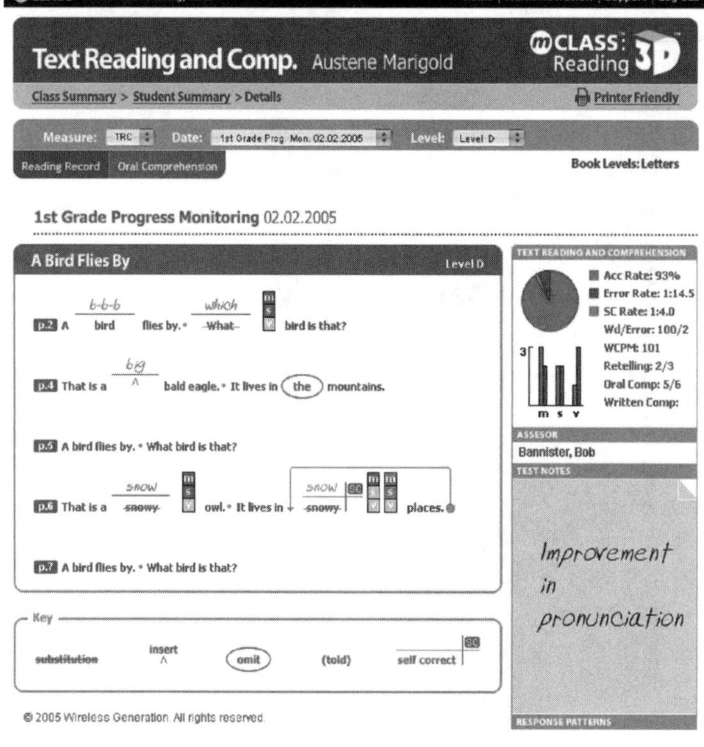

Source: Wireless Generation.

mCLASS: Reading 3D Product Screenshots: Web Application, Classroom Data

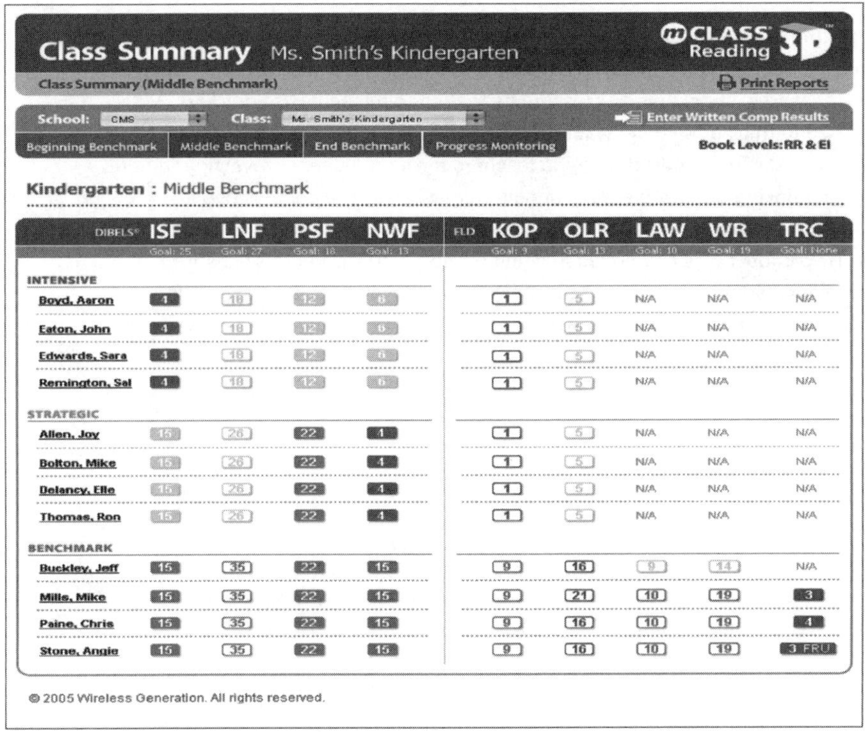

	DIBELS® ISF	LNF	PSF	NWF	FLD KOP	OLR	LAW	WR	TRC
	Goal: 25	Goal: 27	Goal: 18	Goal: 13	Goal: 9	Goal: 13	Goal: 10	Goal: 19	Goal: None
INTENSIVE									
Boyd, Aaron	4	18	12	6	1	5	N/A	N/A	N/A
Eaton, John	4	18	12	6	1	5	N/A	N/A	N/A
Edwards, Sara	4	18	12	6	1	5	N/A	N/A	N/A
Remington, Sal	4	18	12	6	1	5	N/A	N/A	N/A
STRATEGIC									
Allen, Joy	15	26	22	4	1	5	N/A	N/A	N/A
Bolton, Mike	15	26	22	4	1	5	N/A	N/A	N/A
Delancy, Elle	15	26	22	4	1	5	N/A	N/A	N/A
Thomas, Ron	15	26	22	4	1	5	N/A	N/A	N/A
BENCHMARK									
Buckley, Jeff	15	35	22	15	9	16	9	14	N/A
Mills, Mike	15	35	22	15	9	21	10	19	3
Paine, Chris	15	35	22	15	9	16	10	19	4
Stone, Angie	15	35	22	15	9	16	10	19	3 FRU

Source: Wireless Generation.

Exhibit 6

mCLASS: Math Product Description

The mCLASS:Math solution—The mCLASS:Math handheld-to-Web solution is an easy, fast, and effective way to evaluate K–3 students' math skills and thinking. It includes screening and progress-monitoring measures, short-timed assessments that enable teachers to quickly identify students at risk and track how those students respond to adjustments in instruction. In addition, it includes diagnostic interviews that guide teachers through a deeper investigation of children's mathematical thinking and problem-solving strategies. Data and conclusions are linked directly to instruction through recommended teaching strategies and research-based classroom activities. The product was developed in collaboration with Dr. Herbert Ginsburg, professor of psychology and education at Columbia University's Teachers College, a leading researcher on development of mathematical thinking and assessment of cognitive function.

Exhibit 7

Professional Services Product Description

Wireless Generation Professional Services (WGPS)—WGPS helps school systems develop highly skilled educators committed to continuous improvement and the use of formative data in their instruction. Offerings are tailored to the needs of each audience, from teachers to coaches to administrators. Professional Services workshops include Data Analysis for Instructional Leaders; Taking Action with DIBELS Data; Using the mCLASS:Direct System to Analyze Data; Response to Intervention; and Early Mathematics Institutes. WGPS also offers Data Analysis and Action Consulting, a year-long engagement in which Wireless Generation's highly trained consultants partner with a district to build lasting internal capacity in analyzing and using formative assessment data to improve outcomes in the classroom. Finally, WGPS offers customized data analysis and reporting, in which Wireless Generation's analysts conduct in-depth analysis of a district or state's data to help them draw conclusions based on the data.

Source: Wireless Generation.

Stacey Childress ■ Tonika Cheek Clayton

Focusing on Results at the New York City Department of Education

The 2007–2008 academic year would mark a turning point for the New York City Department of Education (DOE). For the first time, the DOE would publicly release progress reports for each of New York City's 1,456 public schools. The reports would evaluate schools along two dimensions. First, each school would receive a letter grade from "A" to "F" based on its demonstrated ability to improve student achievement. Second, each school would be given one of five ratings ranging from "undeveloped" to "well-developed" to evaluate the school team's ability to use and manage data to improve student outcomes. Senior managers at the DOE expressed a wide range of predictions about how parents, teachers, and principals would react to the results, but all agreed that transparency of school performance data was a necessary step in dramatically improving student achievement.

Chief Accountability Officer Jim Liebman was the primary architect of the DOE's new performance management system. He knew Chancellor Joel Klein's citywide strategy and massive restructuring plan depended on the DOE's ability to build the capacity of school teams to improve their performance without heavy oversight from a central bureaucracy and to hold principals accountable for their schools' performance. Liebman and his team in the Office of Accountability were focused on both of these tasks.

As Liebman reflected on the design and initial implementation phases of the performance management system, he knew there was an inherent tension in simultaneously implementing an accountability system with strong consequences and a set of organizational learning processes that encouraged school teams to collaboratively use performance data to improve their own practice. He also believed that achieving the optimum balance between the two tasks could accelerate the shift to the results-oriented culture that was already under way in New York. (See **Exhibits 1a** and **1b** for performance data.)

Background and Context

Serving 1.1 million students in over 1,456 schools with a budget of $15 billion, the New York City school system was the largest in the United States (**Exhibit 2**). After 32 years of governance by a seven-member appointed Board of Education in conjunction with 32 locally elected boards, the system came under the aegis of the city's mayor, who established the DOE in 2000 and had the power to appoint the chancellor and other key personnel. When Mayor Michael Bloomberg began his first term in January 2002, he inherited what many perceived to be a failing school system In July 2002, Bloomberg appointed Klein as the DOE's new chancellor.

Klein took over the DOE after a successful career in business, law, and politics. His lack of direct experience in education sparked some resistance to his appointment, but others hoped he could offer a fresh perspective on how to improve the troubled system. Following a series of community engagement meetings during his first year, Klein unveiled the Children First reform agenda, named to show his commitment to putting the interests of "children first, not politics or bureaucracy."

Preparing for Empowerment and Accountability

The early years of Children First focused mainly on regaining control of what Klein described as a "chaotic and dysfunctional organizational structure." Klein noted that his administration's "first task was to lock the system down, establish some control, and bring coherence to the system." Klein grouped the 32 community districts into 10 regional offices designed to support schools' operational and instructional needs. Using the regional offices to enforce standards and implement reforms, the DOE instituted a common math and literacy curriculum for grades K–8, ended social promotion, created 150 small schools to replace large failing high schools, and added math and literacy coaches as well as a parent coordinator position to every school (**Exhibit 3**).

Two years after establishing the regional offices, Klein's Children First message began shifting from regional control to school-level empowerment. The refined Children First strategy included three pillars of reform: leadership, empowerment, and accountability. Klein remarked: "Our reform strategy is premised on the core belief that strong school leaders who are empowered to build and support teams and make instructional and managerial decisions and who are prepared to be held accountable for student performance will result in high-functioning schools."

To address the inadequate preparation of principals for NYC schools, Klein created a selective Leadership Academy to train and recruit high-quality principals. Klein believed that if highly competent principals who were closest to the problems were empowered and given the resources needed to make decisions about solving them, this would ultimately be in the best interest of students. In order for empowerment to be effective, Klein also believed that principals needed to be held accountable for student performance. Klein described his theory of change:

> If we empower principals and hold them accountable for school results, we'll do two things—shift the locus of power from central office to the schools, and shift the organizational culture to a focus on results. However, I know that autonomy in and of itself is not going to guarantee success. But it will lead to innovation. And I suspect that if we're tight on accountability and instill an intense focus on student outcomes, we can also build into the equation some variability in terms of problem solving at the school level and learn from it.

The Autonomy Zone

In 2004, the DOE put Klein's theory into practice by launching a pilot program called the Autonomy Zone (the Zone), which gave a self-selected group of schools autonomy from regional control in exchange for more accountability for specific student performance targets. Twenty-six schools volunteered to join the Zone and signed five-year performance contracts that specified targets for a variety of indicators, including state test scores, attendance figures, and graduation rates. As part of the agreement, principals assumed control over all budgetary and decision-making authority that previously resided with regional offices and the DOE (**Exhibit 4**).

Zone schools that met their performance targets were left alone, while those that missed more than a set number of targets entered into what the DOE called the "ladder of consequences." The first year a school missed its targets, the school's leadership was required to develop specific action plans for the following year. If a school missed its performance goals for a second year, the principal could be removed. If things did not improve by the third year, the school could be closed. The principals answered to the DOE's Zone chief executive officer, who was responsible for overseeing all Zone schools and working directly with those who failed to meet their targets.

After the first year of the pilot, four out of 26 schools failed to meet their targets. After the second year of the pilot, these four schools had met their targets. At the beginning of the second year, 20 additional schools joined the Zone. At the end of the second year, two of the 46 Zone schools failed to meet their performance goals for the first time. After three years, it had not been necessary for the DOE to remove any principals or close any schools participating in the pilot.

Empowerment Schools

Pleased with the results of the Autonomy Zone, Klein extended the strategic pillars of empowerment and accountability to all NYC public schools. In 2006, every principal in NYC had the opportunity to join Zone schools in a new structure called "empowerment schools." Becoming an empowerment school was not based on prior performance. As Klein saw it, "Empowerment is a precondition for success, not something that schools should have to earn."

Despite opposition from people in the regional and central offices and from the principals' union, 320 principals from schools across all five NYC boroughs volunteered to become empowerment schools. Some opponents of the reorganization argued that empowerment school principals were giving up too much by signing performance contracts, while other critics felt that the empowerment structure discarded the benefits of the regional structures, such as community relationships, feeder school collaborations, and the sharing of solutions to problems common within regions (**Exhibit 5**).

Klein remarked on the success of the initiative in beginning a cultural change:

> I think if you don't change the culture of public education, you're not going to change the outcomes materially. A culture that doesn't focus on performance is a culture that won't work. And now these principals are saying they want to be held accountable for their performance. It's quite a thing to have 320 principals, over the objection of their union, sign performance agreements saying, "If I don't hit the ball, they'll be sending me to the minors." It's a big, big deal given the objections from the union and the good relationships many of these principals have with their regions. So that, to me, is a really profound change.

Empowerment schools assumed all instructional and budget authority previously held by the regional and central offices and received additional money to compensate for the support services they would no longer receive from the DOE. The DOE created a market for services by allowing empowerment schools to purchase support they needed from regional offices or external vendors.

Because the Zone CEO did not have the capacity to directly oversee all of the empowerment schools, the DOE created a network structure to support schools' instructional and operational needs. Each school self-selected into a network of 20 to 25 schools based solely on the principal's desire to affiliate with other empowerment schools. In practice this meant that there were no geographic patterns, and few schools in any of the networks had similar school-level characteristics. Each network interviewed and selected a network leader from a pool of former principals and regional administrators. The network leader's role was to coordinate common support services for the group of schools, not to supervise network principals. In fact, the network leader was accountable to the network principals for providing the support they needed. The network leader selected and supervised a staff including two achievement coaches to help schools focus on using data to improve instruction, a business manager to provide operational support across the network, and a special education specialist. However, these roles were loosely defined, and it was up to the principals and the network leader to design the team to provide differentiated support based on schools' needs.

Empowerment schools faced a ladder of consequences similar to the one that had been developed during the Autonomy Zone pilot. The first year a school missed its targets, it had to develop an action plan for reaching them the following year. The second year, the principal could be removed, and if the school failed to improve after two more years, it could be closed. During SY 07, the 320 empowerment schools formed networks, built network teams, and exercised their autonomy in a variety of ways. Because they represented nearly 25% of all New York schools, they had a dramatic influence on Klein's thinking about changes to the entire system.

Restructuring the Entire System

In January 2007, Klein announced a fundamental shift away from the regional model he had established at the beginning of his tenure and unveiled a new three-pronged organizational structure that would go into effect in fall 2007. The 10 regional offices would be disbanded, and all schools would choose to participate in one of three structures:

1. *The empowerment support organization:* Additional schools could become empowerment schools by signing performance contracts and forming self-managed networks.
2. *Learning support organizations (four):* Most similar to the old regional structure but not organized geographically, learning support organizations would offer schools service, support, and oversight through four centers run by the DOE in locations around New York.
3. *Partnership support organizations:* Schools that partnered with external nonprofit organizations for support and services would be part of this structure and would sign performance contracts. A number of schools were already partnered with external organizations, and the new structure would formally give those organizations additional support responsibilities, hold them accountable for school results, and open up the option to additional schools and nonprofits.

As with the Autonomy Zone and empowerment schools experiments, all elementary and middle school principals would still have a relationship with one of 32 community superintendents, and high school principals with one of 10 high school superintendents. Both groups of superintendents were responsible for duties specified by law (e.g., hiring, rating, and firing principals) (**Exhibit 6**). The services previously provided by the regions would be supplied, if at all, by the organization with which each school chose to affiliate. Although each of the three organizational structures had distinctive features and benefits, all principals would sign performance contracts and be held accountable for their students' results. With the intentional differentiation of structures and school practices that would result from the dramatic change,

Klein knew the DOE needed a common thread to keep the schools linked to one another and the DOE. As he explained: "Schools will not only be allowed to but encouraged to differentiate their approaches for achieving results for their students. But we need to create integrating mechanisms through accountability and organizational learning systems that are inherently flexible enough to allow for this differentiation while knitting all schools together into a system of great schools."

Creating a Learning Organization

Liebman had been a respected scholar and teacher at Columbia Law School when Klein convinced him to join the DOE in 2005 as the chief accountability officer and charged him with leading the design and implementation of a performance management system. Liebman believed that the success of the performance management system was contingent upon schools' developing into organizations in which the professionals in them were constantly learning with one another about how to solve performance problems. He described the link between accountability and organizational learning:

> Accountability isn't entirely or even mainly about incentives. It's about capacity building, which to me means adult learning based on self- and team evaluation of what's working and what's not, and knowledge management, meaning spreading what works from one student or school to another. If we want the lever of accountability to be as powerful as possible, we have to provide ways for schools to build their capacity to be relatively self-sufficient in evaluating themselves every day and in solving their unique performance problems and, when necessary, in asking for the specific help they need. This will never work if the central bureaucracy behaves as if it has all the answers. Our role is to help professionals in schools ask better questions so that they can craft customized answers based on their own evaluation of their performance problems.

With this philosophy in mind, Liebman's team in the Office of Accountability worked to develop tools and processes that could enable schools to build their capacity to self-evaluate and learn while holding them accountable for student performance and spreading the knowledge their innovations generated. Key elements of the new system were school-quality reviews, periodic assessments, inquiry teams, senior achievement facilitators, a new technology system, and school progress reports.

Quality Reviews

Beginning in SY 07, every school in New York would participate in an annual quality review (QR). The Office of Accountability partnered with Cambridge Education, a United Kingdom–based school review firm, to develop and implement the QR protocols for three years. Modeled in part after public school inspections in the U.K. and Hong Kong, the rubric developed for NYC QRs focused primarily on a school's use of data to adjust teaching practices in order to improve student outcomes. Liebman and his team created five overarching quality statements with detailed secondary points for reviewers to use as a guide when evaluating schools. Before their review, principals received training that covered the quality statements and the QR process (**Exhibit 7**).

Liebman described why he created a rubric focused on the use of data:

> I looked at all of the rubrics that are out there for school reviews and instructional walkthroughs. They all have one section on the use of data to drive strategy and facilitate frequent adjustment, and many other sections on inputs such as specific teaching practices and curricular materials. As I thought about what we are trying to accomplish, I realized that what

> we needed to change most was the emphasis in our schools from "teaching inputs" to "learning outcomes." Until we instill a culture of data-driven instructional differentiation in our schools, I'm not as interested in the parts of these rubrics about inputs.
>
> Secondly, we are not pushing a particular educational philosophy or professional development strategy. The last thing we want to do is to convey the sense that we have an idea in our heads at the central office about what the "right" answer is for each school. So it all came together for me in formulating our school-quality reviews around this notion of school teams organizing themselves to use what they know objectively or can learn about their students to be good self-evaluators and problem solvers.

In spring 2006, the DOE worked with Cambridge Education to pilot the process in 100 schools. Throughout SY 07, after modestly revising the rubric and the process, Cambridge Education consultants performed all of the school-quality reviews and began training DOE principals and administrators to conduct the process by having them observe actual QRs. Since most of the consultants were former school principals and administrators who resided in the U.K., each traveled to NYC for five to six weeks at a time to keep a steady flow of QRs in process.

By June 2007, approximately 140 consultants had conducted school-quality reviews across all 1,456 schools. Starting in SY 08, principals would be held accountable for the results of their QRs. The DOE planned to have enough internal reviewers trained so that many QRs could be conducted without outside consultants by 2010.

Real-Life QR—A Principal's Perspective

Principal Karen Reed perused the QR agenda she had created as she waited for the reviewer to arrive (**Exhibit 8**). The reviewer was set to meet privately with a group of parents, teachers, and students as part of the QR protocol. Following established QR procedure, Reed had also asked two teachers to each present a case study of a student to demonstrate how the school differentiated instruction to improve the student's progress. In addition to the self-evaluation form she had already submitted to demonstrate her school's own assessment of its success in meeting the quality statements, she had prepared several documents that she hoped would shed light on her team's efforts to incorporate the ideas in the quality statements into their day-to-day work. As principal of an empowerment school, she understood the consequences of receiving an "undeveloped" rating because they mirrored those she had agreed to in her performance contract (**Exhibit 9**).

Reed had participated in the Children First Intensive, a two-hour training session to prepare principals for QRs. She learned that reviewers signed a code of conduct stating that they did not have any preconceived notions of the school prior to the QR, but she worried about the reviewer's ability to fairly assess her school during a relatively short visit. Because her school's student population was under 500, only one reviewer would assess the school over a one-and-a-half-day visit. For schools with student populations between 500 and 1,000, one reviewer would visit for three days and be joined by a second reviewer for a day and a half. Schools with enrollments over 1,000 received two reviewers for three days.

She had heard mixed reactions to QRs from her colleagues. While some found their reviewers to be helpful and constructive, others felt as though they were treated harshly or had difficulty connecting personally with the reviewer. If she felt that her QR was conducted unfairly, she knew she had the option to appeal to the Office of Accountability. Appeals could be as simple as language changes in the report or as complicated as direct challenges to the reviewer's final ratings.

Real-Life QR: A Reviewer's Point of View

Scott Abbott had not traveled to NYC much before becoming a Cambridge Education consultant, so he enjoyed walking from subway stops to schools to get a sense of the neighborhood before entering the school. Prior to his job at Cambridge Education, Abbott worked as one of Her Majesty's inspectors, a title given to school inspectors in the U.K., after serving for several years as a U.K. school principal. He was one of the first consultants to administer NYC's QRs during the 100-school pilot, so he had reviewed many empowerment and regional schools across the ratings spectrum.

In preparation for this QR, Abbott reviewed all available student performance data and the self-evaluation form completed by the principal and her team. During the school visit, he would look for evidence of the quality review statements in action. Although the self-evaluation form provided by the principal gave him some of the evidence he was looking for, he still needed answers to several questions. He had also prepared specific questions for his group meetings with teachers, parents, and students absent the principal. Throughout the visit, he would ask the principals and teachers very specific questions in search of evidence to support each quality statement. In some cases, the school leadership provided the evidence needed early on without much effort. In other cases, Abbott felt as though getting the principal to talk in detail about the school's use of data to inform instruction was "like trying to nail jelly to a wall."

At the end of the visit, Abbott would meet privately with the school principal to offer feedback and to discuss ratings on each of the quality statements and the school's overall rating. Depending on Abbott's evaluation of each quality statement, he would give the school an overall rating of well-developed, proficient, or undeveloped. When assigning a rating to a quality statement, Abbott needed to cite specific evidence in support of his assessment. In the following days, he would write a report for the principal and the Office of Accountability detailing his observations and evidence in support of his ratings. Once completed and reviewed by the principals, and barring any appeal, the report would be published on the DOE's public website.

After Cambridge Education had conducted a few hundred QRs, it worked with the Office of Accountability to pull examples from real reports to clarify for principals and reviewers what a well-developed, proficient, or undeveloped school looked like for each of the quality statements in order to try to build consistency across reviewers. After the first round of QRs, the team realized that a small number of schools were rated well-developed or undeveloped, and most schools were designated proficient. However, the range of observed practices within the proficient category was so wide that the Office of Accountability decided to expand from three to five ratings for SY 08 in order to capture more granularity for schools rated at the high and low ends of the proficient category, at the top of the undeveloped category, and at the bottom of the well-developed category.

Periodic Assessments

The Office of Accountability instituted a "no-stakes" periodic assessment program to gather data on students' strengths and needs in support of quality statement number five. The assessments were intended to be used by teachers as a tool for understanding where students were struggling so that they could align instruction accordingly. By "no stakes," the Office of Accountability meant that the data from periodic assessments was solely for the use of school-level employees to improve their own instructional practice, not for the purpose of any external evaluation of how individual teachers or schools were performing. The results of the periodic assessments would not influence a school's quality review rating; however, the school's ability to demonstrate processes and practices for using the data to improve instruction would be a major factor in the QR ratings.

Beginning in SY 07, empowerment schools were required to deliver periodic assessments in math and reading five times per year. In the following academic year, this requirement would expand to all schools regardless of which of the three organizational structures they joined. Some senior managers at the DOE felt that mandating periodic assessments was contrary to empowering school principals to make instructional decisions, while others believed that the assessments were critical to helping schools adopt a continuous improvement cycle in which they used data to improve student learning. Skeptical of the impact of periodic assessments, Randi Weingarten, president of NYC's United Federation of Teachers, remarked, "Our issue is, how much teaching time is this eating up? You're spending a lot of time doing test prep and paperwork associated with test prep instead of teaching."[1]

Acknowledging that schools had different needs with regard to the content and design of the assessments, the Office of Accountability allowed schools to either choose from a menu of DOE-approved assessments or develop assessments of their own. To ensure a certain level of quality, schools that decided to develop their own periodic assessments had to submit a proposal to the Office of Accountability to demonstrate that their own approach equaled or surpassed the rigor of the options approved by the DOE. The proposal also had to explain in detail the school's capacity to design and implement the assessments given competing demands for the school leadership's time. All self-designed assessments had to meet eight criteria:

1. Align with state standards.
2. Demonstrate mastery of curriculum.
3. Break down activity into component parts and identify student strengths and weaknesses.
4. Reveal student progress to teachers, parents, and students.
5. Rely on objective evaluative standards that can be applied by school faculty consistently for different students.
6. Allow progress of students and groups of students to be compared over time.
7. Identify ways to close the gap between where students are now and the learning objectives they need to achieve.
8. Administer assessments approximately five times a year.

The implementation of the periodic assessment program in empowerment schools resulted in significant feedback on the assessment features, both positive and negative. The DOE used this feedback to draft a highly specific request for proposal (RFP) to provide a more flexible and comprehensive assessment program for the citywide application that aligned with educators' requirements. When all schools adopted periodic assessments in SY 08, the vendor chosen through the RFP would provide multiple testing options for schools that would:

- Predict student's performance on state exams and identify areas of weakness
- Assess progress in those targeted areas of weakness
- Align to the most widely used curricula in city schools
- Pinpoint a student's instructional level regardless of grade level (for students performing well below or above grade level)
- Allow for customization of the assessment by schools

In line with Klein's empowerment philosophy, schools could either administer a vendor's assessments that best met their students' needs or design their own tests as long as they met the eight criteria for self-designed assessments.

Inquiry Teams

In an effort to build each school's capacity to use data to improve instruction, the Office of Accountability asked each of the 320 empowerment schools to develop an "inquiry team" during SY 07. Each team included the school's principal and three or four teachers selected by the principal and was charged with identifying a struggling group of students and using data from periodic assessments and school-level observations to develop a targeted instructional approach for each student. Irma Zardoya, leader of the Children First Intensive professional development program, described the process and expectations for each inquiry team:

> Each team selects 15 to 30 students who are outside the school's sphere of success and who share similar academic struggles. Then, the team looks not only at the students' current performance data but also at their histories, looking for patterns. The team conducts low-inference classroom observations to understand how instruction is delivered, how the students respond, and how they are either learning or not learning.
>
> Then, the inquiry team members develop strategies that they feel will help the students learn. These go beyond finding an extra teacher or offering reading recovery. Rather, the team focuses on specific ways that a student's existing teacher could change his or her practice to support the student's progress in developing a particular skill. The team tracks the group of students' progress as a result of these strategies.
>
> We ask the teachers on the inquiry teams to share their findings with their colleagues in the school to lay the groundwork for other teachers to engage in a similar collaborative process of inquiry. We hope the inquiry teams serve to develop a culture of learning, in which the members of each school community continually study what they do and incorporate the learning to make their teaching better and to improve student achievement.

Liebman's team was encouraged that in a survey of inquiry teams, over 85% of respondents felt as though the work was valuable and wanted to continue it in the coming year. In addition to expanding inquiry teams to all 1,456 schools in SY 08, the Office of Accountability planned to extend the range of activities for the existing inquiry teams to include communicating with the school community about the school's results, developing schoolwide protocols for looking at student work, and implementing solutions based on QR findings.

Senior Achievement Facilitator

To provide additional support from the Office of Accountability to each school, Liebman planned to institute a new high-level role called the senior achievement facilitator (SAF). SAFs would support 20–25 schools within the empowerment, learning support, and partner organizations, but they would not supervise principals in the traditional sense. Their chief responsibilities would be to support their schools' efforts to utilize all of the new performance tools and processes to improve student achievement and to provide professional development in support of the inquiry teams. Liebman also expected the SAFs to be a critical part of a feedback loop that would help his team continually refine the tools and processes to best serve schools.

Liebman estimated that the DOE needed 62 individuals in achievement facilitation roles to cover all 1,456 schools. As a key part of their own training to succeed in the new environment, the 32 community and 10 high school superintendents would provide achievement facilitation to a group of 20–25 schools while continuing to oversee a separate group of schools as established by state law. This arrangement was designed to enable the superintendents, during this initial capacity-building period, to separate their support activities from the oversight function. The DOE would fill 20 SAF openings with senior managers such as former regional and deputy superintendents and former principals who had credibility with existing principals. All candidates would be required to demonstrate a solid knowledge of the uses of data to improve instruction.

Achievement Reporting and Innovation System (ARIS)

In order to support the push for schools to use data to solve performance problems, the DOE had to revolutionize its technology infrastructure. To access student achievement data using the existing systems, principals and teachers endured a time-intensive process that required multiple logins to different systems, none of which presented all the relevant data in a single application. Moreover, performance data was not broken down to detail a student's strengths or weaknesses; nor did a student's performance data follow the child from school to school.

As one senior manager described it, the DOE's existing knowledge management system was "based on the old bureaucratic idea that experts would develop knowledge about valuable instructional practices centrally and push it down to schools vertically—often by fiat." She continued:

> The new empowerment structure assumes that most knowledge will be developed locally in individual schools in response to problems presented by individual students and groups of students. Distributing this more granular knowledge horizontally from one school to another both on a voluntary "pull" basis [teachers and schools proactively seeking the information] and on a data-driven "push" basis [automatically informing struggling schools about practices at schools performing better with similar student populations] poses a challenge that school systems all over the country are trying to solve.

To integrate the existing disparate student data systems and use the data to help distribute knowledge horizontally, the DOE signed an $80 million contract with IBM and Wireless Generation to create the Achievement Reporting and Innovation System (ARIS). The goal of ARIS was to provide school professionals with access to all of the district's historical and current student performance data and effective practices through a single Web-based interface. This would require the system to bring together all of the district's past and current student achievement data systems on one application and to provide added functionality for administrators and teachers, including the ability to analyze the new periodic assessment data. The system would also allow teachers, principals, and administrators to publish, retrieve, and receive targeted alerts about effective practices tagged to particular subjects and student populations (**Exhibit 10**).

Office of Accountability Chief of Staff Rajeev Bajaj described the purpose of ARIS:

> Over a period of time, we expect ARIS to become an intelligent engine that links data and content in a way that's meaningful for practitioners. So say there's a fourth-grade teacher who has a specific reading problem [e.g., phonemic awareness] with her ELL students. The teacher will be able to go onto ARIS and look up schools with similar populations of ELL fourth graders that are doing well with that specific reading concept and learn about interventions or other pieces of "small knowledge" they've used to improve performance. We are enabling

> collaboration through Web 2.0 tools so educators can interactively share and refine best practices and describe what worked [or did not] when they tried to solve a similar problem.
>
> In the past, the assumption was that there were only a few big instructional problems and that central experts had the right one-size-fits-all approach. We now know that if you can break down large problems into series of more granular problems, often many of those small problems have already been solved and the best "know-how" is in other schools with the same challenge. This bottom-up approach to harvesting effective practices from educators who are closest to students will allow knowledge flow to be horizontal within and across schools instead of top down from a regional office or the DOE. This has transformed our thinking about one role of the central office as a facilitator and supporter of collaboration.

The first development phase of ARIS would launch to principals and teachers in September 2007. In the fall of 2008, ARIS would be used to distribute school- and student-performance data and quality review reports to parents and periodic assessment reports following the five assessment windows.

Designing and Implementing Progress Reports

In order to achieve a transparent way of evaluating and communicating school performance internally and externally, the Office of Accountability designed a progress report that would give a historical account of a school's overall success in improving student academic outcomes. Progress reports for all schools covered four main components, each with different weights that would contribute to the school's overall letter grade of A, B, C, D, or F: school environment = 15%; student performance = 30%; student progress = 55%; and closing the achievement gap = extra credit (**Exhibits 11a** and **11b**).

To account for differences in curriculum and targets by grade level, two versions of the report were created, one for elementary and middle schools and another for high schools. The DOE would eventually expand the range of reports to include separate reports for schools serving only early-childhood students (grades K–3), special education students taking alternative assessments, and high schools students who were at risk of "aging out" of the school system without graduating.

School Environment

In both versions of the report, the school environment section scored schools based on attendance figures and survey data from parents, teachers, and students in sixth through 12th grades. The DOE used an outside vendor to administer surveys that Liebman's team had designed. The surveys covered four areas: safety, expectations, student engagement, and communication between stakeholders and schools. The section would count 15% toward the overall progress-report score (5% for attendance and 10% for the four areas covered by the surveys). At the end of SY 07, the DOE had conducted the first survey of parents, teachers, and students. Administering almost 2 million surveys posed significant implementation challenges, but the response rates were large enough to allow for reliable data on the four survey areas in a large majority of schools. Overall response rates were close to 25% of the more than 1 million surveyed families, 30% of surveyed teachers, and over 90% of sixth through 12th graders.

Student Performance

The student performance section graded the school based on the percentage of students scoring proficient and above on that year's state mathematics and English-language arts exams for elementary and middle school students. Science and social studies would be added over the next two years. On the high school progress report, this section also scored graduation rates and the percentage of 11th and 12th graders taking the PSAT, SAT, or ACT. This section comprised 30% of the overall progress-report score.

Student Progress

To distinguish the new progress reports from previous "accountability reports" distributed by the city and state, the DOE added a focus on individual student *progress* over time rather than a sole focus on student *performance* at a point in time. The *progress* section measured the longitudinal change in an individual student's performance within one school year. For example, if most students started the school year at a "below-basic" level but ended the year at a "high-basic" level, the school would receive credit for the aggregate gain, even if the students did not reach the "proficient" level. On the flip side, a school could lose points if many students started the year at the "advanced" level and ended the year at the "proficient" level.

In the past, accountability reports only focused on percentages of students at proficient and above at a point in time, not on the gains or losses in a student's performance within and across all of the performance levels. Instead of rewarding schools for the kinds of students they attracted, the DOE hoped this area of the progress report would reward what schools brought to the students—in other words, giving schools credit for "adding value" to their students' performance trajectory. They expected the progress measurement to highlight the schools in which student learning was taking place and to stop giving schools an incentive to screen for higher-performing students in their enrollment processes.

To reflect changes in performance, the elementary and middle school student progress sections measured the average change of student proficiency in mathematics and English-language arts on state exams. For high schools, the student progress section compared schools based on whether students' scores on the New York state high school Regents exams across five subjects were below, at, or above the levels predicted by the same students' eighth-grade scores on state standardized tests in the same subject. The high school version also weighted credit accumulation, the average changes in PSAT scores from 10th to 11th grade, and the average pass rate for Regents exams. To make operational their belief in the importance of a school's ability to add value to its students' learning, Liebman and his team weighted this section as 55% of a school's overall progress-report score.

Closing the Achievement Gap

Lastly, the achievement gap section gave extra credit to elementary and middle schools that raised proficiency levels by half of a proficiency level or more among high proportions of struggling African-American, Hispanic, English-language learner, and special education students. The comparable section on the high school version gave extra credit to schools based on the number of students in those same populations that attained at least a quarter of the credits needed to graduate in each of their first two years of high school. This was based on DOE data that showed that ninth- and 10th-grade credit accumulation predicted graduation.

Overall Grade

In each of the three subcomponents, schools received two scores: one showing how well the school performed in relation to all NYC public schools, and another demonstrating how the school performed relative to "peer" schools with comparable student populations. To determine the overall grade, the city and peer comparisons for each subsection were weighted 33% and 67%, respectively, to derive a total subsection score, and then each subsection score was weighted appropriately (school environment = 15%, student performance = 30%, and student progress = 55%). Then, any extra credit was added for closing the achievement gap. This calculation yielded a numerical score that was converted into a letter grade (**Exhibit 12**). In addition to the letter grades, the rating from the school's QR would be reported on the progress report but would not factor into the progress-report grade.

During SY 07, draft versions of progress-report results were piloted first for empowerment schools and then, after revisions based on the pilot, for all schools. SY 07 results would be publicly released in September 2007 with consequences attached.

Results and Consequences

Although QRs and progress reports were both tools to help the DOE hold schools accountable for results, Liebman viewed the results from each very differently. He described school-quality reviews as leading indicators in predicting the school's future student-performance outcomes. He categorized the letter grades on the various sections of the progress reports as lagging indicators of a school's current and past performance. Because of this difference, it was possible for a school to receive a low grade on its progress report based on current performance indicators but receive a "well-developed" rating as a result of its QR—the opposite was also possible. One member of Liebman's team explained his reaction to this potential outcome:

> In the early years of the implementation of these systems, I imagine we will see some counterintuitive pairings of quality-review ratings and progress-report grades. But what we have to believe is that if our QR rubric and rating process is valid as a leading indicator, then over a few years a school's progress-report grades will change for better or worse consistent with the QR ratings.

To clearly communicate the consequences for schools earning low grades and poor QR ratings, Liebman's team created a matrix that defined a school's standing depending on its results (**Exhibit 9**).

To assist in the enforcement of consequences, Liebman's Office of Accountability team was expanded to include a School Improvement Office, which had previously been housed in the DOE's Division of Teaching and Learning. This office would assist community and high school superintendents in conducting performance conversations and work with school support organizations and senior achievement facilitators to support the structured academic planning required in the first year in which schools failed to meet their goals.

Supported by the chancellor's office, the community and high school superintendents would implement principal removal and school closures if they became necessary and exercise other statutory supervisory roles. Because the DOE was moving to an organizational structure in which principals had more control over their programs and activities, the new emphasis on accountability and on consequences for school success and failure had important philosophical and practical implications. As one senior manager explained:

> When people ask me whom principals will be accountable to, a big part of my answer is that "they are accountable to the data." But to make this stick, we need to be prepared to remove principals from their schools each year based on their students' performance. If we can't effectively enforce that consequence in a disciplined way, we will dilute the power of all the other elements of the system.

Making the Cultural Shift

Chancellor Klein often explained his view of the culture change that had to happen in New York, saying, "If our reforms are to succeed, we'll need to go through three major cultural shifts. We will have to evolve from a culture of excuses to a culture of accountability, from a culture of compliance to a culture of innovation, and from a culture of uniformity to a culture of differentiation." As Liebman reflected on the three shifts, it was clear to him that each piece of the performance management system he and his team were implementing had a role to play in creating a culture of accountability, innovation, and differentiation.

As the school teams used the new tools and processes to improve their performance, Liebman and his team would continue to adapt and refine them based on what they learned during the implementation phases. Accomplishing rapid institutionalization of the new systems and structures to create lasting culture change was a key challenge. Mayor Bloomberg would not run for reelection, so 2009 would be his last year in office. Because Klein reported to the mayor, there would likely be a leadership change at the top of the DOE in 2010. Liebman knew that he and his team had less than three years remaining to contribute to the realization of Klein's vision of cultural transformation.

Notes

1. Julie Bosman, "City Expands Test Program in Schools," *The New York Times*, May 31, 2007.

Exhibit 1a

New York City and State of New York English-Language Arts and Mathematics Assessments Results

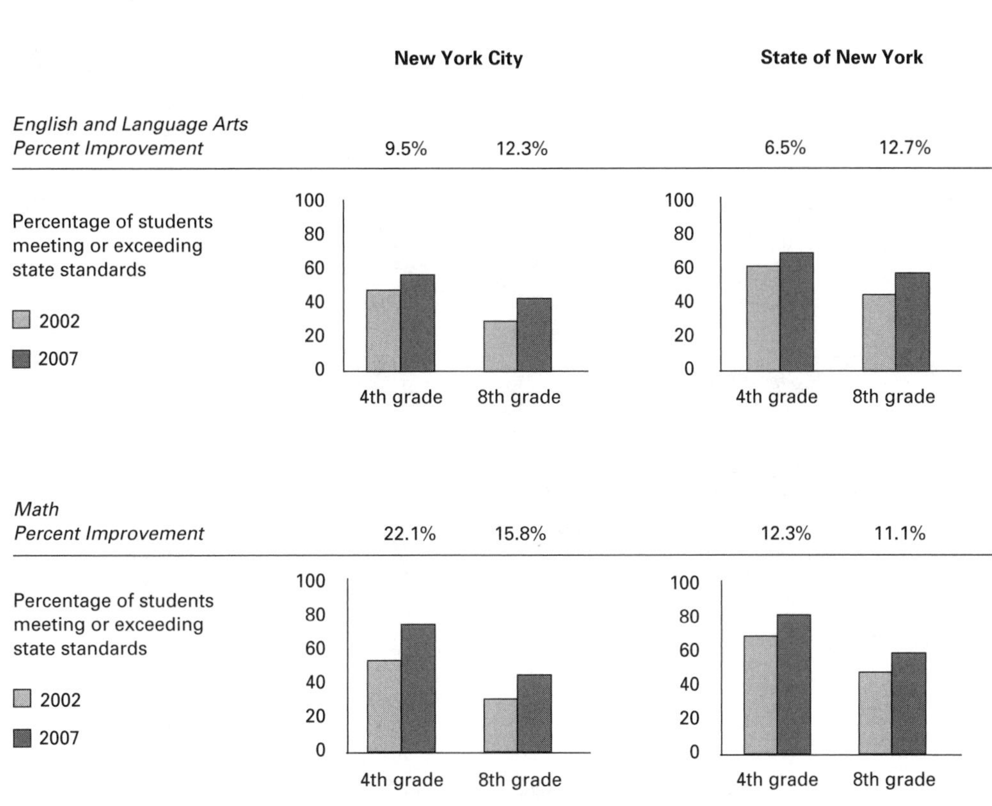

Sources: New York City Department of Education; State University of the State of New York, State Education Department: *2002 English Language Arts Test Results,* http://www.emsc.nysed.gov/irts/ELA4_8_2002/4th8thEnglish2002final.ppt; *2002 Math Test Results,* www.emsc.nysed.gov/irts/Math4_8_2002/Math_Results4th8th_grade_2002.ppt; *2007 English Language Arts Test Results,* http://schools.nyc.gov/daa/2007ela/default.asp, Summary Report on the 2007 Results of the ELA Assessments (Grades 3–8), and http://www.emsc.nysed.gov/irts/ela-math/ela-07/Grade3-8ELAresults2007Final.ppt; and *2007 Math Test Results,* http://www.emsc.nysed.gov/irts/ela-math/math-07/Grade3-8MathTests2007FINAL.ppt.

Exhibit 1b

New York City Mathematics Assessments Results, 1999–2007

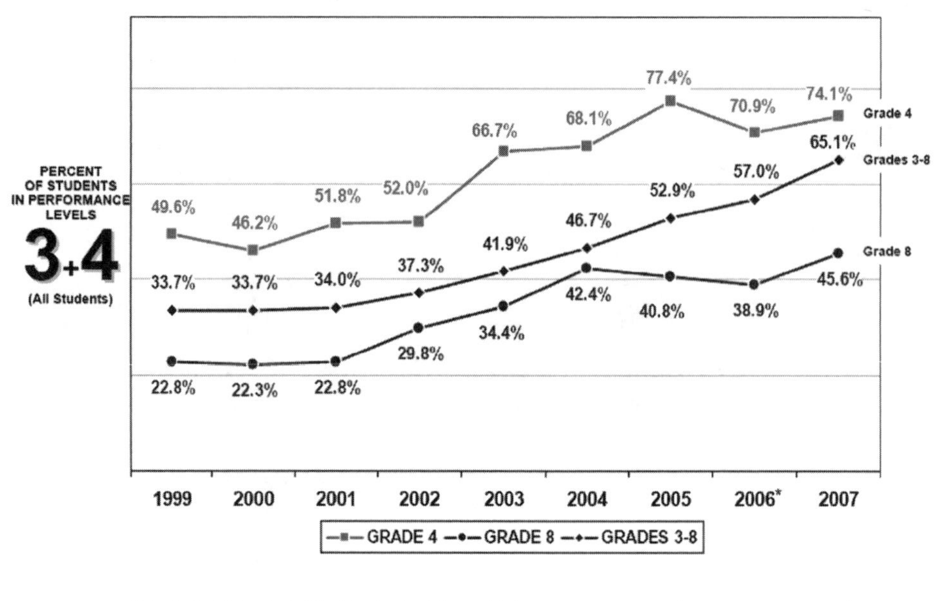

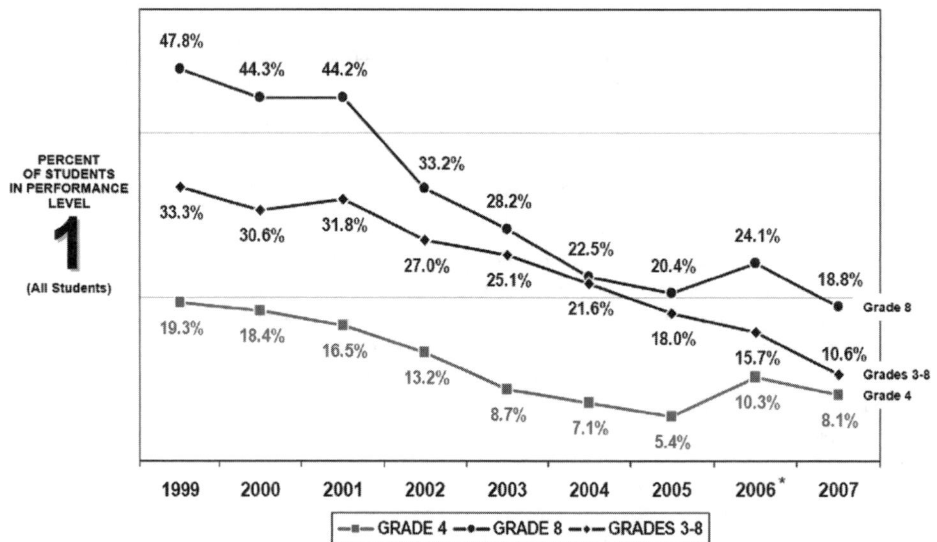

Source: New York City Department of Education.

Note: New York state exams have four performance categories, with level one being the lowest and roughly comparable to "below-basic" designations in other states, level two comparable to "basic," level three comparable to "proficient," and level four comparable to "advanced."

Exhibit 2

New York City Public Schools Facts and Figures

Number of K–12 students (as of 10/31/06)	1,042,078
American Indian	4,520
Asian	142,172
Black	336,191
Hispanic	410,016
White	149,179
English Language Learners	135,573
Budget	$15 billion
Number of Schools and Programs (as of 12/31/06, excludes charters)	1,456

Source: New York City Department of Education.

Exhibit 3

Summary of Children First Reforms

Children First Reform Highlights 2002–2005

- DOE management structure reorganized with the creation of regional offices
- A uniform literacy and math curriculum instituted for grades K–8
- Select failing secondary schools closed; 150 new small secondary schools opened
- New parent support system established with a parent coordinator in every school
- Leadership Academy created to train new school leaders
- Autonomy Zone piloted

Three Pillars of Children First

- *Leadership*—Principals as the locus of control
- *Empowerment*—Value exchange between autonomy and accountability
- *Accountability*—Use quantitative and qualitative measures to hold principals accountable for the demonstrated progress of every student

Source: New York City Department of Education.

Exhibit 4

Autonomy Zone Value Exchange Summary

Value Exchange: Summary Autonomy for Accountability

<table>
<tr><th>PRINCIPALS ACCEPT:
5-year Performance Agreements</th><th>PRINCIPALS RECEIVE:
Control and Support</th></tr>
<tr><td>STUDENT ACHIEVEMENT
5-year standards with a minimum annual gap-closure target:
• Average daily attendance: 90% HS; 92% MS/ES
• 80% Regents cohorts pass rate for ELA and Math Regents Exams
• 4-year cohort graduation rate: 70% OR 55% 4-year and 75% 5-year
• 2 or 4-year college acceptance: 90% of graduating students
• Annual drop-out rate: No more than 4% of HS students enrolled
• Annual course pass rate: 75% HS
• Meet AYP targets for ELA, Math & Science in all subgroups for grades 3 through 8</td><td>AUTONOMY (within legal and contractual requirements)
• Choice of curriculum, instructional models and interim assessments
• Membership in school-led networks organized around shared educational philosophies
• Choice of professional development
• Flexibility in scheduling of school day
• Maximum flexibility in staffing decisions within contract
• Greater flexibility in school budget
• Opportunity to develop new approaches to educate special populations</td></tr>
<tr><td>EDUCATIONAL EQUITY
• All student groups (ELL, SPED and Level 1) make educational gains on test scores and graduation rates
• For choice enrollment schools, attract an equitable entering class mix that I close to citywide HS average for ELL, SPED, level 1 (no less than 10% ELL; 10% SPED, no less than 25% Level 1)</td><td rowspan="4">CROSS-FUNCTIONAL SUPPORT
• Dedicated team from ROC/Admin, Human Resources, Youth Development, Special Education/ELL
• Voice in selecting LIS and setting coaching/support priorities
• Reduction in administrative/paperwork burden on principals
• Timely, useful data about all aspects of school performance: accountability metrics and other management information
• Optional attendance in any professional development or other DOE forum</td></tr>
<tr><td>SHARED LEARNING
• Document, share best practices, accept visits</td></tr>
<tr><td>FISCAL INTEGRITY
• Expend resources consistent with education plans and within approved budget levels. In addition, spending must comply with contracting and purchasing procedures</td></tr>
<tr><td>INCENTIVES & CONSEQUENCES
Consequences:
• Renewal/non-renewal with or without conditions
• School closure
Incentives:
• Visibility of results to peers, public</td></tr>
</table>

Source: New York City Department of Education.

Exhibit 5

NYC Schools Old and New Organizational Structures

Disbanded NYC Department of Education and Regional Organizational Structure

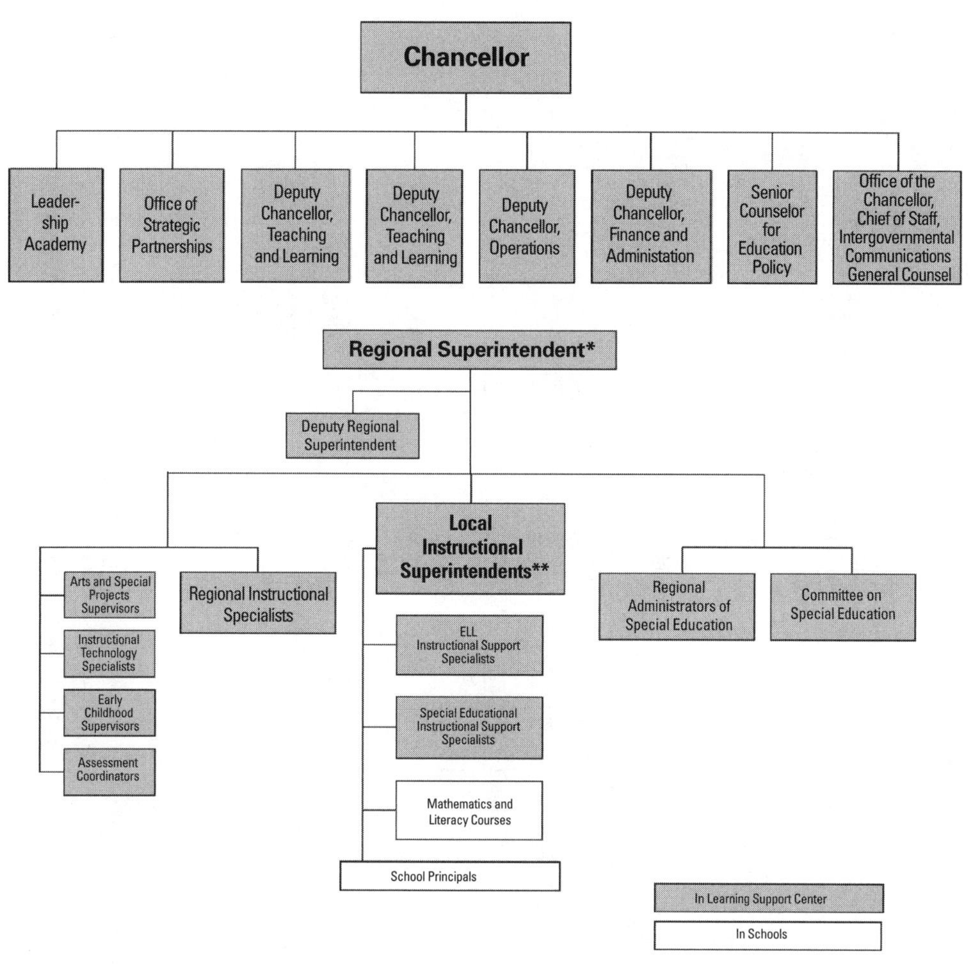

Source: New York City Department of Education.

* Reports to Deputy Chancellor for Teaching and Learning

** 32 Local Instructional Superintendents also serve as Community School District Superintendents, some housed in district offices

NYC Department of Education Organizational Chart (2007–2008)

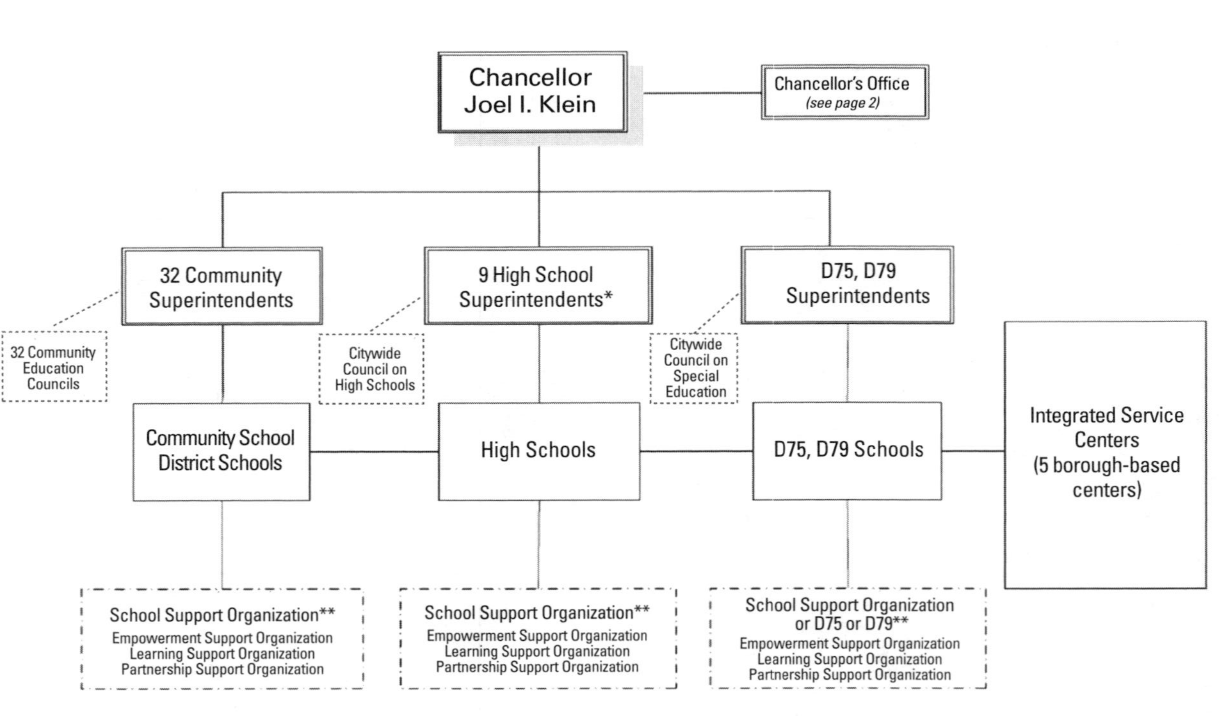

Source: New York City Department of Education.

* There will be 9 certified high school superintendents, which will have schools assigned to them based partly on geographic factors and partly on the school support organization they have chosen to work with.

** School support organizations to be selected by the principal and approved by the appropriate Superintendent.

NYC Department of Education—Chancellor's Office

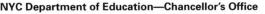

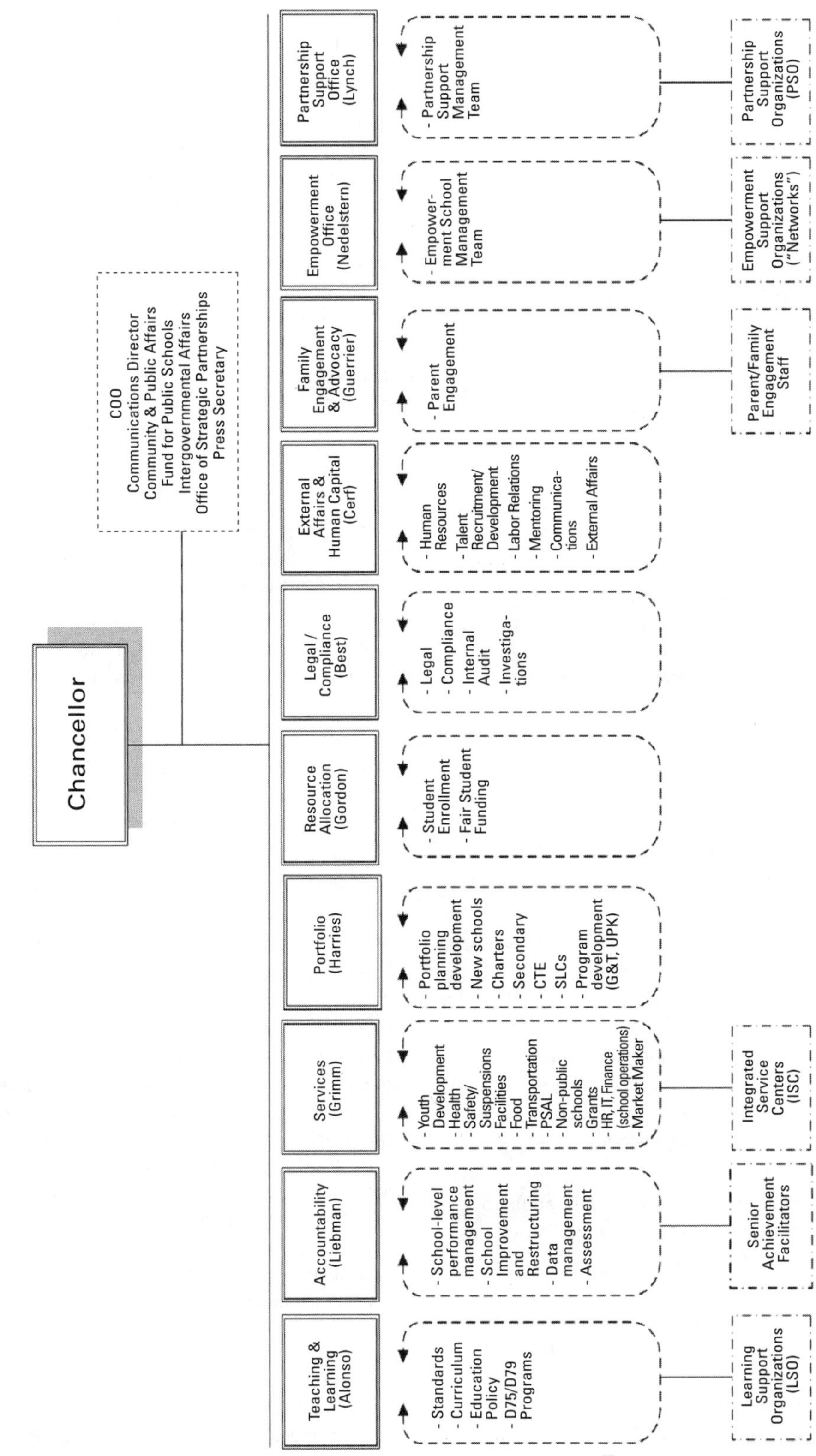

Source: New York City Department of Education.

Exhibit 6

New York State Statutory Powers and Duties of Community Superintendents

1. Appoint and assign principals and supervisory personnel in accordance with chancellor's regulations.
2. Evaluate, at least annually, the performance of every principal in the district with respect to educational effectiveness and school performance, including effectiveness of promoting student achievement and parental involvement and maintaining school discipline.
3. Transfer or remove principals for persistent educational failure, conflicts of interest, and ethics violation.
4. Require principals to participate in training and other remedial programs to address identified factors affecting student achievement and school performance.
5. Retain fiscal officer(s), who shall be selected from qualified fiscal personnel employed by the City Department of Education, to monitor and report on schools' expenditures pursuant to school-based budgets. Fiscal officers may be responsible for more than one district. The fiscal officer may be located as determined by the chancellor.
6. Operate the administrative offices and similar facilities, including social centers and recreational and extracurricular programs, under the district's jurisdiction.
7. Administer district minor repair and purchasing funds and provide for minor repairs to all schools buildings and other sites within the district.
8. Provide relevant data to the Community District Education Council to encourage informed and adequate public discussion on student achievement and the state of each school within the district.
9. Submit zoning lines, consistent with regulations of the chancellor, to the Community District Education Council for approval.
10. Recommend to the Community District Education Council for approval and submission to the chancellor a district annual capacity plan, based on data from the chancellor on enrollment/utilization for each school within the district.
11. Have regular communications with all parent associations in the district and meet at least quarterly with elected officers of the parent associations and provide information so that associations have full factual information concerning matters of pupil achievement, including (but not limited to) annual reading scores, comparison of achievement of pupils in comparable grades and schools, and the record of achievement of such pupils as they progress through schools (in nonidentifiable manner).
12. Take all necessary steps to ensure the integrity of community district operations, consistent with regulations promulgated by the chancellor.
13. Review, modify, and approve school-based budgets proposed by each school in the district.
14. Sign written orders issued by the director of finance of the city for the disbursement of funds credited to a community council.
15. Discontinue teaching and supervisory staff prior to the completion of probation and recommend teaching and supervisory personnel for appointment on tenure.
16. Appoint, define duties of, assign, promote, and discharge all nonsupervisory employees in the district, subject to the terms of any applicable collective bargaining agreements.
17. Initiate charges against teaching and supervisory staff who have completed probation, and where delegated by the chancellor implement any penalties or punishment imposed after a hearing on such charges.
18. Contract for and receive special, federal, state, and private funds, to be transmitted to the city board and disbursed through the chancellor, and use funds and resources obtained to design programs of educational excellence tailored to the needs and peculiar characteristics of the district. Apply to funding agencies as a local educational agency for federal or state funds not allocated to the city on a formula basis and accept such funds. Submit proposals to the chancellor for review as to form only and prompt transmittal to funding agencies for special funds allocated to the city on a formula basis, subject to restrictions on the total amount as determined by citywide formula, and consult with non-public school authorities on a continuing basis with any special funds applicable to non-public school programs and students.

19. Prepare semiannual and end-of-year reports, including an accounting of all funds received and expended by the Community District Education Council to be distributed to the chancellor, the Community District Education Council, and the public.
20. Approve/disapprove matters relating to the instruction of students in all district schools, including school choices with respect to the selection of textbooks and other materials, subject to the chancellor or his designees with authority to, among other things, establish minimum clear educational standards, curriculum requirements and frameworks, and mandatory educational objectives applicable to all schools and programs throughout the city district.
21. Delegate powers and duties to subordinate officers or employees of the district as he/she deems appropriate and modify or rescind such delegation.
22. Attend monthly public meetings of the Community District Education Council and discuss the current state of the schools in the district and progress made toward the implementation of the district's comprehensive education plan required by the chancellor.
23. The community superintendent is the superintendent of schools of the Community School District.
24. Maintain discipline in the educational and other facilities in the district and provide schools with the assistance necessary to maintain discipline. Suspend students from required attendance for specified behaviors and conduct hearings or designate a hearing officer to conduct such hearings for student suspensions that exceed five days.
25. Receive annual School Comprehensive Education Plans aligned with the school-based budget submitted by School Leadership Teams, as required by state education law.
26. Approve plans developed by the principal to enhance teacher and staff development related to increasing student achievement and support extended day programs, school reform programs, and pupil support services.
27. Develop a proposed budget for the administrative and operational expenses of the community superintendent and the Community District Education Council for submission to the chancellor and modify and reallocate monies in the enacted district budget.
28. Consult with the chancellor on the development of objective formulae to be used to allocate funds to the districts for the district's programs and activities, and advise on the educational needs of the community district, so that the formulae may reflect the relative needs of community districts to the maximum extent feasible.
29. With the participation of principals and schools, provide an annual update of the capital plan for the district, addressing health and safety, maintenance, capacity, and technology.
30. Purchase material goods, supplies, and services directly from vendors or suppliers, pursuant to a procurement policy for the city schools established by the chancellor.
31. Develop, in collaboration with administrators, teachers, and parents, a district plan for school-based planning and shared decision making, in accordance with Commissioner's Regulations 100.11.
32. Make an annual report covering all matters relating to schools under the district's jurisdiction including, but not limited to, the evaluation of the educational effectiveness of such schools and programs connected therewith.
33. Employ or retain counsel subject to the powers and duties of the corporation counsel of the city of New York to be the district's attorney and counsel, pursuant to subdivision a of section three hundred ninety-four of the New York city charter.
34. In addition to statutory powers and duties, community superintendents shall follow applicable chancellor's regulations, policies, and procedures, policies of the city boards and regulations on the New York State Commissioner of Education.

Source: New York City Department of Education.

Exhibit 7

School-Quality Review Quality Statements

Quality Review Scoring Key	
Δ	Underdeveloped
➤	Underdeveloped with Proficient Features
✓	Proficient
+	Well Developed
◇	Outstanding

Quality Statement 1 – Gather Data: School leaders and faculty consistently gather and generate data and use it to understand what each student knows and can do, and to monitor the student's progress over time.					
To what extent do school leaders and faculty gather, generate, and utilize data to provide . . .	Δ	➤	✓	+	◇
1.1 an objective, constantly updated understanding of the performance and progress of each student, classroom, grade level?					
1.2 an objective, constantly updated understanding of the performance and progress of special education students?					
1.3 an objective, constantly updated understanding of the performance and progress of English language learners?					
1.4 an objective, constantly updated understanding of the performance and progress of ethnic groups, gender groups and all other categories of interest to the school?					
1.5 a measurement of performance and progress based on the school's own past performance, and among students, classrooms, grades and subject areas?					
1.6 a measurement of performance and progress based on comparisons with similar schools?					
1.7 training, management systems and structures that support teachers in the use of school data to inform planning and instruction and to track the progress of students?					
Overall score for Quality Statement 1					

Quality Statement 2 – Plan and Set Goals: School leaders and faculty consistently use data to understand each student's next learning steps and to set suitably high goals for accelerating each student's learning.					
To what extent do school leaders and faculty . . .	Δ	➤	✓	+	◇
2.1 engage in collaborative processes to set rigorous, objectively measurable goals for improvement, and to develop plans and time frames for reaching those goals?					
2.2 focus on each student, classroom, grade level, academic subject and group of students whose performance or progress has been identified by the school as a particular focus area?					
2.3 identify and improve the performance and progress of those students in greatest need of improvement?					
2.4 share whole school goals with all members of the school community to rigorously improve the performance and progress of students?					
2.5 convey consistently high expectations to students and their parents/caregivers?					
2.6 regularly provide students and their parents/caregivers with information about the goals set for each student, and about each student's progress and performance, and how they can improve?					
2.7 invite and enable parents/caregivers to provide useful information to teachers and the school about the learning needs and capacities of their children ?					
Overall score for Quality Statement 2					

Source: New York City Department of Education.

Quality Statement 3 – Align Instructional Strategy to Goals: The school aligns its academic work, strategic decisions and resources, and effectively engages students, around its plans and goals for accelerating student learning.					
To what extent do the school leaders . . .	Δ	➤	✓	+	◇
3.1 select core curricular approaches that facilitate and provide meaningful interim data about progress towards goals and focus on raising the achievement of students?					
3.2 provide a broad and engaging curriculum, including the arts, to enhance learning both within and outside the school day?					
3.3 hold teachers accountable for the progress and learning of the students in their charge, for making instruction interesting and compelling, and for creating a positive, safe and inclusive learning environment ?					
3.4 ensure that teachers use school, classroom and student data to plan for and provide differentiated instruction that meets the specific needs of all the students in their charge?					
3.5 make budgeting, staffing and scheduling decisions strategically, based on data, to meet the school's academic goals for all students?					
3.6 ensure that there is an environment of mutual trust and respect between all staff and students to support personal and academic development?					
3.7 ensure that there are effective and consistently applied procedures to encourage and monitor student attendance and tardiness?					
Overall score for Quality Statement 3					

Quality Statement 4 – Align Capacity Building to Goals: The development of leadership, teachers and other staff capacity is aligned to the school's collaboratively established goals for accelerating the learning of each student.					
To what extent do the school leaders. . .	Δ	➤	✓	+	◇
4.1 use frequent observations of classroom teaching by the principal and other available information to develop a differentiated strategy for improving the quality of each teacher's instruction?					
4.2 make professional development decisions strategically, based on data, to help meet the improvement goals of students and teachers?					
4.3 provide frequent opportunities for teachers to observe each other's classroom instruction and to meet together in teams to plan, share effective practices, and evaluate one another's instruction in an open and reflective professional environment?					
4.4 develop effective procedures for the induction and support of teachers who are new to the profession or the school?					
4.5 align youth development, guidance/advising and other student support services around stated academic and personal development goals?					
4.6 consistently implement clear procedures that enable the school to run smoothly, encourage effective student learning, and effectively address discipline related incidents?					
4.7 create effective partnerships with outside entities that support the academic and personal growth of the students?					
Overall score for Quality Statement 4					

Quality Statement 5 – Monitor and Revise: The school has structures for monitoring and evaluating each student's progress throughout the year and for flexibly adapting plans and practices to meet its goals for accelerating learning.					
To what extent do . . .	Δ	➤	✓	+	◇
5.1 the school's plans for improving student outcomes include interim goals that are objectively measurable and have suitable time frames for measuring success and making adjustments?					
5.2 the school's plans for improving teacher outcomes include interim goals that are objectively measurable and have suitable time frames for measuring success and making adjustments?					
5.3 teachers and faculty use periodic assessments and other diagnostic tools to measure the effectiveness of plans and interventions for individual and groups of students in key areas?					
5.4 teachers and faculty use the information generated by periodic assessments and other progress measures and comparisons to revise plans immediately in order to reach stated goals?					
5.5 school leaders track the outcomes of periodic assessments and other diagnostic measures and use the results to makes strategic decisions to modify practices to improve student outcomes?					
5.6 school leaders and staff use each plan's interim and final outcomes to drive the next stage of goal setting and improvement planning?					
5.7 the principal and school community have a clear vision for the future development of the school and implement procedures and systems to effect change?					
Overall score for Quality Statement 5					

Source: New York City Department of Education.

Exhibit 8

Sample School-Quality Review Agenda

Day 1

8:00–10:00 a.m.	Arrival and Meeting with Principal
10:00–11:00 a.m.	Classroom Walkthroughs
11:00 a.m.–12:00 p.m.	Teacher Group Meeting/Lunch
12:00–1:00 p.m.	Student Group Meeting
1:00–2:00 p.m.	Classroom Walkthroughs
2:00–3:00 p.m.	Parent Group Meeting
3:00–4:00 p.m.	Observe Instructional Leadership Team Meeting
4:00–4:30 p.m.	Recap day with Principal

Day 2

8:00–9:00 a.m.	Arrival and Meeting with Principal
9:00–9:45 a.m.	Student Case Studies Presentation
10:00–11:00 a.m.	Classroom Walkthroughs
11:00 a.m.–12:30 p.m.	Exit Interview with Principal

Exhibit 9

Consequences for Progress-Report Grades Crossed with Quality-Review Ratings

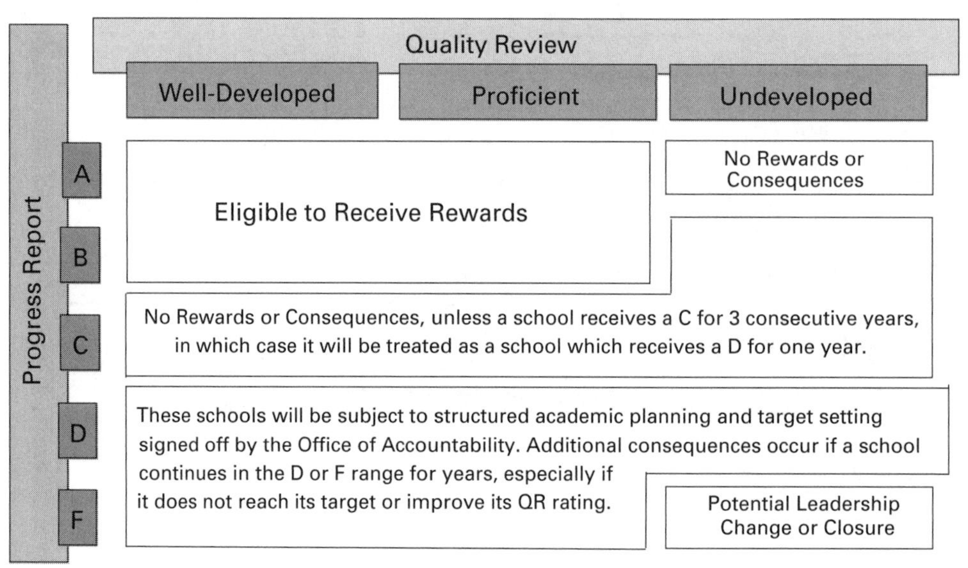

Source: New York City Department of Education.

Exhibit 10

ARIS Objectives and Scope

Objectives

- Ensure access to the information and tools necessary to enable
- Longitudinal and detailed analysis and reporting of achievement and performance data
- Best-in-class assessment design and implementation processes to extract data from multiple sources, including designing own reports and the capability to slice and dice the data
- Tools to improve learning of students with a range of identified needs
- Sharing best practices and collaborating across schools to encourage cultures of continuous school improvement and professional learning

Scope of the ARIS

- Provide principals, teachers, and parents with online information on student achievement, including periodic assessments
- Support development of longitudinal and detailed analysis
- Develop an integrated portal, including a dashboard to analyze key environment factors and achievement metrics
- Enable real-time prediction of school performance against year-end targets
- Generate standard reports for specific end users
- Develop scorecards to enable drill-downs by student, assessment, strand and sub-strand analysis
- Provide knowledge management tools that capture teaching and assessment content generated at school level with an ability to approve, publish and share with the networks or the broader district, as well as capturing new quality review data

Exhibit 11a

Elementary/Middle School Sample Progress Report

MIDDLE SCHOOL

This Progress Report is for:

SCHOOL	**FREDERICK DOUGLASS ACADEMY V MIDDLE SCHO (212273)**
PRINCIPAL	**DEBORAH CIMINI**
ENROLLMENT	**269**
SCHOOL TYPE	**MIDDLE SCHOOL**
PEER INDEX	**3.14**

Your School's Overall Results

Progress Report Grade **A**

What does this grade mean?

Schools are assigned letter grades based on their overall Progress Report score. Schools that get As and Bs are eligible for rewards. Schools that get Ds and Fs, or 3 Cs in a row, face consequences.

How did this school perform?

- This School's overall score for 2006–07 is **66.6**
- This score places the School in the **78.5** percentile of all middle school's citywide (i.e., **78.5** percent of those schools scored lower than this school)
- This School's target score for 2007–08 is **79.1**

Category	Calculated Score	
School Environment	11.1 out of 15	0 – 15
Student Performance	19.4 out of 30	0 – 30
Student Progress	31.6 out of 55	0 – 55
Additional Credit	4.5	
Overall Score	**66.6**	0 – 100; Next year's target **79.1**

How Scores translate to grades:

- Schools receive letter grades based on their overall score
- Schools with an overall score between **65.2 and 93.6** receive a letter grade of **A**
- **25.2%** of schools earned an **A** in 2006–07.

Middle School Table

Grade	Score Range	2006-07 City Summary
A	65.2–93.6	25.2% of schools
B	50.5–65.2	35.5% of schools
C	38.8–50.5	25.5% of schools
D	30.9–38.8	9.7% of schools
F	-0.4–30.9	4.1% of schools

Quality Review Score

This school's 2006–07 Quality Review score is **P**. To see your school's Quality Review Report, locate your school at **http://schools.nyc.gov/**, click 'Statistics', and scroll down to Quality Review Report.

2006-07 State Accountability Status

Based on its 2005–06 performance, this school is **In Good Standing**. This measure, determined by New York State as part of the federal No Child Left Behind (NCLB) Act, is not a factor in the Progress Report Grade.

Inside This Report:

The NYC Progress Report is a new accountability tool. Each school's Progress Report (1) measures student year-to-year progress, (2) compares the school to peer schools, and (3) rewards success in moving all children forward, especially children with the greatest needs. The Progress Report measures four areas:

School Environment uses surveys and other data to evaluate necessary conditions for learning: attendance, safety, academic expectations, engagement, and communication.

Student Performance evaluates student skill levels in English Language Arts and Math.

Student Progress measures average student improvement in English Language Arts and Math from last year to this year.

Closing the Achievement Gap gives schools additional credit for exemplary gains among high-need students.

More information about the Progress Report is on the back page. →

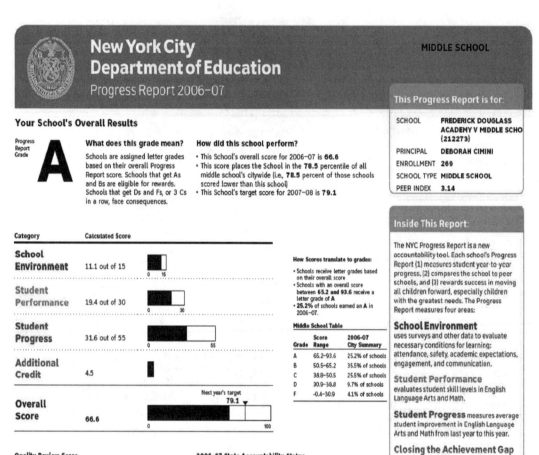

Source: New York City Department of Education.

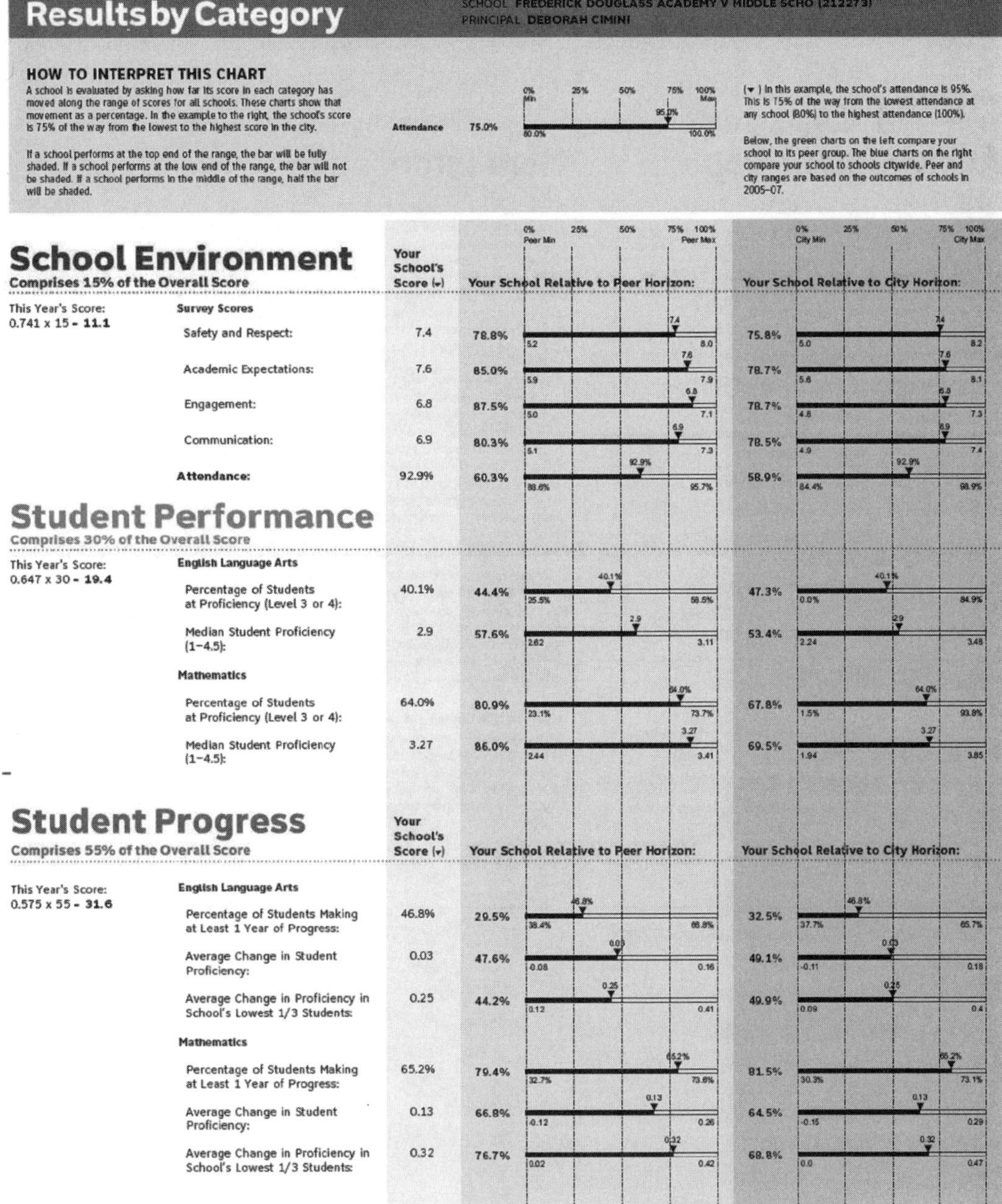

Results by Category
SCHOOL FREDERICK DOUGLASS ACADEMY V MIDDLE SCHO (212273)
PRINCIPAL DEBORAH CIMINI
HOW TO INTERPRET THIS CHART
A school is evaluated by asking how far its score in each category has moved along the range of scores for all schools. These charts show that movement as a percentage. In the example to the right, the school's score is 75% of the way from the lowest to the highest score in the city.
If a school performs at the top end of the range, the bar will be fully shaded. If a school performs at the low end of the range, the bar will not be shaded. If a school performs in the middle of the range, half the bar will be shaded.
Attendance 75.0%
(▾) In this example, the school's attendance is 95%. This is 75% of the way from the lowest attendance at any school (80%) to the highest attendance (100%).
Below, the green charts on the left compare your school to its peer group. The blue charts on the right compare your school to schools citywide. Peer and city ranges are based on the outcomes of schools in 2005–07.
School Environment
Comprises 15% of the Overall Score
This Year's Score: 0.741 x 15 = 11.1
Your School's Score (▾)
Your School Relative to Peer Horizon:
Your School Relative to City Horizon:
Survey Scores
Safety and Respect: 7.4 78.8% 75.8%
Academic Expectations: 7.6 85.0% 78.7%
Engagement: 6.8 87.5% 78.7%
Communication: 6.9 80.3% 78.5%
Attendance: 92.9% 60.3% 58.9%
Student Performance
Comprises 30% of the Overall Score
This Year's Score: 0.647 x 30 = 19.4
English Language Arts
Percentage of Students at Proficiency (Level 3 or 4): 40.1% 44.4% 47.3%
Median Student Proficiency (1–4.5): 2.9 57.6% 53.4%
Mathematics
Percentage of Students at Proficiency (Level 3 or 4): 64.0% 80.9% 67.8%
Median Student Proficiency (1–4.5): 3.27 86.0% 69.5%
Student Progress
Comprises 55% of the Overall Score
This Year's Score: 0.575 x 55 = 31.6
English Language Arts
Percentage of Students Making at Least 1 Year of Progress: 46.8% 29.5% 32.5%
Average Change in Student Proficiency: 0.03 47.6% 49.1%
Average Change in Proficiency in School's Lowest 1/3 Students: 0.25 44.2% 49.9%
Mathematics
Percentage of Students Making at Least 1 Year of Progress: 65.2% 79.4% 81.5%
Average Change in Student Proficiency: 0.13 66.8% 64.5%
Average Change in Proficiency in School's Lowest 1/3 Students: 0.32 76.7% 68.8%

Source: New York City Department of Education.

Additional Information

SCHOOL **FREDERICK DOUGLASS ACADEMY V MIDDLE SCHO (212273)**
PRINCIPAL **DEBORAH CIMINI**

Closing the Achievement Gap

Schools earn additional credit when their high-need students make exemplary gains. These gains are based on the percentage of high-need students who improve by at least one-half of a proficiency level in English Language Arts or Math (e.g., student improves from 2.25 to 2.75 in ELA, or 3.10 to 3.60 in Math). Schools earn this additional credit if the percentage of students, in any of the five high-need categories, who achieve exemplary gains is in the top 40% of all schools citywide.

This component can only improve a school's overall progress report grade. It cannot lower a school's grade.

Credit	Exemplary Proficiency Gains	Student Group
		English Language Arts
☐	-	English Language Learners
☐	16.7%	Special Education Students
☐	23.3%	Hispanic Students Who Are In Lowest Third Citywide
☐	18.2%	Black Students Who Are In Lowest Third Citywide
☐	-	Other Students Who Are In Lowest Third Citywide
		Mathematics
☐	23.8%	English Language Learners
☑	25.0%	Special Education Students
☑	46.5%	Hispanic Students Who Are In Lowest Third Citywide
☑	45.2%	Black Students Who Are In Lowest Third Citywide
☐	-	Other Students Who Are In Lowest Third Citywide

More Information

Each school's Progress Report **(1)** measures student year-to-year progress, **(2)** compares the school to peer schools, and **(3)** rewards success in moving all children forward, especially children with the greatest needs. Each of these steps is a key component of Mayor Michael R. Bloomberg and Chancellor Joel I. Klein's Children First reforms. By taking these steps in a rigorous way that is sensitive to empowered schools' many pathways to success, the Progress Report is designed to assist administrators, principals, and teachers in accelerating the learning of all students. The Progress Report also enables students, parents, and the public to hold the NYC Department of Education and its schools accountable for student achievement and improvement and for ensuring a high quality education for every student in NYC's public schools.

The Office of Accountability (OA) developed the Progress Report in collaboration with parents, teachers, principals, community leaders, and researchers. The report also reflects feedback from a citywide pilot in 2006–07. OA will continue to monitor results, solicit feedback, and refine the report over time.

This Progress Report relies in part on surveys of parents, teachers, and secondary students citywide to evaluate schools' learning environments. Details and analysis of each school's survey results are available at **http://schools.nyc.gov/Surveys.**

Progress Reports will be distributed at the beginning of each school year. Schools are eligible for rewards and consequences based on Progress Report outcomes and scores on annual Quality Reviews. For more information about rewards and consequences, see **http://schools.nyc.gov/Accountability/ProgressReports/Consequences.** Future Progress Reports will compare each school's performance in the current year to the target set for the school in the previous year.

In addition to Progress Reports for Elementary and Middle Schools and general education High Schools, OA is developing Progress Reports for Specialized High Schools, Transfer Schools, Special Education (District 75) School and Early Childhood Schools. Each of these Progress Reports reflects the unique qualities and challenges of the schools it evaluates.

If you have any questions or comments about the Progress Report, please visit **http://schools.nyc.gov/Accountability/ProgressReports** or send us an email at **pr_support@schools.nyc.gov.**

Source: New York City Department of Education.

Exhibit 12

Progress Report Peer Group and Letter Grade Calculations

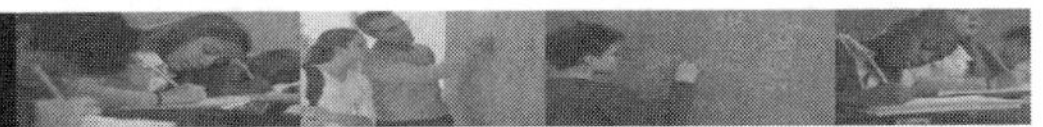

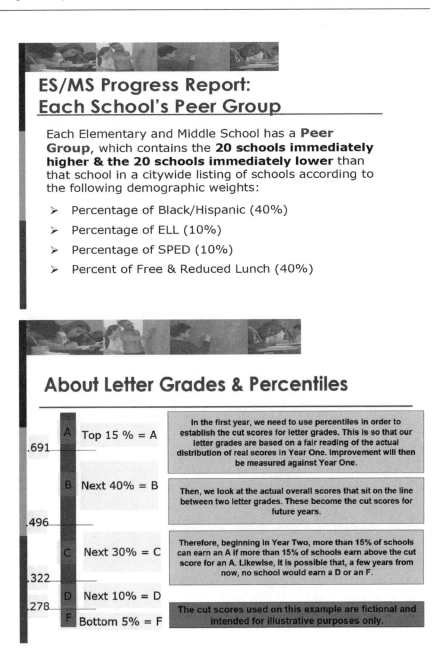

ES/MS Progress Report: Each School's Peer Group

Each Elementary and Middle School has a **Peer Group**, which contains the **20 schools immediately higher & the 20 schools immediately lower** than that school in a citywide listing of schools according to the following demographic weights:

- Percentage of Black/Hispanic (40%)
- Percentage of ELL (10%)
- Percentage of SPED (10%)
- Percent of Free & Reduced Lunch (40%)

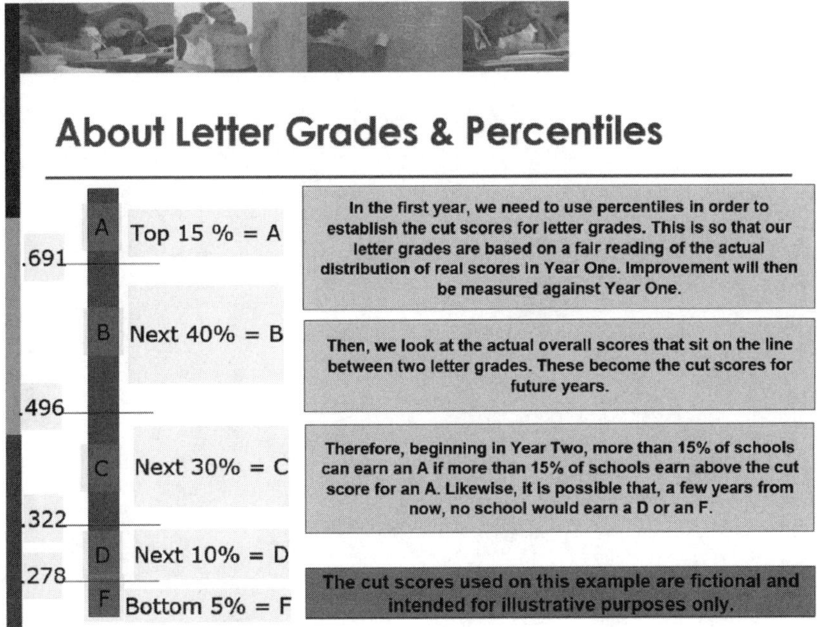

About Letter Grades & Percentiles
A
Top 15 % = A
.691
B
Next 40% = B
.496
C
Next 30% = C
.322
D
Next 10% = D
.278
F
Bottom 5% = F
In the first year, we need to use percentiles in order to establish the cut scores for letter grades. This is so that our letter grades are based on a fair reading of the actual distribution of real scores in Year One. Improvement will then be measured against Year One.
Then, we look at the actual overall scores that sit on the line between two letter grades. These become the cut scores for future years.
Therefore, beginning in Year Two, more than 15% of schools can earn an A if more than 15% of schools earn above the cut score for an A. Likewise, it is possible that, a few years from now, no school would earn a D or an F.
The cut scores used on this example are fictional and intended for illustrative purposes only.

Source: New York City Department of Education.

Launching and Growing New Schools

Launching and growing new schools is a significant area of entrepreneurial activity in public education. At the heart of this opportunity area is the theory of competition—new schools designed for students who are routinely underserved by existing district schools will not only improve the academic outcomes of these students, but exert pressure to improve on the larger system by attracting away students, staff, and funding. Some charter advocates who launched the movement in the early 1990s contend that their aim was simply to give parents options, not to transform the entire system. But the majority of entrepreneurs starting new schools and growing school networks today are interested in systemwide change.

Some new schools and networks are being created inside districts under the sponsorship of entrepreneurial superintendents who see the approach as part of an overall strategy for phasing out chronically low-performing schools and replacing them with a supply of higher-performing schools, whether district-run or charter. However, most charter schools and networks are growing outside the auspices of local school districts. Module IV allows for an exploration of these various approaches.

The module begins with an exercise titled "If We Blew It Up, Then We Could . . ." which forces you to choose between two rather extreme options for re-creating the U.S. education system from scratch. This stylized thought experiment proposes either more radical decentralization of education decisions to families or a more extreme centralization to a national body. This discussion provides a good preface to the cases that follow by helping you examine your own assumptions about families, markets, government, and the overall goals of an education system.

The first case, "Launching the Bronx Lab School," is an example of an in-district start-up in the New York City Department of Education (discussed in Module III). The next two cases are about independent charter schools in Massachusetts, Codman Academy and Frederick Douglass Charter School (FDCS). Codman has had success balancing the academic and social-emotional needs of its students with an innovative model, but an impending change in the definition of "passing" on annual state exams calls its model into question. The case will allow you to examine whether the school has truly been successful so far and how the school leaders might adapt to the new state expectations while preserving parts of its model that the leaders believe have value beyond their direct impact on reading and math scores. FDCS is a struggling school in its fifth year facing a renewal decision from the state board of education. This case will put you in the shoes of the state board chair attempting to evaluate the school's potential to improve should its charter be renewed. The school is performing worse than other charter schools in the area, but better than nearby district schools, where its students will likely enroll should the school shut down. Given the overall charter school theory of change, the case forces the question "How good is good enough?" The case discussion hinges on the choice to extend the school's charter or shut it down.

While the autonomy granted charters brings many benefits, it also poses limitations, as the Frederick Douglass case demonstrates. "New Schools for New Orleans 2008" offers an alternative to the "on your own" model by offering an innovative approach that allows charter schools to take advantage of their independence while still having access to some of the support functions typically provided by a school district, especially in their first few years of operation. The rapid proliferation of charter schools after Hurricane Katrina in New Orleans, a city that before the storm had few of these types of schools, created a market opportunity for an organization to provide some of the benefits of a network without rebuilding the bureaucracy of a large school district. New Schools for New Orleans was launched in response to this market need, and the case allows for an evaluation of strategic choices facing the organization as it attempts to support autonomous schools in New Orleans to increase their chances for success.

As you work through the cases in the first half of the module, you will have an opportunity to practice a diagnostic framework for assessing a school's instructional and organizational strength. The tool has been adapted from the Public Education Leadership Project (PELP) Coherence Framework, developed by the author of this book with colleagues at Harvard Business School and the Harvard Graduate School of Education.[1] The coherence framework was originally designed for school systems interested in developing a districtwide improvement strategy and creating an organization that would support its effective implementation. Over time, through the writing and teaching of cases at the single-school and network level, the framework was adapted slightly to make it useful for analyzing a school-level instructional model and organization. The components of the framework are a school's learning model, theory of action, culture, systems and structures, resources, stakeholders, and environment. Figure 1 shows the school effectiveness framework.

The framework works from the inside out, starting with the most important aspect of a school—its approach to teaching and learning, or its *learning model*. Is the school practicing a back-to-basics approach focused on building skills in the core content areas such as reading, math, and science? Is it pursuing a more progressive approach in which concepts are integrated across content areas and students are engaged in inductive learning and project-based work? Or is there a more nontraditional strategy grounded in a particular point of view about human development such as expeditionary learning? Regardless of which learning model a team has adopted, is it grounded in a clear *theory of action* about how students will learn, and is it understood by school leaders and staff alike?

Once you have diagnosed this aspect of the school, how do all the other pieces fit together to make the strategy more successful? *Culture* is a good place to start. What are some descriptors that would describe a culture necessary for implementing the instructional model effectively (tight discipline? flexible and friendly? high expectations? no excuses? egalitarian?)? Does the observable culture of the school seem consistent with these attributes?

How well do the school's *systems and structures* seem to fit the strategy and the culture? How is the day organized? The week? How are courses arrayed across the year? Is the system

Figure 1

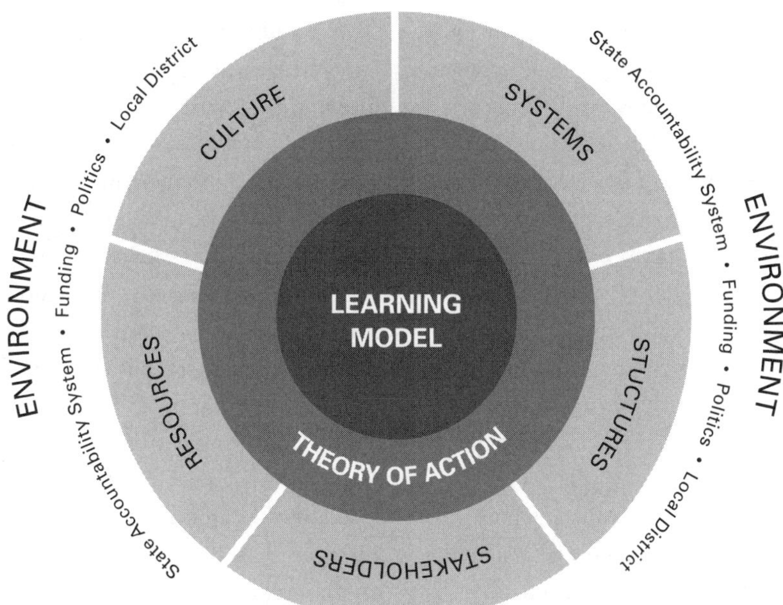

for managing student discipline a good match for the desired culture? What about staff hiring and compensation systems? Do they reinforce the learning model and culture? Are there processes in place to help teachers work together to effectively deliver the model?

Does the school allocate its *resources* (people, technology, money) in a way that is likely to best support the model? How are teachers assigned to courses and students? How is technology used to strengthen teachers' effectiveness and students' learning? Do dollars flow to high-priority activities and away from low-impact projects? Is the team proactive about seeking funding to supplement the per-student allocation from the state? Is this external funding aligned with the school's goals and model?

A school has many *stakeholder* groups, and managing the various *relationships* in ways that are consistent with the learning model can be difficult. Are students engaged in the governance and management of the school? What is the leadership team's stance toward parents? Are they seen as a force to be mitigated so that a student can be more successful during the school day? Or are they fully integrated into the life of the school? What about the board of directors—do they have the information and level of engagement they need to fully support the school's success? Has the membership been built for particular areas of expertise or simply as supporters of the school leader's vision?

Schools exist in a community, regulatory, and policy *environment*. How effectively are the school leaders managing their interaction with the environment? Is the learning model likely to produce the results required by the prevailing accountability structure? Is the available funding sufficient to run the learning model? Does the school have the relationships and social capital necessary to navigate the current context as well as potential shifts?

Increasingly, as school operators achieve results (or are pressed to grow by funders or other stakeholders), they are looking to expand their reach by running multiple schools. The cases in the second half of the module allow for a discussion of three approaches to growth in school networks at various stages of maturity. The framework for evaluating growth opportunities that was explained in Module II overview on page 75 will be helpful in analyzing the cases in the rest of the module. The categories of the framework are impact, market, organizational capacity, and risks.

In St. HOPE Academy, the Sacramento-based organization has built a preK–12 footprint, first with a K–8 charter school, followed by the conversion of a district high school into a charter school, and finally the launch of an early learning center. The case focuses on the decision faced by the founder about whether to accept an invitation to launch a new school in Harlem, 3,000 miles away. By evaluating the network's current state in Sacramento and the various aspects of the expansion opportunity using the growth framework introduced in Module II, the case discussion opens up a wide range of issues related to the growth of a school network.

Green Dot Public Schools is focused on transforming education in one city—Los Angeles. The nonprofit school network starts new charter high schools in neighborhoods with existing district high schools that have underperformed for decades. At the time of the case, Green Dot has ten schools—five in full operation and five more about to open. The choice facing the organization is about how to launch its next set of schools. Should it continue to compete head-to-head with the Los Angeles Unified School District (LAUSD) by opening new charters in distressed neighborhoods, attracting students and talented staff away from district schools, or should it formally collaborate with LAUSD, helping the district transform an existing low-performing high school using the Green Dot educational model? Using the growth framework as a diagnostic tool, the case allows for a discussion of which option is most consistent with the Green Dot theory of change and vision for long-term impact.

The last case in the module, and therefore in the book, is "KIPP 2007: Implementing a Smart Growth Strategy." The exploration of education entrepreneurship comes full circle, from the first case in Module I, in which KIPP's founders have two successful schools and are beginning to think about expansion, to this last case, in which the network has grown organically to nearly 60 schools and now faces new questions about growth. With a high-profile brand, a far-flung network of loosely connected schools, and a new CEO, the organization has formalized its approach to opening new sites and now must begin to make decisions based on the new criteria. The approach has significant implications for the culture of the organization, as well as its potential for system-level impact. The case hinges on a real decision about whether to approve the growth plans of a local school leader and allows you to use the various tools and ideas that have been introduced throughout the book.

Module Questions

1. How do the various aspects of the schools and school networks in the module (culture, systems and structures, resources, stakeholder relationships, and environment) fit together to make the learning model more effective?
2. How might the effectiveness of the various schools in the module be evaluated?
3. Is it possible to create systemwide impact by creating schools and networks?

Notes

1. Stacey Childress et al., "Note on the PELP Coherence Framework," PEL-010, Harvard Business School Press, Boston, 2004.

Stacey Childress

If We Blew It Up, Then We Could . . .

A Thought Experiment for Students of Entrepreneurship in Education

Over the years many of my students have wondered about the implications of "blowing up" the current education system in the United States. In other words, what would we do if we could start over from scratch? In the real world, the options that could be pursued in place of the existing system fall along a continuum. For purposes of this thought experiment, let us avoid any middle ground and work from the poles. Below I describe the two extremes and pose some questions for class discussion.

The Continuum

←——————————→

Nationalize education decisions about standards, curricula, financing, accountability, etc.	Completely decentralize education decisions and funding to families and allow a demand-driven market to emerge

Nationalization

At the left end of the continuum, some make the case for "nationalizing" educational and resource allocation decisions by stripping the states and local entities of their decentralized role in U.S. public education (see **Exhibit 1** for relevant excerpts from the U.S. Constitution).

Suspend what you know about the current constitutional and statutory limitations regarding this end of the continuum. What are the practical implications of a national education system, in terms of curriculum, standards, financing, accountability, and human capital? How might it look different from the current system? Who would make the national decisions? Assume the current average spending of $10,000 per student would remain the same. How would the money work? What are the biggest risks? Would this increase the quality of education? Why? Why not?

What would you have to assume about families, educators, government, incentives, etc., to believe that this is an effective approach to improving educational outcomes for all students?

Further Decentralization

At the right end of the continuum, some propose further decentralizing from the current state and local entities to private citizens. In other words, this point of view includes putting education resources directly into the hands of families, and giving them the responsibility to decide how to spend this allocation by providing the service themselves or choosing from among other providers to educate their children.

What would be the implications of abolishing all education revenues to institutions, and instead giving parents $10,000 annually per child (approximate current national average) to spend on his/her education, with limited restrictions? As in the "nationalization" example, suspend your concerns about constitutional and statutory limitations and consider the consequences of a system that operated this way.

What kinds of choices might spring up? Would they be for-profit, non-profit, or public sector entities (would districts still exist and get paid by parents for their services)? What might the effects on innovation be? How might parents behave? What kinds of decisions would they make? What would accountability look like in this environment? What are the biggest risks? Would this increase the quality of education? Why? Why not? What would you have to assume about families, educators, government, incentives, etc., to believe that this is an effective approach to improving educational outcomes for all students?

Creating the Necessary Change

In order to change the current system (regardless of which end state on the continuum you are more inclined to support), what kind of action is necessary? Would a bottom-up grassroots movement by parents and educators have more power, or would a top-down effort, led by elected officials such as the president or congressional leaders, be more effective? How might each work in practice? For this question, we must re-introduce the constitutional and statutory constraints, because creating dramatic change toward either pole of the continuum would require overturning existing rules of the game and/or introducing new ones.

Final Instructions

Free your mind from the current constraints posed by the system in place, think deeply and creatively about both extremes, take a position, and come to class ready to have a provocative discussion.

Exhibit 1

Excerpts from the United States Constitution

Amendment 10: Powers of the States and People. Ratified 12/15/1791.

> The powers not delegated to the United States by the Constitution, nor prohibited by it to the States, are reserved to the States respectively, or to the people.

Notes on Amendment 10: This amendment is also known as the States' Rights Amendment. Anything not expressly granted to the federal government is reserved for the states or the people. It was part of the original 10 amendments ratified all at once as the Bill of Rights. Public education is not mentioned in the body of the constitution, and therefore is under the purview of the states under the 10th amendment.

Amendment 14: Citizenship Rights. Ratified 7/9/1868.

> 1. All persons born or naturalized in the United States, and subject to the jurisdiction thereof, are citizens of the United States and of the State wherein they reside. No State shall make or enforce any law which shall abridge the privileges or immunities of citizens of the United States; nor shall any State deprive any person of life, liberty, or property, without due process of law; nor deny to any person within its jurisdiction the equal protection of the laws.

Notes on Amendment 14: This first clause of the 14th amendment is also known as the Equal Protection Clause. Prior to the 14th, states were free to ignore the Bill of Rights; a series of Supreme Court rulings made it clear that the bill was to apply to acts of the federal government only. With the establishment of the 14th after the Civil War, the Bill of Rights is made to apply to state law, too. This clause has been used as the basis for legislation such as the Voting Rights Act of 1965 and legal decisions such as *Brown vs. The Board of Education of Topeka, Kansas* in 1954.

Source: Direct quotes from the U.S. Constitution; notes are adapted from http://www.usconstitution.net/ and expanded by the case author.

Stacey Childress

Launching the Bronx Lab School

> We will provide students with real opportunities to think, to learn, to question, to explore, to create, to solve, to achieve, to evaluate, to imagine, to realize, to reflect, and to dream.
>
> —*Bronx Lab vision statement, 2004*

"Hi, Marc!" shouted a student in a Roger Clemens baseball jersey as he walked quickly past the school office on his way to class.

"Good morning, Rafael. Get over here! Nice shirt. What's the latest on your Global project that's due Thursday?" Marc asked, stepping into the hallway.

"I should have it done in time," the student offered as the two shook hands quickly.

"Remember, absolutely no late projects, Rafael!" Marc reminded him as he hurried off to class.

Marc Sternberg, the founding principal of the Bronx Lab School, believed that every interaction between students and staff in the new small high school in New York was an opportunity to reinforce the culture of success that he and his team were trying to build among their school community. He turned back into the office.

"Marc, who is the girl sitting in the staff room with her mother?" Michelle Brochu, the director of instruction, was concerned that another student was being transferred in at the request of the district office. At 110 ninth-graders, Bronx Lab had already exceeded their official capacity by two students.

"That's Mariana. She's struggling in a nearby large high school because some older boys have been harassing her—she and her mother think Bronx Lab would be a good fit. Would you talk with them and see what you think?" Marc shared the capacity concerns, but this was a tough one to turn away. As Michelle moved toward the staff room, the school's social work intern entered the office.

"Guys, a fight has spread from Evander's third-floor to our space. Someone's going to get hurt. I can't find our guard—should I call security to come up?" Evander Childs was the name of the 2,600-student public high school within which Bronx Lab operated.

As Marc nodded his assent, he thought about the challenges he and his team faced in implementing their vision. Was it really possible to build a culture of success as a new small school inside one of the largest, lowest-performing high schools in the largest urban district in the United States? With no security guard in sight, Marc ran down the hall to break up the fight.

Background

The New York City Department of Education (NYCDOE) was the largest public school system in the United States in SY05,[1] serving over 1.1 million students in approximately 1350 schools with a teaching force of over 65,000. The district had an annual budget of over $12 billion. Mayor Michael Bloomberg took control of the system when he was inaugurated in early 2002. He dismissed the elected school board and announced that he would be personally accountable to the voters for the performance of the city's schools. Bloomberg hired Chancellor Joel Klein, the former Chairman and CEO of Bertlesmann, Inc., as chief executive of the district. Klein reported directly to the mayor. Klein consolidated 32 community school districts into ten geographic regions, each with its own regional superintendent who supervised the principals within their regions.

The district had over 190 high schools in SY02, the vast majority of which were large and comprehensive. That year, Bloomberg and Klein announced that the district would create 200 small high schools by launching standalone new schools or breaking up large existing schools. In SY03, the Bill and Melinda Gates Foundation announced a $51 million grant to support the creation of 67 small schools as part of the district's overall small high school reform effort. The grant was awarded to seven nonprofit intermediaries that would partner with NYCDOE in opening the 67 schools. By SY05, the district had over 300 high schools, with approximately 150 of those classified as small schools.

The Bronx Lab School was launched as part of this effort in SY05 and served 110 ninth grade students from 22 zip codes, primarily from the Bronx, but also from upper Manhattan. Ninety-one percent of the student body qualified for free or reduced-price meals, and approximately 60% were Latino, 33% African American, 2% White, and 1% Asian. Nine students were identified as English Language Learners, and two were classified as special education students. Bronx Lab planned to accept a new ninth grade class each year, eventually becoming a ninth through twelfth grade school of over 430 students.

Founding Principal Marc Sternberg led a team of six full-time teachers who taught English/Language Arts, Integrated Math and Science, Global History, and Art. The teachers operated under the contract of the New York City teachers' union, the United Federation of Teachers (UFT). Other staff members included a director of instruction, a director of operations, a school social worker, a director of student programming, and a school aide. The full-time staff was 54% white, 23% African American, 15% Latino, and 8% Southeast Asian. In addition, a number of interns and part-time and contract staff conducted electives, special programs, and other support services.

Bronx Lab operated on an annual budget of approximately $900,000 and had two primary revenue streams—the NYCDOE and the Gates Foundation. The Gates funds were administered by the Institute for Student Achievement (ISA), one of the seven nonprofit intermediaries that received grants in 2003. In addition to serving as fiscal agent for the Gates money, ISA also played an active role in advising the school team. Bronx Lab received additional resources in the form of in-kind staff support and part-time elective instructors from the Federal Employment Guidance Services (FEGS). FEGS also provided money for career development programming for students. (**Exhibit 1** contains Bronx Lab financial data.)

Bronx Lab was located inside Evander Childs High School (Evander), an existing five-story, 326,000-square-foot public school building in the central Bronx, constructed in 1929. Evander housed a comprehensive high school serving approximately 2,600 students on the first, third, and fourth floors of the building, and was part of Region 2. Bronx Lab and four other small schools operated separately on the second floor. Although no hierarchy existed among the six principals, the Evander principal was ultimately in charge of the physical facility and the associated support staff.

Evander had failed to meet Adequate Yearly Progress (AYP) in any year since the inception of the federal No Child Left Behind Act in 2001. In SY04, Region 2 announced a desire to close the school in SY08, and that as a first step it would not enroll its usual 1,250 student ninth grade class in SY05. Students who had already matriculated at Evander would be allowed to remain there to complete high school, but there would be no new freshman class. Although NYCDOE had not announced the closure, the Chancellor was strongly inclined to support the region's request. Before the beginning of SY05, however, NYCDOE allowed 500 students to enroll in the ninth grade at Evander. Even though this was a markedly smaller class than usual, the move generated some uncertainty regarding NYCDOE's willingness to close Evander. In the meantime, the small schools currently occupying the second floor planned to take over more of the building each year as they admitted new ninth grade classes. Eventually, Region 2 planned for the Evander building to exclusively house six separate small high schools. (See **Exhibit 2** for data on NYCDOE high schools and Evander Childs.)

Getting Started

"We wanted to create a school in which everyone believed that with the right supports, expectations and culture, all students can excel," explained Marc, who had both an MBA and an M.Ed. from Harvard University. Michelle Brochu, Bronx Lab's director of instruction, recalled meeting Marc in 2003 at the suggestion of a FEGS staff member who believed they shared a mutual approach to educating disadvantaged students: "When Marc shared an early version of his start-up plan, I saw nuggets of ideas that I had prior success with as a teacher and instructional consultant in New York and around the country. I was excited that we could combine our ideas and expertise to build a school that would focus on delivering high-level instruction for kids who needed it the most." Marc and Michelle agreed to join forces to launch the Bronx Lab School. The school's name signaled a focus on progressive, student-centered instruction and learning by doing. At the core of the school's plan were high expectations not only for students, but for teachers and parents as well. As Marc put it, "Building a culture of success for everyone involved in this community is fundamental to our approach—and everyone is a part of the community of learners, adults and students alike."

Working with Partners

The Institute for Student Achievement (ISA) was an important partner for Bronx Lab. Dr. Gerry House, a former urban superintendent, was CEO of ISA and was best known for her innovative work in the 1990s in the public school system in Memphis, TN. ISA had received a $6 million grant from the Gates Foundation to start 10 new small high schools over five years inside the New York City public school system. ISA was required to give $4 million directly to the new schools and was allowed to use $2 million to build its own organizational capacity to support the schools. Bronx Lab received $25,000 from ISA for its planning phase and was guaranteed $100,000 per year in its first three years, and $75,000 in its fourth year. In addition to this funding, ISA brought expertise in instructional design, professional development, and school leadership, as well as help in navigating "the system."[2] House explained ISA's process for launching new schools:

> We first recruit a prospective principal with the vision, values, and skills to identify and lead a team to design and open a school in partnership with ISA. After gaining the regional superintendent's approval of and support for the school leader, we work closely with the team

> to create the school vision and design the implementation plan. School design plans that are endorsed by the NYCDOE Office of New Schools are then recommended to Chancellor Klein for approval. Marc and I had known each other for a few years through our common network and had many discussions about school leadership. Having observed his vision, passion and commitment, I knew he would make and excellent leader of a new small school; and I encouraged him to pursue the process. It has been exciting to work with Marc and his team to design and implement Bronx Lab School and to continue serving as an advocate and supporter as the school develops.

The Bronx Lab team developed a strong relationship with Laura Rodriguez, the superintendent for Region 2, and their plan to open a small school within an existing large high school building was approved by NYCDOE in early spring of 2004. The Gates Foundation assigned a program director to provide oversight and support from their organization.

As part of the planning process, Marc and Michelle also worked closely with FEGS to provide students with social services and health care referrals, along with career development programs, all areas in which FEGS had particular expertise. FEGS had been serving Bronx individuals and families for over 100 years, and was among the most well-regarded human and social services agencies in the city, with an annual operating budget of over $150 million. Michelle had been affiliated with FEGS previously through her work conducting instructional workshops on their behalf around New York City. Eric Weingartner, the assistant vice president for employment training, education, and youth services for FEGS, had been the executive director of the New York affiliate of Teach For America (TFA) while Marc was a TFA corps member in the Bronx from 1995 to 1998, and they had stayed in touch. In fact, it was Weingartner who initially suggested that Marc and Michelle meet each other.

FEGS funded a full-time director of student programming through a U.S. Department of Labor contract called PAVE, an acronym for Program for Adolescents' Vocational Exploration. Dehvi Kumar filled this role and created a career development program at Bronx Lab that included workshops, field trips, speakers, and internships. Dehvi also developed Bronx Lab's elective curriculum. FEGS provided an on-site social work intern named Joel Sanchez to work with Bronx Lab's full-time social worker, Raymond Godwin, in serving students and their families. FEGS was interested in building its own capacity to provide teacher professional development to schools and formed a reciprocal relationship with Bronx Lab in which FEGS provided partial financial support for Michelle's role as director of instruction, and in return would observe and learn from her intensive coaching and professional development work with the Bronx Lab teaching staff. Because the NYCDOE provided funding for an assistant principal (AP) only when a school reached 300 students, Bronx Lab would not have a budget allocation for an AP until year three. Therefore, FEGS's support of Michelle dramatically increased Bronx Lab's managerial capacity during its critical first year.

Recruiting a Student Body

High school students in New York could choose which high school they attended by listing up to twelve preferences, and in turn each school ranked its list of interested students. NYCDOE then ran a matching process. In SY05, 84% of NYCDOE students were matched with one of their choices, and about a third received their top pick. As a start-up, Bronx Lab had to attract a new crop of students to the school. The Bronx Lab team made it clear to potential students and their parents that the following characteristics were necessary for success in their new school: a natural curiosity; a desire to explore and collaborate; dependability and promptness; an ability to listen and be coached; a desire to contribute positively; courage, compassion, and creativity; humor; and passion. Prospective students were also advised of an important non-negotiable: students at Bronx Lab were expected to attend classes through 5:00 p.m. each day and would participate in a compulsory, three-week residential summer program.

The NYCDOE published a guide to small high schools to acquaint parents with their options, but Marc knew that he needed to build relationships and trust with families to interest them in choosing Bronx Lab: "I spent months spreading the word about Bronx Lab. I invited myself into any and all middle schools I could get in touch with. I was like a traveling salesman. I'd have an appointment with one middle school, and on my way back to Manhattan, if I passed another I'd park the car, go inside and introduce myself to the principal, and ask to speak to any potential applicants. I was ruthless. Week after week, I did anything I could to get in front of eligible 8th graders."

Beyond his work at Bronx middle schools, Marc attended community meetings, visited local churches, and contacted parent organizations to get the word out about Bronx Lab. "We fielded a thorough grass-roots effort to let families know about our vision and our commitment to students in the Bronx, as well as the types of students we felt were best suited to our model. When applications came to us in May, almost 300 kids had applied for our 100 seats. We were pleased, but wondered if parent concerns about safety at Evander dampened our numbers." From the applicant pool, NYCDOE assigned 100 students for the inaugural class through the matching process. Shortly before school started, NYCDOE increased Bronx Lab's capacity to 108 students and assigned students to fill the seats through over-the-counter enrollment.

Building a Team

Marc, Michelle, and their partners knew that assembling a committed team of teachers and support staff with a passion for working in a start-up environment to increase the academic achievement of all students was critical, but also a considerable challenge. In describing the key characteristics necessary for their teachers, Michelle cited "respect for kids, passion for teaching, and a willingness to reflect and work on their own instructional practice." With six classroom teachers and 108 students, it was also important for staff members to be comfortable in a small, intimate environment. After culling through dozens of resumes and combing their networks for viable candidates, Marc and Michelle hired two English/Language Arts teachers, two Integrated Math and Science teachers, a Global History teacher, and an Art teacher. (See **Exhibit 3** for staff bios and **Exhibit 4** for organizational chart.) The staff spent significant time together before school opened getting to know one another and jointly developing an integrated curriculum for the first year.

In addition, Marc hired Carrie Lynch as director of operations. On the official roster, Carrie filled the school secretary slot, but her duties were much broader than the secretary title implied.

A former third grade teacher in a Bronx school, she was responsible for student records, payroll, financial reporting and accounts payable, scheduling, maintenance, fire drills, and other operational duties. She described her main responsibility as trying to "maneuver" within the system to get things done for their small school inside the larger structure of Evander and the NYCDOE. "We have to build bridges within the district and particularly here at Evander—they have resources that we need but don't have control over. It's not always easy, but we find ways to cooperate and get it done." Given the hierarchical nature of the district, Carrie found it necessary to introduce herself with a variety of titles when calling around for assistance. "People in the system are accustomed to dealing with each other in their assigned roles. So depending on what I'm trying to get done, I might have to introduce myself as the secretary, the payroll clerk, the attendance person, or the maintenance manager, depending on who I'm talking to. I'm learning as I go about how big schools work by trying to get resources for our small school." Marc explained that Carrie's previous experience in a small Bronx school was of critical importance, saying, "Carrie has been there before, and she gets things done with grace and wit. Frankly, she does the work of five people, and we're lucky to have her."

Joining the Autonomy Zone

In August 2004, the NYCDOE announced the creation of the "autonomy zone." Thirty high schools of various types—large, small, traditional, charter, existing, and new—had opted into the city-wide zone, and out of their assigned regions. No longer accountable to their regional superintendents, these high school principals agreed to sign performance contracts in exchange for more freedom to design curriculum and instruction programs tailored to the needs of their students, as opposed to using required materials and methods prescribed by the district.

Expressing her frustration that the unions were not consulted in the design of the new policy, Randi Weingarten, the president of the United Federation of Teachers, called the zone another "unilateral, top-down experiment on autonomy."[3] Principals gained some flexibility in hiring teachers at the site level, but schools in the zone would operate under the same labor contract provisions as all other schools. However, some principals publicly expressed hope that over time, hiring constraints related to teacher seniority would be loosened or removed for principals who joined the zone and subsequently met their performance agreements. The first year was considered a pilot, and the only consequence for schools not meeting their performance targets would be to drop out of the zone. Afterwards, schools failing to meet performance targets over a five-year period could be shut down. About half of the schools that joined the zone were new small schools.

For some critics, the creation of the autonomy zone called into question the effectiveness of the massive reorganization that the district underwent in 2002, when 32 community school districts were consolidated into 10 areas led by regional superintendents. Others, such as Jill Levy, president of the district's principals' union, asserted that the move was related to pressure from the Gates Foundation to release new small schools from the organizational structure that all other schools were required to participate in, asking, "Must we take these chests of silver and gold that come our way and pander to the people donating?" Jim Shelton of the Gates Foundation countered this notion and called the autonomy zone a proactive move by the district to balance the right level of autonomy with the optimal support necessary for schools to be held accountable for results.[4]

Eric Nadelstern, NYCDOE's chief academic officer for new schools, was in charge of the autonomy zone and encouraged Marc to apply. Marc explained, "Eric was one of the first to contact me about starting a school when he was the deputy superintendent for Region 2 back in 2003, so we had a good relationship and a foundation of trust. When he contacted me about the autonomy zone, I was intrigued and excited." After seeking input from his staff and partners, Marc decided to join the zone. "One of the most compelling reasons to join was the caliber of some of the other schools that had opted into the autonomy zone—these were some of the premier public schools in the city. Even though many of the advantages associated with this new construct were unclear, the network I would be joining was a deciding factor." One of the risks was the potential damage to the positive relationship with Rodriguez, the Region 2 superintendent who had been a valuable supporter of Bronx Lab. With the help of Gerry House, Marc worked to preserve Rodriguez's support and good will in explaining his desire to join the zone. Because of the role of ISA, House would be a co-signer to the performance agreement. In signing the agreement, Bronx Lab and ISA committed to a set of targets that include an annual attendance rate of 90%, a student retention rate of 80%, a course pass rate of 80%, and positive growth in student assessment scores in English and mathematics. (See **Exhibit 5** for performance agreement.) In order to create a baseline for student performance, the autonomy zone administered pre-tests to students in zone schools at the beginning of school. (See **Exhibit 6** for mathematics baseline for autonomy zone schools and Bronx Lab.)

The 30 schools in the autonomy zone were divided into four networks, and principals opted into one of the networks based on a combination of geography and school design. The principals in each group met twice a month to compare their experiences, identify common challenges, and share best practices. As Marc described, "We are a self-directed group of principals. We develop our own meeting agendas, and decide on the pace and content of our discussions. The meetings are a forcing function for me to develop a network of other principals in similar situations, some rookies like me and some very seasoned principals, so in that way they have been helpful." Marc also commented on the freedom the autonomy zone offered from what he termed "the vaunted NYCDOE bureaucracy," saying, "I look around at other principals in my building and in my circle of friends and see them mired in meetings, reports, and other work that takes them away from instructional leadership. Because the autonomy zone is peer-led, our dynamic is radically different." The participation in the zone did not come without cost, however. Because it was new and controversial, and took him out of the circle of principals within the Evander campus, Marc often felt that Bronx Lab was ostracized by others not participating in the autonomy zone.

Opening School

After spending more than a year building a team of school staff and external partners, designing the instructional core of the school, mobilizing the resources needed to support this vision, and recruiting a student body, Marc and the Bronx Lab team welcomed students to the first day of school in September 2004.

Process and Schedule

The Bronx Lab student body was divided into four cohorts. Cohorts moved together between four classrooms for their daily schedule of English/Language Arts (ELA), Integrated Math & Science (IMS), Global History (Global), and Art. The two ELA teachers and two IMS teachers each taught two cohorts of students, so that their student load was approximately 54. Because Bronx Lab staffed only one Global and one Art teacher, each taught their subjects to all students, but in fewer 75-minute blocks per week than ELA and IMS teachers. (See **Exhibit 7** for daily schedule.)

The faculty created an integrated curriculum to respond to NYCDOE standards for each content area, and focused on student-centered inquiry as a common approach to learning across subjects. This approach was designed to develop independent thinking, deep investigation, meaningful discourse, and frequent and varied demonstrations of learning by students. The school employed a workshop model, wherein faculty acted primarily as facilitators of student discourse as an alternative to a lecture format. In classrooms, students were organized around small tables in groups of four to six for activities that required interactions with each other around content, guided by the teachers.

In addition to the four cohorts, students were grouped into eight "colleges" that met every day but Wednesday. Each college had 13 or 14 students led by a staff member. In addition to traditional homeroom activities such as information sharing and administrative tasks (field trip announcements, permission slip collection, etc.), the colleges opened each session with a "bridging circle" in which everyone, including staff, was encouraged to share their thoughts and feelings. Student comments ranged from reactions to class content from earlier in the day, to reactions to last night's Yankees game, to concerns about Bronx Lab community issues. Two of the four college sessions each week were dedicated to quiet, independent reading by both the students and the adult leader.

Every morning except Wednesday, the entire Bronx Lab community met for "Gathering" from 8:45 to 9:00 a.m., a time to focus on the goals for the day. On Wednesday afternoons, Gathering was scheduled from 12:30 to 1:20 p.m. and often featured outside speakers who focused on college, career, and inspirational topics. After Wednesday gathering, students were dismissed for the day. On the other weekdays, students finished classes at 3:15 and then attended elective curriculum courses from 3:20 to 4:40 p.m.

On the third Thursday of every month, Bronx Lab held a parent gathering. This event was an opportunity for parents and teachers to get to know each other and for students to present their learning in both the required and the elective curriculum. Bronx Lab also engaged parents when student discipline or attendance became a problem. If a student was "dinged" three times in a week (written up for a discipline infraction) or was absent three times in a trimester, a "problem-solving conference" was held with Marc or Raymond, the student, and at least one parent. In addition to reducing discipline problems and absenteeism, the conferences reinforced the culture of success the school was trying to build with students and their families.

Once each trimester, the entire staff and student body participated in a five-day off-campus retreat for learning activities and community building. In November 2004, the group spent a week camping and hiking in upstate New York. Two other retreats were planned before the end of school, one to participate in the Model United Nations program and another to tour colleges in the northeast. Students would also attend a three-week summer academy at the Lawrenceville School, a renowned private boarding school in New Jersey.[5] These activities required support from private philanthropy.

Content

Bronx Lab's curriculum focused on four core subjects and a variety of electives for students. The electives included activities such as yoga instruction, a quilting circle, a dance troupe, piano and drum classes, and a documentary film class. The core courses were ELA, IMS, Global, and Art. Dalia Hochman taught Global and focused on building integrated knowledge through investigation of historical figures, such as the Greek philosophers, as well as challenging students to apply that knowledge through project-based demonstrations of learning. Art teacher Kristen Smith combined art history with hands-on art projects and led schoolwide field trips to New York institutions such as the Metropolitan Museum of Art, the Whitney Museum, and the Studio Museum of Harlem. Because of the need to build both basic skills and critical thinking in ELA and IMS, the Bronx Lab teams developed specific strategies for each of these areas.

ELA Strategy

ELA teachers Chris Bernard and Steve Pyle focused on building literacy skills as well as critical thinking through challenging novels such as Toni Morrison's *The Bluest Eye,* literature circles, guided reading, large group discussions of assigned works, and writing projects. Many students had literacy skills that were well below the ninth grade level, and teachers had to focus on what they termed "language recovery" and basic skills in addition to focusing on independent inquiry and critical thinking as planned. Students were required to complete multiple writing assignments each week focused on the ELA content as well as personal expression. Students presented many of their writing projects to their classmates and learned to effectively critique each other's work.

IMS Strategy

The IMS course was subtitled "Life by Numbers." Faculty integrated concepts from district standards in math and science in order to build specific skills, and challenged students to make the conceptual link between two disciplines that were typically separated in the schools that the students attended before coming to Bronx Lab. On a representative day in IMS, a geometry lesson on angle measurement in the Cartesian plane was paired with a physical science lesson on finding and plotting direction using a compass. IMS required students to complete projects to demonstrate their learning; for instance, students presented projects entitled "Can I take your order (of magnitude), please?" to demonstrate their understanding of exponents. Teachers Kari Ostrem and Adam Kerzner had developed the curriculum for the entire year before school started, and much of it was adapted from Kari's previous experience at the Lawrenceville School.

Staff Development

Michelle and Marc employed an instructional planning model called "purposeful planning." Michelle visited each teacher's classroom for a full session at least once a week and met weekly with each teacher one on one for individualized planning and development. She used the individual meeting time to reflect on the teacher's instructional practice, collaboratively plan upcoming lessons using student data, and discuss challenges the teacher might be experiencing in the classroom. This intense interaction with an instructional coach was unusual in high schools and new for most of the Bronx Lab staff.

Teachers had at least 75 minutes of individual planning time each day and common planning time with the other teacher in their subject area at least once a week. As the first year progressed, teachers began using some of their planning time to visit each others' classrooms to pick up new techniques and learn from each other. Discussions about these visits spilled into the weekly Faculty Gathering that took place for two hours each Wednesday after students were dismissed at 1:20 p.m. The team used this meeting for professional development led by Michelle and best-practice sharing among the teachers, and for identifying common student challenges across the cohorts and subject areas. The gathering was also a time for the staff to participate in the continual shaping of the culture of Bronx Lab by explicitly discussing the school's progress toward the established vision.

Early Challenges

Teacher Turnover

One week before school started, one of the ELA teachers quit Bronx Lab. Their alternate candidates from the first search process had already committed to other jobs, so Marc and Michelle decided to share responsibility for teaching cohorts one and two while they rushed to find a new pool of candidates. With school starting in a few days they knew it would be difficult to fill the spot in time for the first day of school. Combing their own contacts and using the ISA network, they were able to find a few applicants, whom they quickly interviewed. With no perfect candidates, Michelle and Marc weighed the strengths and limitations of each; ultimately they decided to bring someone in on a trial basis. Marc recalled, "It wasn't clear to us that she was ready to commit to our instructional model or deal with the intense interaction with the kids and with us, but she expressed a willingness to adapt to our environment, so we went with it. It was a disaster."

After a few days in the classroom, it was clear that this teacher was not committed to student-centered instruction, and unwilling to adjust her practice to adapt to the model. Other staff members expressed doubt that she even liked kids. Her students were having a very different experience than those in the other ELA cohort, and as a consequence, their performance was falling behind. Marc and Michelle decided to release her, and reentered the classroom while they conducted another search. As a consequence of sharing the ELA teaching load, they struggled to balance their administrative and coaching duties with the added teaching responsibilities. Marc explained, "Even though it meant we weren't able to be in the other classrooms observing and giving feedback as much as we planned, we felt it was more important to keep faith with our families and other teachers by refusing to compromise on our instructional model or our culture. Even though it was painful, in retrospect I wonder if the time in the classroom wasn't a good thing for Michelle and me." At the end of September, they hired Steve Pyle, believing he was a good fit. The early evidence was positive. On October 12, in Steve's first bridging circle with his college, two students used their time to express hope that he would stay for the whole year, given the uncertainty they experienced up to that point.

Systems

The NYCDOE data systems were cumbersome, and it often took months for changes in enrollment to show up in the system. As a result, data regarding attendance in particular was inaccurate. By the beginning of the second trimester, Bronx Lab had fewer actual students than reflected in the system because of transfers, long-term absences, and students who had never appeared. However, attendance percentages were still calculated based on the original enrollment. With the autonomy zone performance contract goal of 90% average attendance, this presented a potential accountability problem for Marc. To address this, he implemented a data tracking system on salesforce.com to manually track attendance and other indicators using up-to-the-minute student data. (**Exhibit 8** includes selected attendance data.)

Facilities

Facilities challenges were part of daily life at Bronx Lab. With only four classrooms, the students and teachers rotated between classrooms throughout the day for required and elective courses. In addition to a small office, the school had one small common room that was used as a staff conference room, an elective course room, and a teacher-parent conference room, among other things. Bronx Lab had two community computers available for teachers and students located in the common room, making it a hub of activity throughout most of the day. Teachers generally used the space for their planning time, as they had no space of their own.

Students had lunch in the fourth-floor cafeteria, and Bronx Lab elected a late lunch time in order to separate their students from the Evander student body. This created a need to provide a morning snack to keep students energized and focused between the beginning of school and 1:20 p.m. In order to provide physical activity for students, Bronx Lab staff had to negotiate with the Evander coaching staff for use of the gyms, weight room, and other athletic department facilities. These spaces were well maintained and included two swimming pools. Through most of the first trimester, access to the space was sporadic and the relationship with the coaching staff problematic, although by November the Bronx Lab staff had achieved some cooperation with the Evander coaches. Bronx Lab students were eligible to try out for some Evander sports teams, including girls' track and boys' and girls' basketball, although the Bronx Lab staff wondered if they would be fully accepted by the Evander coaches and students.

Evander operated in lock-down mode, with only one way to enter and exit the building. All entering students and visitors were required to place their backpacks and other belongings on a conveyor belt through an X-ray machine, and then proceed through metal detectors. Security guards were posted at the four corners on each floor, including the second-floor small-schools enclave. Bronx Lab staff considered the guards an unfortunate necessity. As one teacher observed, "The guards could be a positive force on the floor, but they often reflect the culture of Evander rather than Bronx Lab. Their default attitude is that the kids are a problem, and the tone they use in normal interactions with them is threatening. I've seen some of them try to goad students into confrontations. We're still trying to figure out how to make them a part of our culture and community, but I'm not sure it's possible."

Looking Ahead

As Marc and his team worked to refine and stabilize their model, they also began planning for their second class of ninth graders. By January 2005, Bronx Lab had received approximately 1,000 applications for the 108 seats available for SY06. They also had to recruit new teachers, plan the 10th grade curriculum for their existing students, and resolve the facilities challenges associated with doubling their student body. Marc understood that increased scale would bring additional operational challenges that would make it more difficult to maintain the culture, instructional coherence, and focus to which he and his team were committed. Retaining the existing staff was a key factor in building on the initial success.

With many of their students lacking basic literacy and math skills, could the team stick with their founding philosophy that focused on building critical thinking and independent inquiry? An outside supporter noted that as the first group of students moved up a grade level, the staff would be forced to recommit to the vision of graduating kids "college ready." She wondered, "As the time to graduation shortens, if students continue to have serious deficits in basic literacy and math skills, will it be possible not to renege on the initial vision? Will the team be able to sustain a focus on inquiry and critical thinking while addressing these basic skills deficits? The team is young, smart and energetic, but the kids are real, and it will require enormous energy and dedication." (**Exhibit 9** contains first trimester academic results.)

The cycle of new entering classes and grade-level promotions would continue until Bronx Lab graduated its first senior class. This milestone would also mark the end of the initial commitment from Gates and ISA. By then, Bronx Lab needed to be financially and programmatically sustainable within the NYC-DOE system. Marc knew he had significant work to do to address all of these challenges and deliver on the vision he and his team had set for the students of Bronx Lab. But first, he had a fight to break up, and a decision to make about Mariana.

Notes

1. "SY" is used to denote "school year." For example, the academic year spanning 2004–2005 is identified as SY05.

2. For more on the Institute for Student Achievement, see their website at www.isa-ed.org.

3. Caroline Hendrie, "30 NYC Schools gain autonomy from rules by promising results," *Education Week,* September 29, 2004.

4. Adapted from Ellen Yan, "High School Autonomy Plan," *New York Newsday,* August 20, 2004.

5. For more information on the Lawrenceville School, see www.lawrenceville.org.

Exhibit 1

Bronx Lab School Financial Data, SY05

Revenues	
City Tax Levy	$634,288
Other City sources	27,613
State	29,007
City and State Special Education	35,504
Federal Title One	70,761
ISA – Gates Allocation	100,000
Total Revenues	$897,173
Expenses	
Administrative staff	$171,168
Pedagogical staff	366,488
Support staff	51,184
Total Salaries	$588,840
Absence coverage	$1,500
Curriculum development	42,640
Professional Development	12,637
Tutoring	5,533
Professional/Curriculum Development Total	$62,310
Consultants	8,222
Elective Curriculum/Athletics	44,000
Computer Equipment and Software	25,000
Equipment	75,964
Library books	706
Parent Involvement	3,693
Supplies	36,347
Textbooks	23,586
Explore Week (A)	13,801
ISA Summer Institute (B)	9,000
Miscelaneous staff expenses	5,704
Total Other Services and Supplies	$246,023
Total Expenses	$897,173

Source: Bronx Lab School internal documents and case writer analysis.

Notes: (A) Item utilizes NDOE and Gates funding; (B) Item uses Gates funding only

Exhibit 2

Selected Data for NYCDOE High Schools and Evander Childs High School, SY03

Student Characteristics as Percentage of Enrollment

		NYDOE	*Evander Childs*
Ethnicity	White	16	1
	Black	35	56
	Hispanic	35	40
	Asian & Others	14	3
Gender	Male	50	55
	Female	50	45
Free & Reduced Lunch		54	81
Recent Immigrants		10	16
Special Education		11	15
Attendance (as % of days)		85	72

Discpline Data as Number per 1000 Students

	NYDOE	*Evander Childs*
Suspensions	59	78
Involved in Police Incidents	25	68

Student Achievement Data, Class of 2003

			NYDOE	*Evander Childs*
Passed Regents English Exam (A)			61%	45%
	by ethnicity	African American	n/a	45%
		Hispanic	n/a	32%
		Asian	n/a	57%
		White	n/a	0%
Passed Regents Math Exams (A)			43%	33%
	by ethnicity	African American	n/a	42%
		Hispanic	n/a	29%
		Asian	n/a	57%
		White	n/a	0%
Average SAT scores		Verbal	443	374
		Math	472	384
		Total	915	758
% of entering 12th graders who graduated that year (B)			57%	40%
% of entering 9th graders who graduated in four years (B)			53%	30%

Notes: (A) Represents students scoring 65 and above on Regents exams; (B) Includes recipients of both Regents and local diplomas.

Sources: NYCDOE public documents: "Evander Childs 2003 School Report Card" and "The Class of 2003 Four-Year Longitudinal Report," March 2004.

Exhibit 3

Bronx Lab Staff Biographies

Christine Bernard has a B.A. in Africana studies and Spanish literature from Cornell University, and an M.A. in English education from the Steinhardt Graduate School of Education at New York University. She has been teaching English and technology courses in New York City's public high schools for nearly a decade. Before coming to Bronx Lab, she taught at Satellite Academy High School in Manhattan for seven years.

Michelle Brochu is a co-founder of the Bronx Lab School and passionate school reformer. She serves as Bronx Lab's Director of Instruction, working full time with staff to develop and refine instructional practice. Before collaborating on the conceptual design and development of Bronx Lab, Michelle worked as a literacy consultant at public high schools throughout the city of New York. She is a former high school teacher of English, art, and drama. She holds a B.A. from the University of New Hampshire, and is presently pursuing her Master's in Education from Baruch College.

Raymond Godwin has more than 15 years of experience as a social worker in the areas of child welfare, program management, and direct youth services. He is a native of New York City and a graduate of the New York City public school system. Before joining the Bronx Lab School, Ray worked in elementary schools and middle schools, and is excited to be again working with young adults. He holds an M.S.W. from Hunter College School of Social Work and received his B.A. in psychology from Hunter College.

Dalia Hochman is a fourth-year social studies teacher. Before coming to Bronx Lab, she taught global history at the LaGuardia High School of Music, Art and Performing Arts in New York City. She holds a B.A. in history from Yale University and is currently a Ph.D. candidate in educational policy at Teachers College, Columbia University.

Adam Kerzner is a native of the Bronx. He teaches Integrated Math Science and coaches the Bronx Lab swim team. He taught science for three years at a public middle school in Washington Heights. Adam is a graduate of Bronx Science High School and Cornell University. He is currently pursuing a Master's in middle and high school science education at Lehman College.

Dhevi Kumar works in the Education and Youth Services Division at Federation Employment Guidance Services (F.E.G.S), a founding partner of Bronx Lab. She manages the school's elective and athletics programming, and helps to provide auxiliary health and human services for students and their families. Dhevi is a graduate of Johns Hopkins University.

Carrie Lynch is Director of Operations for Bronx Lab. Prior to joining the Bronx Lab team, she served as the administrative coordinator for the Bronx High School of Visual Arts, a small New York City public high school founded in 2002.

Karena Ostrem comes to the Bronx Lab School from the Lawrenceville School in New Jersey, where she taught science and math for five years and was a founding teacher of the Island School in Eleuthera, Bahamas. Her degrees in engineering (a B.S.E. from Princeton University and an M.S. from Columbia University) have led her to design and teach integrated math and science curricula rooted in experiential education.

Steve Pyle is a third-year teacher. Last year he taught at I.S. 240 in the Midwood section of Brooklyn, NY. He holds a B.A. in English from Brown University and is working toward his M.A. in secondary English education at Fordham University.

Joel Sanchez is the social work intern for Bronx Lab, and is currently in the Smith School for Social Work program. Joel holds an M.F.A. in Theater from Columbia University and was an actor and teaching artist for many years before dedicating himself to clinical social work.

Kristin Smith is a first-year New York City public school teacher. She has her B.A. and B.F.A. from Colorado State University and an M.A. in arts education from Teachers College, Columbia University. Before launching her career as a classroom teacher, Kristin spent several years as a museum educator at the Frye Art Museum and Henry Art Gallery in Seattle, Washington.

Marc Sternberg is a first-year New York City high school principal. After graduating with a B.A. in politics from Princeton University, he joined the 1995 corps of Teach For America and taught in a Bronx middle school for three years. Marc holds a Master's in Business Administration and Master's in Education from Harvard University and is a doctoral candidate in education policy at Teachers College, Columbia University. Prior to founding Bronx Lab, he served as Vice President of Victory Schools, a New York–based charter school management organization.

Maritza Alvarez Tineo, a school aide at Bronx Lab School, started working at Evander Childs High School in 1997 as an attendance secretary. In July 2004 Mrs. Tineo left Evander to join the Bronx Lab team. She is a native of Puerto Rico and has maintained a professional career as a hair stylist is upper Manhattan for the last 24 years. She is the mother of two and has a four-year-old granddaughter.

Exhibit 4

Bronx Lab School Organizational Chart, SY05

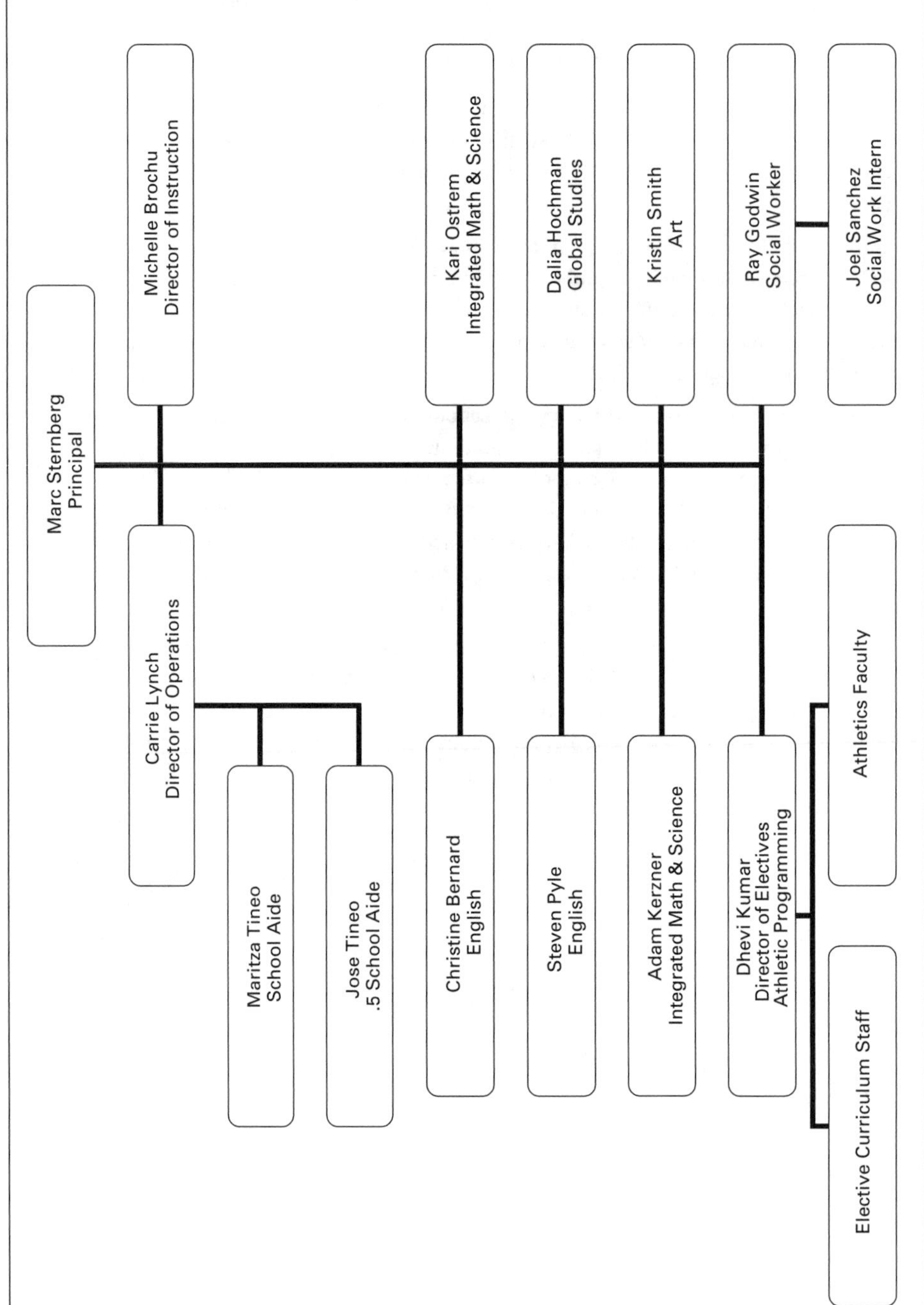

Source: Bronx Lab School internal document.

Exhibit 5

Autonomy Zone Performance Agreement, SY05

Schools whose principals agree to participate in the pilot year of the zone (2004–05) will be part of a strategic planning and research project. The goal is to explore how increased autonomy and accountability will lead to improved school and student performance. The opportunity for schools to continue to participate in this initiative beyond the pilot year will be predicated upon the achievement of the student performance targets outlined below. As the targets relate to voluntary participation in a strategic planning project, they will not be used to evaluate principal performance except to the extent they are part of the existing Principal Performance Review.

Student Achievement: For the pilot year of this research initiative, principals of participating schools must agree to the following student performance goals:

1. Existing schools will either meet the following six targets or at the very least close the gap between actual performance and the targets by making progress over the year of at least 20% toward each of these goals:
   a. Attendance rate of at least 90%
   b. Retention rate of at least 80%
   c. Course pass rate of at least 80%
   d. Regents examination pass rate of at least 80%
   e. Graduation rate of at least 80% of 12th grade students and 70% of the cohort
   f. College acceptance rate of at least 90%
2. New schools must achieve the following targets:
   a. Attendance rate of at least 90%
   b. Retention rate of at least 80%
   c. Course pass rate of at least 80%
   d. Demonstrated positive growth on value-added assessment examinations in ELA and Math

In addition to agreeing to meet the student performance goals outlined above, principals of schools participating in the zone should be aware of the following:

- Education equity will be an important area of consideration in the strategic planning process. Ultimately, schools would be expected to serve a population that reflects the full range of students throughout the city.
- Fiscal integrity will be an important area of consideration in the strategic planning process. Schools will be accountable for expending resources in the best interest of the students enrolled and subject to standard budget audits.

School Name	Intermediary Organization (if applicable)
Principal Name	Intermediary Representative Name
Principal Signature	Intermediary Representative Signature
Date	Date

Source: Bronx Lab School internal document.

Exhibit 6

Incoming Students' Mathematics Proficiency, Autonomy Zone Schools and Bronx Lab School, SY05

Standard/Topic	*Zone Schools* *Tests: 1155* *Pre-test*	*Bronx Lab School* *Tests: ~94* *Pre-test*
Total:	43%	49%
Number and Numeration	36%	37%
Understanding of the uses of numbers in the real world, to communicate mathematically & to develop ideas.	36%	37%
Students apply the properties of the real numbers to various subsets of numbers.	36%	37%
Modeling/Multiple Representation	47%	55%
Students use math modeling/multiple representation to present, interpret, convey & link information & relationships.	47%	55%
Students represent problem situations symbolically by using algebraic expressions, sequences, tree diagrams, geometric figures and graphs.	60%	73%
Students justify the procedures for basic geometric constructions.	43%	44%
Students investigate transformations in the coordinate plane.	38%	46%
Measurement	42%	48%
Students use metric & English measure to link mathematics & the real world to describe & compare objects & data.	42%	48%
Students derive and apply formulas to find measures such as length, area, volume, weight, time and angle in real-world contexts.	30%	32%
Students use statistical methods including measures of central tendency to describe and compare data.	45%	52%
Students apply proportions to scale drawings, computer-assisted design blueprints and direct variation in order to compute indirect measurements.	51%	58%
Uncertainty	41%	48%
Students use ideas of uncertainty to illustrate that mathematics involves more than exactness in everyday situations.	41%	48%
Students use experimental or theoretical probability to represent and solve problems involving uncertainty.	41%	48%
Patterns/Functions	45%	51%
Students use patterns & functions to develop math power, appreciate mathematics & make generalizations of patterns.	45%	51%
Students use function vocabulary and notation.	43%	45%
Students represent and analyze functions using verbal descriptions, tables, equations and graphs.	61%	83%
Students apply and interpret transformations to functions.	44%	50%
Total:	43%	49%

Source: Bronx Lab School internal data.

Exhibit 7

Bronx Lab School Daily Schedule, SY05

COHORT 1 — Trimester 2

	Monday	Tuesday	Wednesday	Thursday	Friday
8:00 - 8:45	Consultation	Consultation	Consultation	Consultation	Consultation
8:45 - 9:00	Gathering	Gathering	A 236	Gathering	Coffee House
9:00 - 10:15	IMS 240	E 236		Movement 236	A 236
10:15-10:20	Snack	Snack	Snack	Snack	Snack
10:15-11:30	G 242	G 242	IMS 240	G 242	IMS 240
11:30-12:45	E 236	IMS 240	E 236	IMS 240	E 236
12:45-1:20	Colleges	Colleges	Community Gathering	Colleges	Colleges
1:20-2:00	Lunch	Lunch		Lunch	Lunch
2:00-3:15 Week 1	E 240	A 236		E 236	Athletics
Week 2	IMS 237				
3:20-4:40	Athletics	EC		EC	

COHORT 3 — Trimester 2

	Monday	Tuesday	Wednesday	Thursday	Friday
8:00 - 8:45	Consultation	Consultation	Consultation	Consultation	Consultation
8:45 - 9:00	Gathering	Gathering	E 242	Gathering	Coffee House
9:00 - 10:15	E 242	E 242		IMS 237	E 242
10:15-10:20	Snack	Snack	Snack	Snack	Snack
10:15-11:30	IMS 237	A 236	IMS 237	A 236	IMS 237
11:30-12:45	G 242	IMS 237	G 242	Movement Auditorium	G 242
12:45-1:20	Colleges	Colleges	Community Gathering	Colleges	Colleges
1:20-2:00	Lunch	Lunch		Lunch	Lunch
2:00-3:15 Week 1	A 236	E 237		E 242	Athletics
Week 2		IMS 240			
3:20-4:40	Athletics	EC		EC	

COHORT 2 — Trimester 2

	Monday	Tuesday	Wednesday	Thursday	Friday
8:00 - 8:45	Consultation	Consultation	Consultation	Consultation	Consultation
8:45 - 9:00	Gathering	Gathering	E 240	Gathering	Coffee House
9:00 - 10:15	A 236	IMS 240		E 240	E 240
10:15-10:20	Snack	Snack	Snack	Snack	Snack
10:15-11:30	E 240	E 240	G 242	Movement Auditorium	G 242
11:30-12:45	IMS 240	A 236	IMS 240	A 236	IMS 240
12:45-1:20	Colleges	Colleges	Community Gathering	Colleges	Colleges
1:20-2:00	Lunch	Lunch		Lunch	Lunch
2:00-3:15 Week 1	IMS 237	G 242		IMS 240	Athletics
Week 2	E 240				
3:20-4:40	Athletics	EC		EC	

COHORT 4 — Trimester 2

	Monday	Tuesday	Wednesday	Thursday	Friday
8:00 - 8:45	Consultation	Consultation	Consultation	Consultation	Consultation
8:45 - 9:00	Gathering	Gathering	IMS 237	Gathering	Coffee House
9:00 - 10:15	IMS 237	IMS 237		G 242	IMS 237
10:15-10:20	Snack	Snack	Snack	Snack	Snack
10:15-11:30	A 236	E 237	A 236	IMS 237	A 236
11:30-12:45	E 237	G 242	E 237	E 237	E 237
12:45-1:20	Colleges	Colleges	Community Gathering	Colleges	Colleges
1:20-2:00	Lunch	Lunch		Lunch	Lunch
2:00-3:15 Week 1	G 242	IMS 240		Movement Auditorium	Athletics
Week 2		E 237			
3:20-4:40	Athletics	EC		EC	

Legend: A = Art; E = English; EC = Elective Curriculum; G = Global History; IMS = Integrated Math and Science.

Source: Bronx Lab School internal documents.

Exhibit 8

Bronx Lab School's Selected Attendance Data, SY05

Date	*BLS Portal Data*[a] *% present*	*NYCDOE ATS Data*[b] *% present*
12/13/2004	93	89.5
12/14/2004	96	90.4
12/15/2004	94	88.5
12/16/2004	86	85.6
12/17/2004	85	79.8
1/10/2005	91	88.6
1/11/2005	94	89.5
1/12/2005	92	88.6
1/13/2005	96	91.4
1/14/2005	83	80
1/18/2005	93	89.5
1/19/2005	92	88.6
1/20/2005	91	86.7
1/21/2005	91	87.6

Source: Bronx Lab internal documents.

[a] Data as tracked and entered manually into the Bronx Lab portal on salesforce.com by Bronx Lab staff using current enrollment data.

[b] Data as tracked by NYCDOE using the Automate the Schools (ATS) IT system using beginning-of-year enrollment data.

Exhibit 9

Bronx Lab School's Academic Results, First Trimester, SY05

Eagle and Owl Roll by Cohort

	Cohort				
	I	*II*	*III*	*IV*	*Total*
Eagle Roll	1	3	2	1	7
Owl Roll	2	1	7	5	15
Total/Cohort	3	4	9	6	22

Note: Eagle Roll students achieved an average of 92.5% and above across their courses; Owl Roll students achieved an average between 85% and 92.5%.

Students with Failing Course Grades by Cohort and Subject

Student #	*Cohort*	*IMS*	*English*	*Global*	*Art*	*Totals by Student*
1	1	1				1
2	1			1		1
3	1			1		1
4	1	1				1
5	1			1		1
6	1			1		1
7	1	1		1		2
8	1	1		1		2
9	1	1			1	2
10	1	1	1	1	1	4
	Total Cohort One	6	1	7	2	
11	2				1	1
12	2		1			1
13	2			1		1
14	2	1		1		2
15	2		1	1		2
16	2	1		1		2
17	2	1	1			2
18	2	1	1	1		3
	Total Cohort Two	4	4	5	1	
19	3	1				1
20	3			1		1
21	3	1			1	2
22	3		1	1		2
23	3		1	1		2
24	3	1	1		1	3
	Total Cohort Three	3	3	3	2	
25	4			1		1
26	4		1	1		2
27	4	1		1		2
28	4		1	1		2
29	4	1		1		2
30	4		1	1		2
31	4	1	1	1		3
32	4		1	1	1	3
33	4	1	1	1		3
	Total Cohort Four	4	6	9	1	
	Total Bronx Lab	17	14	24	6	

	# Courses Failing			
	1	2	3	4
# of Students	12	15	5	1

Source: Bronx Lab School internal documents.

CASE 4.3

Stacey Childress ■ Tiffany K. Cheng

Codman Academy: Beyond the Start-Up Phase

Principal Thabiti Brown had been taking notes in the back of the classroom when he paused to reflect on the question being asked by Peter Dutton: "How do we know this is a recursively defined sequence?" Several students raised their hands and offered responses. Listening intently from one of the group clusters, math teacher Karen Crounse looked puzzled and, raising her hand, asked, "Peter, I don't know if I understand how this sequence is represented algebraically. Can you explain to me how you and your team came up with the equation you have on the board?"

As Peter and his teammates explained their work and continued teaching, Thabiti slipped out of Karen's classroom to observe a science lab down the hall. He thought, "When students own the work, those are really beautiful moments."

Although it was Thabiti's first year as principal at Codman Academy Charter Public School, he had been a part of the school since its founding in 2001—first as a humanities teacher, and most recently as the academic dean. In six years, he had seen Codman Academy grow from a single ninth-grade class of 34 students to an established high school that had succeeded in helping each member of the 2007 graduating cohort enter four-year colleges and universities around the country. But he knew critical challenges lay ahead.

In 2006, the state's board of education passed into law a new regulation requiring a "proficient" score on the reading and mathematics portions of the Massachusetts Comprehensive Assessment System (MCAS) as a prerequisite for graduation beginning with students in the class of 2010. Previously, "needs improvement" scores were considered passing. State board chairman Jim Peyser explained the rationale for the change: "We have largely succeeded in ensuring that all high school graduates in [Massachusetts] acquire certain basic skills in reading, writing and math. However, we have not yet ensured that all high school graduates are ready for success in college or the global labor market. We must set our sights higher."[1]

The new standard worried Thabiti and the rest of his staff. In 2007, 94% of Codman students passed the English portion of the MCAS, and 88% passed the mathematics portion. Under the new standards, the same results would have meant that only 61% passed the English exam and only 48% the mathematics exam.

Thabiti explained, "The conceptual understanding we're able to give students across the board is much stronger than their foundations coming in. Their higher-order thinking skills allow them to perform well—they'll talk credibly about the things they're learning but have trouble formulating a solid written paragraph."

Codman Academy cofounder Meg Campbell acknowledged, "Over the years, we were happy if they passed the MCAS—we declared victory if they got over the needs improvement hurdle. When they changed the rules, it was a sock in the stomach because our students are coming in really low and we want to make this test work for us without having it destroy our culture and curriculum." (See **Exhibit 1a–1c** for student performance data.)

Background

Charter Schools in the U.S.[2]

Charter schools were defined as public schools of choice operating free from many of the rules and regulations that apply to district schools. Although local, state, or other authorities authorized and oversaw charter schools, the schools themselves determined their own academic mission, instructional model, budget, human capital management, and most other operational issues. In 2007, 40 states and the District of Columbia had charter school legislation with about 4,000 charter schools serving 1.5 million students. In Massachusetts, 59 schools enrolled over 23,000 students.

One of the founding tenets of the charter school movement was to link autonomy with accountability. In return for operational freedom from local school districts, charter schools were expected to offer high-quality alternatives for resource-limited families and could be shut down if they failed to meet the goals specified in the performance contracts they signed. A number of advocates of charters supported them because they believed they could replicate academic results that could catalyze reform in existing public schools.

Dorchester

Up until the 1960s, Dorchester was a vibrant Jewish and Irish-Catholic community with a bustling commercial district. Prominent local leaders, including Mayor John Fitzgerald, his daughter Rose Kennedy, and three Harvard University presidents, among others, called Dorchester home. Over the next decade, African Americans began moving into the neighborhood in large numbers as whites left for the suburbs. Boston's overall population suffered a net loss of almost 250,000 people—most of whom had lived in communities like Dorchester. This dramatic decrease was quickly followed by a real estate collapse, economic depression, and escalating violence borne of racial tensions.

Bill Walczak arrived in Codman Square in 1972 as a college dropout working in a factory and organizing for Cesar Chavez's lettuce boycott. He remarked, "In those days, Dorchester was literally burning down—people found nothing worth salvaging here. On average, we had a house fire every day through the middle of the 1970s." Along with other community leaders, Bill founded Codman Square Community Health Center (CSCHC) and became its director in 1974 as a way to address neighborhood challenges. He recalled, "The creation of a health center was a way to give residents a reason to hope. To me, urban redevelopment is about changing people's attitudes toward the community."

Over the next three decades, community leaders and nonprofit organizations like CSCHC helped to improve and develop Codman Square into a more vibrant center. Concurrently, Dorchester became Boston's largest and most diverse community, with over 50 different racial and ethnic groups. Significant numbers of Caribbean Americans, African Americans, Vietnamese Americans, and Latinos lived in the area.

Yet, despite development improvements and its close proximity to the economic hub of the region, Dorchester had an unemployment rate three times Boston's average. Dorchester also continued to face chronic violence and public health crises. According to a Boston Public Health Commission report,[3] residents were more than twice as likely to be victims of nonfatal shootings as in Boston as a whole. Homicide incidents in Dorchester were four times the overall rate in Boston for youths age 18–24. Sexually transmitted diseases, diabetes, and HIV also affected Dorchester's community in disproportionate rates.

Codman's Founding Team

In the fall of 2000, Meg Campbell, Bill Walczak, and George Brackett delivered a charter school application to the Massachusetts Department of Education (DOE) with great anticipation. As a former community organizer, policy analyst, and executive director of Expeditionary Learning Outward Bound (ELOB), Meg had long dreamed of opening a school in Dorchester, where she had lived for over 20 years. She recalled, "Back then, before the Boston Public Schools reorganized district high schools into small learning communities, Dorchester's families did not have strong local options for their children. The two worst high schools in the city were also the only district high schools in Dorchester. Gang activity, high dropout rates, you name it—these schools were in crisis."

From the beginning, Meg knew she wanted to create a small high school using Expeditionary Learning's design principles (see **Exhibit 2**). Developed in 1992, ELOB sought to improve schools using five core practices: learning expeditions, active pedagogy, school culture and character, leadership and school improvement, and structures that promote student and adult learning. Drawing heavily from Outward Bound's philosophy of personal transformation through adventure, service, and other direct experiences, Expeditionary Learning schools brought experts into the classroom, took students into the field, and engaged students in real-world experiences.

Much of her initial philosophy was based on her training in early childhood education and community organizing principles. When she visited other charter schools across the country, she looked for evidence of strong programs and relationships. She said, "I was struck by how preoccupied they seemed with facilities, which raised many questions for me. None of them were doing anything different from traditional high schools. It was clear to me that if a school is dedicated to breaking the cycle of poverty and creating opportunities for families, then it cannot do it alone." Having known Bill through various community activist efforts, Meg approached him about starting a school together. Bill remembered, "I couldn't believe it. I had written down my personal goals in relation to my job four months before she contacted me. One of them was, in fact, starting a school."

George had led the technology in education program at Harvard Graduate School of Education for nine years. He had since begun working with Bill at CSCHC to create a technology center that would disseminate health information to the community at large. George recalled, "A certain Meg Campbell came and sat on my desk and wouldn't leave until I agreed to help with this school she was imagining. Her vision of what the school could be was very compelling. I was a little skeptical, but it sounded exciting to integrate what I knew about technology into a small high school."

Launching the School: Codman's Beginnings

In February 2001, the DOE granted a charter to the founding team. Codman Academy was designated as a high school serving grades 9–12 with a funding maximum capped at a total of 125 students. "There was a lot of push back that the school shouldn't be that small, but I was about quality and proving what was possible," recalled Meg.

The founding team quickly mobilized for the school's launch and raised funding to help build out a 2,100-square-foot section inside the health center that had been unused. After a lottery yielded 34 aspiring ninth-grade students, Meg conducted a focus group to find out what students considered the three most important traits in their future teachers. In the group, 22 students were African American, seven were Latinos, and six were of Caribbean descent. She was surprised to discover that not a single student indicated their preference for teachers of color: "Instead, they told me how they wanted teachers who knew the material they were teaching. They also asked for teachers who liked students. Finally, they insisted that there not be any first-year teachers, because they had experienced classes where the entire first semester was wasted because of classroom management issues."

Among her first hires was Thabiti Brown, whose previous teaching experiences were in New York City and Panama. Codman Academy's emphasis on project-based learning and the opportunity of working with students from a community that was very similar to his home in central Brooklyn drew Thabiti to apply for a humanities teaching position. He said, "I also loved the Expeditionary Learning philosophy of educating the whole child. Meg's big push around health education and wellness was very important to me. It seemed to be a strong theoretical model for how to create a school."

Meg also hired a dean of enrichment and a math/science teacher to round out the first-year teaching staff. As Codman Academy's doors opened in fall 2001, the daily challenges of teaching and running a start-up school became real. Families resisted the idea of students calling adults by their first name, citing the need for a hierarchy in relationships. "Having students call us by our first names was purposely symbolic in that we were trying to change the relationship between adults and students," said Meg. "We wanted to extend that privilege of closeness to children."

Moreover, integrating a brand-new school into a well-established community health center created a number of challenges. Bill explained, "Most people on my staff theoretically like the idea of having a school here, but they're health-care people and turf oriented—they don't want students walking into the health center without an adult." Thabiti added:

> We had a really tough time with the health center the first couple of years because students run around, break things, and make a lot of noise. The staff looked on us negatively. With Bill's leadership and insistence that we were as much a part of the health center as anything else, the relationship slowly began to change. People have become used to the idea of having high school students around all the time and are much more welcoming.

Meg summarized the various challenges of launching a school embedded in a health center:

> That first year wasn't all about instructional leadership. It was about building culture. The students and families needed a paradigm shift about what school was going to be in their lives. It was hard figuring out a balance between having firm, explicit expectations and yet not wanting to be a school that was joyless. I was always saying, "Upstairs, they might be finding out they have cancer. They don't want to hear a lot of screaming down here." By embedding ourselves in a health center and having the adults in the building outnumber the children, I hoped the culture of professionalism would dominate.

Codman Academy's Evolution

As Codman Academy grew, it enrolled a new ninth-grade class by lottery each year until it reached its capacity. Meg continued to increase her staff and looked to hire additional teachers who could thrive in the entrepreneurial environment and complement her weaknesses. Thabiti explained, "Meg is an incredible visionary with a huge heart for students. She knows her flaws and weaknesses. I think the majority of the folks she's hired are people who can build and implement her ideas with attention to detail." Those early years presented a myriad of difficulties, especially since the school was still in its start-up stages and struggling to adjust to each additional class. Thabiti recalled, "We ran out of space, had to hire new teachers every year, and began dealing with the incredible challenges of the college planning process and SATs. Meg tried hard to hire support staff that could take over some of the more difficult aspects that teachers may not be trained for. The link to the health center also helped us remove some of that chaos." Not only did CSCHC's mental health professionals work with students based on referrals, but they also provided behind-the-scenes support in the form of valuable repair and maintenance services.

In 2007, the majority of the student population lived in Dorchester, but some also commuted from neighboring areas such as Jamaica Plain, Hyde Park, and Roxbury. Sixty-nine percent of the student body qualified for free or reduced-price meals, and 86% were African American, 13% Latino, and 1% white. Codman Academy's special education population stood at 21%.

School days officially ran from 9:00 a.m. to 5:00 p.m. Monday through Friday and 9:00 a.m. to 12:00 p.m. Saturdays, but many students participated in physical education classes before or after school, as well as art and music enrichment classes. School grounds were open and staffed until 7:00 p.m., offering students a safe place to work in groups or receive additional assistance from teachers and volunteer tutors. Every Friday, students completed fieldwork or internships at various sites across the city. On Saturdays, students participated in elective curriculum that included subject areas such as marine biology, youth justice, urban design, filmmaking, and taxes. (See **Exhibits 3, 4,** and **5** for a daily schedule, sample student transcript, and selected staff biographies.)

Codman Academy Culture

Drawing inspiration from Outward Bound founder Kurt Hahn's assertion "We are crew, not passengers," students were organized into 10 single-sex, multigrade crews. Crews met three times a week after lunch for a 30-minute block. In addition to providing opportunities for crew leaders and students to discuss academic and behavioral issues, crews addressed leadership and personal development through a variety of student- and crew-leader-initiated activities. Meg discussed the underlying theory of organizing students in this manner: "One of the reasons we did the multiage crews was to use the power of the older students in shaping the younger ones." One male student who had recently transferred from a large Boston district school commented, "The biggest change I noticed is that here, I can't tell who the seniors are. At my old school, they used to pick on us. Here at Codman, they want to help you."

Every October, the entire staff and student body participated in a three-day off-campus retreat for learning activities and community building. There, students formulated "intentions" in crews. Science teacher and crew leader Emily Simpson recalled this process: "Students thought about their best qualities and created visual representations of their intentions, things they wanted to accomplish, to hang up throughout the school. Younger students' intentions tend to focus on academics. Older students get deeper and reflect more about who they want to become."

Incoming ninth graders were welcomed via letters written by their immediate predecessors. "Letters to the 9th Graders" described life at Codman Academy and offered advice to students (see **Exhibit 6**). In addition, ninth graders met in single-sex groups with clinical social worker Shelby Derissaint once a week in "talking circles," a place where issues of wellness, academics, communication, and health were addressed. During their senior year, students were given the opportunity to reflect on their learning at a community event called "senior talks" (see **Exhibit 7**).

Learning Expeditions

Codman Academy students engaged in project-based learning and demonstrated their mastery of content through portfolios, exhibition/performances, and by passing MCAS tests. Faculty created "learning expeditions" across subject areas consistent with state curriculum standards. According to ELOB design principles, learning expeditions placed a high value on rigorous academic content and authentic, real-world projects.

Portfolio Gateways

Codman Academy's course programming centered around three core subjects: humanities, math, and science. Students only received credit for courses in which they obtained a grade of 70 or higher.

Students completed two major portfolio examinations. The portfolio in the 10th grade required students to create one major project in each core subject. Thabiti explained the reasoning for this first gateway: "We wanted to have a strong distinction between what it meant to do ninth- and 10th-grade work, and then what it meant to do up to 12th-grade work." Typically, students presented one of their three projects to a panel consisting of their teacher, a member of the community, and a peer. Humanities Department chair Susan Barrett described how one group of students studied the AIDS epidemic in Haiti: "They selected this topic based on our curriculum theme of justice and injustice. They learned to write expository pieces, interview primary sources, and present facts." Her students ultimately wrote and performed a series of monologues based on the information they had researched together. They also decided to raise funds for these causes and to involve audience members in a collective effort. Susan reflected on her students' growth, saying, "The energy around the project and the way the students developed a greater motivation for themselves was amazing. In the end, their sense of accomplishment is really what expeditionary learning is all about."

Thabiti agreed and emphasized the importance of this experience in preparing students for 11th- and 12th-grade work: "We want the students to know that when they get to the 12th grade, they're going to be required to do these rigorous, ongoing, extended projects. The onus for learning will be fully on them."

For their second portfolio examination, students in 11th and 12th grade worked toward a graduation portfolio that was typically presented senior year. This process required students to write and speak on various academic disciplines studied at Codman Academy, with special emphasis on topics they investigated deeply. Susan commented, "All of us want our students to leave Codman with a sense of agency—that they can go out into the world and be who they want to be." One of Codman Academy's first graduates had recently returned to the school to share his leadership and activism experiences as an elected student senator at the University of Massachusetts Amherst. He had been part of the student-led efforts to reduce public college fees in order to ensure greater access for all. Susan remarked, "Our students are creating things that have an impact not just on their peers or school community. They are truly impacting the world."

Addressing MCAS Demands

Teachers at Codman Academy were cognizant of the real demands of the state's accountability exam, the MCAS. As with the rest of the state, students at Codman Academy were required to pass the grade-10 tests in English language arts (ELA) and math as one condition for graduation. Susan remarked, "As much as possible, I try to integrate explicit lessons about test-taking and multiple-choice strategies into our work products. It's not as if skill building isn't part of expeditionary learning—it's just that given the choice, I wouldn't do five-paragraph essays all the time."

Math Department chair Karen Crounse offered her thoughts: "Every expedition starts with the standards. Expeditionary learning isn't separate from what students need to know for the MCAS. The big difference is that they learn about linear equations in the context of staircases."

On the heels of the state's decision to raise the bar for passing the MCAS, the school instituted several interventions. In addition to a three-week, ninth-grade "boot camp"—focused on basic skills and learning how to be a "Codman" student—students began using a workbook series designed to build computation skills as a supplement to their math and science classes. All students were given a diagnostic assessment that identified weakness areas. Ninth- and 10th-grade students spent 90 minutes once a week in classroom work sessions, whereas 11th- and 12th-grade students worked on assignments at home to strengthen their skills. Emily commented, "For most students, it's an opportunity for them to take control of their own education in a very concrete manner. They could feel very successful in a relatively short period of time." The Humanities Department decided to focus more on grammar instruction and pay specific attention to essay writing. Thabiti explained, "We're trying to teach our students how to write a strong piece in five revisions and wean them off the 38-revision process." As he considered what Codman Academy had put in place, Thabiti said, "In the end, I think we could quickly get to 100% proficiency if we torched our entire curriculum and decided we were just going to focus on the MCAS. But, I just refuse to do it."

Co-Curricular Programs

Consistent with the principles of expeditionary learning, students had many opportunities to learn from the world around them. Meg explained, "The entire city—really the world—is their classroom."

Health and Wellness Program

Codman Academy was the only high school in the country located within a community health center. Students were introduced to an array of health careers, and several seniors held internships at CSCHC. Codman Academy also taught students wellness habits and knowledge of healthy living. For example, incoming ninth graders enrolled in a required nutrition course, which addressed prevention, recognition, and treatment of common diseases such as obesity, asthma, and diabetes. All students participated in at least one physical education class, which ranged from soccer and basketball to personal fitness and dance. Bill asserted the importance of this health focus: "Many of our students believe that diabetes is something you get when you're older. It's our job to educate them so, at minimum, they understand the causes and solutions to diseases and talk to their families about these issues." Moreover, he hoped that exposure to health careers would bridge the divide between Boston's medical schools, its hospitals, and its youth. He commented:

> Here at the health center, we train medical students and residents from all the teaching hospitals and medical schools, but all of them are

> white suburbanites. We have to make sure that some of the people that eventually come through places like CSCHC for training are non-white students from the city. So many jobs in health care guarantee a middle-class salary. We hope that some day, our medical and nursing students will wind up coming from Dorchester.

Huntington Theatre Company

Every other Friday, all 9th- and 10th-grade students participated in theater education at the Huntington Theatre Company, located at Boston University. Students engaged in improvisation exercises, built sets, and learned about stage management. In collaboration with visiting artists, students learned and performed pieces from William Shakespeare, Alfred Hitchcock, and James Joyce. All ninth graders prepared to participate in a yearly national poetry contest, whereas 10th graders compete in a nationally recognized Shakespeare competition.

One student described his experience in the Huntington program:

> At first, I didn't want to be an actor. I wanted to be behind the scenes, but because the teachers have a good sense of who you are and what you can accomplish, they push you. Now, I'm getting compliments about my acting, and without me even realizing it, it's building up my character for the future. We're responsible for getting ourselves there, and the school has enough trust in you not to chaperone you on the train. And, everybody comes. I can't remember the last time anybody skipped out on a Friday at the Huntington.

Supported by various grants, the program had grown to incorporate 11th graders, who participated in hip-hop opera with another local arts project. The Huntington's director of education, Donna Glick, explained the goal of these collaborations:

> The point isn't to turn out actors necessarily. Students are getting real-life skills that they can use in their professions or community. They begin to see that they need each other. They learn the importance of communication, how to listen, walk across a stage, use one's voice, and be part of an audience. Of course, there's a lot of pressure, but this intensive process imparts a real sense of "I did this."

Some staff wondered if these Fridays spent off campus distracted from the instructional priorities of preparing students for college success. One said, "It's eight hours every other Friday. Is that the right use of time? I don't always feel like it is, when someone can't add. I would love to increase their level of academic preparation so that they have more choices in what they can study."

South Africa Study Tour

Eleventh-grade students were given the opportunity to learn about South Africa through a Saturday course. Students could apply for one of 12 spots on the yearly Codman Academy delegation to South Africa after completing this course, writing an essay, and passing all classes. Similar to the Huntington Theatre program, this was funded in part by additional grants and private donations.

Each year, students visited AIDS hospices, schools, the Apartheid Museum, and other notable cultural landmarks. One student reflected on his involvement:

> When people used to say South Africa, I would think of cheetahs and trees. But once I started learning about apartheid, I became passionate and so upset. I went around the school preaching about this oppression. I thought about it and realized that if I learned about this years ago, I wouldn't have been mature enough to take it in. I used to think that my world was

> where I went to school, but now, I realize it's much bigger than that.

Social and Emotional Support

Clinical social worker Shelby Derissaint, who had been at Codman Academy for four years, had led the Talking Circles groups since her arrival. She noted the effects of this ongoing support:

> Talking Circles groups have been healing—over time, students learn to become supportive of one another. When one of the students wasn't doing well academically, another student said to her, "I'm really concerned about you. I think you've been hanging around this boy too long, and your grades have been slipping." Everybody started giving their opinions on how she needed to improve her grades.

Shelby also witnessed and supported one student's decision to announce her bisexuality to her classmates in this space: "I remember how supportive the other students were. They asked her questions like, 'How do you know? How do you feel about this?' I thought it was amazing that the students had built up so much trust."

Meg commented, "Ninth graders come in with such a bravado and toughness because that's what it took to survive in their other schools. When they come here, they get younger because we back up and let them be students again. We strive to create a culture where girls and boys can talk about their feelings and acknowledge when they don't know something and how to ask for help."

In addition, Shelby provided individual counseling and facilitated a peer mediation training course for aspiring student leaders: "At first, students weren't that interested in it. Now, students will come to my office and say, 'I need some peer mediation before I beat this other kid up.' They really want to have a dialogue and understand their peers."

Shelby had various interaction points within the school to understand the needs of Codman Academy's students. Once a week, she met with Thabiti and special education teachers to conduct deep assessments of several students who presented social, emotional, and academic needs. Shelby also conducted intake interviews with students and families once they were accepted to Codman Academy to understand their interests, home life, and medical histories (see **Exhibit 8**).

Susan, Codman Academy's Humanities Department chair, said, "The hardest thing to navigate as a teacher is seeing our students fight against the racist expectations of an urban society. There's the expectation that our girls are going to get pregnant or that our boys will get involved in gangs." She continued, "Some students come to me with problems that are so immediate. They've been falsely arrested, or they think they're pregnant. It's so clear that students' social and emotional needs have an impact on the classroom." Crisis intervention was central to Shelby's role at the school. "Even now, when I hear of a student getting shot, I hold my breath until I hear the name and see the face. I grew up in this community, but things are so different now."

Ongoing Challenges

Resources

Codman Academy's founding team had been very deliberate in managing the school's finances in spite of their ongoing facility challenges. Cofounder and former board member George said, "Finances typically kill charter schools because they don't get space from the state—many schools spend money on debt service before operational needs. We were unwilling to go into debt, which is why facilities have been more of a struggle than perhaps at other schools." (See **Exhibit 9** for school financial statements.) But the challenges had created inefficiencies. He added, "We're not only struggling to find enough space but to devise how much space one needs to support the kind of education we're still figuring out how to do." Science teacher Emily agreed: "My classroom is in the basement with bad ventilation, and while I had a lot of input on the things that went in there, I couldn't put fume hoods in because there just wasn't space. There are experiments that are a little dangerous because we just don't have the space to do them properly."

Staff hoped that Meg's transition into a role that was primarily focused on fund-raising would allow them to utilize Meg's strengths as a leader. "We would prefer Meg to be more outwardly directed because she's very good at building relationships," said George. Emily commented, "This transition is going to be so hard for Meg because she'll be outside the school and not as involved. But most of us felt that this would be the best for her, Thabiti, and the school going forward." (See **Exhibit 10** for an organizational chart.)

Staff Retention

Some staff wondered if their peers were satisfied with their roles at the school and the amount of support they received. The school's demanding pace and intense culture had attracted young, aspirational teachers, but a steady number had left the school after a few years (see **Exhibit 11**). One teacher said, "I love becoming a better teacher and find this work personally fulfilling, but I don't think I'll be here for 10 or 15 years." Another reflected, "I think some people give future years off their life to this job. Codman can be an incredibly stressful place, especially when students are working towards their portfolio performances. It's easy to look at those projects and marvel at the quality of work, but when you've got teachers sitting in the back row dying because they've been up until 10 o'clock at night for three weeks straight, working with these students to get them to this point, I think, 'We just can't keep doing this.'"

Meredith Liu, the dean of enrichment, credited her colleagues for the growth students experienced at the school: "What Codman does for students is unbelievable. Teachers are very thoughtful about the curriculum—it's brilliant." However, the demands on staff had consequences. She added, "Staff retention is pretty bad. We're expected to deliver so much and, in the process, people kill themselves in that effort and burn out." Although teachers and staff met monthly for full-day professional development provided by Expeditionary Learning coaches, some staff members worried that these skill-building activities did not keep pace with the expertise and content knowledge that left with departing teachers. One commented, "Codman needs to develop and keep its master teachers. Most of us are young, still learning, naïve, very creative—all of those things are good. But we need stability and people who are teaching the same thing over in order to improve curriculum and instruction."

Thabiti offered his thoughts: "The majority of teachers who have left leave to pursue other opportunities—law school, doctoral programs, or other roles in education. But I think people stay because teachers and staff have a lot of freedom to create pieces of their own vision within the larger vision." Emily agreed that autonomy was one of the primary reasons for her continued role at the school but also thought the pace was, at times, unmanageable: "Right now, in order to feel successful at my job, the amount I have to give of my life is too high to sustain long term. But as long as I'm here, it is part of my responsibility to help the school become more sustainable so that we retain teachers for

10 or 15 years." Meg looked at staff retention from this perspective: "It's one thing if they're burned out and decide to be an investment banker. My goal is to have talented people stay in the field of education. We're a talent factory, and I don't see that as a problem."

Student Outcomes

The work environment for students was demanding, and those who did not meet the high expectations were not promoted. At times, students left Codman Academy for other high schools where they could enter the next grade level. Some chose to remain at Codman Academy, but overall, staff took great care to communicate expectations and numerous warnings before making the decision to withhold promotion. (See **Exhibit 12** for enrollment and graduation data.) Cofounder George acknowledged the high attrition numbers but asserted, "We've got a very fluid neighborhood and sometimes, students leave for reasons that have nothing to do with their experiences. The school bends over backwards to keep students whom it thinks it can reach. That's one of Meg's strongest qualities. She is like a bull terrier—she just doesn't let go."

Still, its senior class was just 12 students, a dramatic decrease from the 43 who had entered in 2004 as ninth graders. Meredith reflected, "It's awful to lose students, but Codman is not a great fit for everyone. In fact, it's such an unusual school—the quantity of work, the rules, and the hours they spend here are so much more than other high schools." Emily added, "Some of our students come in several grade levels behind, and we explain that we are trying to get them through eight grade levels in four years. Those who stay at Codman are better prepared for college, but they have to want to be here that extra year."

Codman Academy graduates were provided alumni support. The school hoped that this additional guidance would improve college graduation rates among alumni. Staff sourced additional financial aid, facilitated transfers between schools, and referred out-of-school students to employment and job-training opportunities. In 2007, 80% of Codman Academy's three alumni cohorts were pursuing degrees at four-year colleges and 7% were enrolled in two-year colleges. The remaining 13% were not enrolled in school. (See **Exhibit 13a** for alumni college attendance data, **Exhibit 13b** for state and national high school graduation rates by race, and **Exhibit 13c** for proportion of students nationally who graduate with college-ready transcripts.)

Although the school aimed to prepare all students for success in college, one staff member voiced concerns about the trade-off between advancing students' skills and understanding and following the teaching principles of Expeditionary Learning:

> The idea behind Expeditionary Learning is to get students to understand content more deeply, but it causes the curriculum to move very slowly. We want our students to be ready for college, but I worry that even our most driven students will struggle in college-level courses because their academic preparation is not where it needs to be. It's unfortunate, but I think they'll be limited in what they are able to study.

Looking Ahead

Thabiti recognized that the school faced numerous challenges, especially as it sought to prepare students to meet the new MCAS standards. In order to survive, he knew Codman Academy would need to respond to the state's accountability mechanism. How could the school preserve its identity as an Expeditionary Learning school and meet the MCAS challenge? He struggled with the implications of the new standards. He believed, "If our students continue to go out into the community and speak their minds, speak truth to power, and are educated, thoughtful citizens who are interested in giving back to the larger community, then in the long run, we'll have achieved success."

Notes

1. "New MCAS Regulations Require All Students to Strive for Proficiency," Massachusetts Department of Education, October 24, 2006, http://www.doe.mass.edu/news/news.asp?id=3120, accessed November 12, 2007.

2. This section is drawn from Stacey M. Childress and Christopher C. Kim, "Green Dot Public Schools: To Collaborate or Compete?" HBS No. 307-086 (Boston: Harvard Business School Publishing, 2007).

3. "Boston Public Health Commission: Status Report on Youth in Dorchester," October 22, 2007.

Exhibit 1a

MCAS Annual Performance Comparison for Codman Academy

	Grade 10 English Language Arts				*Grade 10 Mathematics*			
	A %	*P* %	*NI* %	*W/F* %	*A* %	*P* %	*NI* %	*W/F* %
2007	0	61	33	6	15	33	42	12
2006	0	45	50	5	5	30	50	15
2005	18	36	46	0	7	32	36	25
2004	10	65	25	0	10	10	62	19
2003	0	44	56	0	8	16	44	32

Source: Massachusetts Department of Education and case writer analysis.

Legend: MCAS Performance Categories: A = Advanced; P = Proficient; NI = Needs Improvement; W/F = Warning/Failing.

Exhibit 1b

MCAS Performance Comparisons: Codman Academy with Boston Public Schools and Comparable Boston Charter High Schools, 2007

	Grade 10 English Language Arts				*Grade 10 Mathematics*			
	A %	*P* %	*NI* %	*W/F* %	*A* %	*P* %	*NI* %	*W/F* %
Codman Academy	0	61	33	6	15	33	42	12
Neighboring Boston Public High Schools								
Academy of Public Service	0	23	48	29	3	0	53	44
Noonan Business Academy	0	22	66	12	5	17	51	27
Social Justice Academy	2	28	55	16	13	20	41	26
Community Academy of Science & Health	0	28	40	32	7	26	33	34
Engineering School	0	38	56	6	12	22	52	14
Boston Charter High Schools								
City on a Hill	6	66	29	0	38	38	25	0
MATCH	11	72	17	0	76	24	0	0
Boston Collegiate	14	69	14	3	55	35	10	0
Academy of the Pacific Rim	11	61	28	0	72	19	6	3

Source: Massachusetts Department of Education and case writer analysis.

Legend: MCAS Performance Categories: A = Advanced; P = Proficient; NI = Needs Improvement; W/F = Warning/Failing.

Exhibit 1c

Math Diagnostic Assessment Results for Incoming Ninth Graders (Class of 2011)

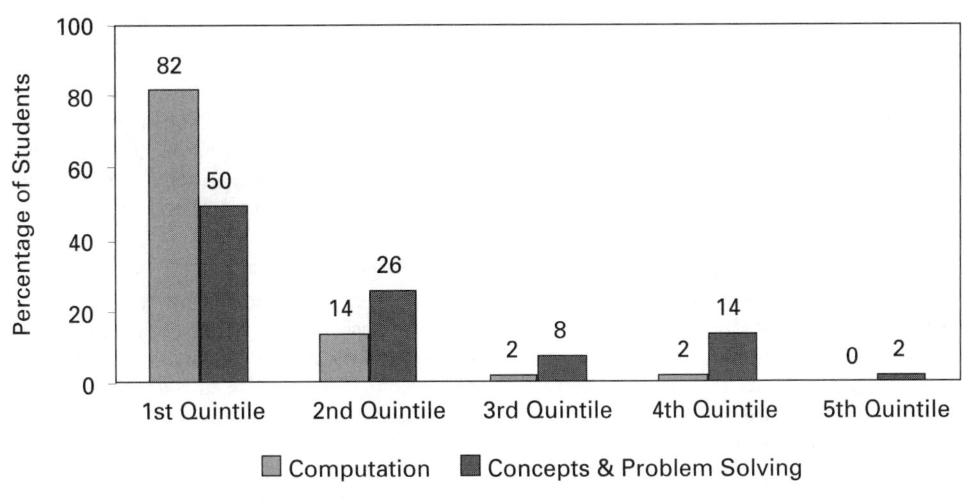

Source: School files and case writer analysis.

Note: Data represent percentiles on a national norm-referenced assessment, which compares an individual's performance to a sample of peers. The first quintile represents the lowest 20% of performance, and the fifth quintile represents the highest 20% of performance on the norm-referenced assessment.

Exhibit 2

Expeditionary Learning Outward Bound (ELOB) Design Principles

Overview:

Expeditionary Learning is built on ten design principles that reflect the educational values and beliefs of Outward Bound. These principles also reflect the design's connection to related thinking about teaching, and the culture of schools.

1. The Primacy of Self-Discovery

Learning happens best with emotion, challenge and the requisite support. People discover their abilities, values, passions, and responsibilities in situations that offer adventure and the unexpected. In Expeditionary Learning schools, students undertake tasks that require perseverance, fitness, craftsmanship, imagination, self-discipline, and significant achievement. A teacher's primary task is to help students overcome their fears and discover they can do more than they think they can.

2. The Having of Wonderful Ideas

Teaching in Expeditionary Learning schools fosters curiosity about the world by creating learning situations that provide something important to think about, time to experiment, and time to make sense of what is observed.

3. The Responsibility for Learning

Learning is both a personal process of discovery and a social activity. Everyone learns both individually and as part of a group. Every aspect of an Expeditionary Learning school encourages both children and adults to become increasingly responsible for directing their own personal and collective learning.

4. Empathy and Caring

Learning is fostered best in communities where students' and teachers' ideas are respected and where there is mutual trust. Learning groups are small in Expeditionary Learning schools, with a caring adult looking after the progress and acting as an advocate for each child. Older students mentor younger ones, and students feel physically and emotionally safe.

5. Success and Failure

All students need to be successful if they are to build the confidence and capacity to take risks and meet increasingly difficult challenges. But it is also important for students to learn from their failures, to persevere when things are hard, and to learn to turn disabilities into opportunities.

6. Collaboration and Competition

Individual development and group development are integrated so that the value of friendship, trust, and group action is clear. Students are encouraged to compete not against each other but with their own personal best and with rigorous standards of excellence.

7. Diversity and Inclusion

Both diversity and inclusion increase the richness of ideas, creative power, problem-solving ability, and respect for others. In Expeditionary Learning school, students investigate and value their different histories and talents as well as those of other communities and cultures. Schools and learning groups are heterogeneous.

8. The Natural World

A direct and respectful relationship with the natural world refreshes the human spirit and teaches the important ideas of recurring cycles and cause and effect. Students learn to become stewards of the earth and of future generations.

9. Solitude and Reflection

Students and teachers need time alone to explore their own thoughts, make their own connections, and create their own ideas. They also need time to exchange their reflections with others.

10. Service and Compassion

We are crew, not passengers. Students and teachers are strengthened by acts of consequential service to others, and one of an Expeditionary Learning school's primary functions is to prepare students with the attitudes and skills to learn from and be of service to others.

Source: "Expeditionary Learning Schools Outward Bound Design Principles," Expeditionary Learning, http://www.elschools.org/design/DesignPrinciples.pdf, accessed December 2, 2007.

Exhibit 3

Codman Academy Class Schedule

CACPS Class Schedule 2007-2008

Monday Schedule								
Block/Class	9A	9B	10A	10B	11A	11B	12A	12B
7:00-8:45	PE	PE	PE	PE	PE	PE	PE	PE
9:00-9:30	M	H	S	H	M (202)	F (Rm. B)	H (204)	H (204)
9:30-10:00	M	H	S	H	M	F	H	H
10:00-10:30	M	H	S	H	M	H (Rm. B)	H	H
10:30-11:00	S	H	TAI	H	S (204)	H	F (202)	F (202)
11:00-11:30	S	Nutrition	TAI	PP (H)	S	H	SI/F	SI/F
11:30-12:00	S	Nutrition	TAI	PP (H)	S	H	Sr. Intern	Sr. Intern
12:00-12:45	Lunch	Lunch	Lunch	Lunch	Lunch	Lunch	Lunch	Lunch
12:45-1:15	Crew	Crew	Crew	Crew	Crew	Crew	Crew	Crew
1:15-1:45	WB/TCG	S	H	M	H (Rm. B)	S (204)	M (202)	M (202)
1:45-2:15	WB/TCG	S	H	M	H	S	M	M
2:15-2:45	H	S	H	M	H	S	M	M
2:45-3:15	H	M	H	S	H	M (202)	S (204)	S (204)
3:15-3:45	H	M	WB	S	F (Rm. B)	M	S	S
3:45-4:15	H	M	WB	S	F	M	S	S
4:15-5:15	PE	PE	PE	PE	PE	PE	PE	PE
5:15-6:15	PE	PE	PE	PE	PE	PE	PE	PE

Tuesday Schedule								
Block/Class	9A	9B	10A	10B	11A	11B	12A	12B
7:00-8:45	PE	PE	PE	PE	PE	PE	PE	PE
9:00-9:30	H	M	H	S	F (Rm. B)	S (204)	TAI (202)	TAI (202)
9:30-10:00	H	M	H	S	F	S	TAI	TAI
10:00-10:30	H	S	H	PP (M/S)	H (Rm. B)	TAI (202)	H (204)	H (204)
10:30-11:00	H	S	H	PP (M/S)	H	TAI	H	H
11:00-11:30	Nutrition	WB/TCB	PP (M/S)	TAI	H	F (202)	H	H
11:30-12:00	Nutrition	WB/TCB	PP (M/S)	TAI	H	F	H	H
12:00-12:45	Lunch	Lunch	Lunch	Lunch	Lunch	Lunch	Lunch	Lunch
12:45-1:15	Crew	Crew	Crew	Crew	Crew	Crew	Crew	Crew
1:15-1:45	S	H	M	H	S (204)	H (Rm. B)	F (202)	F (202)
1:45-2:15	S	H	M	H	S	H	F	F
2:15-2:45	M	H	S	H	TAI (202)	H	S (204)	S (204)
2:45-3:15	M	H	S	H	TAI	H	S	S
3:15-3:45	CC	CC	CC	CC	CC	CC	CC	CC
3:45-4:15	CC	CC	CC	CC	CC	CC	CC	CC
4:15-5:15	PE/AM	PE/AM	PE/AM	PE/AM	PE/AM	PE/AM	PE/AM	PE/AM
5:15-6:15	PE/AM	PE/AM	PE/AM	PE/AM	PE/AM	PE/AM	PE/AM	PE/AM

Source: School files.

Codman Academy Class Schedule (continued)

Wednesday Schedule								
Block/Class	9A	9B	10A	10B	11A	11B	12A	12B
7:00-8:45	PE	PE	PE	PE	PE	PE	PE	PE
9:00-9:30	TAI	H	S	H	S (204)	F (Rm. B)	M (202)	M (202)
9:30-10:00	TAI	H	S	H	S	F	M	M
10:00-10:30	TAI	H	S	H	S	H (Rm. B)	M	M
10:30-11:00	S	H	M	H	M (202)	H	S (204)	S (204)
11:00-11:30	S	Nutrition	M	WB	M	H	S	S
11:30-12:00	S	Nutrition	M	WB	M	H	S	S
12:00-12:30	Lunch	Lunch	Lunch	Lunch	Lunch	Lunch	Lunch	Lunch
12:30-1:15	Club/WB	Club/WB	Club/WB	Club/WB	Club/WB	Club/WB	Club/WB	Club/WB
1:15-1:45	WB/TCB	S	H	M	H (Rm. B)	M (204)	F (202)	F (202)
1:45-2:15	WB/TCB	S	H	M	H	M	F	F
2:15-2:45	H	S	H	M	H	M	H (202)	H (202)
2:45-3:15	H	M	H	S	H	S (204)	H	H
3:15-3:45	H	M	PP (H)	S	F (Rm. B)	S	H	H
3:45-4:15	H	M	PP (H)	S	F	S	H	H
4:15-5:15	PE	PE	PE	PE	PE	PE	PE	PE
5:15-6:15	PE	PE	PE	PE	PE	PE	PE	PE

Thursday Schedule								
Block/Class	9A	9B	10A	10B	11A	11B	12A	12B
7:00-8:45	PE	PE	PE	PE	PE	PE	PE	PE
9:00-9:30	H	TAI	H	S	H (Rm. B)	M (202)	S (204)	S (204)
9:30-10:00	H	TAI	H	S	H	M	S	S
10:00-10:30	H	TAI	H	S	H	M	S	S
10:30-11:00	H	S	H	M	H	S (204)	M (202)	M (202)
11:00-11:30	Nutrition	S	WB	M	F (Rm. B)	S	M	M
11:30-12:00	Nutrition	S	WB	M	F	S	M	M
12:00-12:45	Lunch	Lunch	Lunch	Lunch	Lunch	Lunch	Lunch	Lunch
12:45-1:15	Crew	Crew	Crew	Crew	Crew	Crew	Crew	Crew
1:15-1:45	S	WB/TCG	M	H	M (204)	H (Rm. B)	F (202)	F (202)
1:45-2:15	S	WB/TCG	M	H	M	H	F	F
2:15-2:45	S	H	M	H	M	H	H (202)	H (202)
2:45-3:15	M	H	S	H	S (204)	H	H	H
3:15-3:45	M	H	S	WB	S	F (Rm. B)	H	H
3:45-4:15	M	H	S	WB	S	F	H	H
4:15-5:15	PE	PE	PE	PE	PE	PE	PE	PE
5:15-6:15	PE	PE	PE	PE	PE	PE	PE	PE

Friday Schedule								
Block/Class	9A	9B	10A	10B	11A	11B	12A	12B
	FIELDWORK		FIELDWORK		FIELDWORK		INTERNSHIP	

Key:

H	Humanities	Specials	Nutrition, Portfolio, Sr.Intern.
M	Mathematics	PE	Physical Education
S	Science	AM	Art/Music
F	French	WB	Work Block
CC	Community Circle	TCG	Talking Circle Girls
Crew	Crew	TCB	Talking Circle Boys

The School day is 9:00-5:00. Most blocks are 30 minutes long.

Source: School files.

Exhibit 4

Sample Student Transcript

Secondary School Transcript

CODMAN ACADEMY

Charter Public School
637 Washington Street
Dorchester, MA 02124
617-287-0700
617-287-9064 (fax)
www.codmanacademy.org

To Learn, to Lead, & to Serve

Name: DOB:

Address:

Grading & Graduation Requirements

Codman Academy does not rank students.
All core academic courses are honors level and receive letter grades. To receive credit a student must earn at least 70%. Because of our size we do not offer AP classes.
Electives are graded Pass/No Credit.

Grading Scale		Graduation Requirement
A	93-100	4 years Humanities
A-	90-92	4 years Math
B+	87-89	4 years Science
B	83-86	2 years Foreign Language
B-	80-82	4 years Physical Education
C+	77-79	1 year Art
C	73-76	Senior Year Internship
C-	70-72	2 Portfolios (10th and 12th grades)
NC	69 and below	2 summers of an approved program
P	Pass	

Year-long courses.

9th Grade		10th Grade		11th Grade		12th Grade	
Humanities 9	B+	Humanities 10	A	Humanities 11	A-	Humanities 12	B+
Algebra	B	Geometry	A-	French	A-	Sr. Internship	B-
Biology	B+	Physics	C+	Algebra 2	C+	French 2	B+
				Chemistry	B	Pre-Calculus	B-
						Biology	C
						Social Action Project	A

Selectives
One semester/trimester classes.

Wellness	P	Wellness	P	Basketball	P	Basketball	P	Softball	P
Saturday Course - Girls History	P	Saturday Course - School Newspaper	P	Youth Justice	P	Basketball	P	Health	P
Wellness	P	Wellness	P	Basketball	A-			Softball	P
		Saturday Course - Intro-Figure Drawing	P	Legal Studies	P			Health	P

Cumulative GPA: 3.433
Graduation/Transfer Date: 6/14/2007

Margaret M. Campbell, Head of School

Date

Source: School files.

Exhibit 5

Selected Codman Academy Staff Biographies

Kari Abdal-Kallaq, Math Teacher. Kari is a graduate of Prairie View A & M University, where he earned a Bachelor of Science in Electrical Engineering. He is enrolled in the Master's program at Tufts University and completed a year-long internship at Codman as part of his studies during the 04–05 year. Previously, Kari has worked for Citizen Schools as the High School Placement Coordinator for 8th Grade Academy, one of the campuses in the Citizen Schools network.

Susan Barrett, Humanities Teacher. Susan Barrett teaches Humanities 10. She is a graduate of the University of Colorado at Boulder (B.A. in history, minor in French) with a Master of Arts in Teaching from Tufts University. Susan has worked with students of all ages, including having an internship at Codman last year. She is excited to be teaching Humanities to sophomores at Codman this year.

Ken Bowers, French Teacher and Senior Internship Coordinator. Ken received his B.A. from St. Lawrence University in 2001 with a music and sociology double major. He later moved to Québec, where he taught English and picked up his French fluency. Ken graduated from Lesley University in 2006 with a Master's in Education as part of a National Teaching Fellowship through Citizen Schools. He runs the French program at Codman Academy and also coordinates Senior Internships.

Sydney Chaffee, Humanities Teacher. Sydney comes to Codman Academy from the Citizen Schools National Teaching Fellowship, where she taught eighth graders, coordinated the Boston Public Library's citywide Homework Assistance Program, and earned a Master's in Education from Lesley University. Before that, she graduated from Sarah Lawrence College with a concentration in women's history and writing. When she's not teaching (and sometimes when she is), Sydney enjoys making people laugh with improv comedy.

Karen Crounse, Math Teacher. Previously a computer programmer, Karen made a career change to teaching to share her passion for and excitement about mathematics with students. She returns to Codman for her third year, working with students in grades 9 and 10. When she's not immersed in mathematics, Karen also enjoys running and knitting (but not at the same time). Karen is a graduate of Wesleyan University and Harvard School of Education.

Ellie Goldberg, Math Teacher. Ellie Goldberg is originally from Chicago, where she was born, raised, and educated, receiving a Bachelor of Arts in both Mathematics and Psychology from the University of Chicago. She has spent the past four years teaching high school mathematics as a part of the Baltimore City Public School System, originally as a Teach For America Corps Member. At the end of her second year in Baltimore, Ellie received a Master of Arts in Teaching from the Johns Hopkins University. She is excited to grow professionally this year at Codman teaching 10th grade mathematics.

Niki Janus, Dean of Alumni. Niki is Midwestern born, California educated, and a Boston resident for 30 years and counting. Graduated from Mills College (Oakland, CA), she has an M.Ed. from Tufts. Her career in higher educational administration included work at Harvard and Wheaton. She has also been a partner in a home renovation business, run summer lacrosse camps for girls, and worked in development for Parents Helping Parents and Boston Baroque.

Meredith Liu, Dean of Enrichment. Meredith graduated Phi Beta Kappa from Dartmouth College with a degree in Economics and Education Public Policy. She is a native of Washington, D.C., where she spent her entire primary and secondary education in the D.C. Public Schools. Prior to joining Codman, she worked at Bain & Company, a global management consulting firm.

Lorigiana Meneide, Humanities Teacher. Lorigiana Meneide is proud to be a Boston College double eagle, returning to her alma mater in 2006 to earn an M.Ed. in Secondary Education with a concentration in instructing English Language Learners. Most recently, she was named a Donovan and Sharp Scholar, honors given to individuals who demonstrate fervent commitment to urban education and school excellence. As the 11th grade Humanities teacher, she is excited to become part of Codman Academy's community of learners!

Carrie-Anne Sherwood, Science Teacher. Carrie-Anne graduated Phi Beta Kappa from Fairfield University with a B.S. in Chemistry and minor in Mathematics. Having been accepted to a Ph.D. program for chemistry at the University of California, San Diego, she headed out west to sunny southern California. Why did she leave California without an advanced degree in science or a tan? To pursue science teaching as a NYC Teaching Fellow in the Bronx. After two years at Middle School 80 and with a Masters in Secondary Science Education from City College of New York, Carrie-Anne headed up to Codman Academy.

Emily Simpson, Science Teacher. Emily Simpson teaches Chemistry and Biology. She received her bachelor's degree in Biology and Environmental Studies from Williams College, and a Master of Arts in Teaching from Tufts University. She brings a wealth of experience to Codman having taught science in a variety of settings including West Africa, the Boston Museum of Science, Fenway High School, and the Willauer School on Thompson Island Outward Bound Education Center here in Boston. She is excited to use Expeditionary Learning as a means to develop students' passion and skills in all areas of science.

Katy Tooke, Science Teacher. Katy graduated Phi Beta Kappa from Dartmouth College with a degree in civil engineering and studio art, and has just finished a Master's in Education at Lesley University. She has taught in a wide variety of experiential settings, most recently bringing hands-on engineering science to life after school with the Citizen Schools program. Katy is excited about the opportunity to share her love of physics and the way things work with the Codman community. When not immersed in the world of education, Katy loves to hike, run and paint.

Source: School files.

Exhibit 6

Excerpts of Letters to the 9th Graders

Dear Freshmen,

The organization in your classes has to be on point. For Math class, your teacher will give you a folder and you will keep your papers in order when they are handed out to you. In Science, you have a binder and your teacher will give you binder checks for all three trimesters. For Humanities, you have to keep your papers where you want to find it.

Procrastination is not an option in this school. You shouldn't procrastinate in this school because if you don't work it means more work that you will have to do in the end to try and get your grade up. If you stay on top of your work in trimester 1 and 2, you don't have to worry about trimester 3. I was worried if I was going to summer school or if I was going to get kept back in trimester 3. I'm telling you now so you won't make the mistake that I made, DO NOT PROCRASTINATE!!!

This school year is going to be fun. The school day will fly by when you get here, and you won't even know it. If you want to take my advice, take it seriously. If you don't want to take my advice in this letter, you will be in the same scenario I was in and you will be sorry. Peace.

Dear Freshmen,

As far back as I can remember my first year at any new school has been difficult. Unfortunately, this year was my first at Codman; my grades were not as good as they could have been, I was in Thabiti's office one too many times and my relationships with classmates were filled with so much drama. I do not want my sophomore year to be like my freshman one.

As a student at Codman Academy I have learned to get my work done and appreciate the people and friends that I have. You have to do your work! When I first came to this school I was like: "SCREW MY WORK," but what really helped me was that I always had this one girl in my ear just bugging me. She would say, "Do your work," "Stop slacking off," or "Get your points up!" I realized that she was just doing it for my own good, and I love and thank her for that because it has made me who I am today.

Dear Freshmen,

Let me explain how things work at this school. Codman is a school that has numerous opportunities and hands-on teaching that makes things easier to learn. Also, what I like is that you don't always stay at the school. You're always somewhere, especially on Fridays. It's either we're at the Huntington or visiting colleges or learning more about colleges back at school.

Besides all of the good qualities there are things that make me not want to be at Codman. Let's get started with the fact that you must wear uniform at all times and if you don't I must warn you, you will get points taken off. Also we go to school from 9-5 Monday thru Saturday. You don't know how many times I had to blow off numerous plans and tell my peoples: "Sorry, I can't, I got school."

I've met a lot of cool students and learned that the teachers are not like regular teachers. If its one thing I can admit, it's that this school is not like any normal school and at most times you will have fun. For now, welcome to Codman and I wish you the best.

Source: School files.

Exhibit 7

Excerpt from *Senior Talks*

Cornel West once said in a speech that our task in education is not so much to become "successful" but to become "great." Again and again, we are told that greatness lies within us. But how can we become great when the odds are so against us? That is my question today: How can we become great?

The odds have certainly been against me.

I will start when I am about 3 years old. I walk up the street to the yellowish, brow-stained apartment. Three flights of stairs. I get sent to the back room to play with the other students. Some days I get tired and need some juice. In the kitchen, I see them playing cards. Drinking liquor. Laughing while they talk about others. I can see the rings of white powder around their noses. The red tents in the eyes. Razorblades. Open plastic baggies and money on the table. One day someone shouts, "Call the ambulance for G-baby!" I run into the front room. She is breathing hard, clutching her chest. Where is her asthma pump? A few minutes later, the ambulance arrives. The men in brown uniforms come up the stairs. They lay her on the stretcher. She looks up at me and winks. Winks. Down the stairs they go. It was the last time I saw my mother. She died three days later.

My father had long been incarcerated, so I lived with my grandparents. I always knew that my father's collect call promises were empty. When he was released, he became a stranger to me. He chose the street life—fast money, women, and a three-inch needle—over me. Once again, I was abandoned. My grandmother, who I had been living with, died when I was in the 3rd grade and I moved in with my cousin, who has cared for me ever since.

I was pregnant at 14. But I was so ashamed and embarrassed, so afraid of becoming like my own parents, of being a failure, that I kept my pregnancy a secret from everyone. It wasn't until I was 8 months pregnant that I let myself face the truth. I felt intense self-hate. I would become like my mother. I put a shield between myself and the world, hoping my heart would become invisible.

My son was born on April 30, 2003. Everything changed that day. That night, I finally got the chance to be with him alone, to hold him, to look into his little brown eyes. I promised him I would dedicate my whole life to him, that I would never let him want for anything. Still, I was terrified I was going to fail him. Indeed, I am still afraid of this. I don't think this is a fear that's ever going to go away. But I felt courage, too.

So, I began to do everything I could so as not to fail him and repeat the errors of my own past. I decided to let my aunt, who lived first in Providence and then in Atlanta, raise my son. I realized that the most important thing for me to do both for my son, and me was to stay in school, excel academically, and develop myself as a person.

Sometimes, I look back on my past and am thankful for every second of it. It's not in spite of my struggles but because of them that I have learned what it means to fight to excel. More than that, everyone who has hurt me has also taught me what it means to love. Sometimes, I think about my mother. I hope she is proud of me. Even more than this, I hope my son is proud of me.

I always wondered if I could make it to college and if that was the right road for me. This year, I decided I would go to college. I was accepted at Holy Cross University and was offered, essentially, a full scholarship.

I will prove wrong all those who did not believe in me and who gave up on me. Cornel West told me that my task in education is not so much to become "successful" but to become "great." Against all odds, I will become great.

So, my seniors, I am with all of you. We are not weak. We are not failures. We are free to cry. We are free against all the odds to be great.

It is ironic how all my life I wanted to be loved and yet this one thing I really wanted, was not there. I was not loved and that is what I am here to talk to you about today. Love.

There are so many ways that I see people not loving, or failing to love in our streets, in our community, even in our school. People are throwing up gang signs, people are fighting their own people, people are killing their own people and people are disrespecting their own people. Why do we not love? Because we haven't been loved. It's a horrible cycle.

I grew up on Draper Street in Dorchester, a neighborhood in Boston. Violence seemed like everyone's answer to most questions. I remember young men hiding underneath cars, people running away from the cops, and police dogs barking all through the night. I thought this was everyone's America—gun shots going off, houses being broken into, drive-by shootings, childhood acquaintances arrested for attempted murder. Funerals. And always questions, too many questions running through my head. This was D-Block, where no one loved at all. The funny and tragic thing is, I used to think I loved my street. But now I realized that my street had no love. This was everyone against everyone. Why? Because of the absence of love.

I remember being in seventh grade, watching TV late one night. The phone's ring frightened me. I grabbed it clumsily and answered in a tired voice, "Hello?"

I hear on the other end, "This is the Boston Police. Danny has just been sent to the hospital after a shooting that occurred on Wendover Street." My brother . . . shot. It was the violence in the community that caused this. The people were not loved and so they acted without love—violently, with guns and fists and hate.

Watching my brother get shot taught me that I wanted peace in my community. Ever since the day my brother was shot, I have wanted to become a person who can stop, or at least reduce, the violence in my community. Instead of seeking revenge, I drove to the hospital and offered my support. I offered my love.

And I didn't offer my love because I had come to feel loved. No, I came to realize that, even when there was no love, I had to love anyway.

Sometimes I lose myself and don't even know if I want to deal with my own issues. I figure I could just give up the fight for love and follow the path of some people in my family. I could do drugs, carry guns, and go to jail. Sometimes I feel I should give up and go to prison. Prison sometimes feels like the best place for me. I fear these thoughts. I fear being alone.

But I fight this fear. I love anyway. When fear is present, I do what I have to do to continue my day. I fight to believe I am who I am and I am going to live my life the way I want to. I fight to believe that maybe one day, someone will just love me.

Source: School files.

Exhibit 8

Excerpts of Family Intake Information Survey

Family Routines Questions

What is your current school day routine?

- Morning (When do you wake up? How do you get to school?):
- Daytime (What is the school day like? What do you do at lunch? What do you enjoy/dislike about school?):
- After-school (What do you do when school finishes? How do you get home? When do other family members get home? What happens at dinner? Where/when do you do homework?):</BL>

What is your current weekend routine (friends, family, activities, homework)?

What did you do last summer?

Student Goals Questions

We're interested in hearing about your goals for being a student at Codman Academy. During your time here, we'll adjust and revisit these goals periodically to make sure you're reaching your dreams.

- What are your goals as a student at Codman Academy?
- What are your goals for being a leader at Codman Academy?
- What are your goals for contributing to the community while at Codman Academy?
- What do you consider to be your greatest strengths?
- How would you like most to improve?

Information Survey for Parents

We have prepared the following survey to collect information about Codman Academy students and their families. Our aim is to evaluate how the school can best meet the needs of the children and families we serve. Any information you offer will be kept CONFIDENTIAL and will NOT be used to assess your student's performance. Thank you for your honesty in answering the following questions.

1. Does your family currently have a library card? (Circle one) Yes No

   If yes, to which library? ______________________________
2. How many visits has your family made to the library in the past year? (Check one)

   ❑ None ❑ 1 to 2 ❑ 3–5 ❑ Once every month ❑ Once every week ❑ Once every day
3. Does your family currently subscribe to any periodicals (magazines, journals or newspapers)?

   If yes, please list: ____
4. On average, how many hours per week does your family spend reading (books, magazines, newspapers)? ____________hours/week
5. On average, how many hours per week is the TV on in your home? ________hours/week
6. On average, how many hours per week does your student watch TV? ________hours/week
7. Do you currently have a computer at home? (Circle one) Yes No
8. Do you have internet access at home? (Circle one) Yes No
9. On average, how many hours per week is the computer used in your home? ________hours/week
10. How many people use the computer in your home? _____people out of _____members of the household

11. How is your home computer used? (For example: to play computer games; to do homework; to browse the Internet . . .)
12. Does your family currently have a fitness center membership (Circle one) Yes No
13. How many visits has your family made to the fitness center in the past year? (Check one)

    ❑ None ❑ 1 to 2 ❑ 3–5 ❑ Once every month ❑ Once every week ❑ Once every day
14. Does your family have a membership to any museums or other educational or cultural institutions? (Circle one) Yes No
15. How frequently has your family visited a museum or other educational or cultural institution in the past year? (Check one)

    ❑ None ❑ 1 to 2 ❑ 3–5 ❑ Once every month ❑ Once every week ❑ Once every day
16. Has anyone in your family attended or contributed to a community event or project over the past year? (Circle one) Yes No

    If yes, please describe the event or project: (For example: community dinner, fund drive, workshop, lecture, town meeting . . .)
17. Did you or another parent/guardian visit your student's school this year (during 8th grade)?

    If yes, how many times this year? _______times this year

    If yes, what was the nature of your visit(s)? (For example: Parent conference, parent's night, student performance, conference with guidance counselor, conference with special needs counselor . . .)

    If no, do you have any suggestions for how Codman Academy could better involve you in your student's educational experience?

    How many children in your family currently receive free or reduced lunch? _________

Source: School files.

Exhibit 9

Codman Academy Financial Statements

	Fiscal Year Ended June 30		
	2005	*2006*	*2007*
		(All numbers in US dollars)	
Revenue			
State and federal sources	1,118,436	1,195,950	1,356,899
Government grants	161,924	177,272	131,166
Private support	105,000	112,759	129,897
Program fees	12,371	14,067	17,742
General revenue and capital grants	105,981	287,208	493,535
Total revenue	1,503,712	1,787,256	2,129,239
Operating Expenses			
Salaries and wages	646,573	889,516	1,017,406
Payroll taxes and benefits	56,877	70,606	114,035
Recruitment and staff development	14,066	43,666	40,250
Instructional and program expenses	109,659	183,934	227,590
Consultants and service contractors	232,048	182,745	131,936
Administrative expenses	126,257	122,072	119,961
Facilities	51,936	66,003	70,945
Furniture and equipment	21,718	38,389	19,821
Depreciation	86,343	107,152	127,136
Total operating expenses	1,345,477	1,704,083	1,869,080
Increase in net assets	158,235	83,173	260,159

Source: Annual reports and case writer analysis.

Exhibit 10

Codman Academy Organizational Structure

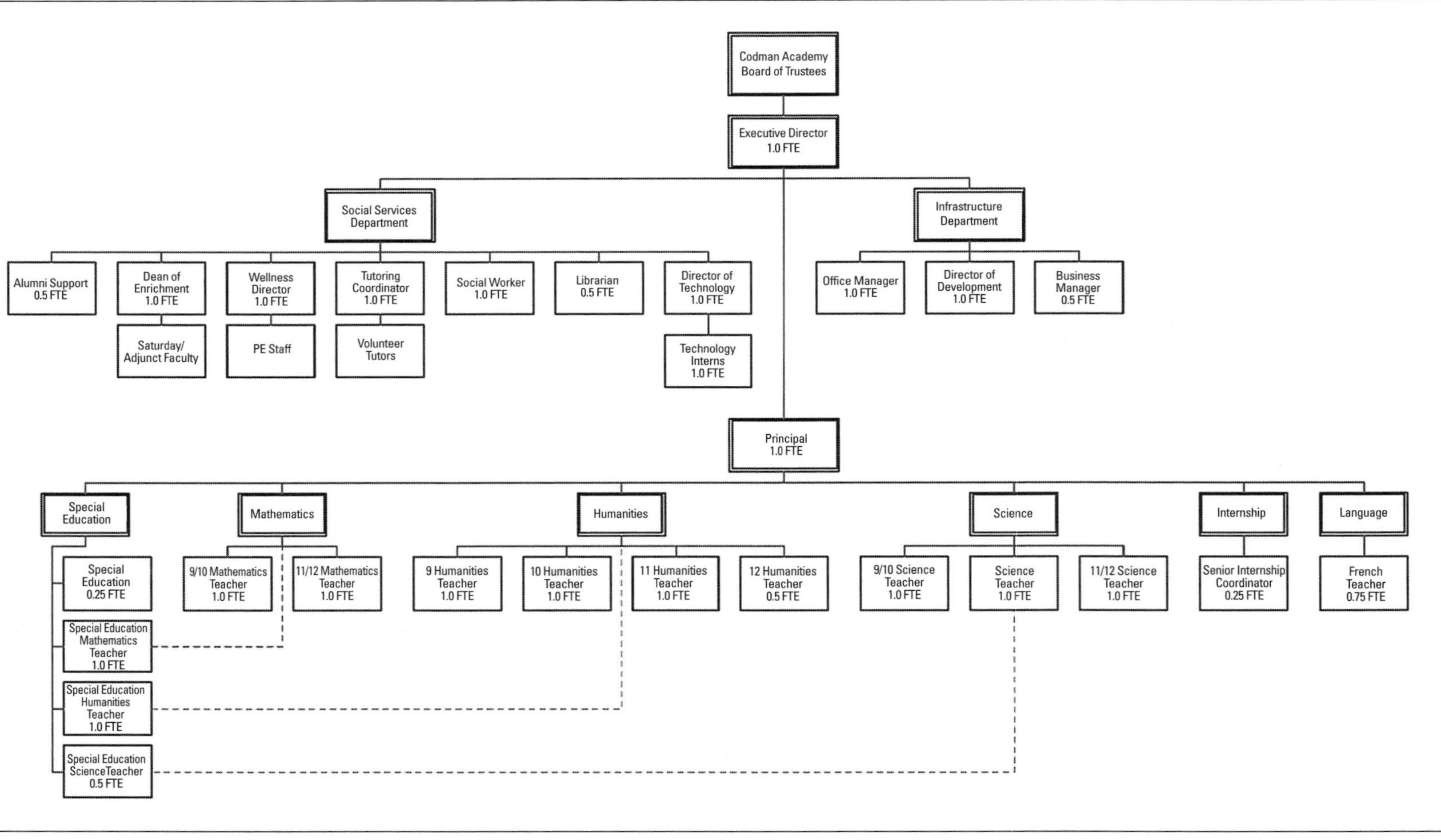

Source: School files.

Exhibit 11

Codman Academy Teaching Staff Data

Teaching Staff Data (School Year 2007-2008)

Total Number of Teaching Staff	13
Percent Certified	80%
Teacher Experience Level	
0-2 years	23%
2-4 years	16%
4-6 years	33%
6-8 years	0%
8-10 years	0%
10+ years	23%

Teacher Retention

School Year	*Total Number of Teachers*	*Total Number Who Left the School*
2004-2005	8	2
2005-2006	9	2
2006-2007	11	2

Source: School files and case writer analysis.

Exhibit 12

Codman Academy Student Enrollment and Graduation Data

	Class of 05	*Class of 06*	*Class of 07*	*Class of 08*	*Class of 09*	*Class of 10*	*Class of 11*
Lottery/Entry Year	2001	2002	2003	2004	2005	2006	2007
Admitted	34	40	40	43	40	40	40
Waitlisted	6	10	22	23	27	28	68
Graduated	**12**	**17**	**19**	**12***			

Source: School files and case writer analysis.

*Expected.

Exhibit 13a

Codman Academy Alumni College Attendance

College	*Class*	*Total*
Anna Maria College	2006	1
Bates	2007	1
Boston College	2006	1
Boston University	2006	1
Bowdoin College	2005	1
Brandeis	2006	1
	2007	1
College of Eastern Nazarene	2006	1
Emmanuel College	2006	1
Hesser College	2005	2
Holy Cross	2006	1
	2007	2
Johnson and Wales University	2005	1
	2006	1
Kentucky State University	2006	2
Landmark College	2007	1
Marietta	2007	1
Mills	2007	1
Mount Holyoke	2007	1
North Carolina A & T University	2005	1
Northeastern University	2005	1
	2007	1
Regis College	2006	2
	2007	3
Roxbury Community College	2005	1
	2007	1
Simmons College	2005	1
Trinity College	2007	2
UMASS Amherst	2005	4
	2006	1
UMASS Boston	2005	1
	2006	2
Utica	2007	2
Wentworth Institute of Technology	2005	1
Wheelock College	2005	1
Bunker Hill Community College	2007	1
Grand Total		48

College Type	*Class*	*Total*
Four-year	2005	14
	2006	15
	2007	16
Four-year Total		45
Two-year	2005	1
	2007	2
Two-year Total		3
Grand Total		48

Source: School files.

Exhibit 13b

Massachusetts and National High School Graduation Rate by Subgroup, Class of 2001

	Total %	*American Indian* %	*Asian American* %	*Latino* %	*Black* %	*White* %
Massachusetts	73	I	76	49	65	78
National	70	54	79	52	51	72

Source: J. Greene and G. Forster, "Public High School Graduation and College Readiness Rates in the United States," September 2003, http://www.manhattan-institute.org/pdf/ewp_03.pdf, accessed December 3, 2007, and case writer analysis.

Legend: I = Insufficient data to calculate graduation rate.

Exhibit 13c

Proportion of Students Who Graduate with College-Ready Transcripts, Class of 2001

	Total %	*American Indian* %	*Asian American* %	*Latino* %	*Black* %	*White* %
Massachusetts	41	M	38	21	35	47
National	36	21	46	22	25	39

Source: J. Greene and G. Forster, "Public High School Graduation and College Readiness Rates in the United States," September 2003, http://www.manhattan-institute.org/pdf/ewp_03.pdf, accessed December 3, 2007, and case writer analysis.

Legend: M = Missing high school graduation rate.

CASE 4.4

Stacey Childress ■ Debbie Kozar

Frederick Douglass Charter School: The Renewal Decision

> If there is no struggle, there is no progress. Those who profess to favor freedom, and deprecate agitation, are men who want crops without plowing up the ground, they want rain without thunder and lightning.
>
> —*Frederick Douglass*

On a late afternoon in March 2005, Jim Peyser, chair of the Massachusetts Board of Education, prepared for a final hearing on the future of the Frederick Douglass Charter School (FDCS). Opened in 2000 in Boston's Hyde Park neighborhood, the school served nearly 350 students by the fifth and final year of its charter. FDCS leaders had applied for a renewal to operate the school for another five years. Peyser considered the decisions the board made about the fate of charter schools an important element of the state's overall accountability system for its public schools.

For Peyser, deciding whether or not to renew a school's charter required more than just looking at test scores. He explained, "My framework for thinking about whether or not to renew a school's charter comes down to two variables. One is the strength of the organization, and the other is the strength of the educational program. The latter is primarily demonstrated by MCAS[1] results, but I'm open to considering other factors in evaluating the impact a school has on students."

Through his full-time job as a partner in the NewSchools Venture Fund, Peyser was familiar with the national debate about how to effectively measure charter school performance. He also knew that after an extremely rough start, FDCS supporters claimed the school was turning itself around and experiencing real pockets of success. Even so, the school had not achieved the ambitious performance aspirations that the founders committed to when they received their original charter in 2000.

As the meeting time drew near, FDCS parents and students began filling the boardroom. Some wore pins inscribed, "I love my charter school." Others carried pictures of the school's namesake, famed abolitionist Frederick Douglass. Having turned down renewal requests before, Peyser understood the potential repercussions: "The hardest thing about closing a school is the dislocation it creates for students. It's difficult for kids, but also for their families, because generally speaking, they like their schools. All schools have success stories, so some kids thrive, even in a bad school. And if they weren't thriving in their previous school, closing their charter school is really a harsh loss."

As he called the meeting to order, Peyser knew that the decision would boil down to one question: How good is good enough?

The Charter School Phenomenon

Charter schools were nonsectarian public schools of choice that operated with freedom from many of the regulations that applied to traditional public schools. The "charter" establishing each school was a performance contract detailing the school's mission, program, goals, students served, and measures of success.[2] The theory of change underpinning the charter movement asserted that if schools received increased autonomy from district bureaucracies, union contracts, and credentialing requirements for teachers and principals, then they would produce better results for the students who chose to attend them. Charter school advocates believed that improved results would be driven by increased accountability to a variety of stakeholders and by the competition created when families could choose from multiple high-quality, publicly funded options for their children's education.

The charter movement began in 1991, when the state of Minnesota passed legislation supporting the formation of charter schools. By 2005, 40 states, Puerto Rico, and Washington, D.C., had similar laws that formed the foundation for the over 3,400 charter schools that served nearly one million American students by 2005 (**Exhibit 1**).

The dramatic growth of charter schools was partially due to the broad bipartisan political support they received. Presidents Bill Clinton and George W. Bush each supported charter schools vocally and financially during their administrations, increasing yearly grants available to charter schools from the U.S. Department of Education to over $200 million by 2005. In addition to federal support, charters received wide-scale support at the grassroots level. Charter schools were typically founded by parents, teachers, community organizations, social entrepreneurs, or leaders of existing schools converted to charter status. Founders were often motivated by the desire to implement an alternative vision of schooling, serve a specific target population, or gain autonomy from district regulations.

Charter Schools in Massachusetts

Massachusetts had a rich education history dating back to the seventeenth century. The state had been the first in the United States to open a public school, establish a university, and provide a free education for all its children. The passage of the Massachusetts Education Reform Act of 1993 marked a turning point in modern education for the state. With this act, Massachusetts embraced two forms of education reform: statewide standardized tests and charter schools.

On the testing front, the Massachusetts Comprehensive Assessment System (MCAS) was developed to hold students and schools accountable for their academic performance. The MCAS, a standards-based test administered to all Massachusetts students, became the benchmark for measuring students, schools, and districts. Noted as "exceptionally, clear, specific, and measurable," Massachusetts's standards were viewed by some outside observers as the "best in the nation."[3]

Following the 1993 law, the first charter school opened its doors in Massachusetts in 1994, and over the next 10 years charters experienced varying degrees of success and support. Massachusetts law provided for two categories of charter schools: Commonwealth and Horace Mann. Commonwealth charter schools were start-up schools that operated with legal and financial autonomy from local school districts. Horace Mann charters allowed existing district-run schools to convert to charter status and, unlike Commonwealth charters, were subject to some of the same educational policies and labor agreements as traditional district schools. Massachusetts was a "single-authorizer" state, meaning that aspiring charter founders applied directly to the state department of education (DOE), the only agency able to grant charters. Many other states followed a "multi-authorizer" model, in which other entities such as universities, local school districts, or various nonprofits were able to issue charters to founding teams.

Massachusetts charter schools experienced slow but steady growth, and by 2005, 57 were operating in the state, with an enrollment that was mostly low-income and minority students. The relatively slow growth was partially attributed to legislation that capped the number of charters available each year, a concern for many charter school advocates. One analyst noted that these caps had "the effect of blocking future charter school growth in several urban areas, including Boston."

The approval process for receiving a new charter in Massachusetts was also considered one of the most rigorous in the nation. The DOE developed a Charter School Office (CSO), which supported applicants throughout the approval process, conducted rigorous screening of applications, and recommended charter applicants for approval to the DOE. One national charter law analyst described receiving a Massachusetts charter as akin to passing through the eye of a needle.

Even so, Massachusetts law was considered generous in the amount of freedom schools received. According to Shaka Mitchell, director of policy at the Center for Education Reform,[4] "The Massachusetts law gives schools a lot of autonomy, so it gives them room to breathe. In some ways, that means it also gives them enough rope to hang themselves." The majority of charter schools embraced their independence and succeeded over the term of their charters. Only a handful of charters closed due to financial, managerial, or academic reasons (**Exhibit 2**).

Founding the Frederick Douglass Charter School (FDCS)

The five founders of FDCS (Ben Anderson, Joyce Coleman, Mike Flaherty, Dennis McCoy, and Jackie Walsh) met in the winter of 1997 through their involvement in an intensive summer and after-school program run by Anderson (see **Exhibit 3** for founder bios). The program focused on preparing elementary students for the entrance exams for three of Boston's premier high schools: Boston Latin School, Boston Latin Academy, and the John D. O'Bryant School of Mathematics and Science.

In early October 1998, Walsh and her husband, McCoy, became interested in the idea of creating a charter school during a dinner party they attended. Another dinner guest ran a charter school in Boston's Hyde Park area and encouraged the couple to act immediately. The political environment added fuel to their fire: Boston was nearing its cap of available charters. Once Walsh and McCoy committed to securing a charter, the other three founders quickly came aboard.

While their backgrounds ranged from politics to parenting, the founders were united by their concern over the shortcomings of urban education. Anderson explained, "We saw the broader system as failing students. We can prepare the most underserved students to get into Boston Latin, but it's a zero-sum game. One student gets in, another student doesn't. We wanted to start up a school to address the lack of supply of college preparatory paths."

With the application prospectus due by mid-October, the founders had no time to waste. Through long nights of discussions, frequent e-mails, and heated debates, they determined a mission, focus, and name for the school. The founders knew they wanted to build a college preparatory school for urban youth focused on research and communication skills. In famed abolitionist Frederick Douglass, they found the embodiment of their vision. The founders developed a mission "to prepare students for college through a rigorous curriculum focused on research, writing and public speaking." They also aimed "to foster the values of justice, integrity and personal responsibility which Frederick Douglass himself so effectively modeled in his lifetime."

The team wrote the entire proposal the weekend before the deadline, without time to proofread the document. Walsh recalled that after the application was submitted she had the horrifying realization that she had misspelled "Massachusetts." Yet, even with the typographical errors, FCDS was "the top-rated applicant" of the 32 teams that submitted proposals, and was granted one of six charters that the DOE issued that year. The charter designated FDCS as a fifth through twelfth grade school, and the team's goal was to open in fall of 2000 with fifth and sixth grade classes, and add a grade in each subsequent year, graduating its first class from high school in 2007.

The Planning Year

While overjoyed to have received the charter, "the honeymoon ended abruptly," remembered cofounder Joyce Coleman. For the five entrepreneurs, the planning year was life-changing in many ways, beyond founding FDCS. Some changes, such as Anderson's and Flaherty's engagements, were celebrated. Others, such as Coleman's divorce and the separation of Walsh and McCoy, created challenges for the founders and the school. Yet they all agreed that whatever the status of their personal lives, building the school could not wait.

Without a facility, principal, teaching staff, curriculum, or a single student, the goal of opening in September 2000 loomed ominously. Securing a principal was the first priority. The founders cast a broad net and landed a candidate who was surprising to some observers. Jim Bower, a 61-year-old Caucasian educator who built a career in suburban schools, had applied for the job. Assuming the school would "be looking for black educators,"[5] Bower was surprised and excited when he received an offer to lead the school. For the founders, race and age did not matter—they wanted the best candidate for the job, and because charter schools were so new, they had not expected to attract someone with Bower's history of excellence in school leadership.

With a principal in place, the team turned its attention to recruiting a student body. They held coffee chats for potential students and parents to learn about the school. During these open houses, Bower spoke passionately about the school, saying, "This isn't my school, or the founders' school. It's our school."[6] By February of 2000, FDCS recruited 102 incoming students—51 fifth-graders and 51 sixth-graders—on the promise that the school would have a home by September.

After a few unsuccessful leads, the team finally secured a location in May, renting the second floor of a Catholic archdiocese building. Because the facility was small and a considerable distance from many of the students, it was only a temporary solution. The founding team planned to continue their search for a more permanent home. At the time, Bower explained, "We will be underserved the first year, both the students and the faculty, but there is no choice. . . . We will paint it and we will clean it and we will make it shine so when the kids come, they will be proud."[7]

A Bumpy Start

When FDCS opened its doors, the founders and staff were unable to predict how turbulent the first year would be. The principal, a dean, and 11 teachers struggled to establish a culture of learning and respect among the student body. Without a set of working norms, FDCS struggled to build its educational and operating plans while simultaneously implementing them. Most importantly, the school's educators needed to develop a comprehensive curriculum, but few teachers had time to focus on long-term planning due to the daily challenges of teaching in a start-up school.

Facilities

The school worked hard to use its space effectively, but the facilities created various operating challenges. Because of space limitations, classrooms were separated by temporary partitions, and often students and teachers could access their classrooms only by walking through other classrooms. Disruptions happened often. One teacher remembered how "students liked to stand up and peek over the partitions into the other classrooms," often distracting students in both classes.

The shared space also had an impact on the school's culture. Purnima Kochikar, a board member, observed that the facilities situation created a sense of limbo for students and faculty. "People always felt like it was a temporary place while they were waiting for a permanent home." Maintaining order throughout the school remained a challenge for students and teachers as they learned to adjust to one another and their new surroundings.

School Culture and Safety

In order to build a sense of culture, the school held a community meeting in which the first-year class selected the school's core values as the foundation for their Citizenship Code. The students chose compassion, respect, tolerance, cooperation, honesty, and responsibility as the pillars of the school. While many students embraced these values, a number of students struggled to live up to them because, as the school noted in its first annual report, "breaking old habits does not come easy."

Longer school days and small class sizes of 16 to 18 students per teacher were considered critical to building a school that fostered an atmosphere of community and safety. Having teachers and staff who knew students by name promoted a sense of unity. For many parents, Frederick Douglass was viewed as a safe alternative to Boston's district schools. Looking back, teacher Melinda Fernandez observed, "When you send your kid to a Boston public school, you never know what everyone else has. There are police officers. There are metal detectors. Here at Frederick Douglass, you didn't have that. It was pretty much a safe haven. Parents felt like it was safe for their kids to go here."

The founding vision was to prepare students for college. From the beginning, school leaders worked to position college as a viable option for all students. Wings of the school were names for different colleges such as Howard and Vassar, and students went on field trips to visit neighboring universities. The school created "a culture of not *if*, but *where* one is going to go to college."[8]

Leadership Transition

During the spring of the first year, Headmaster Bower decided to leave the school. While the separation was mutual, some speculated that the principal's "top-down view" of education was ill suited for an urban start-up. Although Bower officially finished the first year, for practical purposes board member and founder Ben Anderson and the two deans took over the operations of the school. The uncertainty about the school's leadership and the challenges of the start-up phase took its toll on the staff. Only three of the 11 original teachers decided to stay for a second year.

The start of FDCS's second year was marked by continued uncertainty. With no headmaster in place, Anderson and the deans were forced to continue leading the school. While Anderson focused on strategic issues facing the school such as finding a permanent home, securing funding, and recruiting teachers, the two deans managed daily operations. For the deans, the arrangement was particularly challenging because neither had experience leading a school, much less one in start-up mode. As one teacher recalled, "neither of them were very good leaders for this sort of situation."

Finally, in November 2001, after an exhaustive search, Wanda Speede was named Head of School. Anderson recalled, "Wanda came in when there was a leadership vacuum, and people were thrilled to have her. But there was a very short honeymoon because she had to quickly make some things happen to get the school back on track."

Speede, an accomplished African American educator, described coming to FDCS "like being home."[9] The challenge of moving the school forward was her key priority. Speede recalls, "Pretty much everyone described the place [as] having had an unfortunate false start the first time around. They needed to be redirected, organized, and managed effectively." Speede immediately focused on understanding the strengths and weaknesses of the school, engaging parents in an open dialogue about their children's education, and establishing an accountability plan with a set of operating guidelines to turn the school around (**Exhibit 4**).

Ongoing Operations

FDCS attracted students from the Dorchester section of Boston. During the first five years of operation, enrollment and retention remained high with waiting lists ranging from 30 to 130 students (**Exhibit 5**). Ninety percent of the students were African American, and 60% qualified for free or reduced-price lunch. FDCS was viewed by some as serving a population of students who "would easily get lost in the larger system" of Boston Public Schools. Anderson remarked, "FDCS was an environment for children who had had unsuccessful, unsatisfactory experiences in other schools. I think our children were behind and really put off by education. I think we got good at serving those kinds of children, ones that usually are the most underserved."

Ensuring that students were engaged in education and focused on social and academic progress remained a constant problem for the school. Behavior was often described by observers and staff as "chaotic." For instance, in the 2003–2004 school year, of the 270 students at FDCS, 134 students committed at least one "suspendable" infraction for a total of 328 suspensions. The reasons for suspension ranged from minor disruptive horseplay to rare but serious fights.

Some teachers believed the disciplinary problems were caused by continual growth. According to teacher Christina Farese, "We had a difficult range of students. We had grades six through ten by 2004. There's quite a developmental difference between middle schoolers and high schoolers, but high schoolers were supposed to follow the same rules that the middle schoolers followed."

The divide between the middle school and high school was a point of contention for some students who felt that the school favored the lower grades. One year, the principal revoked the high school students' cafeteria privileges and sports. According to one staff member, with little left to lose, the students became more "rebellious," further escalating their behavior problems.

Adding to the school's operational challenges was a midyear move during its fourth year. Having outgrown its Hyde Park facility, the school community welcomed the move to a larger space in Roslindale. While the new building had many new benefits such as science laboratories and a gymnasium, it was a suboptimal solution because FDCS was again forced to share the facility with another school. Even after the move, Speede and the board continued to explore opportunities for a permanent home, since FDCS would outgrow the new building within three years.

School Staff

Within the first two years of operations, FDCS had three different headmasters. Under Speede, the school's leadership finally began to stabilize. To some within the school, Speede was a "strong leader" who was "extremely visionary" and "passionate" about the school and the staff. Others saw her as a "strong personality" who ran the school as if "it was her way or no way." Regardless of people's perceptions of her leadership, everyone agreed that one of the biggest challenges she faced was dealing with staff retention.

Under FDCS's model of adding a grade each year, the school was continually recruiting staff. This task was compounded by faculty attrition of nearly 70% in the first two years. One administrator noted the impact that the staff exodus had on FDCS: "When you hire a new teacher, it takes a year, at least, for them to become part of the culture of the school. If they're only staying for one or two years, you don't have a staff that has the culture built into it. We suffered from that."

While attrition had a noticeable effect on the school, not everyone was surprised by the staff departures. Farese explained, "A lot of schools have attrition. Fifty percent of new teachers leave the profession in five years. It's really hard, and at a charter school, I think it's harder, because they expect more of you."

To combat teacher attrition, FDCS worked to create programs that supported teachers. In 2004, Speede decided to shorten the school day on Fridays so faculty could meet from 1:15 to 3:15 for professional development. Inexperienced teachers were also enrolled in The Skillful Teacher, a 36-hour graduate course focused on classroom management and instruction. Internally, the school began to focus time and attention on encouraging senior faculty to support junior faculty. Bi-monthly departmental meetings were held to discuss classroom difficulties, potential curriculum integrations, and students' performance.

Curriculum and Instruction

The school opened in 2000 without an organized curriculum. Instead, teachers remembered being left alone with "some vague guidelines." Over time, the school focused on building a coherent curriculum across grades and subjects based on the Massachusetts Curriculum Frameworks. Observers noted that the curriculum became "more articulated" and "clearer" through the use of standard syllabi for each class and the predetermined exit skills for each grade. Students' academic achievement was assessed based on both internal standards of student effort, citizenship, and academics, and external standardized tests such as the MCAS and the SAT 9.[10]

The typical classroom at FDCS had 17 students with varying academic backgrounds and performance. The school made the decision to employ an inclusion model, placing high-performing students in the same classroom as students with learning needs, to encourage students to help one another learn. While the varying skill levels complicated lesson planning, some faculty enjoyed the challenge of teaching students with various needs.

In order to manage classroom dynamics, the school utilized "Lorraine Monroe's Blackboard Configuration" (BBC) to provide structure to lessons. The BBC was a widely adopted instructional organization model designed to provide structure by establishing expectations and routines for students through elements called "Do Now," "Aim," and "Assignment." Written on the blackboard before class, the "Do Now" was a 5–7 minute warm-up activity that students were expected to begin on their own upon entering the classroom. "Aim" was an explicit skill-development goal for the day, and the "Assignment" represented the day's new work. FDCS's modified BBC allowed teachers to structure class into three parts: a 3–4 minute opening activity, a formal lesson plan with stated learning objectives and core skills, and a discussion of the night's homework assignment. While the system was implemented in every classroom, some felt it was more form than function. Yet, for Melinda Fernandez, a high school teacher, the approach "worked because it showed the students what they needed to do in class." However, she noted that "you really need to have students do something that is going to mentally challenge them . . . not all teachers did this."

In addition to providing traditional classroom instruction, the school offered additional support and learning opportunities. FDCS offered a summer program for students who needed or wanted remedial academic help, and during the school year offered peer and faculty tutoring and weekly MCAS review sessions. These supplemental services were instituted to improve student academic achievement and ultimately prepare students for success in college.

FDCS also created innovative programs focused on its mission of public speaking. In 2004, the school began a symposium on elocution and public speech writing. This elective class focused eighth-grade students on the research and study of speeches from the abolitionist and civil rights movement. For many of the students, the class was their first opportunity to study African American leaders and "learn more about their own history." Speede, the creator of the speech academy, explained the rationale for the program: "The abolitionist connection was because of Frederick Douglass. Kids always think the abolitionist movement was 300 years ago, and that the civil rights movement was hundreds of years ago. We wanted to have kids bring it alive."

The program culminated with an end-of-the-year celebration in which students wrote speeches and presented them in front of their peers and parents. According to Kim Joyce, the program's instructor, the performance was "powerful" and those in attendance were "inspired to see how much the young people had to say."

Funding

Like all charter schools in Massachusetts, FDCS received funding from the district, state, and federal governments. On average, the school received just over $10,000 per pupil in entitlements and grants. In addition to government support, FDCS actively sought grants from foundations and individuals. With its unique vision for urban education, the school was successful in securing donations from the Walton Family Foundation, the Nellie Mae Foundation, and numerous small foundations and individuals.

In addition to traditional sources of funding, the school used creative events both to bring the community together and to raise money. Through a partnership with Walden Media, FDCS held auctions and private screenings of movies. In 2004, a showing of *Around the World in 80 Days* brought together 500 community members and school supporters to raise over $30,000.

While the school experienced some success raising funds, many within the school felt it was not enough. According to one teacher, "There are certainly schools out there that have more money as a result of fundraising, and I don't think we did a good enough job of that. We had one big fundraiser per year. That's not enough."

Some school staff felt that the board composition was suboptimal for major fundraising. According to Speede:

> I know boards of other charter schools. They have people who are connected business-wise in the city. We had community-based people who cared about kids rather than people with deep pockets. We had a working board of people who were not terribly high profile but were committed to the vision, as opposed to a board made up of very high-profile people who could therefore bring in money.

FDCS leaders were always concerned with balancing the annual budget (**Exhibit 6**). Most years, the school was able to break even or have a surplus. However, in the 2003–2004 academic year, FDCS ran a deficit of just over $250,000. School leaders attributed the shortfall to overlapping rent, moving costs, and renovation expenses associated with school's midyear move to a new facility in Roslindale. Although many FDCS supporters understood the reasons for the increased expenses, the deficit nevertheless highlighted the difficulties of the school's financial situation.

Approaching the Renewal Horizon

During their fourth year of operation, FDCS leaders were convinced that their most turbulent times were behind them, and looked forward to petitioning the state to renew the school's charter beyond the initial five-year term. The process included interaction with the state's charter school office and outside reviewers, along with creating a renewal application that addressed the school's progress to date and its plans for the future.

State Review Process

For the lucky few charter school applicants who received charters from the DOE, the relationship between the school and the state's Charter School Office (CSO) became one marked by oversight and accountability. While helpful in connecting charter school applicants to resources during the application process, once the school was operating, the staff of the CSO could not be "too much of a friend or an advocate to the charter school because ultimately we are reviewing them," remarked Hannah Richman, director of Charter School Development. This transition from promoter to reviewer was felt acutely by some charter school leaders. One charter administrator observed that "the CSO was not designed to support charter schools. It was not providing us with technical assistance, not providing us with resources. They were, in fact, a group that was really judging us."

The perception of a shift to oversight was not without merit. Charters were required to submit an initial accountability plan and annual reports to the DOE through the CSO. The CSO was charged with reviewing the performance of charter schools on a regular basis, beginning with mandatory site visits in the second and third year of a new school's operations. The CSO could perform an optional fourth-year site inspection of schools judged to be struggling with academic or management problems. Because charters carried five-year terms, schools wishing to continue operations beyond the initial term submitted renewal applications to the CSO at the end of their fourth year. As part of the renewal decision process, an independent third party conducted an evaluation during the fall of the fifth year. The CSO then synthesized the inspection and evaluation information, along with the renewal application, and recommended a course of action to the state education commissioner. The commissioner then advised the state board of education on whether to reject the application, or to renew the school's charter outright, or with conditions.

First Warning

In April 2004, members of the CSO decided to conduct a fourth-year site visit at FDCS, given the findings from routine inspections in years two and three. Using an established protocol, the CSO team assessed the school based on the three pillars of the Massachusetts charter school accountability program: academic success, organizational viability, and faithfulness to the original charter. According to a member of the review team, the decision to perform a site visit at FDCS was a "result of concerns about the school's ability to provide affirmative evidence in these three key areas as the school moved towards the renewal process."

The site visit did not come as a surprise to FDCS staff members who had experienced the school's turbulent first years. Instead, it became a rallying point for the school's most vocal supporters. Speede and other staff members welcomed the opportunity to show the CSO how far the school had come in the last year. Even though the school still struggled to achieve consistent academic success, many of the issues raised in prior visits had been addressed (**Exhibit 7**). School leaders hoped that this visit would be an opportunity to begin building the case for renewal.

While both the school and the CSO had good intentions coming into the inspection, the site visit did not meet the expectations of either side. Administrators, faculty, board members, and parents complained that they felt "uncomfortable" with the inspection team. Some characterized a few members of the team as "having their own agenda" against the school. Some CSO staffers noted hostility toward their inspection. One member of the inspection team explained that while "there were never explicitly accusations of racism," they felt "undertones" that the school did not think the predominately Caucasian team could understand and assess urban education.

Preparing for Renewal

In June 2004, FDCS formally applied for a five-year renewal of its charter. In documents sent to the CSO, the school both highlighted its successes and acknowledged areas for improvement. The application explained some of the challenges FDCS had experienced during its first charter term—specifically, leadership and staff turnover and facilities. The school also included its plan for the next five years detailing enhancements and changes in academic standards, facilities, and staff support.

The next step in the renewal process was an impartial inspection of the school by a third-party reviewer that would produce a report on its findings, but not make a recommendation about the renewal decision. The board of education would use the inspection report as part of a portfolio of information when deciding the fate of FDCS. In October 2004, the CSO hired SchoolWorks, an independent education consulting company, to conduct an in-depth, four-day, on-site assessment. Aretha Miller, project manager for SchoolWorks, described the rationale for the inspection:

> There are three primary purposes for the charter renewal visit. First, the renewal inspection provides current information about the school from an external, independent source. Second, the renewal inspection is the only in-depth, on-site study of the school that looks closely at teaching, curriculum, and management. Third, the renewal inspection visit maintains the balance between internal and external accountability that characterizes the Massachusetts public charter school accountability system. Most charter schools tend to be isolated and tend to reflect in a vacuum. There is no one on the outside holding up the mirror to them to see if there is another way they could do this. At the end of the visit people start thinking about new ways to tackle problems.

Miller tried to stress to leaders at the school that inspectors were "not coming in to catch them doing badly" but rather to "collaborate" with them. During the inspection, the group of four consultants became deeply ingrained in the operations of the school. The team observed 48 lessons, held focus groups with 10 parents and 20 students, and conducted one-on-one interviews with 25 teachers, 7 board members, and 8 administrators. At the end of the inspection, the team wrote an inspection report which was shared with both the school and the CSO (**Exhibit 8**).

The team reported that, organizationally, the school was improving, but teacher attrition remained a factor that "adversely affected the school's ability to establish a sound, cohesive culture." However, SchoolWorks saw the school as "well positioned to structurally deal with a growing school and increasing curriculum demands."

The report found that the school had "established a sound and viable framework for improving teaching and learning through a standards-based curriculum, teacher-developed syllabi and lesson plans to build a rigorous academic program in line with its mission." But the report also found that the quality of instruction and classroom management was dramatically uneven across classrooms, which weakened the school's ability to implement the academic program it had established. The team observed evidence that student behavior was a major obstacle to improving the quality of the classroom experience, including multiple instances of students directly insulting their teachers, and teachers responding in kind.

In terms of academic performance, SchoolWorks reported that FDCS "failed to achieve its accountability plan goals in math and reading." The school founders had set a goal of students achieving at the 50th percentile in reading and math on the SAT 9. FDCS had not achieved the goal at any grade level in either math or reading. The report elaborated on SAT 9 scores:

> In the sixth grade, results over the four years generally indicate very few dramatic gains either within the course of a year or during the full testing period. Generally, the seventh grade results do not vary substantially over the three years of testing. The figures for eighth grade in both reading and math demonstrate little variance between fall and spring scores or over the two years of test administrations.

On the MCAS test, FDCS had achieved its targets in English from 2002 to 2004, but failed to make its goals in mathematics. The school scored below state and Boston district averages in the proficiency category in both subjects in all grades.

Even though the inspection report highlighted both the positive and negative aspects of the school, some within the school felt too much emphasis was placed on the challenges. One faculty member described the inspection as "witch-huntish." One of the deans summed up the school's opinion of the experience with SchoolWorks:

> They came in and were very professional. They went about their job in a professional way. They were very data-driven. Am I pleased with the report they put out? No. I don't think their report was balanced. I felt they dwelled on the negative and did not dwell on the positive. There was no recognition of the fact that this was a school that was, in fact, looking at what it meant to be a black kid in Boston.

The Beginning of the End?

By the end of 2004, it became clear that the school's chance for renewal was in jeopardy. Some within the school blamed the CSO for not setting clearer standards for student achievement. Although the CSO admitted that there "was inconsistent communication from this office" due to "a changing staff," it refused to say that standards had changed. The office stated it was simply measuring the school against its own accountability plan (**Exhibit 4**). Yet, in the eyes of many FDCS supporters, the school appeared to be penalized for setting high goals. Anderson explained, "We were being held against the highest standard of where we wanted to be. And on another level we were being compared to the average scores in Boston public schools. The failure in the process is that it doesn't take into account your starting point. It only takes into account your ending point."

In February 2005, the commissioner of education recommended not to renew the charter, citing low academic performance and lack of progress over time, continuing high staff turnover, and concerns relating to instructional practice and curriculum. School supporters were outraged by the recommendation and believed that many of the problems FDCS was experiencing were problems other charter schools that were renewed faced as well, such as unstable financial conditions. Speede, who sometimes referred to the experience as the "non-renewal process" rather than the "renewal process," explained, "I think we are moving in the right direction. We need more time. Other schools that are 10 years old had similar data in their tenth year. I feel that we are being treated as a sacrificial lamb to show that the state is being tough in their treatment of charter schools."

On February 7, a special meeting of the board of education was held to allow supporters of FDCS to present evidence in support of renewal. Administrators, faculty, and students attended the hearing to show their support for the school. Some who could not attend wrote letters of support (**Exhibit 9**). Emotions ran high as parents and students fought for the school they loved. Melissa Clarke-Ferguson, whose eighth-grade daughter testified at the hearing, praised the school and stressed, "It takes a whole community to education a child. Frederick Douglass is a community school."

Speakers, including Ben Anderson, presented evidence comparing FDCS to Boston district schools (**Exhibit 10**). He stressed that FDCS's African American students outperformed most African American students in BPS middle schools. Analysis by the Massachusetts Charter School Association comparing students at FDCS to African American students in Boston's 32 open-enrollment schools revealed that if FDCS students were dispersed into these schools, they would have a two in three chance of attending a school with lower MCAS scores for African American students.

Additional testimony focused on comparing FDCS to other charter schools that had been renewed, but showed little difference between their academic performance and the performance of FDCS (**Exhibit 7**). For supporters, this was the overwhelming evidence in the case for renewal.

According to Sally Bachofer, coordinator of charter school accountability for the CSO, "Every school has its own yardstick. They have their own accountability plan. Every school has its own progress over time. These schools are independent schools. They should not be compared to each other. They should be evaluated independently in order for us to make the best decision."

The Final Decision

As Peyser settled into his seat and prepared to call the meeting to order, he ran through the four potential options for FDCS one last time:

Full Renewal

Historically, the DOE renewed charters even if they had not met all of their accountability goals, as long as they had shown substantial improvement over time. FDCS clearly struggled in its first two years but experienced increased stability in the later years. However, even though the school outperformed the majority of public schools in Boston among African American students, it still lagged Boston averages and most other charter schools.

Conditional Renewal

Conditional renewal allowed the DOE to increase oversight and require FDCS to reapply for renewal in two years instead of five. This option allowed the school to try to leverage the positive changes it had made, but ensured that if the school did not meet strict academic standards quickly, it would be shut down. On the other hand, the board realized it might be postponing the inevitable by choosing this option.

Conditional Renewal for Middle School Only

This option would require that the school stop serving high school and focus solely on middle school, and had similar benefits to the two-year conditional renewal. It would force the school to focus on existing grades instead of further expansion, potentially curbing some of its behavior problems. However, shrinking the school's size would significantly reduce its revenue and create unused capacity within the facility.

Non-renewal

Rejecting the renewal application would send a signal to Massachusetts charter schools that marginal performance was not enough to merit continued existence. Yet, by rejecting FDCS's renewal but renewing another Boston charter with similar data, the board ran a serious risk of backlash if it was perceived to be more lenient to some schools than others. Also, if the leaders of FDCS decided to fight the decision, the DOE would have to enter an expensive and lengthy hearing process.

By the end of the meeting, the fate of FDCS would be settled, and the state would have one more precedent to look back on when facing future renewal decisions.

Notes

1. The MCAS are criterion-referenced tests delivered as part of Massachusetts's public school accountability system.

2. Adapted from the U.S. Charter Schools website, http://www.uscharterschools.org/pub/uscs_docs/o/index.htm, accessed October 2005.

3. Richard W. Cross, Theodor Rebarber, and Justin Torres, editors, *Grading the System: The Guide to State Standards, Tests, and Accountability Policies* (Thomas B. Fordham Foundation, 2004), p. 20.

4. The Center for Education Reform is a national nonprofit research and advocacy organization focused on issues such as school choice, standards, and accountability.

5. Dick Lehr, "Birth of a School," *The Boston Globe Magazine,* September 3, 2000.

6. Ibid.

7. Ibid.

8. 2002 Site Visit Report (Malden, MA: Massachusetts Department of Education, 2002).

9. Adrian Walker, "The Boston Globe Adrian Walker Column" *The Boston Globe*, February 17, 2005, via Factiva, accessed September 2005.

10. The SAT 9 is a norm-referenced achievement test structured by grade level and content area, and is independent of state testing regimes.

Exhibit 1

Charter School Growth in the United States, 1991–2004

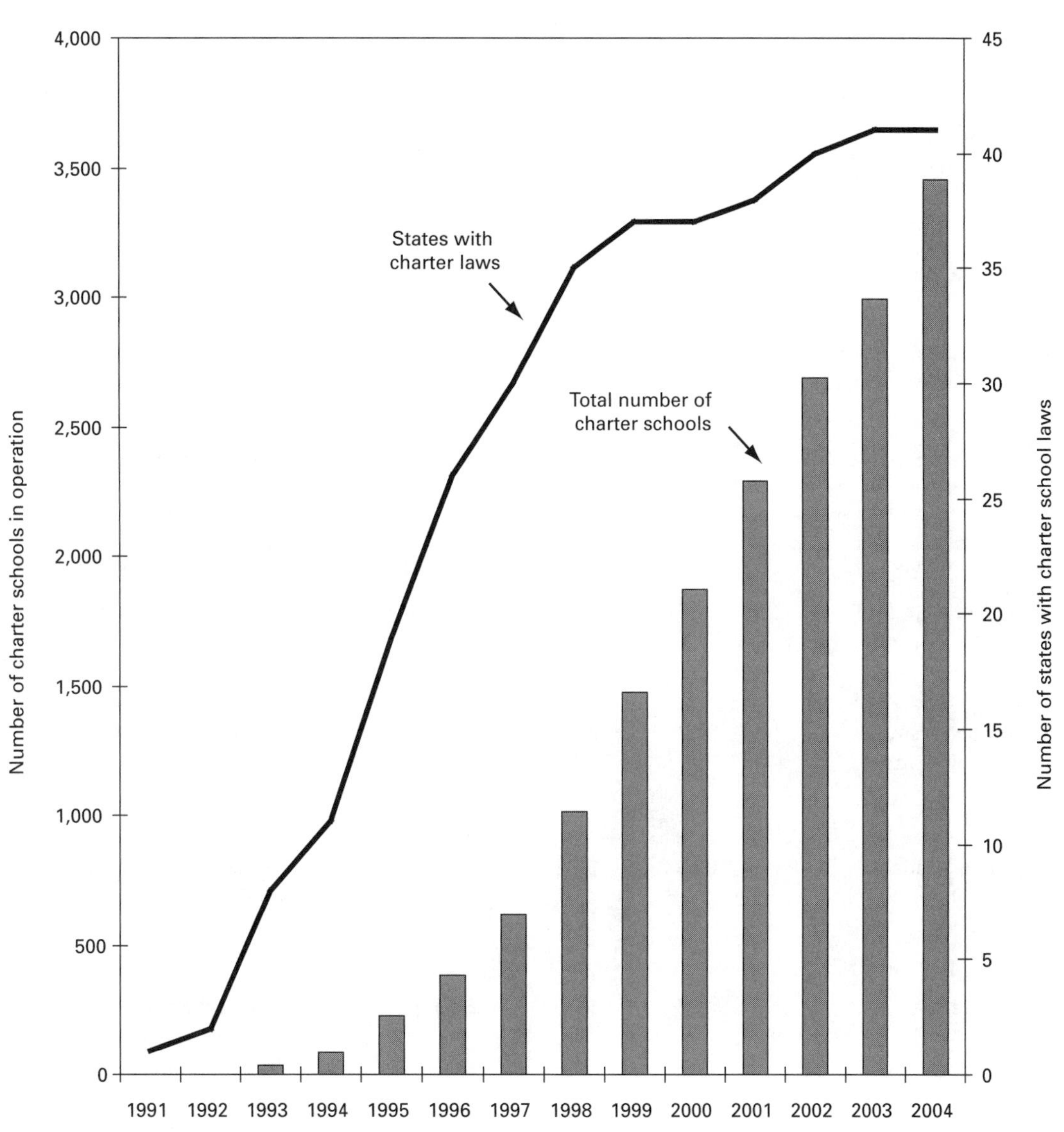

Source: Center for Education Reform and case writer analysis.

Note: Totals include charter schools and states within the 50 U.S. states and the District of Columbia.

Exhibit 2

Charter School Closures in Massachusetts, 1999–2004

Charter School	*Charter Granted*	*Charter Removed*	*Charter Status*	*Explanation*
Roxbury Charter High School for Business, Finance and Entrepreneurship[a]	2002	2004	Revoked	Financial instability Insufficient governance and administrative oversight
South End College Preparatory	2002	2002	Relinquished	Never opened
Northern Bristol County Regional Charter School	2002	2002	Relinquished	Never opened
Horace Mann High School of Essential Studies	1999	2000	Relinquished	Never opened
Lynn Community Charter School	1997	2002	Not renewed	Persistent academic problems Inability to meet accountability plan
Boston University Residential Charter School	1997	2000	Relinquished	Financial instability Low enrollment
North Star Academy Charter School	1996	2001	Relinquished	Persistent academic problems Low enrollment
YouthBuild	1995	1999	Relinquished	Persistent academic problems Insufficient management

Source: Center for Education Reform; Massachusetts Department of Education; case writer analysis.

[a]As of 2005, Roxbury Charter High was operating without a charter from the state.

Exhibit 3

Founders' Biographies as Represented in FDCS Charter Application

Ben Anderson is Director of The Magnet Program at The Steppingstone Foundation. In the last year, Ben developed a successful academic program that prepares under-served Boston schoolchildren to gain admissions to Boston Latin School and Boston Latin Academy. Prior experience included positions as a Site Director and Evaluator at Citizen Schools and as a Consultant at Mercer Management Consulting. He has recently served as an Allocation Committee Member for The United Way, as a Programming Committee Member for Citizen Schools and as a Class Agent for several schools.

Joyce Coleman is Director of Community Outreach and Volunteer Services at Carney Hospital. She is a lifelong resident of Dorchester and has three children in the Boston Public School system. She served on the advisory board to the School-To-Career office at BPS. She also has been involved in the development stages of another charter school.

Mike Flaherty is currently an Industrial Designer with the Learning System Group at GTE Internetworking. Mike served as the Special Assistant to former Massachusetts Senate President William M. Bulger for the last four years of the Senate President's tenure, acting as Chief Speech Writer and advisor on all educational issues. Since the Senate President's departure in early 1995, Mike has been involved in a number of innovative educational projects. He served as the chief content author and creative director for the *BusinessWeek* "Inside the GMAT" CD-ROM. He also developed a curriculum to prepare students in The Magnet Program at The Steppingstone Foundation to achieve the necessary score to attend one of Boston's open-enrollment schools.

Dennis McCoy is an experienced venture capitalist currently working with a small start-up company that merges medical devices with biotechnology. After graduating from Yale in 1988, he worked for a venture capital industry, Alex Brown and Sons, in Baltimore, MD. He has played an integral part in the planning of two startup companies (Dyax and Belmont Research), where he developed and wrote strategic plans.

Jacquelyn Walsh is a teacher at The Steppingstone Foundation in Dorchester and a regional representative for World Learning/The Experiment in International Living. She expects to receive her doctoral degree in Comparative Literature from New York University in August of 1999. After graduating Cum Laude with Distinction in Literature from Yale University in 1989, she taught English in Guatemala and Indonesia. From 1995–1998, she taught writing and research at New York University, Boston University, and Bentley College. She has received several awards and grants for academic excellence at NYU, including the Henry Mitchell McCracken Fellowship.

Source: FDCS internal documents.

Exhibit 4

Excerpts from Frederick Douglass Charter School Accountability Plan, January 2002

Charter School	*Expectation/Performance Standard*	*Method(s) of Assessment*
1.1a	FDCS students will show annual progress is establishing and sustaining subject grades of 80% or better; effort grades of 3 or better, and citizenship grades of 3 or better.	Link and summarize in-class formative assessment in academic subjects, progress and report cards, IEP recommendations and monitoring to support student growth and development.
1.1b	Students will score in the 50th percentile or above, and a minimum of 50% will score at level 3 or 4 (strong or mastery) on Standard 9 reading tests. 60% of students will score in the advanced, proficient, or needs improvement categories of MCSA ELS subtest.	Analysis of Standard 9 Reading performance results. Item analysis of MCAS ELS results.
1.1c	Students will score in the 50th percentile or better, and a minimum of 50% will score at level 3 or 4 (strong or mastery) on Standard 9 math tests. 60% of students will score in the advanced, proficient, or needs improvement categories of MCSA math subtest.	Annual comparison of Fall and Spring Stanford 9 Math results; analysis of student cohorts based on tenure at FDCS.
1.2a	Students will produce 80% of homework assignments on time. Students will demonstrate conduct consistent with the Code of Conduct. Students will attend school a minimum of 80% of each term. The number and range of students performing at honor roll status will increase quarterly.	Quarterly analysis of increases and decreases in attendance, disciplinary action, homework production and honor roll achievement.
2.1b	The school will meet all of its required expenses. The Board will achieve a balanced budget for each of its five years of operations.	Review monthly financial reports with the Board. Review enrollment data (also see section 2.2a).
2.2a	Maintain enrollment within 5% of target annually. On average, retain 90% or more of student body during its first five years of operations.	Enrollment analysis through application monitoring and attrition analysis.
2.4a	The school will retain 60% of its teaching staff over the first five years of its operations. The School will attract a balance of experienced and new teachers and staff.	Annual statistics will be compiled with an analysis of candidate pools, hiring process, and the reasons for attrition as documented by the Head of School in letters of resignation.
2.4d	Engage in collaborative partnership relationships with universities, other schools and organizations. Develop ongoing institutional relationships. Share expertise and resources. Focus partnership relationships on areas of need such as faculty mentoring, student support, parent/guardian training and leadership development, student exposure to college options, and technology development.	Assess development of partnerships annually. Quantify in-kind support.

Source: FDCS internal documents.

Exhibit 5

Frederick Douglass Operating Statistics for School Years 2001 through 2004

	Academic Year			
	2000-2001	*2001-2002*	*2002-2003*	*2003-2004*
School statistics				
Grades	5th-6th	6th-7th	6th-8th	6th-9th
Average enrollment	97	123	188	270
Waiting list at year end	54	91	37	129
Student statistics				
Student retention	80%	80%	63%	89%
Attendance rate	97%	95%	95%	93%
Staff retention				
Total teaching faculty	27%	21%	50%	50%
Instructional, specialists, and support staff	N/A	N/A	33%	70%
Core teachers	N/A	13%	58%	37%
Teacher qualifications				
Average years of experience	5.1	9.3	2.8	6.3
Total staff	11	14	18	28
Staff holding Master's	10	10	9	18
Staff certified	8	3	9	16
Highly qualified per NCLB	N/A	N/A	N/A	25
Administrator qualifications				
Average or range of years of experience	20 (avg)	18 (avg)	2 to 32	3 to 33
Total administrators	4	4	5	6
Administrators holding Master's	4	4	4	6
Administrators certified	3	1	2	3

Source: FDCS annual reports, SchoolWorks Inspection Report, and case writer analysis.

Exhibit 6

Frederick Douglass Charter School Income Statements, FY 2001–2004

	Fiscal Year Ended June 30			
	2001	*2002*	*2003*	*2004*
	(All numbers in US dollars)			
Revenue				
State and federal sources	1,077,514	1,482,551	1,975,175	2,763,870
Grants	213,056	113,627	182,125	39,700
Other revenue	146,412	36,553	41,439	56,260
Total revenue	1,436,982	1,632,731	2,198,739	2,859,830
Operating Expenses				
Salaries and wages	583,526	805,696	1,293,564	1,707,711
Payroll tax	22,984	35,520	37,733	116,165
Benefits	36,707	79,700	145,589	132,965
Instructional expenses	261,754	178,508	108,837	202,048
Student services	50,256	55,873	53,282	79,816
Administrative expenses	58,749	81,831	127,419	323,311
Facilities	81,387	145,007	392,914	490,472
Furniture and equipment	143,010	116,681	18,759	65,232
Total operating expenses	1,238,373	1,498,816	2,178,097	3,117,718
Increase in net assets	198,609	133,915	20,642	(257,888)

Source: FDCS annual reports and case writer analysis.

Exhibit 7

MCAS Performance Comparisons: Frederick Douglass with Boston Public Schools and Comparable Massachusetts Charter Schools, 2004

	Boston Total District 2004				*Boston African American 2004*				*Frederick Douglass 2004*				*Boston Renaissance[a] 2004*				*City on a Hill[b] 2004*			
	A %	*P* %	*NI* %	*W/F* %	*A* %	*P* %	*NI* %	*W/F* %	*A* %	*P* %	*NI* %	*W/F* %	*A* %	*P* %	*NI* %	*W/F* %	*A* %	*P* %	*NI* %	*W/F* %
Grade 3—Reading	—	35	46	18	—	33	48	18	—	—	—	—	—	37	46	17	—	—	—	—
Grade 4—English Language Arts	4	26	46	23	2	23	48	26	—	—	—	—	4	26	49	22	—	—	—	—
Grade 4—Mathematics	6	16	48	31	3	12	48	37	—	—	—	—	1	8	53	39	—	—	—	—
Grade 5—Science and Technology	5	17	42	36	2	13	44	42	—	—	—	—	1	12	48	39	—	—	—	—
Grade 6—Mathematics	6	12	29	54	2	9	28	61	0	9	37	54	6	13	26	55	—	—	—	—
Grade 7—English Language Arts	3	44	37	15	1	41	52	17	0	42	49	8	0	35	46	19	—	—	—	—
Grade 8—Mathematics	7	17	29	47	2	11	29	58	0	11	39	50	1	18	32	48	—	—	—	—
Grade 8—Science and Technology	1	9	27	63	0	4	23	73	0	1	27	71	0	6	30	64	—	—	—	—
Grade 10—English Language Arts	9	29	37	25	4	26	41	29	—	—	—	—	—	—	—	—	0	42	56	4
Grade 10—Mathematics	21	21	31	27	10	20	37	33	—	—	—	—	—	—	—	—	3	39	38	20

Source: Massachusetts Department of Education and case writer analysis.

Legend: MCAS Performance Categories: A = Advanced; P = Proficient; NI = Needs Improvement; W/F = Warning/Failing.

[a]Boston Renaissance opened in 1995 and served grades K–8. In 2004, 84% of the student population was African American. The Massachusetts DOE renewed the school's charter in 2000. In 2005, the DOE conditionally renewed the school's charter but limited it to grades K–6 and required academic improvements by 2007.

[b]City on a Hill Charter School opened in 1995 and served grades 9–12. In 2004, 84% of the student population was African American. The DOE renewed the school's charter unconditionally for full five-year terms in 2000 and 2005.

Exhibit 8

Excerpts from SchoolWorks' Report on Inspection of Frederick Douglass Charter School

Renewal Question 1: Is the academic program a success?

1. FDCS failed to make its external MCAS goals in mathematics in grades six and eight during the testing period 2001–2004, but did achieve its target goals in English language arts from 2002–2004.
2. For the most part, FDCS failed to achieve its accountability plan goals in math and reading on the SAT 9. In many cases, student achievement declined within a given school year and when tracked within unmatched cohort groups from year to year.
3. The school has established a sound and viable framework for improving teaching and learning through a standard-based curriculum, teacher-developed syllabi and lesson plans to build a rigorous academic program that is in alignment with its mission.
4. The observed quality of instruction and classroom management at FDCS is dramatically uneven and weakens the school's ability to implement a rigorous academic program.

Renewal Question 2: Is the school a viable organization?

1. FDCS is in the early stages of developing processes to monitor the implementation of its initiatives and to accurately assess the efficacy of its programs in raising students' overall performance to meet the goals outlined in its accountability plan.
2. The high teacher attrition rate appears to be a factor that adversely affects the school's ability to establish a sound, cohesive culture and compromises the academic and social aspects of the school's mission.

Renewal Question 3: Is the school faithful to the terms of the charter?

1. FDCS has not met its student performance math goals on the MCAS or the Stanford 9, as outlined in the accountability plan. FDCS achieved its stated English language arts goal on MCAS but did not reach the ELA objective on the Stanford 9 exam. While many of the plan's non-academic student goals are difficult to assess, the school has created a framework to promote their accomplishment.
2. With the exception of staff and student retention, FDCS has been faithful to the terms of its charter in meeting a majority of its organizational performance goals.
3. The Head of School reported that FDCS does not currently have a dissemination plan because the school has focused all its efforts on building its internal systems and processes.

Renewal Question 4: If the school's charter is renewed, what are its plans for the next five years?

1. The proposed Accountability Plan does not reflect the newly issued guidelines of the DOE and, as such, is not yet a clear road map for guiding school improvement.
2. While the school's administration has expanded and appears well positioned to structurally deal with a growing school and increasing curriculum demands, the long-term vision of how to address these issues, particularly at the high school level, has not yet been concretized.

Source: SchoolWorks Inspection Report—Frederick Douglas Charter School, 2004.

Exhibit 9

Letters from FDCS Supporters

Exhibit 9a

The Commonwealth of Massachusetts

HOUSE OF REPRESENTATIVES
STATE HOUSE, BOSTON 02133-1054

SHIRLEY OWENS-HICKS
REPRESENTATIVE
8TH SUFFOLK DISTRICT
ROOM 134, STATE HOUSE
TEL. (617) 722-2400
FAX (617) 722-2850

Chairwoman
Committee on Local Affairs and
Regional Government

February 1, 2005

Ms. Robin Walker, Chairperson
Frederick Douglass Charter School
190 Cummins Highway
Roslindale, MA 02131

Dear Ms. Walker:

I understand that the Frederick Douglass Charter School is currently undergoing the Department of Education review for the renewal of your school charter.

Please accept this letter as an expression of support for all of the hard work performed by the board and staff of the Frederick Douglass Charter School. As a former elected member of the Boston School Committee and as a former House Chairwoman of the Legislature's Joint Committee on Education, Arts and Humanities, I am impressed by your commitment to developing young minds so that they will be better prepared to meet the many challenges of life. Essential to this development is the school's goal of increasing the supply of quality college-preparatory public education available for Boston's children of color and underserved youth.

I hope that the school will succeed in its quest to renew its charter. I encourage you to contact me if I may be of service.

Sincerely,

Shirley Owens-Hicks

Representative Shirley Owens-Hicks
Chairwoman, Committee on Local Affairs
and Regional Government

cc: Ms. Wanda A. Speede, Head of School

Exhibit 9b

January 25, 2005

To: Mr. David Driscoll, Commissioner
Massachusetts Department of Education
350 Main Street
Malden, MA 02148-5023

Dear Mr. Driscoll:

I am the mother of three children who attended private school. My third child is now attending the Frederick Douglass Charter School in Roslindale. I find the Frederick Douglass Charter School to be comparable in education, discipline and social values as that of the private school he previously attended.

The educational curriculum is well prepared by the teachers and the students are learning in a well organized and structured environment, and at a greater pace. The school is well equipped and the principal is organized, highly visible, very intelligent, and strives to achieve anything and everything that is in the best interest for the student's education in the school.

I believe it would **not** be in the best interest of my child and fellow students not to have this opportunity for a good and valuable education taken away from him by not renewing the school's charter.

Sincerely

Monica Washington
Parent

Cc: James Peyser
Marian Walsh, State Senator
Dianne Wilkerson, State Senator
Gloria Fox, State Rep.
Angelo Scaccia, State Rep
Marie St. Fleur, State Rep
Martin Walsh, State Rep

Exhibit 9c

January 21, 2005

Frederick Douglass Charter School
190 Cummins Hgwy.
Roslindale, MA 02131

Department of Education
350 Main Street
Malden, MA 02148-5023

To Whom It May Concern:

I am a 7th grader at the Frederick Douglass Charter School. The purpose of this letter is that I want you to do everything in your power to keep my school open. For seven years I attended the Saint Williams School, which was very good. Then we discovered the Frederick Douglass Charter School, which has what I am looking for in a school.- education, preparation for college, and extra help.

I want the school to stay open because I am very serious about my education. The teachers are strict. What matters are my grades on report cards and the Charter Renewal. I've never been to a school with the MCAS but this school is preparing me for it. The after-school programs are helpful and they help me raise my grades. The advisory teachers prepare me for college. I've learned so much in my first year at the Frederick Douglass Charter School and I want to continue being consistent in my grades. This school has done so much for me and if it stays open it will continue to help me so that I can become the best scholar that I can be.

Thank you for your time and help.

Sincerely,
Nicholas Doyle

Signature: Nicholas Doyle

Exhibit 9d

Jan. 21, 2005

F.D.C.S
190 Cummins Hgwy
Roslindale MA 02131

Department of Education
250 Main Street
Malden, MA 02148

To Whom It May Concern.

I am a 7th grader at the Frederick Douglass Charter School. I am writing to you because I do not want the School to Shut down. I want the School to be renewed for 5 more years.

I you to renew the School. because if you close down FDCS there will be no where for the kids to go. They would have to go to the public Schools and that is where a lot of people get beat up.

Thank you for your time and help.

Sincerely,
Richard Maurice 7D

Source: Frederick Douglass Charter School internal documents.

Exhibit 10

Comparison of FDCS Students to Other Charter and District School Students in Boston, as Presented by FDCS Supporters to the Massachusetts Board of Education in February, 2004

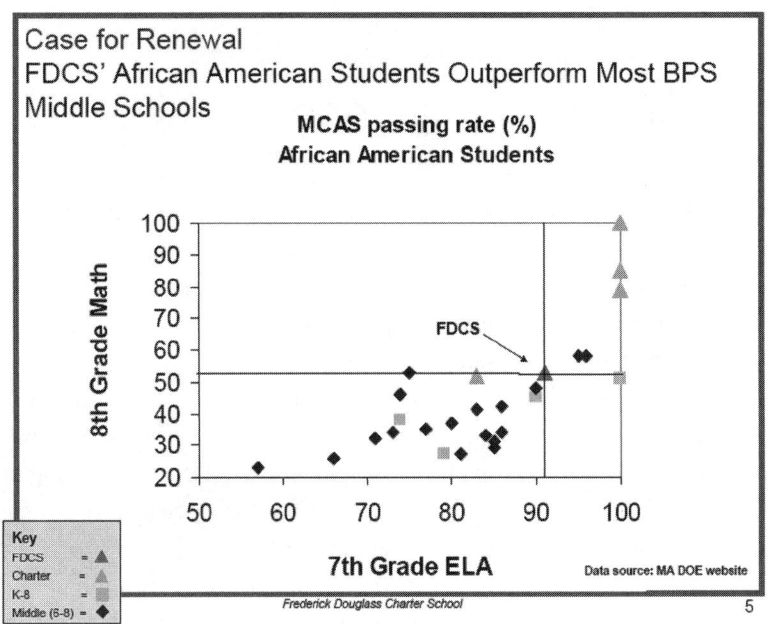

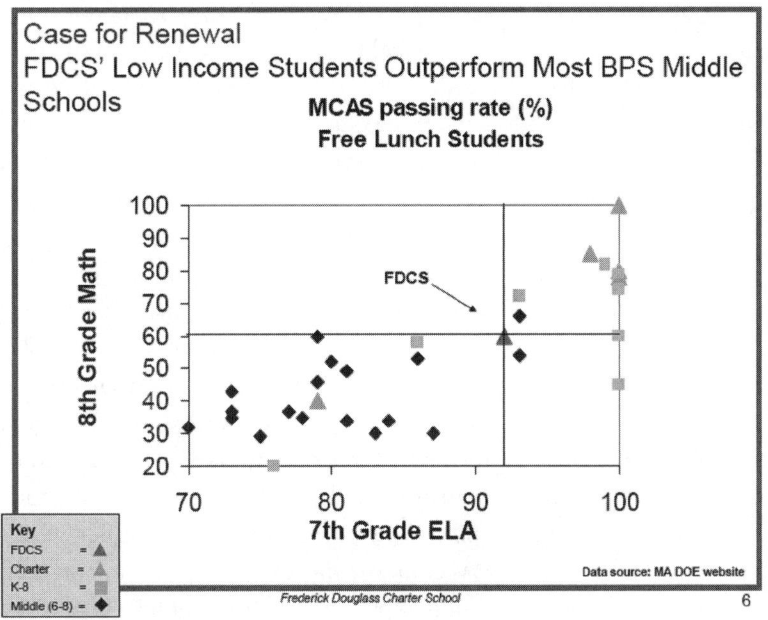

Source: FDCS internal documents.

CASE 4.5

Stacey Childress ■ Scott Benson ■ Sarah Tudryn

New Schools for New Orleans 2008

On December 13, 2007, Sarah Usdin and Matt Candler celebrated with their staff and fielded countless congratulatory phone calls from education reform leaders around the country. The Bill & Melinda Gates Foundation, the Doris and Donald Fisher Fund, and the Broad Foundation had just announced a joint $17.5 million investment to support public education reform in New Orleans, Louisiana. New Schools for New Orleans (NSNO), the organization that Usdin had founded in March 2006 and now co-led as President with CEO Candler, received $10 million of the total.

In its August 2005 devastation, Hurricane Katrina had created the opportunity to entirely redesign New Orleans' low-performing public school system from scratch. In the wake of the disaster, the state of Louisiana took control of the vast majority of city schools from the Orleans Parish School Board (OPSB) through an organization called the Recovery School District (RSD). With the state in control, charter schools proliferated in New Orleans to a degree that no other large urban school system had yet experienced. By 2007, over half of the city's public schools were charter schools. The remainder had been opened as schools run directly by a much smaller OPSB or the RSD (**Exhibit 1**).

NSNO emerged as a recognized supporter of charter schools, based on Usdin and Candler's belief that New Orleans would benefit more from a network of autonomous schools than a centralized school system. They also believed that though charter schools were independent, the schools and the other parts of the reform movement needed a support structure. NSNO aimed to meet this need by focusing on three pillars: starting new schools, developing human capital for schools, and engaging in advocacy on behalf of the charter movement at the city and state levels.

The $10 million gift was premised on NSNO's 2008 operating plan, which relied on spring 2007 forecasts of families with children returning to New Orleans. Based on these forecasts, 24 additional charter schools would be needed by 2010. NSNO planned to incubate, launch, and support up to 16 of these schools and partner with other organizations to recruit and train the necessary principals and teachers.

However, by the time the grant was awarded, the context had changed. Families were returning more slowly than expected, and the RSD claimed that its non-charter schools already had more than enough seats to meet demand. Usdin and Candler wondered whether there was still a need for NSNO to direct the bulk of its energy and resources toward creating and staffing new charter schools. If not, what was the most effective strategy to support their vision to provide excellent public schools for every child in New Orleans?

Sarah Usdin: An Accidental Entrepreneur

As Sarah Usdin explained it, "I didn't intend to start an organization. It just happened." By supporting others who were working to re-open schools after Hurricane Katrina, Usdin said she founded New Schools for New Orleans "almost by accident."

On August 29, 2005, Hurricane Katrina had made landfall in south Louisiana. The storm's powerful winds and rain caused significant damage in and around New Orleans, but the majority of the devastation in the city resulted from three major levee breaches that poured millions of gallons of water into the city. Parts of the city sat beneath as much as 20 feet of water, and approximately 450,000 New Orleans residents were forced to seek refuge throughout the United States. All schools were closed indefinitely.

The New Orleans Public School District (NOPS) was considered a disaster by many education experts prior to Hurricane Katrina. In 2004, the state academic ranking system categorized 47% of NOPS schools as "academically unacceptable" and another 27% as under "academic warning." Nearly half of New Orleans' 125 schools failed to meet their annual progress targets as required by the federal No Child Left Behind Act (**Exhibits 2 and 3**).

In response, the Louisiana Department of Education (LADOE) created an entity called the Recovery School District (RSD) through which the state could take control of any school labeled as "academically unacceptable" for four consecutive years. Prior to Hurricane Katrina, LADOE had already used the RSD to transfer control of the five worst-performing schools to independent operators such as non-profits and universities.

On top of the performance challenges the district faced, it was struggling with a crippling debt burden. An independent study showed that the district was nearly bankrupt with $270 million in bond debt, $30 million in annual debt service obligation, and only $40 million of cash on hand when Hurricane Katrina hit.

When Usdin and her family evacuated ahead of Katrina she could not have predicted that the storm would create an opportunity for her to play an integral role in completely rebuilding a school system that she had already devoted much of her career to improving. After graduating from Colgate University in 1991, she taught for a year in Germany on a Fulbright Scholarship and then was a Teach For America corps member in Baton Rouge, Louisiana. Appalled that some of her fifth graders could not read or write, Usdin abandoned her plans for law school to remain in education. She said, "I needed to focus on changing public education. For me there was no other choice."

After three years in the classroom, Usdin became executive director of TFA's Louisiana region, managing teacher placement and development in New Orleans and 20 other communities throughout the state. In 2000, she left TFA to become a partner of The New Teacher Project (TNTP), a TFA spin-off that consulted to school districts and states in recruiting, selecting, training, and hiring "exceptional teachers." During her five years with TNTP, she worked to recruit hundreds of certified teachers for school districts in the southeastern United States, including New Orleans.

After the chaos that initially followed the storm subsided, Usdin and others in New Orleans's education community began to realize the enormity of the challenge of rebuilding the public school system. All but eight of the 125 school buildings had been damaged, and principals and teachers were displaced throughout the country. The school district paid all employee salaries for work done up until the storm but then was out of money and laid off everyone.

The Rebuilding Begins

Frustrated over years of poor performance and ineffective governance, the state of Louisiana seized the opportunity to take control of the majority of schools away from the local school board. On November 23, 2005, the Louisiana state legislature passed a law that gave the state-controlled RSD every New Orleans public school with performance below the state average. In total, 107 of 125 public schools in New Orleans came under the jurisdiction of the RSD. This legislation also named the state Board of Elementary and Secondary Education (BESE) as the sole chartering authority, effectively stripping the local school board of its ability to issue additional charters (**Exhibit 4**).

When Usdin and her family returned to New Orleans from Louisville, Kentucky, in January 2006, only 17 schools had reopened, all in neighborhoods that had experienced minimal flood damage. Fifteen of these had organized themselves as charter schools in order to reopen quickly, given the disarray of the local district. Usdin was a board member at a public high school trying to reopen, and she urged the school leader to apply for charter status. Although her experience with charter schools was limited, Usdin "was adamantly for chartering" because she was convinced that an independent governance model would not only allow schools to reopen quickly, but would enable them to rise above the political rancor and operational dysfunction of the pre-Katrina school system.

Many other NOPS schools expressed interest in taking advantage of the chartering process, but for many it seemed a bold leap to transition from a district school to an independent charter school. Usdin knew many of these school leaders from her past work with TFA and TNTP and was eager to help them on a range of issues, from the application itself to teacher and board member recruitment. As she continued to invest more energy into the charter movement, she became convinced that a system of independent charter schools could dramatically improve school performance in New Orleans, and she joined the broader movement to redesign public education in the city.

As she attended conferences around the country and spoke with people in the education sector, Usdin discovered that many people wanted to help New Orleans but did not know how. "There were many national players trying to figure out what to do, but there was not a logical place for them to go," Usdin said. Because she had been immersed in New Orleans' complex local politics for years, Usdin emerged as a respected authority from which non-profits and foundations sought guidance.

The formal launch of New Schools for New Orleans grew out of Usdin's informal involvement with local and national education reformers. By April 2006, just three months after Usdin returned to New Orleans, she had incorporated NSNO as a 501(c) 3 nonprofit organization and raised $500,000 of seed capital from the Greater New Orleans Foundation. When asked about why the foundation gave NSNO the money to get started, Usdin shrugged, "I didn't even have a business plan, but they must have believed in our ideas."

The Birth of New Schools for New Orleans

With the money she needed to get started, Usdin turned her attention to recruiting a core team. One of her first hires was Neerav Kingsland, a Yale law student who had arrived in New Orleans as a volunteer right after the storm. He helped file NSNO's incorporation papers and offered to work for Usdin while finishing his third year of law school. In order to draw educational leaders from outside of New Orleans, Usdin positioned NSNO as an incubator for talent. With this philosophy, Usdin hired John Alford (HBS 2001) from the KIPP Foundation and Ben Kleban (HBS 2005) from the Building Excellent Schools (BES) program. BES recruited high-potential leaders into a one-year residency program that prepared them to open their own charter schools in 15 communities around the country, from Massachusetts to California. Even though Alford and Kleban both intended to start their own schools in New Orleans the following year, Usdin knew that in the meantime NSNO could leverage their talent in support of others who were launching charters.

By July 2006, NSNO had a team of six people. NSNO was committed to supporting open-enrollment charter schools from the beginning, but had not determined what services it would offer. Usdin decided to start with what she knew best—human capital. To provide schools with qualified teachers, NSNO partnered with The New Teacher Project to create a recruiting organization called teachNOLA. A few months later, NSNO successfully convinced New Leaders for New Schools to consider New Orleans as a placement city for its school leaders. Charter schools eagerly embraced these services and requested many more as they struggled to meet the needs of returning students.

Hiring a CEO

Although she had worked in education reform for over a decade, Usdin's entire experience was in recruiting teachers to traditional school systems. Though human capital was a vital component of NSNO's strategy, Usdin believed she needed a partner with significant experience in the charter movement. She admitted, "I didn't know charter schools, and because there were only a few charters in New Orleans before Katrina, there wasn't really anyone in the city who was an expert."

Usdin and the NSNO board began actively searching for a candidate with significant charter experience. Matt Candler, co-founder and chief operating officer of the New York Center for Charter School Excellence, attended a meeting of national charter school experts convened by Louisiana's state superintendent in January 2006. Usdin was impressed with his background and insights, and asked him to become NSNO's CEO after visiting him in New York and seeing his operation. Candler had been active in the charter movement since 1996 and, before his current role, had spent several years at KIPP. The New York Center for Charter School Excellence supported charter schools throughout New York City and had many attributes that Usdin hoped NSNO could emulate.

Although Candler enjoyed his position in New York, the opportunity excited him. He explained, "The offer to become CEO of New Schools for New Orleans was ultimately too hard to pass up. Given my work with KIPP and in New York, I believed that charter schools had enormous potential to transform urban education in New Orleans and that the city could become a national model for how to turn around a failing school system." He accepted the job, and eventually relocated his family to New Orleans in October 2006.

To accommodate Candler's arrival and Usdin's ongoing role, NSNO's board created a dual leadership arrangement, naming Candler as CEO and Usdin as President, with both reporting directly to the board. Both were satisfied that the reporting structure supported Usdin's desire to remain an integral part of the organization while acknowledging Candler's role as chief executive. (See **Exhibit 5** for biographical information.)

Adding Value in the First Post-Katrina School Year

At the start of the 2006–2007 school year, 54 schools had been reopened, of which 31 were charters. In fact, at 57% of the total, New

Orleans charter schools had a larger share of the local public school market than in any other major school district in the country. Washington, D.C., came closest with charters representing approximately 25% of total schools. The proliferation of independent school models throughout New Orleans did not go unnoticed. Local residents had a range of reactions toward the new environment. Some were cautiously optimistic, while others were opposed to the reform movement because of their sense that "outsiders" were trying to take over the school system. Nationally, the system received an enormous amount of publicity not only from education reformers, but also from mainstream media. New Orleans had become what Time Magazine described as the nation's "greatest education lab."

Given this environment, NSNO was in a position to accelerate the effectiveness of charter schools in New Orleans. At his former organization in New York, Candler had provided a robust set of services to charter schools and was eager to replicate these activities in New Orleans. These services included leadership development; student performance evaluation, assessment, and data management support; services and systems to ensure successful operations; start-up technical assistance and financial grants; and advocacy for systemic education reform.

Because of the lack of infrastructure in the re-emerging public school system, NSNO received requests for these services and many more from all types of schools, not just charter schools. Candler was clear that they "could not be everything to everyone," at least not initially. It took discipline to deny services when schools urgently needed them, but Candler and Usdin were adamant that they did not want NSNO to "become a surrogate district office" for all the schools in New Orleans. Instead, they believed that NSNO would be most effective if it focused on independent charter schools and offered a defined set of services to help those target schools improve and expand.

Even for the target schools, Candler acknowledged that NSNO's services "came at a price." Principals and their boards had to be comfortable letting NSNO be intimately involved in many aspects of their schools in order to receive support. For this reason, some school leaders were hesitant to work with NSNO in the early days. To strengthen ties to these schools, Candler outlined a plan for an investment fund through which NSNO would offer targeted grants to individual schools. This investment-centric model would require a large source of external funding that only a small number of national foundations could provide. Candler knew that convincing these foundations to entrust their money to NSNO as an intermediary investor would be difficult, but he believed that this feature was necessary to ensure that NSNO remained relevant to schools once they were stable.

In the meantime, NSNO built strong relationships with a number of charter schools, including eight newly launched schools, by providing critical services such as operations, IT, and financial training, board member orientation, and free office and meeting space. In addition, NSNO successfully recruited four leaders to incubate new schools for the 2007–2008 academic year who otherwise would not have come to New Orleans.

NSNO also played a critical role in attracting national education organizations such as TFA and New Leaders for New Schools to join the New Orleans rebuilding effort. The relationships with NSNO were instrumental in the willingness of these organizations to commit resources not only to charter schools, but also to the schools run by the RSD. The staffing challenges were significant, but the city made great strides in recruiting teachers for all of its schools through teachNOLA, and TFA committed to dramatically expand its New Orleans corps to serve both charter and district schools.

NSNO initially made a strategic decision not to pursue advocacy on behalf of the charter movement in Louisiana, but rather to focus on more concrete support for schools. Yet, by the end of their first full year, NSNO was clearly perceived as a "voice for charters" at the city and state level. Usdin and Candler were able to build and maintain relationships with key leaders in the Louisiana State Legislature, the state Board of Elementary and Secondary Education (BESE), and the RSD. NSNO had a fundamental role with other partners in creating the first-ever parent's guide for all New Orleans schools, distributing more than 35,000 copies, and had implemented an outreach campaign to more than 500 families who had inquired with the RSD about school openings for their children. Usdin said, "To be an independent voice that is constant over time—that is very important to who we are."

"We must focus on what we do best and say no to what is beyond the scope of our mission," explained Usdin. This meant doing a better job in the recruitment and selection process of school leaders as well as accelerating the entire timeline for starting new schools. Usdin and Candler also believed that going forward they should improve the understanding of and support for charter schools, strengthen ties with key politicians, and continue outreach to parents.

At the end of the 2006–2007 academic year, the enrollment of all New Orleans public schools was 26,156—approximately 45% of what it was prior to Katrina. To support the continued repopulation and rebuilding of New Orleans, ten additional charter schools were scheduled to open for the 2007–2008 academic year. Reflecting on NSNO's first full year of operation, Candler noted, "We realized that the education environment had shifted from one of crisis to greater stability and that we needed to better understand NSNO's evolving role in the changing context, even as we quickly transition from a start-up into a more mature stage of development."

Due to the shifting context, NSNO recognized they needed to formalize their strategic partnerships and support other organizations' expansion efforts to ensure better quality and consistency of programs throughout the city. In particular, they saw the potential for greater collaboration and coordination with the RSD.

After a rocky first year under the direction of a staff member from the Louisiana Department of Education, the state had hired Paul Vallas away from the School District of Philadelphia to be the new superintendent of the RSD. His early impressions of Usdin and Candler were positive, and as he saw it, "NSNO has been the principal organization responsible for creating the nonprofit and charter movement that characterizes the rebuilding efforts in New Orleans." Now that he was in place as the chief executive of the state-run traditional and charter schools in the city, it was unclear what the nature of the relationship between the entrepreneurial reform organizations and the school district would be and what role NSNO might play in that relationship.

The 2008 Operational Plan

In preparation for their second year of operation, Usdin and Candler launched an intensive, two-month strategic planning process. Usdin commented, "Matt and I agreed early on that staff involvement was critical. Everyone invested an incredible amount of thought, energy, and passion. We were able to build consensus around considerable areas of disagreement, uncertainty, and ambiguity and create a clear vision for the 2008 school year."

The result of the team's effort was the NSNO 2008 Operational Plan—a 30-page playbook designed to guide NSNO, specifically Usdin, Candler, and the Board of Directors. As Usdin explained, "The plan provided alignment and structure for our team, allowing us to be as responsive, reflective, and effective as we could possibly be. We reaffirmed our three focus areas—launching and supporting charter schools, attracting and preparing talent to teach and lead, and advocating for high-quality public schools—and set clear objectives for each" (**Exhibits 6, 7,** and **8**).

Launching and Supporting Open-Enrollment Public Charter Schools

Usdin and Candler created the School Incubation Program, a 12-month residency-based training program that prepared promising educators to open their own charter schools, as the vehicle for starting new schools. As Usdin described it, the incubator was "a major investment—both financial and timewise. We incorporated into the plan opening three to five of these schools each year."

NSNO also continued its partnership with Building Excellent Schools by providing fellowship funding, giving BES fellows work space, and assisting with the acclimation of BES fellows to the New Orleans environment. NSNO benefited by integrating parts of BES's well-established charter school leader training into its own incubator program.

Prioritizing Support for Schools

The 2008 plan took into account what NSNO learned in 2007 about supporting different types of schools, and as a result prioritized schools based on two variables: the school's actual or potential academic achievement and its board of directors' level of commitment to academic achievement. By assessing schools along these two dimensions, Usdin and Candler devised four priority levels for schools that determined the types of services NSNO would provide to charter schools (see Table A).

New and existing charter schools that scored high on both variables commanded the most attention and were categorized as Priority One schools. Schools with a strong board commitment but weak performance were considered Priority Two schools. NSNO would provide the boards of schools in this category an assessment of the school leadership in hopes it would lead to corrective action. NSNO would support the board in replacing school leadership should it be necessary.

Schools with weak performance and low commitment from their boards to academic performance were considered Priority Three schools. "If we are to realize our vision of citywide excellence," explained Candler, "we have to take a more active role to insure that these lower-performing schools are held accountable for results, and in the case of school closures, that families, teachers and students have the support they need to find another school quickly."

All other charter schools were categorized as Priority Four schools. These schools would benefit from NSNO advocacy on behalf of all charter schools, be invited or self-select on a case-by-case basis to attend trainings, and referred to competent partners if they desired, but NSNO would provide no direct services.

NSNO made a conscious decision to work less intensively with non-charter schools. Usdin confessed, "Matt and I agreed on most issues throughout the planning process. The one major issue that we debated was how to interact with non-charter schools. Matt felt we should provide fewer services to these schools than I did. We agreed that our human capital work would extend to non-charters, but had good debate about to what degree non-charters would have access to our other services. In the end, we made the decision not to focus our direct service efforts there." (See **Exhibit 9** for 2008 school launch and support objectives.)

Table A
NSNO School Prioritization Matrix

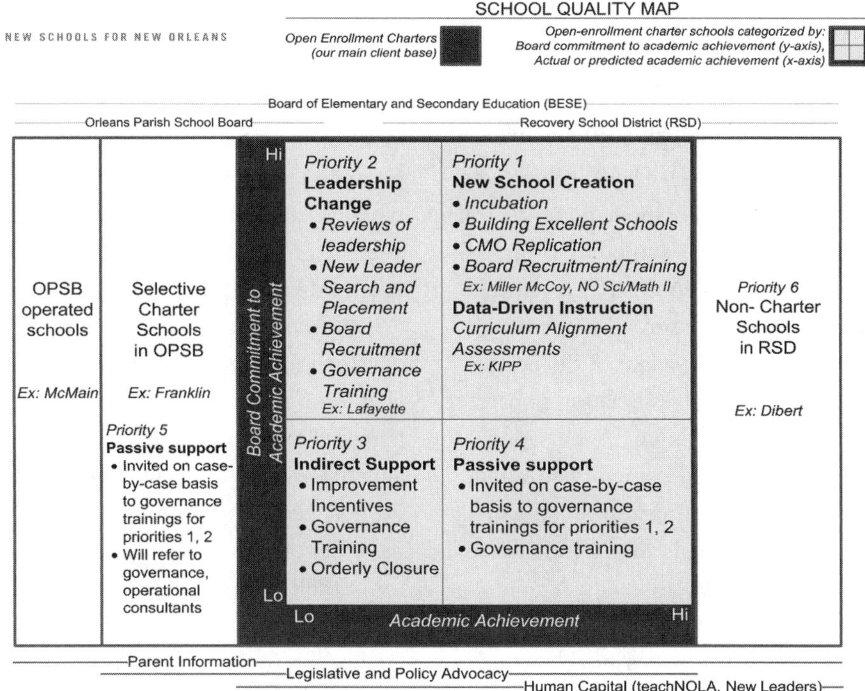

Source: NSNO 2008 Operating Plan.

Attracting and Preparing Talent to Teach and Lead

Usdin described how NSNO's human capital efforts mapped to the school prioritizations:

> We committed to increase the alignment of our human capital efforts with the needs of our priority one and two schools. Attracting well-prepared talent is the most important task for new schools or struggling schools. The New Teacher Project and New Leaders for New Schools will continue to be key partners in meeting the demand for teachers and school leaders in these schools.

The operational plan also included support for TFA's efforts to double the number of New Orleans corps members to approximately 250 annually. This included leveraging their relationships with national contributors to help TFA fund their expansion efforts. Members of the expanded corps would teach in charter schools in all four priority areas as well as in non-charter RSD schools. Kira Orange-Jones, the executive director for TFA in New Orleans and a graduate of the Harvard Graduate School of Education, estimated that within three years, one in three New Orleans students would be taught by a TFA corps member or alumnus.

In 2008, NSNO committed to exploring the possibility of incubating a new local organization licensed to train teachers. This "teacher training university" would focus on creating a pipeline of teachers for Priority One and Two schools as a collaborative effort with TNTP, TFA, charter management organizations, local universities, and national reformers. (See Exhibit 10 for 2008 human capital objectives.)

Advocating for Accountability and Sustainability of High-Quality Public Schools

"We finally admitted that we had a role in advocacy for the charter school movement. We had done a lot before, but we wanted to formalize it," explained Usdin. NSNO advocacy would be implemented in three ways. First, through Candler's role as vice president of the Louisiana State Charter School Association's board of directors and in partnership with the national foundations that invested in the organization, NSNO would provide direction to the association to ensure state legislative efforts were responsive to New Orleans' needs.

Second, at the state and city level, NSNO would represent charter issues and challenges to the relevant leadership teams. "We meet regularly with Paul Vallas, the new superintendent of the RSD, to build momentum for the charter movement and to align our visions," explained Usdin. NSNO did not see a need to engage the OPSB with advocacy efforts during 2008 as charters under their purview were not Priority One or Two schools.

Finally, when discussing key success factors for rebuilding the New Orleans public school system, NSNO board member Cathy Pierson voiced the opinion of many, saying, "Success depends on bringing entire families into the system." In theory, parents had the opportunity to choose which school their children attended. However, there was some evidence that parents were still tied to the old reputations of their neighborhood schools, whether charter or traditional, and did not understand what being a charter school meant. As one parent noted, "Everybody's a charter now, post-Katrina. Everybody has the word 'charter' behind their name."

A study conducted by the Boston Consulting Group in spring 2007 found that only half of the city's parents thought they had a choice about where their children could enroll in school. Some long-time residents were suspicious of "outsiders" coming to the city to "fix" education. As a local pastor described, "You just see these new people constantly coming into your neighborhood, coming in to help your kids, and you get a little scared."

With these concerns in mind, NSNO developed a partnership with the New Orleans chapter of the Urban League to bring a local perspective and respected brand to the first annual Parent's Guide for Public Schools. NSNO began incubating the Parent Organizing Network, led by Aesha Rasheed, the editor of the Parent's Guide, which was focused on building families' capacity to measure school quality and to share the information publicly. (See Exhibit 11 for 2008 advocacy objectives.)

Creating Value in a Fluid Environment

"The 2008 Operational Plan was an excellent tool because it provided discipline and direction to our work. However, the fluidity of the New Orleans public school system required that New Schools for New Orleans, and Sarah and Matt more specifically, have the ability to shift gears quickly," explained NSNO board member Tony Recasner. He continued, "With so many constituencies—partner organizations, BESE, the RSD, schools, parents, students, and funders—NSNO must balance putting a stake in the ground with maintaining the flexibility to change with the environment."

Under the legislation that established the Recovery School District, the RSD had three years remaining of its original five-year mandate. Afterward, the state would decide which local entity would be responsible for overseeing schools and what form this entity would take. "The role we might play in ensuring New Orleans public schools achieved our vision of excellence in the long term and how we would remain relevant as an organization is always top of mind for us," said Usdin.

Ongoing Relationships with Incubated Schools

In the next three years, there could be as many as fifteen schools under the NSNO umbrella as a result of their school leader incubation efforts. A number of charter management organizations (CMOs) had emerged around the country, with an aim to start and run networks of charter schools under the same management and support structure. Among other things, CMOs aimed to achieve economies of scale in back-office and strategic functions, leverage best practices across groups of schools, and implement a common accountability framework in order to achieve higher performance than individual schools could on their own.

Though NSNO had not explicitly intended to become a CMO, Usdin observed that many of their activities were similar, saying, "We are already a quasi-CMO with an advocacy arm. The hardest strategic question in my mind is to what degree should we become like a CMO, rather than having a more informal relationship with the schools we incubate as they become more mature?" (See Exhibit 12 for comparison of NSNO services with those typically provided by districts and CMOs.)

Given its vision of ensuring excellent public schools for all children in New Orleans, should NSNO commit more of its resources to developing more formal connections and robust support to the charter schools it helped launch?

Evolving Relationship with the Recovery School District

The dynamic nature of the New Orleans environment at times made operational decisions seem more art than science. For instance, in an effort to ensure an adequate supply of seats for students coming back to New Orleans, a number of groups had made a concerted effort to estimate the population inflow and to open new schools accordingly. As New Orleans continued its transition from crisis to stability, the growth in students did not meet projections and now was expected to stagnate. The result was an oversupply of seats. "We already have more schools this year than we had kids to fill them," explained RSD superintendent Vallas. "NSNO should recognize that its longer-term vision has to adjust to the constraints of the system. They cannot continue opening schools if the market does not support it."

After taking over the RSD in fall of 2007, Vallas developed a five-prong vision for the RSD that he planned to implement over two years. Rather than simply run the non-charter schools it was responsible for, Vallas aimed for the RSD to:

- Create a central entity to solicit and manage all new school proposals
- Support the opening of high-quality schools as needed based on demand
- Provide support services to schools (i.e., busing, janitorial, food service)
- Assess and evaluate schools
- Hold schools accountable for performance

Vallas shared the NSNO vision for ensuring excellent public schools for all children in New Orleans. Usdin and Candler recognized, however, that the charter movement was only one part of Vallas's overall reform strategy. As Vallas explained it, "A core strategy for non-charter RSD schools that are failing is to gradually transition them, one grade at a time, to a more independent model. Within a couple of years, all RSD schools should be charter-like." (See Exhibit 13 for 2007 performance data.)

With this in mind, Vallas imagined a different role for NSNO than was currently captured in the 2008 Operational Plan. Specifically, he stated, "I would like to see NSNO move beyond charter schools to also support non-charters within the RSD. Similar to the situation I had in Philadelphia with the Public Education Fund, I would like to see NSNO become a contract service agency to the RSD to support schools, charter and non-charter, within the district."

Usdin knew the sustainability of NSNO was dependent on a healthy collaboration with the RSD and recognized that Vallas's leadership presented a great opportunity for New Orleans public schools. But the kind of relationship Vallas described also posed challenges to NSNO's strategic intent. Usdin explained, "Our commitment to students in New Orleans is long-term. Paul is a great, innovative partner, but with urban superintendent tenures somewhere between three and five years, we have to be careful to make decisions for NSNO that will allow us to achieve our vision regardless of who is the superintendent of the RSD."

The Future of New Schools for New Orleans

The 2008 Operational Plan had proved an effective document for attracting financial commitments to the rebuilding efforts. The support from the Bill & Melinda Gates Foundation, the Doris and Donald Fisher Fund, and the Broad Foundation provided the resources NSNO needed to execute the operational plan. As Usdin explained, "We felt we made the right decisions in the development of the operational plan. We were confident about our strategy for prioritizing schools and about working to get new, high-quality schools up and running."

But Usdin and Candler were more concerned with creating value in the shifting context than hitting all of the marks laid out in the planning document. Contemplating the changes in the environment, they were determined to adapt the organization's strategy effectively. Specifically, what were the implications for the type of support they should provide to priority schools as they matured? Should they stick to their decision to limit their work with the non-charter RSD schools to human capital, or should they engage more intensively in other direct services to these schools? Ultimately, what was the best course of action for ensuring excellent public schools for all children in New Orleans?

Notes

1. Walter Isaacson, "The Greatest Education Lab," *Time* Magazine, September 6, 2006.

2. Erik W. Robelen, "No Easy Road to Choice," *Education Week*, February 27, 2008.

3. "The State of Public Education in New Orleans," The Boston Consulting Group, June 2007.

4. Robelen, "No Easy Road to Choice."

Exhibit 1a

New Orleans Student Enrollment Data by Type of School, 2007–2008

Type	*No. of Schools*	*No. of Students*	*% Total Enrollment*	*% Low-Income*	*% White*	*% Black*	*% Other*
Open-Enrollment Charter[a]	32	13,154	41%	94%	2%	93%	5%
Selective-Enrollment Charter[a, b]	8	4,757	15%	56%	31%	58%	11%
OPSB Direct-Operated[c]	7	2,630	8%	74%	1%	94%	5%
RSD Direct-Operated[d]	33	11,608	36%	77%	1%	98%	1%
Total	80	32,149	100%	80%	5%	90%	5%

Source: Case writer analysis of Louisiana Department of Education enrollment data for New Orleans.

[a] Of the 40 total charter schools, 12 were chartered by the Orleans Parish School Board (OPSB), 26 by the Recovery School District (RSD), and 2 by the state Board of Elementary and Secondary Education (BESE). The 32 open-enrollment charters were open to all students, and the 8 selective-enrollment charters had admissions criteria. All 26 RSD charters were open-enrollment.

[b] Selective-enrollment charters required students to meet a variety of academic and non-academic criteria to be eligible for enrollment. Of the 8 selective enrollment charters, 7 were chartered by the OPSB, and 1 was chartered by BESE. The selective enrollment charters accounted for 84% of the white students enrolled in all 80 New Orleans public schools.

[c] Four of seven OPSB direct-operated schools had selective-admissions policies.

[d] None of the 33 RSD operated direct-operated schools had selective-admissions policies.

Exhibit 1b

New Orleans Enrollment and Performance Data by Type of Governance, 2007–2008

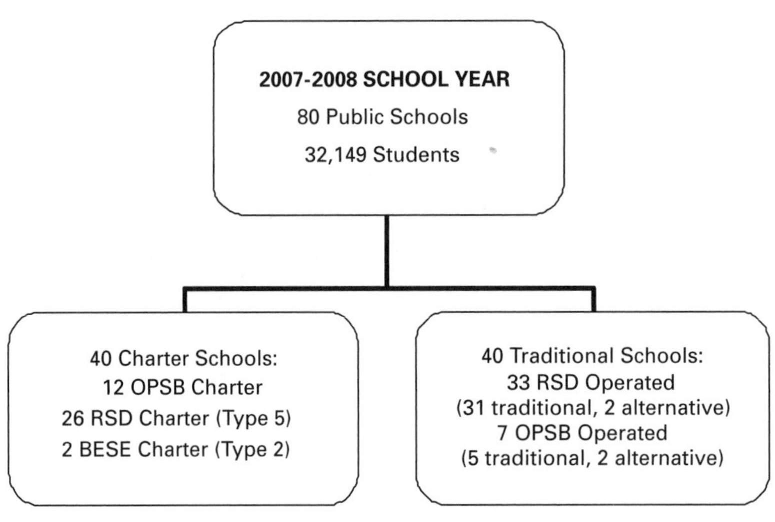

School Type	*Performance Score*[a]	*% of Total Students*	*% Low-Income*	*% Minority*
OPSB Traditional	75.46	8%	74%	99%
OPSB Charter	89.45	22%	68%	79%
RSD Traditional	29.11	36%	77%	99%
RSD Charter	52.29	31%	94%	99%
BESE Charter	75.95	3%	57%	84%

Sources: Chart is an NSNO document; table was created by the case author using NSNO and Louisiana State Department of Education data.

[a] Performance score is an unweighted average of individual school performance scores (SPS) in each category for 2007. Each school's SPS is determined by the Louisiana Department of Education and is an index rating based on a variety of weighted performance metrics, including Louisiana Education Assessment Program (LEAP) exams, graduation exit exams, student attendance, and drop-out rates. The index is a 200-point scale with the following categories: 0–49 = unsatisfactory; 50–99 = approaching basic; 100–149 = mastery; 150–200 = advanced. The highest-scoring elementary school in Louisiana in 2006 had an SPS of 150.7, and the top-scoring high school had an SPS of 149.9.

Exhibit 2

Selected School Performance Data for New Orleans Public Schools, 2004

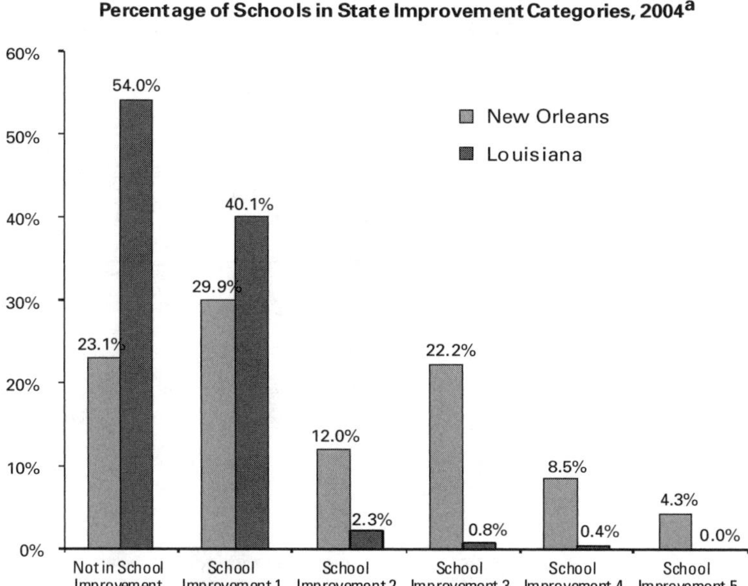

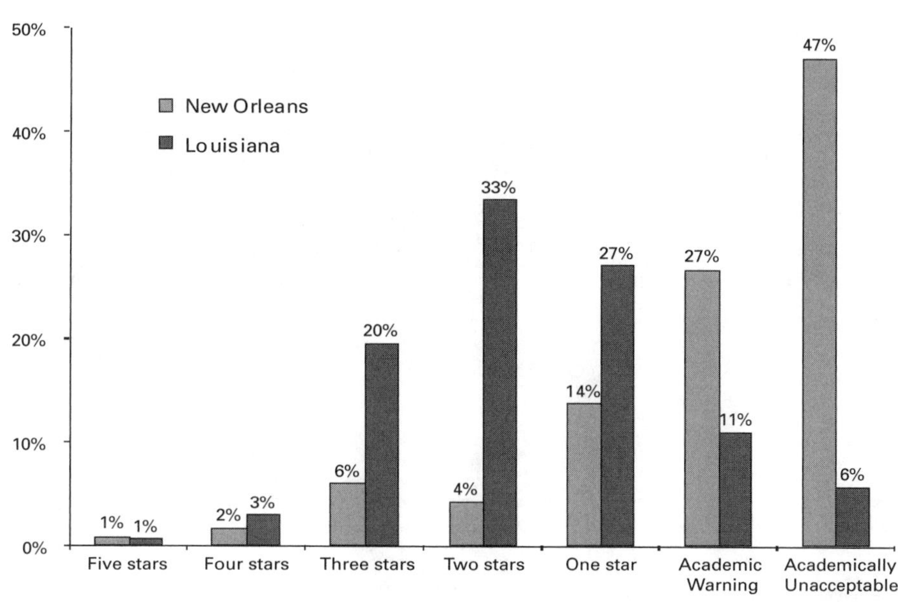

Source: "District Composite Report: Orleans Parish," Louisiana Department of Education, April 2005, and case writer analysis.

[a] The school improvement categories are determined by a set of criteria, including a school's performance and growth on specified standardized tests by sub-groups of students, and schools can move between each category at the end of every academic year. "Not in School Improvement" is the highest ranking, and "School Improvement 5" is the lowest ranking on this chart.

[b] The "star" ranking system is based on performance on a number of criteria, including aggregate performance on the Louisiana Assessment of Basic Skills, The Iowa Test of Basic Skills, student attendance rates, and drop-out percentages.

Exhibit 3

Selected Student Performance Data for New Orleans Public Schools, 1999–2004 (Pre-Katrina)

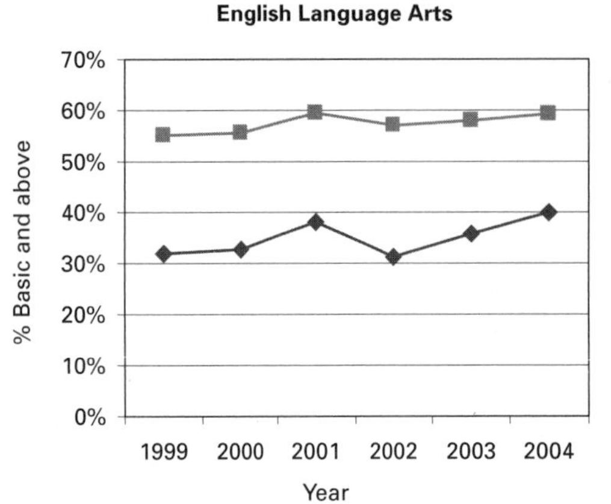

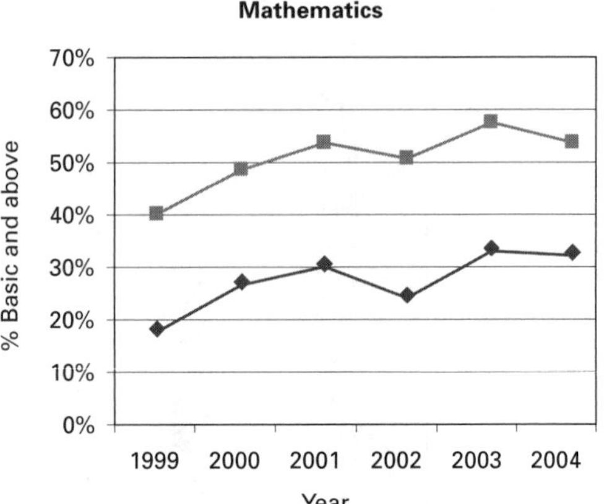

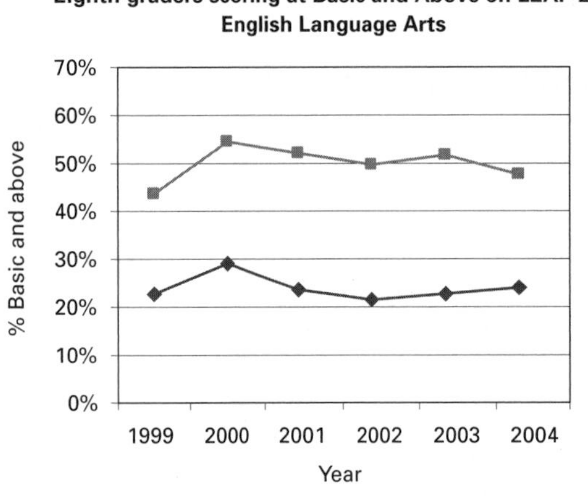

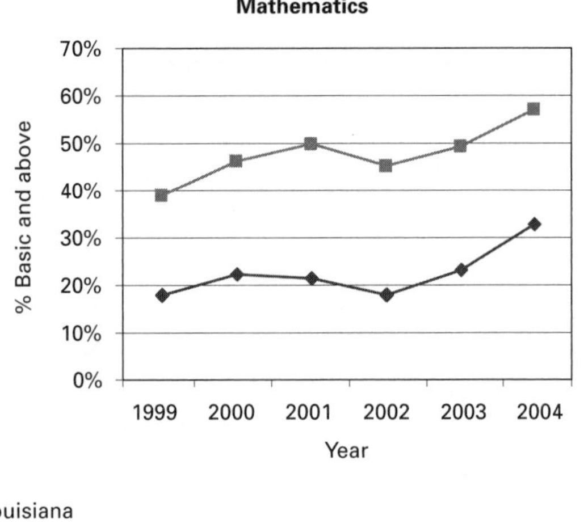

Louisiana

New Orleans

Source: "District Composite Report: Orleans Parish," Louisiana Department of Education, April 2005, and case writer analysis.

Note: Louisiana Education Assessment Program (LEAP)

Exhibit 4

New Orleans Public School Governance, 2006–2007

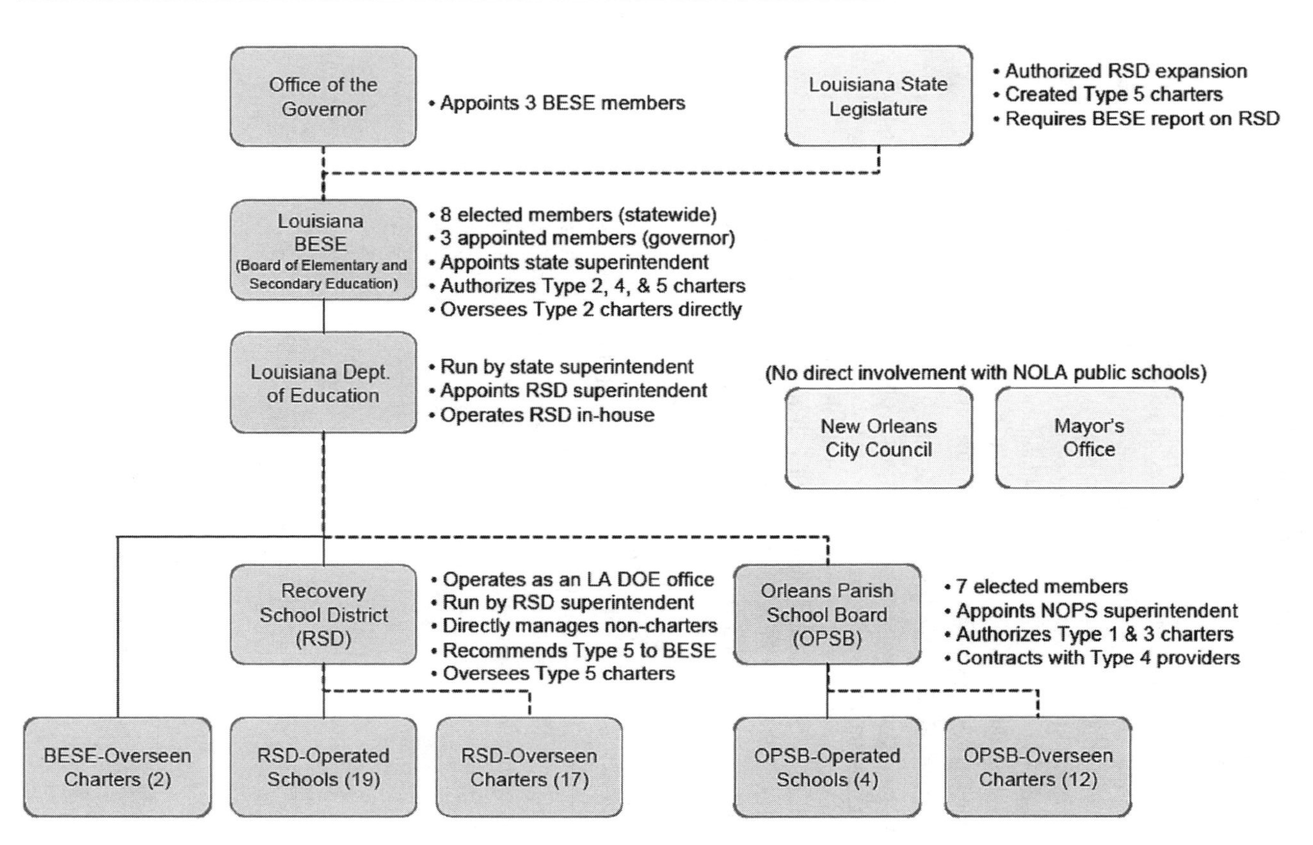

Source: Stig Leschly, "New Orleans Charter School Sector: 5-Year Plan and Investment Recommendation," prepared by NSNO.

Exhibit 5

New Schools for New Orleans Leader Biographies

Sarah Newell Usdin, Founder and President, has been involved in the education reform movement since 1992. After teaching in Germany on a Fulbright Scholarship, she joined Teach For America, a national corps of recent college graduates who teach in our nation's lowest-income communities. Usdin spent the next three years teaching in Baton Rouge before becoming Teach For America's Executive Director in Louisiana. Believing that more needed to be done to systemically impact the quality of teachers in public schools, she became a Partner with The New Teacher Project, a national nonprofit teacher recruiting and training organization. In the aftermath of Hurricane Katrina, Sarah formed New Schools for New Orleans to assist in the recovery and reformation of public education. Because of an early interest in social justice, Sarah majored in religion and German at Colgate University. Sarah also holds a Master's in Curriculum and Instruction from Louisiana State University. She has two children, Lyle (5) and Cecile (1), and is married to Tommy.

Matt Candler, CEO, has been involved in the charter school movement since 1996 and has taught and coached and at the elementary, middle, and high school levels. Candler worked for Paul Vallas in Chicago on the nation's first large-scale program designed to combat social promotion, co-founded a K–5 charter school in North Carolina and started a consulting practice specializing in start-up support for charter school founders. In 2001, Candler joined the KIPP Foundation in San Francisco as the Vice President of School Development. His team established 37 new charter schools across the country and was responsible for recruiting school leaders, securing contractual and charter relationships with school districts, and securing facilities and financing for each school. In 2004, Candler became the Chief Operating Officer of the New York City Center for Charter School Excellence, where he co-managed a $40M endowment to help open, operate, and sustain successful charter schools throughout the City. He joined New Schools for New Orleans as the CEO in October of 2007. Candler has an MBA from Northwestern University's Kellogg School of Management with a concentration in education management, managerial economics, and decision making.

Source: NSNO.

Exhibit 6

New Schools for New Orleans—Vision, Mission and Core Values

Our Vision for the Future:

Excellent public schools for every child in New Orleans.

Our Mission Statement:

The mission of New Schools for New Orleans is to achieve excellent public schools for every child in New Orleans by:

- Attracting and preparing talent to teach and lead
- Launching and supporting open-enrollment public charter schools
- Advocating for accountability and sustainability of high-quality public schools

Core Values by everyone on the New Schools for New Orleans team:

No Excuses in the Pursuit of Excellence

- We have a sense of urgency about our work
- We commit to having goals that measure the impact of our work
- We are tenacious and constantly strive to improve

Humility and Respect

- We seek first to understand and then be understood
- We are not in the trenches each day, and therefore must reflect a sense of respect, service and humility when engaging with teachers, principals and parents
- We expose ourselves to diverse opinions to deepen our understanding of the public education landscape
- Our recognition will be based on the successes of schools

Sense of Possibility

- We stay focused on the mission even in the face of daily obstacles
- We think boldly and greet new ideas openly
- We choose our profession every day

Integrity

- We demonstrate coherence between our core values and our actions
- We are good stewards of the resources entrusted to us
- We make tough choices rooted in our mission

Teamwork

- We believe that a diverse team is more effective than an individual
- We depersonalize disagreements and do not hold grudges
- We actively seek feedback on our actions, thoughts, and words and their impact on our teammates
- We cultivate an open and joyful work environment

Source: NSNO 2008 Operational Plan.

Exhibit 7

New Schools for New Orleans—Organization Chart

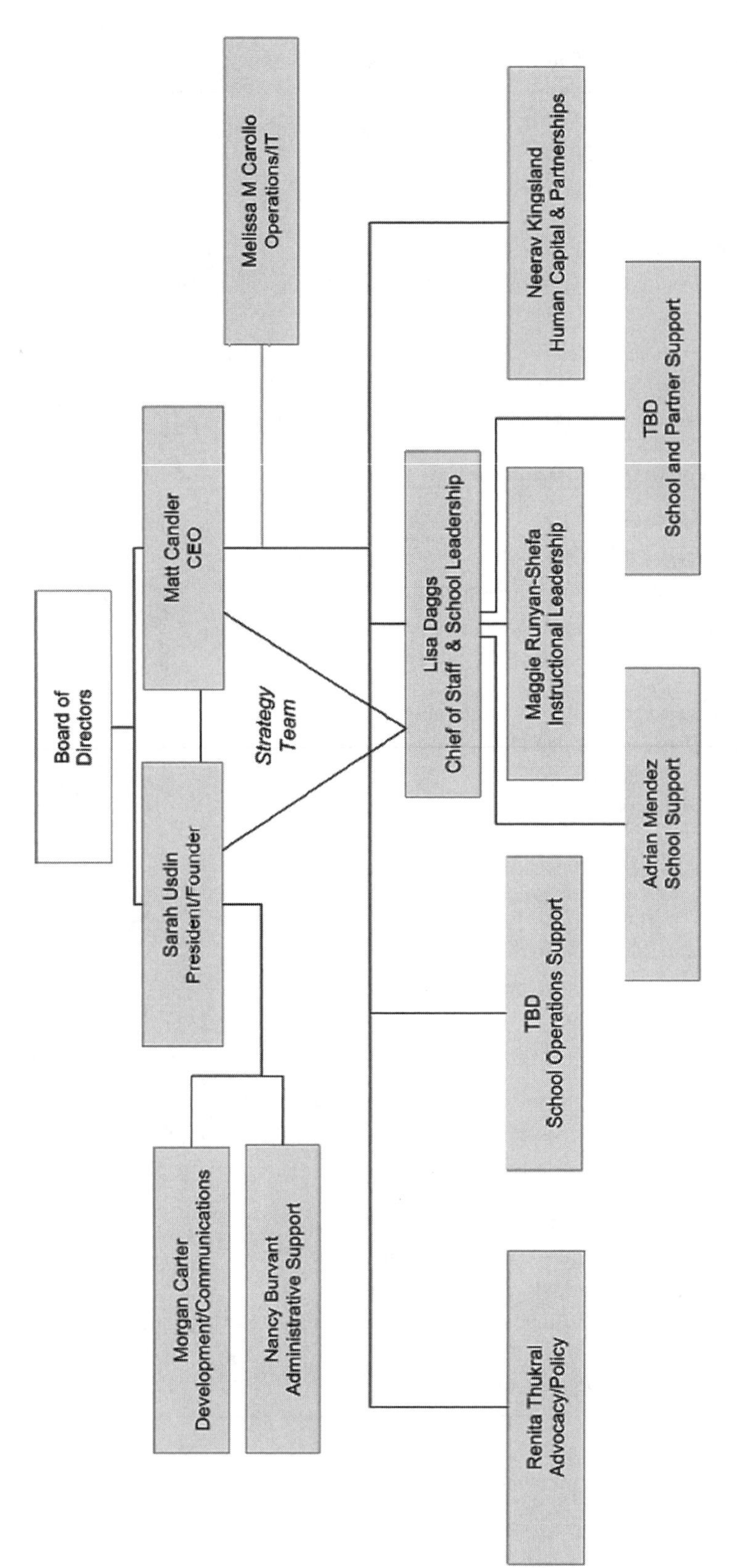

Source: NSNO 2008 Operational Plan.

Exhibit 8

New Schools for New Orleans—Allocation of Staff Priorities

	G and A		Teach and Lead			Launch and Support				Advocate			
	General and Admin	Development	The New Teacher Project	New Leaders for New Schools	TFA Expansion/New Teacher Development	Priority 1: Incubate, BES	Priority 1: Data-Driven Instruction	Priority 1: School Start-Up	Priority 2/3: Leadership Change and Closure	Legislation	Policy (BESE/LDE/RSD/OPSB)	Parent Choice and Information	Public/Community Outreach
Chief Executive Officer	10	10				25	5	10	20	10	10		
President/Founder	10	50			5						10		25
Chief of Staff, New School Development	20					70	10						
Human Capital and Partnerships Director			15	15	15	25			10	10	10		
School Operations Support Director						20		60			20		
Instructional Quality Director						80	20						
Advocacy and Policy Director										40	30		30
Data-Driven Instruction Director						20	80						
Development / Communications Director		40	5	5		10	5	5	5				25
NSNO Operations Director	40	10	5	5		15		5	5		5	5	5
School Support Manager						70		15					15
School Support Manager						40			40		20		
Administrative Assistant to Founder	10	50			5						10		25
Incubating Parent Advocacy Founder												*80*	*20*
Incubating School of Ed Founder					*100*								

Source: NSNO 2008 Operational Plan.

Exhibit 9

2008 School Launch and Support Objectives

Priority One—Incubation Program: New high-performing charter schools aligned with NSNO's core values

1. Develop comprehensive recruitment strategy to attract excellent local and national school founders

2. Finalize TFA alumni recruitment partnership

3. Finalize selection process that identifies great leaders and captures emerging leaders and teachers to be placed in existing schools

4. Develop training program that covers charter application writing, instruction, governance, operations, and organizational leadership

5. Build and maintain diverse board bank of community and business leaders, and place effectively

6. Help schools build high-quality parent engagement

7. Create board member training that ensures all new board members understand roles and responsibilities

8. Arrange site visits for incubators

9. Create efficient grant processes

10. Attract high-quality charter management organizations to the city

11. Partner with BES on training

12. Partner with NYC Center for Charter School Excellence on emerging leaders program

13. Define "milestones" throughout grant period (i.e., 501c3 application, corporation filing, monthly financial reporting in line with budget)

Owner: Chief of Staff/School Leadership Director

Support, Instructional Portion: Instructional Leadership Director

Assistance During Pilot Year: Human Capital and Partnerships Director

Grant Processes and Reporting: Director of NSNO Operations

Recruitment: School Support Manager

General Support: School Support Manager

Board Training/Governance: Meetinghouse Solutions, Inc.

CMO Interaction: CEO

Priority One—Building Excellent Schools: New schools founded through year-long residency program

14. NSNO partner in selection process with ultimate veto power over candidates

15. Coordination and participation in trainings

Owner: Chief of Staff/School Leadership Director

Support: CEO

Priority One—Data-Driven Instruction: Assist schools with curriculum alignment and assessment development and use (consider expanding to priority two schools in future—post leadership change)

16. Develop assessments for 4th, 5th, and 6th grades

17. Create training program with pilot schools

18. Clarify Massachusetts Project for School Performance role and sign partnership agreement

19. Create plan for additional schools and grades; evaluate and determine additional grade levels to be developed in the next phase of the pilot

20. Hire full-time Director of Data

Owner: Chief of Staff/School Leadership Director

Support: CEO

Owner, Short-Term: Instructional Leadership Director

Long-Term: Data-Driven Instruction Director

Support: Heather Caudill, Former Data-Driven Instruction Director, NYC CCSE, MAs Project for School Performance

Priority One—Start-Up Program: Operations support to newly approved charter schools not already part of the Incubation or BES programs

21. Design operational and financial trainings for initial year of operation
22. Rework grant agreement to better align with NSNO expectations, outcomes
23. Develop efficient Operations and Finance Training Program
24. Decide what level of governance support to provide
25. Assist each school with each financial and operations hire
26. Assist with procurement, facilities, other start-up
27. Conduct post-opening audit
28. Coordinate Walton funds
29. Coordinate with advocacy team on RSD issues

Owner, Short-Term: Charter School Business Management

Long-Term: School Operations Support Director

Support: Chief of Staff/School Leadership Director

School Support Manager

Priority Two—Board Support and Leader Change: In schools where boards are highly invested in achievement, we will work with the board to diagnose and quickly address weak leadership

30. Assist existing schools with active searches already under way
31. Rank schools to determine Priority Two candidates
32. Reach out to most significant Priority Two school boards
33. Conduct leadership audits on five schools
34. Conduct training on how to evaluate and hold school leader accountable once leader is chosen
35. Provide recruitment and selection support for three schools seeking new leaders
36. Hire Director of School Operations

Owner, Short-Term: CEO

Long-Term: School Operations Support Director

Support: Human Capital and Partnerships Director

School Instructional Leadership Director

Priority Three—Improvement Incentives and Closure

37. Offer support to authorizers when the weakest schools refuse to improve
    - 37.1. Propose standards to BESE on annual oversight and orderly escalation process
    - 37.2. Develop parent support and information program
    - 37.3. Pilot charter school self-policing program
38. Offer improvement incentives to schools that create largest improvements in academic achievement
    - 38.1. Develop clear process for school eligibility, rigor of award process
39. Develop best-practice awards for schools with highest levels of academic achievement to share with schools receiving improvement awards

Owner: Advocacy and Policy Director

Support: Human Capital and Partnerships Director

CEO

Source: NSNO 2008 Operational Plan.

Exhibit 10

2008 Human Capital Objectives

The New Teacher Project: Certified and alternate-route teachers for RSD-operated and charter schools

1. Recruitment and selection
    1.1. Assess number of teachers (certified and alt route) needed for 2008–2009 school year
    1.2. Develop understanding of link between teacher cash flow needs and quality recruitment
    1.3. Work with teachNOLA to increase quality of selectors
    1.4. Increase selectivity for certified teacher process
    1.5. Work with teachNOLA to measure the effectiveness of teachers and to use this data in the following years' selection process
    1.6. Encourage teachNOLA to ease teacher introduction to New Orleans and increase retention
    1.7. Increase efforts to encourage recruitment of local teachers
    1.8. Increase number of NSNO staff acting as selectors
2. Placement
    2.1. Ask TNTP to poll charters to develop understanding of buy-in and acceptance of teachNOLA
    2.2. Attend all major RSD/teachNOLA meetings
    2.3. Develop incentives to motivate placements in Priority One and Two schools
3. Other support to schools
    3.1. Explore model school initiative with TNTP

Owner: Human Capital and Partnerships Director

Support: CEO supports as necessary with RSD, TNTP National

New Leaders for New Schools: Principals for RSD-operated and charter schools

4. Recruitment and selection
    4.1. Increase efforts to encourage recruitment of local leaders
    4.2. Ensure high quality by becoming a part of the selection and placement process
    4.3. Define and communicate relationship with NLNS and how we are contractually able to participate in recruitment and selection
5. Placement
    5.1. Develop relationships with residents by attending their meetings at least once a month
    5.2. Recruit exceptional candidates for incubation
    5.3. Match other high-quality candidates with Priority One and Two schools

Owner: Director of Human Capital and Partnerships

Support: CEO supports with Charter Management Organizations and NLNS National

Teacher Training University: A local teacher training institution focused on Priority One and Two schools

6. Continue talks with New Schools Venture Fund

7. Collaborate with TNTP/TFA/CMOs

8. Research viability of teacher development organization: legal constraints, attendance estimates, funding, etc.

9. Meet with local university leaders and national reformers to discuss potential collaborative efforts

10. Discuss this idea thoroughly with the Cowen Institute and flesh out our joint roles in the development of such an organization

Owner: Human Capital and Partnerships Director

Support: CEO and Founder support

Partnership with TFA: Assist TFA in doubling number of corps members to approximately 250 annually

11. Work with TFA to increase funding for both TFA and NSNO

12. Support TFA in their efforts to recruit more highly effective teachers

Owner: Founder

Support: Development and Communications Director

Source: NSNO 2008 Operational Plan.

Exhibit 11

2008 Advocacy Objectives: Advocacy with Legislature/Louisiana Department of Education/BESE/RSD

Legislative

1. Lift charter cap
2. Manage campaign to expose legislature to long-term options for protecting charters from OPSB

BESE

3. Ensure that NACSA remains in charge of authorization, uses experts not bureaucrats
4. Propose clear and transparent policies for school oversight, renewal and closure
5. Provide legal assistance in closure proceedings
6. Make sure BESE members are aligned with our vision
7. Play role in facility master plan—including how to use facilities to group and roll out new charters

RSD

8. Monitor funding streams going through RSD (incentive fund, etc.)
9. Push for consolidation of existing RSD schools
10. Determine plan for charter advisory council

Community Leaders

11. Map out which groups we need to build relationships with—both pro and anti charter
12. Create strategy to influence all un-aligned organizations

Owner: Advocacy and Policy Director

Support: CEO, Founder/President

Strategy: Human Capital and Partnerships Director, School Operations Support Director

Empower Parents: Make parents the driving force of choice and accountability

13. Ensure *Parents' Guide* remains high quality and expands to include data about school quality
14. Determine role Urban League will play in ownership of *Parents' Guide*; make orderly transition
15. Develop plan for new data collection methods (at the state level if necessary) to achieve access to key data that is not already collected
16. Support parent empowerment process that:
    a) trains parents on how to choose the best school setting for their students
    b) educates parents about school choice
    c) ensures parents understand the power they have to close bad schools through choice
17. Coordinate RSD registration and charter lottery processes
18. Pilot feedback system for parents to report violations and irregularities in open-enrollment processes
19. Create program to assist parents during school closure

Owner: Parent Advocacy Organization Founder

Support: Business Plan—Human Capital and Partnerships Director

Parents' Guide: Urban League

Open-Enrollment Oversight: Advocacy and Policy Director

Source: NSNO 2008 Operational Plan.

Exhibit 12

Comparison of Services

Service Provided to Individual Schools	*Traditional Districts*	*Charter Management Organizations*	*New Schools for New Orleans*
Teacher Recruitment	Y	Y	Y
Teacher Training	Y	S	N
School Leader Recruitment	Y	Y	Y
School Leader Training	Y	S	Y
Board Member Recruitment	N	S	Y
Board Member Training	N	S	Y
Student Assessments	Y	Y	Y
School Assessments	Y	S	Y
Transportation	Y	S	N
Food Service	Y	S	N
Custodial Service	Y	S	N
Facilities	Y	S	N
Maintenance	Y	S	N
Legal Assistance	Y	Y	Y
Political Advocacy	Y	S	Y

Source: Case writer analysis.

Legend: Y = yes; S = some organizations provide the service and others do not; N = no.

Exhibit 13

New Orleans Schools Student Performance Data, 2006–2007

Percentages of Students Scoring at Basic and Above on the 2007 Louisiana Educational Assessment Program Test, Organized by Governing Body and Compared to State of Louisiana Averages

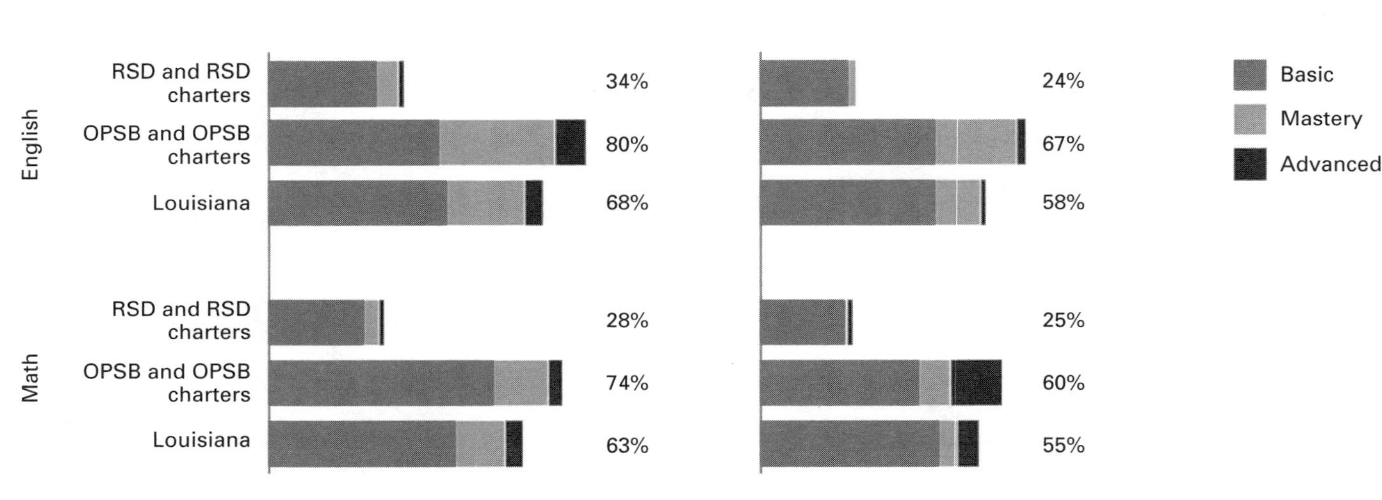

Source: "The State of Public Education in New Orleans," June 2007. Prepared by the Boston Consulting Group for The Greater New Orleans Education Foundation, The Scott S. Cowen Institute for Public Education Initiatives, and the New Orleans City Council Education Committee, http://www.tulane.edu/cowen_institute/stateofnola.pdf, p. 23.

Stacey Childress ■ Alison Berkley Wagonfeld

St. HOPE Academy: The Expansion Decision

In October 2006, Kevin Johnson was preparing to teach the first session of his new Leadership 101 class at Sacramento High School (Sac High). The former NBA all-star hoped his daily presence at the school would inspire the students to work a little harder on academics and personal development. In 2003, Johnson's nonprofit organization, St. HOPE Academy, had re-opened the 147-year-old Sac High as an independent charter school. In 2008, Johnson and his team would need to prove to the Sacramento City Unified School District (SCUSD) that the school's charter should be renewed.

Johnson started St. HOPE Academy (SHA) in 1989 as an after-school program for kids in his native Oak Park neighborhood of Sacramento, California. By 2006, Johnson had expanded the organization to include civic leadership, economic development, the arts, and public education. Johnson described St. HOPE as a "faith-based organization," but staff members were not required to belong to a specific religion. Instead, Johnson defined faith as "good values and strong character." He espoused "practical theology," which he described as "applying religion outside of the walls of the church." He believed that faith should draw people together, not divide them.

Until the summer of 2006, Sac High was the most ambitious project in the St. HOPE portfolio. But that year, the New York City Department of Education had asked Johnson to transform the struggling Choir Academy of Harlem into a charter school. To do so, Johnson and his team would have to decide if their model was transferable to New York, and master the unique aspects of the New York education system. St. HOPE had always planned to include economic development, arts, and civic leadership activities as it expanded, but had not yet figured out how to adapt these elements to a new city. As Johnson left his office to travel the few blocks to Sac High, he was excited by the prospect of improving the lives of students in New York as well as Sacramento, but he knew that a successful St. HOPE expansion was not a "slam dunk."

Sacramento and Oak Park

Sacramento, with a population of 460,000, was located approximately 100 miles northeast of San Francisco. The city was one of the first incorporated cities on the West Coast in 1849, and its population exploded with the discovery of gold in 1850. Sacramento became California's state capitol in 1854. Like any major city, Sacramento consisted of a variety of neighborhoods. The Oak Park neighborhood was located in the southeast section of the city, near a major highway.

In the 1950s the community was considered a "white, working class suburb" of Sacramento. This shifted in the 1960s, when the area "received an influx of African Americans and other minorities after the city tore down many low-income housing units near the Sacramento River."[1] According to a Sacramento State urban geography professor, "Racial change coincided with a change in the local economy—people moving in had a lower income than people moving out. Many businesses left, taking jobs with them. All this led to more poverty and the problems that often come with it: crime, drugs, prostitution and absentee landlords."[2] By the 1990s, the neighborhood developed a reputation for being one of the most dangerous areas in Sacramento. Oak Park's population of 29,000 was diverse: Whites represented 41%, Hispanics accounted for 36%, and African Americans 23%.

Kevin Johnson and St. HOPE Academy

St. HOPE's founder Kevin Johnson was raised in Oak Park by his mother and his maternal grandparents. (Johnson's father died in a boating accident when he was three.) Johnson's grandfather played an active role in his upbringing, influencing him to think broadly about his role in the community. Johnson remembered his grandfather as someone "who always stopped if there was a driver on the side of the road that needed help."

Like his parents and grandfather, Johnson had attended Sac High, where he played basketball and baseball. Upon graduation he attended the University of California at Berkeley on a sports scholarship. Johnson described Berkeley as an "eye-opening experience." He felt ill-prepared for the academic rigor and the conditioning required for college basketball. He rose to the challenge, however, breaking the school's basketball scoring record and graduating in 1987 with a BA in political science. He was drafted to play baseball for the Oakland A's, but decided to play professional basketball with the Cleveland Cavaliers. He was traded to the Phoenix Suns in 1988 where he was selected as an NBA All-star three times. Johnson played for the Suns until he retired in 2000, advancing to the playoffs almost every year. Johnson was one of only four players in NBA history to have averaged at least 20 points and 10 assists a game during three different seasons.

Johnson founded St. HOPE in 1989 during his summer break from the Phoenix Suns. Johnson explained his motivation: "I went home and saw people I went to school with who were in jail, on drugs, unemployed or dead. Many had kids and the cycle was repeating itself. I saw these 8, 9, 10 year olds headed down that same path and I said, 'I've got to do something.'"[3] Johnson selected 12 young men (ages 9–16) to mentor and named the program St. HOPE (Helping Others Pursue Excellence). He met with the group each afternoon in a portable classroom outside of Sac High. In exchange for tutoring the boys, Johnson required them to abide by his rules and promise to "give their best effort to profit from the experience." Johnson incorporated more than academics—he also wanted to teach morality, responsibility and self-esteem.[4] He crafted a mission for St. HOPE:

> St. HOPE Academy is a youth organization that is committed to providing young people with opportunities for educational, cultural, spiritual and social edification. We aim to build self-confidence and promote character development within the context of a cohesive and nurturing family environment. It is our goal to indoctrinate the members of St. HOPE with the belief that no problem is insurmountable, and the willingness to try and the desire to improve will lead to fulfillment and success.[5]

After the first summer session, Johnson wanted to expand SHA. He asked a friend from college, Lori Mills, to work with him to lay the foundation for a year-round program. Johnson combined his personal money and donations from community members to construct a new 7,000-square-foot multi-use facility located in the middle of Oak Park. In January 1992, St. HOPE celebrated the opening of its new facility, and later that year, the organization expanded its after-school and summer program to include girls. (See **Exhibit 1**.) The programs continued to combine academic elements with character development. During the 1990s, Mills headed up the day-to-day activities of St. HOPE while Johnson provided guidance and continued to play basketball for the Phoenix Suns.

St. HOPE Development Corporation: Economic Development and the Arts

Johnson knew he wanted to do more in Oak Park than guide kids in an after-school and summer program. He explained, "Better education cannot exist in a vacuum. Healthy schools thrive in healthy economic environments."[6] In 1994, Johnson founded St. HOPE Development Corporation (SHDC) to focus on improving Oak Park's outward appearance with a goal of inviting new businesses into the community. SHDC started by renovating a historic bank building on Broadway and then turned its attention to three additional projects: a dilapidated Victorian house on a prominent corner, a new headquarters for St. HOPE at the center of the "old Oak Park," and a 25,000-square-foot art gallery and retail complex next to the St. HOPE headquarters. The Victorian was completed in 2001, and the first phase of the headquarters was ready for use in 2002. (See **Exhibit 2**.)

The commercial complex was a difficult project, ultimately requiring three years, many permits, and millions of dollars to complete. The property included the run-down Woodruff Hotel that was being used for prostitution and drugs, and the dilapidated Guild Theater that dated back to the early 20th century but had been abandoned for decades. St. HOPE renovated the entire complex, and renamed it the 40 Acres Art Gallery and Cultural Center, in reference to the unfulfilled pledge by the U.S. government in the 1860s that emancipated slaves would receive 40 acres of farmland and the loan of a mule. The center opened in May 2003 with the art gallery, a Starbucks, a bookstore, a barbershop, 12 upscale lofts, and an impeccably renovated 200-seat Guild Theater.

The arts program was a critical element of St. HOPE's mission because Johnson believed that it was important to integrate art into business and education. In addition, art curator Kim Curry-Evans explained, "People of color have traditionally been under-represented in many art galleries. The 40 Acres gallery gives us an opportunity to showcase some great black artists." The Guild Theater, used for hundreds of speakers, shows, and other performances, was an integral part of the arts program.

Johnson saw SHDC as a channel for "shifting the paradigm from receiving social services (e.g., welfare and food bank) to stimulating economic growth." Ultimately, he hoped that SHDC would generate revenue that could be reinvested in the community. Because so many of the redevelopment projects focused on iconic buildings, Johnson believed they served a "symbolic purpose of showing the community that a small group of people can make a difference." He described his overall philosophy of community redevelopment as "taking what was, and making it so again."

Civic Leadership—Neighborhood Corps

Johnson's vision also included developing community leaders because he believed that many inner city communities, including Oak Park, lacked sustainable leadership. In response, he launched Neighborhood Corps (or "Hood Corps") in 1998, with a "mission to recruit, train and mobilize an army of civic leaders committed to revitalizing inner-city communities." In addition to short-term volunteer projects,

Hood Corps included a one-year residential fellowship program that involved long hours, hard work, physical exercise, college classes, community service, awareness of current events, and spiritual growth. Johnson modeled aspects of the program on his early experience at UC Berkeley. He explained, "I don't want our kids to be shocked at college the way I was." High school graduates and college students could apply to be one of up to ten Hoods Corps fellows each year. Some participants quickly dropped out due to the rigorous schedule and discipline, but Johnson believed that the students who completed the program "would be prepared for anything."

Expansion into Public Schools

In the late 1990s, Johnson became aware of the burgeoning charter school movement. Charter schools were nonsectarian public schools of choice that operated without many of the regulations that applied to traditional public schools. For example, most charter schools were not required to hire unionized teachers. Advocates claimed that charter schools were granted this increased operating autonomy in return for more accountability for results. The "charter" that established each school served as a performance contract detailing the school's mission, program, goals, students served, methods of assessment, and ways to measure success. Most charters were granted for three- to five-year terms, at the end of which it could be renewed or terminated by the entity that had granted it.[7] Charter schools received funding from the state, and were not allowed to charge tuition or discriminate against any pupil on the basis of ethnicity, national origin, gender, or disability. By 2006, there were charter school laws in 40 states, Puerto Rico, and Washington, D.C., and more than 3,500 charter schools serving over 1,000,000 students.[8] (See **Exhibit 3**.)

Each state had its own regulations governing charter schools. California required charter schools to participate in the same statewide testing as other public schools, and the results were used as one of the measures to determine if a school's charter should be renewed. California's charter schools received approximately $7,500 in per pupil operating revenue, which was comparable to its regular public schools, but they did not receive public money for capital expenditures such as facility construction or renovation. California instituted a "cap" of 250 charter schools in 1999, with an additional 100 allowed per year. At 470 charter schools, the state was operating below its cap of 850 in 2006. California had two types of charter schools—independent and dependent. Independent charter schools operated as autonomous legal entities and were not restricted by local collective bargaining agreements. Dependent charter schools were legally part of the school district or county office of education that granted their charter, and usually had to recognize existing collective bargaining agreements. Johnson kept his eye on the charter school movement as it gained momentum, wondering if it was another way that St. HOPE could make a difference in Oak Park.

Sacramento and Oak Park Schools

The Sacramento City Unified School District (SCUSD) served approximately 52,000 students in 83 schools from grades kindergarten (K) through 12. Hispanics made up approximately 29% of the student body, with African-American and White students accounting for 22% each, and Asians 23%. Approximately 63% of students were low-income. California schools were evaluated in part by their scores on an Academic Performance Index (API) (ranging between 200 and 1,000), which was based on student performance on a variety of standardized tests. The statewide API performance target for all schools was 800. A school's growth was measured by how well it was moving toward or beyond that goal. The district-wide API score for SCUSD was 700 in 2005 and 706 in 2006. The overall score for the state of California was 709 in 2005 and 720 in 2006. (See **Exhibits 4** and **5**.)

SCUSD was run by a superintendent who was hired by an elected seven-member school board. According to the SCUSD website, "Among its many responsibilities, the Board establishes a long-term vision for the district and sets district policies and goals, while the Superintendent carries out the policies and manages the day-to-day operations of the district."[9] The Board was also responsible for reviewing and approving requests for charter schools.

In 2001, SCUSD Superintendent Jim Sweeney asked Johnson if he could help underserved elementary students in Oak Park, many of whom were African-American. Oak Park had three elementary schools, Bret Harte (Bret), Father Keith B. Kenny (Kenny), and Oak Ridge, but African-American students as a group did not perform well in any of them. Sweeney knew that St. HOPE effectively served African-American students in its after-school program for older students, and he thought Johnson might be able to help younger children as well. Johnson agreed to partner with the district to create a new charter school, Public School 7 (PS7), in an empty SCUSD building in Oak Park.

Public School 7

Johnson pulled together a task force to create a charter petition for PS7, which he submitted to SCUSD in 2002. The school was designed as a K–8 model, but the team planned to start with K–4 before expanding into the higher grades. The educational program included year-round classes, low student-to-teacher ratios, music and art education as well as hands-on learning, leadership training, and parental involvement. St. HOPE received an independent charter for PS7 in 2002, and Johnson hired Herinder Pegany, a long-time Sacramento educator, as the school's first principal.

St. HOPE recruited students throughout 2003, and the school opened its doors to 200 students on August 4, 2003. All PS7 families were required to sign a commitment contract that stipulated the responsibilities of the families attending the school, including attendance at year-round classes, extended class days, and minimum parent volunteer hours. In addition, families had to agree to the "five pillars" of the school: (1) high expectations; (2) choice and commitment; (3) more time; (4) focus on results; and (5) power to lead. (See **Exhibit 6** for details about each of these pillars.)[10]

By 2006, the school had grown to 370 students with a waiting list. Although the PS7 student body reflected the socioeconomic mix of Oak Park, the school's ethnic composition did not—approximately 90% of the PS7 students were African American. Lisa Serna-Mayorga, director of public relations for St. HOPE, attributed this ratio to Johnson's involvement in the initial recruitment for the school. She explained, "When St. HOPE decided to open PS7, members of Kevin's church were excited to send their kids to the school. Then word of mouth took over, particularly in the African-American community, and some families wanted to come to PS7 even though it meant driving 15–20 minutes to get there." Lori Mills added, "PS7 does not discriminate and would be happy to have more diversity in its student body. We have tried to recruit in the whole community, but many people associate St. HOPE with the original after-school program that predominantly served black students."

PS7's student API score jumped from 638 in 2004 to 737 in 2005, representing one of the largest one-year gains in the state of California. In 2006, PS7's API score rose to 746. By way of comparison, the 2006 API score for Harte was 721, for Kenny was 627, and for Oak Ridge was 642. Students reported they were excited to attend school and began thinking of themselves as college-bound—a major shift for many of the students and their families. Mills reported that St. HOPE believed that "Sweeney and the SCUSD board were pleased with the results." (See **Exhibit 7** for performance data.)

Nevertheless, challenges remained. One of the biggest issues was the need for additional space. By 2006, PS7 had expanded to K–7, but it was overcrowded and there was no space to add 8th grade. The facility was owned by SCUSD, which had to approve any changes to the building, including the addition of portable classrooms. As of late 2006, St. HOPE and SCUSD had been in discussions about space expansion for nearly six months without resolution. The district had to approve minor upgrades as well—when PS7 wanted to add air conditioning to classrooms that were used during the summer, they had to ask for SCUSD's permission. Chief Financial Officer Tom Bratkovich (HBS '01) observed, "Our lack of control over PS7 facilities could put our growth plans at risk."

Sacramento High School

Sac High was one of the oldest high schools on the West Coast, having first opened its doors in 1856. When Johnson attended the school in the early 1980s, it was considered a strong high school, but by 2002 it was faltering. The school's API score was 568, and graduation rate had slipped to 84% of students who started their senior year. During an October 2002 meeting, Sweeney told Johnson that the school was at risk of being shut down and restructured into five smaller schools. A week later, when Johnson heard that yet another principal was resigning, he became even more concerned about the fate of his alma mater and its students. As Johnson thought of the challenges facing the school, he decided that St. HOPE could help. Although they were busy with the start-up of PS7 and the opening of 40 Acres, Johnson believed that the situation at Sac High presented a rare opportunity to turn around a troubled school in the middle of Oak Park. Sweeney indicated that the SCUSD board was open to a proposal from St. HOPE for a charter school to replace the existing Sac High.

By January 2003, Johnson had raised seed money from the Gates Foundation[11] and pulled together a group that drafted a petition to reopen Sac High as an independent charter school. There was deep community support for St. HOPE, but there was also strong opposition, particularly from the Sacramento City Teachers Association (SCTA). SCUSD held many heated meetings about St. HOPE's petition, but finally voted in March 2003 to award the charter to St. HOPE. The SCTA opposed the decision and filed a lawsuit against the district. One practical implication of the lawsuit was that St. HOPE was not allowed access to Sac High for planning purposes. SCUSD and St. HOPE fought the lawsuit during the spring and summer, while preparing to re-open Sac High in the fall of 2003.

After a contentious battle, Johnson and his team prevailed just three weeks before the opening of school in fall of 2003. On short notice, the teachers and staff scrambled to pull together a comprehensive curriculum. Johnson explained, "St. HOPE had little time to hire teachers and plan classes before school started, so everyone had to plan on the fly more than they would have liked."

On September 2, 2003, Sac High opened as a charter school with 1,450 students. The new Sac High consisted of five small schools on one campus: School of the Arts, School of Business and Communications, School of Health Sciences, School of Law and Public Service, and School of Math, Engineering and Science. Each of the schools had its own principal and focus areas, although all shared a standardized curriculum (e.g., English, math, science, social studies). Students attended classes at their small school and met up with the broader student body during lunch periods. St. HOPE believed the small-school environment would help create more accountability for students, teachers, and administrators.

Johnson admitted that it took some time for students to get accustomed to the new organization, particularly students who had attended the "old" Sac High. In addition to the new small-schools model, St. HOPE ran the school in a more disciplined manner than before, which proved challenging for students who were used to fewer enforced rules. Students and their families were required to sign a "Commitment to Excellence" form before starting school that included behavior requirements for attending Sac High. (See **Exhibit 8**.)

Johnson promoted Herinder Pegany from principal of PS7 to chief academic officer for St. HOPE Public Schools, with responsibility for the educational programs at the elementary and high schools. Pegany described Sac High's first two years as a time of "unrelenting focus on culture and expectations," which he believed was critical to improving learning. By 2006, the school had improved on some measures, but not on others. The one-year graduation rate reached 96%, and more students indicated an interest in attending a four-year college—both of which were seen as positive developments. However, Sac High did not meet its state API growth targets in 2006—the school's API score dropped from 615 in 2005 to 610 in 2006. (See **Exhibit 9** for additional data.)

Pegany explained:

> The 2006 API data that came out in August was a wake up call for Kevin and our whole organization. From 2003 to 2005, we focused on culture and classroom management, but we were not able to focus on teaching to the California standards as much as we would have liked. Teachers did the best they could with what they had.
>
> We are now making a conscious effort to acquire resources to help us focus on improving our teaching and ensuring that our students are learning what they need to learn. We now have assessment software to help us track student progress during the year, and we have arranged for professional development for our teachers. We hired coaches that can train teachers, demo lessons, co-teach and provide immediate feedback in the spirit of improvement as opposed to evaluation. Of course we were disappointed with our scores, but we don't make excuses at St. HOPE. Instead, we look for solutions.

In addition to improving its scores, it was also important for St. HOPE to maintain enrollment, which had dropped from 1,450 to 1,200 by 2006. The Sac High campus could accommodate 1,800 students, and SCUSD wanted to see St. HOPE using the building to its capacity. As an independent charter, St. HOPE was responsible for recruiting its students without the help of the district—it was not even listed as a high school option on the SCUSD website or in its publications. Sac High had to recruit all of its students through mailings, word of mouth, and other methods. St. HOPE struggled to educate the community about what it meant to be a charter school and how the "small schools" worked inside of the bigger school. In addition, in 2006 Sac High adopted a year-round school calendar, longer class days, and uniforms, all of which had to be explained to potential families.

St. HOPE knew that the coming year would be critical in demonstrating progress on test scores and enrollment. The Sac High charter would be up for renewal in 2008, and the state required specific evidence of academic success (e.g., hitting API growth targets) in order to grant the renewal. Johnson was prepared to rise to the challenge of turning around the school. He explained, "There are educators who believe that it is impossible to fix a troubled school without shutting it down for at least a year and starting fresh. We are going to prove them wrong." However, Sacramento seemed less hospitable to charter schools in 2006 than it had been in the past. Superintendent Sweeney had retired, and his successor was less enthusiastic about charters. Also, the current SCUSD school board had no strong charter advocates.

In addition to preparing for the Sac High charter renewal, St. HOPE planned to open the Triumph Center for Early Childhood Education in partnership with the school of education at UC Davis and the M.I.N.D. Institute. Triumph would serve 90 children aged three to five beginning in September 2007. The school was designed to accommodate approximately 20–25 children with special needs, including autism, speech and language disorders, and learning disabilities. The new focus on preschool and special needs children required technical expertise that did not currently reside in the organization. Johnson hired an expert to lead the school, but many parts of the organizational infrastructure had to learn how to integrate this new school into the St. HOPE portfolio.

Organization and Management

St. HOPE was a nonprofit umbrella organization that consisted of three separate legal entities: St. HOPE Academy, St. HOPE Public Schools, and St. HOPE Development Corporation. Johnson served as CEO/President and Chairman of all three groups, yet each maintained its own Board of Directors. In 2006, there were approximately 140 employees across all three entities, with 120 of these employed by St. HOPE Public Schools and the remaining 20 by St. HOPE Academy.

St. HOPE Academy (SHA) served as a headquarters office and was responsible for fundraising, programming, and managing shared services such as human resources, information technology, finance/accounting, and legal. SHA's operating budget was approximately $2 million, the majority of which came from donations and grants. (See **Exhibits 10a** and **10b** for SHA financials.)

SHA was run by a loyal management team who described themselves as being "irresistibly drawn to Johnson's vision." Mills, one of Johnson's first employees, served as chief operating officer in 2006. Dana Gonzalez, the chief program officer, joined in 2003 during the planning of Sac High. Pegany, the chief academic officer since 2005, was initially hired as an educational consultant in 1999, and then became the first principal of PS7 in 2003. Chief financial officer Bratkovich was the newest member of the St. HOPE management team, having joined in July 2006.

St. HOPE Public Schools (SHPS) was responsible for overseeing PS7, Sac High, the Triumph Center for Early Childhood Education, and any future education efforts outside of California. It had its own board of directors, bylaws, rules and procedures. SHPS had a 2005–2006 operating budget of $12 million, the majority of which came from local and state funding on a per-student basis. SHPS supplemented its public funding with private grants. (See **Exhibits 11a** and **11b** SHPS financials.)

St. HOPE Development Corporation (SHDC) was the nonprofit vehicle for the organization's real estate transactions. As of September 2006, SHDC owned several buildings in Oak Park, and served as a landlord to the building's tenants. SHDC generated revenue through rent and lease payments. SHDC had approximately $5 million of assets. No employees worked directly for SHDC. (See **Exhibits 12a** and **12b** for SHDC financials.)

Although each of the three entities had its own focus, there was also some overlap in activities and some financial transfers between them.

(See **Exhibit 13** for cash flow between entities.) As Gonzalez described, "Each of our employees works for one of the legal entities, but we think of ourselves as one big organization with functional responsibilities. In the past, our organizational structure was a bit confusing, and we are in the process of figuring out if there is a better way to organize, particularly as we position ourselves for growth outside of Sacramento." Bratkovich believed there were specific aspects of the organization structure that were likely to be addressed in the coming months. He elaborated:

> For years we were structured as three separate legal entities, each of which had its own staff. We are now establishing functional groups that work across all three of the entities. We just created a new organization chart, but we are still getting used to working this way. [See **Exhibit 14.**] We are also figuring out the best way for functional areas such as Finance and Operations, Programs and Educational Services to connect with each school run by SHPS.

Expansion Beyond Sacramento

From the time St. HOPE opened its first charter school in 2003, Johnson received requests to expand into other communities. Starting in April 2006, the expansion invitations increased after St. HOPE was profiled on *The Oprah Winfrey Show* in two episodes about U.S. public schools. Johnson was wary of expanding too quickly, but thought that the St. HOPE model might work in other regions as long as certain prerequisites were met. For example, Johnson required that parents and students in a new community be able to articulate a desire for a different educational experience than the one they currently had; otherwise, it would be difficult for them to embrace the high expectations set by St. HOPE. He required a 12- to 18-month planning phase leading up to the opening of a new school, along with a commitment of adequate planning money. He believed that dedicated, high-quality staff in the new locale was essential, as was support from the school board and superintendent. And finally, the local superintendent had to agree to appoint someone on his or her staff who had a strong belief in charter schools to serve as an advocate for St. HOPE in the charter petition and start-up processes.

These prerequisites were bolstered by a list of operational "non-negotiables" (the "Four Fs"):

- Funding ($10,000–$13,000 per student, primarily from the city and state)
- Facilities (Exclusive use of a building that could accommodate 900–1,200 students with access to nearby fields and playground facilities, at little or no cost to St. HOPE)
- Freedom (Independence to develop programs and hire staff, unfettered by unions)
- Fellows (Assistance in finding leaders who could participate in a one-year fellowship program to conduct the planning process in the ramp-up to the opening of a new school)

The combination of these prerequisites and non-negotiables were designed to help Johnson and his team analyze various opportunities as they arose. As of early 2006, St. HOPE had yet to find a situation that met all of the organization's criteria.

In the meantime, board member Michelle Rhee was concerned that the organization might not be ready to expand when the time came. She felt that St. HOPE was "woefully understaffed" for growth. Johnson agreed with her and with her help convened an external task force in May 2006 for a six-month project focused on "enhancing the performance of St. HOPE Public Schools and positioning the organization for significant growth in the future." Johnson recruited five members for the task force from around the country. He had been inspired by a story in Jim Collins' book *Good to Great* about the philosophy of former Vietnam POW Admiral Jim Stockdale. The admiral recounted the importance of keeping faith that you will reach your goals in the long run, while all the time confronting the brutal facts of the present situation. In honor of this concept, Johnson named the external group the Stockdale task force, and gave it two goals:

1. Develop the capacity, processes and infrastructure necessary for SHPS to be able to guarantee results for students including:
    a. Having undeniable evidence of success for charter renewal
    b. Being the top-rated elementary and high school in Sacramento
    c. Becoming a long-standing institution in the community
2. Determine a long-term model for success and sustainability of SHPS (including proper alignment between SHA and SHPS)

The group talked several times a month and focused on six areas: Curriculum and Instruction, Data and Accountability, Human Resources, Finance and Operations, Organization and Governance, and Student Recruitment. They developed a list of deliverables, and made great strides on all fronts by the SHPS September board meeting. The group made recommendations about strengthening the academic program at Sac High, implementing a new accountability system, and designing a new organizational structure, among others. Commenting on the group's dedication to St. HOPE's success, Rhee observed, "St. HOPE has an amazing culture in which everyone involved goes above and beyond, even volunteers. The task force completed a massive amount of concrete work that made the organization stronger—their output was incredibly impressive."

The Harlem Opportunity

In May 2006 Johnson received a call that gave the task force an even greater sense of urgency. A group of parents from New York City with children at the Choir Academy of Harlem (Choir Academy) contacted Johnson about becoming involved in revitalizing their struggling public school. The Choir Academy of Harlem, a school serving grades 5–12, had long been affiliated with the Harlem Boys Choir, a well-known boys singing group. In 2005, the New York City Department of Education (NYCDOE) severed the ties between the school and the singing group due to fiscal issues and alleged sexual abuse. The school's parents were looking for a new partner, and sought out Johnson after seeing him on *Oprah*.

Johnson began discussions with the Choir Academy parents and the NYCDOE to determine if there was a fit with St. HOPE's prerequisites and non-negotiables. His initial discussions were encouraging, and he received a commitment from New York City Chancellor Joel Klein and Deputy Mayor Dennis Walcott that they would help him work through any issues. After a series of meetings, St. HOPE and the NYDOE set forth the terms of a partnership under which St. HOPE might "revitalize" the Choir Academy, if Johnson and his team decided an expansion made sense.

St. HOPE wanted to reopen the Choir Academy as a charter school serving grades K–12; however, that depended on New York lifting its state cap on new charter schools. The New York charter school law imposed a cap of 100 new charters state-wide due to a compromise with the state teachers union. When the cap was reached in 2005, only "charter conversions" of existing public schools were allowed; however, conversion schools often did not have the same degree of control over the teachers and curriculum as a new charter school. New charter schools could be authorized by the State University of New York board of trustees, the New York State Board of Regents, or the NYCDOE.

Though charter advocates engaged in significant lobbying activities, as of October 2006 the cap was still in effect. As a result, St. HOPE was working with the NYCDOE to determine ways to run the school either as a conversion charter or as a "contract school." As a contract school, Choir Academy would remain a regular NYCDOE public school bound by district policies and union contracts, but the chancellor would hire St. HOPE as an outside provider to manage the school on a day-to-day basis. However, as a contract school St. HOPE would not be able to enforce aspects of its operating model such as requiring students to wear uniforms.

Building a Team

Within days of first talking to parents at the Choir Academy, Johnson began thinking about staffing the Harlem school. He knew that "finding the right high-level leaders would be a critical factor in the ultimate success of the school, and therefore our willingness to go to New York." In advance of a final decision about expansion, Johnson decided to put people on the ground to assess the opportunity and plan for the potential school. Johnson knew that one of his former employees—Jill Gibson—was living in New York. Gibson had worked with St. HOPE from 1990 to 1994 as the head of program development and fundraising, and then she left for law school. She returned for a short period of time in the mid-1990s, but then left again, this time to work as a consultant for IBM.

Johnson called Gibson in June 2006 and convinced her to take a leave of absence from IBM and return for a third time—this time to run "new site development" for Harlem. Gibson agreed to serve as a "trailblazer," which entailed working on the new charter application, spending time in the existing school, building relationships with the parents and teachers, and assessing who might be interested in staying if St. HOPE assumed operation of the school. In addition, Gibson worked with the current school administration to establish new systems, policies, and procedures that reflected St. HOPE's approach to education. Gibson was surprised by "the lack of discipline and structure in the school," which she attributed to having five principals in five years, and the distractions stemming from the conflict with the Harlem Boys Choir. She discovered that the community was frustrated with the school's lack of improvement over several years. One parent had asked, "We've had all these people come in to the school, but it never seems to get any better. Why will St. HOPE be any different?" Gibson knew St. HOPE had to answer that question satisfactorily to gain the trust of students, teachers, and parents.

Johnson also hired Tanya Morgan to begin planning the academic program. Johnson had heard of Morgan through the Teach For America network—she had a strong background in New York City public education and was also a 1995 graduate of Sac High. In June 2006, Johnson had sent her an email inquiring if she would be interested in discussing St. HOPE. Morgan was familiar with St. HOPE and its initiatives in Sacramento, and happened to be at a career transition when Johnson contacted her. They talked later that week for over two hours, and within a month, Morgan was hired as "Principal in Training" for Harlem and received a Peat Fellowship[12] to help cover her expenses while she planned the new school.

Morgan had high expectations for the Choir Academy—if St. HOPE took over, she wanted the school to represent "a renaissance in public education through a blending of academics and the arts." She knew, however, that the transition from the current state of the school to her vision would require a lot of hard work by everyone involved, as well as a charter school policy change at the state level. Given the uncertainty around the "charter" status of the school, it was unclear just how much control SHPS would have when it came to hiring (and firing) teachers and administrators. Gibson expressed concern: "Many of the teachers and administrators in place right now do not have the skills that we need, and we require more accountability than they are accustomed to. If we do not have the right educators to implement our model, it will hamper our success."

Although SHPS ideally would run a K–12 program at the Choir Academy facility, the team considered starting with K–3 or K–4 and scaling up from there, both because it was easier to manage a smaller group of students and because it could be easier to get a charter approved for an elementary school. Also, if the charter was denied, St. HOPE could operate the school under a management contract with the NYC-DOE, which allowed a school with less than 250 students to operate outside of the union contract. However, fewer students meant less money from the NYCDOE, as New York provided approximately $10,000 per pupil. If the school was run as a contract or conversion charter, the students would likely come from the existing school in the facility. If it was a new charter, St. HOPE would need to actively recruit new students.

Morgan, Gibson, and the rest of St. HOPE hoped to have more clarity about the charter status of the school by early 2007. They realized, however, that even if the charter cap was lifted in 2007, it might be another one to two years before St. HOPE could open a charter school at the Choir Academy site. In the meantime, the St. HOPE team was working on several contingency plans that would enable them to "fully engage" with the school during the transition. St. HOPE budgeted for approximately $400,000 of expenses (e.g., salaries, supplies, travel) in 2007 to explore the Harlem opportunity. The organization received a $120,000 donation earmarked for New York expansion to offset a portion of the costs, and SHA was actively seeking additional sources of funding.

Exporting the St. HOPE Model

Morgan and Gibson spent a great deal of time thinking about what parts of St. HOPE in Sacramento they would implement in New York if the expansion became a reality. Most importantly, Morgan believed that they needed to capture the "spirit of St. HOPE," which she described as a "belief that you can make changes . . . a belief that individuals can make a difference." Morgan and Gibson were working with the St. HOPE board of directors and managers on how to codify the culture of St. HOPE in a way that could be integrated into the Harlem school. Along those lines, the St. HOPE team felt strongly that they needed exclusive use of the existing facility in order to control the "feel" of the school. Fortunately, the NYCDOE was willing to help make that happen, and even offered to shoulder the costs of the facility.

In thinking about the curriculum, Morgan considered a number of "best practices" from PS7. For example, she believed the extended day seemed to be working, as did the method of engaging parents. She thought that PS7 handled remediation effectively, bringing kids up to their grade level by pulling them out of class in small groups and increasing their time in school.

Gibson wanted to replicate the small-school environment, even if they eventually became a K–12 school. However, she questioned Morgan's assumption that the California curriculum was necessarily the right one for New York. She wondered, "How much we should dictate the details to the Choir Academy administration and teachers, as opposed to letting them make their own choices based on their knowledge of New York standards?"

As St. HOPE worked through the many complicated details of the decision to open a school in Harlem, the team also discussed how they might include the civic leadership and economic development aspects of the organization. The Harlem school was already grounded in the arts due to its historic relationship with the Boys Choir, and St. HOPE planned to build on that foundation. Rhee believed that "the St. HOPE educational model in Sacramento is based on the Hood Corps tenets, particularly the importance of high expectations for everyone, and it's important that those beliefs help define our academic and arts agenda in Harlem. The real question is whether to undertake a building renovation or other symbolic project to reflect the economic development piece of our mission."

Johnson also knew that St. HOPE had to have the right organizational infrastructure in place to expand. Bratkovich agreed: "St. HOPE has a compelling vision, and we are now at the stage in which we need to structure the organization for growth. We must define what can and should be shared among communities, and what should be specific to each community. In order to scale, we need to share infrastructure costs whenever we can—a challenge we are just starting to tackle."

Ready to Grow or Stretched Too Thin?

Even though Johnson was described as a "workaholic," he did not have enough time to do everything he wanted each day. He believed it was critical to be personally involved at the beginning of any new initiative, but once a framework was in place, Johnson thought he could pull back and rely on strong leaders "on the ground." He explained, "I need to make sure that the uniqueness of St. HOPE does not stop with me."

Johnson knew that expanding to New York was a risk. But he also believed St. HOPE would "never perfect our model—there will always be room for improvement. But with the right attitude and leaders, along with well-thought-out controls and systems, we can make a positive impact on hundreds, or even thousands, of kids." Amidst the pressure to move fast, Johnson was committed to being as rigorous as possible in assessing the New York opportunity. As he often did, he relied on advice that his grandfather, a steel worker, had given him repeatedly over the years: "Measure twice, and cut once."

Before making a formal commitment to NYCDOE, St. HOPE needed to answer several questions: Was the Sacramento model replicable? If it was replicable, how much should they implement in Harlem, and to what extent should the school be unique to the community? Whatever the answers, did the organization have the capacity to successfully manage a new site 3,000 miles from home? And were the conditions on the ground in New York favorable enough for expansion, particularly with respect to the uncertainty around the charter regulations? "Measure twice, cut once."

Notes

1. Oak Park information from article in the *Sacramento State Bulletin*. "Project Has Students Probing Memories of Oak Park Residents," *Sacramento State Bulletin,* October 31, 2005, http://www.csus.edu/bulletin/bulletin103105/bulletin103105oakpark.htm, accessed October 19, 2006.

2. Ibid.

3. Interview: "Oprah's Special Report: American Schools in Crisis," *The Oprah Winfrey Show,* August 1, 2006, excerpt found through Factiva, accessed September 5, 2006.

4. "Fifteen Years of Hope," excerpt from St. HOPE Story, upcoming book provided by St. HOPE Academy, page 10.

5. Ibid.

6. Ibid., page 12.

7. Ibid.

8. Adapted from the U.S. Charter Schools website, http://www.uscharterschools.org/pub/uscs_docs/o/index.htm, accessed October 31, 2006.

9. Sacramento City Unified School District Website, http://www.scusd.edu/board_of_education/index.htm, accessed October 20, 2006.

10. Johnson had a strong relationship with KIPP (Knowledge is Power Program), another prominent charter school organization, and elements of the commitment contract and the pillars were borrowed from KIPP.

11. The Bill & Melinda Gates Foundation provided grants to improve public education, with an emphasis on small high schools.

12. Johnson developed the Peat Fellowship Program in memory of his grandparents. Recipients were given a stipend to spend a year learning about best practices and planning for the future.

Exhibit 1

St. HOPE Timeline (1989–2006)

July 1989:	St. HOPE founded by Kevin Johnson
April 1990:	First Annual St. HOPE Benefit Dinner
November 1990:	Groundbreaking for St. HOPE Academy Building
July 1992:	Girls join St. HOPE Academy
1994:	Johnson creates St. HOPE Development Corporation
August 1999:	Hoods Corp Fellowship Program started
August 2001:	Opening of Oak Park Victorian
May 2002:	SCUSD approves charter for PS7 Elementary School
March 2003:	SCUSD approves charter for Sac High
May 2003:	40 Acres Art Gallery and Cultural Center opens
August 2003:	PS7 opens
September 2003:	Sac High re-opens as a charter school
January 2006:	Planning begins for Early Childhood Education Center
July 2006:	Agreement reached with New York City Department of Education for St. HOPE involvement at the Choir Academy of Harlem

Source: St. HOPE.

Exhibit 2

Map of Oak Park Region in Sacramento

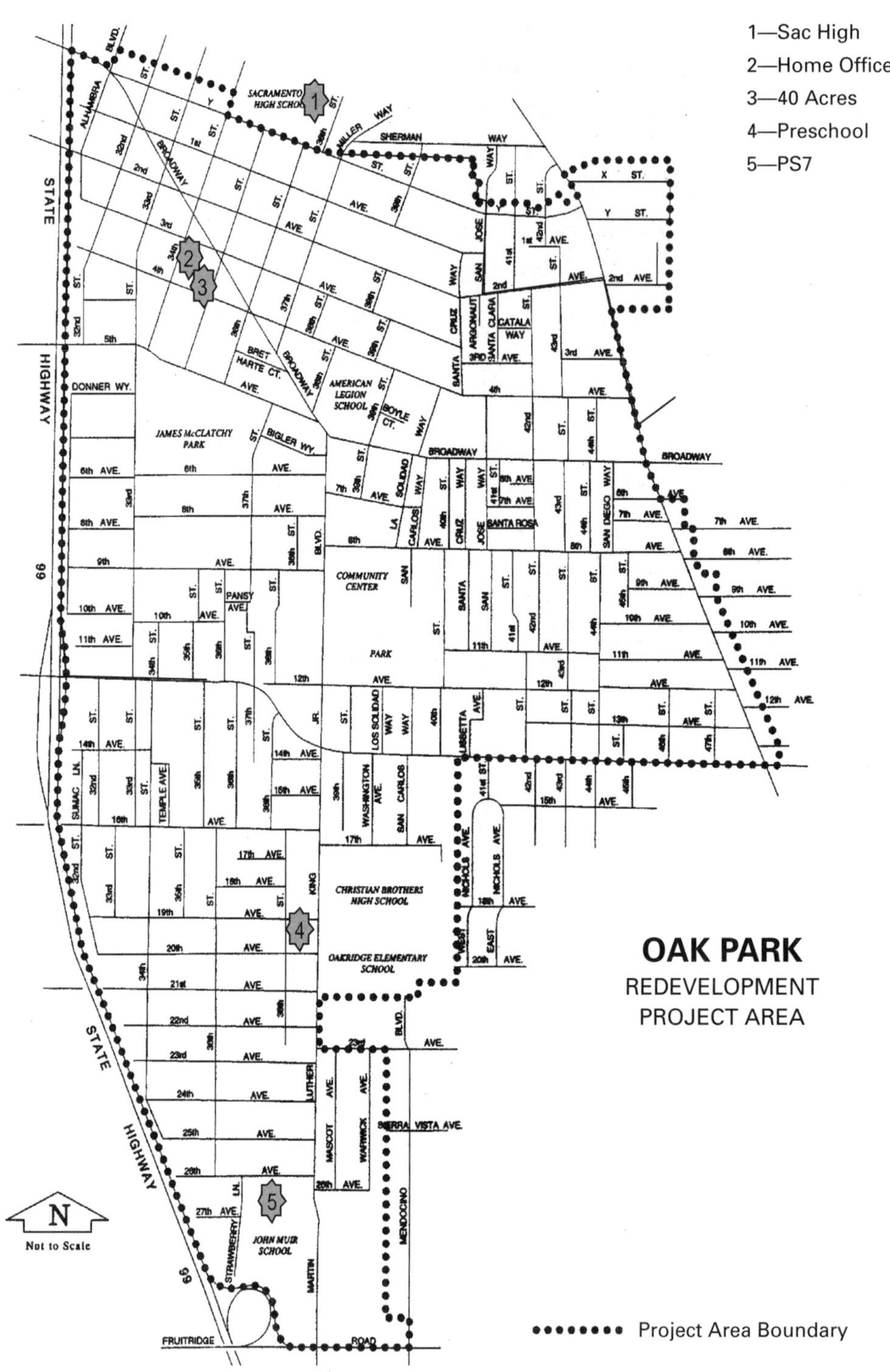

Source: St. HOPE Academy.

Exhibit 3

Charter School Trends

A comprehensive 2004–2005 study by the National Charter School Research Project (NCSRP) drew eight major conclusions about trends in charter schools:

1. Nationally, the number of charter schools grew faster in 2004–2005 than in any of the previous four years;
2. Future growth is limited in many states by legislative caps on numbers and/or location of charters;
3. Nationally, charter schools serve a larger proportion of minority and low-income students than is found in traditional public schools, a characteristic due largely to the disproportionate number of charter schools in urban areas;
4. Charter schools differ from traditional public schools in size and grade span;
5. Alternate authorizers, such as state agencies or universities, are more likely to sponsor brand new charter schools than to sponsor existing schools that convert to charter status;
6. Few charters are operated by management organizations;
7. Few states provide facilities funding, a fact that limits the number of charter schools that can be opened in a majority of states;
8. Charter schools are creatures of state policy and therefore differ from one state to another and are as diverse as the states and the legislation that permit them.

Source: "Hopes, Fears and Reality: A Balanced Look at Charter Schools in 2005," Robin J. Lake and Paul T. Hill, *National Charter School Research Project Center on Reinventing Public Education,* Daniel J. Evans School of Public Affairs, University of Washington, November 2005, Chapter 1.

Exhibit 4

Sacramento City Unified Schools—Schools by Type

Number	*Type of School*
54	Elementary—K to 6
6	Kindergarten to 8
8	Middle—7 to 8 (two have grades 6 to 8)
6	High
1	Continuation
1	Independent Study K–12
1	Alternative Schools
6	Charter Schools
5	Adult Education Centers

Source: Compiled from SCUSD website, accessed October 20, 2006.

Exhibit 5

Comparative Data for Selected California Urban School Districts

	Sacramento Unified	*Los Angeles Unified*	*San Diego Unified*	*Long Beach Unified*	*Fresno Unified*	*San Francisco Unified*	*Oakland Unified*
Enrollment	51,420	741,367	134,709	96,319	80,760	57,144	49,214
Number of Schools	83	721	190	86	85	108	123
Student Demographics (Race)							
African American	22%	12%	14%	18%	11%	14%	41%
American Indian	1%	0%	1%	0%	1%	1%	0%
Asian	23%	4%	9%	9%	16%	42%	17%
Filipino	1%	2%	7%	4%	0%	6%	1%
Hispanic or Latino	29%	73%	43%	49%	54%	22%	33%
Pacific Islander	1%	0%	1%	2%	0%	1%	1%
White (not of Hispanic origin)	22%	9%	26%	17%	16%	10%	6%
Student Demographics (Other)							
Low-Income	63%	78%	54%	61%	82%	54%	71%
English Learners	31%	42%	28%	24%	30%	28%	28%
Designated Gifted and Talented	6%	9%	21%	7%	11%	16%	9%
API							
2002 API	644	595	677	648	579	683	568
2003 API	666	622	697	682	610	706	592
2004 API	679	633	710	694	623	724	601
2005 API	700	649	728	713	644	745	634
2006 API	706	658	735	724	659	755	653
Four-Year Growth (2002–2006)	62	63	58	76	80	72	85

Source: California Department of Education.

Exhibit 6

St. HOPE Public School Pillars of Education

1. High Expectations. St. HOPE Public Schools has high expectations for academic achievement and conduct that are clearly defined, measurable, and make no excuses based on the background of students. Students, parents, teachers, and staff create and reinforce a culture of achievement and support, through a range of formal and informal rewards and consequences for academic performance and behavior.

2. Choice and Commitment. Students, their parents, and the staff of St. HOPE Public Schools choose to participate in the program. No one is assigned or forced to attend. Everyone must make and uphold a commitment to the school and to each other to put in the time and effort required to achieve success.

3. More Time. St. HOPE Public Schools knows that there are no shortcuts when it comes to success in academics and life. With an extended school day, week, and year, students have more time in the classroom to acquire the academic knowledge and skills that prepare them for competitive colleges, as well as more opportunities to engage in diverse extracurricular experiences.

4. Focus on Results. St. HOPE Public Schools focuses relentlessly on high student performance through standardized tests and other objective measures. Just as there are no shortcuts, there are not exceptions. Students are expected to achieve a level of academic performance that will enable them to succeed in the nation's best colleges and the world beyond.

5. Power to Lead. St. HOPE Public Schools strongly believes the measure of a person's success is in what he or she gives to others. Through community service, students develop a strong sense of civic responsibility and establish the foundation for a lifetime of meaningful community involvement. Students also deepen and demonstrate their learning, are empowered to become leaders, and benefit the community in which they live.

Source: St. HOPE Academy.

Exhibit 7

Performance Data, St. HOPE PS7

Percentage of Students Scoring Proficient or Above on California Standards Exam

	Math			*ELA*		
Grade	*2004*	*2005*	*2006*	*2004*	*2005*	*2006*
2	40%	69%	63%	31%	56%	42%
3	25%	45%	46%	29%	26%	37%
4	18%	38%	50%	3%	43%	38%
5	-	23%	49%	-	33%	40%
6	-	-	57%	-	-	48%

Comparison of St. HOPE PS7 and Nearby Elementary Schools, 2006

Schools in the 95820 Zip Code	*Grades*	*Enrollment*	*Pupil Teacher Ratio*	*Largest Ethnic Group*	*% Minority*	*State API Ranking*	*% Proficient ELA All Grades*	*% Proficient Math All Grades*
Earl Warren Elementary	K-6	498	21.9	Hispanic	90.8	4	35.6	45.1
Ethel Phillips Elementary	K-6	486	22.8	Hispanic	92.2	2	19.9	45.1
Fruit Ridge Elementary	K-6	478	21.9	Hispanic	91	1	27	39.4
Joseph Bonnheim Elementary	K-6	464	22.2	Hispanic	77.2	2	30	46.5
Mark Twain Elementary	K-6	447	21.9	Hispanic	74.8	2	32.4	39.2
Oak Ridge Elementary	K-6	469	21.3	Hispanic	94.7	1	22.7	35.4
St. HOPE Public School 7 (PS7)	K-6	287	19.1	African American	98.6	5	38.6	51.1
Tahoe Elementary	K-6	318	21.6	Hispanic	73.6	3	35.9	41.3
The Language Academy of Sacramento	K-7	264	22	Hispanic	95.1	2	25.7	40.6

Source: Adapted by case writer from California Department of Education.

Exhibit 8

Sacramento High Commitment to Excellence Form

Student Commitment

I fully commit to Sacramento High School in the following ways:

1. I will give my best effort to be the best learner I can be. This means I will not take shortcuts. I will come to school every day prepared to learn and will work, think, and behave in the best way I know how.
2. I am responsible for my own behavior. If I make a mistake, this means I will tell the truth to my teachers and accept responsibility for my actions.
3. I will always behave so as to protect the safety, interests, and rights of all individuals in the classroom. This also means that I will always listen to all my Sacramento High School teammates and give everyone my respect.
4. I will put forth my best effort toward my fellow students and my learning. I will take charge of my own learning by making sure I get help, asking questions in class or after class, and completing my homework.
5. I will take pride in our school by respecting the facility and helping keep it clean.
6. I will treat my classmates, the staff, and visitors with kindness, courtesy, and respect.
7. I will arrive at Sacramento High School every day by 8:00 a.m. (Monday–Friday) and, if necessary, I will dedicate time beyond the school day to learning, including after school, Saturdays, and summer school.
8. I will always make myself available to parents, teachers, and staff and will address any concerns they might have.
9. I will follow the Sacramento High School dress code.
10. I will abide by the policies and regulations as explained in this student-parent handbook or I will be subject to disciplinary action.

I understand that failure to adhere to these commitments can cause me to lose various Sacramento High School privileges.

Parent(s)/Guardians(s) Commitment

We fully commit to Sacramento High School in the following ways:

1. I will help my child in the best way I know how to take no shortcuts in preparing for college and life. I will do whatever it takes to help him or her to learn.
2. I will partner with the teachers and staff to help my child excel in school, both academically and behaviorally.
3. I will make sure my child arrives at Sacramento High School every day by 8:00 a.m. (Monday–Friday) and, if necessary, I will make arrangements so my child can dedicate time beyond the school day to learning, including after school and summer school.
4. I will meet and talk with my child's teachers on a regular basis and make myself available to my child and the school. This also means that if my child is going to miss school, I will notify the school as soon as possible, and I will read carefully all the papers that the school sends home to me.
5. I will support other parents, students, and the staff by volunteering and supporting school initiatives and activities.
6. I will make sure my child follows the Sacramento High School dress code.

7. I understand that my child must follow the Sacramento High School rules as explained in this student-parent handbook so as to protect the safety, interests, and rights of all individuals in the classroom. I, not the school, am responsible for the behavior and actions of my child.
8. I will help create a safe space for all Sacramento High School families, students, and staff by respecting the diversity found in the school and the community.

I understand that failure to adhere to these commitments can cause my child to lose various Sacramento High School privileges.

Faculty/Staff Commitment

We fully commit to Sacramento High School in the following ways:

1. We will hold high expectations for all students, parents, and each other and foster a sense of pride, respect, and teamwork in our words, deeds, and actions.
2. We will make every effort to "be the constant, not the variable" in our students' lives.
3. We will embrace diversity and protect the interests and rights of all individuals, creating a safe and caring space for all of our students to learn.
4. We will help students, staff, faculty, parents, community members, and visitors feel welcome by focusing on excellent customer service and treating one another with kindness, courtesy, and respect.
5. We will meet and talk regularly with parents, providing them with updates on the progress of their child(ren) and make ourselves available to students and parents, and any concerns they might have.
6. We will always strive to be the best teachers we can be and do whatever it takes to prepare our students to excel in college and in life.
7. We will lesson plan, unit plan, and work with colleagues to design and implement the best classroom teaching experiences possible.
8. We commit to ongoing professional development and constant learning to ensure we continue to refine our craft and learn the best practices that will ensure all of our students learn at high levels.

I understand that failure to adhere to these commitments can lead to my removal from Sacramento High School.

Source: St. HOPE Public Schools.

Exhibit 9

Performance Data, St. HOPE Sacramento High School

Sacramento High School
Students scoring proficient and above on English/Language Arts California Standards Exam

	Before St. HOPE	*St HOPE*			
ELA	*2003*	*2004*	*2005*	*2006*	
9	54%	40%	40%	63%	White
	19%	24%	25%	27%	African-American
	22%	8%	32%	37%	Asian
	17%	22%	14%	15%	Hispanic
10	43%	39%	58%	45%	White
	3%	23%	25%	24%	African-American
	12%	15%	9%	21%	Asian
	11%	19%	17%	20%	Hispanic
11	48%	43%	51%	53%	White
	17%	20%	20%	26%	African-American
	18%	12%	20%	15%	Asian
	16%	19%	18%	23%	Hispanic

Sac High Students Passing the California High School Exit Exam (CAHSEE), 2006	
10th Graders	70%
11th Graders	33%
12th Graders	39%

Percentage of Students Graduating with UC/CSU Required Courses, 2006	
Sac High	55.3%
SCUSD	44%
State-wide	35.7%

Comparison of St. HOPE Sac High with all SCUSD High Schools
2005–2006 School Year Data

			Students			*Teachers*	*Performance*		
School Name	*Grade Span*	*Enroll-ment*	*% Free Meals*	*Largest Ethnic Group*	*% Minority*	*Pupil-Teacher Ratio*	*API Statewide Rank*	*AYP Lang Arts % Proficient*	*AYP Math % Proficient*
America's Choice	9-12	177	54	Hispanic	69	13.6	1	17.9	21.4
C. K. McClatchy High	9-12	2429	38	Hispanic	71.4	21.5	6	59.1	51.7
Genesis High	9-12	287	60	Hispanic	93.7	20.4	1	16.1	11.1
Health Professions High	9-9	150	0	African American	78	14.2	5	48.8	9.5
Hiram W. Johnson High	9-12	2060	53	Hispanic	84.5	19.7	1	27.3	27.3
John F. Kennedy High	9-12	2488	33	Asian	80.2	22.1	6	59.6	52.5
Luther Burbank High	9-12	2199	69	Asian	91.8	18.6	2	29.7	41
Met Sacramento Charter High	9-12	120	26	White	41.7	17.1	2	56.7	20.7
New Technology High	9-12	358	69	White	71.2	17.5	5	58.3	48.2
Rosemont High	9-12	1524	30	White	51.3	21.3	4	54.6	42.5
Sacramento Charter High	9-12	1318	81	African American	82.2	20.1	2	36.5	27.1
Visual and Performing Arts Charter	7-12	439	0	Hispanic	61.7	22.1	-	45	33.5
West Campus	9-12	797	35	Asian	68.6	23.4	10	88.2	74.2

Source: Adapted by case writer from California Department of Education.

Exhibit 10a

St. HOPE Academy Financials—Income Statement (2005–2006)

	July 2005–June 2006
Ordinary Income/Expense	
Income	
CONTRIBUTIONS	$ 448,692
SHPS Small School Pledge	300,000
GRANTS	610,975
INTEREST INCOME	5,774
DIVIDENDS	11,774
REIMBURSEMENT FROM SHPS	140,472
RENTAL INCOME	39,695
SPECIAL EVENTS AND DINNER INCOME	254,171
ST. HOPE ACADEMY FOUNDATION	120,000
Total Income	$1,936,036
Cost of Goods Sold	
Total 6000 · THEATER EVENT COSTS	3,506
Total 7000 · DINNER	68,167
Total COGS	71,673
Gross Profit	1,864,364
Expense	
MANAGEMENT/ADMINISTRATION	229,039
PROGRAM EXPENSES	1,280,403
EDUCATIONAL GRANTS	206,968
INTERNSHIP	787
GALLERY EXPENSES	79,061
STUDENT STORE—SAC HIGH	47,422
CHILD DEVELOPMENT CENTER	41,918
PRESCHOOL	9,890
BLACK HISTORY MONTH	5,106
Total Expense	$1,900,595
Net Ordinary Income	(36,231)
Net Income	$ (36,231)

Source: St. HOPE.

Exhibit 10b

St. HOPE Academy Financials—Balance Sheet as of June 30, 2006

	June 30, 2006
ASSETS	
Current Assets	
Total Checking/Savings	$1,006,686.31
Total Accounts Receivable	1,387,608.15
Other Current Assets	
INTERCOMPANY ACCOUNT	
Due from SHDC	699,088.06
Due from SHPS	525.00
INTERCOMPANY ACCOUNT	$ 699,613.06
MERRILL LYNCH	$ 175,695.13
Total Other Current Assets	$ 875,308.19
Total Current Assets	3,269,602.65
Total Fixed Assets	$1,647,282.95
Total Other Assets	6,853.60
TOTAL ASSETS	$4,923,739.20
LIABILITIES AND EQUITY	
Liabilities	
Total Current Liabilities	$ 32,739.42
Total Long-Term Liabilities	$1,215,589.17
Total Liabilities	$1,248,328.59
Equity	
NET ASSETS—UNRESTRICTED	3,094,588.66
Retained Earnings	617,053.00
Net Income	-36,231.05
Total Equity	$3,675,410.61
TOTAL LIABILITIES AND EQUITY	$4,923,739.20

Source: St. HOPE.

Exhibit 11a

St. HOPE Public Schools Financials—Income Statement (2004–2006)

Description	*June 30, 2006 Unaudited*	*June 30, 2005 Audited*	*June 30, 2004 Audited*
REVENUES			
Revenue limit sources (State aid portion of general purpose block grant)	$ 6,328,782	$ 7,035,842	$ 6,062,507
Federal revenues	1,340,308	957,008	307,862
Other state revenues	924,053	988,621	808,693
Other local revenues	2,974,827	2,481,862	2,944,796
Private Grants and Contributions	n/a	150,700	2,969,666
Donated services and property	n/a	11,501	n/a
Release of temporarily restricted net assets	n/a	1,088,373	n/a
TOTAL REVENUES	$11,567,970	$12,713,907	$13,093,524
EXPENSES			
Certificated salaries	4,676,243	5,103,605	4,566,389
Classified salaries	1,582,773	1,590,735	1,612,058
Employee benefits	1,684,717	1,985,111	1,764,086
Books and supplies	874,546	1,153,707	798,024
Services, other operating expenses	3,380,438	3,566,431	2,579,865
Depreciation	$ 158,380	$ 116,713	$ 27,876
TOTAL EXPENDITURES	$12,357,098	$13,516,302	$11,348,298
NET DECREASE IN NET ASSETS	(789,128)	(802,395)	1,745,226
TEMPORARILY RESTRICTED NET ASSETS			
Private grants		176,696	2,222,569
Release of temporarily restricted net assets		1,088,373	n/a
INCREASE (DECREASE) IN RESTRICTED NET ASSETS		$ (911,677)	$ 2,222,569
INCREASE (DECREASE) IN NET ASSETS	(789,128)	(1,714,072)	3,967,795
NET ASSETS, Beginning of Year	2,253,723	3,967,795	
NET ASSETS, End of Year	$ 1,464,595	$ 2,253,723	$ 3,967,795

Source: St. HOPE.

Exhibit 11b

St. HOPE Public Schools Financials—Balance Sheet

Description	*June 30, 2006 Unaudited*	*June 30, 2005 Audited*	*June 30, 2004 Audited*
ASSETS			
Current Assets			
Cash	$218,154	$630,558	$2,550,891
Accounts receivable	1,318	66,172	10,226
Private grants receivable, current	815,000	600,000	726,982
Due from grantor government	599,375	751,875	784,671
Prepaid expenditures	51,337	80,991	15,330
Total current assets	$1,685,184	$2,129,596	$4,088,100
Private Grants Receivable	260,091	630,892	1,495,587
Property and Equipment, Net	474,647	555,226	345,392
TOTAL ASSETS	$2,419,922	$3,315,714	$5,929,079
Current Liabilities			
Accounts payable	$750,164	$892,985	$1,716,884
Accrued liabilities	134,063	110,910	133,217
Due to student groups	59,128	40,693	78,968
Capital lease, current	n/a	17,403	14,812
Due to grantor governments	10,980	n/a	n/a
Deferred revenue	993	n/a	n/a
Total current liabilities	$955,328	$1,061,991	$1,943,881
Capital Lease	n/a	n/a	17,403
NET ASSETS			
Unrestricted	940,514	942,831	1,745,226
Temporarily restricted	524,081	1,310,892	2,222,569
Total net assets	$1,464,595	$2,253,723	$3,967,795
TOTAL LIABILITIES AND NET ASSETS	$2,419,922	$3,315,714	$5,929,079

Source: St. HOPE.

Exhibit 12a

St. HOPE Development Corp. Financials—Income Statement (2005–2006)

	July 2005–June 2006
Ordinary Income/Expense	
Total Income	$263,683
Expense	
Total ADMINISTRATIVE EXPENSES	25,644
Total MAINTENANCE EXPENSES	75,776
Total RENTING EXPENSES	49
Total TAXES AND INSURANCE	62,138
Total UTILITY EXPENSES	21,235
Total Expense	$184,842
Net Ordinary Income	78,841
Other Income/Expense	
Total Other Income	61,261
Total Other Expense	95,816
Net Other Income	$ (34,554)
Net Income	$ 44,287

Source: St. HOPE.

Exhibit 12b

St. HOPE Development Corp. Financials—Balance Sheet as of June 30, 2006

	June 30, 2006
ASSETS	
Total Current Assets	$ 120,199
Fixed Assets	
40 ACRES PROJECT	
BUILDING—40 ACRES	3,711,063
COMMISSIONS—STARBUCKS	11,000
CONSTRUCTION LOAN INT—40 ACRE	25,701
FURNITURE AND FIXTURES—40 ACRES	64,509
IMPROVEMENTS—40 ACRES	85,881
LAND—40 ACRES	230,000
Total 40 ACRES PROJECT	$4,128,154

	June 30, 2006
ACCUMULATED AMORTIZATION	(138)
ACCUMULATED DEPRECIATION	(201)
DON JU PROPERTY	
LAND/BLDG—3402-3406 BROADWAY	397,556
Total DON JU PROPERTY	$ 397,556
LAND—34TH BROADWAY	56,000
LAND—STRAWBERRY LANE	114,784
VICTORIAN	
BUILDING—VICTORIAN	703,132
LAND—3418 3RD AVE	71,376
Total VICTORIAN	$ 774,508
Total Fixed Assets	$5,470,663
Total Other Assets	$ 750
TOTAL ASSETS	$5,591,612
LIABILITIES AND EQUITY	
Liabilities	
Total Current Liabilities	$ 77,441
Long-Term Liabilities	
CALNET BANK	326,924
DUE TO SHA	648,717
LOAN—KMJ	1,136,172
LOAN—NEHEMIAH	1,028,356
NOTES PAYABLE—KDC—VICTORIAN	188,412
SHRA LOANS	2,606,887
Total Long-Term Liabilities	$5,935,467
Total Liabilities	$6,012,908
Equity	
Retained Earnings	2,595
UNRESTRICTED FUND BALANCE	(468,178)
Net Income	44,287
Total Equity	(421,296)
TOTAL LIABILITIES AND EQUITY	$5,591,612

Source: St. HOPE.

Exhibit 13

Cash Flows Between St. HOPE Entities

Current Situation, Late 2006

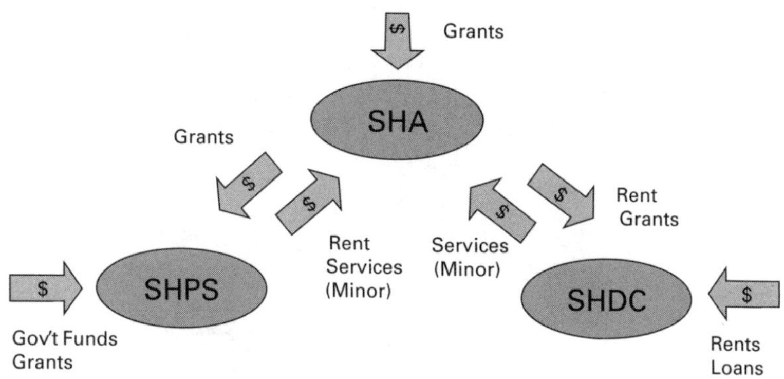

Future Situation, Late 2007

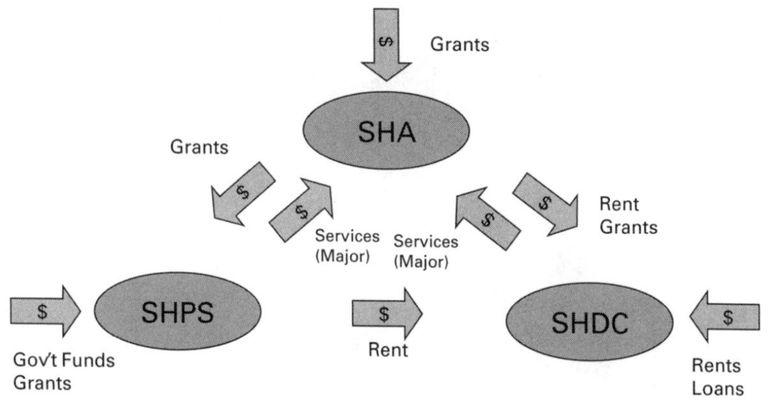

Source: St. HOPE.

Exhibit 14

St. HOPE Functional Organizational Structure

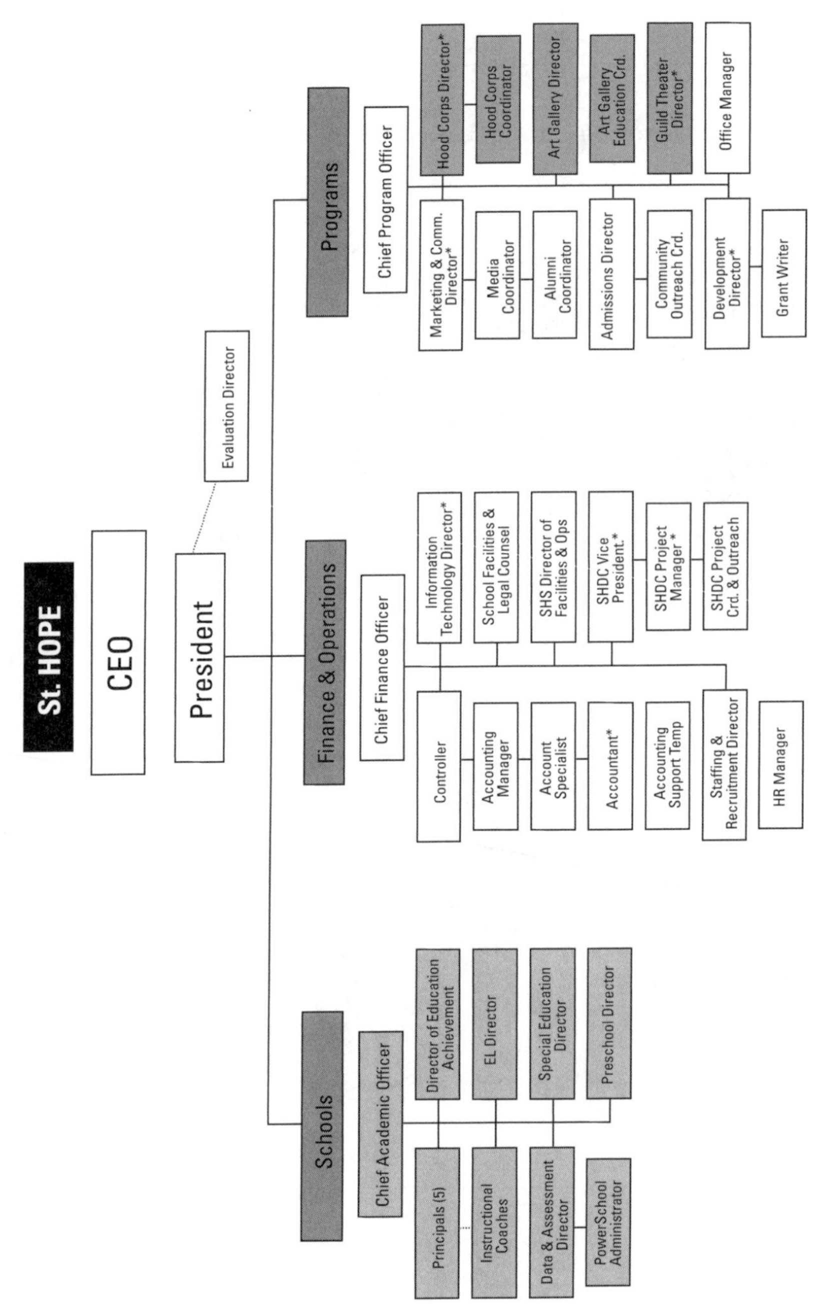

Source: St. HOPE.

Stacey Childress ■ Christopher C. Kim

Green Dot Public Schools: To Collaborate or Compete?

On a Friday afternoon in late 2006, Steve Barr, founder and chief executive officer of Green Dot Public Schools, prepared to leave his downtown Los Angeles office. According to the previous year's standardized test scores, Green Dot charter high schools had outperformed other similar high schools in Los Angeles. Barr was on his way to celebrate at a party for teachers from all of the schools.

The scores were just one of several reasons that the last few months had been an exciting time for Green Dot, a nonprofit charter management organization. Earlier that spring, Green Dot had tried to collaborate with the Los Angeles Unified School District (LAUSD) to transform the 3,000-seat Jefferson Senior High School into five or six smaller schools. When efforts to collaborate failed, Green Dot decided to pursue the transformation without LAUSD's cooperation by opening five new independent charter schools in the same neighborhood to draw away Jefferson's students.

Having previously opened five high schools over several years, Green Dot simultaneously launched the five new schools in September 2006. Doubling its portfolio of schools had gone relatively smoothly, and two areas of perennial concern for charter schools—finding adequate facilities and attracting students and teachers—had not been major barriers. In fact, Green Dot had 10 applications for every teaching slot, and many more families had applied to enter their children into the new Green Dot schools than there were available seats. The waiting list extended into the hundreds. However, not everyone in Los Angeles, including Superintendent Roy Romer, was happy that Green Dot had moved forward so aggressively.

Only six weeks into the new school year, Barr was already faced with important growth questions for 2007. With the Jefferson transformation in full swing, should Green Dot move forward with another transformation in September 2007 or spend a year strengthening its capacity to run its existing 10 schools with high quality? If it moved ahead, should Green Dot pursue a transformation of Crenshaw Senior High or Locke High School? The schools presented different opportunities: Crenshaw would signal an alignment with the Los Angeles mayor's high-profile efforts to wrest control of a number of schools away from LAUSD's elected school board, while Locke would allow Green Dot to attempt another collaboration with LAUSD. Each path had significant implications for the organization's long-term strategy, and Barr wanted the next move to maximize the full potential of Green Dot to transform the performance of all schools in Los Angeles.

The Los Angeles Unified School District[1]

The Los Angeles Unified School District (LAUSD) was the second-largest school district in the United States, with a K–12 enrollment of 727,000 students in 854 schools. LAUSD's SY06[2] budget was $13.2 billion, and its largest expense was the payroll and benefits for its 42,000 teachers and 35,000 nonteaching staff, including school-based and central office administrators and clerical support staff. Because LAUSD included not only the City of Los Angeles but also a number of neighboring cities and towns, the geographical area covered by the district was 710 square miles.

Like many urban school districts, most LAUSD students belonged to an ethnic minority. Almost 75% of the students were Hispanic, and 11% were African American. White students made up approximately 10% of enrollment, and the remaining students were of other minority descent. Seventy-seven percent qualified for free or reduced-price lunch, and 40% were designated as "English-language learners" (ELL), meaning English was not their primary language.

Retention and academic performance problems plagued LAUSD. According to a Harvard study,[3] only 45% of LAUSD students who had entered the ninth grade in 1998 had completed high school by 2002, compared with a national graduation rate of 68%. The fate of Hispanic students was even worse, with a four-year graduation rate of 39%.

In 2005, less than half the students had fulfilled the minimum course requirements necessary for the University of California or California State University systems, and district test scores from the statewide California Standards Test (CST) consistently indicated that most students in the district were not proficient in English language arts or mathematics. Only 25% of high school students tested proficient or advanced in English language arts, and less than 20% tested proficient or advanced in mathematics.

The CST results also indicated a persistent and significant achievement gap between white, African-American, and Hispanic students. The percentage of Hispanic and African-American high school students scoring proficient or advanced in English language arts was 36 points lower than that of whites. The gap in mathematics was 22 points. (See **Exhibit 1** for LAUSD and state data.)

LAUSD was governed by a seven-member board of education elected to serve four-year terms. Superintendent Romer, the former governor of Colorado, announced in the spring of 2006 that he would step down in December after six years of service. The board launched a national search for the next superintendent.

Also in spring of 2006, Los Angeles Mayor Antonio Villaraigosa had launched a controversial initiative with the state legislative assembly to wrest control of LAUSD from the popularly elected board and assume the power to delegate authority directly to a district superintendent.[4] New York, Chicago, and Boston already used this governance model, but opposition to Villaraigosa's plan was fierce. The issue was complicated by the fact that LAUSD served students in over 20 separately incorporated municipalities, each with its own mayor.

Charter Schools in California

Charter schools were defined as public schools of choice operating free from many of the rules and regulations that apply to traditional schools. Although local, state, or other authorities provided authorization and oversight of charter schools, the schools themselves determined their own academic mission, instructional model, budget, human capital management, and most other operational issues. In 2006, 40 states and the District of Columbia had charter school legislation with about 3,500 charter schools serving nearly 1 million students. Student enrollment at charter schools was increasing at approximately 15% per year.[5]

One of the founding tenets of the charter school movement was to link autonomy with accountability. In return for operational freedom from local school districts, charter schools were expected to offer high-quality alternatives for resource-limited families and could be shut down if they failed to meet the goals specified in the performance contracts they signed. A number of advocates of charters supported them because they believed they could produce replicable academic results that could catalyze reform in existing public schools.

California was the second state in the nation to enact legislation in 1992 authorizing charter schools. By 2006, California had over 550 charter schools serving almost 200,000 students.[6] Of those, 86 charter schools spanning grades K–12 were located within LAUSD.

Green Dot's First Five Schools: 2000–2004

Green Dot Public Schools started with one school in 2000 and grew to five schools by 2004. Founder Steve Barr had been an author, television journalist, founder of Rock the Vote, and an operative for the state Democratic Party in California. Growing up in modest circumstances and raised by his single mother, he turned his attention to public education in his late 30s after his younger brother died from a combination of pain pills and alcohol. Barr considered himself lucky to have survived his youth, and he began thinking about what had made the difference. He decided it had been his experience in a good public school in a suburb of San Jose. Barr became interested in the charter school movement in 1997 after attending an event hosted by then President Bill Clinton highlighting charter schools in the state. Meeting several education entrepreneurs spurred his thinking about the state of public education: "In my lifetime it seems we've gone from the best schools in the world to almost the worst, and the political and policy debate has been framed by the Left saying, 'Give us more money for a failed centralized system,' and the Right saying, 'Scrap it, privatize it, let's go get the unions.' I thought there had to be another way."

He spent a year visiting schools in the Los Angeles area looking for effective practices and then launched Green Dot in September 2000. Each Green Dot school was located in a low-income, high-need neighborhood. The name of the school always included the word "Animo"—Spanish for "courage." Of the over 2,000 students enrolled across the five schools, approximately 97% were Latino or African American and 83% were low income.

School Model

All five of the schools were based on Green Dot's "Six Tenets of High Performing Schools":

1. Small, Safe, Personalized Schools
2. High Expectations for All Students
3. Local Control
4. Parent Participation
5. Get Dollars into the Classroom
6. Keep Schools Open Later

The six tenets were considered the "non-negotiables" that schools were required to adopt. Specific requirements included maximum school size of 540 students, school uniforms, curriculum aligned with state standards, site control over budgeting and hiring, parent or family volunteering for at least 35 hours per year, parent representatives on key committees, and school facilities open until 5:00 p.m.

In addition to the six tenets, the schools were provided with a set of recommended practices in the areas of curriculum, student intervention, professional development, parent participation, and school operations. For example, within the student intervention area, recommended practices included advisory groups, guided study during lunch, and a homework club after school. While principals had discretion over which recommended practices to adopt; the majority of practices were implemented across all five schools. (See **Exhibit 2** for explanation of the six tenets.)

Home Office

Barr had single-handedly founded Animo Leadership Charter High School (Animo Leadership) in 2000 but realized immediately that he would need help if he wanted to open more schools. Prior to opening the second school in 2002, Animo Inglewood Charter High School (Animo Inglewood), he hired Marshall Tuck (HBS 2000) as his chief operating officer. Tuck had spent most of his career in the private sector in banking, consulting, and e-commerce but had also spent a year before graduate school teaching in Thailand.

Tuck made the transition from an enterprise software company, where he had been a general manager, to a nonprofit start-up environment. He recalled, "I joined Steve and quickly realized that we were opening a new school in two months but had nowhere to put it. We still had a few staff members to hire and there was no home office, so no services were being provided to Animo Leadership. And there were really no operating funds outside the per pupil money the school received from the state, so there was no money to invest in facilities or growth planning."

Tuck continued, "We didn't know a whole lot, but I think that actually allowed us to be successful. Our lack of knowledge freed us to do things differently than traditional public schools." Forgoing salaries and living off beer and takeout pizza, Tuck and Barr worked to obtain the necessary permits and funds needed to start up the second school. They were newcomers to the charter school landscape, but Barr was politically well connected and Tuck drew upon his experiences in the private sector, and they were able to find a facility for Animo Inglewood as well as relocate Animo Leadership to allow for its expansion. With Animo Inglewood up and running, Tuck had time to reflect on longer-term plans for the Green Dot home office:

> Once we got through the first three months, we started working at how do you actually build a real organization out of this? How do we develop a solid business plan? How do we think about growth? How do we think about replicating our model with quality? We started pulling together a team that could actually carry out the vision of what we wanted to do with the existing schools, as well as help us grow a lot more effectively and rapidly.

By 2006, the home office had grown to 20 people supporting five Green Dot schools. The home office team included staff in finance, human resources, school operations, facilities development, information technology, knowledge management, fund-raising, and public relations. (See **Exhibits 3, 4,** and **5** for student and home office data.)

Academic Approach

Rounding out the executive team of CEO Barr and President and COO Tuck, Chief Academic Officer Sandy Blazer oversaw an instructional support team at the home office that included the founding principal of Animo Inglewood and other staff in charge of pupil services such as special education. Blazer had been on the senior leadership team at Long Beach Unified School District before Barr recruited her as Green Dot's chief academic officer.

Blazer thought of her role as building on the early success of Green Dot to ensure that it produced student outcomes in the midst of rapid growth. She explained, "We got this far on adrenaline, and you can only go so far on adrenaline, and then that dries up, and you actually have to have an educational model." She described her approach as a balance between consistency and experimentation, explaining, "If you walked into any of the 10 schools or the home office, you know you're at Green Dot. It's about an integrated, shared set of values and practices." But, she added, "If we made everybody do the same thing, we'd never learn anything."

Together with a team of experienced education specialists in the home office, Blazer worked closely with the school principals on curriculum development, teacher supervision, and student management. Since the principals were freed of many administrative worries that were the domain of the home office staff, Blazer was able to coach them on how to use their time to better strengthen their teachers' classroom skills. This was especially important since most of the Green Dot school leaders were first-time principals.

In addition, Blazer was the person most directly responsible for quality control in each of the schools. The six tenets were well defined, but Blazer considered the recommended practices a work in progress. Part of her responsibility was to continually develop the practices for the benefit of all the schools, which meant giving the schools enough autonomy to experiment with different practices within certain areas such as curriculum or teacher professional development.

This did not mean that principals and teachers were left completely alone to innovate. Blazer kept close track of what was going on in each school. For example, one of the schools decided not to use the home office's recommended math intervention program and to have a weekly advisory for students instead of a study skills class. Blazer described her approach to such situations, saying, "I'm finding myself in kind of a balancing act and saying to schools, 'OK, here's the recommended practice—it's not mandatory. If you choose not to do it, that's fine right now, but you are still accountable for results. If your data comes back and it's not up to expectations, then I'm going to take away some of your autonomy, because you didn't use it well.'"

Union Relations

Charter schools were criticized by teachers unions across the country because the provisions of charters usually did not require a collective bargaining agreement between management and the teachers. Because of the relatively small size of the schools and the young age of the teachers, charter schools rarely unionized. Barr expressed a different view, saying, "If you're going to create change, why can't union reform be part of that—especially in a heavily unionized industry like education? It drives me crazy that the myth out there is that teachers just want to get tenure so you can't fire them if they don't perform. I know most teachers work hard and don't think like that."

Green Dot was the only independent charter management organization with its own teachers union. Barr had encouraged his teachers to organize, and they did. They created *Asociacion de Maestros Unidos* and affiliated with the California Teachers Association (CTA) and the National Education Association (NEA). The union and Green Dot signed a three-year agreement in 2003 that included the following provisions: teacher input into school policy and curriculum; no tenure and no seniority preference in assignments; and the flexibility to adjust the contract as needed over time. Teachers were paid more than what they would have been paid in LAUSD. (See **Exhibit 6** for salary information.)

The CTA embraced the Green Dot teachers and featured the organization in an issue of its statewide membership magazine. Barr was quoted as saying, "Teachers need to know they have some stability. And if you are bent on systemic change within the urban school environment, the biggest player is the teachers union. I want us to be partners with the union at all our schools."[7]

Because Green Dot schools were small to begin with, the total size of the faculty at each school did not allow for large-scale organizing. Instead, union representation at each school was often informally appointed. Union leaders at Green Dot were different from their counterparts at the United Teachers of Los Angeles (UTLA): they were younger, much less experienced, and much more open to collaboration with management. However, Green Dot was aware that its relationship with the Green Dot teachers union would continue to evolve and, with a growing number of teachers on the payroll, there could potentially be a different dynamic in the relationship in the future.

A home office staff member wondered how important the union actually was to Green Dot teachers, saying, "The engagement of our teachers in their own union is not extremely strong. Not many people actually have run for union leadership, and not many people actually vote in union elections. And so that tells me that so far our teachers aren't extremely engaged in the union."

Despite the positive connection to the state and national teachers unions, Green Dot faced heavy criticism from the local UTLA. It had been widely publicized that hundreds of teachers and administrators were leaving LAUSD and UTLA to join charter schools across the city, including Green Dot. One UTLA representative complained, "It is not healthy competition. It's not healthy for us at all. We have groomed these teachers and they have risen up with us," and then the charters "come in and harvest them."[8]

Student Performance

California measured school-level academic success in terms of an Academic Performance Index (API). Scaled from a low score of 200 to a high of 1,000, the API was based on a battery of standardized tests administered annually to students, including the California Standards Test (CST), California Achievement Test (CAT/6), and California High School Exit Examination (CAHSSE).

In 2005 each of the Green Dot schools had higher API scores—an average difference of 113 points—than comparable high schools in their geographical areas. On an aggregate basis, the combined average API score of 672 for all Green Dot schools was 74 points higher than the average of all LAUSD high schools throughout the city, including the city's wealthier neighborhoods.

Green Dot's student population was similar to LAUSD's in terms of key demographics such as racial composition, parental education levels, and percentages of low-income and non-native English speakers. Yet Green Dot's graduation rate was 80%, compared with LAUSD's 47%. Green Dot's overall pass rate for the English language arts portion of the CAHSEE was 74%, compared with 56% for LAUSD; for mathematics it was 61% for Green Dot, compared with 50% for LAUSD. (See **Exhibits 7** and **8** for student performance data.)

New Strategy, New Schools: 2005–2006

From the time of Green Dot's founding in 1999, Barr had always envisioned 100 Green Dot charter high schools in Los Angeles. The organization had consistently communicated this vision, but after opening its fourth and fifth schools (Animo South Los Angeles and Animo Venice) in 2004, the team began to question the future of Green Dot.

Tuck recalled asking, "How can we scale as quickly as possible? What structure does that scale actually take? If you just operate as a charter school entity, just open charter schools in the City of Los Angeles, you can't scale fast. And if you can't scale fast, you won't have a significant impact on the majority of kids in Los Angeles." He recognized that there were significant operational challenges to scaling fast; foremost among them was the difficulty of finding and securing appropriate school facilities. Green Dot's operations team estimated it already spent 50% of its time and energy on real estate issues. Also, the capital investment required to convert newly acquired space into a school could typically cost upwards of $500,000 or more.

Green Dot board member Marco Petruzzi, at the time a partner in the Los Angeles office of the consulting firm Bain & Company, wondered, "Where are we really going with this? Green Dot's website said it would build 100 high schools in L.A. But I had some Bain folks do some math that showed this was highly unlikely. That led Steve to start thinking, 'I don't know if I can build 100 high schools. Maybe that's not really who we are.'"

Petruzzi and a case team from Bain followed up with a *pro bono* strategy project. Within a few weeks, everyone realized that there was no way Green Dot was going to have the kind of impact it wanted by growing one or two schools at a time. Petruzzi said, "We are really a change agent for LAUSD. And so we focused on the question, how do we transform LAUSD using the Green Dot model, and how can Green Dot be a partner to LAUSD to help them transform themselves?"

As a result of the work with Bain, Green Dot outlined an ambitious plan in which it would operate on a district transformation model in collaboration with LAUSD. Within 10 years, LAUSD could transform its 46 comprehensive high schools into 500 high-performing small schools, with each one adopting Green Dot's Six Tenets of High-Performing Schools. Green Dot did not envision every school looking the same. Instead, local control—one of the six tenets—would ensure that "principals, teachers, parents, and students [would] customize their schools to meet their unique needs."[9]

The proposed mechanism by which Green Dot and LAUSD would transform the city's comprehensive high schools involved a four-year process. Incoming ninth graders would be redirected into new small schools off-site in "incubator" facilities that would expand by one grade level per year. The existing upperclassmen would remain in the legacy high school until it was phased out as each class graduated. As space in the legacy high school became available, most of the new small schools would move out of the incubator facilities and back into the old building. Due to increased retention and smaller class sizes, some of the new small schools would remain permanently housed in the incubator facilities. (See **Exhibit 9** for transformation model.)

School transformation would require a significant capital investment in new facilities. Green Dot figured that LAUSD could leverage its recent $19 billion in bond funding to acquire incubator facilities instead of building its old style of large, comprehensive high schools. In addition, school transformation would require an additional 500 school principals and 5,000 teachers because of the lower student-teacher ratio and increased student retention. (See **Exhibit 10**.)

Despite the considerable challenges, Barr felt strongly about Green Dot's transformation strategy. As he explained, "We felt confident that 75% of the kids in LAUSD could be going to these small autonomous Green Dot–like schools—not charter schools, hopefully district schools—within 10 years, and we would seed a dramatic sea change in urban reform across the country."

Transforming Jefferson

The Green Dot/Bain proposal had deliberately used Jefferson Senior High as the hypothetical example for a transformation project. Jefferson was one of the lowest-performing high schools in the state of California, was severely overcrowded, and recently had suffered violent incidents between the Latino and African-American students. For these reasons, Barr found Jefferson a highly attractive first candidate for transformation:

> Jefferson High has been an awful school for 40 years. If you're not going to do something bold there, where the hell are you going to do it? We actually spent time with a lot of community groups in the area around Jefferson, and people were just desperate. We wanted to disprove the notion that we're just a charter school group and the only answer is charter schools. We were offering collaboration with the district. And we also wanted to prove that our results aren't based on the fact that we get certain kinds of kids. We wanted to show what can happen when you take most of the kids in an underserved community and give them a better educational option.

Superintendent Romer and his staff had provided input to Bain's strategy project and signaled initial interest in collaborating on a Jefferson transformation project. But after a promising start, the talks between Green Dot and LAUSD ended without an agreement to collaborate. According to published reports, LAUSD officials insisted that they were not interested in collaborating because they were already making significant progress at Jefferson: new uniforms for students, improved class schedules, and the creation of six small learning communities called "academies."[10]

Petruzzi, who had helped Green Dot present the transformation project to Romer, saw it differently: "Romer was initially doing back flips over it, I mean he was really excited about the prospect of collaborating. But the reality was that there was no political support around him for the plan, and he didn't have the power to push it alone in the face of fierce opposition from the UTLA."

In August 2005, Green Dot announced its plans to transform Jefferson Senior High without the cooperation of LAUSD. The reaction from the establishment was swift and negative. Romer responded publicly, "We want to cooperate with the charter school community. We need them to help our schools, and I look forward to that collaboration. But what I do not look forward to is a hostile takeover."[11]

An LAUSD board member added, "What I don't want is a lone ranger coming in and trying to pull something off. Then we'll just have more conflict at a school that has already had enough." UTLA president A. J. Duffy expressed his organization's position by saying, "I'm not in favor of charters. As far as I'm concerned, they are just private schools in a different suit or a fancy dress."

Competition, Not Collaboration

Barr and his senior team decided they would transform Jefferson using a different approach. Barr maintained that his preference was to collaborate, but his reaction to Romer's refusal to cooperate was aggressive: "I thought to myself, okay if that's how you want to play it, now I'm going to have to build five charter schools around Jefferson and take away your ninth-grade class."

In January 2006, the Green Dot home office staff walked into the conference room for a meeting. On the white board was the statement "We will open five schools this year." Tuck and Blazer asked the staff to write down their reactions on a piece of paper. One staff member recalled, "My reaction at the time was, 'Are you serious? We're going to open five schools after the most we've ever opened in a year was two? That's nuts. It doubles our size. That's nuts.'"

Although it was the first time the senior team had explicitly expressed Green Dot's intentions to the full staff, the idea was not a complete surprise to them. Everyone knew Barr's intention to transform Jefferson through other means, and it had been a year and a half since Animo South Los Angeles and Animo Venice had opened. But the statement signified an unambiguous commitment to proceed with Green Dot's new strategy. School transformation was going to take place with or without the support of LAUSD or UTLA, and the Green Dot home office was going to make it happen in nine short months.

When Green Dot announced its plans to apply to open five charter schools in the neighborhood around Jefferson, the UTLA organized teachers at Jefferson to start a counter-petition to the proposal. A Jefferson administrator who openly supported Green Dot's transformation efforts was suddenly given notice by the LAUSD central office that she was being transferred to a school across town.

However, community support was strong. When the school board met to discuss Green Dot's charter applications, the meeting was packed with parents from Jefferson wearing green T-shirts that said, "Transform Jefferson." After the board approved the charters, over 1,000 students filed applications for the 640 ninth-grade spaces in the new schools. Of the five schools, three had student bodies with incoming test scores similar to Jefferson's average and the other two had student bodies with slightly lower scores. More than 800 educators vied to fill the 80 open teaching and administrative positions. Most of those hired came from the staff at Jefferson Senior High.

In order to open the schools within such a short period of time, the Green Dot staff faced a number of operational hurdles, not the least of which was securing five suitable school facilities and preparing them for occupancy. The home office team worked around the clock with the leaders of the schools to hire staff, acquaint them with Green Dot's philosophy, and prepare schedules for incoming students.

Ultimately, the five schools opened in September 2006. Although it had been a very busy summer, a staff member in the home office reflected, "We opened five schools simultaneously this fall, and it was very successful, and it was actually relatively smooth. Compared to 2004 when we opened two schools at once, we had more people and more experience under our belt. We also had more resources. So it actually seemed easier to do five than it was to do two."

However, one new principal remarked, "I do think that the summer was probably a little bit hard for Green Dot in terms of scaling up so fast. People were really responsive, but we struggled with things like our air conditioning not working . . . it still doesn't really."

The Challenges Ahead

"I think from a business standpoint, we're doing fine. But every charter school we open is a failure in forging political collaboration," observed Barr. With a new superintendent search under way and continued uncertainty over the mayor's efforts to control the school district, it was difficult to predict how the next few years would play out for Green Dot's relationship with LAUSD.

Some predicted that since Villaraigosa had been a union organizer earlier in his career, he would be conflicted about charter schools if he won his battle to take control of LAUSD. But early indications were that he would be a strong supporter of charters in general and Green Dot in particular. At a summer rally in support of the legislation to grant him control of the schools, Villaraigosa surrounded himself with Green Dot students, calling them "brilliant and beautiful. They are defining what is possible for all of L.A.'s children."[12] He was also on the record as saying, "I believe we need to abandon the one-size-fits-all approach and give educators the freedom to innovate." He stressed more charter schools "both to give families more choices and to keep positive pressure on the school bureaucracy."[13]

A senior team member mused about the key to keeping the mayor's support should he take over the schools: "The most critical success factor for us is going to be a very vocal, broad, and diverse army of support demanding that the mayor work with Green Dot. Huge demand from the community will, I think, offset any sort of misgivings that the mayor may feel because of the UTLA."

It was impossible to predict whether Romer's successor as superintendent—to be appointed by the school board and not the mayor—would support charter schools. Most staff members in the home office thought that Green Dot would have to continue to push LAUSD hard. Tuck commented, "Without really intense, aggressive leverage, we're not going to accomplish a major shift in LAUSD policy, whether we are running charter schools or trying to transform district schools." Another staff member agreed, saying, "We're the guys that put the pressure on the system. We try to look for every single crack to push the district to the brink so that it will change the way it operates, both as a whole system and as individual schools."

But the senior team realized that playing too aggressively would be seen as antagonistic and therefore contrary to Green Dot's desire for collaborative transformation. It also had practical implications—securing additional charters and facilities required the LAUSD school board's support. As one staff member explained, "We can probably find three sites on our own, but not 10, and certainly not 14. The only way to do that is in partnership with the district."

Sustaining High Performance While Growing

The success of Green Dot depended ultimately on its ability to provide a better academic experience for the students in all its schools. As Tuck described, "The most important question for us is, how do we dramatically improve our student performance results? Because that, at the end of the day, is the business we are in." Petruzzi felt Green Dot's success depended specifically upon the academic success of the Jefferson transformation. He noted, "Now that our growth plans have become high profile, they have to deliver amazing results. It's all over the local news. These five schools have to deliver."

In order to deliver results, the home office needed to continue to support all 10 schools, plus any additional schools in the coming years, without building a cumbersome bureaucracy. One staff member worried about the capacity of a lean home office to support an ever-increasing number of schools: "We have to service our existing schools, because we can't succeed unless our existing schools succeed. If we can't accomplish that, we will get real tired of growth real soon."

Another staff member expressed concern about the ability of Green Dot to continue attracting top-notch principals if it grew rapidly every year, saying, "If we don't have really strong leaders in our schools who hold people accountable and give them the best professional development, our great teachers will become good teachers, and good teachers will become bad teachers. It just happens."

Other staff members worried about the supply of teachers: "I sometimes wonder if it's possible to really have this kind of a school for every kid. Is it possible to have that many adults who are good enough at their jobs and who care that much, whether it's adults at the school or people in the home office? Is there the human resource capacity to really do this? I don't know."

Up Next: Crenshaw or Locke?

The senior team was weighing whether or not to embark on another transformation project in 2007, and Barr recognized that if they decided to proceed, Green Dot only had the capacity to attempt one transformation, even though there were two attractive target schools, each representing different types of opportunities: Crenshaw Senior High and Locke High School (see **Exhibit 11**).

Crenshaw Senior High was well-known throughout the city as one of the district's only high schools with a predominantly African-American student population. Barr observed, "Crenshaw is the jewel of the black community." However, the school had recently fallen on hard times. The loss of its accreditation had devastated community leaders and parents, and Barr wanted to revive their pride and hope in the school.

Barr considered Crenshaw the kind of high-profile school that was ripe for transformation, similar to Jefferson. Mayor Villaraigosa was specifically interested in designating Crenshaw a "demonstration school" in which the city—presumably with Green Dot's help—would take over management of Crenshaw from the LAUSD School Board. Taking on Crenshaw would put Green Dot squarely in the mayor's camp. As a senior staff member remarked, "Being aligned with the mayor is good because it has a game-changing quality to it, but it definitely puts us at odds with the powers that be in LAUSD."

But much of the future success of a Crenshaw transformation would depend on several variables that were difficult to predict. First, the mayor's legislative initiative—state bill AB 1831—needed to pass major legal hurdles for the mayor to truly take control of some LAUSD schools, and serious court battles loomed ahead. Second, working with the mayor could ultimately mean losing some operational independence if he decided to work closely with the UTLA, and even worse, the UTLA could demand that the mayor halt Green Dot's work on Crenshaw if it was not satisfied with the organization's labor practices. And finally, the Green Dot team worried about the availability of facilities near Crenshaw. Finding affordable real estate in that part of town was extremely difficult, and they would probably not have access to the Crenshaw building, given it was LAUSD property.

On the other hand, Locke High School presented another potential collaboration with LAUSD. Located in the city's Watts neighborhood, Locke was high on the district's list of high schools in need of a radical overhaul. In 2005, the district had hired a new principal, Frank Wells, and given him a mandate to turn around the school. However, Wells found significant obstacles to his efforts in his dealings with the LAUSD bureaucracy and the UTLA. He explained, "It is criminal to allow a school to continue on year after year, the way this one has. I went to Locke thinking I could turn it around, but I ran into a brick wall."[14]

In January 2007, LAUSD hired retired U.S. Navy admiral David Brewer to succeed Romer as superintendent of schools. Brewer was an outsider to public education, and many of those involved in education reform in Los Angeles, including the Green Dot team, hoped he would be more open to innovation than his predecessor. Brewer was specifically interested in sharpening the district's focus on the performance of African-American boys, and Locke's demographics made it a priority for him. Green Dot already had two charters approved for the area around Locke but had yet to open a school or develop a specific plan for entering the neighborhood.

Choosing Locke as its next transformation project meant that Barr and his team would immerse themselves in negotiations with Brewer, the LAUSD School Board, and the UTLA about how to implement the Green Dot model inside Locke's physical structure and how to transition teachers to a work arrangement in keeping with Green Dot's teachers contract. The opportunity to create change inside the district and UTLA was consistent with Green Dot's long-term goals—as Barr often said, "We want systemic change, not to create oases in the desert."

But the path to Locke was high risk, and Green Dot had traveled it before during the Jefferson negotiations. As a new superintendent, it was unclear how willing Brewer would be to move ahead with Green Dot if the UTLA opposed its involvement in Locke or insisted that the teachers there remain covered by the existing union contract. For Barr, this would be a nonstarter. Also, with so many parties involved, the negotiations could take several months, disrupting Green Dot's ability to begin a transformation project in the 2007–2008 school year.

Barr knew that the choices that he and his senior team made about Green Dot's next steps would have consequences for many years, but he felt they could not wait for all of the pending decisions that were outside of their control to play themselves out. There would always be unknowns. The most important question was, given all of their options, how could the Green Dot team take the best next step toward moving from a charter school operator that opened a few schools at a time to a true force for the transformation of every school in Los Angeles?

Notes

1. Data in this section accessed and adapted from Los Angeles Unified School District (LAUSD) and California Department of Education (CDE) websites.

2. SY denotes school year. For example, SY06 refers to the 2005–2006 school year.

3. Dan Losen and Johanna Wald, "Confronting the Graduation Rate Crisis in California," The Civil Rights Project, Harvard University, March 24, 2005.

4. "The Mayor Takes Charge: Los Angeles Schools," *The Economist*, April 29, 2006.

5. California Charter Schools Association, "About Charter Schools," http://www.charterassociation.org/cnt_about_charter_description.asp, accessed October 29, 2006.

6. California Department of Education, "Charter Schools FAQ," http://www.cde.ca.gov/sp/cs/re/qandasec1mar04.asp, accessed October 29, 2006.

7. Sherry Posnick-Goodwin, "Animo High Empowers Its Teachers," *California Educator*, October 2003.

8. Joel Rubin, "L.A. Unified Losing Staff to Charters," *Los Angeles Times*, July 3, 2006.

9. Green Dot Public Schools and Bain & Company, "The School Transformation Plan," April 2006.

10. Jean Merl, "Takeover Plan Sparks New Debate," *Los Angeles Times*, August 12, 2005.

11. Jean Merl and Joel Rubin, "Troubled L.A. Campus May Be Taken Over," *Los Angeles Times*, August 11, 2005.

12. Office of the Mayor, City of Los Angeles, "A New Day for Our Schoolchildren," Press Release, August 30, 2006.

13. "The Mayor Takes Charge: Los Angeles Schools," *The Economist*, April 29, 2006.

14. Joel Rubin, "Locke Principal Rips LA Unified," *Los Angeles Times*, May 4, 2007.

Exhibit 1

LAUSD and California Demographic and Performance Data

	LAUSD	*State*
Student Demographics		
Number of students (K-12)	727,319	6,312,103
Hispanic	73%	48%
African American	11%	8%
White	9%	30%
Asian	4%	8%
Other Minority	3%	6%
Eligible for free or reduced-price lunch	77%	50%
English-language learners	40%	25%
Schools and Staffing		
Number of schools	768	9,553
Number of teachers (FTE)	34,033	295,184
Pupil-Teacher Ratio	21.4	21.4
Charter Schools		
Number of schools	86	560
Enrollment	35,436	199,916
Number of teachers (FTE)	1,636	9,525
Pupil-Teacher Ratio	21.7	21.0
Student Achievement (SY05)		
Graduates with UC/CSU Required Courses	48%	35%
Students Taking SAT	46%	36%
Average Math Score	458	521
Average Verbal Score	443	499
Academic Performance Index (API)		
2006 API Growth	658	720
2005 API Base	649	709
California High School Exit Exam (CAHSEE)		
Passing Math	50%	59%
Passing English Language Arts	55%	61%

Source: Adapted by case writer from the California Department of Education.

Note: All data is from SY06 unless otherwise noted.

Exhibit 2

Green Dot's Six Tenets of High-Performing Schools

The Six Tenets	*School Requirements ("Non-negotiables")*
Small, Safe Schools	• Target student population of 525 students. Maximum number of students is 540. • No classes will have a class size greater than 33. • Students must wear uniforms.
High Expectations	• All students take a curriculum aligned to UC A-G requirements and California State Standards. • Schools must provide intervention programs based on proven practices in the 9th grade for English and Math. • Schools are opened one grade at a time, starting with the 9th grade, to allow for the development of a culture of high expectations and to ensure that all students receive strong support in the 9th grade.
Local Control	*Local Control* • School sites have ultimate autonomy over budgeting, hiring, and curriculum. • School leaders and lead teachers are trained on effective practices for budgeting, hiring, and curriculum. *Professional Development* • 10 professional development days built into the school year and time for staff professional development is built into the school week. • Principals, assistant principals, and lead teachers must observe teachers regularly (at least once a month). • Extensive professional development based on proven practices must be provided to all teachers and school-site staff. *Accountability* • Goals and expectations set annually with schools and employees. • Stakeholders (staff, parents, students, etc.) surveyed annually, and the feedback is integrated into school plans. • Student performance measured and reviewed annually to ensure that student achievement is occurring at each school site. • All employees evaluated at least once a year. • Extensive development is provided when student achievement is not meeting expectations in a particular school or classroom. • Consistently poor results that are below expectations will result in the home office requiring that the recommended practices be followed and in potential personnel changes.
Parent Participation	• Parents or other family members must perform 35 hours of service for the school each year. • Parents/guardians must be able to directly reach any school staff member via phone or e-mail and receive a prompt response. • Parent representatives must be a part of school-site committees including hiring, fund-raising, and strategic planning. • Green Dot parents have access to their students' grades and other information online through the school's student information.
Get Dollars into the Classroom	• Schools must operate within their budgets. • $0.94 of each public dollar must make it to the school site.
Keep Schools Open Later	• School facilities kept open until 5:00 p.m. • Wide array of after-school programs must be offered. • School facilities should be available for community use after school if space and management capacity exists.

Source: Green Dot Public Schools.

Exhibit 3

Green Dot Organizational Growth, 2000–2006

As of October 31	*2000*	*2001*	*2002*	*2003*	*2004*	*2005*	*2006*
New Schools Open	1	0	1	1	2	0	5
Total Schools	1	1	2	3	5	5	10
Student Enrollment	140	280	552	940	1,482	1,993	3,075
School Staff FTE	10	18	39	65	110	136	217
Home Office FTE	1	1	2	9	14	16	21
Budget Expenses (,000) (FY ended June 30)	$1,270	$1,572	$3,751	$8,700	$13,994	$20,005	$33,990

Source: Green Dot Public Schools and California Department of Education.

Exhibit 4

Green Dot Enrollment, 2001–2007

For School Year Ended	*2001*	*2002*	*2003*	*2004*	*2005*	*2006*	*2007*
Animo Leadership	140	280	412	520	516	511	526
Animo Inglewood	0	0	140	280	411	523	519
Oscar De La Hoya Animo	0	0	0	140	274	411	518
Animo South LA	0	0	0	0	140	268	393
Animo Venice	0	0	0	0	141	280	409
Animo Ralph Bunche	0	0	0	0	0	0	151
Animo Pat Brown	0	0	0	0	0	0	144
Animo Jackie Robinson	0	0	0	0	0	0	143
Animo Justice	0	0	0	0	0	0	140
Animo Film & Theater Arts	0	0	0	0	0	0	132
Totals	140	280	552	940	1,482	1,993	3,075

Source: Green Dot Public Schools.

Exhibit 5

Green Dot Organizational Design

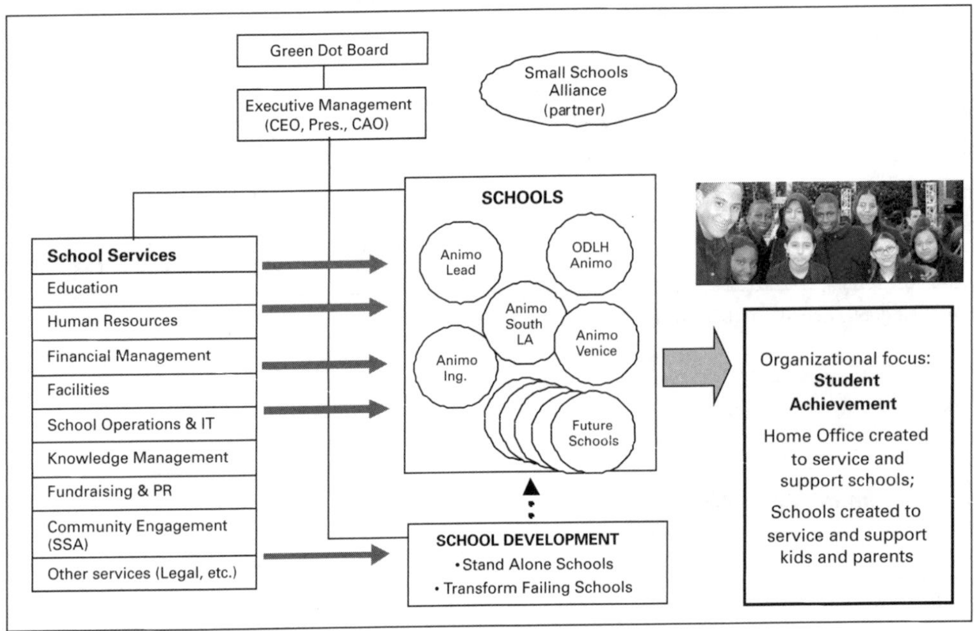

Source: Green Dot Public Schools.

Exhibit 6

Green Dot Salary Schedule

Teacher Salary Schedule (SY07)

	Lane					
Step	*I*	*II*	*III*	*IV*	*V*	*VI*
1	$44,683	$45,092	$47,121	$48,299	$49,748	$50,991
2	$44,906	$45,362	$47,710	$49,265	$50,743	$52,011
3	$45,131	$45,656	$48,903	$50,926	$52,900	$54,222
4	$45,357	$46,000	$50,125	$52,670	$55,102	$56,480
5	$45,357	$46,000	$51,629	$54,961	$57,352	$58,785
6	$45,357	$46,000	$53,823	$57,908	$59,645	$61,137
7	$45,357	$46,000	$56,111	$60,178	$61,984	$63,534
8	$45,357	$46,000	$58,495	$62,490	$64,365	$65,974
9	$45,357	$46,000	$60,835	$64,843	$66,788	$68,459
10	$45,357	$46,000	$63,116	$67,235	$69,252	$70,984
11			$65,483	$69,757	$71,850	$73,646
12			$67,939	$72,373	$74,543	$76,407

Lane Requirements

I	Bachelor's Degree
II	Bachelor's Degree, plus 15 semester units beyond B.A.
III	Bachelor's Degree, plus 30 semester units beyond B.A. including Valid Subject area Teaching Credential; or Emergency Credential with Subject Area Masters
IV	Bachelor's Degree, plus 45 semester units beyond B.A. including Valid Subject area Teaching Credential; or Masters Degreee w/ Valid Subject area Teaching Credential; or National Board Certification w / Valid Subject area Teaching
V	Bachelor's Degree, plus 60 semester units beyond B.A. including Valid Subject area Teaching Credential; or Masters Degree / National Board Certification plus 15 units and Valid Subject area teaching Credential
VI	Bachelor's Degree, plus 75 semester units beyond B.A. including Valid Subject area Credential; or Masters Degree / National Board Certification plus 30 units and Valid Subject area teaching Credential

Other Salary Information

Starting Green Dot salary:	$44,683
Starting LAUSD salary:	$44,346
Average Green Dot salary:	$52,736
Equivalent average LAUSD salary:	$48,106

Source: Adapted from Green Dot Public Schools and California Department of Education.

Exhibit 7

API Results for Green Dot Public Schools vs. Comparable Schools (SY05, SY06)

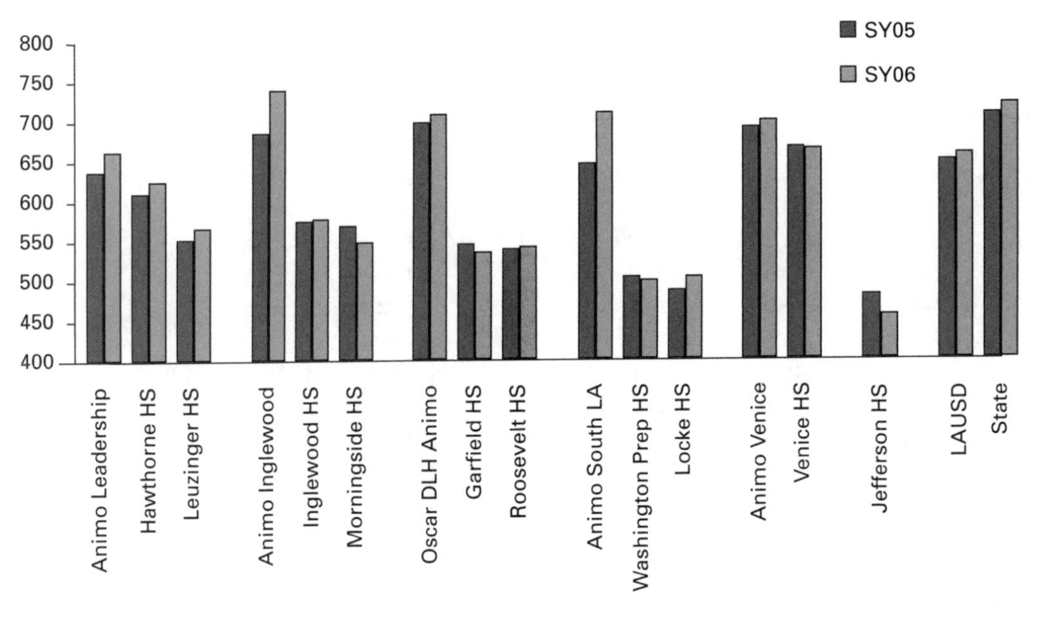

Source: Adapted by case writer from California Department of Education.

Exhibit 8

Green Dot Public Schools and Comparables Schools, 2006

	Animo Leadership	Hawthorne HS	Leuzinger HS	Animo Inglewood	Inglewood HS	Morningside HS	Oscar DLH Animo	Garfield HS	Roosevelt HS	Animo South LA	Washington Prep HS	Locke HS	Animo Venice	Venice HS
Year Founded	2001			2003			2004			2005			2005	
Academic Performance Index (API)														
2006	662	624	567	739	577	547	708	535	542	711	500	505	700	665
2005	638	610	553	686	566	568	697	546	539	645	504	488	691	666
05-06 Growth target	8	10	12	6	11	12	5	13	13	8	15	16	5	7
05-06 Growth actual	24	14	14	53	11	-21	11	-11	3	66	-4	17	9	-1
Student Demographics														
Enrollment	511	2925	3384	523	1949	1535	411	4830	5126	258	3041	3122	280	3210
Hispanic	99.6%	76.1%	59.7%	60.8%	49.1%	59.7%	100.0%	99.2%	99.0%	42.9%	43.3%	64.2%	77.1%	67.7%
African American	0.4%	14.8%	27.7%	34.8%	49.5%	38.6%	0.0%	0.2%	0.4%	57.1%	56.1%	35.5%	15.0%	10.5%
White	0.0%	4.7%	2.4%	0.8%	0.7%	0.5%	0.0%	0.3%	0.2%	0.0%	0.1%	0.1%	5.4%	12.9%
Asian	0.0%	1.6%	5.7%	0.0%	0.2%	0.1%	0.0%	0.2%	0.1%	0.0%	0.1%	0.0%	2.5%	6.7%
Low-income	93.9%	70.6%	58.8%	71.7%	49.7%	57.9%	92.0%	85.6%	85.1%	76.5%	75.4%	79.7%	64.0%	64.3%
English Language Learners	37.0%	30.9%	29.3%	4.7%	20.2%	25.2%	51.2%	38.6%	41.7%	9.6%	16.7%	29.1%	28.4%	24.7%

Source: Adapted by case writer from California Department of Education.

Exhibit 9

School Transformation Project Overview

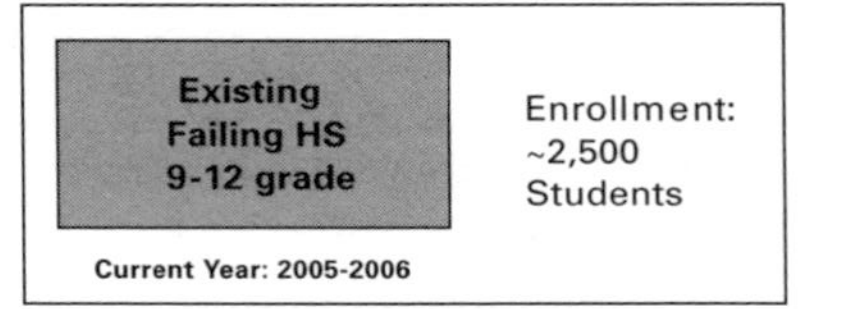

Year 0: Stakeholders, including school-site staff, district representatives, partners, parents, and students, convene regularly to develop the plans to transform the failing high school. Offsite facilities must be secured to incubate the new Schools and the level of partnership between Green Dot and LAUSD is determined. The partnership level will determine if facilities being built as a part of LAUSD's new school construction program will be used, as well as the appropriate mechanism to allow Green Dot to manage the Transition School.

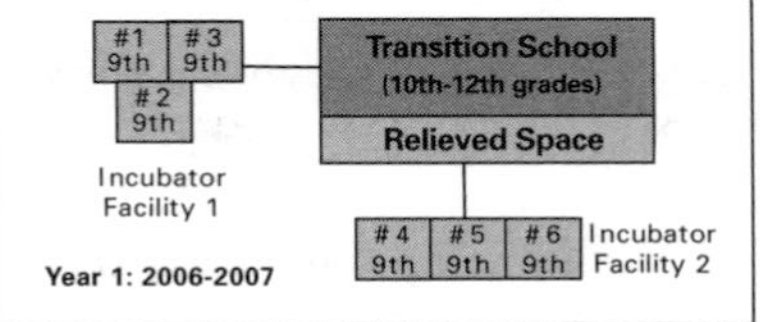

Year 1: All 9th graders are admitted into one of the six New Schools that are located in separate incubator facilities of the main campus (two incubator facilities are used in this example). The six New Schools are all created with the Six Tenets as the foundation for the school models. Existing 10th–12th graders stay on the main campus in the Transition School. The Transition School is provided with extensive resources to help 10th–12th grade students get on track to graduate. The New Schools and the Transition School operate on a traditional school calendar. The relieved space on the main campus is retrofitted to better accommodate the New Schools.

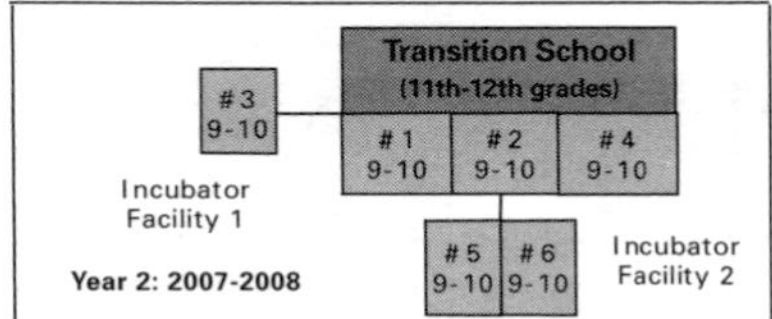

Year 2: New 9th-grade classes are admitted into each of the six New Schools, which now serve 9th and 10th graders. Three of the new Schools are transferred back onto the main campus to the relieved space that was retrofitted during the first year of the project. The Transition School now serves only 11th and 12th graders, as it has graduated one class. Extensive interventions and supports continue to be given to the Transition School.

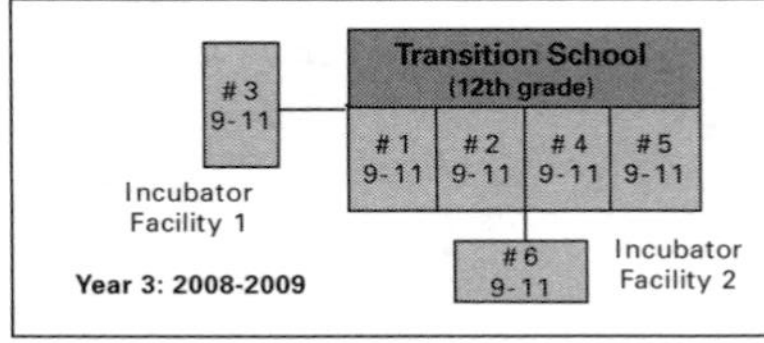

Year 3: Another new set of 9th-grade students are admitted to the six New Schools, which now serve 9th–11th graders. One additional New School is moved back on campus. The Transition School serves only 12th graders, as it has graduated two classes. Extensive interventions and supports continue to be given to the Transition School.

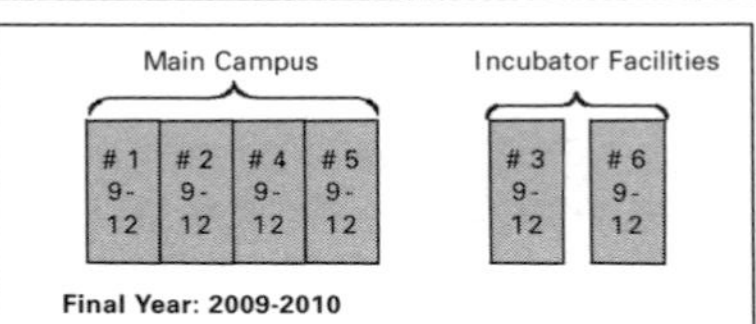

Year 4: After four years, the school transformation will be complete. Six New Schools serving approximately 525 9th–12th graders will have been created. All of the New Schools will follow the Six Tenets and have a strong likelihood of success. Four of the New Schools will be back on the main campus and two of the New Schools will remain offsite in the incubator facilities. The need for additional facilities comes as a result of the increased retention due to the success of the New Schools.

Source: Green Dot Public Schools.

Exhibit 10

Green Dot Consolidated Operating Projections, FY07–FY11

Green Dot Consolidated Projections	*FY 2007*	*FY 2008*	*FY 2009*	*FY 2010*	*FY 2011*
New Schools Opened	6	7	14	0	0
Total Schools	11	18	32	32	32
Students Served	3,235	5,285	9,005	12,565	15,190
Public Revenues					
State Per-Pupil Funds (ADA)	$ 19,881,189	$ 32,877,344	$ 55,949,573	$ 78,525,707	$ 94,251,294
Special Education Entitlement	$ 1,068,470	$ 1,888,387	$ 3,359,874	$ 4,769,140	$ 5,795,515
Federal Revenue	$ 1,967,295	$ 3,195,524	$ 5,431,441	$ 7,573,232	$ 9,128,135
Other State Revenue	$ 1,959,476	$ 3,254,660	$ 5,587,486	$ 7,822,003	$ 9,445,435
Local Revenue	$ 544,156	$ 689,272	$ 996,880	$ 1,388,547	$ 1,672,834
Committed State-start up grants (new schools)	$ 2,430,000	$ -	$ -	$ -	$ -
Committed Philanthropy - Foundations	$ 3,350,000	$ 2,350,000	$ 1,000,000	$ -	$ -
Other Revenue	$ 787,840	$ 237,840	$ 237,840	$ 237,840	$ 237,840
Total Public Revenues	$ 31,988,426	$ 44,493,028	$ 72,563,095	$100,316,469	$ 120,531,053
Expenses					
School Personnel & Benefits	$ 15,729,952	$ 25,994,318	$ 45,231,813	$ 59,125,689	$ 69,735,114
Education Related Expenses (books, training, etc.)	$ 4,601,852	$ 7,168,893	$ 12,722,108	$ 14,455,820	$ 17,002,201
School Facilities & Facilities Related Expenses	$ 4,673,374	$ 7,330,460	$ 11,808,720	$ 15,842,413	$ 18,625,250
School Operations and other School Related Costs	$ 2,838,546	$ 4,232,893	$ 7,038,697	$ 7,976,160	$ 8,779,276
Corporate Salaries & Overhead	$ 4,175,428	$ 4,737,088	$ 6,189,808	$ 6,295,345	$ 6,295,345
De La Hoya Youth Center	$ 235,101	$ -	$ -	$ -	$ -
Total Expenses	$ 32,254,253	$ 49,463,652	$ 82,991,146	$103,695,427	$ 120,437,186
Annual Net Income	$ (265,826)	$ (4,970,624)	$(10,428,051)	$ (3,378,958)	$ 93,867
Adjustments for non-cash items, cap ex and financing costs	$ 101,245	$ 156,883	$ 232,947	$ 325,251	$ 62,628
Reserve for Economic Uncertainty	$ (476,931)	$ (824,230)	$ (1,471,810)	$ (1,436,862)	$ (1,031,270)
Annual Surplus / (Shortfall) after reserve	$ (641,513)	$ (5,637,972)	$(11,666,915)	$ (4,490,570)	$ (874,776)
Beginning Cash for Operations (net of reserve)	$ 446,246				
Surplus / Shortfall Before Equity for Facilities	$ (195,267)	$ (5,833,239)	$(17,500,154)	$ (21,990,724)	$ (22,865,499)
Capital Expenditures for Facilities	$ (1,700,000)	$ (3,500,000)	$ (3,500,000)	$ -	$ -
Surplus / Shortfall Including Capital for Facilities	$ (1,895,267)	$(11,033,239)	$(26,200,154)	$ (30,690,724)	$ (31,565,499)
Total Cash Reserve	$ 1,271,029	$ 2,095,259	$ 3,567,069	$ 5,003,931	$ 6,035,202
New Philanthropy Required through Fiscal 2011	$ (31,565,499)				
Years to Sustainability	5				

Source: Green Dot Public Schools.

Exhibit 11

Selected Data from Target High Schools for Green Dot Transformation Projects

SY06 Data	*Jefferson*	*Crenshaw*	*Locke*	*LAUSD*
Students	2,997	2,501	3,122	
% African American	8%	66%	34%	11%
% Hispanic	91%	33%	65%	73%
% English Learners	46%	14%	31%	40%
Free/Reduced Lunch	90%	82%	80%	77%
Teachers	137	121	141	
Per Pupil Ratio	22.3	21.7	23.5	20.8
% Non-White	67%	78%	67%	54%
Academic Performance Index (API) Score	482	505	504	649
Scale of 200–1,000				
California High School Exit Exam (CAHSEE)				
% Passing Mathematics	22%	36%	37%	50%
% Passing English Language Arts	26%	50%	41%	55%
SAT I				
% Taking Test	17%	60%	60%	50%
Verbal	387	377	356	442
Math	385	359	362	446
Writing	390	374	353	445
Reported Four-Year Drop-Out Rate	35.2%	29.1%	46.2%	25.5%
Enrollment by Grade[a]				
9th Grade	1,129	790	1,406	72,344
12th Grade	575	392	317	30,115

Source: Adapted by case writer from California Department of Education.

[a] Enrollment by grade for Jefferson is for SY05, the last complete school year before Green Dot opened five charters nearby and drew significantly from the entering 9th-grade class. All other schools and the LAUSD data are from SY06.

Stacey Childress ■ Maura Marino

KIPP 2007: Implementing a Smart Growth Strategy

Richard Barth, CEO of the KIPP Foundation, wrapped up his speech and walked off stage, energized by the crowd of 1,200 that was crammed into the ballroom of the Fairmont Scottsdale Princess for the 2007 KIPP School Summit. Since being named CEO in November 2005, Barth had overseen an expansion from 44 schools to 57 schools, in keeping with the network's opportunistic approach to growth. This approach had yielded success; most KIPP schools performed well (**Exhibit 1**). But as Barth explained in his speech, he believed the network needed a more strategic approach to growth in order to continue serving students with the greatest need, while preserving the Foundation's limited resources and ensuring the quality of the KIPP brand.

Barth had articulated two basic principles of "smart growth" in his speech: 1) expanding in regions where KIPP already had a presence, and 2) finding high-quality executive directors for each region before expansion. The strategy included two additional principles: having a single governing board for each region and the centralized provision of shared services for all schools in a region. Now Barth and his team would have to execute on those principles and determine which regions would get the "green light" for future growth, as well as which regions' growth plans would be halted.

The issue was more than academic, since KIPP University Prep Academy[1] was eager to grow and would be the first region to enter the new "stage-gate process" under the smart growth initiative. University Prep had opened in 2003 and its students had shown tremendous growth over the previous four years. The current school leader was aggressively pursuing expansion and had outlined a plan to open an additional middle school, two elementary schools, and a high school in the next six years. But were they ready for that kind of expansion? Barth knew that this test case for the new strategy would send a signal to the rest of the network about growth at KIPP. He was pleased that his verbal explanation had been well received, but he understood that a concrete decision about one region's actual growth plan could have consequences that would outweigh the excitement generated by his speech. (See **Exhibit 2** for additional KIPP strategic priorities.)

Background[2]

Dave Levin had graduated from Yale University only weeks before he met Mike Feinberg in the summer of 1992. Both had decided to join Teach For America (TFA), a national teaching corps that placed recent college graduates in two-year teaching assignments in some of the most challenging schools across the country. After a summer of training, Feinberg and Levin drove together from Los Angeles to Houston, and on that trip they recognized their philosophical similarities about what it took to make a great teacher and a great school. Despite an exhausting, frustrating two years teaching in Houston, they finished their TFA commitment convinced that they could make an impact and improve the educational experience for youth in Houston. Through their own experience and observations of other master teachers who were successful with low-income students, they came to believe that there were no excuses for low performance. They agreed that setting high expectations for students, gaining commitment from families, and working hard as teachers could produce results that many people thought were impossible for low-income students of color.

Dissatisfaction with the status quo in Houston schools led Feinberg and Levin to launch an experimental program in the summer of 1994 in the school in which Feinberg had been teaching. They called it the Knowledge Is Power Program (KIPP) and walked house-to-house to sign up their initial cohort of 50 fifth graders, almost all of whom were low-income Latino students. Parents and students were required to sign learning pledges committing the students to attend school from 7:30 a.m. to 5:00 p.m. on weekdays and a half-day on Saturdays. At the end of a grueling year of co-teaching the 50 students in a single classroom, Feinberg and Levin had delivered results to families and to the district: although 50% of their students had failed the Texas Assessment of Academic Skills (TAAS) in the prior year, 98% passed after a year in KIPP.

Despite the students' impressive progress, Feinberg and Levin recognized the daunting reality that was ahead for their students when they returned to the local public schools; Feinberg and Levin wanted to build students' academic skills over a sustained period and give them an opportunity to go to college. They worked to convince district officials in Houston and New York (Levin's home) to let them open middle schools on the KIPP model. Ultimately, they opened schools in both locations in the fall of 1995, KIPP Academy Houston and KIPP Academy New York.

KIPP School Model

The initial KIPP schools were built on the lessons learned by Feinberg and Levin during their time together in Houston, and from the outset had a trademark style. Students arrived at KIPP at 7:30 a.m. and were greeted by slogans throughout the building such as "Work Hard, Be Nice" and "No Excuses." KIPPsters were not referred to as 5th or 6th graders, but as the "Class of 2003," signifying the year they would enter college. The school community was considered a "team and family" that solved problems collectively.

KIPP classrooms exhibited high levels of student engagement. It was not uncommon for every hand in a classroom to be raised when a teacher posed a question to students. Teachers led students in chants and rhymes to generate excitement about classroom content. In fact, the KIPP name was taken from a chant that Feinberg and Levin learned from Houston teacher Harriet Ball. The chant was commonly heard in KIPP classrooms: "You've gotta read, baby, read! You've gotta read, baby, read! The more you read, the more you know! Knowledge is power! Power is freedom! You gotta want it!"

Character lessons were emphasized as much as academic lessons, and students learned that they had to treat other KIPPsters well in order to "climb the mountain to college." Feinberg explained what it meant to be a KIPPster:

> It means to work hard and be nice . . . to realize that there are no shortcuts, that you're going to do whatever it takes, and whether you're a teacher or student or bus driver or the lunch lady, you're going to work very hard at your job and take pride in it. And I think being

> nice refers to the life skills. At the end of the day it's about being nice to yourself and being nice to your neighbors and being a responsible and respectful and contributing person in this world.[3]

Teachers lived the "Work Hard, Be Nice" maxim and were committed to "do whatever it takes" to help students learn. In addition to putting in long hours at school, teachers were available to students on their cell phones at night for help with homework. While many KIPP teachers were Teach For America alumni—often in their twenties, unmarried and without children—Levin recruited more veteran teachers in New York in order to support and coach newer teachers more effectively.

KIPP schools were also notable for their disciplined environment. Students earned a weekly school "paycheck" based on their ability to follow school rules. If their paychecks totaled a sufficient amount at the end of the year, they were rewarded with a major field trip such as visiting a national park. The founders believed they had carefully aligned school culture with the developmental stage of middle school students. For example, KIPP Houston students who did not behave properly were "benched," which Feinberg explained:

> The bench [is] the metaphor that comes from one of our values, which is teammates and teamwork. You know, at KIPP we say all the time that we are a team and a family, and that team always beats individual. And so the bench has become, basically, one of the consequences when kids are making bad choices and not following the rules. They're "on the bench," as in, they're not part of the team playing the game, they're on the sidelines watching . . . on the bench. What we've taken away is the social aspect, which the kids at the middle school level so crave. So they're still in the classroom, they're still learning, but they have to sit apart from their teammates.[4]

The KIPP Academies were founded on a philosophy that there was no single solution to improving the performance of low-income students of color, but that hard work and unwillingness to accept failure would create a climate of success. By 1999, KIPP New York and KIPP Houston celebrated their first class of graduates, most of whom continued on to highly competitive high schools. KIPP New York was named the best performing public middle school in the Bronx. KIPP Houston's students had made an average gain of 7.3 grade levels in just four years.

The KIPP Foundation[5]

In the fall of 1999, KIPP New York and KIPP Houston appeared in a segment on the television newsmagazine *60 Minutes*. Soon after, KIPP caught the attention of Don and Doris Fisher, the founders of GAP, Inc. and funders of the Pisces Foundation. The Fishers collaborated with Levin and Feinberg to discuss national expansion by committing $15 million to launch the KIPP Foundation. The goal of the KIPP Foundation was to train school leaders to replicate the success of the original KIPP Academies nationally in order to impact public education broadly (**Exhibit 3**).

While there was much debate on what the role of the Foundation should be and the optimal way to build KIPP to scale, ultimately, the Fishers, Levin, Feinberg, and Scott Hamilton, executive director of the Pisces Foundation, determined that human capital was the critical ingredient for opening high-quality schools. Rather than create a cookie-cutter model for schools, the KIPP Foundation sought school leaders whom they described as "visionary, idealistic, competitive" entrepreneurs committed to education reform. These entrepreneurs would be trained by the Foundation and then allowed to operate a KIPP school. School leaders would have freedom to open their school wherever they chose, which would support the founders' belief that their "no excuses" philosophy transcended geographic location and cultural differences.

Feinberg moved from Houston to San Francisco to become founding CEO of the KIPP Foundation, while Levin stayed in the Bronx as the leader of KIPP Academy New York. The KIPP Foundation was ultimately set up to support schools in five core ways:

- *Recruiting, selecting and training Fisher Fellows:* The Fisher Fellowship was the year-long training program for new KIPP school leaders. Fellows spent a summer studying under Levin, Feinberg, and other Foundation staff members. In the fall they observed other KIPP schools through a "residency" program, before spending the final six months of their Fellowship year in their city of choice getting ready to open their school.
- *Providing "trailblazing" services:* A team of KIPP Foundation staff members were dedicated to performing critical tasks to open each new school, such as writing charter applications, finding school facilities, and ensuring legal compliance.
- *Conducting performance evaluations:* The KIPP Foundation partnered with an educational consulting firm to conduct first-, second- and fifth-year school inspections of each KIPP school to determine whether schools were financially sound and delivering on their promise of academic achievement.
- *Supporting high-quality instruction:* While KIPP schools were free to determine their own curriculum, an Instructional Support Team helped share best practices across the network, provided guidance on curricular choices, and coached schools looking to improve in certain areas.
- *Building an alumni network:* Since most KIPP schools were 5th–8th grade, keeping in contact with alumni was critical to support their "climb up the mountain to college" and to assess the success of the KIPP school model.

Initial Growth: 2000–2007

The KIPP Foundation officially opened in April 2000, and Feinberg, Levin, and Hamilton set to work, eager to train school leaders to open schools in the fall of 2001, rather than waiting for an entire additional school year to pass before they could begin. They chose three Teach For America alumni as founding school leaders—Susan Schaeffler, Caleb Dolan, and Dan Caesar. In the fall of 2001, following their Fisher Fellowship year, Schaeffler opened a school in Washington, DC, serving predominantly urban African-American students; Dolan opened a school in Gaston, NC, serving predominantly rural African-American students; and Caesar opened a school in Houston, TX, serving predominantly urban Mexican-American students.

The experience of replicating KIPP schools led the Foundation to better articulate what it meant to "be KIPP." These ideas became codified in KIPP's Five Pillars (**Exhibit 4**). The Five Pillars included high expectations for all students; choice and commitment of students, parents, and faculty; more time in school; power to lead for principals; and a focus on results. In practice, while there was variation among schools, there was strong evidence of the Five Pillars throughout the network. KIPPsters around the country could be found in school from 7:30 a.m. to 5:00 p.m. and on Saturday mornings. Parents, students, and teachers all signed the "Commitment to Excellence." Principals had control over their budgets and created a data-driven culture in their schools in which teachers regularly gave benchmark assessments and tracked student progress over time. Another common element of KIPP schools was the fact that they were launched the same way: each school started with 5th grade and grew one grade at a time. Feinberg explained the rationale for starting in 5th grade:

> Our idea of fifth grade is like the fourth quarter—the two-minute warning, we're down by a touchdown. . . . You can still win the game but now every second counts; there's a tremendous sense of urgency and there's no more margin for error. . . . After fifth grade it's simply a matter of less than eight years of time to prepare the kids to be ready to succeed in college as well. And less than eight years, when you're starting from close to scratch, is not enough time on the clock. So even if you are a great teacher and if you're running a great school, the variable of not enough time still weighs heavily on you and we want to eliminate that variable.[6]

The vast majority of KIPP schools were charter schools—publicly funded, but independently run by local 501(c)(3) organizations and accountable to a charter authorizer such as a local school board or state department of education. Some KIPP schools were contract schools—managed by KIPP and operated with the Five Pillars, but typically subject to all other regulations of the local districts, including collective bargaining agreements and requirements to use district services.

With common philosophical underpinnings, Five Pillars as a platform for school design, and similarities in school structures, the KIPP network began to expand quickly. In 2003 alone, KIPP opened 17 schools in communities such as Buffalo, San Francisco, Philadelphia, Chicago, San Antonio, and Los Angeles to bring the size of the network to 32 schools.

Evolving Leadership

Developing formal structures and systems to support both new and existing schools became an increasing priority for the Foundation. In 2003, Feinberg recognized that this was neither where his strength nor interest lay. He considered himself "very good at starting things . . . at dealing with the craziness . . . with lots of ambiguity" but simultaneously saw that KIPP was "about to double in size. A lot was coming down the road. And I knew that we were going to need leadership at a level, at a skill set that I was not good at doing." Feinberg decided to return to Houston to manage the network of KIPP schools that were emerging there.

Scott Hamilton of the Pisces Foundation stepped in to serve as executive director of the KIPP Foundation in late 2003. As he was stepping into this role, the Foundation was also shifting its position with respect to the network. Clusters of schools were beginning to develop in New York and Houston, which made it possible to aggregate services across a region.

Fundraising, for example, had always been handled by individual schools or at the Foundation, but clusters made it possible to regionalize fundraising across multiple New York City schools. Fisher Fellows could be selected from a pool of strong teachers at existing schools to seed new schools in a given region. The Foundation, therefore, could transfer some of its responsibility for recruiting fellows onto the regions, thus freeing up the Foundation's capacity to deal with other issues. Managing a network of school clusters was a fundamentally different challenge than the Foundation was initially set up to support.

This new model changed the nature of leadership at school sites as well. While initial school leaders at KIPP did everything on their own, this was not the case for school leaders in regions. Mike Wright, Director of Network Growth, explained that "the next generation of school leaders didn't need to be superheroes anymore. They could be great school leaders, but they could leave facilities issues, talent recruitment, board development, and fundraising up to their regional office. School leaders could focus on kids and families and less on the business side than in the past."

Due to a serious motorcycle accident in the fall of 2005, Scott Hamilton was succeeded as CEO by Levin, who agreed to step into the role on a temporary basis. Levin remained in New York, managing the Foundation from a distance while continuing to run the New York network of schools. The Foundation did an extensive search for a leader capable of bringing the network to scale in a sustainable way. In November 2005, Richard Barth was named CEO of the KIPP Foundation. Barth's past experience as one of the founding staff members of Teach For America and later as president of the District Partnership business for Edison Schools gave KIPP Foundation staff members the confidence that Barth would be a strong fit to move KIPP forward.

School Closings

Between 2001 and 2007, KIPP opened 64 schools across 17 states and the District of Columbia, making it the largest network of nonprofit charter schools in the country (see **Exhibits 5, 6,** and **7**). Ninety percent of schools started by the KIPP Foundation were still in operation and part of the network as of the summer of 2007. However, the KIPP team had also learned some difficult lessons about managing growth, which resulted in five schools closing and two schools leaving the KIPP network but continuing to operate as independent charters. In particular:

1. KIPP Chicago Youth Village Academy opened in 2003 and was under contract to Chicago Public Schools. It ultimately closed in 2005 due to low enrollment and lack of flexibility and control stemming from its contract-school status.
2. KIPP Achieve opened in Atlanta in 2003, and lost its license to use the KIPP name in February 2006 as a result of financial difficulties.
3. KIPP PATH opened in 2002 in DeKalb County, GA, near Atlanta. In 2004, due to "philosophical differences," KIPP Path became an independent public charter school no longer affiliated with the KIPP network.
4. KIPP Sac Prep opened in Sacramento, CA, in 2003, and its charter was held by the KIPP Foundation itself, as opposed to a local nonprofit organization. In November 2005, the charter was transferred to a local organization in response to the board and principal's desire for local autonomy.
5. KIPP Harbor Academy opened in 2005 in Annapolis, MD, and closed in summer 2007 when it could not find suitable facilities to house its students.[7]
6. KIPP Sankofa Charter School opened in Buffalo, NY, in 2003, and it closed in the spring of 2007 because the school was not meeting KIPP standards.
7. KIPP Asheville Youth Academy in Asheville, NC, opened as a contract school with Asheville City Schools in 2002, and enrolled fewer than 80 students in grades 5 through 8. The school merged with another public school in May 2006.

Lessons Learned

KIPP's success attracted national attention and was highlighted by *The Oprah Winfrey Show, The New York Times, Time* magazine, *ABC World News,* and other national and local media outlets. While KIPP was being heralded as a success, though, staff at the KIPP Foundation recognized that their continued success would depend on growing strategically in the future. Barth, drawing on his experience at Edison Schools and Teach For America, spent time at the outset of his tenure as CEO understanding what the major challenges were for existing schools, and what it would take to get to greater scale without sacrificing quality.

Later, in order to clarify organizational imperatives for KIPP, Barth engaged a consulting firm to perform an in-depth analysis of the common challenges throughout the network. Through interviews with school leaders, regional leaders, Foundation staff, funders, parents, and other stakeholders, a growing consensus was uncovered about the state of the network. Barth described one striking finding:

> It turns out that every time we had a school in trouble, either academically or financially, that school was out on its own. It wasn't in an area with other KIPP schools. These were the places that the Foundation staff was spending 80% of their time. Sometimes we could rescue the school, and sometimes we shut it down or severed our ties, but the common theme was that these were single-site schools. To be clear, not all of our single sites were in trouble, but all of our struggling schools were single sites.

KIPP recognized several fundamental challenges for single-site schools:

- *Role of school leader:* Founding school leaders served as the instructional, operational, and financial leader of their school, in addition to being an entrepreneur, fundraiser, public relations director, and political strategist. When asked about his job, one principal said he "[acted] as the instructional leader of the school, liaison to the Board of Trustees, [oversaw] the operations of the school, [handled outreach] to funders and to the community, [ran] breakfast and lunch, [taught] a 5th grade class called 'Life' as well as a Tae Kwon Do elective, [plunged] an occasional toilet, [rode] the bus, etc." Given the variety of hats that school leaders wore, their ability to focus on academics, professional development of staff, and school culture was limited.[8]
- *Succession planning:* The role of a founding school leader required tremendous intensity, and many only stayed in that role for four to five years. Finding and developing talented leaders to replace school leaders was a challenge throughout the network. Very few school leaders successfully built "bench depth" to plan for their eventual departure.
- *Governance and oversight:* Each school was governed locally by a board of directors composed of volunteers. While some board members had extensive backgrounds in education and were able to dedicate significant time to KIPP, many were unfamiliar with charter school operations and did not understand the role of such schools. Few resources were dedicated to training and developing the board, and consequently school leaders in some cases were not able to rely heavily on their board for direction.

Yet the answer to the challenges that single-site schools were experiencing seemed to exist in the emerging regions. Regional offices in New York City and Houston were managing facilities, finance, charter compliance, development, and recruiting. Wright described the benefits of geographic density "not necessarily in bringing financial economies of scale—that is yet unproven in charter schools—but in creating stable, sustainable regions with local resources to support school leaders."

For KIPP New York, reaching greater scale meant the ability to create its own teacher credentialing and master's degree program to stabilize its teacher recruitment and training pipeline. Developed in collaboration with two other New York charter-management organizations, Achievement First and Uncommon Schools, the Teacher YOU program at Hunter College was tailored to meet the unique teacher training needs of urban, "high expectations" charter schools and was projected to enroll 500 students by 2011. Barth was hopeful that more of these types of partnerships would develop as KIPP regions grew.

Regional structures also provided opportunities for improved communication and sharing of best practices. In addition to network-wide events such as the KIPP School Summit and the annual KIPP School Leader retreat, regional offices would allow opportunities for local KIPP schools to share their challenges and successes. Barth considered this sharing the key to KIPP's success moving forward:

> When we gathered for KIPP School Summit, I challenged us, as a network, to set a new standard for sharing . . . to set a new standard for the entire world of K–12 public education. I put this goal out there before all of us because I am convinced that we cannot achieve our aspirations unless we truly become great at sharing. Key to all of this is investing in creating a culture of sharing, a culture in which we are not governed by fear or insecurity, but one in which we celebrate each other and personal growth . . . Technology certainly has a role to play in all of this, a not insignificant one. But it starts with a culture that—in its focus on our kids—recognizes the need for people to be able to share openly and without unnecessary anxiety.

By 2007, the KIPP network had grown rapidly to $170 million in annual public revenue, with an 83% compound annual growth rate over the previous two years. As it grew, KIPP had developed a two-pronged goal: provide a great education to its students and change societal beliefs about what minority and low-income children can achieve when adults invest in them. To communicate this goal, the organization developed a motto: "The actual proves the possible." In order to continue to serve more students while pursuing both parts of its goal, Barth felt it was now essential to systematize KIPP's approach to growth and promote the benefits of a regional structure.

Designing a Smart Growth Process

In the spring of 2007, the KIPP Foundation's board of directors approved funding for an internal team that would be responsible for growth management. Wright, then the director of school finance, was named director of the network growth team and was charged with both crafting and executing the processes for growth management.

The network growth team looked to other education-reform organizations for best practices in strategic growth management, but as the market leader in nonprofit charter schools, KIPP was in a unique position. No other organization had reached its scale or geographic footprint, so the group also drew on team members' private-sector experience to consider how companies managed growth. After researching and talking to people both inside and outside the network, the group determined that the Foundation would still pursue strategic growth in new areas if there was a strong leader, community support and a market that could support multiple sites. For KIPP's current cities, the group created a stage-gate process for green-lighting growth applications from leaders of existing KIPP schools.

Stage-Gate Process

The stage-gate process was designed to balance the pace of growth with associated risks in order to ensure that high-quality, sustainable schools were opened in existing KIPP regions. Barth explained that "the Foundation's role in growth management is not as a growth driver, but actually to ensure that we grow in a way that reflects our core belief that the quality of what we do matters more than anything else." Wright was concerned that the process not be overly bureaucratic, but instead simply ensure that schools/regions were well-positioned to grow.

The process involved four stages at which regions interested in growth crafted specific deliverables, and four associated gates at which the regions were evaluated. Regions signaled their desire to grow with an initial letter of interest, which was followed by a detailed examination of the academic, financial, and operational performance of existing schools; a market analysis; a strategic business plan; and finally, establishment of milestones for new school openings (see Table 1).

At each gate, the network growth team convened appropriate Foundation staff members to review the materials submitted by a region and determine whether or not to pass them through the gate and on to the next stage. A cross-functional team of Foundation staff members was created to handle these evaluations, and included members with expertise in data analysis, legal issues, governance, and school finance. In addition, the director of school inspections and a former KIPP school leader were also members of the evaluation team in order to provide a more holistic assessment.

The process was designed to counsel regions that were not ready for growth and steer them out of the process early. Presumably, regions writing strategic business plans in Stage 3 would be well-positioned for growth, and were unlikely to be denied permission to grow at that point. The early stages, however, required a much more critical lens in order to discern which regions should continue in their growth process.

Growth Decision: University Prep Academy

Barth returned to New York after the KIPP School Summit and reviewed the data that the network growth team had sent to him about University Prep Academy. University Prep had submitted its letter of interest and performance data and was now ready for its Gate 1 evaluation meeting. The network growth team would convene the evaluation team the next day, and Barth reflected on what his recommendation should be about growth. He knew that the team would review four key areas: student achievement, governance, operations, and finance.

Student Achievement

University Prep's first class graduated in June 2007 and went on to top private, boarding, and magnet schools throughout the region. The 300 KIPPsters who attended University Prep had a 96% attendance rate, beating the local district's average of 89%. The first class had seen 30% attrition over its four years; attrition rates now seemed to be stabilizing at 10% per year, resulting mainly from families moving out of the area.

Students at University Prep had shown growth over time on state examinations and had outperformed the local district. The school had demonstrated "Adequate Yearly Progress" according to the No Child Left Behind Act in each year since the school opened. Barth was concerned, however, that students were scoring at the 61st percentile nationally in reading. Although this meant that students performed around KIPP's national average, the Foundation believed that students with higher scores were more likely to be well-prepared to succeed in college (**Exhibit 8**).

Governance

University Prep had a nine-member board of directors consisting of local business leaders, philanthropists, and civic leaders, most of whom had been personally recruited by Jose Villegas, University Prep's founding school leader. The board had raised an average of over $250,000 each year to supplement the state and federal funding that University Prep received. Although the first board chair had managed the board informally, a new board chair had been named four months earlier and had instituted regular board meetings; the chair was now

Table 1
KIPP Stage-Gate Process

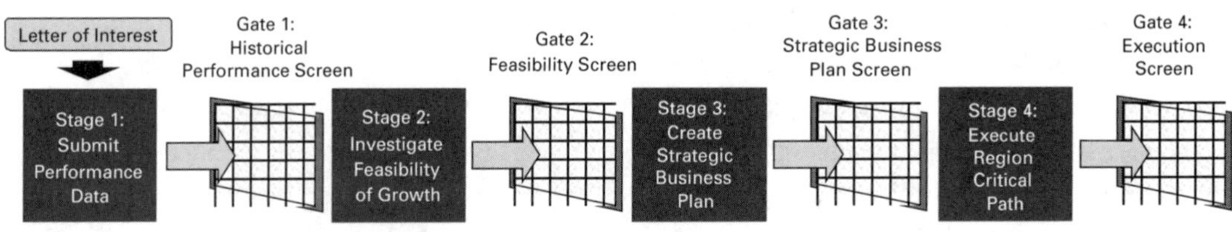

Stage	*Purpose*	*Evaluation Questions at Associated Gate*
Letter of Interest	• Signal to the KIPP Foundation a Region's interest in growth • Demonstrate alignment between the Board and the Regional Leader in terms of growth plans • Articulate initial growth plans	

Stage 1: Submit Performance Data	• Examine historical performance of school/ region to determine:
	  • if past performance establishes a strong platform for growth
	  • if replicable systems and structures are in place
		• Does historical performance indicate a strong platform for growth?
		• Are replicable systems and structures in place?

Stage 2: Investigate Feasibility of Growth	• Ensure that expansion of KIPP is both necessary and viable given the local environment and the performance of the existing school(s) • Set the process and resource allocation framework for strategic business planning in Stage 3	• Is there a need for new KIPP schools? • Are the preliminary plans for growth consistent with KIPP's smart growth principles? • Has the region created a reasonable framework to guide its strategic planning process? • Have existing obstacles been addressed to ensure that growth is feasible?
Stage 3: Create Strategic Business Plan	• Develop strategic clarity around desired impact of region • Determine strategic priorities in order to achieve desired impact • Understand resource implications of pursuing these priorities • Establish performance measures to assess progress toward desired impact	• Is the strategic business plan compelling? • Is the operational plan executable? • Is the plan humanly and financially sustainable? • Have external and internal risks and obstacles been adequately addressed?
Stage 4: Execute Region Critical Path	• Monitor ongoing implementation of strategic business plan based on milestones created jointly by regional leaders and KIPP Foundation • Ensure delivery of adequate support to school leaders and successful launch of new schools	• Are all milestones consistently met and, if not, is a contingency plan in place?

Source: KIPP internal document.

in the process of implementing a committee structure.

Villegas was well-respected by his board, as well as by students, parents, and community members; the board described him as a charismatic, inspirational leader. He was generally the first to arrive in the morning and the last to leave at night. He had studied history as an undergraduate at Harvard University and taught 7th grade social studies for five years before becoming a Fisher Fellow and leading University Prep. Although the board had never conducted a formal evaluation of Villegas, there was wide consensus that he had a vision for University Prep and buy-in from students, families, and teachers to execute on that vision.

Operations Management

University Prep's business manager, Jessica Dixon, was responsible for the non-academic side of the organization—primarily finance, facilities management, and human resources. In its most recent KIPP Foundation evaluation, University Prep had received high marks across the board in operations and finance for adhering to KIPP's Standards of Operational Excellence.

The school was currently housed in a strip mall due to lack of available space in district buildings. Villegas hoped that it was a temporary situation, but after four years, University Prep had not been able to secure a less expensive, more permanent site that was better suited for the school. In fact, facilities costs had been rising each year (**Exhibit 9**).

Human resource practices had been well-developed over the previous four years, including a recently announced collaboration with a local teacher certification program that would allow University Prep to train student teachers. Dixon felt that this would help build a stronger teacher pipeline and allow for future expansion. Currently, University Prep had 24 staff members (21 teachers plus Villegas, Dixon, and an office manager) and an annual turnover rate of 20% among teachers.

University Prep's charter was granted by the state board of education, and it had maintained impeccable compliance with its charter. A charter cap was in place, however, which meant that the state was currently unable to grant new charters. Villegas hoped he could open new KIPP schools under the auspices of his current charter, but to date there was no precedent in the state for doing so.

Financial Management

University Prep had established a clear process for budgeting and ongoing financial reporting, which served as a model for other schools in the KIPP network. Due to low per-pupil funding in the state, however, University Prep anticipated that it would always have an annual shortfall of $1,350 per student, which needed to be filled by local fundraising. The board had stepped up to this challenge, and each year had raised more than was necessary to cover the shortfall. Villegas was concerned, however, about donor fatigue. In particular, over $120,000 in annual support had come from one private foundation. On numerous occasions Villegas and Barth had talked about strategies to diversify this funding base, but it would be a gradual process to cultivate new donors. The local community foundation was already an active supporter of University Prep, and Villegas hoped to use that relationship to establish a larger base of individual contributors and make inroads into local corporate donation programs. According to its projections of enrolling 1900 students in 2013, University Prep would then have a funding need of over $2.5 million per year.

The Decision

The University Prep decision was anything but clear to Barth. He tried to separate his review of the data from his knowledge about the leadership of the school. Villegas was interested in becoming executive director of the region, but he would have to go through a separate process with his board in order to be named to that position. The question at hand was whether the school was ready to grow based on its existing performance, regardless of who was chosen to lead it. Still, Barth wondered who would run University Prep if Villegas became the executive director. Villegas had hired young, energetic teachers, but none of them had been groomed specifically to take a leadership role in the near future. Was anyone ready to step up?

Reviewing University Prep's plan also raised some concerns for Barth about "off-pattern" growth. While KIPP had always started schools at 5th grade and grown one grade at a time, Villegas intended to start the elementary school with both a kindergarten and first grade in its first year. And he planned to start the new middle school with a 5th and 6th grade simultaneously. Additionally, the high school called for a 700-student capacity, but the two middle schools could feed a maximum of only 600 students (**Exhibit 10**). How would students from non-KIPP middle schools fit into KIPP culture if they entered in high school?

Barth also thought about the signal that the evaluation team's decision would send to the rest of the network. Villegas had been very well-liked in his cohort of Fisher Fellows and had kept in touch with them regularly. Villegas had also supported many new school leaders as they opened their schools. Historically, school leaders had been able to grow whenever they wanted, and saying "no" at the Foundation level would be a huge cultural shift for KIPP. If Villegas was told that his region was not ready to grow, how would other school leaders in the network react to the decision? On the other hand, if University Prep was greenlighted before it was fully ready to grow, not only would the legitimacy of the smart growth process be compromised, but it could potentially have an adverse impact on the school's current students.

Barth knew that early growth decisions such as those being made at University Prep would have long-term consequences for the impact of the KIPP network.

Notes

1. University Prep Academy is a fictional school that was created by the case writers using data from multiple KIPP schools that had entered the first stage-gate process.

2. This section draws from Stig Leschly, "KIPP National, 1999 (A): Designing a School Network," HBS Case 803-124 (Boston: Harvard Business School Publishing, 2002).

3. PBS, "Making Schools Work," PBS website, http://www.pbs.org/makingschoolswork/sbs/kipp/feinberg.html, accessed November 2007.

4. Ibid.

5. This section was adapted from Howard Husock, "The KIPP Schools: Deciding How to Go to Scale," Kennedy School of Government, Case C16-06-1847.0, Copyright 2006, President and Fellows of Harvard College.

6. PBS, "Making Schools Work."

7. Kimberly Marselas, "Last Charter School Defends Its Performance," *Baltimore Sun*, December 2, 2007, http://www.baltimoresun.com/news/local/annearundel/bal-ar.charter02dec02,0,7889885.story, accessed December 2007.

8. Josh Zoia biography, HBS Social Enterprise Conference Program, 2008.

Exhibit 1

KIPP Network-wide Performance

1a: Students Scoring Proficient and Above on State Exams, KIPP Schools Founded 2004 and Prior, Organized Alphabetically by State

School	*Percent Proficient +*		*Low-Income*	*Location*	*Year Opened*
	Math	*Reading*			
KIPP Delta College Preparatory	66	78	87%	Helena, AR	2002
KIPP Academy Fresno	80	81	81%	Fresno, CA	2004
KIPP Academy of Opportunity	53	73	73%	Los Angeles, CA	2003
KIPP LA Prep	22	51	93%	Los Angeles, CA	2003
KIPP Bridge College Preparatory	32	44	65%	Oakland, CA	2002
KIPP Adelante Preparatory Academy	72	80	90%	San Diego, CA	2003
KIPP Bayview Academy	29	57	67%	San Francisco, CA	2003
KIPP SF Bay Academy	73	70	84%	San Francisco, CA	2003
KIPP Heartwood Academy	95	99	86%	San Jose, CA	2004
KIPP Summit Academy	79	54	62%	San Lorenzo, CA	2003
KIPP Sunshine Peak Academy	65	67	90%	Denver, CO	2002
KIPP DC: KEY Academy	100	79	70%	Washington, D.C.	2001
KIPP South Fulton Academy	100	97	69%	Atlanta, GA	2003
KIPP WAYS Academy	100	100	73%	Atlanta, GA	2003
KIPP Ascend Charter School	100	94	92%	Chicago, IL	2003
KIPP Indianapolis College Preparatory	41	47	79%	Indianapolis, IN	2004
KIPP Academy Lynn	68	83	84%	Lynn, MA	2004
KIPP Ujima Village Academy	98	83	81%	Baltimore, MD	2002
KIPP Gaston College Preparatory	97	100	62%	Gaston, NC	2001
Freedom Academy Charter School, A KIPP School	20	68	88%	Camden, NJ	2004
TEAM Academy Charter School, A KIPP School	42	63	77%	Newark, NJ	2002
KIPP Academy New York	84	82	86%	New York, NY	1995
KIPP STAR College Preparatory School	77	63	76%	New York, NY	2003
KIPP Reach College Preparatory	98	100	77%	Oklahoma City, OK	2002
KIPP Philadelphia Charter School	91	91	84%	Philadelphia, PA	2003
KIPP Diamond Academy	86	88	79%	Memphis, TN	2002
KIPP Austin College Prep	95	100	93%	Austin, TX	2002
KIPP Truth Academy	86	96	82%	Dallas, TX	2003
KIPP 3D Academy	100	100	86%	Houston, TX	2001
KIPP Academy Middle School Houston	98	100	91%	Houston, TX	1995
KIPP Houston High School	98	100	86%	Houston, TX	2004
KIPP Aspire Academy	88	96	72%	San Antonio, TX	2003

Source: Adapted by case writers from KIPP: Report Card 2007, released April 21, 2008.

1b: Comparison of KIPP Schools to Their Local Districts on 2007 State Exams for All Schools Founded 2004 and Prior, Organized by Year Founded.

		Difference in % Proficient +	
Year Founded	*School*	*Math*	*Reading*
1995	KIPP Academy New York	62	59
1995	KIPP Academy Middle School Houston	27	11
2001	KIPP DC: KEY Academy	69	43
2001	KIPP Gaston College Preparatory	42	17
2001	KIPP 3D Academy	36	14
2002	KIPP Delta College Preparatory	58	44
2002	KIPP Bridge College Preparatory	19	20
2002	KIPP Sunshine Peak Academy	43	29
2002	KIPP Ujima Village Academy	74	38
2002	TEAM Academy Charter School	7	13
2002	KIPP Reach College Preparatory	34	38
2002	KIPP Diamond Academy	10	3
2002	KIPP Austin College Prep	31	16
2003	KIPP Academy of Opportunity	39	47
2003	KIPP LA Prep	8	25
2003	KIPP Adelante Preparatory Academy	52	38
2003	KIPP Bayview Academy SF	-6	8
2003	KIPP SF Bay Academy	38	21
2003	KIPP Summit Academy	59	31
2003	KIPP South Fulton Academy	15	4
2003	KIPP WAYS Academy	31	21
2003	KIPP Ascend Charter School	29	16
2003	KIPP STAR College Preparatory School	45	37
2003	KIPP Philadelphia Charter School	47	42
2003	KIPP Truth Academy	29	15
2003	KIPP Aspire Academy	29	14
2004	KIPP Academy Fresno	63	52
2004	KIPP Heartwood Academy	53	65
2004	KIPP Indianapolis College Preparatory	-6	4
2004	KIPP Academy Lynn	40	34
2004	Freedom Academy Charter School	3	34
2004	KIPP Houston High School	21	15

Source: Adapted by case writers from KIPP: Report Card 2007, released April 21, 2008.

Note: Data is for highest grade served.

1c: Change in Students' National Percentile Rankings on Norm-Referenced Exams from Entry in a KIPP School Through Final Year of Available Data, Organized Alphabetically by State

	Math			Reading				
School	*Beginning Year*	*Final Year*	*Change*	*Beginning Year*	*Final Year*	*Change*	*Low-Income*	*Location*
KIPP Delta College Preparatory	23	72	49	23	42	19	87%	Helena, AR
KIPP Academy Fresno	47	94	47	37	66	29	81%	Fresno, CA
KIPP Academy of Opportunity	39	87	48	29	69	40	73%	Los Angeles, CA
KIPP LA Prep	49	71	22	38	48	10	93%	Los Angeles, CA
KIPP Bridge College Preparatory	39	67	28	37	48	11	65%	Oakland, CA
KIPP Adelante Preparatory Academy	41	89	48	34	75	41	90%	San Diego, CA
KIPP Bayview Academy	25	80	55	19	56	37	67%	San Francisco, CA
KIPP SF Bay Academy	35	85	50	30	66	36	84%	San Francisco, CA
KIPP Heartwood Academy	66	96	30	44	74	30	86%	San Jose, CA
KIPP Summit Academy	57	81	24	45	63	18	62%	San Lorenzo, CA
KIPP Sunshine Peak Academy	29	72	43	29	48	19	90%	Denver, CO
KIPP DC: KEY Academy	40	91	51	35	57	22	70%	Washington, D.C.
KIPP South Fulton Academy	53	67	14	47	60	13	69%	Atlanta, GA
KIPP WAYS Academy	48	73	25	47	60	13	73%	Atlanta, GA
KIPP Ascend Charter School	35	61	26	20	45	25	92%	Chicago, IL
KIPP Indianapolis College Preparatory	28	58	30	20	45	25	79%	Indianapolis, IN
KIPP Academy Lynn	56	91	35	44	68	24	84%	Lynn, MA
KIPP Ujima Village Academy	38	91	53	30	43	13	81%	Baltimore, MD
KIPP Gaston College Preparatory	50	92	42	47	66	19	62%	Gaston, NC
Freedom Academy Charter School	30	57	27	20	38	18	88%	Camden, NJ
TEAM Academy Charter School	30	67	37	15	44	29	77%	Newark, NJ
KIPP Academy New York	50	90	40	35	74	39	86%	New York, NY
KIPP STAR College Preparatory School	44	88	44	28	67	39	76%	New York, NY
KIPP Reach College Preparatory	26	77	51	28	68	40	77%	Oklahoma City, OK
KIPP Philadelphia Charter School	35	55	20	41	57	16	84%	Philadelphia, PA
KIPP Diamond Academy	26	55	29	18	34	16	79%	Memphis, TN
KIPP Austin College Prep	46	89	43	34	72	38	93%	Austin, TX
KIPP Truth Academy	32	75	43	30	51	21	82%	Dallas, TX
KIPP 3D Academy	56	93	37	47	71	24	86%	Houston, TX
KIPP Academy Middle School Houston	70	82	12	50	64	14	91%	Houston, TX
KIPP Houston High School	83	86	3	54	67	13	86%	Houston, TX
KIPP Aspire Academy	40	89	49	31	60	29	72%	San Antonio, TX

Source: Adapted by case writers from KIPP: Report Card 2007, released April 21, 2008.

Exhibit 2

KIPP Strategic Imperatives, 2007

- Leveraging the power of the KIPP "Team & Family" to deliver on the promises we have made to children and families;
- Executing a smart growth strategy to achieve geographic density;
- Explicitly defining the decision-making process and roles of the KIPP Foundation, clusters of schools, and individual schools with respect to governance, expansion, and evaluation of schools;
- Building a world-class organization and operating model that are equal to the scope of our aspiration;
- Maximizing the influence of the KIPP network by sharing our results, insights, and lessons learned.

Source: KIPP organization documents.

Exhibit 3

KIPP Foundation Mission Statement

KIPP's mission is to create a respected, influential, national network of public schools that are successful in helping students from educationally underserved communities develop the knowledge, skills, character, and habits needed to succeed in college and the competitive world beyond.

Source: KIPP organization documents.

Exhibit 4

The Five Pillars

KIPP schools share a core set of operating principles known as the Five Pillars:

- **High Expectations**. KIPP schools have clearly defined and measurable high expectations for academic achievement and conduct that make no excuses based on the students' backgrounds. Students, parents, teachers, and staff create and reinforce a culture of achievement and support through a range of formal and informal rewards and consequences for academic performance and behavior.
- **Choice and Commitment**. Students, their parents, and the faculty of each KIPP school choose to participate in the program. No one is assigned or forced to attend a KIPP school. Everyone must make and uphold a commitment to the school and to each other to put in the time and effort required to achieve success.
- **More Time**. KIPP schools know that there are no shortcuts when it comes to success in academics and life. With an extended school day, week, and year, students have more time in the classroom to acquire the academic knowledge and skills that will prepare them for competitive high schools and colleges, as well as more opportunities to engage in diverse extracurricular experiences.
- **Power to Lead**. The principals of KIPP schools are effective academic and organizational leaders who understand that great schools require great School Leaders. They have control over their school budget and personnel. They are free to swiftly move dollars or make staffing changes, allowing them maximum effectiveness in helping students learn.
- **Focus on Results**. KIPP schools relentlessly focus on high student performance on standardized tests and other objective measures. Just as there are no shortcuts, there are no excuses. Students are expected to achieve a level of academic performance that will enable them to succeed at the nation's best high schools and colleges.

Source: KIPP organization documents.

Exhibit 5

KIPP Expansion by Year

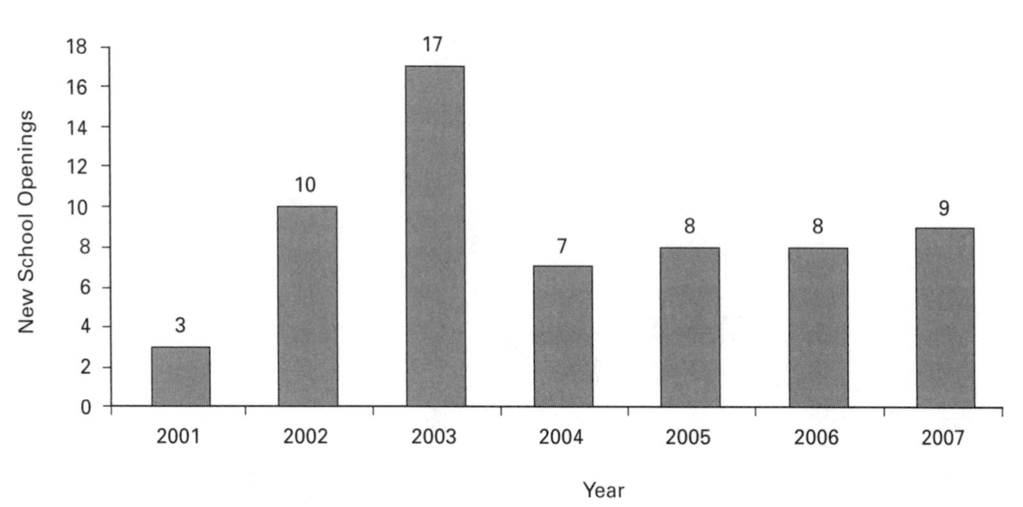

Source: KIPP organization documents.

Exhibit 6

KIPP Network Map, Fall 2007

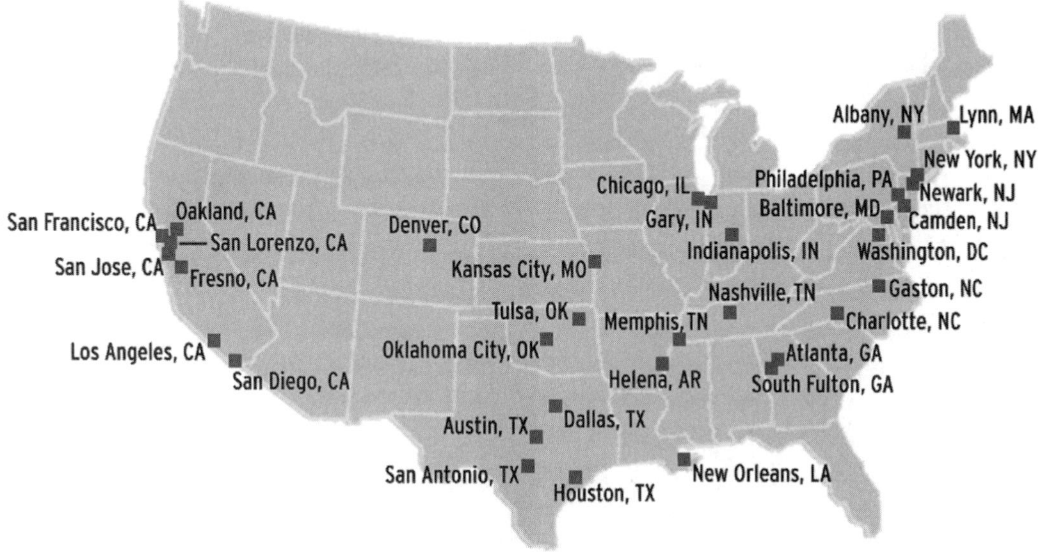

Source: KIPP organization documents.

Exhibit 7

KIPP Geographic Density, 2007–2008 School Year

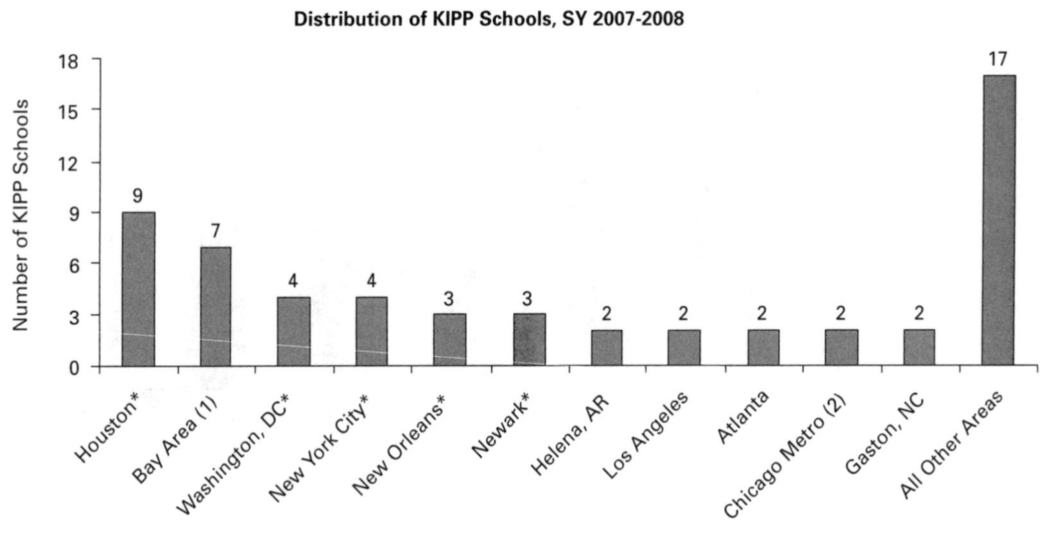

Source: KIPP organization documents.

[1] Bay Area includes schools in Oakland, San Francisco, San Lorenzo, and San Jose.

[2] Chicago Metro includes Chicago and Gary, IN.

* Indicates that the schools in this area already act as a region, with a single governing board, shared service center, and executive director.

Exhibit 8a

National Norm-Referenced Exam Results for All KIPP Schools

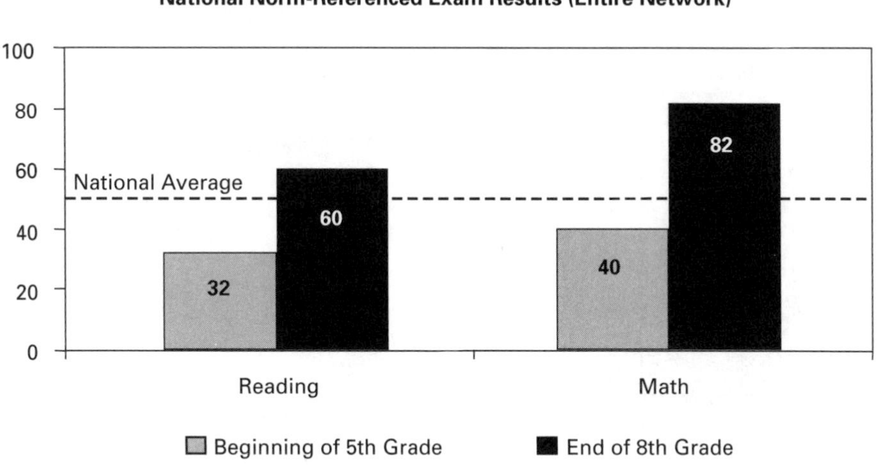

Note: Data reflects achievement gains by all KIPP students who entered KIPP in 5th grade in or after 2000, and who completed the 8th grade at KIPP schools. National norm-referenced exams used by the KIPP network include the Stanford 9, Stanford 10, TerraNova, and Iowa Test of Basic Skills.

Exhibit 8b

National Norm-Referenced Exam Results for KIPP University Prep

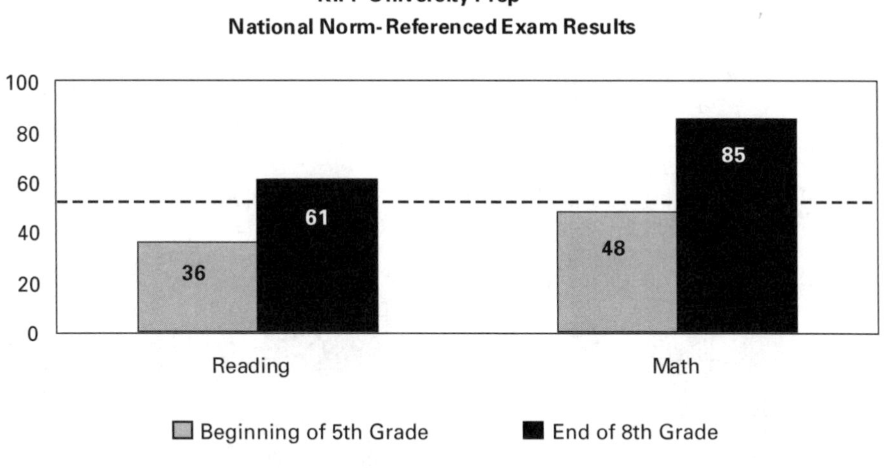

Note: Data reflects achievement gains for KIPP University Prep students who entered the KIPP program in 5th grade in 2003 and completed the 8th grade at KIPP in the spring of 2007.

Exhibit 8c

University Prep State Exam Results, 2006–2007

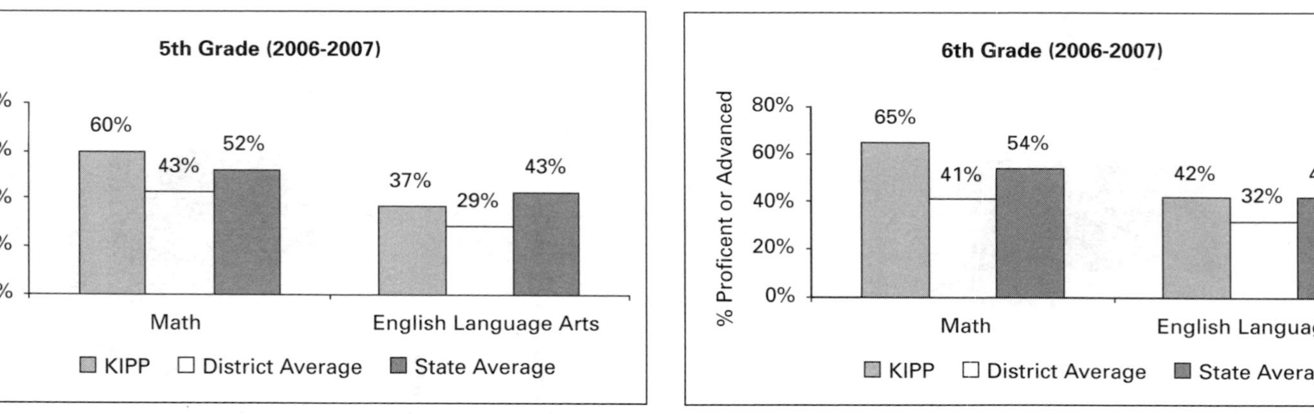

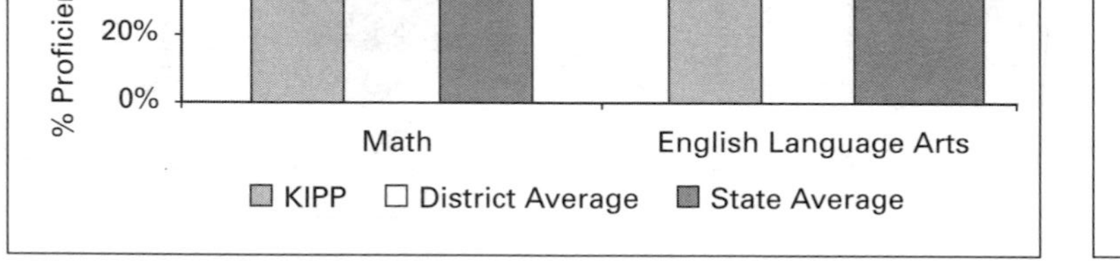

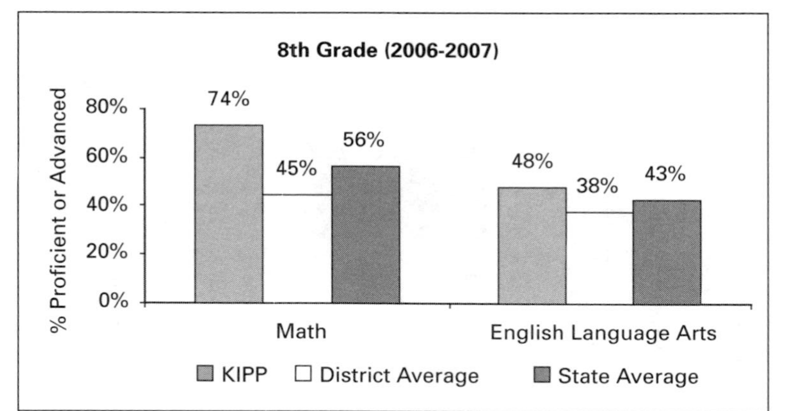

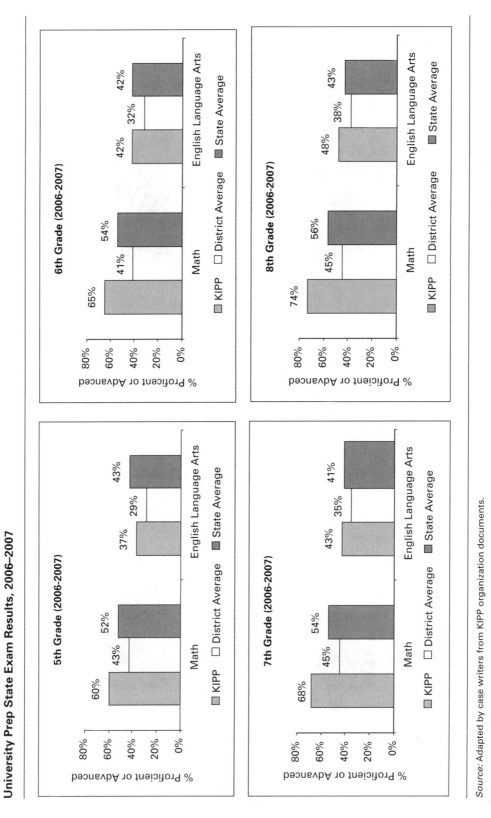

Source: Adapted by case writers from KIPP organization documents.

Note: KIPP data represents the combined network-wide performance on exams in various states; "District Average" data is an aggregate of the performance of local school districts in cities that KIPP schools operate; "State Average" data is an aggregate of the results in all states that have KIPP schools.

Exhibit 9

University Prep Financial Statements

KIPP University Prep Budget 2003-2009

									Projected			
School Year	*2003-2004*		*2004-2005*		*2005-2006*		*2006-2007*		*2007-2008*		*2008-2009*	
Enrollment	75		150		225		304		300		300	
	$(000)	%	$(000)	%	$(000)	%	$(000)	%	$(000)	%	$(000)	%
Revenues												
State Allocation[1]	485	58%	993	65%	1,505	73%	2,054	73%	2,067	72%	2,126	72%
Federal Entitlements[2]	118	14%	154	10%	103	5%	152	5%	144	5%	167	6%
Meal Reimbursement	55	7%	111	7%	166	8%	224	8%	221	8%	221	8%
Grants and Donations[3]	176	21%	261	17%	295	14%	389	14%	441	15%	430	15%
Total Revenues	835	100%	1,519	100%	2,069	100%	2,819	100%	2,874	100%	2,944	100%
Expenses												
Teacher Salaries	301	38%	722	49%	973	48%	1,373	50%	1,475	52%	1,509	52%
Administrative Salaries	238	30%	243	16%	249	12%	255	9%	261	9%	267	9%
Facilities	80	10%	161	11%	241	12%	326	12%	345	12%	355	12%
Instructional Materials	140	18%	284	19%	438	22%	610	22%	614	21%	626	21%
Administrative Expenses	34	4%	72	5%	114	6%	158	6%	164	6%	171	6%
Total Expenses	793	100%	1,482	100%	2,016	100%	2,722	100%	2,859	100%	2,928	100%
Reserve	41	5%	38	3%	53	3%	97	4%	15	1%	16	1%

Source: Created by case writer from analysis of actual KIPP school financial reports.

1 State allocation includes per student allotment for both regular and special education students.

2 Federal entitlements include categorial grants, such as Title I funding, technology grants, and start-up funding for charter schools.

3 Includes contributions from individuals, corporations, and local and national foundations.

Exhibit 10

Proposed Feeder Pattern for University Prep Schools

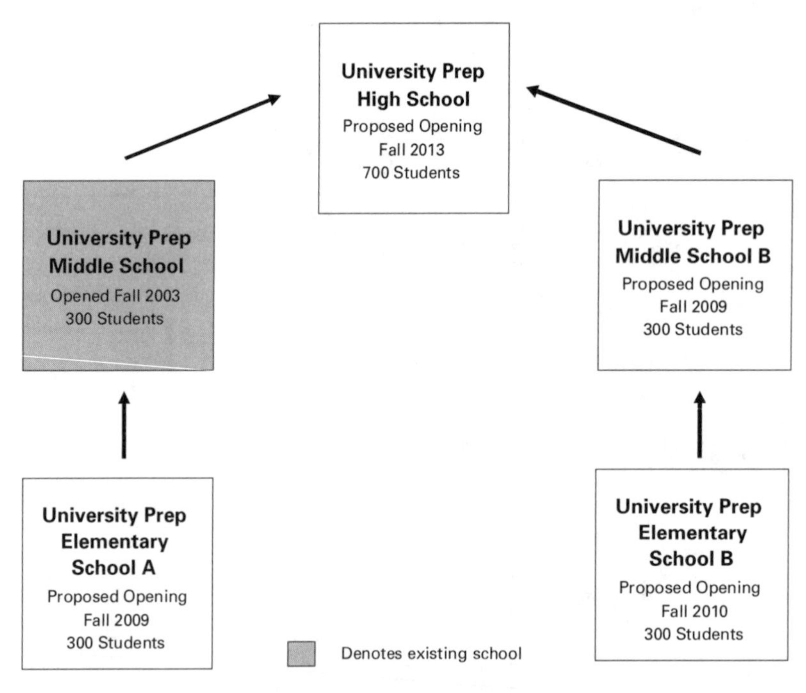

Source: Case writer analysis.

Acknowledgments

Transforming Public Education is a collection of cases used in a similar sequence in Entrepreneurship in Education Reform (EER), a successful course at Harvard Business School. Though I was involved in the writing of most of the cases, many were coauthored with fantastic students and research associates. A number of my faculty colleagues granted permission to use their cases in the course and this book, including Stig Leschly, John Gabarro, Allen Grossman, and Jim Honan. I'm grateful to them for their generosity. The HBS Division of Research and Faculty Development provided the financial resources that made possible the extensive field work and case development represented in these pages. Caroline Chauncey from Harvard Education Press deserves the credit for the vision that led to this project.

This collection would not exist were it not for my six-year-long conversation with the nearly one thousand students from HBS and other graduate programs around Harvard who have taken EER. Because the course is discussion based, on balance my students learned much more from each other than from me over the years. It also means that I learned a great deal from them as they wrestled aloud with the difficult problems in the cases and tried to apply both their intellectual gifts and their deeply held values to some of the most important issues of our time. This book is as much theirs as it is mine.

About the Editor

Stacey M. Childress is a senior lecturer in the General Management Unit at Harvard Business School and a cofounder of the Public Education Leadership Project at Harvard University. She studies entrepreneurial activity in public education in the United States. This includes the behavior and strategies of leadership teams in urban public school districts, charter schools, and nonprofit and for-profit enterprises with missions to improve the public system. Childress is also interested more generally in a range of social enterprise topics, including international social entrepreneurship.

She has authored more than two dozen case studies about large urban districts and entrepreneurial education ventures. Stacey is also a coauthor of *Leading for Equity: The Pursuit of Excellence in Montgomery County Public Schools,* Harvard Education Press, 2009, and a coeditor of *Managing School Districts for High Performance: Cases in Public Education Leadership*, Harvard Education Press, 2007.

Childress teaches in Harvard Business School's MBA program, where she has won the Student Association teaching award from the students in her Entrepreneurship in Education course. In 2008, she was an inaugural recipient of the Charles M. Williams Award for excellence in teaching, named in honor of one of the School's most celebrated case method teachers.

Permissions

Module I

KIPP National (A) (Abridged)

This case was originally prepared by Lecturer Stig Leschly, "KIPP National, 1999 (A): Designing a School Network," HBS No. 803-124. This version was prepared by the same author. Copyright © 2004, 2005, 2008 President and Fellows of Harvard College. Harvard Business School Case 805-068.

Thurgood Marshall High School

Professor John J. Gabarro prepared this case. This case is a revised and redisguised version of "Robert F. Kennedy High School," HBS No. 474-183. Copyright © 1993 President and Fellows of Harvard College. Harvard Business School Case 494-070.

Finding a CEO for the School District of Philadelphia: Searching for a Savior?

This case was prepared by Lecturer Stacey Childress with the assistance of Purnima Kochikar (MBA 2000), and Lecturer Stig Leschly. Copyright © 2003 President and Fellows of Harvard College. Harvard Business School Case 803-072.

Module II

Teach For America 2005

This case was prepared by Lecturer Stacey Childress. Copyright © 2005 President and Fellows of Harvard College. Harvard Business School Case 805-094.

Boston Teacher Residency: Developing a Strategy for Long-Term Impact

Lecturer Stacey Childress and Research Associates Geoff Marietta and Sara Suchman prepared this case. Copyright © 2008 President and Fellows of Harvard College. Harvard Business School Case 309-043.

New Leaders for New Schools

This case was prepared by Lecturer Stig Leschly with the assistance of Research Associate Jessica Boer. Copyright © 2002 President and Fellows of Harvard College. Harvard Business School Case 803-073.

Memphis City Schools: The Next Generation of Principals

This case was prepared by Research Associate Tonika Cheek Clayton under the supervision of HBS Lecturer Stacey Childress and HGSE faculty member Robert Peterkin. Copyright © 2005, 2007 Public Education Leadership Project at Harvard University. Public Education Leadership Project at Harvard University Case PEL-027.

Module III

Learning to Manage with Data in Duval County Public Schools: Lake Shore Middle School (A)

This case was prepared by Research Associate Caroline King under the supervision of HBS Professor Allen Grossman and HGSE faculty member James P. Honan. Copyright © 2004 President and Fellows of Harvard College. Public Education Leadership Project at Harvard University Case PEL-008.

SchoolNet: Pursuing Opportunity Beyond Federal Mandates

This case was prepared by Lecturer Stacey Childress with the assistance of Kristen Campbell (MBA 2005). Copyright © 2005, 2007, 2008 President and Fellows of Harvard College. Harvard Business School Case 806-050.

Wireless Generation

This case was prepared by Lecturer Stacey Childress and Research Associate Sophie Lippincott. Copyright © 2006, 2008 President and Fellows of Harvard College. Harvard Business School Case 307-409.

Focusing on Results at the New York City Department of Education

This case was prepared by Lecturer Stacey Childress and Research Associate Tonika Cheek Clayton. Copyright © 2007 President and Fellows of Harvard College. Public Education Leadeership Project at Harvard University Case PEL-054.

Module IV

If We Blew It Up, Then We Could . . . A Thought Experiment for Students of Entrepreneurship in Education

The case was prepared by Lecturer Stacey Childress. Copyright © 2008 by the President and Fellows of Harvard College. Harvard Business School Case 309-042.

Launching the Bronx Lab School

This case was prepared by Lecturer Stacey Childress. Bronx Lab School student names have been disguised for confidentiality reasons. Copyright © 2005 President and Fellows of Harvard College. Harvard Business School Case 805-093.

Codman Academy: Beyond the Start-Up Phase

This case was prepared by Lecturer Stacey Childress and Research Associate Tiffany K. Cheng. Copyright © 2008 President and Fellows of Harvard College. Harvard Business School Case 308-072.

Frederick Douglass Charter School: The Renew Decision

This case was prepared by Lecturer Stacey Childress and Debbie Kozar (MBA 2006). Copyright © 2006 President and Fellows of Harvard College. Harvard Business School Case 806-063.

New Schools for New Orleans 2008

Harvard Business School Case 9-308-074. Copyright © 2009 President and Fellows of Harvard College. All rights reserved. This case was prepared by Lecturer Stacey Childress, Scott Benson, and Sarah Tudryn.

St. HOPE Academy: The Expansion Decision

This case was prepared by Lecturer Stacey Childress and Alison Berkley Wagonfeld, Executive Director of the HBS California Research Center. Copyright © 2007 President and Fellows of Harvard College. Harvard Business School Case 307-080.

Green Dot Public Schools: To Collaborate or Compete?

The case was prepared by Lecturer Stacey Childress and Christopher C. Kim (HBS MBA 2007). Copyright © 2007 by the President and Fellows of Harvard College. Harvard Business School Case 307-086.

KIPP 2007: Implementing a Smart Growth Strategy

This case was prepared by Professor Stacey Childress and Maura Marino (MBA 2008). Certain details have been disguised. Copyright © 2008 President and Fellows of Harvard College. Harvard Business School Case 308-073.